Federal Estate & Gift Taxes Explained

Quick T

Unified Rate Schedule: Gift and Estate Ta

Column A *Taxable amount over*	Column B *Taxable amount not over*	Column C *Tax on amount in column A*	Column D *Rate of tax on excess over amount in column A* *Percent*
$ 0	$ 10,000	$ 0	18
10,000	20,000	1,800	20
20,000	40,000	3,800	22
40,000	60,000	8,200	24
60,000	80,000	13,000	26
80,000	100,000	18,200	28
100,000	150,000	23,800	30
150,000	250,000	38,800	32
250,000	500,000	70,800	34
500,000	750,000	155,800	37
750,000	1,000,000	248,300	39
1,000,000	1,250,000	345,800	41
1,250,000	1,500,000	448,300	43
1,500,000	2,000,000	555,800	45
2,000,000	2,500,000	780,800	49
2,500,000	3,000,000	1,025,800	53
3,000,000	....	1,290,800	55

An additional 5% tax is levied on amounts transferred in excess of $10 million but not exceeding $17,184,000.

State Death Tax Credit

Adjusted Taxable Estate is over*	*Adjusted Taxable Estate is not over*	*Credit =*	*+ %*	*Of Excess over*
$ 0	$ 40,000	$ 0	0	$ 0
40,000	90,000	0	.8	40,000
90,000	140,000	400	1.6	90,000
140,000	240,000	1,200	2.4	140,000
240,000	440,000	3,600	3.2	240,000
440,000	640,000	10,000	4	440,000
640,000	840,000	18,000	4.8	640,000
840,000	1,040,000	27,600	5.6	840,000
1,040,000	1,540,000	38,800	6.4	1,040,000
1,540,000	2,040,000	70,800	7.2	1,540,000
2,040,000	2,540,000	106,800	8	2,040,000
2,540,000	3,040,000	146,800	8.8	2,540,000
3,040,000	3,540,000	190,800	9.6	3,040,000
3,540,000	4,040,000	238,800	10.4	3,540,000
4,040,000	5,040,000	290,800	11.2	4,040,000
5,040,000	6,040,000	402,800	12	5,040,000
6,040,000	7,040,000	522,800	12.8	6,040,000
7,040,000	8,040,000	650,800	13.6	7,040,000
8,040,000	9,040,000	786,800	14.4	8,040,000
9,040,000	10,040,000	930,800	15.2	9,040,000
10,040,000	....	1,082,800	16	10,040,000

* "Adjusted Taxable Estate" is the decedent's taxable estate less $60,000.

Key Transfer Tax Figures

Annual Gift Tax Exclusions

Per Donee	$ 10,000**
Split Gifts by Spouses	20,000**
Gift to Noncitizen Spouse	100,000

Unified Estate & Gift Tax Credit

Year	*Applicable Credit*	*Applicable Exclusion*
1997	$192,800	$ 600,000
1998	202,050	625,000
1999	211,300	650,000
2000 and 2001	220,550	675,000
2002 and 2003	229,800	700,000
2004	287,300	850,000
2005	326,300	950,000
2006 and thereafter	345,800	1,000,000
Nonresidents Not Citizens (no treaty provision)	13,000	60,000

Credit for Estate Tax on Prior Transfers

If the transferor predeceased the decedent by a period exceeding ***	*But not exceeding*	*Percent allowable*
0 years	2 years	100
2 years	4 years	80
4 years	6 years	60
6 years	8 years	40
8 years	10 years	20
10 or more years		0

Generation-Skipping Transfer Tax

GST Tax Exemption (1999)	$1,010,000
GST Tax Rate	55%
Effective GST Tax Rate on Direct Skips at Death	33.48%

Transfer Tax Return Filing Deadlines and Extensions

Filing of gift tax return and payment of gift tax	April 15 after calendar year of gift****
Filing of estate tax return and payment of estate tax	9 months after date of death
Filing extension for gift and estate tax return	Up to 6 months
Payment extension for gift tax	Up to 6 months
Payment extension for estate tax for reasonable cause	Up to 10 years
Deferred payment of estate tax on closely held business interests	Up to 14 years

** Indexed for inflation for decedents dying and gifts made after 1998.

*** A credit of 100% is also allowed for transfers to a decedent within two years after the decedent's death.

**** For gifts made in the year of death, the due date for the gift tax return is the earlier of (1) the due date of the estate tax return or (2) April 15 after calendar year of gift.

Federal Estate and Gift Taxes *Explained*

32nd Edition

CCH Editorial Staff Publication
Eric M. Brown, J.D., LL.M.,
Revision Editor

CCH INCORPORATED
Chicago

Editorial Staff

Editors .... Bruno Graziano, J.D., M.S.A., Robert K. Kauffman, J.D., LL.M.
Production .... Kathleen M. Higgins, Clarissa Hinojosa

ISBN 0-8080-0375-5

4025 W. Peterson Ave.
Chicago, IL 60646-6085
1-800-248-3248
http://www.cch.com

Preface

Federal Estate and Gift Taxes Explained (32nd Edition) is designed as a guide for tax advisors, estate representatives, and estate owners involved in federal estate and gift tax return preparation and tax payment. The explanations and coordinated filled-in form excerpts reflect major federal estate, gift, and generation-skipping transfer tax developments occurring to the date of publication. This edition reflects the provisions of the Internal Revenue Service Restructuring and Reform Act of 1998 (P.L. 105-206), which enacted several technical corrections to the estate and gift tax law.

This book reproduces filled-in specimens of the July 1998 revision of Form 706 (United States Estate (and Generation-Skipping Transfer) Tax Return). The book also includes filled-in specimens of Form 709 (For gifts made after December 31, 1997), the federal gift tax return; Form 706-NA (Rev. September 1993), the federal estate tax return for nonresidents not U.S. citizens; Form 706-A (Rev. March 1997), the return for reporting the additional tax owing on recapture of the benefits of a special use valuation election; Form 709-A (Rev. December 1996), the short form gift tax return; and Form 706-QDT (Rev. January 1996), the estate tax return for qualified domestic trusts.

In addition, the book includes filled-in specimens of the March 1995 revisions of the following generation-skipping transfer tax forms: Form 706-GS(D), Form 706-GS(D-1), and Form 706-GS(T).

The rules and principles explained in this book are accompanied by citations to the Internal Revenue Code, regulations, IRS rulings and court decisions. These features will enable practitioners to further research the estate and gift tax law. Also included are a topical index and finding lists of forms reproduced and Code sections cited.

Eric M. Brown, J.D., LL.M.
Aronberg Goldgehn Davis & Garmisa
Chicago

April 1999

Preface

Table of Contents

UNIFIED ESTATE AND GIFT TRANSFER TAX

Paragraph

GIFT TAX

GENERATION-SKIPPING TRANSFER TAX

SPECIAL VALUATION RULES

Unified Estate and Gift Transfer Tax

Chapter 1

RATES AND CREDITS

¶ 11 Unified Rate Schedule

A single unified transfer tax applies to estate and gift taxes effective for the estates of decedents dying, and for gifts made, after December 31, 1976.[1] The rates are progressive on the basis of cumulative lifetime transfers and those transfers occurring at death. Currently, the unified transfer tax rates range from 18 percent on cumulative transfers of $10,000 or less to a maximum rate of 55 percent, applicable to cumulative transfers over $3 million.[2] Prior to January 1, 1977, estate and gift taxes were computed by using separate rate schedules (see ¶ 2640 and ¶ 2650).

For estates of decedents dying, and gifts made, before 1982, the maximum transfer tax rate is 70 percent for cumulative transfers exceeding $5,000,000. For 1982 and 1983, respectively, the maximum transfer tax rates are 65 percent and 60 percent for cumulative transfers over $4,000,000 and $3,500,000. The minimum rate of tax for estates of decedents dying, and gifts made, after 1980 is 18 percent. However, due to the operation of the unified credit (see ¶ 15), the effective minimum rate of tax for estates of decedents dying, and gifts made, in 1981 and 1982 is 32 percent. It increases to 34 percent for 1983–1986, 37 percent for 1987–2003, 39 percent for 2004–2005 and 41 percent for 2006 and thereafter. The benefits of the graduated rates and the unified credit under the unified transfer tax system are phased out beginning with cumulative transfers rising above $10,000,000 (see ¶ 16).

¶ 12 Application of Unified Rate Schedule

In computing the gift tax liability for any calendar period (year or quarter, as applicable), the unified rate schedule is applied to the transferor's cumulative lifetime taxable gifts (see Chapter 42). The term "taxable gifts" means gross gifts, minus the annual exclusion (see Chapter 44) and any allowable charitable or marital deduction (see Chapter 45). Taxable gifts for the current period are aggregated with those for all prior periods (see ¶ 2355) and a tentative gift tax is computed. From this amount, a second tentative tax on only the gifts from prior periods is subtracted. In both cases, the current unified rate schedule is used to compute the tentative tax.[3] The applicable credit amount (see ¶ 15) and

---

[1] Code Sec. 2001 and Code Sec. 2502; Reg. § 20.0-2 and Reg. § 25.2502-1.

[2] Code Sec. 2001(c)(1).

[3] Code Sec. 2502(a).

¶ 2376), and the credit for foreign gift taxes, if any, are subtracted to arrive at the current period's gift tax liability.

In computing the estate tax liability under the unified transfer tax system, the unified rate schedule is applied to a decedent's cumulative transfers, both during life and at death. A tentative estate tax is computed on what is sometimes referred to as the "estate tax base," which is composed of the taxable estate (the gross estate minus allowable deductions (see Chapter 6 through Chapter 27 and Chapter 29)) plus all taxable gifts made after 1976, other than gifts includible in the gross estate (see Chapter 30).[4] The gross estate tax is then calculated by subtracting the gift tax payable on the post-1976 taxable gifts (using the current unified rate schedule).[5] The applicable credit amount (see ¶ 15) and additional allowable credits (see Chapter 31 through Chapter 33) are then applied against the gross estate tax liability to arrive at the net estate tax due.

Special phaseout rules apply with respect to both the gift tax and the estate tax for certain large transfers (see ¶ 16 and ¶ 2378).

The estate tax base does not include the value of lifetime transfers that are already included in the decedent's estate, such as transfers where the decedent retained certain interests, rights or powers in the property (see ¶ 30). This precludes having the same lifetime transfers taken into account more than once for transfer tax purposes. The gift tax payable on these transfers is later subtracted in determining the correct estate tax.

Special rules apply in the case of nonresidents not citizens (¶ 1635) and for certain split gifts (¶ 1426). See also ¶ 2350.

¶ 15 Unified Credit

The unified credit is a one-time credit in life and at death against taxes payable on certain transfers.[6] The unified credit replaced the pre-1977 $30,000 lifetime gift tax exemption and the $60,000 estate tax exemption.[7] Although the credit must be used to offset gift taxes on lifetime transfers, regardless of the amount so used, the full credit is allowed against the tentative estate tax. The rationale for such full application is that, under Code Sec. 2001(b)(2), the estate tax payable is calculated using the cumulative transfers at life and at death and is then reduced by the amount of gift tax paid by a decedent. If a portion of the unified credit was used to avoid the payment of gift taxes, the gift tax paid reflects the amount subtracted under Code Sec. 2001(b)(2). The estate tax payable is necessarily increased by the amount of the gift tax credit used. However, the credit for estate tax purposes cannot exceed the amount of the estate tax. In addition, the unified tax credit, for both estate and gift tax purposes, is subject to reduction in accordance with the transitional rule discussed at ¶ 18, below.

It should be noted that, because of the nature of the gift tax, the computation of the unified credit for gift tax purposes is different from that for estate tax purposes (see ¶ 2007 and ¶ 2376).

---

[4] Code Sec. 2001(b).

[5] Code Sec. 2001(b)(2).

[6] Code Sec. 2010 and Code Sec. 2505.

[7] Code Sec. 2010 and Code Sec. 2505.

● *Post-1997 Unified Credit*

For the years 1998–2006, the unified credit is gradually increased to $345,800 and is determined by reference to the "applicable credit amount" and "the applicable exclusion amount" (formerly the exemption equivalent). The increase is phased in as follows:

Year	*Applicable Credit Amount*	*Applicable Exclusion Amount*
1998	$202,050	$ 625,000
1999	211,300	650,000
2000 and 2001	220,550	675,000
2002 and 2003	229,800	700,000
2004	287,300	850,000
2005	326,300	950,000
2006 and thereafter	345,800	1,000,000

As shown in the table above, the applicable credit amount for 1999 will shield $650,000 in transfers from tax. When fully phased in, the applicable credit will shield $1,000,000 in transfers from tax.

● *Pre-1998 Unified Credit*

The unified estate and gift tax credit was $192,800 for decedents dying after 1986 and before 1998. Prior to 1987, the unified credit was phased in as follows:

Year	*Credit*	*Exemption Equivalent*
1981[8]	$ 47,000	$175,625
1982............................	62,800	225,000
1983............................	79,300	275,000
1984............................	96,300	325,000
1985............................	121,800	400,000
1986............................	155,800	500,000
1987–1997	192,800	600,000

The estate tax and gift tax return filing requirements reflect the exemption equivalent (see ¶ 22 and ¶ 26).

¶ 16 Benefits of Graduated Rates and Unified Credit Phased Out

The benefits of the graduated rates and the unified credit under the unified transfer tax system are phased out beginning with cumulative transfers above $10 million.[9] This is accomplished by adding five percent of the excess of any transfer over $10 million to the tentative tax computed in determining the ultimate transfer tax liability. For estates of decedents dying, and gifts made, after 1987 and before 1998, the tax is levied on amounts transferred in excess of $10 million but not exceeding $21,040,000 in order to recapture the benefit of any transfer tax rate below 55 percent and the unified credit. Due to mistakes in the wording of the amendment to Code Sec. 2001(c)(2) by the Taxpayer Relief Act of 1997 (P.L. 105-34), the five-percent additional tax phases out the benefits of graduated rates, but not the benefits of the unified credit (applicable credit amount), for estates of decedents dying, and gifts made, after 1997. Therefore, the additional tax is levied on amounts transferred in excess of $10,000,000

[8] See ¶ 2600 for pre-1981 unified credit amounts. [9] Code Sec. 2001(c)(2).

but not exceeding $17,184,000 for decedents dying after 1997. The applicable credit amount is not recaptured.

¶ 18 Transitional Unified Credit Rule

A special transitional rule applies only to gifts made between September 9, 1976, and December 31, 1976. Under this rule, if the $30,000 lifetime exemption was used during this period, the unified credit available for later gifts is reduced, but only to the extent of 20 percent of the exemption—up to a maximum of $6,000.[10] For example, if gifts were made during this period and the lifetime exemption was applied against a gift tax liability of $15,000, the unified credit allowable after January 1, 1977, must be reduced by $3,000. Use of the $30,000 lifetime exemption on gifts made prior to September 9, 1976, does not reduce the unified credit.

In addition, with respect to lifetime gifts made in 1977, only $6,000 of the available $30,000 unified credit may be applied against gifts made after December 31, 1976, but prior to July 1, 1977. See ¶ 2376 for a year-to-year chart of the phase-in of the unified credit.

¶ 20 Unified Rates and Credit for Nonresidents Not Citizens

Effective for the estates of decedents dying after November 10, 1988, the estate and gift tax rates applicable to U.S. citizens are also applicable to the estates of nonresident aliens.[11] With respect to the unified credit, where permitted by treaty, the estate of a nonresident alien is allowed the same unified credit as a U.S. citizen multiplied by the percentage of the total gross estate situated in the United States. In other cases, the estate of a nonresident alien is allowed a unified credit of the greater of $13,000 (which exempts the first $60,000 of the estate from estate tax) or a pro rata share of $46,800 based on the percentage of property located in the United States.[12]

To reflect the fact that in some cases the estate of a nonresident noncitizen does not receive the same unified credit available to U.S. citizens, the additional five-percent recapture rate imposed on decedents dying and on gifts made after 1987 is adjusted.[13] Accordingly, the additional five-percent rate applies to the taxable transfers of nonresident noncitizens in excess of $10 million only to the extent necessary to phase out the benefit of the graduated rates and unified credit actually allowed by statute or treaty.

See ¶ 1615 for a list of countries that have death duty conventions in effect with the United States.

---

[10] Code Sec. 2010(b) and Code Sec. 2505(b). The retroactive application of this transitional rule was upheld by the U.S. Supreme Court in *A. Hemme*, SCt, 86-1 USTC ¶ 13,671, 476 US 1166. The estate of a decedent who had made lifetime transfers after September 8, 1976, and before January 1, 1977, and who had elected to claim the lifetime exemption of $30,000, was required to reduce its allowable unified credit by 20 percent of the claimed exemption. The Court stated that the application of the transitional rule was not unconstitutional because the amount of the credit that the estate was ultimately allotted resulted in no greater a tax than the estate would have owed under prior law. Therefore, the application of the transitional rule to gifts made by the decedent prior to the Tax Reform Act of 1976 (P.L. 94-455) was not so arbitrary and capricious as to violate due process.

[11] Code Sec. 2101(a).

[12] Code Sec. 2102(c).

[13] Code Sec. 2101(b).

Chapter 2
FILING REQUIREMENTS

¶ 22 Estate Tax Returns for U.S. Citizens and Residents

An estate tax return (Form 706, United States Estate (and Generation-Skipping Transfer) Tax Return) is due within nine months after the date of a decedent's death.[1] For estates of U.S. citizens and residents dying after 1976, the filing requirements are triggered for estates that exceed the applicable exclusion amount—i.e., the amount of property sheltered from tax by the unified credit.

For decedents dying after 1986 and before 1998, the representative must file a federal estate tax return if the gross estate exceeds $600,000.[2] However, if lifetime gifts are made and the applicable credit amount is offset against the gift tax, this amount is reduced accordingly (see the unified credit table at ¶ 15).[3] For decedents dying in 1998 and 1999, the applicable exclusion amount is $625,000 and $650,000, respectively, and the filing threshold is increased to that amount.[4]

¶ 24 Estate Tax Returns for Nonresidents Not Citizens

For estates of nonresidents not citizens of the United States, the estate representative must file a return if the value of that part of the gross estate that is located in the United States exceeds $60,000 (¶ 1600 et seq.).[5]

¶ 26 Gift Tax Return Filing Requirements

A gift tax return (Form 709, United States Gift (and Generation-Skipping Transfer) Tax Return) is to be filed, and any gift tax is to be paid, on an annual basis. Generally, the due date for filing the annual gift tax return is April 15 following the close of the calendar year in which gifts are made (see ¶ 2052).[6] However, for a calendar year in which a donor dies, the gift tax return must be filed no later than the due date for the donor's estate tax return, including extensions.[7] These rules apply to U.S. citizens, residents, and nonresident aliens alike.

A gift tax return must be filed if the donor (1) gave gifts to any donee other than the donor's spouse that are not fully excludable from gift tax under one or a combination of the annual, educational, or medical exclusions (see ¶ 2250), (2) gave gifts to charity unless the donor transfers his entire interest in the property transferred and no noncharitable donee

---

[1] Code Sec. 6075(a); Reg. § 20.6075-1. Extensions of time to file may be granted in certain circumstances (see ¶ 66).

[2] Code Sec. 6018(a)(1)

[3] Code Sec. 6018(a)(3)

[4] Code Sec. 2010(c).

[5] Code Sec. 6018(a)(2).

[6] Code Sec. 6075(b)(1)

[7] Code Sec. 6075(b)(3).

receives an interest in the property, (3) gave gifts of terminable interests (other than a life estate with a general power of appointment) to his or her spouse (see ¶ 2318), or (4) gave gifts of any amount that are split with his or her spouse (see ¶ 2200).[8]

A short form gift tax return (Form 709-A, United States Short Form Gift Tax Return) may be filed annually (i.e., by April 15 of the following year) by a husband and wife who elect to split gifts of not more than $20,000 per year per donee (see ¶ 2240).[9]

¶ 27 Generation-Skipping Transfer Tax Return Filing Requirements

IRS regulations detail the filing requirements for generation-skipping transfer tax returns.[10] The return requirements depend on the type of generation-skipping transfer involved. In general, in the case of a direct skip (other than from a trust), a return must be filed on or before the date on which an estate or gift tax return is required to be filed with respect to the transfer.[11] In all other cases, the due date for the return is on or before the 15th day of the fourth month after the close of the tax year of the person required to file such a return. Exceptions to these general rules are set forth in Reg. § 26.2662-1 (see ¶ 2471).

As noted below, the type of generation-skipping transfer involved determines which return is to be used in reporting the tax.

- *Taxable Distributions*

In the case of a taxable distribution (defined at ¶ 2433), the transferee must report the generation-skipping transfer on Form 706-GS(D) (Generation-Skipping Transfer Tax Return for Distributions), and the trust involved in such a transfer must file Form 706-GS(D-1) (Notification of Distribution from a Generation-Skipping Trust) and send a copy to each distributee.[12]

- *Taxable Terminations*

The trustee in the case of a taxable termination (defined at ¶ 2433) is required to report the generation-skipping transfer tax on Form 706-GS(T) (Generation-Skipping Transfer Tax Return for Terminations).[13]

- *Direct Skips*

In specifying the form of return to be used for reporting the generation-skipping transfer tax on direct skips (defined at ¶ 2433), Reg. § 26.2662-1 distinguishes between *inter vivos* direct skips and direct skips occurring at death. For any direct skip that is subject to the federal gift tax and that occurs during the life of the transferor, Form 709 (United States Gift (and Generation-Skipping Transfer) Tax Return) must be filed.[14]

The generation-skipping transfer tax that is imposed on direct skips that are subject to the estate tax and occur at the death of a decedent is reported on Form 706. Schedule R-1 (Generation-Skipping Transfer Tax)

---

[8] Code Sec. 6019.

[9] Instructions for Form 709-A (Rev. December 1996).

[10] Reg. § 26.2662-1.

[11] Code Sec. 2662(a)(2).

[12] Reg. § 26.2662-1(b)(1).

[13] Reg. § 26.2662-1(b)(2).

[14] Reg. § 26.2662-1(b)(3)(i).

of Form 706 must be filed for any direct skip from a trust if such a direct skip is subject to the estate tax.[15]

Certain *inter vivos* transfers may be subject to both gift and generation-skipping transfer taxes. A generation-skipping transfer is subject to the gift tax if it is required to be reported on Schedule A (Computation of Taxable Gifts) of Form 709 under the rules contained in the gift tax portion of its instructions, including the split gift rules.

For a more detailed discussion of the generation-skipping transfer tax return requirements, see Chapter 48, beginning at ¶ 2430.

---

[15] Reg. § 26.2662-1(b)(3)(ii).

Estate Tax

Chapter 3

NATURE OF TAX

¶ 28 Description of Tax

The federal estate tax is an excise tax levied upon the transfer of a person's property at the time of that person's death.[1] It is neither a tax on the property itself nor a tax on the privilege of an heir to receive the property.

The amount of the tax is determined by applying the relevant tax rates to the tax base or the taxable estate (see ¶ 12 and ¶ 29). With only one exception (noted below), the tax is not affected by the relationship of the beneficiaries to the decedent as is the case under inheritance tax laws in effect in many states.

A special deduction for amounts transferred to a surviving spouse reduces the size of the taxable estate of a U.S. citizen or resident if the transferred amounts meet the conditions of such deduction (see ¶ 1000).[2]

¶ 29 Taxable Estate

The taxable estate is determined by subtracting certain deductions (see ¶ 780) from the gross estate (see ¶ 150).[3] A tentative tax applies to the amount of the taxable estate and the amount of taxable gifts made after 1976, using the unified rate schedule (see ¶ 11). The estate tax is computed by determining the amount of the tentative tax and subtracting gift taxes paid on gifts made after 1976.[4] To the extent that the applicable credit amount was not used to offset gift taxes, the amount of estate tax is reduced.[5]

¶ 30 Gross Estate

The value of the gross estate of a decedent is the total value of the interests described in Code Sec. 2033 through Code Sec. 2044, whether real or personal, tangible or intangible, wherever situated.[6] Generally, the gross estate of a decedent is composed of the value of:

(1) all property to the extent of the decedent's interest in it at the time of the decedent's death (see ¶ 150);

(2) any interest of the surviving spouse existing as dower or curtesy, or similar interest (see ¶ 200);

---

[1] Code Sec. 2001(a); Reg. § 20.0-2(a).

[2] Code Sec. 2056(a).

[3] Code Sec. 2051.

[4] Code Sec. 2001(b).

[5] Code Sec. 2010.

[6] Code Sec. 2031 and Reg. § 20.2031-1, detailing certain exceptions to Code Sec. 2033 through Code Sec. 2044.

(3) property transferred by the decedent during life, if: (a) the transfer was made within three years before death for less than adequate and full consideration by a decedent dying before 1982 (see ¶ 555); (b) the decedent had retained the income or enjoyment for life or for a period not determinable without reference to the decedent's death (see ¶ 570); (c) the transfer was not intended to take effect until the decedent's death and the decedent retained a reversionary interest in the property transferred (see ¶ 565); (d) the decedent possessed a power to change the enjoyment through a power to alter, amend, or revoke (see ¶ 580 and ¶ 585); or (e) the decedent had relinquished a right of the type referred to in (b), (c), or (d) within three years before the decedent's death (see ¶ 595); and

(4) certain other types of property interests including: (a) one-half of the value of qualified joint interests (see ¶ 502); (b) jointly held property interests that are not qualified joint interests (the interest being based on the decedent's contribution to the purchase of joint interests) (see ¶ 500); (c) life insurance proceeds if the decedent or the decedent's estate had any interest in the proceeds at the time of death (see ¶ 400); (d) property over which the decedent had a general power of appointment received from another; (e) certain annuities (see ¶ 700); or (f) qualified terminable interest property (see ¶ 773).[7]

The above summary is not all-inclusive and is subject to various qualifications. These qualifications are discussed in more detail at the paragraphs noted above.

¶ 32 Deductions

The items listed below are deductible from the amount of the gross estate in determining the taxable estate of U.S. citizens and residents:

(1) funeral expenses (see ¶ 785);

(2) various expenses incidental to the administration of the estate (see ¶ 790);

(3) losses incurred due to casualty or theft, etc., during administration (see ¶ 900);

(4) debts of the decedent and enforceable claims against the estate, including taxes (see ¶ 800);

(5) mortgages and liens (see ¶ 850);

(6) a marital deduction for qualifying property passing to the decedent's spouse (see ¶ 1000);

(7) the value of property transferred to, or for the use of, charitable, educational, religious or public institutions, or the government (see ¶ 1100); and

(8) the adjusted value of the decedent's qualified family-owned business interests (see ¶ 1150).[8]

---

[7] Code Sec. 2031 and Code Sec. 2033 through Code Sec. 2044.

[8] Code Sec. 2051 and Code Sec. 2053 through Code Sec. 2057.

¶ 35 Rates

The minimum transfer tax rate is 18 percent on cumulative lifetime and at-death transfers. The maximum transfer tax rate is 55 percent for estates of decedents dying after 1983[9] (see ¶ 2600). The effective minimum transfer tax rate is now 37 percent as a result of the operation of the unified credit (see ¶ 15). However, as the applicable credit amount increases (see ¶ 15), the effective minimum transfer tax rate may increase (see ¶ 11). In addition, the benefits of the graduated rates and the unified credit are phased out beginning with cumulative transfers exceeding $10,000,000 (see ¶ 16). The tax may be further reduced by other credits (see ¶ 36).

¶ 36 Credits

A unified credit is subtracted from the amount of estate tax liability (see ¶ 15) for estates of decedents dying after 1976.[10]

In addition to the unified credit, credits are allowed in reduction of federal estate taxes for taxes paid on prior transfers to the decedent by or from a person who died within 10 years before or two years after the decedent (see ¶ 1300), state inheritance, estate and succession taxes (see ¶ 1370), federal gift taxes paid by the decedent on pre-1977 transfers made by the decedent during his lifetime (see ¶ 1382), and foreign death duties paid (see ¶ 1401).[11] The credit allowed against the estate tax for gift tax paid on property included in a decedent's gross estate is eliminated for post-1976 gifts.

In computing the estate tax against which these credits will be allowed, the sum of all gift taxes payable on gifts made after 1976 is subtracted (see ¶ 1426).[12]

¶ 37 Effect of State Law

The question of whether, and the extent to which, particular property interests are owned by a decedent at death, and thus are includible in the decedent's gross estate, generally is determined on the basis of the law of the state where the decedent resided or where the property was located.[13] The federal courts will follow state law in deciding whether something is a property interest. State law, for this purpose, includes both statutes and state court decisions interpreting statutes. Therefore, it is necessary, in many cases, to refer both to the statutes and to state court decisions in determining whether or not to include an interest in a decedent's gross estate.[14]

Where the type and character of property interests held and transferred by a decedent is determined with respect to state court decisions, the decisions of the highest court of a state have binding effect for federal estate tax purposes. The decision of the state's highest court can involve the actual interest to be reported on the decedent's estate tax return or it can involve the estate of another decedent under the same general factual

---

[9] Code Sec. 2001(c)(1).

[10] Code Sec. 2010.

[11] Code Sec. 2010 through Code Sec. 2015.

[12] Code Sec. 2001(b).

[13] *J. Morgan, Exr.*, SCt, 40-1 USTC ¶ 9210, 309 US 78.

[14] Although state law classifies a property interest as a certain type, it is federal law that determines whether that type of interest is includible in the gross estate.

situation. However, in a National Office Technical Advice Memorandum, the IRS refused to follow, for federal estate tax purposes, a decision of the Georgia Supreme Court that a decedent's power of appointment was limited by an ascertainable standard (see ¶ 653).[15] The lawsuit giving rise to the Georgia court's decision was a will construction proceeding filed by a bank as executor of the decedent's estate, and only the IRS, which was notified but declined to intervene, had an interest adverse to that of the estate. In the IRS's view, the decisions of a state's highest court are binding for estate tax purposes only if the underlying lawsuit was adversarial and affected the property rights of the litigants. In a separate National Office Technical Advice Memorandum, involving a Georgia decedent in a factual situation similar to that resulting in the Georgia Supreme Court's decision, the IRS also refused to accept the Georgia court's decision as controlling for estate tax purposes.[16]

Lower state court decisions are not binding for estate tax purposes and their effect is not clear. The U.S. Supreme Court has held that, in the absence of a decision by a state's highest court, a federal court must apply what it finds the state law to be after giving "proper regard" to decisions of other courts of the state.[17] Intermediate state court decisions may be disregarded if the federal court is convinced that the highest state court would decide otherwise. A state trial court decision must also be given "proper regard" by a federal court; however, such a decision cannot have a binding effect for federal estate tax purposes.[18]

The allowance of estate tax deductions for funeral expenses, the expenses of administering a decedent's estate, claims against a decedent's estate, and mortgages on a decedent's property are all governed by the laws of the jurisdiction where the estate is being administered. Otherwise, the allowance of estate tax deductions is generally determined by the Internal Revenue Code.

¶ 38 Decedents Whose Estates Are Subject to Tax

The estate tax applies to the estate of any person who dies leaving property having a taxable situs within the United States. Its application varies in detail, however, between persons who are considered either residents or citizens of the United States and those who are considered nonresidents not citizens. The term "residence," as used with reference to any person for federal estate tax purposes, means the person's domicile, regardless of citizenship.

Generally, *Federal Estate and Gift Taxes Explained* deals with the status of estates of U.S. residents and citizens. Special notes point out the variations applicable to estates of decedents considered nonresidents not citizens.

---

[15] IRS Technical Advice Memorandum 8339004, 6-14-83, CCH IRS LETTER RULINGS REPORTS.

[16] IRS Technical Advice Memorandum 8346008, 8-4-83, CCH IRS LETTER RULINGS REPORTS.

[17] *H.J. Bosch Est.*, SCt, 67-2 USTC ¶ 12,472, 387 US 456 (consolidated with *Second Nat'l Bank of New Haven, Ex'r (Will of F.F. Brewster)*). See also *D.L. Hastings, Pers. Rep.*, DC Md., 86-1 USTC ¶ 13,662.

[18] *H.J. Bosch Est.*, SCt, 67-2 USTC ¶ 12,472, 387 US 456 (consolidated with *Second Nat'l Bank of New Haven, Ex'r (Will of F.F. Brewster)*). See also *D.L. Hastings, Pers. Rep.*, DC Md., 86-1 USTC ¶ 13,662.

Chapter 4

RETURNS—FORMS REQUIRED

¶ 50 Forms Required

The estate tax return, Form 706 (United States Estate (and Generation-Skipping Transfer) Tax Return), is used to report and pay the estate tax in the case of decedents who were U.S. citizens or residents.[1] Form 706-NA (United States Estate (and Generation-Skipping Transfer) Tax Return—Estate of nonresident not a citizen of the United States) is filed for nonresident aliens (see ¶ 85). Form 706-A is to be used to report the recapture of tax benefits previously enjoyed under an election to have farm or closely held business real property valued under the special use valuation provisions of Code Sec. 2032A (see ¶ 80).

The estate tax return must be filed within nine months after a decedent's death unless otherwise extended.[2] Payment of the tax is also due at this time unless one of the provisions for extension of time to pay tax applies (¶ 1685).[3]

If the tax cannot be finally computed within the filing period, arrangement may be made with the IRS for an extension of time for filing and payment. In order to reduce interest liability, the return may be filed with whatever necessary information is available before expiration of the filing period and with a payment of taxes based upon an estimate. If the return is not filed within one year after it is due (including extensions), the right to use the alternate valuation method is lost (see ¶ 105).

¶ 65 Estate Tax Return

An estate tax return must be filed for the estate of every U.S. citizen or resident whose gross estate exceeds the amount of the applicable exclusion amount (based on the applicable credit amount [4]) on the date of death.[5] The value of the gross estate at the date of the decedent's death is used to determine whether a return must be filed, even though the

---

[1] Discussion and examples herein are based on Form 706, as revised in July 1998.

[2] Code Sec. 6075(a); Reg. § 20.6075-1 and Reg. § 20.6081-1.

[3] Code Sec. 6151(a); Reg. § 20.6151-1, Reg. § 20.6161-1, and Reg. § 20.6163-1.

[4] Beginning in 1998, the unified credit is determined by reference to the "applicable credit," and the exemption equivalent is referred to as the "applicable exclusion amount."

[5] Code Sec. 6018(a)(1) and Code Sec. 6018(a)(3).

executor may elect to have the gross estate valued as of the alternate valuation date (see ¶ 107).[6]

The unified credit and, therefore, the exemption equivalent amount that a decedent's gross estate must exceed before a return is required has increased every year from 1977 through 1986 (see ¶ 15). From 1987 through 1997, the unified credit was $600,000. Accordingly, for a decedent dying after 1986 and before 1998, the decedent's representative must have filed a federal estate tax return if the gross estate exceeded $600,000. For decedents dying in 1998 and after, the decedent's representative must file a federal estate tax return only if the gross estate of the decedent exceeds the applicable exemption amount ($625,000 for 1998; $650,000 for 1999) (see ¶ 15). However, such amount is reduced to reflect the amount of adjusted taxable gifts made by the decedent after 1976, plus the aggregate amount allowed as a specific exemption under former Code Sec. 2521 for gifts made by the decedent after September 8, 1976.[7]

An estate tax return must also be filed by the estate of a nonresident alien if the part of his or her estate situated in the United States exceeds $60,000 (after certain adjustments) at the date of death (see ¶ 85).

For decedents dying prior to 1997, an executor was required to file an estate tax return if the special tax on excess retirement accumulations imposed by Code Sec. 4980A applies (see ¶ 775), regardless of whether a return would otherwise have been required to be filed.[8] The tax on excess retirement accumulations was repealed by the Taxpayer Relief Act of 1997 (P.L. 105-34), effective after December 31, 1996.

¶ 66 Time for Filing Return

Estate tax return Forms 706 and 706-NA must be filed within nine months after the date of a decedent's death, unless a six-month extension to file the return is granted.[9] The due date is the day of the ninth calendar month after the decedent's death numerically corresponding to the date of the calendar month on which death occurred. For example, if the decedent died on February 4, 1999, the federal estate tax return must be filed on or before November 4, 1999. If there is no numerically corresponding day in the ninth month, the last day of the ninth month is the due date. Thus, if the decedent died on December 31, 1998, the due date is September 30, 1999. A six-month extension of time for filing the return does not operate to extend the time for payment of the estate tax (but, see ¶ 1685).

Form 706-A (United States Additional Estate Tax Return) must be filed within six months after an early disposition or cessation of qualified use of a specially valued property, that is, real property for which the special use valuation under Code Sec. 2032A is elected (see ¶ 80).

When the due date for the filing of an estate tax return falls on a Saturday, a Sunday, or a legal holiday, the due date for filing the return is the next succeeding day that is not a Saturday, a Sunday, or a legal holiday.[10] The term "legal holiday" means a legal holiday in the District of Columbia and, in the case of any document required to be filed or any

---

[6] Reg. § 20.6018-1.

[7] Code Sec. 6018(a)(3).

[8] Code Sec. 6018(a)(4).

[9] Reg. § 20.6075-1.

[10] Reg. § 301.7503-1.

other act required to be performed at any office of the United States outside the District of Columbia but within an internal revenue district, the term also means a statewide legal holiday in the state where the office is located.[11]

The estate tax return cannot be amended after the expiration of the extension period granted for filing. However, the estate representative may subsequently file supplemental information that may result in a finally determined tax different from the amount indicated on the return.[12]

An extension of time for filing an estate tax return will be granted if it is impossible or impractical for the executor to file a reasonably complete return before the expiration of the due date.[13] The executor must show good and sufficient cause for granting the extension. Unless the executor is abroad, the extension will not be granted for more than six months beyond the due date of the return. Applications for filing extensions must be made with the IRS official in charge of the office where the estate tax return will be filed. Therefore, the estate representative will normally make such applications to the Director of the IRS Service Center at which the return will be filed or to the office of the District Director at which a hand-carried return will be filed (see ¶ 68). The application should be made before the due date and it must contain a full recital of the causes for the delay. An extension of time for filing a return does not operate to extend the time for payment of the tax, unless so specified in the extension.

¶ 67 Penalties

The willful failure to make and file the estate tax return, to pay the tax, or to keep any records or supply any information at the time or times required by law or regulation constitutes a misdemeanor.[14] These offenses are punishable by a fine of not more than $25,000 ($100,000 in the case of a corporation), or imprisonment of not more than one year, or both, with costs of prosecution.

If the estate tax return is not filed within the prescribed time (see ¶ 66), the IRS will impose a penalty of five percent of the estate tax liability per month or part of a month, up to a maximum of 25 percent, until the return is filed, unless the estate representative can show that the failure to file is due to reasonable cause and not to willful neglect.[15] In addition, if the failure to file is shown to be due to fraud, the penalties range from 15 percent to a maximum of 75 percent.[16]

● *Reliance on Accountant or Attorney*

The question of whether an executor's reliance on an attorney, accountant or other tax professional to timely file the estate tax return constitutes reasonable cause for late filing of the return has frequently been the subject of litigation. In resolving this issue, the Tax Court and several U.S. courts of appeal have utilized different approaches and arrived at conflicting results.[17] The U.S. Supreme Court, in an attempt to

---

[11] Reg. § 301.7503-1.

[12] Reg. § 20.6081-1(c).

[13] Reg. § 20.6081-1(a).

[14] Code Sec. 7203.

[15] Code Sec. 6651(a)(1).

[16] Code Sec. 6651(f).

[17] *S.E. Young Est.*, 46 TCM 324, CCH Dec. 40,605(M), TC Memo. 1983-686; *M. Ferrando*, CA-9, 57-2 USTC ¶ 11,702, 245 F2d 582; *C.I. Lillehei Est.*, CA-3, 81-1 USTC ¶ 13,389, 638 F2d 65;

establish a "bright line rule" with respect to this issue, has stated that the delegation of an executor's duty to comply with unambiguous and fixed filing requirements does not relieve the executor of his or her burden to ascertain the relevant filing deadlines and to ensure that they are met.[18] Accordingly, the Court held that where an executor relies upon an attorney, accountant or tax adviser to comply with these filing requirements, the executor's reliance will not constitute reasonable cause for a late filing of the estate tax return.

The Court did recognize that where an executor relies upon the erroneous advice of counsel regarding a substantive question of law (e.g., as to whether or not a tax liability exists), such reliance may constitute reasonable cause for a late filing. However, the Court chose not to define the circumstances in which this would be true. The Tax Court has explored this issue and held that a donor's reliance on the advice of her accountant regarding the necessity for filing gift tax returns was reasonable cause for her failure to file the returns. Although the donor's estate eventually conceded gift tax liability for stock and cash advances she had made to her son and that were never repaid, the Tax Court stated that the donor had justifiably relied on her accountant's advice that no gift tax returns were necessary because the advances were intended to be loans at the time of their making.[19] In a similar case, the Tax Court held that an executrix's reliance on her attorney's advice that no estate tax return was due because the estate was too small constituted reasonable cause that excused the executrix's failure to file.[20] The Tax Court has also held that a personal representative's reliance on the erroneous advice of her attorney that an estate was entitled to a second automatic extension of time to file the estate tax return constituted reasonable cause for the untimely filing of the return.[21]

Additionally, an estate administrator's reliance on his attorney was found by a U.S. district court in Tennessee to be reasonable cause for his failure to timely file an estate tax return. The court held that because of his age (78), poor health and lack of experience in estate administration, the administrator was unable to deal with the "emergency situation" created by the unexpected illness of his attorney shortly before the return was due. The district court noted that the Supreme Court had expressly left open the issue of whether an executor's reliance on his attorney would be reasonable cause for delay when that reliance was due to the executor's incapacity. The court found that the administrator was incapable of exercising ordinary business care and prudence by hiring another attorney to file the return or by obtaining an extension of time in which to file, and therefore the delay in filing was due to reasonable cause.[22]

(Footnote Continued)

and *A. Geraci Est.*, CA-6, 74-2 USTC ¶ 13,024, 502 F2d 1148, cert. denied, 420 US 992, have adopted a *per se* rule that reliance on counsel is not "reasonable cause."

[18] *R. Boyle, Exr.*, SCt, 85-1 USTC ¶ 13,602, 469 US 241, rev'g CA-7, 83-2 USTC ¶ 13,530, 710 F2d 1251.

[19] *S.S. Buring Est.*, 51 TCM 113, CCH Dec. 42,539(M), TC Memo. 1985-610. See also *H.J. Knott*, 55 TCM 424, CCH Dec. 44,653(M), TC Memo. 1988-120.

[20] *F.G. Paxton Est.*, 86 TC 785, CCH Dec. 43,021; *L. Chagra Est.*, 60 TCM 104, CCH Dec. 46,713(M), TC Memo. 1990-352; see also, *C.J. Autin*, 102 TC 760, CCH Dec. 41,906, regarding the gift tax.

[21] *E.E. La Meres*, 98 TC 294, CCH Dec. 48,085.

[22] *C. Brown*, DC Tenn., 86-1 USTC ¶ 13,656.

The unusual factual circumstances in the Tennessee case limit the application of its holding. Recent decisions on this issue have uniformly held that reliance on an attorney or accountant will not excuse late filing.[23] However, another Tennessee court has held that reliance on a qualified professional's erroneous advice as to when the estate tax return was due was reasonable cause.[24]

¶ 68 Place for Filing Return

The estate tax return of a resident decedent must be filed with the IRS Service Center serving the state in which the decedent was domiciled at the date of death.[25] Hand-carried returns may be filed with the District Director of the internal revenue district in which the decedent was domiciled at the date of death.

The return of a nonresident (whether a citizen or not) must be filed with the IRS Service Center, Philadelphia, PA 19255.[26]

¶ 69 Payment of Tax

The estate tax is due and payable at the same time and place the return is due. In other words, the payment must be made with the return.[27] Thus, the estate tax is due nine months after a decedent's death, without regard to extensions of time to file (see ¶ 66).

Failure to pay the tax with the return may result in the imposition of a penalty of one-half of one percent of the estate tax liability for each month or part of a month that the tax remains unpaid, up to a maximum of 25 percent.[28] This penalty is in addition to the late-filing penalty discussed at ¶ 67. Code Sec. 6651(d) provides that in cases where a taxpayer fails to pay the tax due upon notice and demand thereof by the IRS, the penalty is further increased each month. If an addition to tax applies both for failure to file a return on the due date and for failure to pay the tax on the due date, the addition for failure to file is reduced by the amount of the addition for failure to pay for any month or part of a month to which both additions apply.[29] See ¶ 1685 for details concerning extensions of time for paying the tax.

¶ 70 Persons Required to File Return

The duly qualified executor or administrator of a decedent's estate is required to file the estate tax return. If there is more than one executor or administrator qualifying, the return must be verified and signed by all.[30]

---

[23] See *L.F. Blumberg Est.*, DC Cal., 86-1 USTC ¶ 13,658; *G.M. Brandon Est.*, 86 TC 327, CCH Dec. 42,911, rev'd and rem'd on another issue, CA-8, 87-2 USTC ¶ 13,733; *R. Cox Est.*, DC Fla., 86-2 USTC ¶ 13,681; *S.B. Gardner Est.*, 52 TCM 202, CCH Dec. 43,285(M), TC Memo. 1986-380; and *H.E. Rothpletz Est.*, 53 TCM 1214, CCH Dec. 43,998(M), TC Memo. 1987-310; *J.K. Fleming Est.*, CA-7, 92-2 USTC ¶ 60,113, 974 F2d 894; *F.S. Newton Est.*, 59 TCM 469, CCH Dec. 46,546(M), TC Memo. 1990-208; *K.S. Wilbanks Est.*, 61 TCM 1779, CCH Dec. 47,153(M), TC Memo. 1991-45; aff'd, CA-11 (unpublished opinion 1-22-92); *J. Nemerov Est.*, 75 TCM 2344, Dec. 52,709(M), TC Memo. 1998-186; *J.G. Maltaman Est.*, 73 TCM 2163, CCH Dec. 51,917(M), TC Memo. 1997-110.

[24] *W.F. Sharp, Jr. Est.*, DC Tenn., 97-1 USTC ¶ 60,268.

[25] Code Sec. 6091(b)(3).

[26] Reg. § 20.6091-1. Instructions for Form 706 (Rev. July 1998), p. 2, and Instructions for Form 706-NA (Rev. September 1993), p. 1.

[27] Reg. § 20.6151-1.

[28] Code Sec. 6651.

[29] Code Sec. 6651(c)(1).

[30] Reg. § 20.6018-2.

If there is no executor or administrator appointed, qualified and acting in the United States, every person in actual or constructive possession of any property of decedent situated in the United States is considered an "executor" for estate tax purposes and is required to make and file a return.[31]

Where two or more persons are liable for the filing of the return, it is preferable for all to join in the filing of one complete return.[32] If all of them are unable to do so, each person is required to file a return disclosing all the information each has with respect to the return (including the name of every person holding a legal or beneficial interest in the property and a full description of the property). Similarly, in the event the appointed, qualified and acting executor or administrator is unable to make a complete return, every person holding an interest in property comprising the decedent's estate must make a return, upon receipt of notice from the district director, as to the interest held by that person.[33]

The person or persons filing the estate tax return must sign, under penalty of perjury, the first declaration on page 1 of the return. If the return is prepared by an attorney or an agent for the person or persons filing the return, the attorney or agent must also sign the second declaration on page 1 under penalty of perjury.

¶71 Missing Person's Return

A duty to file an estate tax return for a missing person's estate rests on any person who would be an executor or administrator of the estate in the event of the missing person's actual death. The executor or administrator must ascertain from existing facts whether the missing person is a "decedent" for purposes of filing the estate tax return.[34]

Facts establishing a missing person's death for estate tax return purposes include the following:

(1) administration of the absentee's property pursuant to adjudication by a court of competent jurisdiction;

(2) transfer to or vesting of the absentee's assets in a beneficiary pursuant to state law;

(3) taking of or receipt of the absentee's property by any person without court order or statutory authority; or

(4) circumstances indicating that the absentee's property has been disposed of as if he were dead.[35]

The mere appointment of a receiver for the missing person's property does not indicate that person's death for estate tax purposes in the absence of any transfer of title or assets. In any event, if the value of the missing person's estate is such as to otherwise require that an estate tax return be filed (see ¶22), such a return must be filed within nine months following

[31] Reg. §20.6018-2.

[32] Instructions for Form 706 (Rev. July 1998), p. 2.

[33] Reg. §20.6018-2.

[34] Rev. Rul. 66-286, 1966-2 CB 485, as clarified and modified by Rev. Rul. 80-347, 1980-2 CB 342, and by Rev. Rul. 82-189, 1982-2 CB 189.

[35] Rev. Rul. 66-286, 1966-2 CB 485, as clarified and modified by Rev. Rul. 80-347, 1980-2 CB 342, and by Rev. Rul. 82-189, 1982-2 CB 189.

the period of continuous and unexplained absence after which the person may be declared legally dead under applicable state law.

In a National Office Technical Advice Memorandum, the IRS has ruled that, where there is a court adjudication of death based upon a presumption of death and no fixed date thereof, the date of death for federal estate tax purposes is the ending date of the state presumptive period and not the date of adjudication. In the IRS's view, any other rule would leave the determination of the date of death, for federal estate tax purposes, to the discretion of the interested party filing the petition in state court.[36]

¶ 72 Supplemental Documents

If the decedent was a U.S. resident and died testate, a certified copy of the decedent's will must be filed with the estate tax return. The executor may also file copies of any documents that the executor desires to submit in explanation of the return. Various other supplemental documents, required for the several property schedules of the return, are discussed in the following chapters.

If the decedent was a nonresident citizen, the following documents must be filed with the return:

(1) A copy of any inventory of property and any schedule of liabilities, claims against the estate, and expenses of administration filed with the foreign court of probate jurisdiction and certified by a proper official of such court.

(2) A copy of any return filed under a foreign inheritance, estate, legacy, succession, or other death tax act and certified by a proper official of the foreign tax department, if the estate is subject to such a foreign tax.

(3) A certified copy of the will if the decedent died testate.[37]

(4) Form 2848 (Power of Attorney and Declaration of Representative) must be filed in order to grant authority to an individual to represent a taxpayer before the IRS and to receive tax information (see ¶ 79). Form 8821 (Tax Information Authorization) is to be used to authorize any designated individual, corporation, firm, organization, or partnership to inspect and/or receive confidential information in any office of the IRS for the type of tax and years or periods listed on the form (see ¶ 79).

See also the material discussing the following: alternate valuation, ¶ 115; real estate, ¶ 270; stocks and bonds, ¶ 318; life insurance, ¶ 481; business interests, ¶ 527; miscellaneous properties, ¶ 535; transfers during life, ¶ 625; powers of appointment, ¶ 670; attorneys' fees, ¶ 792; marital deduction, ¶ 1075; charitable deduction, ¶ 1140 and ¶ 1141.

¶ 73 Execution of the Return

Form 706 is used to report the estate tax. The current Form 706 (Rev. July 1998) is arranged in the following sequence:

---

[36] IRS Technical Advice Memorandum 8526007, 3-14-85, CCH IRS LETTER RULINGS REPORTS.

[37] Reg. § 20.6018-4.

● Page 1 contains questions dealing with general information pertaining to the decedent, a "Tax Computation" section (Part 2), and a section for signing the return by the executor, administrator or person in possession of the decedent's property and by the preparer of the return. The allowable unified credit is subtracted on Line 11 of the "Tax Computation" section. The credits for state death taxes, federal gift taxes on pre-1977 gifts, foreign death taxes and tax on prior transfers are claimed on Lines 15, 17, 18 and 19, respectively, of the "Tax Computation" section where applicable.

● Page 2 of Form 706 includes an "Elections by the Executor" section (Part 3) in which the executor can make elections to specially value property (see ¶ 280 through ¶ 296), to use the alternate valuation date (see ¶ 107), to pay tax in installments under either Code Sec. 6163 or Code Sec. 6166 (see ¶ 1650 through ¶ 1685). Page 2 also contains "General Information" questions (Part 4), which continue onto page 3. If question number 15 is answered in the affirmative, Schedule I (Annuities) must be completed. Schedule I requires an executor to disclose whether a lump-sum distribution under Code Sec. 2039(f)(2) is being excluded from the gross estate. Question number 16 requires the executor to disclose whether the decedent was a beneficiary of a trust for which the marital deduction was claimed on the estate tax return of a predeceased spouse as qualified terminable interest property (QTIP) and which is not reported as part of the decedent's gross estate. If the answer is "yes," an explanation for the failure to report such property must be attached to the return.

● Page 3 of Form 706 contains a "Recapitulation" (Part 5) that has two sections. The decedent's gross estate (from Schedules A through I) is reported in the first section of the Recapitulation, and the "Total gross estate" for this section is then reported on Line 1 of the "Tax Computation" section (Part 2) on page 1 of Form 706. The second section of the Recapitulation is used to record the deductions (from Schedules J through O and T), and the "Total allowable deductions" are then carried over and deducted on Line 2 of the "Tax Computation" section on page 1.

Form 706 also includes the following schedules:

● Schedules A through I, which are used to report a decedent's gross estate.

● Schedule A-1 (Section 2032A Valuation), which is used to report information required to support the election to value certain farm and closely held business property at its special use value. Schedule A-1 includes the Notice of Election (Part 2) and the Agreement to Special Valuation under Section 2032A (Part 3).

● Schedules J through O, which are used to report deductions.

● Schedule P (Credit for Foreign Death Taxes) and Schedule Q (Credit for Tax on Prior Transfers), which are used to report tax credits. Note that IRS Form 706-CE (Certification of Payment of Foreign Death Tax) must also be filed in order to claim a credit for foreign death tax.

● Schedule R (Generation-Skipping Transfer Tax), which is used to compute the generation-skipping transfer tax payable by an estate, and Schedule R-1 (Generation-Skipping Transfer Tax—Direct Skips from a Trust), which is used for the computation of the tax payable by certain trusts that are includible in the gross estate. Only generation-skipping transfer tax imposed as a result of a direct skip occurring at death is reported using Form 706. See Chapter 50 (¶ 2471 through ¶ 2490) for a discussion of the other forms used for reporting the generation-skipping transfer tax.

- Schedule T (Qualified Family-Owned Business Interest Deduction) is used to report information required to support the election to deduct the adjusted value of qualified family-owned business interests otherwise includible in the decedent's gross estate. For 1998, the deduction is limited to $675,000. The amount of the deduction is entered on Form 706, Part 5, Line 22.

- Schedule U (Qualified Conservation Easement Exclusion) is used to report information required to support the election to exclude a portion of the value of land that is included in the decedent's gross estate and is subject to a qualified conservation easement. The amount of the exclusion is entered on Form 706, Part 5, Line 11.

- A Continuation Schedule is to be used for listing additional assets from Schedules A, B, C, D, E, F, G, H, and I and additional deductions from Schedules J, K, L, M, O, and T if there is no more room on the particular schedule. Totals on a continuation schedule should be carried over to the appropriate line of the main schedule. A separate Continuation Schedule must be used for each main schedule being continued.

Money items may be shown on the return as whole-dollar amounts. The rounding off of amounts to whole-dollar figures requires the elimination of any amount less than 50 cents and an increase of any amount in the range of 50 cents to 99 cents to the next higher dollar amount.[38]

The final computation of the tax must be shown in detail. The estate tax return does not provide a detailed schedule for the purposes of this computation, however. If the executor determines that no estate tax is owed by the decedent's estate, he should enter a zero on Line 27—"Balance due" under "Tax Computation" (Part 2) on page 1 of the return.

- *Total Gross Estates Exceeding the Applicable Exclusion Amount*

In the case of a decedent whose total gross estate exceeds the applicable exclusion amount ($625,000 for 1998; $650,000 for 1999), the first three pages of Form 706 and all required supporting schedules must be filed, in accordance with the following rules:

(1) If the gross estate does not include assets reportable on Schedule A (Real Estate), Schedule B (Stocks and Bonds), Schedule C (Mortgages, Notes and Cash), Schedule D (Insurance on the Decedent's Life), or Schedule E (Jointly Owned Property), it is not necessary to file these schedules and a zero should be entered on the applicable line of the Recapitulation on page 3 of Form 706. However, Schedule D must be filed if it is indicated in the "General Information" portion of Form 706 (Part 4, Question 8(a)) that there was insurance on the decedent's life that was not included on the return as part of the gross estate.

---

[38] Instructions for Form 706 (Rev. July 1998), p. 3.

(2) Schedule F (Other Miscellaneous Property) must be filed with every return.

(3) Schedule G (Transfers During Decedent's Life) must be filed if, as indicated in the General Information portion of Form 706 (Part 4, Questions 11 and 12a), the decedent made certain types of transfers during life or if there existed at the date of death any trusts created by the decedent during his or her lifetime. Schedule H (Powers of Appointment) must be filed if it is indicated in the General Information portion of Form 706 (Part 4, Question 13) that the decedent ever possessed, exercised, or released a general power of appointment.

(4) Schedule J (Funeral Expenses and Expenses Incurred in Administering Property Subject to Claims), Schedule K (Debts of the Decedent, and Mortgages and Liens), Schedule L (Net Losses During Administration and Expenses Incurred in Administering Property Not Subject to Claims), Schedule M (Bequests, etc., to Surviving Spouse), Schedule O (Charitable, Public, and Similar Gifts and Bequests), and Schedule T (Qualified Family-Owned Business Deduction) must be filed only if a deduction is claimed for a particular item. For Schedule M (Bequests, etc., to Surviving Spouse), which is used to list the assets for which a marital deduction has been taken, the qualified terminable interest property (QTIP) election is deemed to have been made if property qualifying for QTIP treatment is listed on Schedule M.

(5) Schedule P (Credit for Foreign Death Taxes) and Schedule Q (Credit for Tax on Prior Transfers) must be filed only if the particular credit is claimed.

(6) Schedule U (Qualified Conservation Easement Exclusion) must be filed if the exclusion is claimed on Part 5, Line 11.

¶74 Estate Beneficiaries

Individuals, trusts, or estates receiving benefits of $5,000 or more from the decedent's estate (other than charitable beneficiaries) are to be listed on page 2 of the Form 706 estate tax return, together with their taxpayer identification numbers (Social Security numbers in the case of individuals and employer identification numbers for trusts and other estates), relationship to the decedent, and the dollar value of property received from the estate.

¶75 Beneficiaries Receiving Specially Valued Property

Individuals who received an interest in specially valued property (see ¶280 through ¶296) must be listed on Schedule A-1 of the estate tax return, along with their taxpayer identification numbers, relationship to the decedent, and addresses. In the case of an individual beneficiary, the identification number is the Social Security number; for trusts and estates, the employer identification number should be used.

¶78 Entering Principal and Income on Schedules

For every item of principal, any income accrued thereon at the date of the decedent's death must be separately entered on the appropriate schedule under the column headed "Value at date of death." If the alternate valuation method is elected, any includible income with respect to each item of principal must be separately entered under the column headed "Alternate value."

The information indicated by the columns headed "Alternate valuation date" and "Alternate value" should not be shown unless the executor elects the alternate valuation method. "Alternate value" information should be omitted in the space provided in the Recapitulation section, Part 4, Form 706, if the alternate valuation method is not elected.

The items must be numbered under every schedule. The total of the items on each schedule should be shown at the bottom of the schedule, but the totals should not be carried forward from one schedule to another. The total for each schedule, however, should be entered under the Recapitulation section.

¶ 79 Representation by Lawyer or Agent

If the executor is to be represented by someone else before the IRS, by correspondence or otherwise, in refund claims and other matters, a power of attorney must be filed on Form 2848 (Power of Attorney and Declaration of Representative) and signed by the fiduciary.

Form 2848 authorizes a person or persons to represent an estate in a proceeding before the IRS and to receive confidential information. It also authorizes the person or persons named as a representative to perform one or more of the four following acts: (1) execute waivers (including offers of waivers) of restrictions on assessment or collection of deficiencies; (2) execute consents extending the statutory period for assessment or collection of taxes; and (3) execute closing agreements. In order to grant additional powers, such as the power to delegate authority, to substitute another representative or to sign the return, specific language designating the additional power must be inserted. Form 8821 (Tax Information Authorization) is to be used to authorize any designated individual, corporation, firm, organization, or partnership to inspect and/or receive confidential information in any office of the IRS for the type of tax and years or periods listed on the form. It will not authorize an individual to represent a taxpayer and/or perform other acts on the taxpayer's behalf such as executing waivers, consents, or closing agreements. Form 2848 must be used for that purpose. A properly executed declaration on page 2 (Part 4) of Form 706 will also authorize an attorney to receive confidential tax information, such as a copy of the closing letter.

Generally, only one power of attorney to represent the estate may be in effect in an IRS office in any one matter. Therefore, the names and addresses of all lawyers or agents to whom the executor has delegated authority to represent the estate in the matter should be included in the power of attorney. The power of attorney should be filed with the IRS District Director in whose office the estate tax return has been, or will be, filed.

Attorneys and certified public accountants are not required to be enrolled to practice before the IRS. However, they must file as evidence of recognition a written declaration stating that they are qualified and are authorized to represent the particular parties on whose behalf they are acting.[39] Attorneys are qualified if they are members in good standing of the bar of the highest court of any state, possession, territory, commonwealth, or the District of Columbia, and are not currently under suspension or disbarment from practice before the IRS. Similarly, certified public accountants are qualified if they are authorized to practice as certified public accountants in any state, possession, territory, commonwealth, or the District of Columbia, and are not currently under suspension or disbarment from practice before the IRS.

In both instances the declarants, of course, must be authorized to act on behalf of their clients.

Form 2848 contains a declaration to be completed, which contains the following information:

(1) A statement that the representative is authorized to represent the taxpayer as a certified public accountant, attorney, enrolled agent, enrolled actuary, unenrolled return preparer, member of the taxpayer's immediate family, officer, full-time employee, etc. An actuary enrolled by the Joint Board for the Enrollment of Actuaries may represent a taxpayer before the IRS. However, the actuary's representation is limited to certain areas of the Internal Revenue Code. See section 10.3(d)(1) of Treasury Department Circular No. 230 for a list of the Code sections involved and the areas covered by them.

(2) The jurisdiction recognizing the representative. For an attorney or certified public accountant: Enter in the "jurisdiction" column the state, District of Columbia, possession, or commonwealth that has granted the declared professional recognition. For an enrolled agent or actuary: Enter in the "jurisdiction" column the enrollment card number.

(3) The signature of the representative, and the date signed.

If the estate is to be represented before the IRS by an agent, the agent must be enrolled to practice in accordance with the regulations contained in the Rules on Administrative Procedure. The requirements for enrollment of agents are contained in Treasury Department Circular No. 230 (Title 31, Part 10, Code of Federal Regulations) which may be obtained from the Director of Practice, U.S. Treasury Department, Washington, D.C. 20009. Unenrolled agents may represent taxpayers only under limited circumstances.[40]

Any person qualified under § 10.5(c) (relating to temporary recognition of an applicant for enrollment) or § 10.7 (relating to limited practice without enrollment in the case of a full-time employee, or a bona fide officer of a corporation, trust, estate, association, or organized group, and certain others) of Circular No. 230 will also be recognized to practice before the IRS.[41]

---

[39] Statement of Procedural Rules § 601.502.

[40] Statement of Procedural Rules § 601.502.

[41] Statement of Procedural Rules § 601.502.

¶ 80 Special Use Valuation Recapture—Form 706-A

Where the election to have farm or closely held business real property valued under the special use valuation provisions is made under Code Sec. 2032A, the tax benefits gained as a result are recaptured as an additional estate tax if the property is disposed of to non-family members or ceases to be used for farming or closely held business purposes within 10 years after the death of the decedent (15 years after the death of a decedent dying before 1982). Form 706-A (United States Additional Estate Tax Return) is used to report the recapture of these tax benefits. For a discussion of the Code Sec. 2032A election, see ¶ 280 through ¶ 296.

The basic Form 706-A (Rev. March 1997) computation of the additional estate tax due under Code Sec. 2032A is made on Part II, Lines 1–15. Lines 16–19 are used to report those dispositions, if any, occurring more than 120 months after the commencement date of the qualified use (reflecting the 15-year recapture period for decedents dying before January 1, 1982). Lines 20–22 incorporate information relating to involuntary conversions or exchanges reported on Schedule B before arriving at the additional estate tax amount on Line 23. If an individual is using Form 706-A to report an exchange or involuntary conversion, he or she should not use the same Form 706-A to report any cessations of qualified use or dispositions of specially valued property that are not exchanges or involuntary conversions.[42] A separate Form 706-A should be used for the cessations or other dispositions. However, involuntary conversions and exchanges may be reported together on the same form.

It should be noted that Form 706-A also includes a Schedule C for purposes of reporting dispositions to family members of the qualified heir.

Form 706-A must be filed with the IRS office where the decedent's estate tax return was filed. Unless an extension for filing is obtained, Form 706-A must be filed within six months after the taxable disposition or cessation of qualified use of the property.

A filled-in Form 706-A appears at ¶ 81.

---

42 Instructions for Form 706-A (Rev. March 1997), p. 2.

¶ 81 Filled-In Form 706-A

→ ***Caution: The filled-in Form 706-A (Rev. March 1997), below, does not relate to the James X. Diversey Estate, the hypothetical facts of which are reflected in various examples appearing throughout this publication.***←

Form **706-A** (Rev. March 1997) Department of the Treasury Internal Revenue Service

United States Additional Estate Tax Return

(To report dispositions or cessations of qualified use under section 2032A of the Internal Revenue Code)

For Paperwork Reduction Act Notice, see page 1 of the separate Instructions.

OMB No. 1545-0016

Part I General Information

1a Name of qualified heir Helen Gower	2 Heir's social security number 279-33-1234
1b Address of qualified heir (number and street, including apartment number, P.O. Box, or rural route) 124 South Elmwood	3 Commencement date (see instructions) 5-30-93
1c City, town or post office, state, and ZIP code Turnlake, WI 51534	

4 Decedent's name reported on Form 706	5 Decedent's social security number	6 Date of death
Henry Gower	315-71-4711	5-1-93

Part II Tax Computation (First complete Schedules A and B — see instructions.)

1	Value at date of death (or alternate valuation date) of all specially valued property that passed from decedent to qualified heir:				
a	Without section 2032A election	1a	700,000		
b	With section 2032A election	1b	450,000		
c	Balance (subtract line 1b from 1a)			1c	250,000.00
2	Value at date of death (or alternate valuation date) of all specially valued property in decedent's estate:				
a	Without section 2032A election	2a	700,000		
b	With section 2032A election	2b	450,000		
c	Balance (subtract line 2b from 2a)			2c	250,000.00
3	Decedent's estate tax:				
a	Recomputed without section 2032A election (attach computation)	3a	363,000		
b	Reported on Form 706 with section 2032A election	3b	255,500		
c	Balance (subtract line 3b from 3a)			3c	107,500.00
4	Divide line 1c by 2c and enter the result as a percentage			4	100.00 %
5	Total estate tax saved (multiply line 3c by percentage on line 4)			5	107,500.00
6	Value, without section 2032A election, at date of death (or alternate valuation date) of specially valued property shown on Schedule A of this Form 706-A	6	700,000		
7	Divide line 6 by line 1a and enter the result as a percentage			7	100.00 %
8	Multiply line 5 by percentage on line 7			8	107,500.00
9	Total estate tax recaptured on previous Form(s) 706-A (attach copies of 706-A)			9	0
10	Remaining estate tax savings (subtract line 9 from line 5) (do not enter less than zero)			10	107,500.00
11	Enter the lesser of line 8 or line 10			11	107,500.00
12	Enter the total of column D, Schedule A, page 2	12	735,000.00		
13	Enter the total of column E, Schedule A, page 2	13	450,000.00		
14	Balance (subtract line 13 from line 12) (but enter the line 12 amount in the case of a disposition of standing timber on qualified woodland)			14	285,000
15	Enter the lesser of line 11 or line 14			15	107,500.00

Note: *Complete lines 16 - 18 only if the decedent died before January 1, 1982, and the taxable event occurred more than 120 months after the commencement date. Otherwise, skip lines 16 - 18 and enter the amount from line 15 on line 19.*

16	Enter the number of full months after the commencement date in excess of 120 months (10 years) when the qualified heir disposed of the interest or discontinued the qualified use	16	
17	Divide line 16 by 60	17	
18	Multiply line 15 by line 17	18	0
19	Subtract line 18 from line 15 (do not enter less than zero)	19	107,500.00

If you completed Schedule B, complete lines 20 - 23. If you did not complete Schedule B, skip lines 20 - 22 and enter the amount from line 19 on line 23.

20	Enter the total cost (or FMV) from Schedule B	20	500,000.00
21	Divide line 20 by line 12 and enter the result as a percentage (do not enter more than 100%)	21	68.03 %
22	Multiply line 19 by percentage on line 21	22	73,132.25
23	**Additional estate tax,** subtract line 22 from line 19 (do not enter less than zero)	23	34,367.75

Under penalties of perjury, I declare that I have examined this return, and to the best of my knowledge and belief, it is true, correct, and complete. Declaration of preparer other than taxpayer is based on all information of which preparer has any knowledge.

Helen Gower — Signature of taxpayer/qualified heir — Date: 2-28-98

Signature of preparer other than taxpayer/qualified heir — Date

Address (and ZIP code)

Form **706-A** (Rev. 3-97)

→ Caution: The filled-in Form 706-A (Rev. March 1997), below, does not relate to the James X. Diversey Estate, the hypothetical facts of which are reflected in various examples appearing throughout this publication.←

Form 706-A (Rev. 3-97) Page 2

Schedule A. — Disposition of Specially Valued Property or Cessation of Qualified Use

List property in chronological order of disposition or cessation

A Item number	B Description of specially valued property and schedule and item number where reported on the decedent's Form 706	C Date of disposition (or date qualified use ceased)	D Amount received (or fair market value if applicable) (see instructions)	E Special use value (see instructions)
1	Form 706, Schedule A, Item 1 Description — Farm, Kenosha County, Wisconsin	2-21-98	735,000	450,000
Totals: Enter total of column D on line 12 of the Tax Computation, and total of column E on line 13 of the Tax Computation.			735,000.00	450,000.00

→ ***Caution: The filled-in Form 706-A (Rev. March 1997), below, does not relate to the James X. Diversey Estate, the hypothetical facts of which are reflected in various examples appearing throughout this publication.*** ←

Form 706-A (Rev. 3-97) Page 3

Schedule B. — Involuntary Conversions or Exchanges Check if for: ☒ Involuntary conversion ☐ Exchange

Qualified replacement (or exchange) property

A Item	B Description of qualified replacement (or exchange) property	C Cost (or FMV)
1	Farm, Real Estate, R.R. 6, Box 15, Kenosha Corners, WI (Northeast quarter, Section 12, Kenosha County, WI)	500,000
Total cost (or FMV) (enter here and on line 20 of the Tax Computation)		500,000.00

→ *Caution: The filled-in Form 706-A (Rev. March 1997), below, does not relate to the James X. Diversey Estate, the hypothetical facts of which are reflected in various examples appearing throughout this publication.*←

Form 706-A (Rev. 3-97) Page 4

Schedule C. — Dispositions to Family Members of the Qualified Heir

Each transferee must enter into an agreement to be personally liable for any additional taxes imposed by section 2032A(c) and the agreement must be attached to this Form 706-A. (See Instructions.)

Transferee #1:	Last name	First name	Middle initial
	Social security number	Relationship to the qualified heir	

Description of property transferred

A Item number	B Description of specially valued property and schedule and item number where reported on the decedent's Form 706	C Date of disposition
1	Form 706, Schedule________, Item__________ Description —	

Transferee #2:	Last name	First name	Middle initial
	Social security number	Relationship to the qualified heir	

Description of property transferred

A Item number	B Description of specially valued property and schedule and item number where reported on the decedent's Form 706	C Date of disposition
1	Form 706, Schedule________, Item__________ Description —	

If there are more than two transferees, attach additional sheets using the same format.

¶ 85 Nonresidents Not Citizens

An estate tax return must be filed for the estate of a nonresident not a citizen if the part of the decedent's gross estate having a situs in the United States exceeded a value of $60,000, after reduction for: (1) taxable gifts made after 1976, and (2) the aggregate amount that was allowable as a specific exemption under Code Sec. 2521, as it existed prior to its repeal by the Tax Reform Act of 1976, for gifts made between September 9, 1976, and December 31, 1976.[43] Form 706-NA (Rev. September 1993) is used for the estates of nonresidents not citizens (see ¶ 1636). This return must be filed and the estate tax paid (in U.S. currency at par) within nine months after a decedent's death. The estates of nonresidents who are not citizens are entitled to the same filing and payment extensions that are available to U.S. citizens and residents. Returns of nonresidents who are not citizens must be filed with the IRS Service Center, Philadelphia, PA 19255. If the decedent died testate, a certified copy of the will must be attached to the return.

Schedule A of Form 706-NA is used to report that portion of the nonresident alien's gross estate that is situated in the United States. See ¶ 1617 and ¶ 1620 for further details. Property reported on this schedule must be valued in U.S. dollars, and the "alternate valuation method," discussed at ¶ 105, can be elected. All property must be separately listed on Schedule A and must be described in such a manner that it can be readily identified. The total value of property listed in Schedule A is reported on line 1 of Schedule B of Form 706-NA.

Schedule E of Form 706 must be attached if, at the time of death, the decedent owned any property located in the United States in joint tenancy with the right of survivorship, as a tenant by the entirety, or with a surviving spouse as community property.

Schedule G of Form 706 must be attached to Form 706-NA if the decedent made certain lifetime transfers (described in detail in the instructions for Form 706, Schedule G) of property that was located in the United States either at the time of the transfer or at the time of the decedent's death. A Form 706 Schedule G must also be filed with Form 706-NA if the decedent created any trusts during his lifetime that were in existence at the time of transfer or at the time of the decedent's death.

Schedule H of Form 706 must be attached to Form 706-NA if the decedent, at the time of his death, possessed a general power of appointment over property located in the United States and/or if the decedent exercised or released such a power at any time.

If the gross estate in the United States includes any interests in property transferred to a "skip person" as defined in the instructions to Form 706, Schedule R (Generation-Skipping Transfer Tax) and/or Schedule R-1 (Generation-Skipping Transfer Tax—Direct Skips From a Trust) must be attached.

Schedule B of Form 706-NA is used to compute the taxable estate of a nonresident alien. This schedule is filled out as follows:

---

[43] Code Sec. 6018(a)(2).

(1) The decedent's gross estate located in the United States, as reported on Schedule A, is entered on line 1. The decedent's gross estate located outside of the United States is then reported on line 2. The total of lines 1 and 2, or the decedent's total gross estate wherever situated, is entered on line 3.

(2) The deduction for administration expenses, claims, etc., is determined and claimed on lines 4 and 5 of Schedule B. A deduction for mortgages will be allowed only if the full value of the mortgaged property was included in the total gross estate reported on line 3.

(3) The charitable deduction is claimed on line 6. Line 6 of Schedule B indicates that Schedule O of Form 706 must be attached to support this deduction. However, the Form 706-NA instructions indicate that, if a charitable deduction is claimed under a treaty, the applicable treaty must be specified and the computation of the charitable deduction must be attached. The marital deduction that is available to the estates of decedents only under certain treaties is also claimed on line 6. Estates of decedents claiming this deduction must attach Schedule M of Form 706 and a sheet showing the computation of the amount of the deduction.

(4) The total deductions, the total of lines 5 and 6, are entered on line 7.

(5) The taxable estate is computed on line 8 by subtracting line 7 from line 1. (See ¶ 1625 through ¶ 1636 for further details concerning the allowance of deductions for the estates of nonresident aliens.)

After Schedules A and B of Form 706-NA have been completed, the "Tax Computation" section (Part II) on page 1 can be completed. The taxable estate, from line 8, Schedule B, is entered on the first line of this section. The sum of the taxable estate (line 1) and the decedent's adjusted taxable gifts of tangible or intangible property located in the United States (line 2) is entered on line 3. Estates that find that the amount on line 3 exceeds $10 million should then complete the worksheets included with the instructions.[44] If the amount on line 3 is $10 million or less, the estate uses the Tax Table on page 3 of the Form 706-NA instructions to determine the amount of tax. The tentative tax on the total of the taxable estate and the total taxable gifts (line 3) and the tentative tax on the total taxable gifts alone (line 2) are then entered on lines 4 and 5, respectively. The amount on line 5 is then subtracted from the amount on line 4, and the resulting amount is entered on line 6.

Effective with respect to decedents dying after November 10, 1988, estate and gift tax rates applicable to the estates of U.S. citizens are also applicable to the estates of nonresident aliens.[45] Also, the additional five-percent rate imposed on decedents dying and on gifts made after 1987 is adjusted to reflect the fact that the estate of a nonresident noncitizen may not receive the unified credit available to U.S. citizens. Accordingly, the additional five-percent rate applies to the taxable transfers of nonresident noncitizens in excess of $10 million only to the extent necessary to phase

[44] Instructions for Form 706-NA (Rev. September 1993), p. 3.

[45] Code Sec. 2101(b).

out the benefit of the graduated rates and unified credit actually allowed by statute or treaty.[46]

The unified credit against estate taxes is entered on line 7 and any credit for state death taxes on line 9. The credit for federal gift taxes is entered on line 11, the credit for tax on prior transfers on line 12 and the total of these two credits is entered on line 13. The net estate tax liability is entered on line 14 after subtracting the line 13 amount from the amount on line 10. The generation-skipping transfer tax (see instructions to Schedules R and R-1 of Form 706 imposed on transfers of interests in property that is part of the gross estate in the United States is entered on line 15 and the increased estate tax on excess retirement accumulations (see instructions to Schedule S, Form 706) is reported on line 16. The addition of lines 14, 15 and 16 results in the amount of total transfer taxes entered on line 17. After reduction for prior payments (line 18) and for U.S. Treasury bonds redeemed in payment of estate tax (line 19), the balance of estate tax due is entered on line 21.

It should be noted that effective for estates of decedents dying after November 10, 1988, where permitted by treaty, the estate of a nonresident alien is allowed the same unified credit as that of a U.S. citizen, multiplied by the proportion of the total gross estate situated in the United States. In other cases, the estate of a nonresident alien is allowed a unified credit of $13,000 (which exempts the first $60,000 of the estate from estate tax).[47]

---

[46] Code Sec. 2101(b).

[47] Code Sec. 2102(c).

Chapter 5

VALUATION—DATE AND METHODS

¶ 100 Election Available

The representative of an estate has an election with respect to the time property included in the gross estate is to be valued. The representative may elect to value property as of the date of the decedent's death or as of an "alternate valuation date." The "alternate valuation date" is, generally, a date six months after the date of the decedent's death. See ¶ 107 for further details. Even property that was transferred some time before death, but that is included in the gross estate because of the retention of certain rights or for other reasons, is valued as of the date of death or as of a date six months after death.

¶ 101 Rules Applicable to Various Types of Property

Even though all property included in the gross estate is valued as of the same date—that is, the date of death or the alternate valuation date—special problems arise in valuing particular types of property. For this reason, special rules apply in valuing the various kinds of property or interests in property that might be included in the gross estate: real estate; stocks and bonds; mutual funds; interests in business; notes, secured and unsecured; cash on hand or on deposit; household and personal effects; annuities, life estates, remainders, and reversions; and certain other property.

¶ 102 Request for IRS Valuation Basis

The IRS may be required to furnish a written statement explaining any determination or proposed determination of the value of an item of property in a decedent's estate. The statement must be furnished no later than 45 days after a written request by the executor or donor or 45 days after the determination or proposed determination, whichever is later.[1]

The statement must (1) explain the basis of the valuation, (2) set forth any computation, and (3) include a copy of any expert appraisal. The method used by the IRS in arriving at the valuation is not binding on the IRS.

A request for such a statement must be filed with the District Director's office that has jurisdiction over the estate tax return by the

---

[1] Code Sec. 7517.

deadline for claiming a refund of the tax that is dependent on the valuation.[2]

¶ 105 Alternate Valuation Method

The alternate valuation method for determining the value of a decedent's estate is authorized by Code Sec. 2032. Although an estate representative could previously elect the use of the alternate valuation method under any circumstances, the use of this method by estates of decedents dying after July 18, 1984, is limited to situations in which the election would reduce both the value of the decedent's gross estate and the federal estate and generation-skipping transfer tax liability of the estate.[3]

The alternate valuation date may be elected on an estate tax return that is filed no more than one year late.[4] Once elected, the use of the alternate valuation date is irrevocable.[5] Further, the alternate valuation method must be elected on the first return filed.[6]

The alternate valuation method is not automatic. It must be expressly elected on the estate tax return by checking the box at line 1 of Part 3 (Elections by the Executor) of Form 706 (Rev. July 1998). However, the mere failure to designate the election on the return will not necessarily preclude the use of alternate valuation. A determination of whether an election has been made must be determined by all the facts on the return.[7]

¶ 107 Applicable Alternate Valuation Dates

If the estate representative chooses the alternate valuation method, all property included in the gross estate is valued as of six months after the decedent's death, except that property sold, distributed, exchanged, or otherwise disposed of during the six months is to be valued as of the date of disposition.[8] If there is no day in the sixth month following the decedent's death that corresponds numerically to the date of death, the alternate valuation date is the last day of the sixth month.[9] The actual selling price of securities sold in arm's-length transactions during the alternate valuation period must be used in valuing such securities by a person electing the alternate valuation method.[10]

The phrase "distributed, sold, exchanged, or otherwise disposed of" includes all possible ways by which property may cease to form a part of the gross estate. Property is considered "distributed," either by the estate representative or by a trustee of property included in the gross estate, on the date upon which the first of the following events occurs:

(1) entry of an order or decree of distribution (if the order or decree subsequently becomes final);

(2) separation of the property from the estate or trust so that it is completely available to the distributee; or

---

[2] Reg. § 301.7517-1.

[3] Code Sec. 2032(c).

[4] Code Sec. 2032(d).

[5] Code Sec. 2032(d).

[6] Temp. Reg. § 301.9100-6T.

[7] Rev. Rul. 61-128, 1961-2 CB 150.

[8] Code Sec. 2032(a).

[9] Rev. Rul. 74-260, 1974-1 CB 275.

[10] Rev. Rul. 68-272, 1968-1 CB 394; Rev. Rul. 70-512, 1970-2 CB 192.

(3) actual distribution of the property to the beneficiary or other distributee.

In order to eliminate changes in value due only to lapse of time, Code Sec. 2032 provides that any interest or estate "affected by mere lapse of time" is to be included in the gross estate under the alternate valuation method at its value as of the date of decedent's death. Adjustments for any difference in value as of the alternate valuation date not due to mere lapse of time are allowed. Property "affected by mere lapse of time" includes patents, estates for the life of a person other than the decedent, remainders and reversions.[11]

¶ 109 Property to Be Valued

The property to be valued as of the alternate valuation date is the property included in the gross estate on the date of the decedent's death. Property interests remain "included property" for the purpose of valuing the gross estate under the alternate valuation method even though they change in form during the alternate valuation period by being actually received or disposed of by the estate.[12] Consequently, it is necessary in every case to determine what property comprised the gross estate at the decedent's death.

The alternate valuation election applies to *all* the property included in the gross estate on the date of a decedent's death. The election cannot be applied to only a portion of such property.[13] However, the IRS has ruled that a decedent's estate could elect both to value the decedent's assets on the alternate valuation date and to value the decedent's qualifying farm property under the special use valuation provisions of Code Sec. 2032A.[14] In addition, an estate electing both the alternate valuation date and special use valuation was required to use the alternate valuation date to determine the special use value of farmland owned by the decedent. For purposes of applying the limit on the aggregate reduction in the value of qualified real property, the alternate valuation date was also to be used to compute the difference between fair market value and special use value.[15]

¶ 110 Income After Death

Rents, dividends, and interest received during the six months following the decedent's death are not includible in a decedent's gross estate by reason of the executor's election to adopt the alternate valuation method. If the right to such income has accrued at the date of death, such income is includible.

Any part payment of the principal of interest-bearing obligations, such as notes and bonds, made between the date of death and the subsequent valuation date is includible in the gross estate at its value on the date of payment. Similarly, any advance payment of interest for a period after the subsequent valuation date made during the alternate valuation period that has the effect of reducing the value of the principal obligation as of the subsequent valuation date will be included in the gross

---

[11] Reg. § 20.2032-1(f).

[12] Reg. § 20.2032-1(d); *N.S. Johnston Est.*, CA-5, 86-1 USTC ¶ 13,655, 779 F2d 1123, cert. denied, 6-23-86.

[13] Reg. § 20.2032-1(b)(2).

[14] Rev. Rul. 83-31, 1983-1 CB 225.

[15] Rev. Rul. 88-89, 1988-2 CB 333.

estate at its value on the date of payment.[16] The principle applicable to interest paid in advance also applies to advance payments of rent.

Ordinary dividends out of earnings and profits declared to stockholders of record after the decedent's death are to be excluded from the alternate valuation method. However, if the effect of the declaration of dividends is that the decedent's shares of stock on the alternate valuation date do not reasonably represent the same property existing at the date of his death, such dividends are includible in determining the alternate valuation to the extent paid from earnings of the corporation prior to the date of decedent's death. For example, a stock dividend received during the alternate valuation period affects the value of the decedent's total shares so that, at the alternate valuation date, his total shares "do not reasonably represent the same property existing at the date of his death." The stock dividend is therefore includible in determining the alternate valuation of the gross estate.[17]

A mutual fund capital-gains dividend declared and paid between the time of death and the alternate valuation date is not includible in the gross estate of a decedent, even though the payment reduces the value of the shares outstanding (and the asset value on the alternate valuation date), because the value of a mutual fund share is equal to a pro rata share of the fund's net assets.[18]

¶ 112 Life Insurance Policies

With respect to policies of insurance on the life of a person other than the decedent, a distinction is made, for alternate valuation purposes, as to the cause of the value increase. When the value of a policy of insurance that had been owned by the decedent on the life of another increases following the date of the decedent's death, and such increase is attributable to the payment of premiums or to interest earned, the increase is excluded from the value of the insurance as determined under the alternate valuation method.[19] However, the appreciation in the value of insurance policies caused by the *death of the insured* during the alternate valuation period after the policy owner's death is not considered property earned or accrued during that period. Therefore, the entire value of the proceeds is includible in the deceased policy owner's gross estate.[20]

¶ 115 Return Information Under Alternate Valuation Method

If the alternate valuation election is exercised, the estate tax return must set forth:

(1) an itemized description of all property included in the gross estate on the date of the decedent's death, together with the value of each item as of that date;

(2) an itemized disclosure of all distributions, sales, exchanges, and other dispositions during the six-month period after the decedent's death, together with the dates of such dispositions; and

---

[16] Reg. § 20.2032-1(d).

[17] Rev. Rul. 58-576, 1958-2 CB 625.

[18] *R.W. Bartram*, DC Conn., 75-1 USTC ¶ 13,041. See also Rev. Rul. 76-234, 1976-1 CB 271.

[19] Rev. Rul. 55-379, 1955-1 CB 449.

[20] Rev. Rul. 63-52, 1963-1 CB 173.

(3) the value of each item of property on the appropriate alternate valuation date.[21]

This information must be reflected under the appropriate columns on *each applicable* property schedule of the return.[22]

Under the column headed "Description" on the applicable schedule, a brief statement explaining the status or disposition governing the alternate valuation date must be shown for each item. For example, the statement could be one of the following: "Not disposed of within six months following death," "Distributed," "Sold," or "Bond paid on maturity." A description of each item of principal and includible income must be separately entered in the same column. The applicable date for each separate entry must be shown in the adjacent column headed "Alternate valuation date."

The amount of principal and includible income must also be shown under the heading "Alternate value." In the case of any interest or estate having a value "affected by mere lapse of time," the value shown under the heading "Alternate value" must be the adjusted value. Under the heading "Value at date of death," the amount of the principal and includible income must again be entered separately.

Examples showing the use of Schedules A (Real Estate) and B (Stocks and Bonds) in Form 706 under the alternate valuation method appear at ¶ 278 and ¶ 335. For comparison purposes, examples illustrating the use of the same schedules for the same decedent where the alternate valuation method is not elected also appear at ¶ 278 and ¶ 335.

¶ 120 Supplemental Documents

Statements as to distributions, sales, exchanges, and other dispositions of a decedent's property within the six-month period after the decedent's death must be supported by evidence. If a court issues an order of distribution during that period, a certified copy of the order of distribution must be submitted with the return. The director of a service center or the district director may require the submission of any additional evidence deemed necessary.[23]

¶ 121 Income Tax Basis of Inherited Property

Generally, the income tax basis of property acquired from a decedent by bequest, devise, or inheritance is its fair market value on the date of the decedent's death. However, if the alternate valuation date has been elected, the basis is the fair market value of the property on the alternate valuation date.[24] If the property was sold, distributed, or disposed of within six months of death, its basis is the fair market value at the date of sale, distribution, or disposition. See ¶ 296 for rules on the basis of special use valuation property acquired from a decedent.

A special rule applies to appreciated property acquired by a decedent as a gift within one year of death if such property passes from the decedent

---

[21] Reg. § 20.6018-3(c)(6).

[22] Instructions for Form 706 (Rev. July 1998), p. 3.

[23] Reg. § 20.6018-4(c). Instructions for Form 706 indicate that only the District Director may require such additional evidence.

[24] Code Sec. 1014.

to the original donor or to the donor's spouse.[25] The basis of such property in the hands of the original donor or his or her spouse is its basis to the decedent immediately prior to death, rather than its fair market value on the date of death. This provision, effective for property acquired after August 13, 1981, by decedents dying after 1981, is intended to prevent individuals from transferring property in anticipation of a donee's death merely to obtain a tax-free step-up in basis upon receipt of the property from the donee's estate.

[25] Code Sec. 1014(e).

Gross Estate

Chapter 6

PROPERTY INTEREST AT TIME OF DEATH

¶ 150 What Is Included

All property owned in whole or in part by a citizen or a resident at the time of his or her death is included in the decedent's estate to the extent of the value of the decedent's interest in the property.[1] Foreign realty involves special rules discussed at ¶ 251.

In the estate tax return (Form 706), four schedules are concerned solely with property and interests in property that are owned by the decedent at the time of death and which pass to others either under the terms of the decedent's will or by intestacy. The four schedules are provided for the reporting of: (1) real estate (Schedule A); (2) stocks and bonds (Schedule B); (3) mortgages, notes, contracts to sell land, and cash (Schedule C); and (4) miscellaneous property (Schedule F).

¶ 155 Tests for Includibility

Although the types of property reported on each of the four schedules vary, the tests for determining whether particular property interests are includible in the gross estate are the same for all. Three questions arise in determining whether property should be reported in one of the above four schedules as part of the gross estate. They are:

(1) What types of property are includible in the decedent's estate?

(2) Did the decedent have an interest in such property sufficient to warrant inclusion in the decedent's gross estate of the value of the interest involved? and

(3) If the decedent had an interest, did the decedent still possess it at the time of death, and to what extent?

The answers to these questions, which determine the character of property interests held and transferred by a decedent, are determined under state laws. See ¶ 37 for further details as to the application of state laws.

Questions concerning valuation are peculiar to the specific type of property involved. They are discussed, therefore, in connection with the individual schedules dealing with the particular type of property. Similarly, the taxability of interests and transfers not governed by the general

[1] Code Sec. 2033; Reg. § 20.2033-1.

taxing statute, Code Sec. 2033, is also discussed in connection with the schedule on which such interests or transfers are reportable.

¶ 156 First Question: Type of Property

As to the first question regarding type of taxable property, there is little for the courts to decide. Usually, because the terms of Code Sec. 2033 are so general, it is conceded that all property of the decedent is taxable, unless a state law, the peculiar nature of the interest, or some other external factor suggests a means for excluding the property from the gross estate. Except where the question involves property subject to a power of appointment, it is almost a certainty that any property in which a decedent has a valuable interest at the time of death will be includible in the decedent's gross estate. Not even property set aside for the surviving spouse by state law escapes inclusion in the decedent's gross estate if it has been established that the decedent had an interest in the property.

Lump-sum Social Security death benefits payable to the decedent's surviving spouse or to any person equitably entitled to such payments are not includible in the gross estate of the decedent. Such amounts are not considered property of the decedent.[2] Uncashed Social Security benefit checks that are payable to the decedent and his or her surviving spouse are also not includible.[3] State and municipal bonds that are exempt from federal income taxation are includible in a decedent's gross estate[4] (see ¶ 329). An exclusion applies to Indian trust lands, royalties and funds held by the United States as trustee under the General Allotment Act of 1887, where the decedent dies before receiving a patent in fee simple.[5] Provisions of death tax treaties with other countries also have some exclusionary effects.

¶ 157 Second Question: Sufficient Interest

The issue involved in the second question, that of the sufficiency of the decedent's interest, has almost always been a question of property law. The cases turn largely on common-law and statutory rights. Most of the cases are decided by the application of property law to the facts.

If the decedent held the property in trust for someone else, it is generally not includible. If the property is in a decedent's name for convenience but the property belongs to another, it is not includible. Conversely, property held in the name of another for convenience but belonging to the decedent is includible in the decedent's gross estate.

¶ 158 Third Question: Possession at Death

The third question, regarding possession of property interest at time of death, presents most of the estate tax difficulties. This question is concerned basically with the duration of the decedent's interest and with interests that have begun to accrue or that have come into existence about the time of the decedent's death, but that have not yet come into the decedent's possession.

From the decisions involving this question certain general conclusions may be drawn. If the interest came into existence prior to the decedent's

---

[2] Rev. Rul. 67-277, 1967-2 CB 322; Rev. Rul. 55-87, 1955-1 CB 112.

[3] Rev. Rul. 75-145, 1975-1 CB 298.

[4] Rev. Rul. 81-63, 1981-1 CB 455.

[5] Rev. Rul. 69-164, 1969-1 CB 220.

death and was not defeated by death, its value at the time of death is includible in the gross estate. Thus, vested remainders are includible, but contingent remainders, defeated by the decedent's death, are not includible. Similarly, where the decedent has only a life interest under a transfer by another, nothing is left to tax at the time of the decedent's death.

If the property interest was accruing to the decedent at the time of death, and was enforceable by the decedent's estate, so much of it as had accrued at the time of death is includible in the decedent's gross estate. Therefore, accrued salary, commissions, and income are includible. But, where these items are not *required* to be paid into the decedent's estate, they are not includible, even though actually paid to the executor.

¶ 165 Community Property

Property in which a decedent had an interest at the time of death is includible in the decedent's gross estate for estate tax purposes to the extent of the value of the decedent's interest in such property. Laws in community property states, however, generally limit the extent of a person's interest in community property to one-half of the value of the property.[6]

The federal estate tax law recognizes these state limitations by purposely failing to provide a distinct, specific method of treating community property. This failure causes the application of the estate tax to be governed by state law. Consequently, only one-half of the value of each item of community property held by a decedent and the decedent's spouse may be included in the gross estate of the decedent. The IRS has ruled, in a National Office Technical Advice Memorandum, that this is true even though the decedent's estate actually received selected community assets with an aggregate date-of-death value equal to the decedent's portion of the total amount of community property.[7]

This limitation applies not only to property in which the decedent still had an interest at the time of death but also to life insurance purchased with community funds and to property which was the subject of certain lifetime transfers. However, one-half of the proceeds of life insurance policies purchased with community funds is not includible in the gross estate of the decedent if, under the facts of a particular case or the applicable state law, it can be shown that such policies were the separate property of another.[8]

With respect to estates of decedents dying before 1982, this limitation appeared to place community property in an especially favorable position; however, its effect was balanced by the applicable marital deduction rules. Prior to amendment by the Economic Recovery Tax Act of 1981 (P.L. 97-34), Code Sec. 2056 authorized a deduction from the gross estate for property passing to a surviving spouse up to a maximum of one-half of the value of a decedent's non-community property (less certain expenses). For

---

[6] See, for example, IRS Technical Advice Memorandum 9018002, 1-17-90, CCH IRS LETTER RULINGS REPORTS.

[7] IRS Technical Advice Memorandum 8505006, 10-19-84, CCH IRS LETTER RULINGS REPORTS.

[8] *A.M. Kroloff*, CA-9, 73-2 USTC ¶ 12,959, 487 F2d 334; *A.G. Kern*, CA-9, 74-1 USTC ¶ 12,979, 491 F2d 436; *V.F. Saia Est.*, 61 TC 515, CCH Dec. 32,428 (CA-5, appeal dismissed pursuant to stipulation, 1-27-75); *E.W. Marks, Jr., Est.*, 94 TC 720, CCH Dec. 46,594.

separate estates of community property residents, there was a minimum marital deduction of $250,000, subject to certain reductions (see ¶ 1005).[9]

A marital deduction unlimited in amount is available for estates of decedents dying after 1981. The rules limiting the marital deduction with respect to community property were eliminated in accordance with this change.[10]

¶ 170 Reciprocal Transfers

Reciprocal trusts receive special consideration. Under a reciprocal trust arrangement, each grantor (usually related to the other grantor) transfers property to a trust, at about the same time, and gives the other grantor the lifetime right to enjoy the property as beneficiary. The trust created for the beneficiary is includible in the beneficiary's gross estate when the trusts are found to be interrelated and leave the grantors in the same economic position they would have been in had they created the trusts and named themselves as beneficiaries.[11] In essence, inclusion will result when: (1) the two trusts are substantially identical in terms; (2) the trusts were created at about the same time under some sort of arrangement; and (3) each grantor gives the other grantor approximately the same economic rights.[12]

In at least one case (*B. Bischoff Est.*),[13] the reciprocal trust doctrine has been applied, even though the trust powers exchanged did not have substantial economic value. The existence of the crossed powers in *B. Bischoff Est.* was held sufficient to cause inclusion of the corpora of two trusts in the estates of a husband and wife, each of whom had created identical trusts for the grandchildren wherein each spouse named the other as trustee. Similarly, the value of stock that a decedent transferred to his wife to hold in custody for their children under a Gifts to Minors Act was includible in his gross estate under the reciprocal trust doctrine because his wife made identical transfers of stock to him to hold in custody for the children.[14] However, in one case, the Tax Court refused to apply the doctrine to reciprocal transfers and held that the value of stock transferred by a decedent's wife to a trust that she had created with the decedent as trustee was not includible in the decedent's gross estate even though he transferred the same amount of stock to a trust that he had created with his wife as trustee. Although the decedent granted a special power of appointment to his wife over the corpus of the trust he had created, he received no such power over the trust created by his wife; however, in all other respects the terms of the trusts were identical. In the court's view, the doctrine was inapplicable because the special power of appointment held by the decedent's wife put her in an economic position different from that of the decedent.[15]

---

[9] Code Sec. 2056(c)(1), prior to amendment by P.L. 97-34.

[10] Act Sec. 403(a)(1)(A), P.L. 97-34.

[11] *J.P. Grace Est.*, SCt, 69-1 USTC ¶ 12,609, 395 US 316.

[12] IRS Letter Ruling 8019041, 2-12-80, CCH IRS LETTER RULINGS REPORTS.

[13] *B. Bischoff Est.*, 69 TC 32, CCH Dec. 34,702.

[14] *Exchange Bank and Trust Co. of Florida, Exr.*, CA-FC, 82-2 USTC ¶ 13,505, 694 F2d 1261.

[15] *H. Levy Est.*, 46 TCM 910, CCH Dec. 40,323(M), TC Memo. 1983-453.

Chapter 7

DOWER AND CURTESY

¶ 200 Inclusion of Dower and Curtesy

The gross estate includes the value of dower, curtesy and all interests created by statute in lieu of dower or curtesy.[1] This is true even though the statutory interest may differ in character from dower or curtesy. Therefore, the full value of the property is required to be included, without deduction of the value of the interest of the surviving husband or wife, and without regard to the time when the right to such an interest arose.[2]

Arguments that dower and curtesy are not transfers by the decedent have been unsuccessful. The right of the surviving spouse to use or enjoy the property during the surviving spouse's lifetime becomes consummate by reason of the decedent's death, and this fact is sufficient support for applying a death tax.

¶ 205 Transfers for a Consideration

Transfers of property in which the decedent retains an interest, for consideration of money or money's worth, are included in the gross estate to the extent that the fair market value of the transferred property at the time of death exceeds the value of the consideration received in exchange by the decedent. The relinquishment of dower or curtesy, or a statutory estate created in lieu of dower or curtesy, is not considered the giving of consideration and may not be used in determining the reduction from the transferred property.[3] See ¶ 610 for further details.

---

[1] Code Sec. 2034.

[2] Reg. § 20.2034-1.

[3] Code Sec. 2043(b); Reg. § 20.2043-1.

Chapter 8

REAL ESTATE

¶ 250 Real Property

The value of all real property owned by a U.S. citizen on the date of death is includible in the decedent's gross estate under Code Sec. 2033. For this purpose, it is immaterial whether the decedent was a resident or a nonresident, or whether the property came into the possession and control of the executor or administrator or passed directly to the heirs or devisees. Real property includes certain types of loans classified as real property under local law, as well as mineral rights and royalties. Real estate owned by a decedent is reported on Schedule A (Real Estate) of Form 706, unless such property is owned by a sole proprietorship. In that case, the real estate should be reported on Form 706, Schedule F (Other Miscellaneous Property) (see ¶ 525). Schedule A does not have to be filed with the estate tax return if the decedent did not own reportable real estate.

¶ 251 Real Property Outside the United States

The value of interests in foreign real estate, regardless of when acquired, must be included in the gross estates of property owners. In addition, the value of foreign real property acquired by a decedent after January 31, 1962, is also includible unless it was acquired by *gift, devise, inheritance or survivorship* and the donor or prior decedent had acquired the interest in the foreign realty (or a power of appointment with respect to it) before February 1, 1962.

Capital additions or improvements to foreign real estate, to the extent they materially increase the value of the property and to the extent they are attributable to construction after January 31, 1962, must be treated in the same manner as real property acquired after that date.[1]

¶ 253 Qualified Conservation Easement Exclusion

The executor of the estate of a decedent dying after 1997 may elect to exclude from the gross estate up to 40 percent (the "applicable percentage") of the value of land that is subject to a qualified conservation easement. The amount that may be excluded from the gross estate is limited as follows: $100,000 in 1998; $200,000 in 1999; $300,000 in 2000; $400,000 in 2001; and $500,000 in 2002 or thereafter. In addition, the exclusion is reduced by the amount of any charitable deduction that was taken with respect to the land under Code Sec. 2055(f).[2]

---

[1] Reg. § 20.2031-1(c).

[2] Code Sec. 2031(c).

The election is made by filing Schedule U (Qualified Conservation Easement Exclusion) and claiming the exclusion on Form 706, Part 5, Line 11, and, once made, is irrevocable.[3]

- *Special use valuation property*

The granting of a conservation easement does not affect specially valued property under Code Sec. 2032A. Thus, the granting of such an easement is not treated as a disposition and does not trigger the additional estate tax. In addition, the existence of a qualified conservation easement does not prevent the property from subsequently qualifying for special use valuation.

- *Partnerships, corporations and trusts*

An interest in a partnership, corporation or trust will qualify for the qualified conservation easement exclusion provided that at least 30 percent of the entity is owned, directly or indirectly, by the decedent, as determined under the rules applicable to the qualified family-owned business deduction under Code Sec. 2057 (see ¶ 1150).[4]

¶ 255 Land Subject to a Qualified Conservation Easement

Land subject to a qualified conservation easement is land which, on the date of the decedent's death, is located (1) in or within 25 miles of a metropolitan area as defined by the Office of Management and Budget, (2) in or within 25 miles of a national park or wilderness area, unless the Secretary of the Treasury determines that such land is not under significant development pressure, or (3) in or within 10 miles of an Urban National Forest as designated by the Forest Service of the U.S. Department of Agriculture. In order to qualify for the exclusion, the land must have been owned by the decedent or a member of the decedent's family during the three-year period ending on the date of the decedent's death. Further, the land must be subject to a qualified conservation easement granted by the decedent or a member of the decedent's family. In addition, a post-mortem conservation easement may be placed on the property, provided the easement has been made no later than the date of the election.[5]

- *Members of the family*

The Code Sec. 2032A(e)(2) definition of "member of the family" applies. Thus, with respect to any decedent, a member of the family is (1) an ancestor of the decedent, (2) the spouse of the decedent, (3) a lineal descendant of the decedent, of the decedent's spouse, or of a parent of the decedent, or (4) the spouse of any individual described in (3).

- *Debt-financed property*

The exclusion does not apply to the extent that the land is debt-financed property. Thus, debt-financed property is eligible for the exclusion, only to the extent of the net equity in the property. Debt-financed property means property with respect to which there is an acquisition indebtedness on the date of the decedent's death. Acquisition indebtedness includes the unpaid amount of (1) indebtedness incurred by the donor in acquiring the property, (2) indebtedness incurred before the acquisition of

---

[3] Code Sec. 2031(c)(6).

[4] Code Sec. 2031(c)(10).

[5] Code Sec. 2031(c)(8)(A).

the property if such indebtedness would not have been incurred but for such acquisition, (3) indebtedness incurred after the acquisition of the property if such indebtedness would not have been incurred but for such acquisition and the incurrence of the indebtedness was reasonably foreseeable at the time of acquisition, and (4) the extension, renewal or refinancing of an acquisition indebtedness.[6]

¶ 257 Qualified Conservation Easement

A qualified conservation easement is a qualified conservation contribution, as defined in Code Sec. 170(h)(1), i.e, a contribution of a qualified real property interest to a qualified organization exclusively for conservation purposes.

A qualified real property interest means a restriction, granted in perpetuity, on the use that may be made of the real property. Conservation purposes are defined in Code Sec. 170(h)(4)(A) and include such things as the preservation of land areas for outdoor recreation or the education of the general public, the protection of natural habitat for fish, wildlife or plants, and the preservation of open space. However, for purposes of the qualified conservation easement exclusion, the preservation of an historically important land area or an historic structure does not qualify as a conservation purpose. In addition, a *de minimis* commercial recreational activity that is consistent with the conservation purpose, such as the granting of hunting and fishing licenses, will not cause the property to fail to qualify for the exclusion.[7]

¶ 259 Exclusion Amount

The exclusion amount is calculated based on the value of the property after the conservation easement has been placed on the property. However, the exclusion amount does not extend to the value of any development rights retained by the decedent or the donor. Development rights are defined as any rights retained to use the land for any commercial purpose that are not subordinate to and directly supportive of the land as a farm or for farming purposes within the meaning of Code Sec. 2032A(e)(5). However, if every person in being who has an interest in the land executes an agreement to extinguish permanently some or all of any development rights retained by the donor, on or before the date the estate tax return is due, the estate tax may be reduced accordingly. If the agreement is not implemented by the earlier of the date that is two years after the decedent's death or the date of the sale of the land, an additional tax is imposed in the amount of the estate tax that would have been due on the retained development rights subject to the agreement.[8]

- *Applicable percentage*

If the executor makes the election, there is excluded from the gross estate the lesser of the applicable percentage of the value of the land subject to the qualified conservation easement or the exclusion limitation. The applicable percentage means 40 percent reduced, but not below zero, by two percentage points for each percentage point (or fraction thereof) by which the value of the qualified conservation easement is less than 30

[6] Code Sec. 2031(c)(4).

[7] Code Sec. 2031(c)(8)(B).

[8] Code Sec. 2031(c)(5).

percent of the value of the land.[9] For this purpose, the value of the land is determined without regard to the value of the easement and reduced by the value of any retained development rights. As a result, if the value of the easement is 10 percent or less of the value of the land before the easement, less the value of any retained development rights, the applicable percentage will be zero.

"Development rights" means any right to use land that is subject to a qualified conservation easement for any commercial purpose that is not subordinate to and directly supportive of the use of the land as a farm for farming purposes (within the meaning of Code Sec. 2032A(e)(5)).[10]

> ***Example:*** Dolores Jones died owning land subject to a qualified conservation easement. She did not retain any development rights in the property. The fair market value of the real property on the date of her death was $500,000 without the conservation easement and $400,000 with the easement. Thus, the value of the conservation easement is $100,000, or 20 percent of the value of real property without the easement. The applicable percentage for the estate is 20 percent (40 percent reduced by twice the difference between 30 percent and 20 percent). Therefore, the exclusion amount is $80,000 (20 percent of $400,000).

¶ 262 Reporting Real Property on Return

In reporting real estate that is taxable under Code Sec. 2033, the property should be described and identified in a manner that permits the IRS to locate it readily for inspection and valuation. The area of each parcel of real estate should be given. If the parcel is improved, a short statement of the character of the improvements should be included. For urban property, the following information should also be given: street and number, ward, subdivision, block, and lot. For rural property, the description should include the township, range, and any landmarks.[11]

If an item of real estate is subject to a mortgage for which the decedent's estate is liable, the full value of such property must be reflected in the relevant value column of Schedule A (alternate or date-of-death value). In other words, if the indebtedness is enforceable against other property of the estate not subject to such mortgage, or if the decedent was personally liable for such mortgage, the full value of the property must be shown. The amount of the mortgage is to be noted in the "Description" column, and it should be deducted on Schedule K, which covers mortgages and liens.

If, however, the decedent's estate is not liable for the amount of the mortgage, only the value of the equity of redemption (or value of the property less the indebtedness) need be included in the "Value" column as part of the gross estate, and no deduction as a mortgage or lien for the indebtedness is allowable. Similarly, "points" that a decedent has agreed to pay to a mortgage lender are not includible in the value of the property for estate tax purposes unless the decedent's estate is liable for payment.[12]

---

[9] Code Sec. 2031(c)(2).

[10] Code Sec. 2031(c)(5)(D).

[11] Instructions for Schedule A, Form 706 (Rev. July 1998), p. 5.

[12] Rev. Rul. 80-319, 1980-2 CB 252.

Real property that the decedent has contracted to purchase should be listed in Schedule A. The full value of the property and not the equity must be reflected in the value column of the schedule. The unpaid portion of the purchase price should be deducted under Schedule K. If the land is subject to a valid contract to sell entered into by the decedent, the contract rather than the land is reportable. It is reportable on Schedule C (Mortgages, Notes, and Cash).

¶ 265 Dower and Curtesy

The value of dower and curtesy (or a statutory estate created in lieu thereof) is taxable (see ¶ 200). The extent of the decedent's interest in real property may not be reduced on account of such interest or on account of homestead or other exemptions in reporting real property on the return.

¶ 270 Valuation

The value of real property, each parcel being unique in the eyes of the law, can never be determined by a set formula. Each valuation must be fixed individually in accordance with the requirements and circumstances of the particular situation.

Expert testimony is desirable in most cases, not only to apply a local or general market situation to the piece of land involved, but often to provide the primary means of establishing value for purposes of the tax. Generally, expert testimony, market activity, local sales, rentals and recent mortgages are important in establishing value, if the same valuation can be obtained by the use of two or more of such factors. The local tax assessment values, or only one of the above factors, will frequently not carry sufficient weight to establish valuation contrary to that set by the IRS.

The value is determined as of the date of decedent's death unless the executor elects to use the alternate valuation date. Whatever the method of valuation employed, the method should be stated on the return. If based upon an appraisal, a copy of the appraisal, together with an explanation of the basis of the appraisal, should be attached to the return.

See ¶ 280 through ¶ 308 for special use valuation of real estate of a farm or other closely held business.

¶ 275 Community Property

If community property is involved, only one-half of the value of each item of community property is to be reported on the decedent's Form 706 (see ¶ 165), with an appropriate explanation. For example, the value of a decedent's one-half interest in a house and lot in Tucson, Arizona (valued at $200,000), would be reported as $100,000 on the date of death and the description would be followed by the following statement:

> (One-half only of value reported because the house and lot were held in community with the surviving spouse.)

Likewise, only one-half of the value of any rental income from the property would be listed.

¶ 278 Filled-In Schedule A

Schedule A must be filed only if the decedent owned real estate.

Example Where Alternate Valuation Is Not Adopted

The filled-in examples of Schedule A, Form 706 (Rev. July 1998), relate to the fact situation of a person who dies on January 1, 1998, with an estate tax return due within nine months (without extensions).

Form 706 (Rev. 7-98)

Estate of: James X. Diversey

SCHEDULE A — Real Estate

- *For jointly owned property that must be disclosed on Schedule E, see the instructions on the reverse side of Schedule E.*
- *Real estate that is part of a sole proprietorship should be shown on Schedule F.*
- *Real estate that is included in the gross estate under section 2035, 2036, 2037, or 2038 should be shown on Schedule G.*
- *Real estate that is included in the gross estate under section 2041 should be shown on Schedule H.*
- *If you elect section 2032A valuation, you must complete Schedule A and Schedule A-1.*

Item number	Description	Alternate valuation date	Alternate value	Value at date of death
1	House and lot, 121 Oleander Ave., Tampa, FL (Lot 8, Square 492). Rent of $5,400 due at the end of each quarter: Feb. 1, May 1, Aug. 1, and Nov. 1. Value based on appraisal (copy attached).			336,000
	Rent due on Item 1 for quarter ending Nov. 1, 1997 but not collected at date of death.			5,400
	Rent accrued on item 1 for Nov. and Dec. 1997 and collected on Feb. 1, 1998			3,600
2	House and lot, 402 Oceanview Dr., Tampa, FL. (Lot 18, Square 40). Rent of $1,900 payable monthly. Value based on appraisal (Copy attached).			388,000
	Rent on Item 2 for Dec. 1997, but not collected at date of death.			1,900
3	Unimproved lot, Elgin, IL (Township 41, Range 10). Value based on appraisal (Copy attached).			99,400
4	Unimproved lot, Schaumburg, IL (Township 57, Range 3). Value based on appraisal (Copy attached).			50,000
	Total from continuation schedules or additional sheets attached to this schedule			
	TOTAL. (Also enter on Part 5, Recapitulation, page 3, at item 1.)			884,300

(If more space is needed, attach the continuation schedule from the end of the package or additional sheets of the same size.)
(See the instructions.)

Schedule A — Page 4

Example Where Estate Qualified for and Elected Alternate Valuation

The amounts shown in the following Schedule are not entered in example of the Recapitulation at ¶ 1225, because the alternate valuation method was not elected by the estate of the hypothetical decedent, James X. Diversey.

Form 706 (Rev. 7-98)

Estate of: James X. Diversey

SCHEDULE A — Real Estate

- *For jointly owned property that must be disclosed on Schedule E, see the instructions on the reverse side of Schedule E.*
- *Real estate that is part of a sole proprietorship should be shown on Schedule F.*
- *Real estate that is included in the gross estate under section 2035, 2036, 2037, or 2038 should be shown on Schedule G.*
- *Real estate that is included in the gross estate under section 2041 should be shown on Schedule H.*
- *If you elect section 2032A valuation, you must complete Schedule A and Schedule A-1.*

Item number	Description	Alternate valuation date	Alternate value	Value at date of death
1	House and lot, 121 Oleander Ave., Tampa, FL (Lot 8, Square 492). Rent of $5,400 due at the end of each quarter: Feb. 1, May 1, Aug. 1, and Nov. 1. Value based on appraisal (Copy attached). Not disposed of within 6 months of death.	7-1-98	340,000	336,000
	Rent due on Item 1 for quarter ending Nov. 1, 1997 but not collected until Feb. 1, 1998.	2-1-98	5,400	5,400
	Rent accrued on Item 1 for Nov. and Dec. 1997 and collected on Feb. 1, 1998.	2-1-98	3,600	3,600
2	House and lot, 402 Oceanview Drive, Tampa, FL (Lot 18, Square 40). Rent of $1,900 paid monthly. Value based on appraisal (Copy attached). Property exchanged for farm on May 1,1998.	5-1-98	382,500	388,000
	Rent on Item 2 for Dec. 1997, but not collected until Feb.1, 1998.	2-1-98	1,900	1,900
3	Unimproved lot, Elgin,IL (Township 41, Range 10). Property sold on Mar.1,1998).	3-1-98	96,000	99,400
4	Unimproved lot, Schaumburg,IL (Township 57, Range 3). Property sold on April 15,1998.	4-15-98	48,900	50,000
	Total from continuation schedules or additional sheets attached to this schedule			
	TOTAL. (Also enter on Part 5, Recapitulation, page 3, at item 1.)		878,300	884,300

(If more space is needed, attach the continuation schedule from the end of the package or additional sheets of the same size.)
(See the instructions.)

Schedule A — Page 4

¶ 279 Schedule U

Sample Qualified Conservation Easement Exclusion

Reproduced below is Schedule U, Form 706 (Rev. July 1998). The Schedule is not filled in because the James X. Diversey estate did not own any land subject to a qualified conservation easement.

Form 706 (Rev. 7-98)

Estate of:

SCHEDULE U. — Qualified Conservation Easement Exclusion

Part 1. — Election

Note: *The executor is deemed to have made the election under section 2031(c)(6) if her or she files Schedule U and excludes any qualifying conservation easements from the gross estate.*

Part 2. — General Qualifications

1 Describe the land subject to the qualified conservation easement (see separate instructions) ____________

2 Did the decedent or a member of the decedent's family own the land described above during the 3-year period ending on the date of the decedent's death? . . . . . ☐ Yes ☐ No

3 The land described above is located (check whichever applies) (see separate instructions)

☐ In or within 25 miles of an area which, on the date of the decedent's death, is a metropolitan area.

☐ In or within 25 miles of an area which, on the date of the decedent's death, is a national park or wilderness area.

☐ In or within 10 miles of an area which, on the date of the decedent's death, is an Urban National Forest.

4 Describe the conservation easement with regard to which the exclusion is being claimed (see instructions).

Part 3. — Computation of Exclusion

5	Estate tax value of the land subject to the qualified conservation easement (see separate instructions)			5	
6	Date if death value of any easements granted prior to decedent's death and included on line 11 below (see instructions)	6			
7	Add lines 5 and 6	7			
8	Value of retained development rights on the land (see instructions)	8			
9	Subtract line 8 from line 7	9			
10	Multiply line 9 by 30% (.30)	10			
11	Value of qualified conservation easement for which the exclusion is being claimed (see instructions) **Note:** *If line 11 is less than line 10, continue with line 12. If line 11 is equal to or more than line 10, skip lines 12 through 14, enter ".40" on line 15, and complete the schedule.*	11			
12	Divide line 11 by line 9. Figure to 3 decimal places (e.g., .123) *If line 12 is equal to or less than .100, stop here; the estate does not qualify for the conservation easement exclusion.*	12			
13	Subtract line 12 from .300. Enter the answer in hundredths by rounding any thousandths up to the next higher hundredth (i.e., .030 = .03; but .031 = .04)	13			
14	Multiply line 13 by 2	14			
15	Subtract line 14 from .40	15			
16	Deduction under section 2055(f) for the conservation easement (see separate instructions)	16			
17	Amount of indebtedness on the land (see separate instructions)	17			
18	Total reductions in value (add lines 8, 16, and 17)			18	
19	Net value of land (subtract line 18 from line 5)			19	
20	Multiply line 19 by line 15			20	
21	Enter the smaller of line 20 or $100,000. Also enter this amount on item 11 Part 5, Recapitulation, Page 3			21	

Schedule U — Page 42

Chapter 9

FARMS AND CLOSELY HELD BUSINESSES

¶ 280 Special Use Valuation

Real property used as a family farm or in a closely held business may be valued on the basis of its "current" use rather than on the basis of "highest and best" use.

The maximum amount by which the value of qualifying real property can be reduced under the special use valuation provision is $750,000 for estates of decedents dying after 1982.[1] If the estate of a decedent dying in 1998 consists of qualifying real property valued at $1,200,000 on the basis of its "highest and best" use, and the property's value under the special use valuation provision is $400,000, the gross estate will be reduced by only $750,000 (although the difference in value is $800,000, the maximum reduction allowed is $750,000). For decedents dying in 1999 and later years, the $750,000 limitation will be indexed for inflation (for 1999, the indexed amount is $760,000).[2]

The IRS has ruled that an estate electing both the alternate valuation date and special use valuation was required to use the alternate valuation date to determine the special use value of farmland owned by the decedent at death. Additionally, in applying the applicable limit on the aggregate reduction in the value of qualified real property as a result of valuing the property for a qualified use, the difference between the fair market value and the special use value was to be determined as of the alternate valuation date.[3]

Real property may qualify for special use valuation if it is located in the United States and if it is devoted to either (1) use as a farm for farming purposes or (2) use in a closely held trade or business other than farming. In either case, there must be a trade or business use.

---

[1] Code Sec. 2032A(a); Reg. § 20.2032A-8.

[2] Code Sec. 2032A(a)(3); Rev. Proc. 98-61, IRB 1998-52, 18.

[3] Rev. Rul. 88-89, 1988-2 CB 333.

¶ 281 Qualifying Conditions

In order to qualify for the special use valuation procedure, the following conditions must be satisfied:

(1) the decedent must have been a resident or a citizen of the United States and the property must be located in the United States;

(2) the property must pass to a qualified heir (see ¶ 282) and a requisite agreement must be filed (see ¶ 289);

(3) the property must be devoted to a qualified use (see ¶ 291) on the date of the decedent's death;

(4) the decedent or a member of the decedent's family must have owned the qualifying property and have materially participated in the operation of the farm or other business for the required period (see ¶ 291 through ¶ 292);

(5) the adjusted value of the real and personal property used in the farm or closely held business must comprise at least 50 percent of the adjusted value of the decedent's gross estate; and

(6) at least 25 percent of the adjusted value of the gross estate must be qualified real property.[4]

For purposes of the 50-percent and 25-percent tests, the special use value is not used in determining the value of property included in the gross estate. With respect to requirement (5), the value of any transfer made within three years of death (see ¶ 555) is includible in the decedent's gross estate for the limited purpose of determining the estate's qualification for special use valuation.[5]

The IRS has allowed an estate to combine the adjusted values of personal property used for farming, farm property and a building used in a business other than farming in order to meet the 50-percent test for special use valuation. The personal property was used in connection with the qualifying farm property, and the real estate was otherwise eligible for special use valuation.[6]

The IRS distinguished its result from a Tax Court decision in which a decedent's estate was not entitled to elect special use valuation for farmland owned by the decedent because personal property owned and used by him in a business unrelated to farming could not be aggregated with the farmland to meet the 50-percent requirement. In the court's view, Congress enacted the special use valuation rules in order to lessen the estate tax burden that might result from valuation of real property used in the family farm or business at its highest and best use rather than at its value to the farm or business. Because the rules were designed to protect family farms and businesses, the court reasoned that personal property should be considered in meeting the percentage requirements only if it is used in the family business together with the real property that is to be specially valued.[7]

---

[4] Code Sec. 2032A(a) and Code Sec. 2032A(b).

[5] Code Sec. 2035(d)(3). See IRS Letter Ruling 8514032, 1-8-85, IRS LETTER RULINGS REPORTS; Rev. Rul. 87-122, 1987-2 CB 221.

[6] Rev. Rul. 85-168, 1985-2 CB 197.

[7] *W.H. Geiger Est.*, 80 TC 484, CCH Dec. 39,936.

¶ 282 Qualified Heir

The term "qualified heir" (to whom special use valuation property must pass) refers to a member of the decedent's family who acquired the real property from the decedent or to whom the property has passed.[8] Where there is a further disposition of any interest in the property from a qualified heir to a member of the heir's family, the family member is to be treated as a qualified heir.[9] However, the IRS has ruled that the post-1981 disposition of specially valued farm property by a qualified heir to his cousin within 10 years of the decedent's death resulted in imposition of the recapture tax (see ¶ 284). For purposes of this exception, the cousin was not considered a member of the qualified heir's family.[10]

For estates of decedents dying after 1981, an individual's family members are: (1) the individual's ancestors, (2) the individual's spouse, (3) lineal descendants of the individual, of the individual's spouse, or of the individual's parents, and (4) the spouse of any descendant mentioned in (3).[11] In interpreting this provision, the Tax Court has held that the nephew of a decedent's predeceased spouse was not a qualified heir because he was not a lineal descendant of the decedent's parents but, rather, was a lineal descendant of the decedent's husband's parents.[12]

With respect to estates of decedents dying before 1982, an individual's family members are: (1) the individual's ancestors or lineal descendants, (2) lineal descendants of the individual's grandparents, (3) the individual's spouse, and (4) spouses of any descendants mentioned in (1) and (2).[13]

For purposes of the preceding discussion, a legally adopted child of an individual is treated as the individual's child by blood.

All interests in the property to be specially valued must pass to qualified heirs. Thus, if successive interests are created in the property such as, for example, a life estate followed by a remainder interest, qualified heirs must receive all interests.[14] The IRS has ruled that an estate could elect special use valuation for farm property in which a qualified heir received a life estate under the decedent's will, even though the heir also received the power to appoint the remainder interest in the property to a nonqualified heir. The election was allowed because the heir executed a qualified disclaimer (see ¶ 2009) of the power of appointment, thus causing the remainder interest to vest in another qualified heir.[15] However, the IRS has also disallowed special use valuation elections because not all successive interests in otherwise qualifying real property passed to qualified heirs.[16]

In 1986, two Tax Court cases held that Reg. § 20.2032A-8(a)(2) is invalid to the extent that *all* successive interests are required to go to qualified heirs.[17] In the *Davis* case, the court held that *de minimis* successive interests that do not go to qualified heirs will not prevent

---

[8] Code Sec. 2032A(e)(1).

[9] Code Sec. 2032A(e)(1).

[10] Rev. Rul. 89-22, 1989-1 CB 276.

[11] Code Sec. 2032A(e)(2).

[12] *I.M. Cone Est.*, 60 TCM 137, CCH Dec. 46,722(M), TC Memo. 1990-359.

[13] Code Sec. 2032A(e)(2), prior to amendment by P.L. 97-34.

[14] Reg. § 20.2032A-8(a)(2).

[15] Rev. Rul. 82-140, 1982-2 CB 208.

[16] IRS Letter Rulings 8337015, 6-7-83, and 8346006, 7-29-83, CCH IRS LETTER RULINGS REPORTS.

[17] See *D. Davis IV, Est.*, 86 TC 1156, CCH Dec. 43,105, and *C.M. Clinard Est.*, 86 TC 1180, CCH Dec. 43,106.

special use valuation for otherwise qualified property. Similarly, the *Clinard* case limited Reg. § 20.2032A-8(a)(2) by holding that special use valuation is permitted where a qualified heir possesses a life estate with a special power of appointment. In other words, the fact that a qualified heir could direct that an unqualified heir receive a remainder interest would not preclude the use of special use valuation for the interest in question. Both cases recognize that where unqualified heirs are in a position to receive an interest, special use valuation will not be precluded if those interests are exceedingly remote. This principle has also been followed by the U.S. Court of Appeals for the Seventh Circuit in affirming a decision of a U.S. district court in Illinois which allowed special use valuation despite a remote possibility that the contingent remainder interest in the property could pass to nonqualified heirs.[18]

¶ 283 Valuation Methods

Two valuation methods are used for farms or closely held businesses that qualify for the special use valuation.

- *Farm Method*

If a farm qualifies for special use valuation, it is valued on the basis of a formula of cash rentals, real estate taxes and effective interest rates. Under the formula, the value of a farm is determined as follows:

(1) the average annual gross cash rental for comparable land, used for farming purposes and located in the same region as such farm, less the average annual state and local real estate taxes for such comparable land, divided by

(2) the average annual effective interest rate for all new Federal Land Bank loans.

Each average annual computation described in the formula is to be made on the basis of the five most recent calendar years ending before the date of the decedent's death.[19] "Net-share" rentals (i.e., crop-share rentals) may be used in the formula valuation method if cash rentals for comparable land in the same locality are not available. The amount of a net share is equal to the value of the produce received by the lessor of the comparable land on which such produce is grown minus the cash operation expenses (other than real property taxes) of growing the produce paid by the lessor.[20]

- *Multiple Factor Method for Closely Held Businesses*

If a closely held business or a farm that does not use the farm method described above qualifies for special use valuation, its valuation generally is determined by the following factors:

(1) capitalization of income;

(2) capitalization of fair rental values;

(3) assessed land values in a state which provides a differential or use value assessment law;

---

[18] *L. Smoot, Exr.*, CA-7, 90-1 USTC ¶ 60,002, aff'g DC Ill., 88-1 USTC ¶ 13,748.

[19] Code Sec. 2032A(e)(7)(A).

[20] Code Sec. 2032A(e)(7)(B).

(4) comparable sales of other farm or closely held business land where nonagricultural use is not a significant factor in the sales price; and

(5) any other factor which fairly values the farm or closely held business value of the property.[21]

However, in applying special use valuation to farm property the IRS has ruled that a fiduciary could not select only one of the factors enumerated in Code Sec. 2032A(e)(8) as the exclusive basis of valuation. Each factor that was relevant to the respective valuation was to be applied although, depending on the circumstances, certain factors could be weighed more heavily than others.[22]

● *Change in Method*

The IRS has ruled that an estate that had made a valid special use valuation election with respect to farmland included in the decedent's gross estate could amend the election in order to substitute the farm method of valuation for the multiple factor method that was originally applied. The executor valued the decedent's farm under the multiple factor method because he was unable to obtain the information (rentals for comparable farmland) necessary for computing value under the formula method until after the return was filed. Although the special use valuation election is irrevocable, the IRS did not bar the estate from changing the method of valuation once the election was made. In addition, the IRS noted that a change from the multiple factor method is allowable even where information regarding comparable farmland was available but the executor nevertheless originally applied the multiple factor method.[23]

¶ 284 Recapture of Taxes

Tax benefits realized by an estate that elects special use valuation may be fully or partially recaptured if the qualified real property passes out of the family or ceases to be used as a farm or closely held business within a "recapture period" measured from the decedent's death (but before the death of the qualified heir). For estates of decedents dying before 1982, the recapture period was 15 years from the date of death; [24] however, this period is shortened to 10 years from the date of death for estates of decedents dying after 1981.[25] Tax liability incurred as a result of such a disposition or cessation of qualified use is to be reported on Form 706-A (see ¶ 81).

A second disposition of the property or cessation will not trigger a second tax on the same qualified interest.[26] Thus, where a qualified heir ceases to use the property for its qualified purpose and later sells the property within the recapture period, a recapture tax will be imposed as to the first event that triggers recapture (cessation of use), but not as to the second event (sale of the property).

The amount of the tax benefit potentially subject to recapture is the excess of the estate tax liability that would have been incurred had the

---

[21] Code Sec. 2032A(e)(8).

[22] Rev. Rul. 89-30, 1989-1 CB 274.

[23] Rev. Rul. 83-115, 1983-2 CB 155.

[24] Code Sec. 2032A(c)(1), prior to amendment by P.L. 97-34.

[25] Code Sec. 2032A(c)(1).

[26] Code Sec. 2032A(c)(3).

special use valuation procedure not been used over the actual estate tax liability based on the special use valuation. In other words, the maximum additional or "recapture" tax is the amount that the special use valuation has saved the estate. This is called the "adjusted tax difference."

The tax will be less than the maximum if the excess of the fair market value of the interest or the proceeds of an arm's-length sale over the value of the interest determined with the special use valuation is less than the "adjusted tax difference." It will also be less than the maximum if the recapture event occurs more than 10, but less than 15, years after the decedent's death (but prior to the death of the qualified heir) in the case of a decedent dying before 1982.[27] In such case, the tax is reduced by one-sixtieth for every full month by which the recapture event occurs more than 120 months after the decedent's death. Thus, if the event occurs 12 full years (144 months) after the decedent's death, the tax is reduced by 40 percent (one-sixtieth times 24). This partial recapture provision was repealed, effective for estates of decedents dying after 1981.

The IRS National Office has ruled that the fair market value of farmland sold in 1982 to an individual who was not a qualified heir could be adjusted in determining the amount of recapture tax, even though the statute of limitations had run for assessing a deficiency with respect to the decedent's estate tax. In the view of the IRS, the imposition of the recapture tax was distinct from the levy of the estate tax upon the decedent's death and, accordingly, the IRS determined that it was not bound by the facts relating to the property's value as stated on the estate tax return or by the time limitations on assessing an estate tax deficiency. However, the difference between the special use value determined on the estate tax return and the fair market value as adjusted by the IRS in computing the recapture tax could not exceed $500,000. This was true because the decedent died in 1977 when $500,000 was the maximum amount by which the fair market value of qualifying property could be reduced pursuant to a special use valuation election.[28]

● *Qualified Use*

As noted above, the tax recapture provision applies if the property ceases to be used for the qualified use (see ¶ 291) under which the property qualified for the special use valuation. However, a qualified heir may begin qualified use of the property at any time within two years of the decedent's death without triggering recapture tax; the recapture period does not begin until the qualified use begins.[29] For tax recapture purposes, a qualified use may cease even if the property continues to be used for its qualifying purpose. A cessation occurs if within the recapture period, during any eight-year period ending after the decedent's death and before the qualified heir's death, there have been periods aggregating more than three years during which there has been no "material participation" (see ¶ 292) by the decedent or family member in the case of property held by the decedent. In the case of property held by a qualified heir, like periods of no such participation by the qualified heir or a family member will result in a cessation of qualified use.[30] However, "active management" (see

---

[27] Code Sec. 2032A(c)(3), prior to repeal by P.L. 97-34.

[28] IRS Technical Advice Memorandum 8403001, 9-9-83, CCH IRS LETTER RULINGS REPORTS.

[29] Code Sec. 2032A(c)(7).

[30] Code Sec. 2032A(c)(6). See also IRS Letter Ruling 8939031, 6-30-89, CCH IRS LETTER RULINGS REPORTS.

¶ 293) will constitute material participation in the case of "eligible qualified heirs." Such heirs are the decedent's spouse or a qualified heir who is under the age of 21, a full-time student, or disabled.[31] This "active management" provision is effective for estates of decedents dying after 1981.

The decedent's surviving spouse and lineal descendants may rent special use property to a family member on a cash rental basis without triggering the recapture tax.[32] Similarly, a family trust's lease of farmland to a family farming corporation for fixed cash payments did not trigger the special use valuation recapture tax for a decedent's children, who were trust beneficiaries. They necessarily retained the financial risks of farming, as owners of the farmland and of the family farming corporation.[33] The rule allowing net cash rental to a family member was extended to lineal descendants by the Taxpayer Relief Act of 1997 (P.L. 105-34) and applies retroactively to leases executed after December 31, 1976. Although the retroactive effect of the Act contemplates that qualified heirs who paid recapture taxes due to a net cash lease of the property to a family member may obtain a refund of such taxes, no guidance is provided by the Act and none has been provided by the IRS as of the date of publication.

The additional tax on recaptured property is due on the day that is six months after the recapture event (premature disposition of the property or cessation of qualified use).[34] As noted at ¶ 288, each heir remains expressly liable for the recapture tax with respect to his or her interest in the property.

The three-year statute of limitations for assessing the recapture tax does not begin to run until the IRS is notified of the disposition or cessation.[35] In one case decided prior to the enactment of the Taxpayer Relief Act of 1997, a qualified heir's cash rental of qualified farm property to her brother constituted a cessation of qualified use resulting in liability for additional estate tax. The heir's alleged participation in the farming operations with her brother was insufficient to change the substance of the arrangement between the parties from that of a landlord-tenant relationship. However, the disclosure of the cash rental arrangement in response to a questionnaire provided by the IRS served as notification to the IRS of the cessation of qualified use and commenced the Code Sec. 2032A(f) three-year statute of limitations on assessment and collection. Accordingly, notices of deficiency that were issued more than three years after the IRS received notification of cessation of qualified use precluded the IRS from assessing and collecting the additional tax.[36]

¶ 285 Pecuniary Bequests and Purchases

Normally, property qualifying for special use valuation is acquired by a qualified heir from a decedent by bequest, devise, or inheritance. However, a special use valuation election also may be allowed where property is acquired by two other methods.

(1) A distribution of qualified property by an estate or trust in satisfaction of a pecuniary bequest, and

---

[31] Code Sec. 2032A(c)(7).

[32] Code Sec. 2032A(b)(5).

[33] *M. Minter*, CA-8, 94-1 USTC ¶ 60,160, 19 F3d 426, rev'g unpublished DC N.D. decision.

[34] Code Sec. 2032A(c)(4).

[35] Code Sec. 2032A(f).

[36] *M.E. Stovall*, 101 TC 140, CCH Dec. 49,183.

(2) The purchase of qualified property by a qualified heir from a decedent's estate.[37]

An estate recognizes gain upon such a distribution or sale only to the extent of the post-death appreciation of the property. This appreciation is equal to the difference between the property's fair market value on the date of the distribution or sale and its estate tax value as determined *without* regard to Code Sec. 2032A. In computing the gain on distribution or sale, therefore, the estate tax value will be the property's fair market value on the date of the decedent's death or the alternate valuation date.[38]

Specially valued property that is transferred to a qualified heir in satisfaction of a pecuniary bequest or that is purchased from the decedent's estate by a qualified heir is deemed to meet the holding period requirement for long-term capital gain treatment upon a subsequent sale of the property to another qualified heir.[39]

¶ 286 Involuntary Conversions and Tax-Free Exchanges

No recapture tax (see ¶ 284) will be imposed where farm or closely held business property that has been specially valued is involuntarily converted. However, the proceeds from the involuntary conversion must be reinvested in real property that is used for the same qualified use as was the involuntarily converted property.[40]

No recapture tax will be imposed on an exchange of specially valued real property to the extent that the exchange qualifies as tax free under Code Sec. 1031 so long as the property received is employed in the same qualified use as was the property exchanged. Real property received in an exchange that is employed in the qualified use is known as "qualified exchange property." If both qualified exchange property and other property are received, the recapture tax is reduced by an amount bearing the same ratio to the recapture tax as the fair market value of the qualified exchange property bears to the fair market value of the property that was exchanged [41] (see ¶ 80 through ¶ 81).

The special use valuation provision permits the aggregation ("tacking") of ownership, qualified use, and material participation periods in the case of replacement property acquired pursuant to like-kind exchanges under Code Sec. 1031 or involuntary conversions under Code Sec. 1033.[42] This tacking is available only if the replacement property is employed in the same qualified use as was the original property, and only for that portion of the replacement property equal in value to the original property.

¶ 287 Special Lien on Qualified Property

A government lien is imposed on all qualified property for which an election to use the special use valuation procedure has been made. The lien applies to the extent of the adjusted tax difference attributable to the qualified real property. The lien arises at the time an election is filed and is to continue until the tax benefit is recaptured, until the time limit for

[37] Code Sec. 2032A(e)(9); Rev. Proc. 82-9, 1982-1 CB 413.

[38] Code Sec. 1040(a).

[39] Code Sec. 1223(12).

[40] Code Sec. 2032A(h)(1)(A).

[41] Code Sec. 2032A(i)(1).

[42] Code Sec. 2032A(e)(14)(A).

collecting the potential liability ceases (that is, the qualified heir dies or the recapture period (see ¶ 284) lapses) or until it can be established to the satisfaction of the IRS that no further liability will arise. In addition, if qualified replacement property is purchased following an involuntary conversion of special use valuation property (see ¶ 286), the lien that was applicable to the original special use valuation property attaches to the qualified replacement property. Similarly, if specially valued property is exchanged for qualified exchange property (see ¶ 286), the lien attaches to the qualified exchange property.[43]

The IRS can issue a certificate of subordination of the government's lien that arose on any part of the qualified property for which the special use valuation election was made if it determines that the interests of the United States are adequately protected thereafter.[44]

¶ 288 Personal Liability for Recapture Tax

A qualified heir is personally liable for the portion of recapture tax that is imposed with respect to his or her interest in specially valued property. A qualified heir's liability is extinguished in two instances: (1) where the recapture period lapses, and (2) where the heir dies without converting or disposing of the property.[45] Additionally, a sale or other disposition by one qualified heir to another of specially valued property is not considered a recapture event and the second heir is treated as if he or she received the property from the decedent, rather than from the first heir. The second heir then becomes liable for the recapture tax and the other qualified heir (the seller) is released of further recapture tax liability.[46] Even if the second heir has paid full consideration for the property, the special estate tax lien (see ¶ 287) remains on the property.

- *Discharge from Liability*

An heir may be discharged from personal liability for future potential recapture taxes imposed on the heir's interest in the qualified property by furnishing a bond for the maximum additional tax that could be imposed on the interest.[47]

The qualified heir must make written application to the IRS for determination of the maximum additional tax that could be imposed. The IRS is then required to notify the heir within one year of the date of the application of such maximum amount.

¶ 289 Election and Agreement

An election to use special use valuation is to be made on Form 706 (Rev. July 1998) by checking the box marked "Yes" on line 2 of part 3, the "Elections by the Executor" section on page 2 of the return (see ¶ 1225). With respect to the estate of a decedent dying after 1981, such an election may be made on a late-filed return so long as it is the first return filed.[48]

In order to make a valid election, an estate must file Schedule A-1 of Form 706 and attach all of the required statements and appraisals.[49]

---

[43] Code Sec. 6324B; Reg. § 20.6324B-1.

[44] Code Sec. 6325(d)(3).

[45] Code Sec. 2032A(c)(1).

[46] IRS Letter Ruling 8115085, 1-16-81, CCH IRS LETTER RULINGS REPORTS.

[47] Code Sec. 2032A(c)(5) and Code Sec. 2032A(c)(11).

[48] Code Sec. 2032A(d)(1).

[49] Instructions for Form 706 (Rev. July 1998), p. 3.

Schedule A-1 contains the Notice of Election and the Agreement to Special Valuation Under Section 2032A. The Notice of Election provides information such as the fair market value of the property to be specially valued, its special use valuation, and the method used in computing special use valuation.[50]

An estate may elect special use valuation for less than all of the qualified property included in the gross estate. However, property for which an election is made must have an adjusted value of at least 25 percent of the adjusted value of the gross estate.[51]

● *Agreement*

An estate executor making the election must also complete and file with the return Schedule A-1, Part 3 (Agreement to Special Valuation Under Section 2032A) signed by each person having an interest in the qualified real property for which the election is made.[52] It is immaterial whether such person is in possession of the property. In the case of a qualified heir, the agreement expresses consent to personal liability in the event of recapture of additional estate tax due to premature cessation of qualified use or disposition of the property. Signatories other than qualified heirs must express consent to collection of any such additional estate tax from the qualified property.

The IRS National Office has ruled that farmland owned by a decedent in his capacity as shareholder of a corporation could not be valued under the special use valuation provisions because the agreement filed with the election did not contain a signature that bound the corporation. The decedent had bequeathed his estate assets, including stock of the corporation, to his children. Rather than signing the agreement as representatives of the corporation, the children, who were also corporate officers, had signed it in their individual capacities.[53]

Similarly, the IRS ruled that a decedent's interest in farmland that was to pass to a testamentary trust created for the benefit of her two minor grandchildren was not eligible for special use valuation because the beneficiaries did not consent to be personally liable for the recapture tax. Although the recapture agreement was signed by the decedent's daughter in her capacity as trustee, she did not have the right to execute a lien in favor of the government and lacked the capacity to legally bind the two minor beneficiaries of the trust. Thus, the agreement failed to include the required signatures of qualified heirs.[54]

The Tax Court has held, however, that Reg. § 20.2032A-8(c)(2) is invalid insofar as it requires that individuals having tenancy in common interests in property that is subject to a special use election sign the required recapture agreement.[55] The court noted that, although all persons having an interest in property to be specially valued must sign the

[50] Reg. § 20.2032A-8(a)(3).

[51] Reg. § 20.2032A-8(a)(2). But see *M.S. Miller, Exr.*, DC Ill., 88-1 USTC ¶ 13,757, holding Reg. § 20.2032A-8(a)(2) invalid insofar as it imposed an additional substantive requirement to the statutory rules governing qualification for special use valuation.

[52] Reg. § 20.2032A-8(c). Also see *R.H. Lucas, Pers. Rep.*, CA-11, 96-2 USTC ¶ 60,247, barring an estate from electing under Code Sec. 2032A because the estate failed to file the recapture agreement.

[53] IRS Technical Advice Memorandum 8602007, 9-7-85, CCH IRS LETTER RULINGS REPORTS.

[54] IRS Technical Advice Memorandum 8802005, 9-29-87, CCH IRS LETTER RULINGS REPORTS.

[55] *M.F. Pullin Est.*, 84 TC 789, CCH Dec. 42,060; *W.C. Bettenhausen Est.*, 51 TCM 488, CCH Dec. 42,887(M), TC Memo. 1986-73.

recapture agreement, the surviving tenants in the instant case did not have such an interest since only the decedent's tenancy in common interests were includible in his gross estate and subject to the election.

● *Protective Election*

Where it is not certain that property meets the requirements for special use valuation, an estate may make a protective election to specially value qualified real property, contingent upon the property values as finally determined meeting the requirements of Code Sec. 2032A.[56] This election is made by filing a notice of protective election with a timely estate tax return. If it is finally determined that the property qualifies for special use valuation, the estate must file an additional notice of election within 60 days of such determination. The IRS National Office has ruled that an estate could make a protective election with respect to a decedent's farmland even though, at the time the estate tax return was filed, the estate met the percentage requirements for special use valuation.[57] However, in another National Office ruling, the IRS has pointed out that neither Code Sec. 2032A nor the regulations thereunder sanction the use of a protective election as a substitute for a timely special use valuation election.[58]

● *Cure of Technically Defective Elections*

For elections made prior to August 6, 1997, if a timely special use valuation election was made and the estate tax return, as filed, evidenced substantial compliance with the requirements of the regulations relating to special use valuation, the executor of the decedent's estate had a reasonable period of time (not exceeding 90 days) in which to cure any technical defects or flaws in the form of the election that would prevent it from being valid otherwise.[59] The 90-day period commenced following the IRS's notification to the estate that a defect existed. Examples of technical defects or flaws in the election include the failure to include all required information in the notice of election and the failure to include the signature of all persons having an interest in the qualifying property.

The Taxpayer Relief Act of 1997 (P.L. 105-34) expanded the ability of the executor to correct omissions. For elections made after August 5, 1997, the executor must file a timely notice of election and a recapture agreement, but need not have substantially complied with the regulations in order to be entitled to submit missing information or signatures.[60] Upon filing, if the election or agreement fails to include all the required information or signatures, the executor may cure the omission by providing the missing information or signatures within 90 day after receiving written notice from the IRS.

Under prior law,[61] an election of special use valuation was considered timely even if made on a return filed late, so long as the return was the first return filed. Corrected notices and agreements pertaining to the special use valuation election could be filed late if two conditions were met: (1) the estate must have filed those documents to the extent requested by

---

[56] Reg. § 20.2032A-8(b).

[57] IRS Technical Advice Memorandum 8407005, 11-8-83, CCH IRS LETTER RULINGS REPORTS.

[58] IRS Technical Advice Memorandum 9013001, date not given, CCH IRS LETTER RULINGS REPORTS.

[59] Code Sec. 2032A(d)(3), prior to amendment by P.L. 105-34.

[60] Code Sec. 2032A(d)(3), as amended by P.L. 105-34.

[61] Act Sec. 1421(a) and (b), P.L. 99-514.

Form 706 and (2) upon the initial filing, it must have indicated the election of the special use valuation. With respect to this issue, the U.S. Court of Appeals for the Seventh Circuit has held that an estate was entitled to special use valuation, even though no recapture agreement was filed with the federal estate tax return. In this case substantially all the information required for making the election was provided with the estate tax return, and the executed agreement was filed four months later.[62] However, the U.S. Court of Appeals for the Seventh Circuit later ruled that an estate's failure to submit a recapture agreement with the estate tax return could not be corrected subsequent to the due date of the return by operation of the substantial compliance doctrine because relief under that doctrine is limited to correcting minor errors in a recapture agreement. In addition, the application of Section 1421 of the Tax Reform Act of 1986 was not available to the estate because it had not raised that issue before the Tax Court or the appellate court.[63]

The U.S. Court of Appeals for the Fifth Circuit has held that where an election and recapture agreement were signed by the executrix of an estate but not by any of the beneficiaries of a testamentary trust, the lack of the beneficiaries' signatures could be perfected on an amended recapture agreement filed within 90 days of the IRS's notification to the estate's representative of the defect.[64] Similarly, the U.S. Court of Appeals for the Tenth Circuit has held that an executor's failure to attach to the decedent's federal estate tax return a previously obtained appraisal of the fair market value of certain property for which a special use value election was made was not an incurable defect.[65]

In contrast, however, the U.S. Court of Appeals for the Eighth Circuit has held that the omission of the signatures of the decedent's children (who received an interest as a result of the surviving spouse's disclaimer) from a recapture agreement did not constitute substantial compliance with the requirements for special use valuation.[66] This was also found to be the case, according to the Tax Court, where the estate failed to attach any notice of election or a signed recapture agreement to a decedent's estate tax return.[67]

¶ 290 Qualified Real Property

Real property may be eligible for special use valuation if it is located in the United States and used as a farm for farming purposes or in a trade or business other than farming. Additionally, the property must satisfy the qualified use (see ¶ 291) and material participation (see ¶ 292) requirements.

A "farm," for purposes of the special valuation procedure, includes stock, dairy, poultry, fruit, fur-bearing animal, and truck farms, plantations, ranches, nurseries, greenhouses or other similar structures used primarily for the raising of agricultural or horticultural commodities, and orchards and woodlands.[68] The term "farming purposes" includes cultivation of the soil, raising agricultural or horticultural commodities and

---

[62] *L. Prussner, Exrx.*, CA-7, 90-1 USTC ¶ 60,007.

[63] *C. Grimes Est.*, CA-7, 91-2 USTC ¶ 60,078.

[64] *M. McAlpine, Jr., Est.*, CA-5, 92-2 USTC ¶ 60,109, 968 F2d 459.

[65] *L. Doherty Est.*, CA-10, 93-1 USTC ¶ 60,125, 982 F2d 450.

[66] *G.L. McDonald*, CA-8, 88-2 USTC ¶ 13,778, cert. denied, 4-3-89.

[67] *G. Merwin Est.*, 95 TC 168, CCH Dec. 46,817.

[68] Code Sec. 2032A(e)(4).

preparing such commodities for market, as well as the planting, cultivating, caring for, cutting down and preparing for market of trees.[69]

Qualified property includes residences, and related improvements located on the qualifying real property and occupied on a regular basis by the owner, his lessee or employees for occupational or maintenance purposes. Also considered qualified real property are roads, buildings, and other structures and improvements functionally related to the qualified use of the property.[70]

- *Qualified Woodlands*

An executor may elect special use valuation for standing timber as part of "qualified woodlands," which are identifiable areas of real property (for which business records are normally maintained) used for growing and harvesting timber.[71] A recapture tax will be imposed when the qualified heir severs or otherwise disposes of the timber during the recapture period.

¶ 291 Qualified Use Requirement

Real property for which a special use valuation election is made must be devoted to a qualified farm or business use for five of the eight years prior to the decedent's death. This requirement is satisfied if either the decedent or a member of the decedent's family is utilizing the property for the qualified use.[72] The IRS National Office has interpreted the qualified use requirement to mean that the decedent or a family member must bear some of the financial risk associated with an active farm or other business.[73] In another example of this concept, the U.S. Court of Appeals for the Seventh Circuit has held that a cash lease of farm property to a nonrelative did not constitute a qualified use.[74] However, the Taxpayer Relief Act of 1997 (P.L. 105-34) provides that a qualified heir may enter into a cash lease of farm property with a member of the heir's family without triggering recapture. The provision is retroactive to apply to all leases entered into after December 31, 1976.

¶ 292 Determination of "Material Participation"

The decedent or a member of the decedent's family must materially participate in the farm or business operations for a certain period of time during the decedent's life in order to qualify the property for special use valuation. With respect to estates of decedents dying before 1982, material participation must have continued for five of the eight years prior to the decedent's death.[75] In the case of decedents dying after 1981, the eight-year period is measured from the earliest of (1) the date of the decedent's death, (2) the date that the decedent became disabled, or (3) the date that the decedent retired.[76] Whether there has been "material participation" by the decedent or family members in a farm or other closely held business is determined in a manner similar to that set forth in the income tax provisions relating to whether income is subject to self-employment

---

[69] Code Sec. 2032A(e)(5).

[70] Reg. § 20.2032A-3(b)(2).

[71] Code Sec. 2032A(e)(13).

[72] Code Sec. 2032A(b)(1)(A)(i).

[73] IRS Technical Advice Memorandum 8201016, 9-22-81, CCH IRS LETTER RULINGS REPORTS.

[74] *T.S. Heffley, Exrx. (O. Heffley Est.)*, CA-7, 89-2 USTC ¶ 13,812; *M.L. Brockman, Admr. (S. Donahoe Est.)*, CA-7, 90-1 USTC ¶ 60,026.

[75] Code Sec. 2032A(b)(1)(C).

[76] Code Sec. 2032A(b)(4).

taxes.[77] However, regulations adopted under Code Sec. 2032A [78] provide additional factors to be considered in making this determination for estate tax purposes. The standards for material participation under Code Sec. 469, governing passive activity losses, are similar to the material participation standards under Code Sec. 2032A. Consequently, the estate of a decedent who reported her losses from a ranch as passive activity losses, rather than as losses from an active trade or business, could not elect special use valuation for ranch property because the decedent had not materially participated in ranching during her lifetime.[79]

● *Employment and Management*

Although no single factor determines whether a decedent or family member has materially participated in a farm or closely held business, physical work and participation in management decisions are the principal factors to be considered. The involvement of such an individual on a full-time basis, or to any lesser extent necessary to allow the individual to manage fully the farm or business, is considered material participation. Payment of self-employment taxes on income derived from the farm or closely held business is also an indicator of material participation. Although payment of such taxes is not conclusive evidence of material participation, if no such taxes have been paid material participation is presumed not to have occurred unless the executor demonstrates otherwise and explains why no self-employment tax was paid. In addition, all such tax determined to be due must be paid before an effective special use valuation election may be made. For this purpose, "tax determined to be due" does not include tax assessments that are barred by the statute of limitations on collection or assessment.[80]

At a minimum, an individual must regularly advise or consult with the other managing party with respect to the operation of the business, and participate in making a substantial number of management decisions.[81] According to the regulations, passive collection of rents, salaries, draws, dividends, or other income does not constitute material participation, nor does the mere advancement of capital and review of crop plans or other business proposals.[82] Thus, for farmland to qualify for special use valuation when all or a portion of it is leased to nonqualified heirs, a decedent's financial stake or other involvement must be more than that of a landlord passively collecting a fixed rental from an unrelated tenant.[83]

The U.S. Court of Appeals for the Seventh Circuit has held that farmland rented pursuant to a cash lease containing a rent adjustment clause providing for a 20-percent downward adjustment of the annual rent if gross income from farm production fell below a specified amount qualified for special use valuation. The appellate court stated that the adjustment clause allocated a portion of the risk of poor yield or low crop prices to the decedent and, therefore, the income derived from the lease of the

---

[77] Code Sec. 2032A(e)(6), referring to Code Sec. 1402(a)(1).

[78] Reg. § 20.2032A-3.

[79] IRS Technical Advice Memorandum 9428002, 3-29-94, CCH IRS LETTER RULINGS REPORTS.

[80] Reg. § 20.2032A-3(e) and Rev. Rul. 83-32, 1983-1 CB 226.

[81] Reg. § 20.2032A-3(e). See also *C.E. Coon Est.*, 81 TC 602, CCH Dec. 40,478.

[82] Reg. § 20.2032-3(a).

[83] *H.F. Sherrod Est.*, 82 TC 523, CCH Dec. 41,084, rev'd, CA-11, 85-2 USTC ¶ 13,644, 774 F2d 1057, cert. denied, 10-6-86. See *M.J. Martin et al.*, 84 TC 620, CCH Dec. 41,998, aff'd, CA-7, 86-1 USTC ¶ 13,659, 783 F2d 81.

farmland was substantially based upon production. However, the court noted that, as the owner of only moderately productive farmland, the decedent was subject to a higher degree of risk than would be the owner of very productive farmland because it was more likely that the rent adjustment clause would be triggered.[84]

- *Financial Risk*

Another factor considered in the determination of material participation is the extent to which an individual has assumed financial responsibility for the farm or other business. This includes the advancement of funds, and, in the case of a farm, the provision of a substantial portion of machinery, livestock, and implements used in production.

- *Residence*

For farms, hotels, or apartment buildings operated as a trade or business, an individual's maintenance of the individual's principal place of residence on the premises is a factor to be considered in determining material participation.

- *Other Considerations*

The activities of at least one family member must amount to material participation at a given time because the activities of a number of family members cannot be considered in the aggregate as material participation. Finally, if nonfamily members participate in the farm or other business, part-time activities by the decedent or family members must be pursuant to a provable oral or written arrangement providing for actual participation by the decedent or family members. For example, the hiring of a professional farm manager will not prevent satisfaction of the material participation requirement if the decedent or family member materially participates under the terms of such an arrangement.[85]

¶ 293 Active Management by Surviving Spouse

A special rule applies to liberalize the material participation requirement with respect to a surviving spouse who receives qualifying property from a decedent in whose estate the property was eligible for special use valuation (whether or not such valuation was actually elected). "Active management" by the surviving spouse will satisfy the material participation requirement for purposes of electing special use valuation in the surviving spouse's gross estate. The Internal Revenue Code defines active management as the making of management decisions of a business (other than daily operation decisions).[86] Combinations of activities such as inspection of crops, review of crop plans, and marketing decisions constitute active management in farming operations.[87]

The "tacking" of active management by a surviving spouse with material participation by a retired or disabled spouse is allowed in order to qualify the property for special use valuation in the spouse's estate, effective for estates of decedents dying after 1981.[88] This provision is

---

[84] *M. Schuneman*, CA-7, 86-1 USTC ¶ 13,660, 783 F2d 694, rev'g DC Ill., 83-2 USTC ¶ 13,540, 570 FSupp 1327.

[85] Reg. § 20.2032A-3(e).

[86] Code Sec. 2032A(b)(5) and Code Sec. 2032A(e)(12).

[87] *General Explanation of the Economic Recovery Tax Act of 1981*, Staff of the Joint Committee on Taxation, p. 246.

[88] Code Sec. 2032A(b)(5).

applicable only if the spouse died within eight years of the retired or disabled spouse, according to the House Committee Report on the Technical Corrections Act of 1982 (P.L. 97-448).

¶ 294 Qualifying Property Passing in Trust

The rules for the special valuation procedure apply to qualifying property that passes in trust. However, future interests in trust property will not qualify for the special use valuation. Trust property will be considered to have passed from the decedent to a qualified heir only to the extent that the qualified heir has a present interest in that trust property. Real property otherwise qualifying for special use valuation passing to a trust may be specially valued even if the trustee has the discretionary power to fix the amounts receivable by any individual beneficiary, so long as all potential beneficiaries are qualified heirs.[89] If the decedent created successive interests in the trust property that is to be specially valued, all of these interests must be received by qualified heirs (see ¶ 282). This provision is generally retroactive to estates of decedents dying after 1976.

¶ 295 Community Property

Community-owned property may be valued under the special valuation rules. For purposes of determining whether community-owned real property meets the two percentage tests necessary to qualify real property for special use valuation (see ¶ 281), the entire value of the property must be taken into account.[90] This ensures equal treatment of community and individually owned property under the special valuation rules.

¶ 296 Basis of Special Use Valuation Property

The basis of specially valued property in the hands of the qualified heir is its value as determined under the special use valuation provisions.[91] In the case of a pecuniary bequest or purchase (see ¶ 285), the basis of the property to the qualified heir is the estate's basis in the property immediately before the distribution or sale (generally, the property's special use value) plus the amount of post-death appreciation recognized as gain by the estate.[92]

● *Basis Increase on Recapture*

A qualified heir may make an irrevocable election to increase the income tax basis of special use valuation property to its fair market value on the date of the decedent's death (or on the alternate valuation date, if the estate so elected) if recapture tax is paid.[93]

---

[89] Code Sec. 2032A(g).

[90] Code Sec. 2032A(e)(10); Rev. Rul. 83-96, 1983-2 CB 156.

[91] Code Sec. 1014(a)(3).

[92] Code Sec. 1040(c).

[93] Code Sec. 1016(c).

¶ 308 Schedule A-1

Reproduced below is Schedule A-1, Form 706 (Rev. July 1998), and the Checklist for Section 2032A Election. The schedule is not filled in because the James X. Diversey estate did not elect special use valuation.

Form 706 (Rev. 7-98)

Checklist for Section 2032A Election. — *If you are going to make the special use valuation election on Schedule A-1, please use this checklist to ensure that you are providing everything necessary to make a valid election.*

To have a valid special use valuation election under section 2032A, you must file, in addition to the Federal estate tax return, **(a)** a notice of election (Schedule A-1, Part 2), and **(b)** a fully executed agreement (Schedule A-1, Part 3). You must include certain information in the notice of election. To ensure that the notice of election includes all of the information required for a valid election, use the following checklist. The checklist is for your use only. Do not file it with the return.

1. Does the notice of election include the decedent's name and social security number as they appear on the estate tax return?

2. Does the notice of election include the relevant qualified use of the property to be specially valued?

3. Does the notice of election describe the items of real property shown on the estate tax return that are to be specially valued and identify the property by the Form 706 schedule and item number?

4. Does the notice of election include the fair market value of the real property to be specially valued and also include its value based on the qualified use (determined without the adjustments provided in section 2032A(b)(3)(B))?

5. Does the notice of election include the adjusted value (as defined in section 2032A(b)(3)(B)) of **(a)** all real property that both passes from the decedent and is used in a qualified use, without regard to whether it is to be specially valued, and **(b)** all real property to be specially valued?

6. Does the notice of election include **(a)** the items of personal property shown on the estate tax return that pass from the decedent to a qualified heir and that are used in qualified use and **(b)** the total value of such personal property adjusted under section 2032A(b)(3)(B)?

7. Does the notice of election include the adjusted value of the gross estate? (See section 2032A(b)(3)(A).)

8. Does the notice of election include the method used to determine the special use value?

9. Does the notice of election include copies of written appraisals of the fair market value of the real property?

10. Does the notice of election include a statement that the decedent and/or a member of his or her family has owned all of the specially valued property for at least 5 years of the 8 years immediately preceding the date of the decedent's death?

11. Does the notice of election include a statement as to whether there were any periods during the 8-year period preceding the decedent's date of death during which the decedent or a member of his or her family **(a)** did not own the property to be specially valued, **(b)** use it in a qualified use, or **(c)** materially participate in the operation of the farm or other business? (See section 2032A(e)(6).)

12. Does the notice of election include, for each item of specially valued property, the name of every person taking an interest in that item of specially valued property and the following information about each such person: **(a)** the person's address, **(b)** the person's taxpayer identification number, **(c)** the person's relationship to the decedent, and **(d)** the value of the property interest passing to that person based on both fair market value and qualified use?

13. Does the notice of election include affidavits describing the activities constituting material participation and the identity of the material participants?

14. Does the notice of election include a legal description of each item of specially valued property?

(In the case of an election made for qualified woodlands, the information included in the notice of election must include the reason for entitlement to the woodlands election.)

Any election made under section 2032A will not be valid unless a properly executed agreement (Schedule A-1, Part 3) is filed with the estate tax return. To ensure that the agreement satisfies the requirements for a valid election, use the following checklist.

1. Has the agreement been signed by each and every qualified heir having an interest in the property being specially valued?

2. Has every qualified heir expressed consent to personal liability under section 2032A(c) in the event of an early disposition or early cessation of qualified use?

3. Is the agreement that is actually signed by the qualified heirs in a form that is binding on all of the qualified heirs having an interest in the specially valued property?

4. Does the agreement designate an agent to act for the parties to the agreement in all dealings with the IRS on matters arising under section 2032A?

5. Has the agreement been signed by the designated agent and does it give the address of the agent?

Page 7

Form 706 (Rev. 7-99)

Estate of:	Decedent's Social Security Number

SCHEDULE A-1 — Section 2032A Valuation

Part 1. — Type of Election (Before making an election, see the checklist on page 7.):

☐ **Protective election (Regulations section 20.2032A-8(b)). — Complete Part 2, line 1, and column A of lines 3 and 4. (See instructions.)**

☐ **Regular election. — Complete all of Part 2 (including line 11, if applicable) and Part 3. (See instructions.)**

Before completing Schedule A-1, see the checklist on page 7 for the information and documents that must be included to make a valid election.

The election is not valid unless the agreement (i.e., Part 3. — Agreement to Special Valuation Under Section 2032A) —

- Is signed by each and every qualified heir with an interest in the specially valued property, and
- Is attached to this return when it is filed.

Part 2. — Notice of Election (Regulations section 20.2032A-8(a)(3))

Note: *All real property entered on lines 2 and 3 must also be entered on Schedules A, E, F, G, or H, as applicable.*

1 Qualified use — check one ▶ ☐ Farm used for farming, or
▶ ☐ Trade or business other than farming

2 Real property used in a qualified use, passing to qualified heirs, and to be specially valued on this Form 706.

A Schedule and item number from Form 706	B Full value (without section 2032A(b)(3)(B) adjustment)	C Adjusted value (with section 2032A(b)(3)(B) adjustment)	D Value based on qualified use (without section 2032A(b)(3)(B) adjustment)
Totals			

Attach a legal description of all property listed on line 2.
Attach copies of appraisals showing the column B values for all property listed on line 2.

3 Real property used in a qualified use, passing to qualified heirs, but not specially valued on this Form 706.

A Schedule and item number from Form 706	B Full value (without section 2032A(b)(3)(B) adjustment)	C Adjusted value (with section 2032A(b)(3)(B) adjustment)	D Value based on qualified use (without section 2032A(b)(3)(B) adjustment)
Totals			

If you checked "Regular election," you must attach copies of appraisals showing the column B values for all property listed on line 3.

(continued on next page)

Schedule A-1 — Page 8

Form 706 (Rev. 7-98)

4 Personal property used in a qualified use and passing to qualified heirs.

A Schedule and item number from Form 706	B Adjusted value (with section 2032A(b)(3)(B) adjustment)	A (continued) Schedule and item number from Form 706	B (continued) Adjusted value (with section 2032A(b)(3)(B) adjustment)
		"Subtotal" from Col. B, below left	
Subtotal		Total adjusted value	

5 Enter the value of the total gross estate as adjusted under section 2032A(b)(3)(A). ▶

6 Attach a description of the method used to determine the special value based on qualified use.

7 Did the decedent and/or a member of his or her family own all property listed on line 2 for at least 5 of the 8 years immediately preceding the date of the decedent's death? ☐ Yes ☐ No

8 Were there any periods during the 8-year period preceding the date of the decedent's death during which the decedent or a member of his or her family:

	Yes	No
a Did not own the property listed on line 2 above?		
b Did not use the property listed on line 2 above in a qualified use?		
c Did not materially participate in the operation of the farm or other business within the meaning of section 2032A(e)(6)?		

If "Yes" to any of the above, you must attach a statement listing the periods. If applicable, describe whether the exceptions of sections 2032A(b)(4) or (5) are met.

9 Attach affidavits describing the activities constituting material participation and the identity and relationship to the decedent of the material participants.

10 Persons holding interests. Enter the requested information for each party who received any interest in the specially valued property. **(Each of the qualified heirs receiving an interest in the property must sign the agreement, and the agreement must be filed with this return.)**

	Name	Address
A		
B		
C		
D		
E		
F		
G		
H		

	Identifying number	Relationship to decedent	Fair market value	Special use value
A				
B				
C				
D				
E				
F				
G				
H				

You must attach a computation of the GST tax savings attributable to direct skips for each person listed above who is a skip person. (See instructions.)

11 **Woodlands election. —** Check here ▶ ☐ if you wish to make a woodlands election as described in section 2032A(e)(13). Enter the Schedule and item numbers from Form 706 of the property for which you are making this election ▶

You must attach a statement explaining why you are entitled to make this election. The IRS may issue regulations that require more information to substantiate this election. You will be notified by the IRS if you must supply further information.

Schedule A-1 — Page 9

Form 706 (7-98)

Part 3. — Agreement to Special Valuation Under Section 2032A

Estate of:	Date of Death	Decedent's Social Security Number

There cannot be a valid election unless:

- The agreement is executed by each and every one of the qualified heirs, and
- The agreement is included with the estate tax return when the estate tax return is filed.

We (list all qualified heirs and other persons having an interest in the property required to sign this agreement)

____

____,

being all the qualified heirs and ____

____,

being all other parties having interests in the property which is qualified real property and which is valued under section 2032A of the Internal Revenue Code, do hereby approve of the election made by____,

Executor/Administrator of the estate of ____,

pursuant to section 2032A to value said property on the basis of the qualified use to which the property is devoted and do hereby enter into this agreement pursuant to section 2032A(d).

The undersigned agree and consent to the application of subsection (c) of section 2032A of the Code with respect to all the property described on line 2 of Part 2 of Schedule A-1 of Form 706, attached to this agreement. More specifically, the undersigned heirs expressly agree and consent to personal liability under subsection (c) of 2032A for the additional estate and GST taxes imposed by that subsection with respect to their respective interests in the above-described property in the event of certain early dispositions of the property or early cessation of the qualified use of the property. It is understood that if a qualified heir disposes of any interest in qualified real property to any member of his or her family, such member may thereafter be treated as the qualified heir with respect to such interest upon filing a Form 706-A and a new agreement.

The undersigned interested parties who are not qualified heirs consent to the collection of any additional estate and GST taxes imposed under section 2032A(c) of the Code from the specially valued property.

If there is a disposition of any interest which passes or has passed to him or her or if there is a cessation of the qualified use of any specially valued property which passes or passed to him or her, each of the undersigned heirs agrees to file a Form 706-A, United States Additional Estate Tax Return, and pay any additional estate and GST taxes due within 6 months of the disposition or cessation.

It is understood by all interested parties that this agreement is a condition precedent to the election of special use valuation under section 2032A of the Code and must be executed by every interested party even though that person mat not have received the estate (or GST) tax benefits or be in possession of such property.

Each of the undersigned understands that by making this election, a lien will be created and recorded pursuant to section 6324B of the Code on the property referred to in this agreement for the adjusted tax differences with respect to the estate as defined in section 2032A(c)(2)(C).

As the interested parties, the undersigned designate the following individual as their agent for all dealings with the Internal Revenue Service concerning the continued qualification of the specially valued property under section 2032A of the Code and on all issues regarding the special lien under section 6324B. The agent is authorized to act for the parties with respect to all dealings with the Service on matters affecting the qualified real property described earlier. This authority includes the following:

- To receive confidential information on all matters relating to continued qualification under section 2032A of the specially valued real property and on all matters relating to the special lien arising under section 6324B.
- To furnish the Service with any requested information concerning the property.
- To notify the Service of any disposition or cessation of qualified use of any part of the property.
- To receive, but not to endorse and collect, checks in payment of any refund of Internal Revenue taxes, penalties, or interest.
- To execute waivers (including offers of waivers) of restrictions on assessment or collection of deficiencies in tax and waivers of notice of disallowance of a claim for credit or refund.
- To execute closing agreements under section 7121.

(continued on next page)

Schedule A-1 — Page 10

Form 706 (Rev. 7-98)

Part 3. — Agreement to Special Valuation Under Section 2032A *(Continued)*

Estate of:	Date of Death	Decedent's Social Security Number

• Other acts (specify) ▶ ______________________

By signing this agreement, the agent agrees to provide the Service with any requested information concerning this property and to notify the Service of any disposition or cessation of the qualified use of any part of this property.

Name of Agent	Signature	Address

The property to which this agreement relates is listed in Form 706, United States Estate (and Generation-Skipping Transfer) Tax Return, and in the Notice of Election, along with its fair market value according to section 2031 of the Code and its special use value according to section 2032A. The name, address, social security number, and interest (including the value) of each of the undersigned in this property are as set forth in the attached Notice of Election.

IN WITNESS WHEREOF, the undersigned have hereunto set their hands at ______________________ ,

this __________ day of ______________________ .

SIGNATURES OF EACH OF THE QUALIFIED HEIRS:

Signature of qualified heir	Signature of qualified heir
Signature of qualified heir	Signature of qualified heir
Signature of qualified heir	Signature of qualified heir
Signature of qualified heir	Signature of qualified heir
Signature of qualified heir	Signature of qualified heir
Signature of qualified heir	Signature of qualified heir

____
Signatures of other interested parties

____
Signatures of other interested parties

Schedule A-1 — Page 11

Chapter 10

STOCKS AND BONDS

¶ 310 Inclusion of Stocks and Bonds

Stocks and bonds owned by a decedent at the date of death are includible in the decedent's gross estate under Code Sec. 2033. They are listed on Schedule B of Form 706, which does not have to be filed if the decedent did not own stocks or bonds.

¶ 311 Dividends and Interest

Dividends and interest on stocks and bonds are included in the gross estate along with the securities on which they are paid. They are usually reflected separately in the same schedule used for reporting stocks and bonds.

Dividends payable to the decedent or to the decedent's estate because, on or before the date of death, the decedent was a shareholder of record must be included in the gross estate and listed on the return as separate items.[1] If dividends have merely been declared and are payable to stockholders of record on a date after the decedent's death, they are not includible in the gross estate.[2] However, they are undoubtedly reflected in the value of the stock.

On the other hand, if the stock is traded on an exchange and the stock is selling "ex-dividend" on the date of the decedent's death, the amount of the dividend must be added to the ex-dividend stock price quotation in fixing the value of the stock.[3] It should not be reported as a separate item in the return schedule. Similarly, if the stock is not traded on an exchange, the dividends must be reported when the record date for determining to whom the dividends are to be paid has passed.

Interest on bonds is includible in the bond owner's gross estate if it has accrued at the owner's date of death.[4] In the case of certain government bonds, however, interest cannot accrue between interest payment dates. With respect to these government bonds, no interest should be

---

[1] Reg. § 20.2033-1(b).

[2] Rev. Rul. 54-399, 1954-2 CB 279.

[3] Reg. § 20.2031-2(i).

[4] Reg. § 20.2033-1(b).

included for the period between the last interest payment date and the date of death.

¶313 Reporting Stocks and Bonds on Return

A decedent's stocks and bonds are to be reported on Schedule B of the estate tax return. The description of the stock should indicate: (1) the number of shares, (2) whether the stock is common or preferred, (3) the issue, (4) the par value, (5) the price per share, and (6) the stock CUSIP number, if available. The CUSIP number is a nine-digit number assigned to traded securities by the American Banking Association. If the stocks are listed on a stock exchange, the exact name of the corporation, and the principal exchange upon which the stock is sold, should be included in the description. If the stock is not listed on an exchange, the description should include the company's principal business office.

A description of bonds should include: (1) quantity, (2) denomination, (3) name of the obligor, (4) kind of bond, (5) date of maturity, (6) rate of interest payable, (7) interest due dates, and (8) the bond CUSIP number, if available. The exchange upon which the bond is listed should be given. If the bond is not listed on an exchange, the principal business office of the company must be supplied.

¶315 Stocks and Bonds Subject to Foreign Death Duties

If an estate, inheritance, legacy or succession tax has been paid to a foreign country on any stocks or bonds included in the gross estate, the stocks and bonds subjected to the foreign death tax should be grouped separately on the schedule with a heading "Subjected to Foreign Death Taxes." [5]

¶318 Valuation

Stocks and bonds included in the gross estate are to be reported at their value on the date of death or on an alternate valuation date (generally, six months after death) if the estate representative so elects.

When the alternate valuation method is elected, the selling price of any securities sold during the six-month period will control their valuation, if the sale is an arm's-length transaction.[6] In reporting securities under the alternate valuation method, their value at the date of death, as well as that on the alternate date, should be shown on the return.

If the alternate valuation method has been elected, stock includible in the gross estate and selling "ex-dividend" must be valued at its "ex-dividend" quoted selling price as of the alternate valuation date, increased by the amount of dividends declared during the alternate valuation period and payable to stockholders of record after the alternate valuation date.[7] Although the dividends themselves are not includible in the gross estate of a decedent in such case, the value of such stock on the alternate valuation date includes the value of the right to the declared dividends.[8]

---

[5] See Instructions for Form 706 (Rev. July 1998), p. 8.

[6] Rev. Rul. 70-512, 1970-2 CB 192.

[7] Rev. Rul. 60-124, 1960-1 CB 368.

[8] *C.D. Fleming Est.*, 33 TCM 1414, CCH Dec. 32,873(M), TC Memo. 1974-307.

¶ 319 Separate Appraisal of Tangible and Intangible Assets

If the value of stocks and bonds is determined by the value of the underlying assets, and these assets are both tangible and intangible ones which do not permit a separate appraisal, no general rule is applicable for valuing such assets. Each case will vary and the value of such assets must be determined upon the factors present in that particular case.[9]

¶ 320 Restricted Stock

Certain shares of unregistered stock are "restricted" under federal securities law and may not be sold to the general public but may only be sold to certain types of investors and only in limited amounts. Because of these restrictions, such stock is typically discounted when valued for estate tax purposes. In determining the amount of the discount, the following factors are relevant:

(1) the earnings, net assets, and net sales of the corporation;

(2) the resale provisions found in the restriction agreements;

(3) the relative negotiating strengths of the buyer and the seller; and

(4) the market experience of freely traded securities of the same class as the restricted securities.

All relevant facts and circumstances bearing on the value of the restricted stock must be considered in arriving at the estate tax value of the stock.[10]

The IRS may contend that no discount should be allowed because the corporation could register the stock and, thus, remove the restrictions on its sale. Whether the corporation would register the stock must be resolved on the facts of each case.[11]

¶ 321 Selling Prices

The estate tax value of stocks and bonds is the fair market value per share or bond on the applicable valuation date. If there is a market for stocks or bonds on a stock exchange or in an over-the-counter market, through a broker or otherwise, the mean between the highest and lowest quoted selling prices on the valuation date is the fair market value of each share or bond.

If there were no sales on the valuation date, but there were sales on trading dates within a reasonable period both before and after the valuation date, the fair market value is determined by: (1) taking the mean between the highest and lowest sales on the nearest trading date before and nearest trading date after the valuation date, (2) prorating the difference between such mean prices to the valuation date, and (3) adding or subtracting, as the case may be, the prorated portion of the difference to

---

[9] Rev. Rul. 65-193, 1965-2 CB 370.

[10] Rev. Rul. 77-287, 1977-2 CB 319, amplifying Rev. Rul. 59-60, 1959-1 CB 237. See also *E.O. Sullivan Est.*, 45 TCM 1199, CCH Dec. 40,015(M), TC Memo. 1983-185, and *C. McClatchy Est.*, CA-9, 98-2 USTC ¶ 60,315, rev'g TC, 106 TC 206, CCH Dec. 51,277.

[11] See, e.g., *S. Brownell Est.*, 44 TCM 1550, CCH Dec. 39,459(M), TC Memo. 1982-632, and *F. Stratton Est.*, 45 TCM 432, CCH Dec. 39,597(M), TC Memo. 1982-744, both holding that a discount was allowable.

or from the mean price on the nearest trading date *before* the valuation date.[12]

> ***Example:*** Assume that sales of stock nearest the valuation date (June 20) occurred two trading days before (June 18) and three trading days after (June 25). Assume further that on these days the mean sale prices per share were $10 and $15, respectively. The price of $12 would be taken as representing the fair market value of a share of stock as of the valuation date:
>
> $$\frac{(3 \times 10) + (2 \times 15)}{5}$$
>
> If, instead, the mean sale prices per share on June 18 and June 25 were reversed—$15 and $10, respectively—the price of $13 would be taken as representing the fair market value.

When a decedent dies on a weekend, the stock included in the decedent's gross estate is valued at the average of the mean sale prices for Friday and Monday.[13] Where the stock begins to sell ex-dividend on the following Monday, the amount of the dividend is added to Monday's quotations to determine the mean sales price.[14]

An alternate method is provided for valuing listed bonds if the highest and lowest selling prices for such bonds are not generally available in a listing or publication on the valuation date. Generally, in such case, the fair market value of a bond at the valuation date is the mean price between the closing selling price on the valuation date and the closing selling price on the trading day before the valuation date.

Special rules are provided for cases where: (1) there were no sales on the trading day before the valuation date but there were sales on a date within a reasonable period before the valuation date; (2) there were no sales within a reasonable period before the valuation date but there were sales on the valuation date; or (3) there were no sales on the valuation date but there were sales on dates within a reasonable period both before and after the valuation date.[15]

Stocks and bonds (other than Treasury bonds) that are usually traded in dollars and dollar fractions not smaller than one-eighth are to be reported in dollars and fractions smaller than eighths, for federal estate and gift tax purposes, when the mean of the high and the low quoted selling prices results in a fraction smaller than an eighth on the applicable valuation date. Treasury bonds that are normally traded in dollars and dollar fractions of thirty-seconds are to be valued and reported in dollars and fractions smaller than thirty-seconds, for estate and gift tax purposes, when the mean between the high and low selling prices results in a fraction smaller than a thirty-second.[16]

In valuing listed stocks and bonds, the executor should be careful to consult accurate records to obtain values on the applicable valuation date. If stocks or bonds are listed on more than one exchange, the records of the exchange where the stocks or bonds are principally traded should be used.

---

[12] Reg. § 20.2031-2(b).

[13] Reg. § 20.2031-2(b).

[14] Rev. Rul. 68-610, 1968-2 CB 405.

[15] Reg. § 20.2031-2(b)(2).

[16] Rev. Rul. 68-272, 1968-1 CB 394.

If quotations of unlisted securities are obtained from brokers, copies of the letters furnishing the quotations should be attached to the estate tax return. Similarly, if evidence as to the sale of unlisted securities is obtained from officers of the issuing companies, copies of the letters furnishing the evidence should be attached to the return.[17]

¶ 322 Large Blocks of Stock

An exception to the usual procedures for valuing listed securities can sometimes be sustained if the decedent owned a large block of stock in a single company. For example, if the executor can show that the block of stock to be valued is so large in relation to the actual sales on the existing market that it could not be liquidated in a reasonable time without depressing the market, the price at which the block could be sold outside the usual market—such as through an underwriter—may be a more accurate determination of value than market quotations or a mean between the high and low on the valuation date. On the other hand, if the block of stock to be valued represents a controlling interest, either actual or effective, in a going business, the price at which other lots change hands may have little relation to its true value.[18]

The IRS has ruled that underwriter's fees incurred by an estate in selling a large block of a decedent's stock were not to be considered in determining the allowable blockage discount. The IRS noted that the estate tax value of the block of stock was the price at which it could be sold to the general public even though the estate would receive less than this price because it paid the underwriter's fees. However, because it was necessary to sell the stock in order to pay debts, expenses and taxes of the estate, the fees were a deductible administration expense.[19]

Expert testimony, together with evidence that the stock must be specially handled by one who will discount its value, is usually necessary to establish a valid "blockage" discount.

¶ 323 Lack of Sales

If stock is sold on an exchange or over the counter and there are no sales during a reasonable period beginning before and ending after the valuation date, the valuation may be based upon the bid and asked prices. The fair market value is then determined by taking the mean between the bona fide bid and asked prices on the valuation date.

If there are no bid and asked prices on the valuation date, the value may be determined by: (1) taking the mean between the bona fide bid and asked prices on the nearest date before and the nearest date after the valuation date, (2) prorating the difference between the mean prices to the valuation date, and (3) adding or subtracting, as the case may be, the prorated portion of the difference to or from the mean price on the nearest date before the valuation date.[20]

---

[17] See Instructions for Form 706 (Rev. July 1998), p. 9.

[18] Reg. § 20.2031-2(e).

[19] Rev. Rul. 83-30, 1983-1 CB 224.

[20] Reg. § 20.2031-2(c).

¶ 324 Incomplete Prices

If actual sale prices or quoted bona fide bid and asked prices are available on a date within a reasonable period *before* the valuation date, but are not available on a date within a reasonable period *after* the valuation date, then the mean between such highest and lowest sales or bid and asked prices may be taken as the fair market value. Similarly, if prices are available within a reasonable period after, but not before, the valuation date, the mean between the highest and lowest available sales or bid and asked prices may be accepted as the value.[21]

¶ 325 Inactive and Unlisted Securities

When stock and other securities are not listed on an exchange and their value cannot be determined on the basis of sales or bid and asked prices because of the absence of sales, the value of the unlisted stock and securities is determined by taking into consideration, in addition to all other factors, the value of stock or securities of corporations engaged in the same or similar line of business which are listed on an exchange.[22] If no active market exists, consideration is also usually given (1) in the case of bonds, to the soundness of the security, the interest yield, the date of maturity and other relevant factors, and (2) in the case of stocks, to the company's net worth, earning power, dividend-paying capacity, and other relevant factors.[23]

Complete financial and other data upon which the estate bases its valuation should be submitted with the return. This information must include balance sheets (particularly the one nearest to the valuation date), and statements of the net earnings or operating results and dividends paid for each of the five years immediately preceding the valuation date.

¶ 326 Close Corporation Stock

The term "close corporation" does not appear in the regulations, which establish only general valuation rules in the absence of sales or bona fide bid and asked prices. However, a ruling by the IRS defines closely held corporations as "those corporations the shares of which are owned by a relatively limited number of stockholders. Often the entire stock issue is held by one family. The result of this situation is that little, if any, trading in the shares takes place. There is, therefore, no established market for the stock and such sales as occur at irregular intervals seldom reflect all of the elements of a representative transaction as defined by the term "fair market value." [24]

• *Valuation Factors*

The factors to be considered in determining the value of closely held stock, and of unlisted securities generally, vary with the particular facts involved. The weight to be given any one factor in any given case depends upon the circumstances. Sometimes, earnings are given the greatest

---

21 Reg. § 20.2031-2(d).

22 Code Sec. 2031(b).

23 Reg. § 20.2031-2(f).

24 Rev. Rul. 59-60, 1959-1 CB 237, modified by Rev. Rul. 65-193, 1965-2 CB 370, and amplified by Rev. Rul. 77-287, 1977-2 CB 319, and Rev. Rul. 83-120, 1983-2 CB 170.

weight. At other times, assets of the corporation provide the best test. The existence of special conditions in the industry at the time of valuation may also have some effect.

Although no formula can be devised for the determination of the fair market value of closely held corporations or stock of corporations where market quotations are either lacking or too scarce to be recognized, all available financial data, as well as all relevant factors affecting the fair market value, should be considered.[25] These factors include:

(1) the nature of the business and the history of the enterprise from its inception;

(2) the economic outlook in general and the condition and outcome of the specific industry in particular;

(3) the book value of the stock and the financial condition of the business;

(4) the earning capacity of the company;

(5) the dividend-paying capacity of the company;

(6) goodwill or other intangible value of the company;

(7) sales of the stock and the size of the block to be valued;

(8) the market price of stocks of corporations engaged in the same or a similar line of business having their stocks actively traded in a free and open market, either on an exchange or over the counter; and

(9) the life insurance proceeds received by a corporate beneficiary on a policy covering the sole or controlling stockholder.

Under (9), above, the incidents of ownership in a policy of insurance on the life of a sole surviving shareholder held by the corporation will not be attributed to the insured decedent (the sole or controlling stockholder) through the decedent's stock ownership under Reg. § 20.2042-1(c) because it will be considered a nonoperating asset of the corporation in determining the stock value included in the decedent's gross estate under Reg. § 20.2031-2(f). Thus, life insurance proceeds excluded from the decedent's gross estate are considered a nonoperating asset of the corporation for purposes of valuing the stock of the decedent which is includible in his estate. However, the incidents of ownership will be attributed to the insured decedent who is the sole or controlling stockholder under Reg. § 20.2042-1(c) if such proceeds are not payable to the corporation or a third party for a valid business purpose.[26]

An additional factor to be considered is the degree of control of the business represented by the block of stock being valued.[27] Thus, if the decedent held control over the corporation, the IRS may contend that a control premium should be added to the value of the stock in determining its estate tax value. In the Tax Court's view, "a premium for control is generally expressed as the percentage by which the amount paid for

---

[25] Rev. Rul. 77-287, 1977-2 CB 319; Rev. Rul. 59-60, 1959-1 CB 237.

[26] Reg. § 20.2031-2(f) and Reg. § 20.2042-1(c), respectively.

[27] Reg. § 20.2031-2(f).

controlling block of shares exceeds the amount which would have otherwise been paid for the shares if sold as minority interests . . . ."[28] The IRS National Office has ruled that the majority voting power of shares of preferred stock in a closely held corporation owned by a decedent at death was to be considered in valuing the stock for estate tax purposes even though the voting rights expired at the owner's death.[29] With respect to the control issue, the Tax Court has held that the possibility of protracted litigation over the relative rights of different classes of stock served to limit the date-of-death value of a decedent's interest in a closely held corporation. In addition, the fact that a decedent held the largest block of shares in the company did not necessarily warrant a control premium where the power to unilaterally direct and change the direction of the company was not present.[30]

The IRS National Office has ruled that two blocks of stock includible in a decedent's gross estate under two different Code sections (Code Sec. 2033 and Code Sec. 2038) can be aggregated to determine the fair market value of the stock for estate tax purposes.[31] A control premium could then be applied if the aggregated stock constituted a controlling interest in a closely held corporation.

In another Technical Advice Memorandum,[32] the IRS National Office treated a decedent's voting preferred stock and voting common stock as a single controlling interest in determining the value of a decedent's gross estate under Code Sec. 2033. A control premium was applied, even though the stock passed to two different beneficiaries. However, when it came to determining the amount of the estate tax marital deduction, the block of stock that passed to the decedent's surviving spouse was valued as a separate minority interest.

● *Effect of Buy-Sell Agreements*

Another element may also be important, however, and may limit or nullify the weight to be given to the above factors in determining the value of close corporation stock. This element is the restrictive sales agreement, primarily the mutual buy-sell type of agreement. Mutual buy-sell agreements are those whereby a corporation or individual (usually a co-stockholder) promises to buy stock, and the stockholder promises to sell, upon the happening of a certain contingency, usually the stockholder's death.

The price stated in a buy-sell agreement will not control the estate tax valuation if such agreement does not restrict lifetime transfers. Thus, in the case of a transfer within three years of death, the price stated in the agreement was held not to be determinative of the fair market value of the stock either at the time of the sale or at the decedent's death.[33]

The existence of mutual promises provides the necessary consideration to make such agreement enforceable. Because of the mutuality of such agreements, the courts, in determining valuation of such stock for federal estate tax purposes, have adopted the specified price of the buy-sell

---

[28] *J.E. Salsbury Est.*, 34 TCM 1441, CCH Dec. 33,503(M), TC Memo. 1975-333, at 1451.

[29] IRS Technical Advice Memorandum 8401006, 9-28-83, CCH IRS LETTER RULINGS REPORTS.

[30] *S. Newhouse Est.*, 94 TC 193, CCH Dec. 46,411 (Nonacq.).

[31] IRS Technical Advice Memorandum 9403002, 9-17-93, CCH IRS LETTER RULINGS REPORTS.

[32] IRS Technical Advice Memorandum 9403005, 10-14-93, CCH IRS LETTER RULINGS REPORTS.

[33] *M. Caplan Est.*, 33 TCM 189, CCH Dec. 32,461(M), TC Memo. 1974-39.

agreements.[34] They recognize that the stock subject to such an agreement cannot possibly be sold for more than the agreed price at any time prior to, or at the happening of, the contingency and, therefore, it would be illusory to consider its value to the estate to be anything except such price. However, the U.S. Court of Appeals for the Eighth Circuit reversed the decision of a district court in Missouri that the estate tax value of a decedent's stock in a closely held corporation was controlled by the price set in an agreement giving the corporation the right to purchase the stock upon the decedent's death. The price was zero under a formula set forth in the agreement, and the appellate court noted that the district court failed to consider the possibility that the agreement was an estate tax avoidance device, in which case it would not control the estate tax value of the decedent's stock.[35]

The IRS National Office has refused to be bound by a price set in a buy-sell agreement that it concluded was not a bona fide business arrangement, but a testamentary device to gratuitously transfer the decedent's interest in the corporation to his heirs.[36] In addition, the stock's value would be determined without regard to the formula price of the buy-sell agreement where the agreement is primarily intended to serve as a device to allow shareholders to transfer their stock in the corporation to beneficiaries for less than adequate consideration.[37]

See, also, ¶ 2500 for a discussion of the special valuation rules for estate freezes.

● *Minority Discounts*

For several years, the IRS maintained that no minority discount should apply when shares in a closely held corporation were transferred from a decedent to other family members, if the corporation remained under family control after the decedent's death. Unless there was evidence of hostility among family members or other indications that the family would not cooperate in corporate matters, the IRS generally challenged the application of a minority discount in these circumstances. However, several courts disagreed with the IRS, finding it appropriate, instead, to consider *only* the decedent's shares of stock in valuing the decedent's interest in the corporation for estate tax purposes.[38] The IRS finally reversed its earlier position and announced that it would no longer disallow a minority discount solely because the transferred interest, when aggregated with interest held by other family members, was a controlling interest.[39]

The IRS has apparently focused its attention on other areas involving the valuation of stock in closely held corporations. For example, the National Office treated a decedent's voting preferred stock and voting

---

[34] *O.B. Littick Est.*, 31 TC 181, CCH Dec. 23,221 (Acq.); *M.G. Seltzer Est.*, 50 TCM 1250, CCH Dec. 42,423(M), TC Memo. 1985-519.

[35] *St. Louis County Bank, Exr.*, CA-8, 82-1 USTC ¶ 13,459, 674 F2d 1207.

[36] IRS Technical Advice Memorandum 8710004, 11-21-86, CCH IRS LETTER RULINGS REPORTS. See also *C. Dorn, Exr.*, CA-3, 87-2 USTC ¶ 13,732, rev'g and rem'g DC Pa., 85-2 USTC ¶ 13,701.

[37] *J. Lauder Est.*, 68 TCM 985, CCH Dec. 50,192(M), TC Memo. 1994-527.

[38] *M. Bright Est.*, CA-5, 81-2 USTC ¶ 13,436, 658 F2d 999; *J.A. Propstra*, CA-9, 82-2 USTC ¶ 13,475, 680 F2d 1248; *W. Andrews Est.*, 79 TC 938, CCH Dec. 39,523; and *E. Lee Est.*, 69 TC 860, CCH Dec. 35,017.

[39] Rev. Rul. 93-12, 93-1 CB 202, revoking Rev. Rul. 81-253, 1981-2 CB 187, and substituting acquiescence for the nonacquiescence (1980-2 CB 2) in *E. Lee Est.*, 69 TC 860, CCH Dec. 35,017.

common stock as a single controlling interest in determining the value of the decedent's gross estate under Code Sec. 2033, even though the two blocks of stock passed to different beneficiaries. However, the block of stock that passed to the decedent's surviving spouse was valued as a separate minority interest for purposes of the estate tax marital deduction and a minority discount was applied.[40] However, the U.S. Court of Appeals for the Fifth Circuit has ruled that aggregation is not required for the valuation of fractional interests.[41]

● *Stock Issued Pursuant to an Estate "Freeze"*

The gross estate of the owner of a closely held corporation may include preferred stock in the corporation issued pursuant to a recapitalization designed to "freeze" the value of the individual's interest in the corporation for estate tax purposes. Such a recapitalization is intended to transfer the potential appreciation of the individual's common stock to others active in operating the corporation, often younger members of the individual's family. Typically, this involves the exchange of the individual's common stock for preferred stock that has a stated par value equal to nearly all of the value of the common stock.[42] The individual also receives new common stock having only a low fair market value, and this new stock is then transferred to the younger family members.

The Revenue Act of 1987 (P.L. 100-203) added Code Sec. 2036(c), which was intended to reduce the benefits available from such an "estate freeze." Code Sec. 2036(c) was repealed retroactively by the Revenue Reconciliation Act of 1990 (P.L. 101-508) and was replaced by a series of rules intended to curb perceived valuation abuses by valuing certain interests at the time of transfer rather than by including previously transferred property in the transferor's gross estate.[43] See ¶ 2500 for further description of the limitations on valuation freezes resulting from the Chapter 14 special valuation rules.

Before the Revenue Act of 1987 limited the potential benefits of estate freezes, the IRS had provided factors to be used in valuing preferred and common stock issued pursuant to an estate freeze in a ruling amplifying Rev. Rul. 59-60.[44] Generally, in valuing the preferred stock, the primary factors to be considered are the yield of the stock and the corporation's ability to pay both the stated dividend rate and the liquidation preference. The adequacy of the yield of preferred stock is to be determined by comparing its dividend rates and liquidation preferences with those of preferred stock issued by publicly traded corporations having similar assets and engaging in similar businesses. Additional factors to be considered are the voting rights of the stock, any covenants restricting its transfer, and the corporation's ability to honor any redemption privilege.

The value of the common stock issued in such a recapitalization, according to the IRS, is largely dependent on the corporation's past growth experience, the economic condition of the industry in which the corpora-

---

[40] IRS Technical Advice Memorandum 9403005, 10-14-93, CCH IRS LETTER RULINGS REPORTS.

[41] *L. Bonner, Sr. Est.*, CA-5, 96-2 USTC ¶ 60,237, 84 F3d 196.

[42] The recapitalization is often structured as a tax-free reorganization under Code Sec. 368(a)(1)(E).

[43] Code Sec. 2701 through Code Sec. 2704.

[44] Rev. Rul. 83-120, 1983-2 CB 170, amplifying Rev. Rul. 59-60, 1959-1 CB 237.

tion operates, and general economic conditions. However, under certain circumstances, voting rights of the preferred stock could increase the value of the preferred stock and reduce the value of the common stock, especially if the preferred stock has voting control of the corporation.

¶ 327 Worthless Securities

Securities reported on the estate tax return as without value, with nominal value or obsolete should be listed last on Schedule B of Form 706. The address of the company, the state in which it is incorporated, and the date of incorporation should be stated. Copies of correspondence or statements used as the basis for determining that the stock is without value should be attached.

¶ 328 Mutual Fund Shares

The fair market value of shares in open-end investment companies (mutual funds) is to be set at the "bid" or public redemption price of such shares at the date of death or on the alternate valuation date if the alternate valuation method is elected.[45] In the absence of an affirmative showing of the public redemption price in effect at the time of death, the last public redemption price quoted by the company for the date of death is presumed to be the applicable public redemption price. If there is no public redemption price quoted by the company for the applicable valuation date (for example, where the valuation date is a Saturday, Sunday, or holiday), the mutual shares are valued by using the last public redemption price quoted by the company for the first day preceding the applicable valuation date for which there is a quotation.[46]

¶ 329 Tax-Exempt Bonds

With respect to securities of privately owned corporations, the question of taxability does not arise. If the securities were held by the decedent at the time of death (see ¶ 310), or if the decedent transferred them during life in a manner coming within the definitions of taxable transfers (see ¶ 550), the value of the securities is includible in the decedent's estate. However, where the securities involved are securities of government-created public corporations or entities, another question arises. What is the effect of provisions stating that the securities shall be exempt from tax? The courts almost invariably answer this question by stating that the federal estate tax is a tax on the transfer of property and not upon the property itself—that the exemption granted the securities is an exemption from taxes on the property itself and not an exemption from excise taxes.

The various statutory provisions that exempt bonds, bills, notes, and certificates of indebtedness of the federal government or its agencies (and the interest thereon) from taxation are not applicable to estate and gift taxes. U.S. government bonds, U.S. Treasury bonds, and U.S. savings bonds are all subject to federal estate and gift taxation. Similarly, despite state statutory exemptions, state and municipal bonds are subject to estate and gift taxation. However, such bonds issued prior to March 1, 1941, and beneficially owned by a nonresident who is not a U.S. citizen and is not

---

[45] Reg. § 20.2031-8(b). *D.B. Cartwright,* SCt, 73-1 USTC ¶ 12,926, 411 US 546.

[46] Reg. § 20.2031-8(b).

engaged in business in the United States at the time of death are exempt from tax because they are considered "situated outside the United States."[47]

● *Anti-*Haffner *Provision*

The Tax Reform Act of 1984 provided that nothing in any provision of law exempting any property from taxation will exempt the transfer of such property (or interest therein) from federal estate, gift and generation-skipping transfer taxes.[48] This provision, in effect, reverses the decision of a U.S. district court in Illinois (later affirmed by the U.S. Court of Appeals for the Seventh Circuit) that public housing agency bonds owned by a decedent were exempt from estate taxes under a provision of the Federal Housing Act of 1937.[49] This rule, also referred to as the "anti-*Haffner* provision," is effective with respect to the estates of decedents dying, and gifts and transfers made, on or after June 19, 1984.[50]

Although the anti-*Haffner* provision was ruled unconstitutional by the district court, that decision has been reversed by the U.S. Supreme Court in *Wells Fargo Bank.*[51] The district court had held that the provision was unconstitutional because the amended legislation amounted to the imposition of a wholly new tax and the retroactive application of that tax would constitute a constitutional violation of due process and equal protection. The Supreme Court, however, held that the language of Section 5(e) of the Housing Act of 1937 exempting property from all taxation applied only to direct taxes, such as the federal income tax, but not to excise taxes, such as the federal estate tax. Because it concluded that the Housing Act did not create an estate tax exemption, the Court found it unnecessary to rule on the constitutionality of the 1984 Tax Reform Act provision.

Basing its reasoning on the principle that a tax exemption cannot be implied, the Tax Court has also refused to infer an exemption from the estate tax for public housing agency bonds. The Tax Court has concluded that because public housing agency bonds had never expressly been exempted from the federal estate tax, their value was includible in the decedent's gross estate.[52] According to the Tax Court, the exemption contained in the Housing Act applied to direct taxes (such as the income tax) and not to the federal estate tax on transfers of property.

The 1984 Act also provides that any provision of law enacted on or after June 19, 1984, will not be construed as exempting the transfer of property from federal estate, gift and generation-skipping transfer taxes, unless the provision refers to an appropriate rule under the Internal Revenue Code.[53] The rule denying exemption from estate and gift taxes also applies with respect to any property that was reported on an estate or gift tax return as subject to estate or gift tax.[54] Finally, with respect to a transfer of property (or interest therein) made before June 19, 1984, the

---

[47] Reg. § 20.2105-1.

[48] Act Sec. 641(a), P.L. 98-369.

[49] *C.C. Haffner III, Exr.*, 84-1 USTC ¶ 13,571, 585 FSupp 354, aff'd, CA-7, 85-1 USTC ¶ 13,611.

[50] Act Sec. 641(b)(1), P.L. 98-369.

[51] *Wells Fargo Bank et al.*, SCt, 88-1 USTC ¶ 13,759 (consolidated with *H. Rosenberg*), rev'g DC Cal., 86-2 USTC ¶ 13,703.

[52] *L.G. Egger Est.*, 89 TC 726, CCH Dec. 44,251.

[53] Act Sec. 641(a), P.L. 98-369.

[54] Act Sec. 641(b)(2), P.L. 98-369.

Act provides that no inference is to arise that such transfer is exempt from federal estate and gift taxation.[55]

● *Reporting Requirements*

Taxpayers are required to provide the IRS with relevant information regarding the transfer of public housing bonds of a type that the district court in *Haffner* held were exempt from estate taxes. This provision is effective with respect to transfers of public housing bonds occurring after 1983 and before June 19, 1984.[56]

¶ 330 U.S. Treasury Bonds

Certain issues of U.S. Treasury bonds (listed at ¶ 1665) are redeemable at their par value and accrued interest in payment of a deceased owner's federal estate taxes. If the quoted market price of such bonds is higher than their stated par value, they must be reported at their quoted selling price, plus accrued interest to the date of death.

If the par value is the higher value, all the Treasury bonds that actually can be applied against the tax must be included in the decedent's gross estate at their par value (and accrued interest) whether or not the estate representative elects to redeem them in payment of estate taxes. This is true even if the executor sold the bonds after the estate tax return was filed but before issuance of a notice of a deficiency against which the bonds could have been applied.[57] Those U.S. Treasury bonds in excess of a value that can be applied to the decedent's estate tax may be reported at their mean quoted market price (and accrued interest to the date of death).[58]

> ***Example:*** At the time of his death, X.L. Cant owned, in addition to other properties of substantial value, four U.S. Treasury bonds. Each bond had a redemption and par value of $100,000. All four were of an issue which could be applied, prior to maturity or call redemption date, at par value and accrued interest in payment of federal estate taxes.
>
> On the date of Cant's death, each bond had a current market quotation of $86,562. The executor of his estate, in preparing the estate tax return, determined that taxes amounting to $500,215 were payable by the estate. However, he decided to apply only two of the Treasury bonds (before maturity or call redemption date) in payment of the estate taxes owing. *All four* Treasury bonds are, nevertheless, includible in the gross estate at their par value.

U.S. savings bonds purchased by a decedent with the decedent's own funds are includible in the decedent's gross estate if: (1) the bonds are registered in the decedent's own name, (2) the bonds are registered in the decedent's own name, but are payable to another person on the purchaser's death, or (3) the bonds are registered in the names of the decedent and another person as co-owners. Bonds purchased with the separate funds of two persons and registered in their names as co-owners are includible in the

---

[55] Act Sec. 641(b)(3), P.L. 98-369.

[56] Act Sec. 642(a), P.L. 98-369.

[57] *E.G. Simmie Est.*, CA-9, 80-2 USTC ¶ 13,377, 632 F2d 93, and Rev. Rul. 81-228, 1981-2 CB 171.

[58] Rev. Rul. 69-489, 1969-2 CB 172.

estate of the first co-owner to die, to the extent of the percentage of the purchase price that the decedent provided.[59] However, the "consideration-furnished" test does not apply to qualified joint interests (see ¶ 502).

Where the purchaser registers bonds in the purchaser's own name and in the name of another person as co-owners, the bonds must be surrendered to the Treasury Department and be reissued solely in the name of this other person in order to remove them from the purchaser's estate as joint property. The mere physical delivery of such jointly owned bonds to the other person, with the intent to make a gift, will not be recognized so as to remove the bonds from a purchaser's estate.[60]

¶ 331 Nonresidents Not Citizens

Except as indicated below, only property located in the United States is includible in the gross estate of a nonresident alien decedent.[61] The notable exception to this general situs rule is the stock of domestic corporations, which is includible in a decedent's gross estate, regardless of where it is located. Likewise, except as mentioned below, debt obligations (bonds, etc.) that are owned and held by a nonresident alien are considered property located within the United States if the primary obligor is a domestic corporation or other U.S. person, the United States, a state, a political subdivision of a state, or the District of Columbia.[62] For this purpose, it is immaterial whether the written evidence of the debt obligation is treated as being the property itself. Currency, however, is not to be considered a debt obligation.

Short-term original issue discount obligations will not be treated as U.S. situs property for estates of decedents dying after August 5, 1997. For this purpose, a short-term obligation means an obligation payable 183 days or less from the date of the obligation's issue.[63] Additionally, debts of a domestic corporation deriving less than 20 percent of its gross income from U.S. sources for the three-year period prior to the nonresident's death are not considered as having a situs in the United States. Other debt obligations are not, according to the House Ways & Means Committee Report to the Foreign Investors Tax Act of 1966, to be considered property within the United States even if written evidence of the obligation which is considered as the property itself is located in the United States.[64]

The situs rules may, however, be modified by a death tax treaty with the country of domicile of the decedent (see also ¶ 1615).

---

[59] Rev. Rul. 68-269, 1968-1 CB 399.

[60] *E.G. Chandler, Exr. (M.E. Baum Will)*, SCt, 73-1 USTC ¶ 12,902, 410 US 257.

[61] Code Sec. 2103.

[62] Code Sec. 2104.

[63] Code Sec. 2105(b)(4).

[64] House Ways & Means Committee Report to the Foreign Investors Tax Act of 1966 (P.L. 89-809).

¶ 335 Filled-In Schedule B

Schedule B must be filed only if the decedent owned stocks and bonds. The schedule can be omitted if the decedent did not own property reportable on this schedule (see ¶ 73).

Example Where Alternate Valuation Is Not Adopted

The filled-in Schedule B, Form 706 (Rev. July 1998), relates to the fact situation of a person who dies on January 1, 1998, with an estate tax return due within nine months (without extensions).

Form 706 (Rev. 7-98)

Estate of: James X. Diversey

SCHEDULE B — Stocks and Bonds

(For jointly owned property that must be disclosed on Schedule E, see the instructions for Schedule E.)

Item number	Description including face amount of bonds or number of shares and par value where needed for identification. Give 9-digit CUSIP number.	CUSIP number	Unit value	Alternate valuation date	Alternate value	Value at date of death
1	$60,000 - Midwest Mining Co., first mortgage 8% 20-year bonds, due 2003. Interest payable quarterly on Feb. 1, May 1, Aug. 1 and Nov. 1;	123456789	92			55,200
	Interest coupons attached to Item 1 due and payable Nov. 1,1997 but not cashed at date of death.					1,200
	Interest accrued on Item 1. Nov. 1, 1997 to Jan. 1, 1998.					800
2	1,000 shares Public Service Corp.	987654321	109			109,000
	Dividend on Item 2 of $2 per share, declared on Dec. 10, 1997, payable on Jan. 10, 1998 to holders of record on Dec. 31, 1997.					2,000
	Total from continuation schedules (or additional sheets) attached to this schedule					
	TOTAL. (Also enter on Part 5, Recapitulation, page 3, at item 2.)					168,200

(If more space is needed, attach the continuation schedule from the end of this package or additional sheets of the same size.)

(The instructions to Schedule B are in the separate instructions.)

Schedule B — Page 12

Example Where Estate Qualified for Stocks and Bonds and Elected Alternate Valuation

The filled-in Schedule B, Form 706 (Rev. July 1998), relates to the fact situation of an estate of a person who dies on January 1, 1998, with an estate tax return due within nine months (without extensions). Not entered on sample Recapitulation at ¶ 1225, because the alternate valuation method was not elected by the estate of the hypothetical decedent, James X. Diversey.

Form 706 (Rev. 7-98)

Estate of:

SCHEDULE B — Stocks and Bonds

(For jointly owned property that must be disclosed on Schedule E, see the instructions for Schedule E.)

Item number	Description including face amount of bonds or number of shares and par value where needed for identification. Give 9-digit CUSIP number.	CUSIP number	Unit value	Alternate valuation date	Alternate value	Value at date of death
1	$60,000 - Midwest Mining Co., first mortgage 8% 20-year bonds, due 2003. Interest payable quarterly on Feb. 1, May 1, Aug. 1 and Nov. 1.	123456789	92			55,200
	$30,000 of such bonds distributed to legatees on April 1,1998.		85	4-1-98	25,500	
	$30,000 of such bonds sold by executor on May 1,1998.		85	5-1-98	25,500	
	Interest coupons attached to bonds due and payable Nov. 1,1997 but not cashed at date of death. Cashed by executor on Feb. 1,1998.			2-1-98	1,200	1,200
	Interest accrued on Item 1: Nov. 1,1997 to Jan. 1,1998. Cashed by executor on Feb. 1,1998.			2-1-98	800	800
2	1,000 shares Public Service Corp.	987654321	109			109,000
	Not disposed of within 6 months following death		102	7-1-98	102,000	
	Dividend on Item 2 of $2 per share, declared on Dec. 10, 1997, payable on Jan. 10, 1998 to holders of record on Dec. 31, 1997.			1-10-98	2,000	2,000
	Total from continuation schedules (or additional sheets) attached to this schedule					
	TOTAL. (Also enter on Part 5, Recapitulation, page 3, at item 2.)				157,000	168,200

(If more space is needed, attach the continuation schedule from the end of this package or additional sheets of the same size.)

(The instructions to Schedule B are in the separate instructions.)

Schedule B — Page 12

Chapter 11

MORTGAGES, NOTES, CONTRACTS TO SELL LAND, AND CASH

¶ 350 Inclusion in Gross Estate

As with property interests reportable in schedules concerned with real property and stocks and bonds, the taxability of mortgages, notes, contracts to sell land, and cash is generally determined under Code Sec. 2033. These items must be valued as of the date of decedent's death unless the executor elects to have them valued as of the alternate valuation date. They are reported on Schedule C of Form 706. This schedule does not have to be filed if the decedent did not own property reportable on it.

¶ 355 Mortgages and Notes

In describing mortgages on the estate tax return, the following information should be set out:

(1) face value and unpaid balance;

(2) date of mortgage;

(3) date of maturity;

(4) name of maker;

(5) property subject to mortgage; and

(6) interest dates and rate of interest.

Similar data should be shown when reporting notes.

The value of notes, whether secured or unsecured, is the amount of unpaid principal, together with accrued interest, unless the estate representative establishes a lower value or proves them worthless. If returned at less than face value, plus interest, the lower value must be established by satisfactory evidence. A lower value may be justified because of the interest rate or date of maturity. For example, the IRS National Office has ruled that the estate tax value of an installment note payable to a decedent was less than its face value because the note provided for payment of interest at a rate below the prevailing interest rate on the date of the decedent's death.[1] If a note is wholly or partially uncollectible because of insolvency of the debtors or any collateral for the loan is insufficient to satisfy the debt, a lower valuation is permitted.[2]

If an estate contends that the actual value of mortgages or mortgage participation certificates is less than their face value, the controlling valuation factors include (1) the valuation of real estate and any collateral covered by the mortgages, (2) arrearages in taxes and interest, (3) gross and net rentals, (4) foreclosure proceedings, (5) assignment of rents, (6)

---

[1] IRS Technical Advice Memorandum 8229001, 2-1-82, CCH IRS LETTER RULINGS REPORTS.

[2] Reg. § 20.2031-4.

prior liens or encumbrances, (7) present interest yield, (8) over-the-counter sales, and (9) bid and asked quotations. The existence of an over-the-counter market for mortgage notes and certificates and the quotations and opinions furnished by brokers and real estate appraisers will not be accepted by the IRS as conclusive evidence of their value. Where the mortgage is amply secured, the value will be the mortgage's face value plus accrued interest to date of death. Where the security is insufficient, the mortgage will be valued upon the basis of the fair market value of property less back taxes, estimated foreclosure expenses, and, where justified, the expense of rehabilitation. The estate must prove the lesser value.[3]

¶ 360 Contracts to Sell Land

In reporting a contract to sell land on the estate tax return, it is necessary to provide the following information:

(1) name of purchaser;

(2) date of contract;

(3) description of property to be sold;

(4) sale price;

(5) initial payment;

(6) amounts of installment payments;

(7) unpaid balance of principal; and

(8) interest rate.

The listing of contracts to sell realty is a listing in lieu of the realty. If the decedent has an unpaid mortgage or other indebtedness on the property being sold under the contract and the decedent's estate is liable for it, the full value of the contract must be included as part of the gross estate. The mortgage or indebtedness is allowed as a deduction in such a case. If the decedent's estate is not liable, only the value of the redemption equity (or the value of the contract, less the mortgage or indebtedness) need be reported as part of the value in the gross estate. In no case may the deduction on account of the mortgage exceed the liability actually contracted for. Only interest accrued to the date of the decedent's death is deductible even though the alternative valuation method is elected.[4]

¶ 365 Cash

In reporting cash on the estate tax return, cash in the decedent's possession should be listed separately from cash deposited in banks or other financial organizations.

In reporting cash deposited in financial organizations, the return should show:

(1) the name and address of each organization;

(2) amount in each account;

(3) serial number or account number;

---

[3] Rev. Rul. 67-276, 1967-2 CB 321.

[4] Reg. § 20.2053-7.

(4) nature of accounts (checking, savings, time deposit, etc.); and

(5) unpaid interest accrued from date of last interest payment to the date of death.

If statements are obtained from the financial organizations, they should be retained for inspection by the IRS.

Cash that belongs to the decedent at the time of death must be reported in full, whether in the decedent's or another's possession and whether or not it is on deposit in a bank. Checks outstanding at the time of death may be subtracted from the total if they are subsequently honored and charged against the decedent's account, but only if the obligation is not claimed as a deduction.[5] The amount of any check that was given under circumstances indicating a taxable lifetime transfer cannot be claimed as a deduction.

If interest on a particular savings bank account does not accrue between interest payment dates, no interest between the last interest payment date and the date of decedent's death should be included in the valuation.[6] However, if certificates of deposit can be redeemed without forfeiture of interest upon the death of the owner, the interest accrued but unpaid at death is includible in the value of the certificates for estate tax purposes even if the interest would have been forfeited had the decedent redeemed the certificates prior to death.[7]

U.S. silver coins (or paper currency) that are held by a decedent at the time of death and that are worth more than their face value must be valued at their fair market value for estate tax purposes, even if the decedent had never been a coin collector.[8] If the cash consists of foreign currency or foreign bank accounts, the value should be stated in terms of the official rate of exchange.[9] Restrictions or difficulties concerning convertibility can justify a lower value.

---

[5] Reg. § 20.2031-5.

[6] Rev. Rul. 55-301, 1955-1 CB 442.

[7] Rev. Rul. 79-340, 1979-2 CB 320.

[8] Rev. Rul. 78-360, 1978-2 CB 228.

[9] *A. Fry Est.*, 9 TC 503, CCH Dec. 16,030 (Acq.).

¶ 380 Filled-In Schedule C

Schedule C must be filed only if the decedent owned mortgages, notes and cash. The schedule can be omitted if the decedent did not own property reportable on this schedule (see ¶ 73).

The filled-in Schedule C, Form 706 (Rev. July 1998), relates to the fact situation of a person who dies on January 1, 1998, with an estate tax return due within nine months (without extensions).

Form 706 (Rev. 7-98)

Estate of: James X. Diversey

SCHEDULE C — Mortgages, Notes, and Cash

(For jointly owned property that must be disclosed on Schedule E, see the instructions for Schedule E.)

Item number	Description	Alternate valuation date	Alternate value	Value at date of death
1	Mortgage of $20,000, unpaid balance of $17,824, dated Jan. 1, 1992; Edward Hansen to James X. Diversey; premises 18742 Jameson St., Homewood, IL due Jan. 1, 2005; payable in monthly installments of $202.86 during the first 10 days of each month; interest at a rate of 9% per annum payable out of each installment on unpaid balance; interest to Dec. 31, 1997, paid with last installment on Dec. 3, 1997.			17,824
2	Note for $1,000; unpaid balance of $1,000; given Dec. 1, 1997, by Robert Diversey, 54 Fir St., Homewood, IL to James X. Diversey, payable Dec. 1, 1998 with interest at 8% per annum at maturity.			1,000
	Interest on Item 2 accrued at date of decedent's death.			7
3	Cash in decedent's home			1,562
4	Cash on deposit in savings account in decedent's name. Account No.21-738-0 at State National Bank, Peterson and Pulaski Aves., Chicago, IL			15,410
5	Cash in safe deposit box held in name of decedent at State National Bank, Peterson and Pulaski Aves., Chicago, IL.			750
	Total from continuation schedules (or additional sheets) attached to this schedule			
	TOTAL. (Also enter on Part 5, Recapitulation, page 3, at item 3.)			36,553

(If more space is needed, attach the continuation schedule from the end of this package or additional sheets of the same size.)

(See the instructions.)

Schedule C — Page 13

Chapter 12
LIFE INSURANCE

¶ 400 Inclusion of Life Insurance

Life insurance, for estate tax purposes, includes not only the common forms of insurance taken out by an individual upon the individual's own life but also the proceeds of certain other types of insurance policies. Proceeds of accident insurance policies, including flight insurance of the type commonly purchased at air terminals, are proceeds of life insurance for estate tax purposes.[1] Similarly included are proceeds of War Risk insurance and of National Service Life insurance. Amounts paid under group insurance and under double indemnity clauses by reason of the accidental death of an insured are also treated as the proceeds of life insurance.

The more common forms of insurance that are regarded as life insurance are ordinary life, limited payment life, endowment, term insurance, and retired lives reserves insurance.

Insurance that a decedent may have taken out on the life of another individual is not taxed under the insurance provision of Code Sec. 2042, but, rather, under the general taxing rules of Code Sec. 2033.

The fact that a contract is called an insurance contract does not automatically entitle it to treatment as insurance for estate tax purposes if it is not, in fact, a contract of insurance. To be an insurance contract, an element of risk must be involved. The risk must be an actuarial one under which the premium cost is based upon the likelihood that the insured will live for a certain period of time and under which the insurer stands to suffer a loss if the insured does not, in fact, live for the expected period.

The IRS has ruled that the value of no-fault death benefits payable to the estates of a driver and a passenger who were killed in an automobile accident was includible in their gross estates as the proceeds of life insurance policies. This was so because, under applicable state law, pay-

---

[1] *M.L. Noel Est.*, SCt, 65-1 USTC ¶ 12,311, 380 US 678.

ment of the death benefits did not preclude the decedents' estates or heirs from bringing wrongful death actions. Accordingly, because the insurer was unconditionally bound to make payment in the event of the insureds' death, the no-fault insurance policy had the necessary risk-shifting and risk-distributing elements necessary to be considered life insurance for purposes of Code Sec. 2042.[2]

Insurance on the decedent's life is reported on Schedule D (Insurance on the Decedent's Life) of Form 706. Schedule D does not have to be filed with the return where there is no insurance on the decedent's life. Insurance on another person's life, which is includible in the decedent's gross estate, is not reportable on Schedule D. Rather, it must be reported on Schedule F (Other Miscellaneous Property Not Reportable Under Any Other Schedule).

¶ 403 Group Insurance

Proceeds of group life insurance are treated the same as the proceeds of any other insurance. Generally, they are includible in the estate of the insured because the insured has incidents of ownership, or is regarded as having them, at the time of death.

● *Assignability*

A group-term life insurance policy, the cost of which is paid by the employer, is excludable from the estate of a deceased employee if the decedent has irrevocably assigned all interest in the policy and did not die within three years of making the assignment.[3] The assignment, in order to be valid, must not be prohibited by state law or by the terms of the policy. Most states now have specific laws permitting assignments of group life insurance policies by insured employees. However, where state law fails to affirmatively provide for assignment, but does not expressly prohibit it, it may be possible to assign the policy and to remove it from the employee's estate.[4]

The IRS will recognize assignments made by employees in those cases where the master policy permits assignments and the individual policy certificates issued to employees do not.[5] On the other hand, where the master policy did not permit assignments, an attempted assignment was held to be invalid, and the proceeds of the policy were includible in an insured-employee's gross estate.[6]

Estates of stockholder-employees of closely held corporations may face difficulty if they attempt to exclude previously assigned group life insurance from the decedent's gross estate.[7] The government has argued that a controlling stockholder had incidents of ownership over a group policy because of his right to surrender or cancel the policy while acting as a corporate officer. The Court of Claims rejected this argument in a situation involving a corporation jointly owned by two unrelated officers. However,

[2] Rev. Rul. 83-44, 1983-1 CB 228.

[3] Code Sec. 2035.

[4] *M.J. Gorby Est.*, 53 TC 80, CCH Dec. 29,801 (Acq.); *L. Landorf, Exr.*, CtCls, 69-1 USTC ¶ 12,593, 408 F2d 461.

[5] *M.J. Gorby Est.*, 53 TC 80, CCH Dec. 29,801 (Acq.).

[6] *S.F. Bartlett Est.*, 54 TC 1590, CCH Dec. 30,278 (Acq.).

[7] *L. Landorf, Exr.*, CtCls, 69-1 USTC ¶ 12,593, 408 F2d 461.

the court indicated that this power might exist where the decedent was the sole stockholder or, in effect, had control over minority stockholder-officers. Presently, this question remains unresolved. For corporate-owned group-term life insurance where the decedent is the sole or controlling stockholder, the power to surrender or cancel a policy held by the corporation will not be attributed to the decedent through the decedent's stock ownership to the extent the proceeds of the policy are payable to the corporation.[8] Also, the IRS has privately ruled that the sole shareholder of a closely held corporation did not possess incidents of ownership in a life insurance policy on his own life, despite his ability to terminate the policy beneficiary's employment contract, causing the distribution of insurance proceeds to a trust for the benefit of the shareholder's family.[9]

A post-1976 assignment of a group policy made by an employee within three years of death evidently will be automatically includible in the employee's estate. However, an assignment of a group-term policy within three years of death will not result in inclusion of the policy in the transferor's gross estate if the assignment was necessitated by the employer's change of insurance carrier and was made pursuant to an "anticipatory assignment" of all present and future employer-provided policies executed more than three years before the transferor's death (see ¶ 555).[10]

● *Conversion Privilege*

A group-term life insurance policy can be excluded from the estate of a deceased employee even though neither the policy nor state law gives the employee the right to convert the group-term coverage to individual life insurance upon termination of employment, provided the employee has irrevocably assigned all interest in such policy, and such assignment is not prohibited by state law or the policy.[11] This is true because the power to cancel the group-term policy solely by terminating employment is not considered to be an incident of insurance ownership.

In addition, the Tax Court has held, and the IRS has agreed, that a decedent's right to convert an employer-owned group policy of insurance on his life to individual insurance upon termination of employment is not an incident of ownership in the policy.[12] In the view of the court and the IRS, termination of employment by an employer is not within a decedent's control, and voluntary termination would be so detrimental to an employee's economic position that a conversion privilege should not be considered an incident of ownership. Therefore, if a decedent transfers all incidents of ownership in the policy, but retains the right to convert the group coverage to an individual policy upon termination of employment, the proceeds of the group policy are not includible in the decedent's gross estate.

● *Settlement Options*

It is an open question whether the proceeds of a noncontributory group-term life insurance policy are includible in an employee's gross estate where the employee has the right to vary the time and manner in

---

[8] Reg. § 20.2042-1(c).

[9] IRS Letter Ruling 9421037, 2-28-94, CCH IRS LETTER RULINGS REPORTS.

[10] Rev. Rul. 80-289, 1980-2 CB 270, revoking Rev. Rul. 79-231, 1979-2 CB 323.

[11] Rev. Rul. 72-307, 1972-1 CB 307, modifying Rev. Rul. 69-54, 1969-1 CB 221.

[12] *J. Smead Est.*, 78 TC 43, CCH Dec. 38,722 (Acq.); Rev. Rul. 84-130, 1984-2 CB 194.

which the proceeds are payable to the beneficiaries even though, under the policy, the employee cannot benefit himself or his estate.[13] The IRS maintains that the right to elect optional modes of settlement for the proceeds of life insurance on a decedent's life is an incident of ownership within the meaning of Code Sec. 2042. In addition, the IRS has announced that it will not follow the decision of the U.S. Court of Appeals for the Third Circuit in *Connelly,* which holds that the right to select such optional settlement modes is not an incident of ownership within the meaning of Code Sec. 2042 if the option merely allows the decedent to alter the time of enjoyment of the insurance proceeds.[14]

¶ 405 Death Benefits

Death benefits, payable other than under a life insurance contract, do not ordinarily qualify as proceeds of insurance. Benefits paid by employers, for example, voluntarily or otherwise, usually are lacking in some of the elements essential for qualification as insurance (see ¶ 420 and ¶ 733 for further details).

¶ 410 Insurance on the Life of Another

If a person, at the time of death, owns policies of insurance on the life of another individual, the value of such insurance is includible in the decedent's gross estate, but not as proceeds of insurance. It is included in the decedent's estate under Code Sec. 2033 as property in which the decedent had an interest at the time of death. It must be reported on Schedule F, Form 706, as "Other Miscellaneous Property."

The value of such insurance is the cost of replacement and not the cash surrender value. Replacement cost is the cost of buying another policy of the same value and same status on the life of the same insured. This cost can only be obtained from the insurer. If the policy has been in force for some time at the decedent's death and further premiums are to be paid, the value may be approximated by adding to the interpolated terminal reserve at the date of the decedent's death the proportionate part of the gross premium last paid before the decedent's death that covers the period extending beyond death.[15]

Conflict exists in those cases where a beneficiary-owner and the insured person die simultaneously. The IRS takes the position that the entire proceeds of a policy are to be included in the owner-beneficiary's gross estate. The courts have almost uniformly rejected this view and have held that the policy is to be valued under the interpolated terminal reserve method in accordance with Reg. § 20.2031-8.[16]

If, however, a policy is sold to the insured within six months following the death of the person who owned the policy, and the estate is valued as of a date six months after the death, the amount received upon the sale of the policy will govern its value for estate tax purposes. Likewise, if the policy

---

[13] See *J.H. Lumpkin, Jr., Est.,* CA-5, 73-1 USTC ¶ 12,909, 474 F2d 1092; *J.J. Connelly, Sr., Est.,* CA-3, 77-1 USTC ¶ 13,179, 551 F2d 545.

[14] Rev. Rul. 81-128, 1981-1 CB 469.

[15] Reg. § 20.2031-8(a)(2).

[16] *N. Meltzer Est.,* CA-4, 71-1 USTC ¶ 12,754, rev'g TC, 29 TCM 265, CCH Dec. 30,004(M), TC Memo. 1970-62; *Old Kent Bank,* CA-6, 70-2 USTC ¶ 12,703, 430 F2d 392; *R.M. Chown Est.,* CA-9, 70-2 USTC ¶ 12,702, 428 F2d 1395, rev'g TC, 51 TC 140, CCH Dec. 29,202; *E.M. Wien Est.,* CA-5, 71-1 USTC ¶ 12,764, 441 F2d 32; rev'g TC, 51 TC 287, CCH Dec. 29,238; *E.W. Marks, Jr., Est.,* 94 TC 720, CCH Dec. 46,594.

is actually surrendered for cash during the alternate valuation period after death, the amount received should be the acceptable value. If premiums are paid by the estate preceding the sale, it is likely that the value will be the total proceeds reduced by the portion attributable to the premiums paid after death.

See also ¶ 112 as to appreciation in value of insurance policies during the alternate valuation period.

¶ 415 Life Insurance and Annuity Combination

Persons who cannot pass the physical examination upon which the issuance of the usual type of life insurance contract is predicated may purchase a special type of insurance and annuity combination. The insurance portion of such a combination cannot be purchased separately. It is issued upon the assumption that, if the purchaser does not live long enough to receive full benefits from the annuity portion of the combination, the amount left over from the cost of that portion will make up the difference between the price paid for the insurance portion and the total amount of the death benefit. If the person does live to receive full benefits from the annuity portion, the money paid for the insurance portion will have gathered interest for a period long enough to build up the full amount of the death benefit. The insurance company actually takes no risk.

Formerly, it was generally believed that the insurance portion of such a combination was excludable from an insured decedent's estate where the decedent had irrevocably assigned all rights in the policy to the named beneficiaries.[17] However, this tax-saving technique was apparently eliminated by a 1972 case.[18] In this case, the IRS claimed, and the Tax Court and the U.S. Court of Appeals for the Fifth Circuit agreed, that the insurance and annuity contracts were part of one transaction and that, therefore, the insurance portion was includible in the decedent's estate as an annuity under Code Sec. 2039. Both courts held that the *Fidelity-Philadelphia Trust Co.* case was not controlling because it was decided before Code Sec. 2039 was enacted.

¶ 420 Pension and Profit-Sharing Plan Benefits

The inclusion of payments from a non-qualified employees' plan or contract depends on whether the payment is, in fact, the payment of proceeds of insurance under a policy on the life of the employee or whether the payment, in fact, represents an annuity payment.[19] (Typically, such plans provide for pension payments and for the payment of a death benefit where the employee dies before retirement.) If the payment represents insurance proceeds, the inclusion of the payment depends on whether the decedent employee has retained "incidents of ownership" over the policy (see ¶ 430). If the payment is an annuity, the estate tax treatment of the payment is based on the annuity rules discussed beginning at ¶ 700.

---

[17] *Fidelity-Philadelphia Trust Co., Exr. (M. Haines Est.)*, SCt, 58-1 USTC ¶ 11,761, 356 US 274.

[18] *L. Montgomery Est.*, 56 TC 489, CCH Dec. 30,822, aff'd per curiam, CA-5, 72-1 USTC ¶ 12,840, cert. denied, 409 US 849; *I.T. Sussman, Exr. (J. Sussman Will)*, DC N.Y., 76-1 USTC ¶ 13,126.

[19] Reg. § 20.2039-1(d).

¶ 425 Refunds in Case of Suicide

If an insured commits suicide before a policy becomes incontestable, the beneficiary will receive only a refund of premiums instead of receiving the face amount. This refund does not constitute a payment of insurance proceeds.[20]

¶ 430 Proceeds Payable to Named Beneficiaries

Life insurance payable to named beneficiaries is subject to special rules. If the insured merely names the beneficiary, but disposes of none, or only some, of the rights which the insured normally receives under the terms of a policy, the proceeds will be includible in the decedent insured's gross estate just like any other property. On the other hand, if the insured disposes of all rights over the policy (incidents of ownership), the entire amount of the proceeds may be kept out of the decedent's gross estate.[21]

Insurance is considered payable to a "named beneficiary" (one other than the estate) when the recipient is not required to use any of the proceeds for the benefit of the estate. Therefore, it may be paid to an executor if the executor may keep the proceeds for the executor's own benefit. It may be paid to a trustee if the trustee is not charged with a duty to apply the proceeds in payment of taxes or other estate charges. Likewise, it may be paid to a corporation, a partnership, or a profit-sharing plan.

The term "incidents of ownership" is not limited in its meaning to ownership of the policy in the technical, legal sense. The term refers to the right of the insured or the insured's estate to the economic benefits of the policy. The retention of any of the following will result in inclusion of the insurance proceeds in the gross estate: [22]

(1) the right to change beneficiaries or their shares;

(2) the right to surrender the policy for cash or to cancel it;

(3) the right to borrow against the policy reserve;

(4) the right to pledge the policy as collateral;

(5) the right to assign the policy or to revoke an assignment;

(6) the right to prevent cancellation of an insurance policy owned by an employer by purchasing the policy for its cash surrender value;[23] and

(7) a reversionary interest by which the insured or the estate of the insured may regain one or more of the above rights in the event a beneficiary should predecease the insured or if certain other contingencies should occur. (The chances that the right or rights will return to the insured must exceed five percent of the value of the policy immediately before the death of the insured.)

---

[20] *W.D. Chew, Jr., Est.*, CA-5, 45-1 USTC ¶ 10,181, 148 F2d 76, aff'g TC, 3 TC 940, CCH Dec. 13,953, cert. denied, 325 US 882.

[21] Code Sec. 2042; Reg. § 20.2042-1(c).

[22] Code Sec. 2042; Reg. § 20.2042-1(c).

[23] Rev. Rul. 79-46, 1979-1 CB 303. The Tax Court, however, has indicated that such a right is too contingent to warrant inclusion of policy proceeds in the gross estate; see, e.g., *J.C. Morrow Est.*, 19 TC 1068, CCH Dec. 19,510, and *J. Smith Est.*, 73 TC 307, CCH Dec. 36,443.

The possession of any of the above rights will result in inclusion of the proceeds in the insured's gross estate even if the consent of some other person is necessary to the exercise of the right. Estate tax liability depends on a general, legal power to exercise ownership, without regard to actual ability to exercise it at a particular moment (as on a trans-Atlantic flight).

- *Insured Decedent as Trustee*

Powers held by a decedent as fiduciary with respect to an insurance policy on his or her life will not constitute incidents of ownership in the policy so long as: (1) the powers are not exercisable for the decedent's personal benefit; (2) the decedent did not directly transfer the policy or any of the consideration for purchasing or maintaining the policy to the trust; and (3) the decedent did not retain the powers as settlor of the trust.[24] Where all of the above conditions are met, a decedent-trustee will not be deemed to have incidents of ownership in the policy even if the decedent held, at the time of death, such broad discretionary powers over the policy as the right to elect to have the proceeds made payable according to various plans, to use the loan value to pay the premiums, to borrow on the policy, to assign or pledge the policy, or to elect to receive annual dividends.[25] This IRS position is consistent with the decisions of several appellate courts.[26]

- *Transfers Within Three Years of Death*

The gross estate of a decedent who transferred all rights over an insurance policy on the decedent's life within three years of death and after 1976 includes the entire proceeds of the policy.[27] However, the proceeds are not reported on the life insurance schedule (Schedule D) of the estate tax return; rather, they are reported on the schedule concerning transfers during life (Schedule G).[28]

Some courts have held that, if a policy of insurance on the life of a decedent is issued within three years of death and the decedent pays the premiums, the policy proceeds are includible in the decedent's gross estate even if the decedent did not own the policy.[29] In the view of these courts, the decedent in each case effectively transferred the policy within three years of death by having it issued in the name of some other person (usually a family member) and paying the premiums. Although these cases were decided prior to the amendment of Code Sec. 2035 by the Economic Recovery Tax Act of 1981 (P.L. 97-34), the IRS National Office has adopted the reasoning of these courts and ruled that the proceeds of a policy of insurance on a decedent's life purchased within three years of the decedent's death in 1983 were includible in the decedent's gross estate even though the decedent never actually possessed any incidents of ownership in the policy.[30]

---

[24] Rev. Rul. 84-179, 1984-2 CB 195, revoking Rev. Rul. 76-261, 1976-2 CB 276.

[25] Rev. Rul. 84-179, 1984-2 CB 195, revoking Rev. Rul. 76-261, 1976-2 CB 276.

[26] *H.R. Fruehauf Est.*, CA-6, 70-1 USTC ¶ 12,688, 427 F2d 80, aff'g TC, 50 TC 915, CCH Dec. 29,416; *H.R. Skifter Est.*, CA-2, 72-2 USTC ¶ 12,893, 468 F2d 699; and *S.A. Hunter et al.*, CA-8, 80-2 USTC ¶ 13,362, 624 F2d 833; but see *C.M. Rose*, CA-5, 75-1 USTC ¶ 13,063, 511 F2d 259; and *N.C. Terriberry*, CA-5, 75-2 USTC ¶ 13,088, 517 F2d 286, cert. denied, 424 US 977.

[27] Code Sec. 2035. This rule was not changed by the Economic Recovery Tax Act of 1981 (P.L. 97-34).

[28] See Instructions for Form 706 (Rev. July 1998), p. 11.

[29] *D.M. Bel, Exr. (J.A. Bel Will)*, CA-5, 72-1 USTC ¶ 12,818, 452 F2d 683, cert. denied, 406 US 919; and *First National Bank of Oregon, Exr. (F.M. Slade Est.)*, CA-9, 74-1 USTC ¶ 12,966, 488 F2d 575.

[30] IRS Technical Advice Memorandum 8509005, 11-28-84, CCH IRS LETTER RULINGS REPORTS.

However, the U.S. Court of Appeals for the Tenth Circuit has held that the rule requiring inclusion of transfers within three years of death only applied to a gift of life insurance where the decedent retained incidents of ownership in the insurance policy under the rules of Code Sec. 2042.[31] Even though the decedent's wholly owned corporation paid the premiums on the policy, only his spouse and children, as owners and beneficiaries of the policy, held incidents of ownership. Thus, the proceeds of the life insurance policy purchased within three years of the decedent's death in 1983 were not includible in his gross estate. Other Tax Court decisions with similar fact situations have been affirmed by the U.S. Courts of Appeals for the Fifth and Sixth Circuits as well.[32] In fact, the U.S. Court of Appeals for the Fifth Circuit held that, following the amendment of Code Sec. 2035, the IRS's position was no longer substantially justified.[33]

On the other hand, the Tax Court has also held that an insurance policy on a decedent's life that was purchased by his spouse within three years of his death was includible in his gross estate in proportion to the decedent's interest in the community funds used to pay the policy premium.[34] The court stated that the payment of the policy premiums out of community property funds effected a "transfer" by the decedent of his interest in those funds, and that the ultimate effect of the transaction was similar to that which would have occurred had the decedent purchased the policy himself and then transferred all incidents of ownership to his wife.

A variation of this reasoning has been applied by some courts to require inclusion of proceeds in the gross estate where the decedent transferred funds to a trust within three years of death and the trustee purchased the policy. Two courts have held the proceeds includible in such a situation on the ground that the trustee acted as the decedent's agent in purchasing the policy.[35] Another court held that the proceeds would be includible in the decedent's gross estate if it could be shown that a trustee acted as her agent in purchasing a policy within three years of her death, and remanded the case to a lower court for a factual determination of the agency issue.[36] However, the Tax Court has held that even though a decedent created an irrevocable trust which purchased an insurance policy on her life within three years of her death, and she paid the policy premiums, the insurance proceeds were not includible in her gross estate because she did not possess any of the incidents of ownership in the policy.[37]

The Tax Court has held that when a wife purchased a life insurance policy on the life of her husband within three years of his death and paid for the policy out of a joint checking account, no portion of the policy

---

[31] *J. Leder Est.*, CA-10, 90-1 USTC ¶ 60,001, aff'g TC, 89 TC 235, CCH Dec. 44,093.

[32] *F.M. Perry, Sr., Est.*, CA-5, 91-1 USTC ¶ 60,064, aff'g TC, 59 TC 65, CCH Dec. 46,442(M); *E.L. Headrick Est.*, CA-6, 90-2 USTC ¶ 60,049, aff'g TC, 93 TC 171, CCH Dec. 45,914.

[33] *F.M. Perry Est.*, CA-5, 91-1 USTC ¶ 60,073.

[34] *R.W. Hass Est.*, 51 TCM 453, CCH Dec. 42,874(M), TC Memo. 1986-63. See *M. Baratta-Lorton Est.*, 49 TCM 770, CCH Dec. 41,890(M), TC Memo. 1985-72, aff'd by CA-9, in unpublished opinion, 3-24-86.

[35] *Detroit Bank & Trust Co., Exr. (F.W. Ritter Est.)*, CA-6, 72-2 USTC ¶ 12,883, 467 F2d 964, cert. denied, 410 US 929; and *T. Kurihara Est.*, 82 TC 51, CCH Dec. 40,914. See also *J. Schnack*, CA-9, 88-1 USTC ¶ 13,768, 848 F2d 933, rev'g TC, 52 TCM 1107, CCH Dec. 43,518(M), TC Memo. 1986-570.

[36] *G.H. Hope, Exr.*, CA-5, 82-2 USTC ¶ 13,504, 691 F2d 786.

[37] *M.F. Richins Est.*, 61 TCM 1706, CCH Dec. 47,125(M), TC Memo. 1991-23.

proceeds was includible in the decedent's estate because no agency relationship existed between the decedent and his wife. Therefore, the decedent did not have a transferable interest in the policy that would warrant the inclusion of the insurance proceeds in his gross estate in proportion to his contributions to the joint checking account.[38] In addition, in affirming a decision of the Tax Court, the U.S. Court of Appeals for the Sixth Circuit has held that life insurance proceeds were not includible in a decedent's gross estate where an *inter vivos* trust purchased the policy and paid the premiums pursuant to a trust agreement that permitted but did not require the purchase of the policy. Although the decedent contributed funds to the trust that were used to purchase the policy and pay premiums, this was not considered a sufficient nexus to establish that the decedent was indirectly paying the premiums while the trustee acted as his agent.[39]

The IRS has ruled that premiums paid within three years of death were includible in the estate of a decedent who had transferred the policy more than three years prior to death.[40] Several courts have adopted this view.[41] However the ruling would seem to apply only in the case of a decedent dying before 1982 (see ¶ 555).

Where the decedent-insured transfers a life insurance policy to a transferee within three years of his death and, after the assignment, the transferee pays the insurance premiums, the amount includible in the decedent's gross estate is that portion of the face value equaling the ratio of premiums paid by the decedent to the total premiums paid.[42]

¶ 435 Proceeds Payable for the Benefit of the Estate

Life insurance payable to one's estate, or to an executor or other person for the benefit of the estate, is always includible in the gross estate for estate tax purposes. It is includible, even though it may have been purchased by another who retains complete control over the policy during the lifetime of the insured.[43] It is even taxable when made payable to a trustee if the trustee is required to apply the proceeds to the payment of taxes, claims, or administration expenses. If the trustee is merely *permitted* to pay such charges, however, the insurance is subject to the same rules as insurance paid to named beneficiaries.[44]

If the proceeds of an insurance policy made payable to the decedent's estate are community assets under local community property law and, as a result, one-half of the proceeds belongs to the decedent's spouse, then only one-half of the proceeds is deemed to be receivable by or for the benefit of the decedent's estate.[45] Where the decedent's spouse dies before the decedent and the community property interest is not partitioned at the time of the spouse's death, the community status of the policy is retained up to the

---

[38] *L.J. Clay Est.*, 86 TC 1266, CCH Dec. 43,128. Cf. *J. Schnack*, CA-9, 88-1 USTC ¶ 13,768, 848 F2d 933, rev'g TC, 52 TCM 1107, CCH Dec. 43,518(M), TC Memo. 1986-570.

[39] *E.L. Headrick Est.*, CA-6, 90-2 USTC ¶ 60,049, aff'g TC, 93 TC 171, CCH Dec. 45,914.

[40] Rev. Rul. 71-497, 1971-2 CB 329, revoking Rev. Rul. 67-463, 1967-2 CB 327. For a discussion of continued premium payment under post-1976 rules, see Rev. Rul. 82-13, 1982-1 CB 132.

[41] See cases annotated at ¶ 4845 of the CCH FEDERAL ESTATE AND GIFT TAX REPORTER.

[42] *M.R. Silverman Est.*, CA-2, 75-2 USTC ¶ 13,084, 521 F2d 574, aff'g TC, 61 TC 338, CCH Dec. 32,246 (Acq.).

[43] Reg. § 20.2042-1(b).

[44] *Old Colony Tr. Co., Exr. (Est. of L.E. Flye)*, 39 BTA 871, Dec. 10,687 (Acq. and Nonacq.).

[45] Reg. § 20.2042-1(b).

time of maturity, and a tenancy-in-common is created as of the spouse's date of death.[46] However, the IRS has ruled that the proceeds of a life insurance policy on a Louisiana decedent's life were not includible in the decedent's gross estate, even though the policy had been purchased with community funds, because the decedent's spouse was the sole owner of the policy. Under Louisiana law, the use of community funds to pay the premiums on a life insurance policy held as the separate property of one spouse does not cause any of the incidents of ownership to be attributed to the community and does not affect the separate property status of the policy.[47] But the U.S. Court of Appeals for the Fifth Circuit has held that the entire proceeds of community property life insurance policies on a decedent's life that were designated as payable to his estate were includible in the gross estate.[48] Although premiums were paid with community funds, under Texas law, the entire proceeds of policies made payable to a decedent's estate are includible in the gross estate if designation of the estate as beneficiary was not made in fraud of the decedent's spouse (as found by the Tax Court). The appellate court noted that the insurance proceeds were (1) payable to the decedent's estate, (2) paid to the estate, and (3) allowed to remain in the estate's possession following the surviving spouse's state court challenge regarding her community property interest and, thus, could not be characterized as not "receivable by the executor" as required under Code Sec. 2042(1).

The proceeds of an insurance policy purchased by a decedent in favor of another person or a corporation as collateral security for a loan or other accommodation are also considered to be receivable for the benefit of the estate. However, the amount of the loan outstanding at the date of the decedent's death, with interest accrued thereon to that date, will be deductible in determining the taxable estate.[49]

¶ 440 Proceeds to Pay Estate Taxes

Although attempts have frequently been made to provide an estate tax exemption for the proceeds of insurance that are used to pay estate taxes, none of the attempts in Congress have been successful. If the recipient of the proceeds is required to use them to pay taxes, the proceeds are includible in the gross estate as insurance receivable by the executor. If a person who receives the proceeds would otherwise receive them free of tax, they do not become taxable by that person's election to apply them toward payment of the estate taxes in order to prevent liquidation of other assets.

¶ 445 Marital Deduction

If an insured's spouse is named as the beneficiary under a policy of life insurance and the insured retains no incidents of ownership in the policy, the proceeds will not be included in the insured decedent's gross estate. Consequently, the Code Sec. 2056 marital deduction will not apply.

---

[46] *H.R. Cavenaugh Est.*, CA-5, 95-1 USTC ¶ 60,195, aff'g in part and rev'g in part TC, 100 TC 407, CCH Dec. 49,030.

[47] Rev. Rul. 94-69, 1994-2 CB 241, revoking Rev. Rul. 48, 1953-1 CB 392, and Rev. Rul. 232, 1953-2 CB 268.

[48] *W. Street Est.*, CA-5, 98-2 USTC ¶ 60,327, aff'g TC, 73 TCM 1787, CCH Dec. 51,834(M), TC Memo. 1997-32.

[49] Reg. § 20.2042-1(b).

Insurance proceeds payable to the spouse or to the spouse's estate—either in a lump sum or in installments—on the condition that the spouse survive the insured by as much as six months will qualify for the marital deduction.[50] The proceeds will also qualify if they are left at interest during the life of the surviving spouse but are to be paid to the spouse's estate or to persons he or she may appoint following her death.[51]

If the insurance proceeds are to be paid to persons that the spouse may appoint, the proceeds will qualify even if provision is made for payment to contingent beneficiaries in the event the spouse fails to exercise the power. If the proceeds are to be paid in installments for at least a certain specified period of time, or if there is to be a refund of a part of principal in the event that the spouse fails to recover a specified amount in installments, the proceeds will still qualify if any payments following the death of the surviving spouse are to be made to the spouse's estate or to persons he or she may appoint.

¶ 450 Business Insurance

Life insurance is frequently used in connection with various types of business transactions, including the funding of agreements for purchase of an insured's business interest. It may also be purchased to protect a business against loss that might occur upon the death of a key employee of the business.

In these situations, the treatment of the insurance for estate tax purposes depends upon the terms of the agreement, if any is involved, and upon the terms of the insurance contract. In addition to affecting the treatment of the insurance for tax purposes, agreements for the purchase of a business interest can also affect the treatment of the interest itself.

Special problems arise where a closely held corporation owns insurance on the life of a stockholder-employee. The incidents of ownership held by a corporation on a corporate-owned life insurance policy covering a sole or controlling stockholder will not be attributed to the insured stockholder through his stock ownership under Code Sec. 2042 where the proceeds of such policy are received by the corporation or a third party for a valid business purpose.[52] Such proceeds are considered a nonoperating asset of the corporation in determining the stock value includible in the decedent's estate under Reg. § 20.2031-2(f). The Tax Court has ruled that the regulations do not permit the shareholder's stock to be valued by first finding the value of the stock without the insurance proceeds and then by adding the proceeds.[53] Rather, the proceeds must be taken into consideration as corporate assets in determining the value of the stock.

Except for group-term life insurance, the incidents of ownership will be attributed to the insured decedent who is the sole or controlling stockholder if such proceeds are not payable to the corporation or a third party for a valid business purpose. For this purpose, a decedent is considered to be the controlling stockholder of a corporation if he owned stock possessing more than 50 percent of the total combined voting power of the corporation at the time of his death. In this regard, the IRS has ruled that

---

[50] Reg. § 20.2056(b)-3.

[51] Reg. § 20.2056(b)-6.

[52] Reg. § 20.2042-1(c)(6).

[53] *J.L. Huntsman Est.*, 66 TC 861, CCH Dec. 33,976 (Acq.).

life insurance proceeds were includible in a controlling shareholder's gross estate where, within three years of his death, the corporation assigned the policy for less than adequate consideration and the shareholder then disposed of his controlling interest in the corporation. Under similar circumstances, the proceeds were includible where, instead of the corporation assigning the policy, the controlling shareholder disposed of his interest in the corporation for less than adequate consideration.[54] However, in a private ruling, the IRS did not attribute incidents of ownership to the sole shareholder of a corporation who could terminate the employment contract of the beneficiary of a life insurance policy on the shareholder's life, even though the termination would cause the insurance proceeds to be distributed to a trust for the benefit of the shareholder's family.[55]

Even if the insured person is not the sole stockholder, the policy may be includible if the insured retains incidents of ownership over the policy and the policy is not used to purchase stockholdings. Inclusion resulted in such a case where an insured stockholder had rights of ownership through the policy terms, even though the premiums were paid by the corporation, the policy was assigned by the corporation as collateral for corporate loans, and the cash surrender value was reflected on the corporate books.[56] The terms of the policy should be examined to make sure that the insured has not retained ownership through them. At least one court has ruled that terms of policies could not be rebutted by external evidence which showed that the decedent-insured intended to transfer all ownership rights to a corporation.[57]

¶ 455 Insurance on Stockholder

Life insurance often is used to fund agreements for the purchase and sale of stock in a close corporation following the death of a stockholder. The life insurance proceeds are used to provide part or all of the price for which the stock is to be sold.

The insurance under such an agreement may be purchased by the corporation, the insured, or by other stockholders. The proceeds may be payable to the corporation, to a trustee, to the insured's estate, or to a person or persons designated by the insured. The agreement may give one or both parties an option or it may require that the insured's stock be sold by the insured's estate and purchased by the corporation or other stockholders.

If the agreement requires the purchase and sale of the stock following the death of the insured, there will be included in the insured's estate either the value of the stock which is to be sold, or the proceeds of the sale of the stock. If the insured has no rights in the insurance policy that would have required inclusion of the proceeds in the insured's estate had no stock transaction been involved, only the value of the stock will be included in the insured's gross estate. Only the value of the stock is includible even if a beneficiary or beneficiaries should actually receive insurance proceeds in excess of the value of the stock. Such a situation, however, is very unlikely.

---

[54] Rev. Rul. 90-21, 1990-1 CB 172, amplifying Rev. Rul. 82-141, 1982-2 CB 209.

[55] IRS Letter Ruling 9421037, 2-28-94, CCH IRS LETTER RULINGS REPORTS.

[56] *G.H. Piggot Est.*, CA-6, 65-1 USTC ¶ 12,290, 340 F2d 829, aff'g TC, 22 TCM 241, CCH Dec. 25,985(M), TC Memo. 1963-61.

[57] *H.B. Cockrill, Exr.*, DC Tenn., 69-2 USTC ¶ 12,610, 302 FSupp 1365.

Usually, the insurance proceeds are less than the amount for which the stock is to be sold.

When the agreement for the purchase and sale of the stock is a mandatory one, the agreement serves to limit the amount actually to be included in the estate. The estate tax value is limited to the amount for which the stock is actually sold. This assumes that some fair method of valuation is used to arrive at the selling price and that all elements, including goodwill, are accounted for in fixing the value. Thus, if book value is to be the basis for fixing the price, there should be no litigation concerning some other method of valuation.

In situations where the various stockholders themselves purchase the stock, the one who dies is likely to own insurance upon one or more of the other stockholders. This insurance is not treated as life insurance for tax purposes. It is treated as any ordinary estate asset. Its value is the cost of replacement rather than the cash or loan value, unless it is disposed of within six months after death and the estate is valued as of six months after death (see ¶ 410).

The stockholders whose lives are covered by the policies are the most likely purchasers of such insurance. Sometimes the purchase agreement requires that the insureds be given an opportunity to purchase the insurance upon their own lives. The purchase opportunity is retained because they may no longer be insurable otherwise. In addition, state law may provide that the estate no longer has an insurable interest.

¶ 460 Partnership Insurance

The estate tax treatment of the proceeds of insurance and of the value of the partnership interest is the same as under the stock purchase agreement. It is less likely, however, that the partnership, as opposed to the individual partners, will be the purchaser of the insurance, since premiums have to be paid out of net income after individual taxes whether the partnership or the partners purchase the insurance.

Partners who purchase life insurance on the lives of each other to fund partnership purchase agreements should make sure (1) that they are named as owner-beneficiaries of a policy on the life of an insured partner and (2) that policy terms do give an insured partner incidents of ownership over the policy. In such cases, the IRS has attempted to include the face amount of the policy in the insured partner's gross estate, where the face value exceeded the value of the decedent's partnership interest as agreed upon. In two such cases, the IRS's attempt was unsuccessful because the Tax Court ruled that the partnership agreement controlled over the policy terms. Because the partnership agreements provided that proceeds were to be used to pay for the insured partners' interest, the court concluded that the partners could not exercise any incident of ownership that directly affected the economic benefits arising from the policies.[58]

The IRS has ruled that the proceeds of a policy of insurance on the life of a partner, which policy was owned by the partnership, were includible in the partner's gross estate because they were not payable to, or

[58] *B.L. Fuchs Est.*, 47 TC 199, CCH Dec. 28,186 (Acq.); *H.F. Infante Est.*, 29 TCM 903, CCH Dec. 30,250(M), TC Memo. 1970-206, CA-7, appeal dism'd, 6-2-71.

for the benefit of, the partnership.[59] The IRS concluded that the insured partner, by virtue of his one-third interest in the partnership, held an incident of ownership in the policy at death. This was so because the insured partner in his capacity as partner had the right (exercisable in conjunction with the other partners) to direct the economic benefits of the policy. However, where insurance proceeds were payable to a partnership, the Tax Court has ruled that a deceased partner's estate did not include insurance proceeds under the predecessor to Code Sec. 2042(2), despite the partner's incidents of ownership.[60] The IRS acquiesced in this result based on the fact that the value of the decedent's partnership interest reflected the payment of insurance proceeds to the partnership.

The IRS has also ruled that the proceeds of a partnership group-term insurance policy were not includible in the gross estate of an insured partner who, more than three years before his death, assigned all of the incidents of ownership in the policy to his children.[61] This was true even though the partnership retained the power to surrender or cancel the policy—a power that is an incident of policy ownership under Reg. § 20.2042-1(c)(2). Applying the rationale of regulations promulgated under Code Sec. 79 that deal with attribution of incidents of ownership in group-term policies held by controlled corporations, the IRS ruled that the partnership's power to surrender or cancel the policy was not to be attributed to the partner.

¶ 465 Insurance on Sole Proprietor

Insurance taken out by a sole proprietor on the proprietor's own life has the same status for estate tax purposes as insurance taken out by any individual upon the individual's own life. The presence or absence of rights of ownership determines whether the proceeds are includible in the insured's estate.

The insurance may have been taken out by the employees or other persons with an insurable interest as a means of providing funds for the purchase of all or a part of the business of the sole proprietor. The status of the insurance and the interest to be sold is the same as in the case of the corporation or partnership. Either the value of the business or the proceeds of its sale will be included in the sole proprietor's estate. If the agreement to sell to the employees is a mandatory one, the agreement will serve to limit the amount at which the value of the interest will be fixed.

¶ 470 Key-Employee Insurance

Sometimes a corporation will purchase insurance upon the life of an officer or stockholder, not to implement a purchase agreement, but to protect the corporation against loss that it feels will result from the untimely death of the insured. This insurance is usually referred to as key-employee insurance.

In key-employee insurance policies, the insured persons are personally responsible for a substantial share of the company's success, so that their

---

[59] Rev. Rul. 83-147, 1983-2 CB 158.

[60] *F. Knipp Est.*, 25 TC 153, CCH Dec. 21,311 (Acq.), aff'd on another issue, CA-4, 57-1 USTC ¶ 11,693, 244 F2d 436.

[61] Rev. Rul. 83-148, 1983-2 CB 157.

death may result in a loss of a certain amount of business. The insurance taken out on their lives is calculated to make up for the loss the company expects to incur. The proceeds are made payable to the corporation rather than to any individual.

A person insured under such an arrangement usually has no interest in the insurance. None of its proceeds will be included in the insured's gross estate. Its presence will, however, be felt in fixing a value for any stock which the insured may have owned in the company. The insurance is includible among corporate assets in determining the value of the insured's stock for estate tax purposes.

If, at the time of death, it does appear likely that the key employee's absence will have an adverse effect upon the conduct of the business, that factor can be taken into account in fixing the value of the stock. The estate is also protected against loss resulting from the death by its right to elect to value the estate as of six months after the insured's death. Insurance of this type is sometimes purchased by partnerships or sole proprietorships with similar results.

¶ 475 Valuation

The amount to be reported if insurance proceeds are payable to or for the benefit of the estate is the amount receivable. If the proceeds are payable to a named beneficiary, the amount receivable is again the amount reportable (although not necessarily taxable). Where the proceeds are to be paid in the form of an annuity, for life or for a certain number of years, the amount to be reported is the one sum payable at death under the lump-sum option. If no lump-sum option exists, the amount to be reported is the sum used to determine the amount of the annuity.[62] As to the valuation of reversionary interest in determining taxability, see ¶ 530.

If the estate must sue the insurance company in order to collect policy proceeds, the amount includible with respect to the policy may be less than the face amount of the proceeds. The IRS National Office has ruled that the amount includible in a decedent's gross estate with respect to two policies of insurance on the decedent's life is the fair market value, on the date of the decedent's death, of claims resulting from lawsuits that the decedent's estate filed to obtain the proceeds payable under the policies. Neither the amount of the proceeds nor the amount received by the estate in settlement of the claims was the correct amount includible. Although Code Sec. 2042 controls the includibility of policies in the estate, it does not control the valuation of the policies which, accordingly, must be valued on the basis of all facts and circumstances existing on the date of death.[63]

¶ 480 Description of Insurance on Return

All insurance on a decedent's life is reportable on Schedule D, Form 706. Every policy of insurance on the life of a decedent must be listed, whether or not it is included in the gross estate. The name of the insurance company and the policy number should be listed under "Description." For every policy listed, the decedent's estate should request a statement from

---

62 Reg. § 20.2042-1(a)(3).

63 IRS Technical Advice Memorandum 8308001, 1-21-82, CCH IRS LETTER RULINGS REPORTS.

the company that issued the policy on Form 712 (Life Insurance Statement) (see ¶ 481).

If the policy proceeds are paid in one sum, the value to be entered in the valuation column is the net proceeds received, from Form 712, line 24. However, if the policy proceeds are not paid in one sum, the value to be entered is the value of the proceeds as of the date of the decedent's death, from Form 712, line 25. If part or all of the policy proceeds are not included in the gross estate, an explanation of the reason for their exclusion must accompany the policy description.

In the case of an estate of a nonresident not a citizen, the proceeds of insurance on the nonresident's life are not taxable and need not be included in the schedule.[64]

¶ 481 Life Insurance Statement

The executor of a decedent's estate must file a Form 712 (Life Insurance Statement) with the estate tax return for every policy of life insurance on the decedent's life that is listed on the schedule and that constitutes a part of the gross estate.[65] It is also the duty of the executor to obtain the statement from the insurance company that issued the policy.

An executor should file Form 712 in order to facilitate valuation of insurance owned by the decedent on the life of another person.

¶ 485 Community Property

Special rules apply when insurance is paid for out of community funds. See ¶ 165 and ¶ 435 for a discussion of the status of community property.

---

[64] Code Sec. 2501(a).

[65] Reg. § 20.6018-4. Instructions for Schedule D, Form 706 (Rev. July 1998), p. 16.

¶ 495 Filled-In Schedule D

Schedule D has to be filled out and filed with Form 706 only if there is insurance reportable on this schedule (see ¶ 73).

The filled-in Schedule D, Form 706 (Rev. July 1998), relates to the fact situation of a person who dies on January 1, 1998, with an estate tax return due within nine months (without extensions).

Form 706 (Rev. 7-98)

Estate of: James X. Diversey

SCHEDULE D — Insurance on the Decedent's Life

You must list all policies on the life of the decedent and attach a Form 712 for each policy.

Item number	Description	Alternate valuation date	Alternate value	Value at date of death
1	$10,000 term policy No. N-17-136-43, National Service Life Insurance Co., payable to decedent's widow, Carrie Diversey, as named beneficiary, proceeds of $10,000 payable in one lump sum as per attached Form 712.			10,000
	Accrued dividends on Item 1: none.			
2	$50,000 20-pay life policy No. 10-612-5, Equitable Life Assurance Society of New York, proceeds of $50,000 payable in one lump sum as per attached Form 712.			50,000
	$1,120 in additional insurance paid for by dividends on policy in Item 2 left in for purchase of additional insurance.			1,120
	INSURANCE PROCEEDS NOT INCLUDIBLE IN GROSS ESTATE			
	$50,000 20-pay life policy No. 864325 taken out in Jan. 1945, with Metropolitan Life Insurance Co. and paid up in Jan. 1965, proceeds irrevocably payable to Carrie Diversey as named beneficiary in installments for life or for 20 years certain; proceeds not includible because insured retained no incidents of ownership and because premium costs were paid by beneficiary Carrie Diversey, who became owner of the policy by reason of irrevocable assignment of rights for love and affection (Form 712 attached).			
	Total from continuation schedules (or additional sheets) attached to this schedule			
	TOTAL. (Also enter on Part 5, Recapitulation, page 3, at item 4.)			61,120

(If more space is needed, attach the continuation schedule from the end of this package or additional sheets of the same size.)

(See the instructions.)

Schedule D — Page 15

Chapter 13

JOINTLY OWNED PROPERTY

¶ 500 Interest of Joint Owners

Property in which the decedent at the time of death held an interest either as a joint tenant or as a tenant by the entirety, with right of survivorship, is the subject of special treatment under the estate tax law. Such joint interests are removed from the scope of Code Sec. 2033, which provides for inclusion of property in which the decedent had an interest at death, and are taxed under the even broader concepts of Code Sec. 2040.

Ordinarily, under property law, each participant in a joint tenancy or tenancy by the entirety is regarded as owning an undivided equal share. The estate tax law follows this concept only with respect to property held jointly with right of survivorship and only if acquired by gift, devise, bequest, or inheritance.[1]

However, special rules apply to certain joint interests held by spouses, in which each spouse will be considered as owning a one-half interest in the joint property for estate tax purposes (see ¶ 502). Therefore, in the case of property acquired by a spouse by inheritance as a tenant by the entirety or a joint tenant with right of survivorship, one-half of the value of the property would be included in the gross estate of the first spouse to die. Similarly, in the case of three tenants of property acquired by gift as a joint tenancy, each tenant is regarded as owning one-third of the property.

¶ 501 Property Acquired by Purchase

The estate tax law provides a general rule in the case of property acquired by purchase and held in joint tenancy or by the entirety. The portion to be included in the deceased tenant's gross estate is based upon the percentage of the decedent's contribution to the total cost. This percentage is multiplied by the fair market value of the entire property on the date of the decedent's death.[2] (Different rules apply to property acquired by married joint tenants—see ¶ 502.)

The value of the entire property will be included in the gross estate unless the amount contributed by the survivor is proven. In determining the amount of the survivor's contribution, any part of the contribution which was originally received from the decedent by gift cannot be included.

> ***Example:*** Amy Cooper and her daughter, Julie, buy a residence for $100,000 as joint tenants. Amy contributed $80,000 to the cost and Julie contributed $20,000. Amy will be regarded as having an 80-percent interest in the property. If she dies first and if, on her

[1] Reg. § 20.2040-1(a)(1).

[2] Reg. § 20.2040-1(a)(2).

death, the property is worth $200,000, 80 percent, or $160,000, will be included in her gross estate.

This provision also covers joint bank accounts and jointly held bonds, stock or other instruments, but has no application to property held by the decedent and any other person as tenants in common.[3]

Where property held in joint tenancy was purchased with community property funds in which the spouses had equal vested interests, one-half of the value of the jointly held property is excluded from the decedent's gross estate.[4]

A decedent's interest as a tenant in common is not reportable on Schedule E as jointly owned property. The proper schedule for reporting the property interest is dictated by the nature of the property—realty on Schedule A, stocks and bonds on Schedule B, etc.

In all instances where the executor or administrator seeks to exclude a part of the value of the jointly held property from the gross estate, the executor has the burden of proving a right to include the reduced value and, therefore, should be prepared to prove the extent, origin, and nature of each joint owner's interest.[5]

¶ 502 Spousal Joint Tenancies

The estate of the first spouse to die includes only one-half of the value of a "qualified joint interest" in property regardless of which spouse furnished the consideration for the property. For purposes of this provision, "qualified joint interest" is defined as any interest in property held solely by spouses as joint tenants with the right of survivorship or as tenants by the entirety.[6]

However, the U.S. Court of Appeals for the Sixth Circuit has held that a surviving spouse was entitled to a stepped-up basis for jointly held property created prior to 1977 where her husband had provided all of the consideration for the property. Because the effective date of the Economic Recovery Tax Act of 1981 (P.L. 97-34) (ERTA) (generally applicable to estates of decedents dying after December 31, 1981) did not expressly or by implication repeal the effective date of the Tax Reform Act of 1976, the contribution test as it existed prior to 1977 was applicable in determining the amount of jointly held property includible in the gross estate of the decedent who died after the effective date of ERTA. Accordingly, because 100 percent of the value of the jointly held property was includible in the decedent's gross estate, his surviving spouse was entitled to a stepped-up date-of-death basis for the entire property.[7] (See, also, ¶ 2107 for treatment of pre-1982 lifetime gifts of spousal joint interests.)

• *Special Rule Where Spouse Is Noncitizen*

The creation of a joint tenancy in property is generally treated as a completed gift. Before the effective date of the Technical and Miscellaneous Revenue Act of 1988 (P.L. 100-647) (TAMRA), such a gift between

---

[3] Reg. § 20.2040-1(b).

[4] *J.A. Kammerdiner*, CA-9, 44-1 USTC ¶ 10,084, 140 F2d 569; Rev. Rul. 78-418, 1978-2 CB 236.

[5] Reg. § 20.2040-1(a)(2).

[6] Code Sec. 2040(b).

[7] *M.L. Gallenstein*, CA-6, 92-2 USTC ¶ 60,114, aff'g DC Ky., 91-2 USTC ¶ 60,088; *J. Patten*, CA-4, 97-2 USTC ¶ 60,279; *E.M. Baszto*, DC Fla., 98-1 USTC ¶ 60,305; and *T. Hahn*, 110 TC 140, CCH Dec. 52,606.

spouses qualified for the marital deduction for estate and gift tax purposes and only one-half of the jointly held property was included in the gross estate of the first spouse to die under the "qualified joint interest" rule described above. However, effective for gifts made to noncitizen spouses on or after July 14, 1988, TAMRA repealed the marital deduction (see ¶ 1000) and also provided that the entire value of jointly held property is includible in the deceased spouse's estate, reduced by the portion of the property for which consideration was received.

In determining the federal estate tax, the value of gifts includible in the gross estate is effectively reduced by the value of taxable gifts when made. Thus, for joint tenancies created on or after July 14, 1988, where the donee spouse is a noncitizen, the amount included in the gross estate of the first spouse to die is effectively reduced by the amount transferred when the tenancy was created. In the case of joint tenancies created prior to July 14, 1988, no such reduction occurred because the gift qualified for the marital deduction and was not taxable. A provision of the Revenue Reconciliation Act of 1989 (P.L. 101-239) as modified by the Revenue Reconciliation Act of 1990 (P.L. 101-508) provides that, for purposes of determining the amount of joint tenancy property includible in a decedent's gross estate, a gift made by creating a joint tenancy in property prior to July 14, 1988, is treated as consideration belonging to the surviving spouse if the transfer would have constituted a gift had the donor been a U.S. citizen. Thus, the amount of joint tenancy property included in the gross estate of the first spouse to die is reduced proportionately by the amount of the gift.[8]

¶ 510 Valuation of Jointly Owned Property

If the decedent and any person with whom the decedent held property jointly transferred that property to others during the decedent's lifetime, the transfer is reportable as a transfer made during the decedent's lifetime, rather than as jointly held property.

The principles governing valuation of jointly held property are the same as those governing other types of property. Therefore, reference should be made to the instructions preceding the various schedules for information concerning the valuation of the specific kinds of property held jointly. However, the Tax Court has ruled that fractional interest discount and lack of marketability descount do not apply in the valuation of joint tenancy property.[9]

¶ 515 Description on Return

Property owned at the time of death by a decedent in joint tenancy with the right of survivorship or in a tenancy by the entirety is to be reported on Schedule E (Jointly Owned Property) of Form 706. If the decedent's spouse was the only other co-tenant, the tenancy constitutes a qualified joint interest (see ¶ 502) and is to be reported in Part I of Schedule E. All other joint tenancy property must be reported in Part II of Schedule E, including the names and addresses of the surviving joint owners (see ¶ 520 for further details).

---

[8] Act Sec. 11701(l), P.L. 101-508, amending Act Sec. 7815(d)(16), P.L. 101-239.

[9] *Wayne-Chi Young Est.*, 110 TC 297, CCH Dec. 52,691.

In reporting jointly owned property on Schedule E, a statement under the column headed "Description" must disclose whether the whole or only a part of the property is included in the gross estate. If only a part of the property is included in the gross estate, the fair market value of the whole must nevertheless be shown under "Description."

Property in which the decedent held an interest as a tenant in common should not be listed on Schedule E. The value of the decedent's interest as a tenant in common should be returned under the schedule for real estate, or, if personal property, under such other appropriate schedule. Similarly, community property held by the decedent and spouse should be returned under appropriate other schedules. The decedent's interest in a partnership should be shown under Schedule F (Other Miscellaneous Property) of Form 706.

¶ 520 Filled-In Schedule E

Schedule E must be filed with Form 706 only if the decedent owned property reportable on it. The schedule can be omitted if the decedent did not own property reportable on it (see ¶ 73).

The filled-in Schedule E, Form 706 (Rev. July 1998), relates to the fact situation of a person who dies on January 1, 1998, with an estate tax return due within nine months (without extensions).

Form 706 (Rev. 7-98)

Estate of: James X. Diversey

SCHEDULE E — Jointly Owned Property

(If you elect section 2032A valuation, you must complete Schedule E and Schedule A-1.)

PART 1. — Qualified Joint Interests — Interests Held by the Decedent and His or Her Spouse as the Only Joint Tenants (Section 2040(b)(2))

Item number	Description For securities, give CUSIP number.	Alternate valuation date	Alternate value	Value at date of death
1	Residence, 54 Fir Street, Homewood, IL. Single family dwelling on 1/2 acre lot (Plot 68, page 53, Lot 16, square 10). Value based on appraisal (Copy attached)			160,000
2	Checking account No. 46835, State National Bank, Peterson and Pulaski Ave.s, Chicago, IL.			4,386
	Total from continuation schedules (or additional sheets) attached to this schedule			
1a	Totals			164,386
1b	Amounts included in gross estate (one-half of line 1a)			82,193

PART 2. — All Other Joint Interests

2a State the name and address of each surviving co-tenant. If there are more than three surviving co-tenants, list the additional co-tenants on an attached sheet.

	Name	Address (number and street, city, state, and ZIP code)
A.	Martha Diversey	54 Fir Street Homewood, IL 60430
B.		
C.		

Item number	Enter letter for co-tenant	Description (including alternate valuation date if any) For securities, give CUSIP number.	Percentage includible	Includible alternate value	Includible value at date of death
1	A	Rental building and lot, 8141 Sangmar, Chicago, IL (Plot 16, page 32, Lot 48, square 48). Two-story brick single-family dwelling. Value based on appraisal (copy attached). One-half of the value is includible because Martha Diversey provided one-half of the purchase price of 10,000 in 1955.	50%		65,000
		Total from continuation schedules (or additional sheets) attached to this schedule			
2b		Total other joint interests			65,000
3		Total includible joint interests (add lines 1b and 2b). Also enter on Part 5, Recapitulation, page 3, at item 5			147,193

(If more space is needed, attach the continuation schedule from the end of this package or additional sheets of the same size.)
(See the instructions.)

Schedule E — Page 17

Chapter 14
MISCELLANEOUS PROPERTY

¶ 525 Items Termed "Miscellaneous"

The classification "Other Miscellaneous Property" on the estate tax return relates to property that is includible in the gross estate under Code Sec. 2033 but that does not fall within any of the preceding property-schedule classifications. It includes such items as:

(1) debts due the decedent (other than notes and mortgages included on Schedule C);

(2) interests in business;

(3) insurance on the life of another;

(4) claims (including the value of the decedent's interest in a claim for refund of income taxes, or the amount of the refund actually received);

(5) rights;

(6) royalties;

(7) leaseholds;

(8) judgments;

(9) shares in trust funds;

(10) household goods and personal effects, including wearing apparel;

(11) farm products and growing crops;

(12) livestock;

(13) farm machinery;

(14) automobiles;

(15) reversionary or remainder interests; and

(16) Code Sec. 2044 property (property for which the marital deduction was previously allowed).

¶ 526 Reporting Property Interests

The various property interests that are described at ¶ 525 as being reportable on Form 706, Schedule F, are taxable under Code Sec. 2033 as property in which the decedent had an interest at the time of death. Schedule F must be filed with Form 706.

If any of the property reportable under this category was transferred by the decedent during the decedent's life, that property should not be listed with the "miscellaneous" property. It should be reported in Schedule G (Transfers During Decedent's Life) for transfers during the decedent's lifetime. The method of valuing such property, however, is the same, no matter which schedule is applicable. If the transfer, by trust or otherwise, was made by a written instrument, a copy of such document should be submitted with the return.

¶ 527 Interests in Business

Business interests, other than corporate, are reported on Schedule F as "other miscellaneous property." In determining the fair market value of any business interest or intangible asset for estate tax purposes, the general approach, methods and factors in Rev. Rul. 59-60,[1] pertaining to valuation of stock in closely held corporations, are applicable, but will not control when better evidence of value is available.

The valuation of interests in business requires great care. A fair appraisal should be made of all of the assets of the business, including goodwill. The business should be given a net value equal to the amount that a willing purchaser would pay to a willing seller in view of asset value and earning capacity. Where the decedent's interest in a partnership, for instance, is subject to an agreement to sell to survivors at a price determined by some equitable means, that price will determine the value. In the absence of a purchase agreement, special attention should be given to fixing an adequate figure for the value of the goodwill.

● *Documentation*

All evidence bearing on the valuation of an interest in a business should be submitted with the return. This includes copies of reports in any case in which examinations of the business have been made by accountants, engineers, or any technical experts as of or near the applicable valuation date. If the decedent owned any interest in a partnership or unincorporated business, a statement of assets and liabilities as of the valuation date and for the preceding five years, along with statements of the net earnings for the same five years, should be submitted with the return. In general, the same information should be furnished and the same methods followed as in valuing interests in close corporations.

¶ 528 Limited Interests

Annuities, interests for life or for a term of years, and remainder and reversionary interests present special valuation problems. For a commercial annuity or insurance policy on the life of a person other than the decedent that is payable under a contract with an insurance or other company regularly engaged in selling such contracts, the value is the price of a comparable contract on the applicable valuation date (see ¶ 760). In all other instances, the value is determined by discounting future payments.

---

[1] Rev. Rul. 59-60, 1959-1 CB 237. Additional valuation information is contained in Reg. §20.2031-3; Rev. Rul. 65-193, 1965-2 CB 370; Rev. Rul. 77-287, 1977-2 CB 319, corrected by Ann. 77-168, I.R.B. 1977-51, 22; and Rev. Rul. 83-120, 1983-2 CB 170, which modified and amplified Rev. Rul. 59-60.

The valuation date for such interests is the date of death regardless of whether the alternate valuation date is used. When the alternate valuation date has been elected, the value at death is then adjusted for any difference in value between the date of death and the applicable valuation date which is due to causes other than the mere lapse of time.[2]

Special tables are used to determine the present value of a private annuity, an interest for life or for a term of years, and a remainder or reversionary interest (see ¶ 530 and 531).

¶ 530 Valuation of Limited Interests

The appropriate authority for determining the estate or gift tax value of limited interests in property such as annuities, interests for life or for a term of years, and remainder and reversionary interests depends on the date of the decedent's death or the date of the gift. Limited property interests valued with respect to decedents dying after April 30, 1989, are governed by Reg. § 20.2031-7. For decedents dying before May 1, 1989, Reg. § 20.2031-7A provides the applicable rules for valuing limited property interests, depending on whether the decedent died before 1952 (Reg. § 20.2031-7A(a)), after 1951 and before 1971 (Reg. § 20.2031-7A(b)), after 1970 and before December 1, 1983 (Reg. § 20.2031-7A(c)), or after November 30, 1983, and before May 1, 1989 (Reg. § 20.2031-7A(d)). The regulations provide various tables for valuing these limited interests depending on whether the interest is dependent upon the termination or continuation of one life or upon a certain period of years.

Expanded versions of the tables in the regulations (at interest rates ranging from 2.2 percent to 26 percent) that are applicable to the estates of decedents dying after April 30, 1989, and to gifts and certain transfers made after that date, including two life factors, are contained in the following IRS publications:

(1) Publication 1457, *Actuarial Values, Alpha Volume,* which includes remainder, income, and annuity factors for one life, two lives, and terms certain for income, estate, and gift tax purposes, including valuation of pooled income fund remainder interests;

(2) Publication 1458, *Actuarial Values, Beta Volume,* which includes unitrust remainder factors for one life, two lives, and terms certain for income, estate, and gift tax purposes; and

(3) Publication 1459, *Actuarial Values, Gamma Volume,* which includes tables for computation of depreciation and adjustment factors for income tax purposes only.

Certain tables contained in these publications were published in the *Federal Register,* along with final regulations.[3] These publications, which include examples that illustrate how to compute special factors for more unusual situations, are available from the Superintendent of Documents, U.S. Government Printing Office, Washington, D.C. 20402.

---

[2] Reg. § 20.2032-1(f).

[3] T.D. 8540, adopting Reg. § 20.7520-1 through Reg. § 20.7520-4, Reg. § 20.2031-7 and Reg. § 20.2031-7A, after redesignating Reg. § 20.2031-7 as Reg. § 20.2031-7A(d), was published in the *Federal Register* on June 10, 1994.

● *Decedents Dying After April 30, 1989*

Applicable valuation rules.—Code Sec. 7520 provides that the value of an annuity, an interest for life or for a term of years, or a remainder or reversionary interest is to be determined under valuation tables prescribed by the Secretary of the Treasury. In general, the fair market value of a limited interest is determined by using an actuarial factor that is based on the most recent mortality experience available (the mortality component) in conjunction with the appropriate Code Sec. 7520 assumed rate of return (the interest rate component). A person's age at their nearest birthday is to be used for computation purposes. The Code Sec. 7520 interest rate is computed as 120 percent of the applicable federal midterm rate (rounded to the nearest two-tenths of one percent) and is published each month in an IRS revenue ruling.

The table below sets forth the applicable Code Sec. 7520 interest rates since January 1986.

Month	*Interest factor*	*Month*	*Interest factor*
January 1996	6.8%	September 1997	7.6%
February 1996	6.8%	October 1997	7.6%
March 1996	6.6%	November 1997	7.4%
April 1996	7.0%	December 1997	7.2%
May 1996	7.6%	January 1998	7.2%
June 1996	8.0%	February 1998	6.8%
July 1996	8.2%	March 1998	6.8%
August 1996	8.2%	April 1998	6.8%
September 1996	8.0%	May 1998	6.8%
October 1996	8.0%	June 1998	7.0%
November 1996	8.0%	July 1998	6.8%
December 1996	7.6%	August 1998	6.8%
January 1997	7.4%	September 1998	6.6%
February 1997	7.6%	October 1998	6.2%
March 1997	7.8%	November 1998	5.4%
April 1997	7.8%	December 1998	5.4%
May 1997	8.2%	January 1999	5.6%
June 1997	8.2%	February 1999	5.6%
July 1997	8.0%	March 1999	5.8%
August 1997	7.6%	April 1999	6.4%

The factors set forth at ¶ 531 involving life contingencies are taken from the values of 1(x) from the Life Table for the Total Population appearing in Table 1 in "U.S. Decennial Life Tables for 1971-81" published by the U.S. Department of Health and Human Services. Table 1 is designated Table 80CNSMT in the regulations[4] and is reproduced at ¶ 531.

Ordinary remainder and reversionary interests.—For decedents dying after April 30, 1989, the present value of a remainder or reversionary interest postponed for a term certain is determined by multiplying the fair market value of the property by the appropriate remainder interest factor in Table B of Reg. § 20.2031-7(d)(6). If the interest is postponed until after the death of one individual, the appropriate remainder interest factor in Table S of Reg. § 20.2031-7(d)(6) is used. The appropriate remainder interest factor is that factor which corresponds to the applicable Code Sec. 7520 interest rate and either the Table B term certain or the Table S current age of the individual who is the measuring life.[5]

[4] Reg. § 20.2031-7(d)(6).

[5] Reg. § 20.2031-7(d)(2)(ii).

Example (1): Computation of a Remainder Interest. Assume a donor makes a gift of an interest in a trust for an 8-year term certain after April 30, 1989, and needs to value the remainder interest. Also assume that 120 percent of the applicable federal mid-term rate for the month is 7.4 percent. In Table B under the column for 7.4 percent and opposite 8 years is the figure .564892. Based upon an interest rate of 7.4 percent per annum, the present worth of $1 due at the end of 8 years is $.564892.

Ordinary term-of-years and life interest.—The present value of a right to receive the income of property, or to use nonincome-producing property, for a term of years or for the life of one individual is determined by multiplying the fair market value of the property by the appropriate term-of-years or life interest factor which corresponds to the applicable Code Sec. 7520 interest rate. Although the term-of-years and life interest factors are not included in Table B or Table S in Reg. § 20.2031-7(d)(6), they may be derived mathematically. The term-of-years (income interest) factor is derived by subtracting the correlative Table B term certain remainder factor that corresponds to the applicable Code Sec. 7520 interest rate from 1.000000. Similarly, the factor for the life of one individual (life estate) is derived by subtracting the correlative Table S single life remainder factor that corresponds to the applicable Code Sec. 7520 interest rate from 1.000000.[6] These actuarial factors for income interests and life estates are included in Table B and Table S, respectively, in IRS Publication No. 1457.

Example (2): Computation of an Income Interest. Assume the same facts as in Example 1, except that the donor needs to value the income interest. The income factor equals 1 minus the remainder factor. Thus, if the remainder factor is .564892 the income factor is 1 − .564892, or .435108.

Annuities.—The present value of an annuity that is payable at the end of each year for a term certain or for the life of one individual is determined by multiplying the aggregate amount payable annually by the appropriate annuity factor which corresponds to the applicable Code Sec. 7520 interest rate. These actuarial factors are included in Table B and Table S in IRS Publication No. 1457. Although the annuity factors are not included in Table B or Table S in Reg. § 20.2031-7(d)(6), they may be derived mathematically. The term certain annuity factor is derived by subtracting the correlative Table B term certain remainder factor that corresponds to the applicable Code Sec. 7520 interest rate from 1.000000 and then dividing the result by the applicable Code Sec. 7520 interest rate expressed as a decimal. Similarly, the single life annuity factor is derived by subtracting the correlative Table S single life remainder factor that corresponds to the applicable Code Sec. 7520 interest rate from 1.000000 and then dividing the result by the applicable Code Sec. 7520 interest rate expressed as a decimal.[7]

Example (3): Computation of an Annuity Interest. Assume the same facts as in Example 1. The valuation factor for a term certain annuity interest may be computed by using this formula.

---

[6] Reg. § 20.2031-7(d)(2)(iii).

[7] Reg. § 20.2031-7(d)(2)(iv).

$$\text{Annuity Factor} = \frac{\text{Income Factor}}{i}$$

(Where i equals the applicable interest rate under Code Sec. 7520.) Thus, if 120 percent of the applicable federal midterm rate for the month is 7.4 percent and the income factor, as computed in Example (2) above, is .435108, the valuation factor for an annuity interest for a term of 8 years is .435108 divided by 7.4 percent, or 5.8798.

Certain adjustment factors must be applied to the valuations determined above if the annuity is payable at any time other than the end of each year. Table J (Reg. § 20.2031-7(d)(6)) contains the adjustment factors applicable for term certain annuities if the annuity is payable at the beginning of annual, semiannual, quarterly, monthly, or weekly periods. Table K (Reg. § 20.2031-7(d)(6)) contains the adjustment factors applicable if the annuity is payable at the end of semiannual, quarterly, monthly, or weekly periods. Regardless of which table applies, the product obtained by multiplying the aggregate amount payable annually by the applicable annuity factor is then multiplied by the applicable adjustment factor to obtain the present value of the annuity.[8]

The present value of an annuity or unitrust interest that is payable for a term of years or until the prior death of an individual may be computed by following the examples set forth in Reg. § 25.2512-5(d)(2)(v).

Split interest trusts.—The fair market value of a remainder interest in a charitable remainder annuity trust (CRAT) is the net fair market value of the property placed in trust less the present value of the annuity, which can be computed by using Table S or Table B under Reg. § 20.2031-7(d).[9] The present value of an annuity interest that is payable until the earlier to occur of the lapse of a specific number of years or the death of an individual may be computed using Tables B, K, S and 80CNSMT at ¶ 531. Reg. § 25.2512-5(d)(2)(v)(A) provides an example for computing the value of such an annuity interest using these tables.

The present value of a remainder interest in a pooled income fund as defined in Reg. § 1.642(c)-5 is valued pursuant to Reg. § 1.642(c)-6.

The present value of a remainder interest in a charitable remainder unitrust (CRUT) as defined in Reg. § 1.664-3 is valued pursuant to Reg. § 1.664-4 using Tables F and D or U(1) at ¶ 531. The present value of a unitrust interest that is payable until the earlier to occur of the lapse of a specific number of years or the death of an individual may be computed using Tables D, F, U(1) and 80CNSMT pursuant to the example provided in Reg. § 25.2512-5(d)(2)(v)(B).

Exceptions to the use of standard factors.—The IRS has established situations in which the standard actuarial factors may not be used.[10] These include (1) transfers to high payout annuities if the annuity is expected to exhaust the fund before the last possible annuity payment is made in full; (2) transfers to split-interest trusts in which a grantor retains an income interest in a trust funded with unproductive or underproductive property; and (3) transfers with a retained life interest for which the

---

[8] Reg. § 20.2031-7(d)(2)(iv)(B) and (C).

[9] Reg. § 1.664-2(c).

[10] Reg. § 20.7520-3(b) and Reg. § 25.7520-3(b).

person who is the measuring life has a terminal illness. Thus, the standard factors may not be used if the governing instrument fails to provide an income beneficiary with that degree of beneficial enjoyment of the property that the principles of the law of trusts accord to a person who is unqualifiedly designated as the income beneficiary of a trust.

An individual is deemed to be terminally ill if he or she is known to have an incurable illness or other deteriorating physical condition such that there is at least a 50-percent probability that the individual will die within one year. If the individual survives for at least 18 months after the date the gift is completed, however, the presumption is made that there was no terminal illness at the time of the transfer, unless the contrary is established by clear and convincing evidence.

Transitional rule.—A transitional rule is provided if a decedent was mentally incompetent on May 1, 1989, and dies without having regained competency or dies within 90 days of the date on which the decedent first regained competency. Under the rule, the fair market value of an annuity, interest for life or a term of years, or a remainder or reversionary interest includible in the gross estate may be determined under the above rules or under the corresponding applicable provisions of Reg. § 20.2031-7A(a)—(d) at the time the decedent became incompetent.[11]

● *Decedents Dying Before May 1, 1989*

Valuation of gross estate before January 1, 1952.—In the case of a decedent dying before 1952, the present value of limited interests that are dependent upon the continuation or termination of one or more lives, or upon a term certain concurrent with one or more lives, is computed on the basis of interest at the rate of four percent a year, compounded annually, and life contingencies as to each life involved from values that are based on the Actuaries' or Combined Experience Table of Mortality, as extended.[12] This table and related factors are contained in 26 CFR Part 81 edition revised as of April 1, 1958. The present value of an interest measured by a term of years is also computed on the basis of interest at the rate of four percent a year.

Valuation of gross estate after December 31, 1951, and before January 1, 1971.—In the case of a decedent dying after 1951 and before 1971, the present value of limited interests that are dependent upon the continuation or termination of one or more lives, or upon a term certain concurrent with one or more lives, is computed on the basis of interest at the rate of 3.5 percent a year, compounded annually, and life contingencies as to each life involved are taken from U.S. Life Table 38.[13] This table and related factors are contained in 26 CFR Part 20 edition revised as of April 1, 1984. The present value of an interest measured by a term of years is also computed on the basis of interest at the rate of 3.5 percent a year.

Valuation of gross estate after December 31, 1970, and before December 1, 1983.—In the case of a decedent dying after 1970 and before December 1, 1983, the present value of limited interests that are dependent upon the continuation or termination of one or more lives, or upon a term certain concurrent with one or more lives, is computed on the

---

[11] Reg. § 20.2031-7(d)(3).

[12] Reg. § 20.2031-7A(a).

[13] Reg. § 20.2031-7A(b).

basis of interest at the rate of six percent a year, compounded annually, and life contingencies as to each male and female life involved are taken from Table LN of former Reg. § 20.2031-10.[14] This table and related factors are contained in 26 CFR Part 20 edition revised as of April 1, 1994. The present value of an interest measured by a term of years is also computed on the basis of interest at the rate of six percent a year.

It should be noted that, with respect to interests that are dependent on the continuation or termination of one or more lives, the six-percent tables make a distinction between an interest that is based on the life of a male (Table A(1)) and one that is based on the life of a female (Table A(2)). This is true because the tables use one set of actuarial assumptions for men and a different set for women. Table B is used if the interest is dependent on a term of years.

IRS Publication No. 723, "Actuarial Values I: Valuation of Last Survivor Charitable Remainders," and IRS Publication No. 723A, "Actuarial Values II: Factors at 6 Percent Involving One and Two Lives," contain many special factors involving one or two lives. Although no longer available from the Superintendent of Documents, a copy of each may be obtained from: Internal Revenue Service, CC:DOM:CORP:T:R (IRS Publication No. 723 or 723A), Room 5228, POB 7604, Ben Franklin Station, Washington, D.C. 20044.[15]

Valuation of gross estate after November 30, 1983, and before May 1, 1989.—In the case of a decedent dying after November 30, 1983, and before May 1, 1989, the present value of an annuity, interest for life, or a remainder or reversionary interest that is dependent upon the continuation or termination of a single life is computed using Table A contained in Reg. § 20.2031-7A(d)(6). An annuity, interest for a term of years, or a remainder or reversionary interest that is dependent upon a term certain is valued using Table B of the regulation. These tables, which are based on a 10-percent interest factor and are actuarially gender-neutral, are reproduced at ¶ 532.

If the valuation of the interest involved is dependent upon more than one life or on a term certain that is concurrent with one or more lives, a special factor must be used. The factor is to be computed on the basis of interest at the rate of 10 percent a year, compounded annually, and life contingencies determined, as to each person involved, from the values of 1(x) that are set forth in column 2 of Table LN, contained in Reg. § 20.2031-7A(d)(6). Table LN (see ¶ 532) contains values of 1(x) taken from the life table for the total population appearing as Table 1 of United States Life Tables: 1969-1971, published by the Department of Health and Human Services.[16]

IRS Publication No. 723E, "Actuarial Values II: Factors at 10 Percent Involving One and Two Lives," contains special factors involving one or two lives. Although no longer available from the Superintendent of Documents, a copy of may be obtained from: Internal Revenue Service, CC:DOM:CORP:T:R (IRS Publication No. 723E), Room 5228, POB 7604, Ben Franklin Station, Washington, D.C. 20044. If a special factor is required in the case of an actual decedent, the IRS will furnish the factor

---

[14] Reg. § 20.2031-7A(c).

[15] Reg. § 20.2031-7A(c).

[16] Reg. § 20.2031-7A(d)(5).

to the executor upon request. The request must be accompanied by a statement setting forth the date of birth of each person whose life may affect the value of the interest and copies of the relevant instruments.[17]

If an annuity is payable at the end of each year for the life of an individual, its value is determined by multiplying the amount payable by the applicable factor in column 2 of Table A, taking into consideration the age of the individual whose life measures the duration of the annuity. Similarly, if the annuity is payable annually at the end of each year for a definite number of years, the amount payable is multiplied by the figure in column 2 of Table B corresponding to the number of years for which the annuity is payable.[18]

Certain adjustment factors must be applied to the valuations determined above if the annuity is payable at the end of semiannual, quarterly, monthly, or weekly periods.[19] The product of the Table A or B factors and the aggregate amount to be paid within a year is multiplied by the applicable factor below, depending upon when the payments are made. The factors for the various periods are as follows:

Semiannual payments	1.0244
Quarterly payments	1.0368
Monthly payments	1.0450
Weekly payments	1.0482

If an annuity for the life of an individual is payable at the beginning of annual, semiannual, quarterly, monthly or weekly periods, the general valuation procedure is slightly different. The value of that annuity is the sum of the first payment *plus* the present value of a similar annuity which would not be payable until the *end* of each payment period (determined as above).

If the first payment of an annuity for a definite number of years is payable at the beginning of the annual or other payment period, the *applicable factor* is the *product* of the factor shown in Table B multiplied by the following additional factor, as appropriate: [20]

Annual payments	1.1000
Semiannual payments	1.0744
Quarterly payments	1.0618
Monthly payments	1.0534
Weekly payments	1.0502

The estate of a decedent dying after November 30, 1983, but before August 9, 1984, can use either the 10-percent tables of Reg. § 20.2031-7A(d)(6) or the six-percent tables pursuant to Reg. § 20.2031-7A(c), whichever is more advantageous, to value an annuity, an interest for life or for a term of years, or a remainder or reversionary interest that is includible in the decedent's gross estate. The estate of a decedent dying on or after August 9, 1984, must use the 10-percent tables unless the estate is subject to a special rule relating to the incompetency of the decedent. Under this rule, where the valuation date is before May 1, 1989, and the decedent was subject to a mental disability on December 1, 1983, such that the disposition of his or her property could not be changed,

[17] Reg. § 20.2031-7A(d)(5).

[18] Reg. § 20.2031-7A(d)(2).

[19] Reg. § 20.2031-7A(d)(2)(ii).

[20] Reg. § 20.2031-7A(d)(2)(iii).

and the decedent either dies without regaining competency or within 90 days after doing so, the decedent's estate may use either the six- or 10-percent tables.[21]

¶ 531 Valuation Tables Prescribed by Code Sec. 7520

Reproduced on the following pages are the tables containing actuarial factors to be used in determining the present value of certain limited interests of decedents dying after April 30, 1989, and to gifts of such interests made after that date.[22] The tables are arranged in the following order:

Table 80CNSMT	Mortality Table
Table S	Single Life
Table J	Adjustment Factors
Table K	Adjustment Factors
Table B	Term Certain
Table U(1)	Single Life Unitrust
Table D	Term Certain Unitrust
Table F	Payout Factors

[21] Reg. § 20.2031-7A(d)(1).

[22] Reg. § 20.2031-7(d)(6) and Reg. § 1.664-4(e)(6); Notice 89-60, 1989-1 CB 700. Also see IRS Publications 1457, 1458, and 1459 (available from the Superintendent of Documents, U.S. Government Printing Office, Washington, D.C. 20402).

TABLE 80CNSMT
APPLICABLE AFTER APRIL 30, 1989

Age x	*1(x)*	*Age x*	*1(x)*	*Age x*	*1(x)*
(1)	*(2)*	*(1)*	*(2)*	*(1)*	*(2)*
0	100000	37	95492	74	59279
1	98740	38	95317	75	56799
2	98648	39	95129	76	54239
3	98584	40	94926	77	51599
4	98535	41	94700	78	48878
5	98495	42	94465	79	46071
6	98459	43	94201	80	43180
7	98426	44	93913	81	40208
8	98396	45	93599	82	37172
9	98370	46	93256	83	34095
10	98347	47	92882	84	31012
11	98328	48	92472	85	27960
12	98309	49	92021	86	24961
13	98285	50	91526	87	22038
14	98248	51	90986	88	19235
15	98196	52	90402	89	16598
16	98129	53	89771	90	14154
17	98047	54	89087	91	11908
18	97953	55	88348	92	9863
19	97851	56	87551	93	8032
20	97741	57	86695	94	6424
21	97623	58	85776	95	5043
22	97499	59	84789	96	3884
23	97370	60	83726	97	2939
24	97240	61	82581	98	2185
25	97110	62	81348	99	1598
26	96982	63	80024	100	1150
27	96856	64	78609	101	815
28	96730	65	77107	102	570
29	96604	66	75520	103	393
30	96477	67	73846	104	267
31	96350	68	72082	105	179
32	96220	69	70218	106	119
33	96088	70	68248	107	78
34	95951	71	66165	108	51
35	95808	72	63972	109	33
36	95655	73	61673	110	0

TABLE S
BASED ON LIFE TABLE 80CNSMT
SINGLE LIFE REMAINDER FACTORS
APPLICABLE AFTER APRIL 30, 1989

INTEREST RATE

AGE	*4.2%*	*4.4%*	*4.6%*	*4.8%*	*5.0%*	*5.2%*	*5.4%*	*5.6%*	*5.8%*	*6.0%*
0	.07389	.06749	.06188	.05695	.05261	.04879	.04541	.04243	.03978	.03744
1	.06494	.05832	.05250	.04738	.04287	.03889	.03537	.03226	.02950	.02705
2	.06678	.05999	.05401	.04874	.04410	.03999	.03636	.03314	.03028	.02773
3	.06897	.06200	.05587	.05045	.04567	.04143	.03768	.03435	.03139	.02875
4	.07139	.06425	.05796	.05239	.04746	.04310	.03922	.03578	.03271	.02998
5	.07401	.06669	.06023	.05451	.04944	.04494	.04094	.03738	.03421	.03137
6	.07677	.06928	.06265	.05677	.05156	.04692	.04279	.03911	.03583	.03289
7	.07968	.07201	.06521	.05918	.05381	.04903	.04477	.04097	.03757	.03453
8	.08274	.07489	.06792	.06172	.05621	.05129	.04689	.04297	.03945	.03630
9	.08597	.07794	.07079	.06443	.05876	.05370	.04917	.04511	.04148	.03821
10	.08936	.08115	.07383	.06730	.06147	.05626	.05159	.04741	.04365	.04027
11	.09293	.08453	.07704	.07035	.06436	.05900	.05419	.04988	.04599	.04250
12	.09666	.08807	.08040	.07354	.06739	.06188	.05693	.05248	.04847	.04486
13	.10049	.09172	.08387	.07684	.07053	.06487	.05977	.05518	.05104	.04731
14	.10437	.09541	.08738	.08017	.07370	.06788	.06263	.05791	.05364	.04978
15	.10827	.09912	.09090	.08352	.07688	.07090	.06551	.06064	.05623	.05225
16	.11220	.10285	.09445	.08689	.08008	.07394	.06839	.06337	.05883	.05472
17	.11615	.10661	.09802	.09028	.08330	.07699	.07129	.06612	.06144	.05719
18	.12017	.11043	.10165	.09373	.08656	.08009	.07422	.06890	.06408	.05969
19	.12428	.11434	.10537	.09726	.08992	.08327	.07724	.07177	.06679	.06226
20	.12850	.11836	.10919	.10089	.09337	.08654	.08035	.07471	.06959	.06492
21	.13282	.12248	.11311	.10462	.09692	.08991	.08355	.07775	.07247	.06765
22	.13728	.12673	.11717	.10848	.10059	.09341	.08686	.08090	.07546	.07049
23	.14188	.13113	.12136	.11248	.10440	.09703	.09032	.08418	.07858	.07345
24	.14667	.13572	.12575	.11667	.10839	.10084	.09395	.08764	.08187	.07659
25	.15167	.14051	.13034	.12106	.11259	.10486	.09778	.09130	.08536	.07991
26	.15690	.14554	.13517	.12569	.11703	.10910	.10184	.09518	.08907	.08346
27	.16237	.15081	.14024	.13056	.12171	.11359	.10614	.09930	.09302	.08724
28	.16808	.15632	.14555	.13567	.12662	.11831	.11068	.10366	.09720	.09125
29	.17404	.16208	.15110	.14104	.13179	.12329	.11547	.10827	.10163	.09551
30	.18025	.16808	.15692	.14665	.13721	.12852	.12051	.11313	.10631	.10002
31	.18672	.17436	.16300	.15255	.14291	.13403	.12584	.11827	.11127	.10480
32	.19344	.18090	.16935	.15870	.14888	.13980	.13142	.12367	.11650	.10985
33	.20044	.18772	.17598	.16514	.15513	.14587	.13730	.12936	.12201	.11519
34	.20770	.19480	.18287	.17185	.16165	.15221	.14345	.13533	.12780	.12080
35	.21522	.20215	.19005	.17884	.16846	.15883	.14989	.14159	.13388	.12670
36	.22299	.20974	.19747	.18609	.17552	.16571	.15660	.14812	.14022	.13287
37	.23101	.21760	.20516	.19360	.18286	.17288	.16358	.15492	.14685	.13933
38	.23928	.22572	.21311	.20139	.19048	.18032	.17085	.16201	.15377	.14607
39	.24780	.23409	.22133	.20945	.19837	.18804	.17840	.16939	.16097	.15310
40	.25658	.24273	.22982	.21778	.20654	.19605	.18624	.17706	.16847	.16043
41	.26560	.25163	.23858	.22639	.21499	.20434	.19436	.18502	.17627	.16806
42	.27486	.26076	.24758	.23525	.22370	.21289	.20276	.19326	.18434	.17597
43	.28435	.27013	.25683	.24436	.23268	.22172	.21143	.20177	.19270	.18416
44	.29407	.27975	.26633	.25373	.24191	.23081	.22038	.21057	.20134	.19265
45	.30402	.28961	.27608	.26337	.25142	.24019	.22962	.21966	.21028	.20144
46	.31420	.29970	.28608	.27326	.26120	.24983	.23913	.22904	.21951	.21053
47	.32460	.31004	.29632	.28341	.27123	.25975	.24892	.23870	.22904	.21991
48	.33521	.32058	.30679	.29379	.28151	.26992	.25897	.24862	.23883	.22957
49	.34599	.33132	.31746	.30438	.29201	.28032	.26926	.25879	.24888	.23949
50	.35695	.34224	.32833	.31518	.30273	.29094	.27978	.26921	.25918	.24966
51	.36809	.35335	.33940	.32619	.31367	.30180	.29055	.27987	.26973	.26010
52	.37944	.36468	.35070	.33744	.32486	.31292	.30158	.29081	.28057	.27083
53	.39098	.37622	.36222	.34892	.33629	.32429	.31288	.30203	.29170	.28186
54	.40269	.38794	.37393	.36062	.34795	.33590	.32442	.31349	.30308	.29316

TABLE S
BASED ON LIFE TABLE 80CNSMT
SINGLE LIFE REMAINDER FACTORS
APPLICABLE AFTER APRIL 30, 1989

INTEREST RATE

AGE	4.2%	4.4%	4.6%	4.8%	5.0%	5.2%	5.4%	5.6%	5.8%	6.0%
55	.41457	.39985	.38585	.37252	.35983	.34774	.33621	.32522	.31474	.30473
56	.42662	.41194	.39796	.38464	.37193	.35981	.34824	.33720	.32666	.31658
57	.43884	.42422	.41028	.39697	.38426	.37213	.36053	.34945	.33885	.32872
58	.45123	.43668	.42279	.40951	.39682	.38468	.37307	.36196	.35132	.34114
59	.46377	.44931	.43547	.42224	.40958	.39745	.38584	.37471	.36405	.35383
60	.47643	.46206	.44830	.43513	.42250	.41040	.39880	.38767	.37699	.36674
61	.48916	.47491	.46124	.44814	.43556	.42350	.41192	.40080	.39012	.37985
62	.50196	.48783	.47427	.46124	.44874	.43672	.42518	.41408	.40340	.39314
63	.51480	.50081	.48736	.47444	.46201	.45006	.43856	.42749	.41684	.40658
64	.52770	.51386	.50054	.48773	.47540	.46352	.45208	.44105	.43043	.42019
65	.54069	.52701	.51384	.50115	.48892	.47713	.46577	.45480	.44422	.43401
66	.55378	.54029	.52727	.51472	.50262	.49093	.47965	.46876	.45824	.44808
67	.56697	.55368	.54084	.52845	.51648	.50491	.49373	.48293	.47248	.46238
68	.58026	.56717	.55453	.54231	.53049	.51905	.50800	.49729	.48694	.47691
69	.59358	.58072	.56828	.55624	.54459	.53330	.52238	.51179	.50154	.49160
70	.60689	.59427	.58205	.57021	.55874	.54762	.53683	.52638	.51624	.50641
71	.62014	.60778	.59578	.58415	.57287	.56193	.55131	.54100	.53099	.52126
72	.63334	.62123	.60948	.59808	.58700	.57624	.56579	.55563	.54577	.53617
73	.64648	.63465	.62315	.61198	.60112	.59056	.58029	.57030	.56059	.55113
74	.65961	.64806	.63682	.62590	.61527	.60492	.59485	.58504	.57550	.56620
75	.67274	.66149	.65054	.63987	.62948	.61936	.60950	.59990	.59053	.58140
76	.68589	.67495	.66429	.65390	.64377	.63390	.62427	.61487	.60570	.59676
77	.69903	.68841	.67806	.66796	.65811	.64849	.63910	.62993	.62097	.61223
78	.71209	.70182	.69179	.68199	.67242	.66307	.65393	.64501	.63628	.62775
79	.72500	.71507	.70537	.69588	.68660	.67754	.66867	.65999	.65151	.64321
80	.73768	.72809	.71872	.70955	.70058	.69180	.68320	.67479	.66655	.65849
81	.75001	.74077	.73173	.72288	.71422	.70573	.69741	.68926	.68128	.67345
82	.76195	.75306	.74435	.73582	.72746	.71926	.71123	.70335	.69562	.68804
83	.77346	.76491	.75654	.74832	.74026	.73236	.72460	.71699	.70952	.70219
84	.78456	.77636	.76831	.76041	.75265	.74503	.73756	.73021	.72300	.71592
85	.79530	.78743	.77971	.77212	.76466	.75733	.75014	.74306	.73611	.72928
86	.80560	.79806	.79065	.78337	.77621	.76917	.76225	.75544	.74875	.74216
87	.81535	.80813	.80103	.79404	.78717	.78041	.77375	.76720	.76076	.75442
88	.82462	.81771	.81090	.80420	.79760	.79111	.78472	.77842	.77223	.76612
89	.83356	.82694	.82043	.81401	.80769	.80147	.79533	.78929	.78334	.77747
90	.84225	.83593	.82971	.82357	.81753	.81157	.80570	.79991	.79420	.78857
91	.85058	.84455	.83861	.83276	.82698	.82129	.81567	.81013	.80466	.79927
92	.85838	.85263	.84696	.84137	.83585	.83040	.82503	.81973	.81449	.80933
93	.86557	.86009	.85467	.84932	.84405	.83884	.83370	.82862	.82360	.81865
94	.87212	.86687	.86169	.85657	.85152	.84653	.84160	.83673	.83192	.82717
95	.87801	.87298	.86801	.86310	.85825	.85345	.84872	.84404	.83941	.83484
96	.88322	.87838	.87360	.86888	.86420	.85959	.85502	.85051	.84605	.84165
97	.88795	.88328	.87867	.87411	.86961	.86515	.86074	.85639	.85208	.84782
98	.89220	.88769	.88323	.87883	.87447	.87016	.86589	.86167	.85750	.85337
99	.89612	.89176	.88745	.88318	.87895	.87478	.87064	.86656	.86251	.85850
100	.89977	.89555	.89136	.88722	.88313	.87908	.87506	.87109	.86716	.86327
101	.90326	.89917	.89511	.89110	.88712	.88318	.87929	.87543	.87161	.86783
102	.90690	.90294	.89901	.89513	.89128	.88746	.88369	.87995	.87624	.87257
103	.91076	.90694	.90315	.89940	.89569	.89200	.88835	.88474	.88116	.87760

TABLE S
BASED ON LIFE TABLE 80CNSMT
SINGLE LIFE REMAINDER FACTORS
APPLICABLE AFTER APRIL 30, 1989

INTEREST RATE

AGE	*4.2%*	*4.4%*	*4.6%*	*4.8%*	*5.0%*	*5.2%*	*5.4%*	*5.6%*	*5.8%*	*6.0%*
104	.91504	.91138	.90775	.90415	.90058	.89704	.89354	.89006	.88661	.88319
105	.92027	.91681	.91337	.90996	.90658	.90322	.89989	.89659	.89331	.89006
106	.92763	.92445	.92130	.91816	.91506	.91197	.90890	.90586	.90284	.89983
107	.93799	.93523	.93249	.92977	.92707	.92438	.92170	.91905	.91641	.91378
108	.95429	.95223	.95018	.94814	.94611	.94409	.94208	.94008	.93809	.93611
109	.97985	.97893	.97801	.97710	.97619	.97529	.97438	.97348	.97259	.97170

TABLE S
BASED ON LIFE TABLE 80CNSMT
SINGLE LIFE REMAINDER FACTORS
APPLICABLE AFTER APRIL 30, 1989

INTEREST RATE

AGE	6.2%	6.4%	6.6%	6.8%	7.0%	7.2%	7.4%	7.6%	7.8%	8.0%
0	.03535	.03349	.03183	.03035	.02903	.02783	.02676	.02579	.02492	.02413
1	.02486	.02292	.02119	.01963	.01824	.01699	.01587	.01486	.01395	.01312
2	.02547	.02345	.02164	.02002	.01857	.01727	.01609	.01504	.01408	.01321
3	.02640	.02429	.02241	.02073	.01921	.01785	.01662	.01552	.01451	.01361
4	.02753	.02535	.02339	.02163	.02005	.01863	.01735	.01619	.01514	.01418
5	.02883	.02656	.02453	.02269	.02105	.01956	.01822	.01700	.01590	.01490
6	.03026	.02790	.02578	.02387	.02215	.02060	.01919	.01792	.01677	.01572
7	.03180	.02935	.02714	.02515	.02336	.02174	.02027	.01894	.01773	.01664
8	.03347	.03092	.02863	.02656	.02469	.02300	.02146	.02007	.01881	.01766
9	.03528	.03263	.03025	.02810	.02615	.02438	.02278	.02133	.02000	.01880
10	.03723	.03449	.03201	.02977	.02774	.02590	.02423	.02271	.02133	.02006
11	.03935	.03650	.03393	.03160	.02949	.02757	.02583	.02424	.02279	.02147
12	.04160	.03865	.03598	.03356	.03136	.02936	.02755	.02589	.02438	.02299
13	.04394	.04088	.03811	.03560	.03331	.03123	.02934	.02761	.02603	.02458
14	.04629	.04312	.04025	.03764	.03527	.03311	.03113	.02933	.02768	.02617
15	.04864	.04536	.04238	.03968	.03721	.03496	.03290	.03103	.02930	.02773
16	.05099	.04759	.04451	.04170	.03913	.03679	.03466	.03270	.03090	.02926
17	.05333	.04982	.04662	.04370	.04104	.03861	.03638	.03434	.03247	.03075
18	.05570	.05207	.04875	.04573	.04296	.04044	.03812	.03599	.03404	.03225
19	.05814	.05438	.05095	.04781	.04494	.04231	.03990	.03769	.03565	.03378
20	.06065	.05677	.05321	.04996	.04698	.04424	.04173	.03943	.03731	.03535
21	.06325	.05922	.05554	.05217	.04907	.04623	.04362	.04122	.03901	.03697
22	.06594	.06178	.05797	.05447	.05126	.04831	.04559	.04309	.04078	.03865
23	.06876	.06446	.06051	.05688	.05355	.05048	.04766	.04505	.04265	.04042
24	.07174	.06729	.06321	.05945	.05599	.05281	.04987	.04715	.04465	.04233
25	.07491	.07031	.06609	.06219	.05861	.05530	.05224	.04941	.04680	.04438
26	.07830	.07355	.06918	.06515	.06142	.05799	.05481	.05187	.04915	.04662
27	.08192	.07702	.07250	.06832	.06446	.06090	.05759	.05454	.05170	.04906
28	.08577	.08071	.07603	.07171	.06772	.06402	.06059	.05740	.05445	.05170
29	.08986	.08464	.07981	.07534	.07120	.06736	.06380	.06049	.05742	.05456
30	.09420	.08882	.08383	.07921	.07492	.07095	.06725	.06381	.06061	.05763
31	.09881	.09327	.08812	.08335	.07891	.07479	.07095	.06738	.06405	.06095
32	.10369	.09797	.09267	.08774	.08315	.07888	.07491	.07120	.06774	.06451
33	.10885	.10297	.09750	.09241	.08767	.08325	.07913	.07529	.07170	.06834
34	.11430	.10824	.10261	.09736	.09246	.08790	.08363	.07964	.07592	.07243
35	.12002	.11380	.10800	.10259	.09754	.09282	.08841	.08428	.08041	.07679
36	.12602	.11963	.11366	.10809	.10288	.09800	.09344	.08917	.08516	.08140
37	.13230	.12574	.11961	.11387	.10850	.10347	.09876	.09433	.09018	.08628
38	.13887	.13214	.12584	.11994	.11441	.10922	.10436	.09978	.09549	.09145
39	.14573	.13883	.13237	.12630	.12061	.11527	.11025	.10553	.10109	.09690
40	.15290	.14583	.13920	.13297	.12712	.12162	.11644	.11157	.10698	.10266
41	.16036	.15312	.14633	.13994	.13393	.12827	.12294	.11792	.11318	.10871
42	.16810	.16071	.15375	.14720	.14103	.13522	.12973	.12456	.11967	.11505
43	.17614	.16858	.16146	.15475	.14842	.14245	.13682	.13149	.12645	.12169
44	.18447	.17675	.16948	.16261	.15613	.15000	.14421	.13873	.13355	.12864
45	.19310	.18524	.17780	.17078	.16414	.15787	.15192	.14630	.14096	.13591
46	.20204	.19402	.18644	.17926	.17247	.16604	.15995	.15418	.14870	.14350
47	.21128	.20311	.19538	.18806	.18112	.17454	.16830	.16238	.15676	.15141
48	.22080	.21249	.20462	.19716	.19007	.18335	.17696	.17090	.16513	.15964
49	.23059	.22214	.21413	.20653	.19930	.19244	.18591	.17970	.17379	.16816
50	.24063	.23206	.22391	.21617	.20881	.20180	.19514	.18879	.18274	.17697
51	.25095	.24225	.23398	.22610	.21861	.21147	.20466	.19818	.19199	.18609
52	.26157	.25275	.24436	.23636	.22874	.22147	.21453	.20791	.20159	.19556
53	.27249	.26357	.25505	.24694	.23919	.23180	.22474	.21799	.21154	.20537

TABLE S
BASED ON LIFE TABLE 80CNSMT
SINGLE LIFE REMAINDER FACTORS
APPLICABLE AFTER APRIL 30, 1989

INTEREST RATE

AGE	6.2%	6.4%	6.6%	6.8%	7.0%	7.2%	7.4%	7.6%	7.8%	8.0%
54	.28369	.27466	.26604	.25782	.24995	.24244	.23526	.22839	.22181	.21552
55	.29518	.28605	.27734	.26900	.26103	.25341	.24611	.23912	.23243	.22601
56	.30695	.29774	.28893	.28050	.27242	.26469	.25728	.25019	.24338	.23685
57	.31902	.30973	.30084	.29232	.28415	.27632	.26881	.26161	.25469	.24805
58	.33138	.32203	.31306	.30446	.29621	.28829	.28069	.27339	.26637	.25962
59	.34402	.33461	.32558	.31691	.30859	.30059	.29290	.28550	.27839	.27155
60	.35690	.34745	.33836	.32963	.32124	.31317	.30540	.29792	.29073	.28379
61	.36999	.36050	.35137	.34259	.33414	.32601	.31817	.31062	.30334	.29633
62	.38325	.37374	.36458	.35576	.34726	.33907	.33117	.32356	.31621	.30912
63	.39669	.38717	.37799	.36913	.36060	.35236	.34441	.33674	.32933	.32217
64	.41031	.40078	.39159	.38272	.37415	.36588	.35789	.35016	.34270	.33548
65	.42416	.41464	.40545	.39656	.38798	.37968	.37166	.36390	.35639	.34912
66	.43825	.42876	.41958	.41070	.40211	.39380	.38576	.37797	.37043	.36312
67	.45260	.44315	.43399	.42513	.41655	.40824	.40019	.39238	.38482	.37749
68	.46720	.45779	.44868	.43985	.43129	.42299	.41494	.40713	.39956	.39221
69	.48197	.47263	.46357	.45478	.44625	.43798	.42995	.42215	.41458	.40722
70	.49686	.48760	.47861	.46988	.46140	.45316	.44516	.43738	.42983	.42248
71	.51182	.50265	.49374	.48508	.47666	.46847	.46051	.45276	.44523	.43790
72	.52685	.51778	.50896	.50038	.49203	.48390	.47599	.46829	.46079	.45349
73	.54194	.53298	.52426	.51578	.50751	.49946	.49161	.48397	.47652	.46926
74	.55714	.54832	.53972	.53134	.52317	.51520	.50744	.49986	.49247	.48527
75	.57250	.56382	.55536	.54710	.53904	.53118	.52351	.51601	.50870	.50156
76	.58803	.57951	.57120	.56308	.55515	.54740	.53984	.53245	.52522	.51817
77	.60369	.59535	.58720	.57923	.57144	.56383	.55639	.54912	.54200	.53504
78	.61942	.61126	.60329	.59549	.58787	.58040	.57310	.56596	.55896	.55212
79	.63508	.62713	.61935	.61174	.60428	.59698	.58983	.58283	.57597	.56925
80	.65059	.64285	.63527	.62785	.62058	.61345	.60646	.59961	.59290	.58632
81	.66579	.65827	.65090	.64368	.63659	.62965	.62283	.61615	.60959	.60316
82	.68061	.67332	.66616	.65914	.65226	.64550	.63886	.63235	.62595	.61968
83	.69499	.68793	.68099	.67418	.66749	.66092	.65447	.64813	.64191	.63579
84	.70896	.70213	.69541	.68881	.68233	.67595	.66969	.66353	.65748	.65153
85	.72256	.71596	.70947	.70308	.69681	.69063	.68456	.67859	.67271	.66693
86	.73569	.72931	.72305	.71688	.71081	.70484	.69896	.69318	.68748	.68188
87	.74818	.74204	.73599	.73003	.72417	.71839	.71271	.70711	.70159	.69616
88	.76011	.75419	.74836	.74261	.73695	.73137	.72588	.72046	.71512	.70986
89	.77169	.76599	.76037	.75484	.74938	.74400	.73870	.73347	.72831	.72323
90	.78302	.77755	.77215	.76683	.76158	.75640	.75129	.74625	.74128	.73638
91	.79395	.78870	.78352	.77842	.77337	.76840	.76349	.75864	.75385	.74913
92	.80423	.79920	.79423	.78933	.78449	.77971	.77499	.77033	.76572	.76118
93	.81377	.80894	.80417	.79946	.79481	.79022	.78568	.78120	.77677	.77239
94	.82247	.81784	.81325	.80873	.80425	.79983	.79547	.79115	.78688	.78266
95	.83033	.82586	.82145	.81709	.81278	.80852	.80431	.80014	.79602	.79195
96	.83729	.83298	.82872	.82451	.82034	.81622	.81215	.80812	.80414	.80019
97	.84361	.83944	.83532	.83124	.82721	.82322	.81927	.81537	.81151	.80769
98	.84929	.84525	.84126	.83730	.83339	.82952	.82569	.82190	.81815	.81443
99	.85454	.85062	.84674	.84290	.83910	.83534	.83161	.82792	.82427	.82066
100	.85942	.85561	.85184	.84810	.84440	.84074	.83711	.83352	.82997	.82644
101	.86408	.86037	.85670	.85306	.84946	.84589	.84236	.83886	.83539	.83196
102	.86894	.86534	.86177	.85823	.85473	.85126	.84782	.84442	.84104	.83770
103	.87408	.87060	.86714	.86371	.86032	.85695	.85362	.85031	.84703	.84378
104	.87980	.87644	.87311	.86980	.86653	.86328	.86005	.85686	.85369	.85054

TABLE S
BASED ON LIFE TABLE 80CNSMT
SINGLE LIFE REMAINDER FACTORS
APPLICABLE AFTER APRIL 30, 1989

INTEREST RATE

AGE	6.2%	6.4%	6.6%	6.8%	7.0%	7.2%	7.4%	7.6%	7.8%	8.0%
105	.88684	.88363	.88046	.87731	.87418	.87108	.86800	.86494	.86191	.85890
106	.89685	.89389	.89095	.88804	.88514	.88226	.87940	.87656	.87374	.87094
107	.91117	.90858	.90600	.90344	.90089	.89836	.89584	.89334	.89085	.88838
108	.93414	.93217	.93022	.92828	.92634	.92442	.92250	.92060	.91870	.91681
109	.97081	.96992	.96904	.96816	.96729	.96642	.96555	.96468	.96382	.96296

TABLE S
BASED ON LIFE TABLE 80CNSMT SINGLE LIFE REMAINDER FACTORS APPLICABLE AFTER APRIL 30, 1989

INTEREST RATE

AGE	8.2%	8.4%	8.6%	8.8%	9.0%	9.2%	9.4%	9.6%	9.8%	10.0%
0	.02341	.02276	.02217	.02163	.02114	.02069	.02027	.01989	.01954	.01922
1	.01237	.01170	.01108	.01052	.01000	.00953	.00910	.00871	.00834	.00801
2	.01243	.01172	.01107	.01048	.00994	.00944	.00899	.00857	.00819	.00784
3	.01278	.01203	.01135	.01073	.01016	.00964	.00916	.00872	.00832	.00795
4	.01332	.01253	.01182	.01116	.01056	.01001	.00951	.00904	.00862	.00822
5	.01400	.01317	.01241	.01172	.01109	.01051	.00998	.00949	.00904	.00862
6	.01477	.01390	.01310	.01238	.01171	.01110	.01054	.01002	.00954	.00910
7	.01563	.01472	.01389	.01312	.01242	.01178	.01118	.01064	.01013	.00966
8	.01660	.01564	.01477	.01396	.01322	.01254	.01192	.01134	.01081	.01031
9	.01770	.01669	.01577	.01492	.01414	.01342	.01276	.01216	.01159	.01107
10	.01891	.01785	.01688	.01599	.01517	.01442	.01372	.01308	.01249	.01194
11	.02026	.01915	.01814	.01720	.01634	.01555	.01481	.01414	.01351	.01293
12	.02173	.02056	.01950	.01852	.01761	.01678	.01601	.01529	.01463	.01402
13	.02326	.02204	.02092	.01989	.01895	.01807	.01726	.01651	.01582	.01517
14	.02478	.02351	.02234	.02126	.02027	.01935	.01850	.01771	.01698	.01630
15	.02628	.02495	.02372	.02259	.02155	.02058	.01969	.01886	.01810	.01738
16	.02774	.02635	.02507	.02388	.02279	.02178	.02084	.01997	.01917	.01842
17	.02917	.02772	.02637	.02513	.02399	.02293	.02194	.02103	.02018	.01940
18	.03059	.02907	.02767	.02637	.02517	.02406	.02302	.02207	.02118	.02035
19	.03205	.03046	.02899	.02763	.02637	.02521	.02412	.02312	.02218	.02131
20	.03355	.03188	.03035	.02892	.02760	.02638	.02524	.02419	.02320	.02229
21	.03509	.03334	.03173	.03024	.02886	.02758	.02638	.02527	.02424	.02328
22	.03669	.03487	.03318	.03162	.03017	.02882	.02757	.02640	.02532	.02430
23	.03837	.03646	.03470	.03306	.03154	.03013	.02881	.02759	.02644	.02538
24	.04018	.03819	.03634	.03463	.03303	.03155	.03016	.02888	.02767	.02655
25	.04214	.04006	.03812	.03633	.03465	.03309	.03164	.03029	.02902	.02784
26	.04428	.04210	.04008	.03820	.03644	.03481	.03328	.03186	.03052	.02928
27	.04662	.04434	.04223	.04025	.03841	.03670	.03509	.03360	.03219	.03088
28	.04915	.04677	.04456	.04249	.04056	.03876	.03708	.03550	.03403	.03264
29	.05189	.04941	.04709	.04493	.04291	.04102	.03925	.03760	.03604	.03458
30	.05485	.05226	.04984	.04757	.04546	.04348	.04162	.03988	.03825	.03671
31	.05805	.05535	.05282	.05045	.04824	.04616	.04421	.04238	.04067	.03905
32	.06149	.05867	.05603	.05356	.05124	.04906	.04702	.04510	.04329	.04160
33	.06520	.06226	.05950	.05692	.05449	.05221	.05007	.04806	.04616	.04438
34	.06916	.06609	.06322	.06052	.05799	.05560	.05336	.05125	.04926	.04738
35	.07339	.07020	.06720	.06439	.06174	.05925	.05690	.05469	.05260	.05063
36	.07787	.07455	.07143	.06850	.06573	.06313	.06068	.05836	.05617	.05411
37	.08262	.07917	.07593	.07287	.06999	.06727	.06470	.06228	.05999	.05783
38	.08765	.08407	.08069	.07751	.07451	.07167	.06899	.06646	.06407	.06180
39	.09296	.08925	.08574	.08243	.07931	.07635	.07356	.07092	.06841	.06604
40	.09858	.09472	.09109	.08765	.08440	.08132	.07841	.07565	.07303	.07055
41	.10449	.10050	.09673	.09316	.08978	.08658	.08355	.08067	.07794	.07535
42	.11069	.10656	.10265	.09895	.09544	.09212	.08896	.08596	.08312	.08041
43	.11718	.11291	.10887	.10503	.10140	.09794	.09466	.09154	.08858	.08576
44	.12399	.11958	.11540	.11143	.10766	.10407	.10067	.09743	.09434	.09141
45	.13111	.12656	.12224	.11814	.11423	.11052	.10699	.10362	.10042	.09736
46	.13856	.13387	.12941	.12516	.12113	.11728	.11362	.11013	.10680	.10363
47	.14633	.14150	.13690	.13252	.12835	.12438	.12059	.11697	.11352	.11022
48	.15442	.14945	.14471	.14020	.13589	.13179	.12787	.12412	.12055	.11713
49	.16280	.15769	.15281	.14816	.14373	.13949	.13544	.13157	.12787	.12433
50	.17147	.16622	.16121	.15643	.15186	.14749	.14331	.13931	.13548	.13182
51	.18045	.17507	.16993	.16501	.16030	.15580	.15150	.14737	.14342	.13963
52	.18979	.18427	.17899	.17394	.16911	.16448	.16004	.15579	.15172	.14780
53	.19947	.19383	.18842	.18324	.17828	.17352	.16896	.16458	.16038	.15635

TABLE S
BASED ON LIFE TABLE 80CNSMT
SINGLE LIFE REMAINDER FACTORS
APPLICABLE AFTER APRIL 30, 1989

INTEREST RATE

AGE	8.2%	8.4%	8.6%	8.8%	9.0%	9.2%	9.4%	9.6%	9.8%	10.0%
54	.20950	.20372	.19819	.19288	.18779	.18291	.17822	.17372	.16940	.16524
55	.21986	.21397	.20831	.20288	.19767	.19266	.18785	.18322	.17878	.17450
56	.23058	.22457	.21879	.21324	.20791	.20278	.19785	.19310	.18854	.18414
57	.24167	.23554	.22965	.22399	.21854	.21329	.20824	.20338	.19870	.19419
58	.25314	.24690	.24090	.23512	.22956	.22420	.21904	.21407	.20927	.20464
59	.26497	.25863	.25252	.24664	.24097	.23550	.23023	.22515	.22024	.21551
60	.27712	.27068	.26448	.25849	.25272	.24716	.24178	.23659	.23158	.22674
61	.28956	.28304	.27674	.27067	.26480	.25913	.25366	.24837	.24325	.23831
62	.30228	.29567	.28929	.28312	.27717	.27141	.26584	.26045	.25524	.25020
63	.31525	.30857	.30211	.29586	.28982	.28397	.27832	.27284	.26754	.26240
64	.32851	.32176	.31522	.30890	.30278	.29685	.29111	.28555	.28016	.27493
65	.34209	.33528	.32868	.32229	.31610	.31010	.30429	.29865	.29317	.28787
66	.35604	.34918	.34253	.33609	.32983	.32377	.31788	.31217	.30663	.30124
67	.37037	.36347	.35678	.35028	.34398	.33786	.33191	.32614	.32053	.31508
68	.38508	.37815	.37142	.36489	.35854	.35237	.34638	.34055	.33488	.32937
69	.40008	.39313	.38638	.37982	.37344	.36724	.36120	.35533	.34961	.34405
70	.41533	.40838	.40162	.39504	.38864	.38241	.37634	.37043	.36468	.35907
71	.43076	.42382	.41705	.41047	.40405	.39780	.39171	.38578	.38000	.37436
72	.44638	.43945	.43269	.42611	.41969	.41344	.40733	.40138	.39558	.38991
73	.46218	.45527	.44854	.44197	.43556	.42931	.42321	.41725	.41143	.40575
74	.47823	.47137	.46466	.45812	.45173	.44549	.43940	.43345	.42763	.42195
75	.49459	.48777	.48112	.47462	.46826	.46205	.45598	.45004	.44424	.43856
76	.51127	.50452	.49793	.49148	.48517	.47900	.47297	.46706	.46129	.45563
77	.52823	.52157	.51505	.50867	.50243	.49632	.49033	.48447	.47873	.47311
78	.54541	.53885	.53242	.52613	.51996	.51392	.50800	.50220	.49652	.49094
79	.56267	.55621	.54989	.54369	.53762	.53166	.52582	.52009	.51448	.50897
80	.57987	.57354	.56733	.56125	.55527	.54941	.54366	.53802	.53248	.52705
81	.59685	.59065	.58457	.57860	.57274	.56699	.56134	.55579	.55035	.54499
82	.61351	.60746	.60151	.59567	.58993	.58429	.57875	.57331	.56796	.56270
83	.62978	.62387	.61806	.61236	.60675	.60123	.59581	.59047	.58523	.58007
84	.64567	.63992	.63426	.62869	.62321	.61783	.61253	.60731	.60218	.59713
85	.66125	.65565	.65014	.64472	.63938	.63413	.62896	.62387	.61886	.61392
86	.67636	.67092	.66557	.66030	.65511	.65000	.64496	.64000	.63511	.63030
87	.69081	.68554	.68034	.67522	.67018	.66520	.66031	.65548	.65071	.64602
88	.70468	.69957	.69453	.68956	.68466	.67983	.67507	.67037	.66574	.66117
89	.71821	.71326	.70838	.70357	.69882	.69414	.68952	.68495	.68045	.67601
90	.73153	.72676	.72204	.71739	.71280	.70827	.70379	.69938	.69502	.69071
91	.74447	.73986	.73532	.73083	.72640	.72202	.71770	.71343	.70921	.70504
92	.75669	.75225	.74787	.74354	.73927	.73504	.73087	.72674	.72267	.71864
93	.76807	.76379	.75957	.75540	.75127	.74719	.74317	.73918	.73524	.73135
94	.77849	.77437	.77030	.76627	.76229	.75835	.75446	.75061	.74680	.74303
95	.78792	.78394	.78001	.77611	.77226	.76845	.76468	.76096	.75727	.75362
96	.79630	.79244	.78863	.78485	.78112	.77742	.77377	.77015	.76657	.76303
97	.80391	.80016	.79646	.79280	.78917	.78559	.78203	.77852	.77504	.77160
98	.81076	.80712	.80352	.79996	.79643	.79294	.78948	.78606	.78267	.77931
99	.81709	.81354	.81004	.80657	.80313	.79972	.79635	.79302	.78971	.78644
100	.82296	.81950	.81609	.81270	.80934	.80602	.80273	.79947	.79624	.79304
101	.82855	.82518	.82185	.81854	.81526	.81201	.80880	.80561	.80245	.79932
102	.83438	.83110	.82785	.82462	.82142	.81826	.81512	.81200	.80892	.80586
103	.84056	.83737	.83420	.83106	.82795	.82487	.82181	.81878	.81577	.81279
104	.84743	.84433	.84127	.83822	.83521	.83221	.82924	.82630	.82338	.82048

TABLE S
BASED ON LIFE TABLE 80CNSMT
SINGLE LIFE REMAINDER FACTORS
APPLICABLE AFTER APRIL 30, 1989

INTEREST RATE

AGE	8.2%	8.4%	8.6%	8.8%	9.0%	9.2%	9.4%	9.6%	9.8%	10.0%
105	.85591	.85295	.85001	.84709	.84419	.84132	.83846	.83563	.83282	.83003
106	.86816	.86540	.86266	.85993	.85723	.85454	.85187	.84922	.84659	.84397
107	.88592	.88348	.88105	.87863	.87623	.87384	.87147	.86911	.86676	.86443
108	.91493	.91306	.91119	.90934	.90749	.90566	.90383	.90201	.90020	.89840
109	.96211	.96125	.96041	.95956	.95872	.95788	.95704	.95620	.95537	.95455

TABLE S
BASED ON LIFE TABLE 80CNSMT
SINGLE LIFE REMAINDER FACTORS
APPLICABLE AFTER APRIL 30, 1989

INTEREST RATE

AGE	10.2%	10.4%	10.6%	10.8%	11.0%	11.2%	11.4%	11.6%	11.8%	12.0%
0	.01891	.01864	.01838	.01814	.01791	.01770	.01750	.01732	.01715	.01698
1	.00770	.00741	.00715	.00690	.00667	.00646	.00626	.00608	.00590	.00574
2	.00751	.00721	.00693	.00667	.00643	.00620	.00600	.00580	.00562	.00544
3	.00760	.00728	.00699	.00671	.00646	.00622	.00600	.00579	.00560	.00541
4	.00786	.00752	.00721	.00692	.00665	.00639	.00616	.00594	.00573	.00554
5	.00824	.00788	.00755	.00724	.00695	.00668	.00643	.00620	.00598	.00578
6	.00869	.00832	.00796	.00764	.00733	.00705	.00678	.00654	.00630	.00608
7	.00923	.00883	.00846	.00811	.00779	.00749	.00720	.00694	.00669	.00646
8	.00986	.00943	.00904	.00867	.00833	.00801	.00771	.00743	.00716	.00692
9	.01059	.01014	.00972	.00933	.00897	.00863	.00831	.00801	.00773	.00747
10	.01142	.01095	.01051	.01009	.00971	.00935	.00901	.00869	.00840	.00812
11	.01239	.01189	.01142	.01098	.01057	.01019	.00983	.00950	.00918	.00889
12	.01345	.01292	.01243	.01197	.01154	.01113	.01075	.01040	.01007	.00975
13	.01457	.01401	.01349	.01300	.01255	.01212	.01172	.01135	.01100	.01067
14	.01567	.01508	.01453	.01402	.01354	.01309	.01267	.01227	.01190	.01155
15	.01672	.01610	.01552	.01498	.01448	.01400	.01356	.01314	.01275	.01238
16	.01772	.01707	.01646	.01589	.01536	.01486	.01439	.01396	.01354	.01315
17	.01866	.01798	.01734	.01674	.01618	.01566	.01516	.01470	.01427	.01386
18	.01958	.01886	.01818	.01755	.01697	.01641	.01590	.01541	.01495	.01452
19	.02050	.01974	.01903	.01837	.01775	.01717	.01662	.01611	.01563	.01517
20	.02143	.02064	.01989	.01919	.01854	.01793	.01735	.01681	.01630	.01582
21	.02238	.02154	.02075	.02002	.01933	.01868	.01807	.01750	.01696	.01646
22	.02336	.02247	.02164	.02087	.02014	.01946	.01882	.01821	.01764	.01711
23	.02438	.02345	.02257	.02176	.02099	.02027	.01959	.01895	.01835	.01778
24	.02550	.02451	.02359	.02273	.02192	.02115	.02044	.01976	.01913	.01853
25	.02673	.02569	.02472	.02381	.02295	.02214	.02138	.02067	.01999	.01936
26	.02811	.02701	.02598	.02502	.02411	.02326	.02246	.02170	.02098	.02031
27	.02965	.02849	.02741	.02639	.02543	.02452	.02367	.02287	.02211	.02140
28	.03134	.03013	.02898	.02790	.02689	.02593	.02503	.02418	.02338	.02262
29	.03322	.03193	.03072	.02958	.02851	.02750	.02654	.02564	.02479	.02398
30	.03527	.03391	.03264	.03143	.03030	.02923	.02821	.02726	.02635	.02550
31	.03753	.03610	.03475	.03348	.03228	.03115	.03008	.02907	.02811	.02720
32	.04000	.03849	.03707	.03573	.03446	.03326	.03213	.03105	.03004	.02907
33	.04269	.04111	.03961	.03819	.03685	.03558	.03438	.03325	.03217	.03115
34	.04561	.04394	.04236	.04087	.03946	.03812	.03685	.03565	.03451	.03342
35	.04877	.04702	.04535	.04378	.04229	.04087	.03953	.03826	.03706	.03591
36	.05215	.05031	.04856	.04690	.04533	.04384	.04242	.04108	.03980	.03859
37	.05578	.05384	.05200	.05025	.04860	.04703	.04553	.04411	.04276	.04148
38	.05965	.05761	.05568	.05385	.05211	.05045	.04888	.04738	.04595	.04460
39	.06379	.06165	.05962	.05770	.05587	.05412	.05247	.05089	.04939	.04795
40	.06820	.06596	.06383	.06181	.05989	.05806	.05631	.05465	.05307	.05155
41	.07288	.07054	.06832	.06620	.06418	.06226	.06042	.05868	.05701	.05541
42	.07784	.07539	.07306	.07085	.06873	.06671	.06479	.06295	.06119	.05952
43	.08308	.08052	.07808	.07576	.07355	.07143	.06941	.06748	.06564	.06387
44	.08861	.08594	.08340	.08097	.07865	.07644	.07432	.07230	.07036	.06851
45	.09445	.09167	.08901	.08648	.08406	.08174	.07953	.07741	.07538	.07343
46	.10060	.09770	.09494	.09230	.08977	.08735	.08503	.08281	.08068	.07865
47	.10707	.10406	.10119	.09843	.09579	.09327	.09085	.08853	.08630	.08417
48	.11386	.11073	.10774	.10487	.10213	.09949	.09697	.09455	.09222	.08999
49	.12094	.11769	.11458	.11160	.10874	.10600	.10337	.10084	.09842	.09609
50	.12831	.12494	.12172	.11862	.11565	.11280	.11006	.10743	.10490	.10247
51	.13600	.13251	.12917	.12596	.12288	.11991	.11706	.11432	.11169	.10915
52	.14405	.14044	.13698	.13366	.13046	.12738	.12442	.12157	.11883	.11619
53	.15247	.14875	.14517	.14172	.13841	.13522	.13215	.12919	.12635	.12360
54	.16124	.15740	.15370	.15014	.14671	.14341	.14023	.13717	.13421	.13136

TABLE S
BASED ON LIFE TABLE 80CNSMT
SINGLE LIFE REMAINDER FACTORS
APPLICABLE AFTER APRIL 30, 1989

INTEREST RATE

AGE	10.2%	10.4%	10.6%	10.8%	11.0%	11.2%	11.4%	11.6%	11.8%	12.0%
55	.17039	.16642	.16261	.15893	.15539	.15198	.14868	.14551	.14244	.13948
56	.17991	.17583	.17190	.16811	.16445	.16092	.15752	.15423	.15106	.14799
57	.18984	.18564	.18160	.17769	.17392	.17029	.16677	.16338	.16010	.15692
58	.20018	.19587	.19172	.18770	.18382	.18007	.17645	.17295	.16956	.16628
59	.21093	.20652	.20225	.19812	.19414	.19028	.18655	.18294	.17945	.17606
60	.22206	.21753	.21316	.20893	.20483	.20087	.19703	.19332	.18972	.18624
61	.23353	.22890	.22442	.22009	.21589	.21182	.20788	.20407	.20037	.19678
62	.24532	.24059	.23601	.23158	.22728	.22311	.21907	.21515	.21135	.20767
63	.25742	.25260	.24793	.24339	.23900	.23473	.23060	.22658	.22268	.21890
64	.26987	.26495	.26019	.25556	.25107	.24671	.24248	.23837	.23438	.23050
65	.28271	.27771	.27286	.26815	.26357	.25912	.25480	.25059	.24651	.24254
66	.29601	.29093	.28600	.28120	.27654	.27200	.26760	.26331	.25913	.25507
67	.30978	.30462	.29961	.29474	.29000	.28539	.28090	.27653	.27227	.26813
68	.32401	.31879	.31371	.30877	.30396	.29927	.29471	.29027	.28593	.28171
69	.33863	.33336	.32822	.32322	.31835	.31359	.30896	.30445	.30005	.29576
70	.35361	.34829	.34310	.33804	.33311	.32830	.32361	.31903	.31457	.31021
71	.36886	.36349	.35826	.35316	.34818	.34332	.33858	.33394	.32942	.32500
72	.38439	.37899	.37373	.36858	.36356	.35866	.35387	.34919	.34461	.34015
73	.40021	.39479	.38950	.38432	.37927	.37433	.36950	.36478	.36016	.35565
74	.41639	.41096	.40565	.40046	.39538	.39042	.38556	.38081	.37616	.37161
75	.43301	.42758	.42226	.41706	.41198	.40699	.40212	.39734	.39267	.38809
76	.45009	.44467	.43937	.43417	.42908	.42410	.41921	.41443	.40974	.40514
77	.46761	.46221	.45693	.45175	.44667	.44170	.43682	.43203	.42734	.42274
78	.48548	.48013	.47488	.46973	.46468	.45972	.45486	.45009	.44541	.44082
79	.50356	.49826	.49306	.48795	.48294	.47802	.47319	.46845	.46379	.45922
80	.52171	.51647	.51133	.50628	.50132	.49644	.49166	.48695	.48233	.47779
81	.53974	.53457	.52950	.52451	.51961	.51479	.51006	.50541	.50083	.49633
82	.55753	.55245	.54745	.54254	.53771	.53296	.52828	.52369	.51917	.51472
83	.57500	.57001	.56510	.56026	.55551	.55083	.54623	.54170	.53724	.53285
84	.59216	.58726	.58245	.57770	.57304	.56844	.56391	.55945	.55506	.55074
85	.60906	.60428	.59956	.59492	.59034	.58583	.58139	.57702	.57270	.56845
86	.62555	.62088	.61627	.61173	.60725	.60284	.59849	.59420	.58997	.58580
87	.64139	.63683	.63233	.62790	.62352	.61921	.61495	.61076	.60661	.60253
88	.65666	.65221	.64783	.64350	.63923	.63502	.63086	.62675	.62270	.61871
89	.67163	.66730	.66304	.65882	.65466	.65055	.64650	.64249	.63854	.63463
90	.68646	.68226	.67812	.67402	.66998	.66599	.66204	.65814	.65430	.65049
91	.70093	.69686	.69285	.68888	.68496	.68108	.67725	.67347	.66973	.66604
92	.71466	.71073	.70684	.70300	.69920	.69545	.69173	.68806	.68444	.68085
93	.72750	.72370	.71994	.71622	.71254	.70890	.70530	.70174	.69822	.69474
94	.73931	.73562	.73198	.72838	.72481	.72129	.71780	.71434	.71093	.70755
95	.75001	.74644	.74291	.73941	.73595	.73253	.72914	.72579	.72247	.71919
96	.75953	.75606	.75262	.74923	.74586	.74253	.73924	.73598	.73275	.72955
97	.76819	.76481	.76147	.75816	.75489	.75165	.74844	.74526	.74211	.73899
98	.77599	.77270	.76944	.76621	.76302	.75986	.75672	.75362	.75054	.74750
99	.78319	.77998	.77680	.77365	.77053	.76744	.76437	.76134	.75833	.75535
100	.78987	.78673	.78362	.78054	.77748	.77446	.77146	.76849	.76555	.76263
101	.79622	.79315	.79010	.78708	.78409	.78113	.77819	.77528	.77239	.76953
102	.80283	.79983	.79685	.79390	.79097	.78807	.78519	.78234	.77951	.77671
103	.80983	.80690	.80399	.80111	.79825	.79541	.79260	.78981	.78705	.78430
104	.81760	.81475	.81192	.80912	.80633	.80357	.80083	.79810	.79541	.79273
105	.82726	.82451	.82178	.81907	.81638	.81371	.81106	.80843	.80582	.80322
106	.84137	.83879	.83623	.83368	.83115	.82863	.82614	.82366	.82119	.81874
107	.86211	.85981	.85751	.85523	.85297	.85071	.84847	.84624	.84403	.84182
108	.89660	.89481	.89304	.89127	.88950	.88775	.88601	.88427	.88254	.88081
109	.95372	.95290	.95208	.95126	.95045	.94964	.94883	.94803	.94723	.94643

TABLE S
BASED ON LIFE TABLE 80CNSMT
SINGLE LIFE REMAINDER FACTORS
APPLICABLE AFTER APRIL 30, 1989

INTEREST RATE

AGE	12.2%	12.4%	12.6%	12.8%	13.0%	13.2%	13.4%	13.6%	13.8%	14.0%
0	.01683	.01669	.01655	.01642	.01630	.01618	.01607	.01596	.01586	.01576
1	.00559	.00544	.00531	.00518	.00506	.00494	.00484	.00473	.00464	.00454
2	.00528	.00513	.00499	.00485	.00473	.00461	.00449	.00439	.00428	.00419
3	.00524	.00508	.00493	.00479	.00465	.00453	.00441	.00429	.00419	.00408
4	.00536	.00519	.00503	.00488	.00473	.00460	.00447	.00435	.00423	.00412
5	.00558	.00540	.00523	.00507	.00492	.00477	.00464	.00451	.00439	.00427
6	.00588	.00569	.00550	.00533	.00517	.00502	.00487	.00473	.00460	.00448
7	.00624	.00604	.00584	.00566	.00549	.00532	.00517	.00502	.00488	.00475
8	.00668	.00646	.00626	.00606	.00588	.00570	.00554	.00538	.00523	.00509
9	.00722	.00699	.00677	.00656	.00636	.00617	.00600	.00583	.00567	.00552
10	.00785	.00761	.00737	.00715	.00694	.00674	.00655	.00637	.00620	.00604
11	.00861	.00835	.00810	.00786	.00764	.00743	.00723	.00704	.00686	.00668
12	.00946	.00918	.00891	.00866	.00843	.00820	.00799	.00779	.00760	.00741
13	.01035	.01006	.00978	.00951	.00927	.00903	.00880	.00859	.00839	.00819
14	.01122	.01091	.01061	.01034	.01007	.00982	.00958	.00936	.00914	.00894
15	.01203	.01171	.01140	.01110	.01082	.01056	.01031	.01007	.00985	.00963
16	.01279	.01244	.01211	.01181	.01151	.01123	.01097	.01072	.01048	.01025
17	.01347	.01311	.01276	.01244	.01213	.01184	.01156	.01130	.01104	.01081
18	.01411	.01373	.01336	.01302	.01270	.01239	.01210	.01182	.01155	.01130
19	.01474	.01434	.01396	.01359	.01325	.01293	.01262	.01233	.01205	.01178
20	.01537	.01494	.01454	.01415	.01379	.01345	.01313	.01282	.01252	.01224
21	.01598	.01553	.01510	.01470	.01432	.01396	.01361	.01329	.01298	.01268
22	.01660	.01613	.01568	.01525	.01485	.01446	.01410	.01375	.01343	.01312
23	.01725	.01674	.01627	.01581	.01539	.01498	.01460	.01423	.01388	.01355
24	.01796	.01742	.01692	.01644	.01599	.01556	.01515	.01476	.01439	.01404
25	.01876	.01819	.01765	.01714	.01666	.01621	.01577	.01536	.01497	.01460
26	.01967	.01907	.01850	.01796	.01745	.01696	.01650	.01606	.01565	.01525
27	.02072	.02008	.01948	.01890	.01836	.01784	.01735	.01688	.01644	.01601
28	.02190	.02122	.02057	.01996	.01938	.01883	.01831	.01781	.01734	.01689
29	.02322	.02249	.02181	.02116	.02054	.01996	.01940	.01887	.01836	.01788
30	.02469	.02392	.02319	.02250	.02184	.02122	.02062	.02006	.01952	.01900
31	.02634	.02552	.02475	.02401	.02331	.02264	.02201	.02140	.02083	.02028
32	.02816	.02729	.02647	.02568	.02494	.02423	.02355	.02291	.02229	.02170
33	.03018	.02926	.02838	.02755	.02675	.02600	.02528	.02459	.02393	.02331
34	.03239	.03142	.03048	.02960	.02875	.02795	.02718	.02645	.02575	.02508
35	.03482	.03378	.03279	.03185	.03095	.03009	.02928	.02850	.02775	.02704
36	.03743	.03633	.03528	.03428	.03333	.03242	.03155	.03072	.02992	.02916
37	.04026	.03909	.03798	.03692	.03591	.03494	.03401	.03313	.03228	.03147
38	.04330	.04207	.04089	.03977	.03869	.03767	.03668	.03574	.03484	.03398
39	.04658	.04528	.04403	.04284	.04170	.04061	.03957	.03857	.03762	.03670
40	.05011	.04873	.04741	.04615	.04495	.04379	.04269	.04163	.04061	.03964
41	.05389	.05244	.05104	.04971	.04844	.04721	.04604	.04492	.04384	.04281
42	.05791	.05638	.05491	.05350	.05216	.05086	.04962	.04844	.04729	.04620
43	.06219	.06057	.05902	.05754	.05612	.05475	.05344	.05218	.05098	.04981
44	.06673	.06503	.06340	.06184	.06034	.05890	.05752	.05619	.05491	.05368
45	.07157	.06978	.06806	.06642	.06484	.06332	.06186	.06046	.05911	.05781
46	.07669	.07481	.07301	.07128	.06962	.06802	.06649	.06501	.06358	.06221
47	.08212	.08015	.07826	.07645	.07470	.07302	.07140	.06984	.06834	.06690
48	.08784	.08578	.08380	.08190	.08006	.07830	.07660	.07496	.07338	.07186
49	.09384	.09169	.08961	.08762	.08570	.08384	.08206	.08034	.07868	.07708
50	.10013	.09787	.09570	.09361	.09160	.08966	.08779	.08598	.08424	.08256
51	.10671	.10436	.10209	.09991	.09780	.09577	.09381	.09192	.09009	.08832
52	.11365	.11120	.10883	.10655	.10435	.10222	.10017	.09819	.09628	.09442
53	.12095	.11840	.11593	.11355	.11126	.10904	.10689	.10482	.10282	.10088
54	.12860	.12595	.12338	.12090	.11851	.11619	.11396	.11179	.10970	.10767

TABLE S
BASED ON LIFE TABLE 80CNSMT
SINGLE LIFE REMAINDER FACTORS
APPLICABLE AFTER APRIL 30, 1989

INTEREST RATE

AGE	12.2%	12.4%	12.6%	12.8%	13.0%	13.2%	13.4%	13.6%	13.8%	14.0%
55	.13663	.13386	.13120	.12862	.12613	.12372	.12138	.11912	.11694	.11482
56	.14503	.14217	.13940	.13672	.13413	.13162	.12919	.12683	.12456	.12235
57	.15385	.15089	.14801	.14523	.14254	.13994	.13741	.13496	.13259	.13029
58	.16311	.16004	.15706	.15418	.15139	.14868	.14606	.14352	.14105	.13866
59	.17279	.16961	.16654	.16355	.16066	.15786	.15514	.15250	.14994	.14745
60	.18286	.17958	.17640	.17332	.17033	.16743	.16462	.16188	.15922	.15664
61	.19330	.18992	.18665	.18347	.18038	.17738	.17447	.17164	.16889	.16622
62	.20409	.20061	.19724	.19396	.19078	.18768	.18467	.18175	.17891	.17614
63	.21522	.21165	.20818	.20480	.20152	.19833	.19523	.19221	.18928	.18642
64	.22672	.22306	.21949	.21602	.21265	.20937	.20617	.20306	.20003	.19708
65	.23867	.23491	.23125	.22769	.22423	.22085	.21757	.21437	.21125	.20821
66	.25112	.24727	.24353	.23988	.23632	.23286	.22948	.22619	.22299	.21986
67	.26409	.26016	.25633	.25260	.24896	.24541	.24195	.23857	.23528	.23206
68	.27760	.27359	.26968	.26586	.26214	.25851	.25497	.25151	.24814	.24484
69	.29157	.28748	.28350	.27961	.27581	.27211	.26849	.26495	.26150	.25812
70	.30596	.30181	.29775	.29379	.28992	.28614	.28245	.27884	.27532	.27187
71	.32069	.31648	.31236	.30833	.30440	.30055	.29679	.29312	.28952	.28600
72	.33578	.33151	.32733	.32325	.31925	.31535	.31152	.30778	.30412	.30054
73	.35123	.34691	.34269	.33855	.33450	.33054	.32666	.32286	.31914	.31550
74	.36715	.36279	.35852	.35434	.35024	.34623	.34230	.33845	.33468	.33098
75	.38360	.37921	.37491	.37069	.36656	.36250	.35853	.35464	.35082	.34708
76	.40064	.39623	.39190	.38765	.38349	.37941	.37540	.37148	.36762	.36384
77	.41823	.41381	.40947	.40521	.40103	.39692	.39290	.38895	.38507	.38126
78	.43632	.43189	.42755	.42329	.41910	.41499	.41095	.40698	.40309	.39926
79	.45473	.45032	.44599	.44173	.43755	.43344	.42940	.42543	.42153	.41770
80	.47333	.46894	.46463	.46040	.45623	.45213	.44811	.44414	.44025	.43642
81	.49191	.48755	.48328	.47907	.47493	.47085	.46684	.46290	.45902	.45520
82	.51034	.50603	.50179	.49762	.49351	.48947	.48549	.48157	.47772	.47392
83	.52852	.52427	.52008	.51595	.51189	.50788	.50394	.50006	.49623	.49246
84	.54648	.54228	.53815	.53407	.53006	.52610	.52221	.51836	.51458	.51084
85	.56426	.56013	.55606	.55205	.54810	.54420	.54035	.53656	.53282	.52913
86	.58169	.57764	.57364	.56970	.56581	.56197	.55818	.55445	.55076	.54713
87	.59850	.59452	.59060	.58673	.58291	.57913	.57541	.57174	.56811	.56453
88	.61476	.61086	.60702	.60322	.59947	.59577	.59212	.58851	.58494	.58142
89	.63078	.62697	.62321	.61950	.61583	.61220	.60862	.60508	.60159	.59813
90	.64674	.64302	.63935	.63573	.63215	.62861	.62511	.62165	.61823	.61485
91	.66238	.65877	.65520	.65167	.64819	.64474	.64133	.63795	.63462	.63132
92	.67730	.67379	.67032	.66689	.66350	.66014	.65682	.65354	.65029	.64708
93	.69130	.68789	.68452	.68119	.67789	.67463	.67140	.66820	.66504	.66191
94	.70421	.70090	.69762	.69438	.69118	.68800	.68486	.68175	.67867	.67563
95	.71594	.71272	.70954	.70639	.70326	.70017	.69712	.69409	.69109	.68812
96	.72638	.72325	.72014	.71707	.71403	.71101	.70803	.70507	.70215	.69925
97	.73590	.73285	.72982	.72682	.72385	.72090	.71799	.71510	.71224	.70941
98	.74448	.74149	.73853	.73560	.73269	.72981	.72696	.72414	.72134	.71856
99	.75240	.74948	.74658	.74371	.74086	.73805	.73525	.73248	.72974	.72702
100	.75974	.75687	.75403	.75121	.74842	.74566	.74292	.74020	.73751	.73484
101	.76669	.76388	.76109	.75833	.75559	.75287	.75018	.74751	.74486	.74223
102	.77393	.77117	.76844	.76573	.76304	.76037	.75773	.75511	.75251	.74993
103	.78158	.77888	.77620	.77355	.77091	.76830	.76571	.76313	.76058	.75805
104	.79007	.78743	.78482	.78222	.77964	.77709	.77455	.77203	.76953	.76705
105	.80065	.79809	.79556	.79304	.79054	.78805	.78559	.78314	.78071	.77829
106	.81631	.81389	.81149	.80911	.80674	.80438	.80204	.79972	.79741	.79511
107	.83963	.83745	.83529	.83313	.83099	.82886	.82674	.82463	.82254	.82045
108	.87910	.87739	.87569	.87400	.87232	.87064	.86897	.86731	.86566	.86401
109	.94563	.94484	.94405	.94326	.94248	.94170	.94092	.94014	.93937	.93860

TABLE J
ADJUSTMENT FACTORS FOR TERM CERTAIN ANNUITIES
PAYABLE AT THE BEGINNING OF EACH INTERVAL
APPLICABLE AFTER APRIL 30, 1989

FREQUENCY OF PAYMENTS

INTEREST RATE	*ANNUALLY*	*SEMI ANNUALLY*	*QUARTERLY*	*MONTHLY*	*WEEKLY*
4.2	1.0420	1.0314	1.0261	1.0226	1.0213
4.4	1.0440	1.0329	1.0274	1.0237	1.0223
4.6	1.0460	1.0344	1.0286	1.0247	1.0233
4.8	1.0480	1.0359	1.0298	1.0258	1.0243
5.0	1.0500	1.0373	1.0311	1.0269	1.0253
5.2	1.0520	1.0388	1.0323	1.0279	1.0263
5.4	1.0540	1.0403	1.0335	1.0290	1.0273
5.6	1.0560	1.0418	1.0348	1.0301	1.0283
5.8	1.0580	1.0433	1.0360	1.0311	1.0293
6.0	1.0600	1.0448	1.0372	1.0322	1.0303
6.2	1.0620	1.0463	1.0385	1.0333	1.0313
6.4	1.0640	1.0478	1.0397	1.0343	1.0323
6.6	1.0660	1.0492	1.0409	1.0354	1.0333
6.8	1.0680	1.0507	1.0422	1.0365	1.0343
7.0	1.0700	1.0522	1.0434	1.0375	1.0353
7.2	1.0720	1.0537	1.0446	1.0386	1.0363
7.4	1.0740	1.0552	1.0458	1.0396	1.0373
7.6	1.0760	1.0567	1.0471	1.0407	1.0383
7.8	1.0780	1.0581	1.0483	1.0418	1.0393
8.0	1.0800	1.0596	1.0495	1.0428	1.0403
8.2	1.0820	1.0611	1.0507	1.0439	1.0413
8.4	1.0840	1.0626	1.0520	1.0449	1.0422
8.6	1.0860	1.0641	1.0532	1.0460	1.0432
8.8	1.0880	1.0655	1.0544	1.0471	1.0442
9.0	1.0900	1.0670	1.0556	1.0481	1.0452
9.2	1.0920	1.0685	1.0569	1.0492	1.0462
9.4	1.0940	1.0700	1.0581	1.0502	1.0472
9.6	1.0960	1.0715	1.0593	1.0513	1.0482
9.8	1.0980	1.0729	1.0605	1.0523	1.0492
10.0	1.1000	1.0744	1.0618	1.0534	1.0502
10.2	1.1020	1.0759	1.0630	1.0544	1.0512
10.4	1.1040	1.0774	1.0642	1.0555	1.0521
10.6	1.1060	1.0788	1.0654	1.0565	1.0531
10.8	1.1080	1.0803	1.0666	1.0576	1.0541
11.0	1.1100	1.0818	1.0679	1.0586	1.0551
11.2	1.1120	1.0833	1.0691	1.0597	1.0561
11.4	1.1140	1.0847	1.0703	1.0607	1.0571
11.6	1.1160	1.0862	1.0715	1.0618	1.0581
11.8	1.1180	1.0877	1.0727	1.0628	1.0590
12.0	1.1200	1.0892	1.0739	1.0639	1.0600
12.2	1.1220	1.0906	1.0752	1.0649	1.0610
12.4	1.1240	1.0921	1.0764	1.0660	1.0620
12.6	1.1260	1.0936	1.0776	1.0670	1.0630
12.8	1.1280	1.0950	1.0788	1.0681	1.0639
13.0	1.1300	1.0965	1.0800	1.0691	1.0649
13.2	1.1320	1.0980	1.0812	1.0701	1.0659
13.4	1.1340	1.0994	1.0824	1.0712	1.0669
13.6	1.1360	1.1009	1.0836	1.0722	1.0679
13.8	1.1380	1.1024	1.0849	1.0733	1.0688
14.0	1.1400	1.1039	1.0861	1.0743	1.0698

TABLE K
ADJUSTMENT FACTORS FOR ANNUITIES PAYABLE AT THE END OF EACH INTERVAL APPLICABLE AFTER APRIL 30, 1989

FREQUENCY OF PAYMENTS

INTEREST RATE	*ANNUALLY*	*SEMI ANNUALLY*	*QUARTERLY*	*MONTHLY*	*WEEKLY*
4.2	1.0000	1.0104	1.0156	1.0191	1.0205
4.4	1.0000	1.0109	1.0164	1.0200	1.0214
4.6	1.0000	1.0114	1.0171	1.0209	1.0224
4.8	1.0000	1.0119	1.0178	1.0218	1.0234
5.0	1.0000	1.0123	1.0186	1.0227	1.0243
5.2	1.0000	1.0128	1.0193	1.0236	1.0253
5.4	1.0000	1.0133	1.0200	1.0245	1.0262
5.6	1.0000	1.0138	1.0208	1.0254	1.0272
5.8	1.0000	1.0143	1.0215	1.0263	1.0282
6.0	1.0000	1.0148	1.0222	1.0272	1.0291
6.2	1.0000	1.0153	1.0230	1.0281	1.0301
6.4	1.0000	1.0158	1.0237	1.0290	1.0311
6.6	1.0000	1.0162	1.0244	1.0299	1.0320
6.8	1.0000	1.0167	1.0252	1.0308	1.0330
7.0	1.0000	1.0172	1.0259	1.0317	1.0339
7.2	1.0000	1.0177	1.0266	1.0326	1.0349
7.4	1.0000	1.0182	1.0273	1.0335	1.0358
7.6	1.0000	1.0187	1.0281	1.0344	1.0368
7.8	1.0000	1.0191	1.0288	1.0353	1.0378
8.0	1.0000	1.0196	1.0295	1.0362	1.0387
8.2	1.0000	1.0201	1.0302	1.0370	1.0397
8.4	1.0000	1.0206	1.0310	1.0379	1.0406
8.6	1.0000	1.0211	1.0317	1.0388	1.0416
8.8	1.0000	1.0215	1.0324	1.0397	1.0425
9.0	1.0000	1.0220	1.0331	1.0406	1.0435
9.2	1.0000	1.0225	1.0339	1.0415	1.0444
9.4	1.0000	1.0230	1.0346	1.0424	1.0454
9.6	1.0000	1.0235	1.0353	1.0433	1.0463
9.8	1.0000	1.0239	1.0360	1.0442	1.0473
10.0	1.0000	1.0244	1.0368	1.0450	1.0482
10.2	1.0000	1.0249	1.0375	1.0459	1.0492
10.4	1.0000	1.0254	1.0382	1.0468	1.0501
10.6	1.0000	1.0258	1.0389	1.0477	1.0511
10.8	1.0000	1.0263	1.0396	1.0486	1.0520
11.0	1.0000	1.0268	1.0404	1.0495	1.0530
11.2	1.0000	1.0273	1.0411	1.0503	1.0539
11.4	1.0000	1.0277	1.0418	1.0512	1.0549
11.6	1.0000	1.0282	1.0425	1.0521	1.0558
11.8	1.0000	1.0287	1.0432	1.0530	1.0568
12.0	1.0000	1.0292	1.0439	1.0539	1.0577
12.2	1.0000	1.0296	1.0447	1.0548	1.0587
12.4	1.0000	1.0301	1.0454	1.0556	1.0596
12.6	1.0000	1.0306	1.0461	1.0565	1.0605
12.8	1.0000	1.0310	1.0468	1.0574	1.0615
13.0	1.0000	1.0315	1.0475	1.0583	1.0624
13.2	1.0000	1.0320	1.0482	1.0591	1.0634
13.4	1.0000	1.0324	1.0489	1.0600	1.0643
13.6	1.0000	1.0329	1.0496	1.0609	1.0652
13.8	1.0000	1.0334	1.0504	1.0618	1.0662
14.0	1.0000	1.0339	1.0511	1.0626	1.0671

TABLE B
TERM CERTAIN REMAINDER FACTORS
APPLICABLE AFTER APRIL 30, 1989

INTEREST RATE

YEARS	4.2%	4.4%	4.6%	4.8%	5.0%	5.2%	5.4%	5.6%	5.8%	6.0%
1	.959693	.957854	.956023	.954198	.952381	.950570	.948767	.946970	.945180	.943396
2	.921010	.917485	.913980	.910495	.907029	.903584	.900158	.896752	.893364	.889996
3	.883887	.878817	.873786	.868793	.863838	.858920	.854040	.849197	.844390	.839619
4	.848260	.841779	.835359	.829001	.822702	.816464	.810285	.804163	.798100	.792094
5	.814069	.806302	.798623	.791031	.783526	.776106	.768771	.761518	.754348	.747258
6	.781257	.772320	.763501	.754801	.746215	.737744	.729384	.721135	.712994	.704961
7	.749766	.739770	.729925	.720230	.710681	.701277	.692015	.682893	.673908	.665057
8	.719545	.708592	.697825	.687242	.676839	.666613	.656561	.646679	.636964	.627412
9	.690543	.678728	.667137	.655765	.644609	.633663	.622923	.612385	.602045	.591898
10	.662709	.650122	.637798	.625730	.613913	.602341	.591009	.579910	.569041	.558395
11	.635997	.622722	.609750	.597071	.584679	.572568	.560729	.549157	.537846	.526788
12	.610362	.596477	.582935	.569724	.556837	.544266	.532001	.520035	.508361	.496969
13	.585760	.571339	.557299	.543630	.530321	.517363	.504745	.492458	.480492	.468839
14	.562150	.547259	.532790	.518731	.505068	.491790	.478885	.466343	.454151	.442301
15	.539491	.524195	.509360	.494972	.481017	.467481	.454350	.441612	.429255	.417265
16	.517746	.502102	.486960	.472302	.458112	.444374	.431072	.418194	.405723	.393646
17	.496877	.480941	.465545	.450670	.436297	.422408	.408987	.396017	.383481	.371364
18	.476849	.460671	.445071	.430028	.415521	.401529	.388033	.375016	.362458	.350344
19	.457629	.441256	.425498	.410332	.395734	.381681	.368153	.355129	.342588	.330513
20	.439183	.422659	.406786	.391538	.376889	.362815	.349291	.336296	.323807	.311805
21	.421481	.404846	.388897	.373605	.358942	.344881	.331396	.318462	.306056	.294155
22	.404492	.387783	.371794	.356494	.341850	.327834	.314417	.301574	.289278	.277505
23	.388188	.371440	.355444	.340166	.325571	.311629	.298309	.285581	.273420	.261797
24	.372542	.355785	.339813	.324586	.310068	.296225	.283025	.270437	.258431	.246979
25	.357526	.340791	.324869	.309719	.295303	.281583	.268525	.256096	.244263	.232999
26	.343115	.326428	.310582	.295533	.281241	.267664	.254768	.242515	.230873	.219810
27	.329285	.312670	.296923	.281998	.267848	.254434	.241715	.229654	.218216	.207368
28	.316012	.299493	.283866	.269082	.255094	.241857	.229331	.217475	.206253	.195630
29	.303275	.286870	.271382	.256757	.242946	.229902	.217582	.205943	.194947	.184557
30	.291051	.274780	.259447	.244997	.231377	.218538	.206434	.195021	.184260	.174110
31	.279319	.263199	.248038	.233776	.220359	.207736	.195858	.184679	.174158	.164255
32	.268061	.252106	.237130	.223069	.209866	.197468	.185823	.174886	.164611	.154957
33	.257256	.241481	.226702	.212852	.199873	.187707	.176303	.165612	.155587	.146186
34	.246887	.231304	.216732	.203103	.190355	.178429	.167270	.156829	.147058	.137912
35	.236935	.221556	.207201	.193801	.181290	.169609	.158701	.148512	.138996	.130105
36	.227385	.212218	.198089	.184924	.172657	.161225	.150570	.140637	.131376	.122741
37	.218220	.203274	.189377	.176454	.164436	.153256	.142856	.133179	.124174	.115793
38	.209424	.194707	.181049	.168373	.156605	.145681	.135537	.126116	.117367	.109239
39	.200983	.186501	.173087	.160661	.149148	.138480	.128593	.119428	.110933	.103056
40	.192882	.178641	.165475	.153302	.142046	.131635	.122004	.113095	.104851	.097222
41	.185107	.171112	.158198	.146281	.135282	.125128	.115754	.107098	.099103	.091719
42	.177646	.163900	.151241	.139581	.128840	.118943	.109823	.101418	.093670	.086527
43	.170486	.156992	.144590	.133188	.122704	.113064	.104197	.096040	.088535	.081630
44	.163614	.150376	.138231	.127088	.116861	.107475	.098858	.090947	.083682	.077009
45	.157019	.144038	.132152	.121267	.111297	.102163	.093793	.086124	.079094	.072650
46	.150690	.137968	.126340	.115713	.105997	.097113	.088988	.081557	.074758	.068538
47	.144616	.132153	.120784	.110413	.100949	.092312	.084429	.077232	.070660	.064658
48	.138787	.126583	.115473	.105356	.096142	.087749	.080103	.073136	.066786	.060998
49	.133193	.121248	.110395	.100530	.091564	.083412	.075999	.069258	.063125	.057546
50	.127824	.116138	.105540	.095926	.087204	.079289	.072106	.065585	.059665	.054288
51	.122672	.111243	.100898	.091532	.083051	.075370	.068411	.062107	.056394	.051215
52	.117728	.106555	.096461	.087340	.079096	.071644	.064907	.058813	.053302	.048316
53	.112982	.102064	.092219	.083340	.075330	.068103	.061581	.055695	.050380	.045582
54	.108428	.097763	.088164	.079523	.071743	.064737	.058426	.052741	.047618	.043001

TABLE B
TERM CERTAIN REMAINDER FACTORS
APPLICABLE AFTER APRIL 30, 1989

INTEREST RATE

YEARS	*4.2%*	*4.4%*	*4.6%*	*4.8%*	*5.0%*	*5.2%*	*5.4%*	*5.6%*	*5.8%*	*6.0%*
55	.104058	.093642	.084286	.075880	.068326	.061537	.055433	.049944	.045008	.040567
56	.099864	.089696	.080580	.072405	.065073	.058495	.052593	.047296	.042541	.038271
57	.095839	.085916	.077036	.069089	.061974	.055604	.049898	.044787	.040208	.036105
58	.091976	.082295	.073648	.065924	.059023	.052855	.047342	.042412	.038004	.034061
59	.088268	.078826	.070409	.062905	.056212	.050243	.044916	.040163	.035921	.032133
60	.084710	.075504	.067313	.060024	.053536	.047759	.042615	.038033	.033952	.030314

TABLE B
TERM CERTAIN REMAINDER FACTORS
APPLICABLE AFTER APRIL 30, 1989

INTEREST RATE

YEARS	6.2%	6.4%	6.6%	6.8%	7.0%	7.2%	7.4%	7.6%	7.8%	8.0%
1	.941620	.939850	.938086	.936330	.934579	.932836	.931099	.929368	.927644	.925926
2	.886647	.883317	.880006	.876713	.873439	.870183	.866945	.863725	.860523	.857339
3	.834885	.830185	.825521	.820892	.816298	.811738	.807211	.802718	.798259	.793832
4	.786144	.780249	.774410	.768626	.762895	.757218	.751593	.746021	.740500	.735030
5	.740248	.733317	.726464	.719687	.712986	.706360	.699808	.693328	.686920	.680583
6	.697032	.689208	.681486	.673864	.666342	.658918	.651590	.644357	.637217	.630170
7	.656339	.647752	.639292	.630959	.622750	.614662	.606694	.598845	.591111	.583490
8	.618022	.608789	.599711	.590786	.582009	.573379	.564892	.556547	.548340	.540269
9	.581942	.572170	.562581	.553170	.543934	.534868	.525971	.517237	.508664	.500249
10	.547968	.537754	.527750	.517950	.508349	.498944	.489731	.480704	.471859	.463193
11	.515977	.505408	.495075	.484972	.475093	.465433	.455987	.446750	.437717	.428883
12	.485854	.475007	.464423	.454093	.444012	.434173	.424569	.415196	.406046	.397114
13	.457490	.446436	.435669	.425181	.414964	.405012	.395316	.385870	.376666	.367698
14	.430781	.419582	.408695	.398109	.387817	.377810	.368078	.358615	.349412	.340461
15	.405632	.394344	.383391	.372762	.362446	.352434	.342717	.333285	.324130	.315242
16	.381951	.370624	.359654	.349028	.338735	.328763	.319103	.309745	.300677	.291890
17	.359653	.348331	.337386	.326805	.316574	.306682	.297117	.287867	.278921	.270269
18	.338656	.327379	.316498	.305997	.295864	.286084	.276645	.267534	.258739	.250249
19	.318885	.307687	.296902	.286514	.276508	.266870	.257584	.248638	.240018	.231712
20	.300268	.289179	.278520	.268272	.258419	.248946	.239836	.231076	.222651	.214548
21	.282739	.271785	.261276	.251191	.241513	.232225	.223311	.214755	.206541	.198656
22	.266232	.255437	.245099	.235197	.225713	.216628	.207925	.199586	.191596	.183941
23	.250689	.240073	.229924	.220222	.210947	.202078	.193598	.185489	.177733	.170315
24	.236054	.225632	.215689	.206201	.197147	.188506	.180259	.172387	.164873	.157699
25	.222273	.212060	.202334	.193072	.184249	.175845	.167839	.160211	.152943	.146018
26	.209297	.199305	.189807	.180779	.172195	.164035	.156275	.148895	.141877	.135202
27	.197078	.187317	.178056	.169269	.160930	.153017	.145507	.138379	.131611	.125187
28	.185572	.176049	.167031	.158491	.150402	.142740	.135482	.128605	.122088	.115914
29	.174739	.165460	.156690	.148400	.140563	.133153	.126147	.119521	.113255	.107328
30	.164537	.155507	.146989	.138951	.131367	.124210	.117455	.111079	.105060	.099377
31	.154932	.146154	.137888	.130104	.122773	.115868	.109362	.103233	.097458	.092016
32	.145887	.137362	.129351	.121820	.114741	.108085	.101827	.095942	.090406	.085200
33	.137370	.129100	.121342	.114064	.107235	.100826	.094811	.089165	.083865	.078889
34	.129350	.121335	.113830	.106802	.100219	.094054	.088278	.082867	.077797	.073045
35	.121798	.114036	.106782	.100001	.093663	.087737	.082196	.077014	.072168	.067635
36	.114688	.107177	.100171	.093634	.087535	.081844	.076532	.071574	.066946	.062625
37	.107992	.100730	.093969	.087673	.081809	.076347	.071259	.066519	.062102	.057986
38	.101688	.094671	.088151	.082090	.076457	.071219	.066349	.061821	.057609	.053690
39	.095751	.088977	.082693	.076864	.071455	.066436	.061778	.057454	.053440	.049713
40	.090161	.083625	.077573	.071970	.066780	.061974	.057521	.053396	.049573	.046031
41	.084897	.078595	.072770	.067387	.062412	.057811	.053558	.049625	.045987	.042621
42	.079941	.073867	.068265	.063097	.058329	.053929	.049868	.046120	.042659	.039464
43	.075274	.069424	.064038	.059079	.054513	.050307	.046432	.042862	.039572	.036541
44	.070880	.065248	.060074	.055318	.050946	.046928	.043233	.039835	.036709	.033834
45	.066742	.061323	.056354	.051796	.047613	.043776	.040254	.037021	.034053	.031328
46	.062845	.057635	.052865	.048498	.044499	.040836	.037480	.034406	.031589	.029007
47	.059176	.054168	.049592	.045410	.041587	.038093	.034898	.031976	.029303	.026859
48	.055722	.050910	.046522	.042519	.038867	.035535	.032493	.029717	.027183	.024869
49	.052469	.047848	.043641	.039812	.036324	.033148	.030255	.027618	.025216	.023027
50	.049405	.044970	.040939	.037277	.033948	.030922	.028170	.025668	.023392	.021321

TABLE B
TERM CERTAIN REMAINDER FACTORS
APPLICABLE AFTER APRIL 30, 1989

INTEREST RATE

YEARS	*6.2%*	*6.4%*	*6.6%*	*6.8%*	*7.0%*	*7.2%*	*7.4%*	*7.6%*	*7.8%*	*8.0%*
51	.046521	.042265	.038405	.034903	.031727	.028845	.026229	.023855	.021699	.019742
52	.043805	.039722	.036027	.032681	.029651	.026907	.024422	.022170	.020129	.018280
53	.041248	.037333	.033796	.030600	.027711	.025100	.022739	.020604	.018673	.016925
54	.038840	.035087	.031704	.028652	.025899	.023414	.021172	.019149	.017322	.015672
55	.036572	.032977	.029741	.026828	.024204	.021842	.019714	.017796	.016068	.014511
56	.034437	.030993	.027900	.025119	.022621	.020375	.018355	.016539	.014906	.013436
57	.032427	.029129	.026172	.023520	.021141	.019006	.017091	.015371	.013827	.012441
58	.030534	.027377	.024552	.022023	.019758	.017730	.015913	.014285	.012827	.011519
59	.028751	.025730	.023032	.020620	.018465	.016539	.014817	.013276	.011899	.010666
60	.027073	.024183	.021606	.019307	.017257	.015428	.013796	.012339	.011038	.009876

TABLE B
TERM CERTAIN REMAINDER FACTORS
APPLICABLE AFTER APRIL 30, 1989
INTEREST RATE

YEARS	8.2%	8.4%	8.6%	8.8%	9.0%	9.2%	9.4%	9.6%	9.8%	10.0%
1	.924214	.922509	.920810	.919118	.917431	.915751	.914077	.912409	.910747	.909091
2	.854172	.851023	.847892	.844777	.841680	.838600	.835536	.832490	.829460	.826446
3	.789438	.785077	.780747	.776450	.772183	.767948	.763744	.759571	.755428	.751315
4	.729610	.724241	.718920	.713649	.708425	.703250	.698121	.693039	.688003	.683013
5	.674316	.668119	.661989	.655927	.649931	.644001	.638136	.632335	.626597	.620921
6	.623213	.616346	.609566	.602874	.596267	.589745	.583305	.576948	.570671	.564474
7	.575982	.568585	.561295	.554112	.547034	.540059	.533186	.526412	.519737	.513158
8	.532331	.524524	.516846	.509294	.501866	.494560	.487373	.480303	.473349	.466507
9	.491988	.483879	.475917	.468101	.460428	.452894	.445496	.438233	.431101	.424098
10	.454703	.446383	.438230	.430240	.422411	.414738	.407218	.399848	.392624	.385543
11	.420243	.411792	.403526	.395441	.387533	.379797	.372228	.364824	.357581	.350494
12	.388394	.379882	.371571	.363457	.355535	.347799	.340245	.332869	.325666	.318631
13	.358960	.350445	.342147	.334060	.326179	.318497	.311010	.303713	.296599	.289664
14	.331756	.323288	.315052	.307040	.299246	.291664	.284287	.277110	.270127	.263331
15	.306613	.298236	.290103	.282206	.274538	.267092	.259860	.252838	.246017	.239392
16	.283376	.275126	.267130	.259381	.251870	.244589	.237532	.230691	.224059	.217629
17	.261901	.253806	.245976	.238401	.231073	.223983	.217123	.210485	.204061	.197845
18	.242052	.234139	.226497	.219119	.211994	.205113	.198467	.192048	.185848	.179859
19	.223708	.215995	.208561	.201396	.194490	.187832	.181414	.175226	.169260	.163508
20	.206754	.199257	.192045	.185107	.178431	.172007	.165826	.159878	.154153	.148644
21	.191085	.183817	.176837	.170135	.163698	.157516	.151578	.145874	.140395	.135131
22	.176604	.169573	.162834	.156374	.150182	.144245	.138554	.133097	.127864	.122846
23	.163220	.150432	.149939	.143726	.137781	.132093	.126649	.121439	.116452	.111678
24	.150850	.144310	.138065	.132101	.126405	.120964	.115767	.110802	.106058	.101526
25	.139418	.133128	.127132	.121416	.115968	.110773	.105820	.101097	.096592	.092296
26	.128852	.122811	.117064	.111596	.106393	.101441	.096727	.092241	.087971	.083905
27	.119087	.113295	.107794	.102570	.097608	.092894	.088416	.084162	.080119	.076278
28	.110062	.104515	.099258	.094274	.089548	.085068	.080819	.076790	.072968	.069343
29	.101721	.096416	.091398	.086649	.082155	.077901	.073875	.070064	.066456	.063039
30	.094012	.088945	.084160	.079640	.075371	.071338	.067527	.063927	.060524	.057309
31	.086887	.082053	.077495	.073199	.069148	.065328	.061725	.058327	.055122	.052099
32	.080302	.075694	.071358	.067278	.063438	.059824	.056422	.053218	.050202	.047362
33	.074216	.069829	.065708	.061837	.058200	.054784	.051574	.048557	.045722	.043057
34	.068592	.064418	.060504	.056835	.053395	.050168	.047142	.044304	.041641	.039143
35	.063394	.059426	.055713	.052238	.048986	.045942	.043092	.040423	.037924	.035584
36	.058589	.054821	.051301	.048013	.044941	.042071	.039389	.036882	.034539	.032349
37	.054149	.050573	.047239	.044130	.041231	.038527	.036005	.033652	.031457	.029408
38	.050045	.046654	.043498	.040560	.037826	.035281	.032911	.030704	.028649	.026735
39	.046253	.043039	.040053	.037280	.034703	.032309	.030083	.028015	.026092	.024304
40	.042747	.039703	.036881	.034264	.031838	.029587	.027498	.025561	.023763	.022095
41	.039508	.036627	.033961	.031493	.029209	.027094	.025136	.023322	.021642	.020086
42	.036514	.033789	.031271	.028946	.026797	.024811	.022976	.021279	.019711	.018260
43	.033746	.031170	.028795	.026605	.024584	.022721	.021002	.019415	.017951	.016600
44	.031189	.028755	.026515	.024453	.022555	.020807	.019197	.017715	.016349	.015091
45	.028825	.026527	.024415	.022475	.020692	.019054	.017548	.016163	.014890	.013719
46	.026641	.024471	.022482	.020657	.018984	.017449	.016040	.014747	.013561	.012472
47	.024622	.022575	.020701	.018986	.017416	.015978	.014662	.013456	.012351	.011338
48	.022756	.020825	.019062	.017451	.015978	.014632	.013402	.012277	.011248	.010307
49	.021031	.019212	.017552	.016039	.014659	.013400	.012250	.011202	.010244	.009370
50	.019437	.017723	.016163	.014742	.013449	.012271	.011198	.010221	.009330	.008519
51	.017964	.016350	.014883	.013550	.012338	.011237	.010236	.009325	.008497	.007744
52	.016603	.015083	.013704	.012454	.011319	.010290	.009356	.008508	.007739	.007040
53	.015345	.013914	.012619	.011446	.010385	.009423	.008552	.007763	.007048	.006400
54	.014182	.012836	.011620	.010521	.009527	.008629	.007817	.007083	.006419	.005818
55	.013107	.011841	.010699	.009670	.008741	.007902	.007146	.006463	.005846	.005289

TABLE B
TERM CERTAIN REMAINDER FACTORS
APPLICABLE AFTER APRIL 30, 1989
INTEREST RATE

YEARS	*8.2%*	*8.4%*	*8.6%*	*8.8%*	*9.0%*	*9.2%*	*9.4%*	*9.6%*	*9.8%*	*10.0%*
56	.012114	.010923	.009852	.008888	.008019	.007237	.006532	.005897	.005324	.004809
57	.011196	.010077	.009072	.008169	.007357	.006627	.005971	.005380	.004849	.004371
58	.010347	.009296	.008354	.007508	.006749	.006069	.005458	.004909	.004416	.003974
59	.009563	.008576	.007692	.006901	.006192	.005557	.004989	.004479	.004022	.003613
60	.008838	.007911	.007083	.006343	.005681	.005089	.004560	.004087	.003663	.003284

TABLE B
TERM CERTAIN REMAINDER FACTORS
APPLICABLE AFTER APRIL 30, 1989
INTEREST RATE

YEARS	10.2%	10.4%	10.6%	10.8%	11.0%	11.2%	11.4%	11.6%	11.8%	12.0%
1	.907441	.905797	.904159	.902527	.900901	.899281	.897666	.896057	.894454	.892857
2	.823449	.820468	.817504	.814555	.811622	.808706	.805804	.802919	.800049	.797194
3	.747232	.743178	.739153	.735158	.731191	.727253	.723343	.719461	.715607	.711780
4	.678069	.673168	.668312	.663500	.658731	.654005	.649321	.644679	.640078	.635518
5	.615307	.609754	.604261	.598827	.593451	.588134	.582873	.577669	.572520	.567427
6	.558355	.552313	.546348	.540457	.534641	.528897	.523225	.517625	.512093	.506631
7	.506674	.500284	.493985	.487777	.481658	.475627	.469682	.463821	.458044	.452349
8	.459777	.453156	.446641	.440232	.433926	.427722	.421617	.415610	.409700	.403883
9	.417221	.410467	.403835	.397322	.390925	.384642	.378472	.372411	.366458	.360610
10	.378603	.371800	.365131	.358593	.352184	.345901	.339741	.333701	.327780	.321973
11	.343560	.336775	.330137	.323640	.317283	.311062	.304974	.299016	.293184	.287476
12	.311760	.305050	.298496	.292094	.285841	.279732	.273765	.267935	.262240	.256675
13	.282904	.276313	.269888	.263623	.257514	.251558	.245749	.240085	.234561	.229174
14	.256719	.250284	.244022	.237927	.231995	.226221	.220601	.215130	.209804	.204620
15	.232957	.226706	.220634	.214735	.209004	.203436	.198026	.192769	.187661	.182696
16	.211395	.205350	.199489	.193804	.188292	.182946	.177761	.172732	.167854	.163122
17	.191828	.186005	.180369	.174914	.169633	.164520	.159570	.154778	.150138	.145644
18	.174073	.168483	.163083	.157864	.152822	.147950	.143241	.138690	.134291	.130040
19	.157961	.152612	.147453	.142477	.137678	.133048	.128582	.124274	.120117	.116107
20	.143340	.138235	.133321	.128589	.124034	.119648	.115424	.111357	.107439	.103667
21	.130073	.125213	.120543	.116055	.111742	.107597	.103612	.099782	.096100	.092560
22	.118033	.113418	.108990	.104743	.100669	.096760	.093009	.089410	.085957	.082643
23	.107108	.102733	.098544	.094533	.090693	.087014	.083491	.080117	.076884	.073788
24	.097195	.093056	.089100	.085319	.081705	.078250	.074947	.071789	.068770	.065882
25	.088198	.084289	.080560	.077003	.073608	.070369	.067278	.064327	.061511	.058823
26	.080035	.076349	.072839	.069497	.066314	.063281	.060393	.057641	.055019	.052521
27	.072627	.069157	.065858	.062723	.059742	.056908	.054213	.051650	.049212	.046894
28	.065905	.062642	.059547	.056609	.053822	.051176	.048665	.046281	.044018	.041869
29	.059804	.056741	.053840	.051091	.048488	.046022	.043685	.041470	.039372	.037383
30	.054269	.051396	.048680	.046111	.043683	.041386	.039214	.037160	.035216	.033378
31	.049246	.046554	.044014	.041617	.039354	.037218	.035201	.033297	.031500	.029802
32	.044688	.042169	.039796	.037560	.035454	.033469	.031599	.029836	.028175	.026609
33	.040552	.038196	.035982	.033899	.031940	.030098	.028365	.026735	.025201	.023758
34	.036798	.034598	.032533	.030595	.028775	.027067	.025463	.023956	.022541	.021212
35	.033392	.031339	.029415	.027613	.025924	.024341	.022857	.021466	.020162	.018940
36	.030301	.028387	.026596	.024921	.023355	.021889	.020518	.019235	.018034	.016910
37	.027497	.025712	.024047	.022492	.021040	.019684	.018418	.017236	.016131	.015098
38	.024952	.023290	.021742	.020300	.018955	.017702	.016533	.015444	.014428	.013481
39	.022642	.021096	.019658	.018321	.017077	.015919	.014841	.013839	.012905	.012036
40	.020546	.019109	.017774	.016535	.015384	.014316	.013323	.012400	.011543	.010747
41	.018645	.017309	.016071	.014923	.013860	.012874	.011959	.011111	.010325	.009595
42	.016919	.015678	.014531	.013469	.012486	.011577	.010735	.009956	.009235	.008567
43	.015353	.014201	.013138	.012156	.011249	.010411	.009637	.008922	.008260	.007649
44	.013932	.012864	.011879	.010971	.010134	.009362	.008651	.007994	.007389	.006830
45	.012642	.011652	.010740	.009902	.009130	.008419	.007765	.007163	.006609	.006098
46	.011472	.010554	.009711	.008937	.008225	.007571	.006971	.006419	.005911	.005445
47	.010410	.009560	.008780	.008065	.007410	.006809	.006257	.005753	.005287	.004861
48	.009447	.008659	.007939	.007279	.006676	.006123	.005617	.005154	.004729	.004340
49	.008572	.007844	.007178	.006570	.006014	.005506	.005042	.004618	.004230	.003875
50	.007779	.007105	.006490	.005929	.005418	.004952	.004526	.004138	.003784	.003460
51	.007059	.006435	.005868	.005351	.004881	.004453	.004063	.003708	.003384	.003089
52	.006406	.005829	.005306	.004830	.004397	.004005	.003647	.003322	.003027	.002758
53	.005813	.005280	.004797	.004359	.003962	.003601	.003274	.002977	.002708	.002463
54	.005275	.004783	.004337	.003934	.003569	.003238	.002939	.002668	.002422	.002199
55	.004786	.004332	.003922	.003551	.003215	.002912	.002638	.002390	.002166	.001963

TABLE B
TERM CERTAIN REMAINDER FACTORS
APPLICABLE AFTER APRIL 30, 1989
INTEREST RATE

YEARS	10.2%	10.4%	10.6%	10.8%	11.0%	11.2%	11.4%	11.6%	11.8%	12.0%
56	.004343	.003924	.003546	.003205	.002897	.002619	.002368	.002142	.001938	.001753
57	.003941	.003554	.003206	.002892	.002610	.002355	.002126	.001919	.001733	.001565
58	.003577	.003220	.002899	.002610	.002351	.002118	.001908	.001720	.001550	.001398
59	.003246	.002916	.002621	.002356	.002118	.001905	.001713	.001541	.001387	.001248
60	.002945	.002642	.002370	.002126	.001908	.001713	.001538	.001381	.001240	.001114

TABLE B
TERM CERTAIN REMAINDER FACTORS
APPLICABLE AFTER APRIL 30, 1989
INTEREST RATE

YEARS	12.2%	12.4%	12.6%	12.8%	13.0%	13.2%	13.4%	13.6%	13.8%	14.0%
1	.891266	.889680	.888099	.886525	.884956	.883392	.881834	.880282	.878735	.877193
2	.794354	.791530	.788721	.785926	.783147	.780382	.777632	.774896	.772175	.769468
3	.707981	.704208	.700462	.696743	.693050	.689383	.685742	.682127	.678536	.674972
4	.630999	.626520	.622080	.617680	.613319	.608996	.604711	.600464	.596254	.592080
5	.562388	.557402	.552469	.547589	.542760	.537982	.533255	.528577	.523949	.519369
6	.501237	.495909	.490648	.485451	.480319	.475249	.470242	.465297	.460412	.455587
7	.446735	.441200	.435744	.430364	.425061	.419831	.414676	.409592	.404580	.399637
8	.398160	.392527	.386984	.381529	.376160	.370876	.365675	.360557	.355518	.350559
9	.354866	.349223	.343680	.338235	.332885	.327629	.322465	.317391	.312406	.307508
10	.316280	.310697	.305222	.299853	.294588	.289425	.284361	.279394	.274522	.269744
11	.281889	.276421	.271068	.265827	.260698	.255676	.250759	.245945	.241232	.236617
12	.251238	.245926	.240735	.235663	.230706	.225862	.221128	.216501	.211979	.207559
13	.223920	.218795	.213797	.208921	.204165	.199525	.194998	.190582	.186273	.182069
14	.199572	.194658	.189873	.185213	.180677	.176258	.171956	.167766	.163685	.159710
15	.177872	.173183	.168626	.164196	.159891	.155705	.151637	.147681	.143835	.140096
16	.158531	.154077	.149757	.145564	.141496	.137549	.133718	.130001	.126393	.122892
17	.141293	.137080	.132999	.129046	.125218	.121510	.117917	.114438	.111066	.107800
18	.125930	.121957	.118116	.114403	.110812	.107341	.103984	.100737	.097598	.094561
19	.112237	.108503	.104899	.101421	.098064	.094824	.091696	.088677	.085762	.082948
20	.100033	.096533	.093161	.089912	.086782	.083767	.080861	.078061	.075362	.072762
21	.089156	.085883	.082736	.079709	.076798	.073999	.071306	.068716	.066224	.063826
22	.079462	.076408	.073478	.070664	.067963	.065370	.062880	.060489	.058193	.055988
23	.070821	.067979	.065255	.062646	.060144	.057747	.055450	.053247	.051136	.049112
24	.063121	.060480	.057953	.055537	.053225	.051014	.048898	.046873	.044935	.043081
25	.056257	.053807	.051468	.049235	.047102	.045065	.043119	.041261	.039486	.037790
26	.050140	.047871	.045709	.043648	.041683	.039810	.038024	.036321	.034698	.033149
27	.044688	.042590	.040594	.038695	.036888	.035168	.033531	.031973	.030490	.029078
28	.039829	.037892	.036052	.034304	.032644	.031067	.029569	.028145	.026793	.025507
29	.035498	.033711	.032017	.030411	.028889	.027444	.026075	.024776	.023544	.022375
30	.031638	.029992	.028435	.026960	.025565	.024244	.022994	.021810	.020689	.019627
31	.028198	.026684	.025253	.023901	.022624	.021417	.020277	.019199	.018180	.017217
32	.025132	.023740	.022427	.021189	.020021	.018920	.017881	.016900	.015975	.015102
33	.022399	.021121	.019917	.018785	.017718	.016714	.015768	.014877	.014038	.013248
34	.019964	.018791	.017689	.016653	.015680	.014765	.013905	.013096	.012336	.011621
35	.017793	.016718	.015709	.014763	.013876	.013043	.012261	.011528	.010840	.010194
36	.015858	.014873	.013951	.013088	.012279	.011522	.010813	.010148	.009525	.008942
37	.014134	.013233	.012390	.011603	.010867	.010178	.009535	.008933	.008370	.007844
38	.012597	.011773	.011004	.010286	.009617	.008992	.008408	.007864	.007355	.006880
39	.011227	.010474	.009772	.009119	.008510	.007943	.007415	.006922	.006463	.006035
40	.010007	.009319	.008679	.008084	.007531	.007017	.006538	.006093	.005679	.005294
41	.008919	.008291	.007708	.007167	.006665	.006199	.005766	.005364	.004991	.004644
42	.007949	.007376	.006845	.006354	.005898	.005476	.005085	.004722	.004386	.004074
43	.007084	.006562	.006079	.005633	.005219	.004837	.004484	.004157	.003854	.003573
44	.006314	.005838	.005399	.004993	.004619	.004273	.003954	.003659	.003386	.003135
45	.005628	.005194	.004795	.004427	.004088	.003775	.003487	.003221	.002976	.002750
46	.005016	.004621	.004258	.003924	.003617	.003335	.003075	.002835	.002615	.002412
47	.004470	.004111	.003782	.003479	.003201	.002946	.002711	.002496	.002298	.002116
48	.003984	.003658	.003359	.003084	.002833	.002602	.002391	.002197	.002019	.001856
49	.003551	.003254	.002983	.002734	.002507	.002299	.002108	.001934	.001774	.001628
50	.003165	.002895	.002649	.002424	.002219	.002031	.001859	.001702	.001559	.001428
51	.002821	.002576	.002353	.002149	.001963	.001794	.001640	.001499	.001370	.001253
52	.002514	.002292	.002089	.001905	.001737	.001585	.001446	.001319	.001204	.001099
53	.002241	.002039	.001856	.001689	.001538	.001400	.001275	.001161	.001058	.000964
54	.001997	.001814	.001648	.001497	.001361	.001237	.001124	.001022	.000930	.000846
55	.001780	.001614	.001463	.001327	.001204	.001093	.000991	.000900	.000817	.000742

TABLE B
TERM CERTAIN REMAINDER FACTORS
APPLICABLE AFTER APRIL 30, 1989
INTEREST RATE

YEARS	*12.2%*	*12.4%*	*12.6%*	*12.8%*	*13.0%*	*13.2%*	*13.4%*	*13.6%*	*13.8%*	*14.0%*
56	.001586	.001436	.001300	.001177	.001066	.000965	.000874	.000792	.000718	.000651
57	.001414	.001277	.001154	.001043	.000943	.000853	.000771	.000697	.000631	.000571
58	.001260	.001136	.001025	.000925	.000835	.000753	.000680	.000614	.000554	.000501
59	.001123	.001011	.000910	.000820	.000739	.000665	.000600	.000540	.000487	.000439
60	.001001	.000900	.000809	.000727	.000654	.000588	.000529	.000476	.000428	.000385

TABLE U(1)
BASED ON LIFE TABLE 80CNSMT
UNITRUST SINGLE LIFE REMAINDER FACTORS
APPLICABLE AFTER APRIL 30, 1989

ADJUSTED PAYOUT RATE

AGE	4.2%	4.4%	4.6%	4.8%	5.0%	5.2%	5.4%	5.6%	5.8%	6.0%
0	.06797	.06181	.05645	.05177	.04768	.04410	.04096	.03820	.03578	.03364
1	.05881	.05243	.04686	.04199	.03773	.03400	.03072	.02784	.02531	.02308
2	.06049	.05394	.04821	.04319	.03880	.03494	.03155	.02856	.02593	.02361
3	.06252	.05579	.04990	.04473	.04020	.03621	.03270	.02961	.02688	.02446
4	.06479	.05788	.05182	.04650	.04183	.03771	.03408	.03087	.02804	.02553
5	.06724	.06016	.05393	.04845	.04363	.03937	.03562	.03230	.02936	.02675
6	.06984	.06257	.05618	.05054	.04557	.04117	.03729	.03385	.03080	.02809
7	.07259	.06513	.05856	.05276	.04764	.04310	.03909	.03552	.03236	.02954
8	.07548	.06784	.06109	.05513	.04985	.04517	.04102	.03733	.03405	.03113
9	.07854	.07071	.06378	.05765	.05221	.04738	.04310	.03928	.03588	.03285
10	.08176	.07374	.06663	.06033	.05473	.04976	.04533	.04138	.03786	.03471
11	.08517	.07695	.06966	.06319	.05743	.05230	.04772	.04364	.04000	.03673
12	.08872	.08031	.07284	.06619	.06026	.05498	.05026	.04604	.04227	.03889
13	.09238	.08378	.07612	.06929	.06320	.05776	.05289	.04853	.04463	.04113
14	.09608	.08728	.07943	.07243	.06616	.06056	.05554	.05104	.04701	.04338
15	.09981	.09081	.08276	.07557	.06914	.06337	.05820	.05356	.04938	.04563
16	.10356	.09435	.08612	.07874	.07213	.06619	.06086	.05607	.05176	.04787
17	.10733	.09792	.08949	.08192	.07513	.06902	.06353	.05858	.05413	.05010
18	.11117	.10155	.09291	.08515	.07817	.07189	.06623	.06113	.05652	.05236
19	.11509	.10526	.09642	.08847	.08130	.07484	.06901	.06375	.05899	.05469
20	.11913	.10908	.10003	.09188	.08452	.07788	.07188	.06645	.06154	.05708
21	.12326	.11300	.10375	.09539	.08784	.08101	.07483	.06923	.06416	.05955
22	.12753	.11705	.10758	.09902	.09127	.08426	.07789	.07212	.06688	.06212
23	.13195	.12125	.11156	.10279	.09484	.08763	.08109	.07514	.06973	.06481
24	.13655	.12563	.11573	.10675	.09860	.09119	.08446	.07833	.07274	.06766
25	.14136	.13022	.12010	.11091	.10255	.09495	.08802	.08171	.07595	.07069
26	.14640	.13504	.12471	.11530	.10674	.09893	.09181	.08531	.07937	.07394
27	.15169	.14011	.12956	.11994	.11117	.10316	.09584	.08915	.08302	.07742
28	.15721	.14542	.13465	.12482	.11583	.10762	.10010	.09322	.08691	.08112
29	.16299	.15097	.13999	.12994	.12075	.11233	.10461	.09753	.09104	.08507
30	.16901	.15678	.14559	.13533	.12592	.11729	.10937	.10210	.09541	.08926
31	.17531	.16287	.15146	.14099	.13137	.12254	.11441	.10694	.10006	.09372
32	.18186	.16921	.15759	.14691	.13709	.12804	.11972	.11205	.10497	.09844
33	.18869	.17584	.16401	.15312	.14309	.13384	.12531	.11744	.11017	.10345
34	.19578	.18273	.17070	.15961	.14937	.13992	.13119	.12312	.11565	.10874
35	.20315	.18990	.17767	.16637	.15593	.14628	.13735	.12908	.12142	.11431
36	.21076	.19732	.18490	.17340	.16276	.15291	.14377	.13531	.12745	.12016
37	.21863	.20501	.19239	.18071	.16987	.15982	.15049	.14182	.13377	.12628
38	.22676	.21296	.20016	.18828	.17725	.16701	.15748	.14862	.14037	.13269
39	.23515	.22118	.20820	.19614	.18492	.17448	.16476	.15571	.14727	.13940
40	.24379	.22967	.21652	.20428	.19288	.18225	.17234	.16310	.15447	.14641
41	.25270	.23842	.22511	.21270	.20112	.19031	.18021	.17078	.16197	.15372
42	.26184	.24742	.23395	.22137	.20962	.19864	.18836	.17875	.16975	.16132
43	.27123	.25666	.24305	.23031	.21840	.20724	.19679	.18700	.17782	.16921
44	.28085	.26616	.25241	.23952	.22745	.21613	.20551	.19554	.18618	.17739
45	.29072	.27591	.26203	.24901	.23678	.22530	.21452	.20438	.19485	.18589
46	.30082	.28591	.27191	.25875	.24639	.23476	.22381	.21352	.20382	.19468
47	.31116	.29616	.28204	.26877	.25626	.24449	.23340	.22295	.21309	.20379
48	.32171	.30663	.29241	.27902	.26640	.25449	.24326	.23265	.22264	.21318
49	.33245	.31730	.30300	.28950	.27676	.26473	.25336	.24262	.23246	.22285
50	.34338	.32816	.31379	.30020	.28735	.27521	.26371	.25283	.24253	.23277
51	.35449	.33923	.32479	.31112	.29818	.28593	.27431	.26331	.25287	.24297
52	.36582	.35053	.33603	.32230	.30927	.29692	.28520	.27408	.26352	.25349
53	.37736	.36205	.34751	.33372	.32063	.30819	.29637	.28514	.27446	.26431
54	.38909	.37376	.35921	.34537	.33221	.31970	.30780	.29647	.28569	.27542
55	.40099	.38568	.37111	.35724	.34404	.33146	.31949	.30807	.29719	.28681

TABLE U(1)
BASED ON LIFE TABLE 80CNSMT
UNITRUST SINGLE LIFE REMAINDER FACTORS
APPLICABLE AFTER APRIL 30, 1989

ADJUSTED PAYOUT RATE

AGE	4.2%	4.4%	4.6%	4.8%	5.0%	5.2%	5.4%	5.6%	5.8%	6.0%
56	.41308	.39779	.38322	.36934	.35610	.34348	.33143	.31994	.30898	.29851
57	.42536	.41011	.39555	.38167	.36841	.35575	.34366	.33210	.32106	.31051
58	.43781	.42262	.40810	.39422	.38096	.36828	.35615	.34454	.33344	.32281
59	.45043	.43530	.42083	.40698	.39373	.38104	.36888	.35724	.34609	.33540
60	.46318	.44813	.43372	.41992	.40668	.39400	.38183	.37017	.35898	.34824
61	.47602	.46107	.44674	.43299	.41979	.40713	.39497	.38329	.37207	.36129
62	.48893	.47410	.45986	.44617	.43303	.42039	.40825	.39657	.38534	.37454
63	.50190	.48720	.47306	.45946	.44638	.43379	.42168	.41001	.39878	.38796
64	.51494	.50038	.48636	.47286	.45986	.44733	.43526	.42362	.41240	.40158
65	.52808	.51368	.49980	.48641	.47350	.46104	.44903	.43743	.42624	.41544
66	.54134	.52711	.51338	.50013	.48733	.47496	.46302	.45148	.44033	.42956
67	.55471	.54068	.52712	.51401	.50134	.48908	.47723	.46577	.45467	.44394
68	.56820	.55437	.54100	.52805	.51552	.50339	.49165	.48027	.46925	.45858
69	.58172	.56812	.55495	.54219	.52982	.51783	.50620	.49494	.48401	.47341
70	.59526	.58190	.56894	.55637	.54417	.53234	.52086	.50971	.49889	.48838
71	.60874	.59564	.58291	.57055	.55854	.54687	.53554	.52453	.51382	.50342
72	.62218	.60934	.59685	.58471	.57291	.56143	.55026	.53939	.52882	.51854
73	.63557	.62301	.61078	.59887	.58728	.57600	.56501	.55431	.54389	.53373
74	.64896	.63669	.62472	.61307	.60171	.59064	.57985	.56932	.55906	.54906
75	.66237	.65040	.63872	.62733	.61622	.60538	.59480	.58447	.57439	.56455
76	.67581	.66416	.65279	.64168	.63083	.62023	.60988	.59977	.58989	.58023
77	.68925	.67793	.66688	.65606	.64550	.63516	.62506	.61517	.60551	.59605
78	.70263	.69166	.68093	.67044	.66016	.65010	.64026	.63062	.62119	.61195
79	.71585	.70525	.69486	.68468	.67471	.66495	.65538	.64600	.63681	.62780
80	.72885	.71860	.70856	.69872	.68906	.67959	.67031	.66120	.65227	.64350
81	.74150	.73162	.72193	.71242	.70308	.69392	.68492	.67609	.66742	.65890
82	.75376	.74425	.73490	.72572	.71671	.70785	.69915	.69059	.68219	.67393
83	.76559	.75643	.74744	.73859	.72989	.72134	.71293	.70466	.69652	.68852
84	.77700	.76821	.75955	.75104	.74266	.73441	.72629	.71831	.71044	.70270
85	.78805	.77961	.77130	.76311	.75505	.74711	.73929	.73158	.72399	.71652
86	.79866	.79056	.78258	.77472	.76697	.75933	.75180	.74438	.73707	.72985
87	.80870	.80094	.79329	.78574	.77829	.77095	.76370	.75656	.74951	.74255
88	.81825	.81081	.80348	.79623	.78908	.78202	.77506	.76818	.76139	.75469
89	.82746	.82035	.81332	.80638	.79952	.79275	.78606	.77945	.77292	.76647
90	.83643	.82963	.82291	.81627	.80971	.80322	.79681	.79047	.78420	.77801
91	.84503	.83854	.83212	.82578	.81950	.81330	.80716	.80109	.79509	.78915
92	.85308	.84689	.84076	.83470	.82870	.82276	.81689	.81107	.80532	.79963
93	.86052	.85460	.84875	.84295	.83721	.83152	.82590	.82033	.81481	.80935
94	.86729	.86163	.85602	.85046	.84496	.83951	.83412	.82877	.82348	.81823
95	.87338	.86795	.86257	.85723	.85195	.84672	.84153	.83639	.83129	.82624
96	.87877	.87354	.86836	.86323	.85814	.85309	.84809	.84313	.83822	.83334
97	.88365	.87861	.87362	.86867	.86375	.85888	.85405	.84926	.84450	.83979
98	.88805	.88318	.87835	.87356	.86880	.86409	.85941	.85477	.85016	.84559
99	.89210	.88739	.88271	.87807	.87347	.86890	.86436	.85986	.85539	.85095
100	.89588	.89131	.88678	.88227	.87780	.87337	.86896	.86459	.86024	.85593
101	.89949	.89506	.89066	.88629	.88195	.87764	.87336	.86911	.86488	.86069
102	.90325	.89897	.89471	.89047	.88627	.88209	.87794	.87381	.86971	.86564
103	.90724	.90311	.89900	.89491	.89085	.88681	.88279	.87880	.87484	.87089
104	.91167	.90770	.90376	.89983	.89593	.89205	.88819	.88435	.88053	.87673
105	.91708	.91333	.90959	.90587	.90217	.89848	.89481	.89116	.88752	.88391
106	.92470	.92126	.91782	.91440	.91100	.90760	.90422	.90085	.89749	.89414
107	.93545	.93246	.92948	.92650	.92353	.92057	.91762	.91467	.91173	.90880
108	.95239	.95016	.94792	.94569	.94346	.94123	.93900	.93678	.93456	.93234
109	.97900	.97800	.97700	.97600	.97500	.97400	.97300	.97200	.97100	.97000

TABLE U(1)
BASED ON LIFE TABLE 80CNSMT
UNITRUST SINGLE LIFE REMAINDER FACTORS
APPLICABLE AFTER APRIL 30, 1989

ADJUSTED PAYOUT RATE

AGE	6.2%	6.4%	6.6%	6.8%	7.0%	7.2%	7.4%	7.6%	7.8%	8.0%
0	.03176	.03009	.02861	.02730	.02613	.02509	.02416	.02333	.02258	.02191
1	.02110	.01936	.01781	.01644	.01522	.01413	.01316	.01229	.01150	.01080
2	.02156	.01974	.01812	.01669	.01541	.01427	.01325	.01234	.01152	.01078
3	.02233	.02043	.01875	.01725	.01591	.01471	.01364	.01268	.01182	.01105
4	.02330	.02132	.01956	.01800	.01660	.01535	.01422	.01322	.01231	.01149
5	.02443	.02237	.02054	.01890	.01743	.01612	.01494	.01389	.01293	.01208
6	.02568	.02353	.02162	.01990	.01837	.01700	.01576	.01465	.01365	.01275
7	.02704	.02480	.02280	.02102	.01941	.01798	.01668	.01552	.01446	.01351
8	.02852	.02619	.02411	.02224	.02057	.01906	.01770	.01648	.01537	.01437
9	.03014	.02772	.02554	.02360	.02184	.02027	.01885	.01756	.01640	.01535
10	.03190	.02938	.02711	.02508	.02325	.02160	.02012	.01877	.01755	.01645
11	.03381	.03119	.02883	.02672	.02481	.02308	.02153	.02012	.01884	.01768
12	.03585	.03313	.03068	.02847	.02648	.02468	.02305	.02157	.02023	.01902
13	.03798	.03515	.03260	.03030	.02822	.02635	.02464	.02310	.02170	.02042
14	.04012	.03718	.03453	.03213	.02997	.02801	.02623	.02462	.02315	.02181
15	.04225	.03919	.03644	.03395	.03169	.02965	.02779	.02611	.02457	.02317
16	.04436	.04120	.03833	.03574	.03339	.03126	.02932	.02756	.02595	.02449
17	.04647	.04319	.04021	.03752	.03507	.03285	.03082	.02898	.02730	.02577
18	.04860	.04519	.04210	.03930	.03675	.03443	.03232	.03040	.02864	.02703
19	.05079	.04725	.04404	.04113	.03847	.03606	.03386	.03185	.03001	.02833
20	.05304	.04938	.04604	.04301	.04025	.03773	.03543	.03333	.03141	.02965
21	.05537	.05157	.04811	.04495	.04208	.03945	.03705	.03486	.03285	.03101
22	.05779	.05385	.05025	.04698	.04398	.04125	.03874	.03645	.03435	.03242
23	.06032	.05623	.05250	.04910	.04598	.04313	.04052	.03812	.03592	.03390
24	.06302	.05878	.05491	.05136	.04812	.04515	.04242	.03992	.03762	.03550
25	.06589	.06150	.05748	.05380	.05042	.04733	.04448	.04187	.03946	.03725
26	.06897	.06442	.06025	.05643	.05292	.04969	.04673	.04400	.04148	.03916
27	.07228	.06757	.06325	.05928	.05563	.05227	.04917	.04632	.04369	.04126
28	.07582	.07094	.06646	.06234	.05854	.05504	.05182	.04884	.04609	.04355
29	.07958	.07454	.06990	.06562	.06167	.05804	.05468	.05157	.04870	.04604
30	.08360	.07838	.07357	.06913	.06504	.06125	.05775	.05452	.05152	.04874
31	.08788	.08249	.07751	.07291	.06866	.06472	.06108	.05771	.05457	.05167
32	.09242	.08685	.08170	.07694	.07252	.06844	.06465	.06113	.05786	.05483
33	.09724	.09149	.08617	.08124	.07666	.07242	.06848	.06482	.06141	.05824
34	.10234	.09641	.09091	.08581	.08107	.07667	.07257	.06876	.06521	.06191
35	.10773	.10161	.09594	.09066	.08575	.08119	.07694	.07298	.06928	.06583
36	.11338	.10708	.10122	.09577	.09070	.08597	.08156	.07744	.07360	.07001
37	.11932	.11283	.10680	.10117	.09592	.09102	.08645	.08217	.07818	.07444
38	.12554	.11887	.11265	.10685	.10142	.09636	.09162	.08719	.08304	.07915
39	.13206	.12521	.11880	.11282	.10722	.10198	.09708	.09249	.08818	.08414
40	.13888	.13184	.12526	.11909	.11332	.10791	.10284	.09808	.09361	.08942
41	.14601	.13878	.13201	.12567	.11972	.11414	.10890	.10398	.09935	.09499
42	.15342	.14601	.13906	.13254	.12641	.12066	.11525	.11016	.10537	.10086
43	.16112	.15353	.14640	.13970	.13340	.12747	.12189	.11663	.11168	.10701
44	.16913	.16136	.15406	.14718	.14070	.13460	.12885	.12342	.11830	.11347
45	.17745	.16951	.16202	.15497	.14832	.14204	.13612	.13053	.12525	.12025
46	.18608	.17796	.17030	.16308	.15625	.14981	.14372	.13796	.13251	.12735
47	.19501	.18673	.17890	.17150	.16451	.15790	.15164	.14571	.14010	.13478
48	.20425	.19579	.18780	.18024	.17308	.16630	.15987	.15378	.14800	.14252
49	.21375	.20514	.19698	.18926	.18193	.17499	.16840	.16214	.15620	.15056
50	.22352	.21476	.20644	.19856	.19107	.18396	.17721	.17080	.16470	.15890
51	.23358	.22467	.21620	.20816	.20051	.19325	.18634	.17976	.17350	.16755
52	.24396	.23490	.22628	.21809	.21030	.20288	.19581	.18908	.18267	.17655
53	.25465	.24545	.23670	.22836	.22042	.21285	.20563	.19875	.19218	.18592
54	.26563	.25631	.24742	.23895	.23086	.22315	.21579	.20876	.20204	.19562

TABLE U(1)
BASED ON LIFE TABLE 80CNSMT
UNITRUST SINGLE LIFE REMAINDER FACTORS
APPLICABLE AFTER APRIL 30, 1989

ADJUSTED PAYOUT RATE

AGE	6.2%	6.4%	6.6%	6.8%	7.0%	7.2%	7.4%	7.6%	7.8%	8.0%
55	.27692	.26747	.25846	.24986	.24164	.23379	.22628	.21911	.21225	.20568
56	.28850	.27895	.26982	.26109	.25275	.24476	.23712	.22981	.22281	.21611
57	.30041	.29076	.28152	.27267	.26421	.25610	.24833	.24089	.23376	.22691
58	.31263	.30288	.29355	.28460	.27602	.26780	.25991	.25234	.24508	.23811
59	.32515	.31532	.30590	.29685	.28817	.27984	.27184	.26416	.25677	.24968
60	.33793	.32803	.31853	.30940	.30062	.29219	.28409	.27630	.26880	.26159
61	.35093	.34098	.33141	.32220	.31335	.30483	.29663	.28873	.28113	.27381
62	.36414	.35414	.34451	.33524	.32631	.31771	.30942	.30144	.29374	.28631
63	.37754	.36750	.35783	.34850	.33951	.33084	.32247	.31440	.30661	.29910
64	.39115	.38108	.37137	.36200	.35296	.34422	.33579	.32765	.31978	.31217
65	.40500	.39493	.38519	.37579	.36670	.35792	.34943	.34122	.33328	.32560
66	.41914	.40906	.39932	.38990	.38079	.37197	.36343	.35517	.34717	.33943
67	.43355	.42350	.41376	.40434	.39521	.38636	.37780	.36950	.36145	.35365
68	.44824	.43822	.42851	.41909	.40996	.40111	.39252	.38419	.37611	.36827
69	.46313	.45316	.44348	.43409	.42498	.41613	.40754	.39919	.39109	.38322
70	.47818	.46827	.45864	.44929	.44020	.43137	.42279	.41445	.40634	.39845
71	.49331	.48348	.47391	.46461	.45557	.44677	.43821	.42988	.42177	.41388
72	.50853	.49879	.48930	.48007	.47108	.46233	.45380	.44550	.43741	.42952
73	.52384	.51421	.50482	.49566	.48674	.47805	.46957	.46130	.45324	.44538
74	.53930	.52979	.52050	.51145	.50261	.49399	.48557	.47736	.46934	.46152
75	.55495	.54557	.53641	.52747	.51873	.51020	.50187	.49372	.48577	.47799
76	.57079	.56157	.55256	.54374	.53513	.52670	.51847	.51041	.50253	.49483
77	.58680	.57775	.56890	.56024	.55176	.54346	.53534	.52739	.51960	.51198
78	.60291	.59405	.58537	.57687	.56855	.56040	.55241	.54458	.53691	.52940
79	.61898	.61032	.60184	.59353	.58537	.57738	.56954	.56185	.55431	.54691
80	.63491	.62647	.61819	.61007	.60210	.59428	.58660	.57907	.57167	.56441
81	.65054	.64234	.63427	.62636	.61858	.61094	.60344	.59606	.58882	.58170
82	.66582	.65784	.65000	.64229	.63472	.62727	.61994	.61274	.60566	.59870
83	.68065	.67291	.66530	.65781	.65044	.64319	.63605	.62903	.62212	.61532
84	.69508	.68758	.68020	.67293	.66577	.65872	.65178	.64495	.63821	.63158
85	.70915	.70190	.69475	.68770	.68076	.67392	.66718	.66054	.65399	.64754
86	.72274	.71573	.70882	.70200	.69528	.68865	.68212	.67567	.66931	.66304
87	.73569	.72892	.72224	.71565	.70915	.70273	.69639	.69014	.68397	.67788
88	.74807	.74154	.73509	.72872	.72243	.71622	.71009	.70403	.69805	.69214
89	.76010	.75381	.74759	.74144	.73537	.72937	.72344	.71758	.71179	.70607
90	.77189	.76584	.75985	.75394	.74809	.74230	.73659	.73093	.72534	.71981
91	.78327	.77746	.77171	.76603	.76040	.75484	.74933	.74388	.73850	.73316
92	.79399	.78841	.78289	.77743	.77202	.76667	.76137	.75613	.75093	.74579
93	.80394	.79858	.79328	.78803	.78283	.77768	.77258	.76753	.76252	.75757
94	.81303	.80788	.80278	.79773	.79272	.78776	.78284	.77797	.77315	.76837
95	.82124	.81628	.81136	.80649	.80166	.79687	.79213	.78742	.78276	.77814
96	.82851	.82372	.81897	.81426	.80959	.80496	.80036	.79581	.79129	.78682
97	.83512	.83048	.82588	.82132	.81679	.81230	.80785	.80343	.79905	.79471
98	.84106	.83656	.83210	.82767	.82328	.81892	.81459	.81030	.80604	.80181
99	.84655	.84218	.83785	.83354	.82927	.82503	.82082	.81664	.81249	.80837
100	.85165	.84740	.84318	.83899	.83483	.83070	.82660	.82252	.81848	.81446
101	.85652	.85238	.84827	.84419	.84013	.83611	.83210	.82813	.82418	.82026
102	.86159	.85757	.85358	.84960	.84566	.84174	.83784	.83397	.83012	.82630
103	.86697	.86307	.85920	.85535	.85152	.84771	.84392	.84016	.83642	.83270
104	.87295	.86919	.86544	.86172	.85802	.85434	.85068	.84704	.84341	.83981
106	.89081	.88749	.88418	.88088	.87760	.87433	.87106	.86782	.86458	.86135
107	.90588	.90296	.90005	.89715	.89425	.89137	.88849	.88561	.88275	.87989
108	.93013	.92791	.92570	.92350	.92129	.91909	.91689	.91469	.91250	.91031
109	.96900	.96800	.96700	.96600	.96500	.96400	.96300	.96200	.96100	.96000

TABLE U(1)
BASED ON LIFE TABLE 80CNSMT
UNITRUST SINGLE LIFE REMAINDER FACTORS
APPLICABLE AFTER APRIL 30, 1989

ADJUSTED PAYOUT RATE

AGE	8.2%	8.4%	8.6%	8.8%	9.0%	9.2%	9.4%	9.6%	9.8%	10.0%
0	.02130	.02075	.02025	.01980	.01939	.01901	.01867	.01835	.01806	.01779
1	.01017	.00960	.00908	.00861	.00819	.00780	.00745	.00712	.00683	.00655
2	.01011	.00951	.00897	.00848	.00803	.00762	.00725	.00690	.00659	.00630
3	.01035	.00971	.00914	.00862	.00815	.00771	.00732	.00696	.00663	.00632
4	.01076	.01009	.00948	.00894	.00843	.00798	.00756	.00718	.00683	.00650
5	.01130	.01059	.00996	.00938	.00885	.00836	.00792	.00752	.00714	.00680
6	.01193	.01119	.01051	.00990	.00934	.00883	.00836	.00793	.00754	.00717
7	.01265	.01187	.01116	.01051	.00992	.00938	.00888	.00842	.00800	.00762
8	.01347	.01264	.01189	.01121	.01058	.01001	.00948	.00900	.00856	.00815
9	.01440	.01353	.01274	.01201	.01135	.01075	.01019	.00968	.00921	.00877
10	.01544	.01453	.01369	.01293	.01223	.01159	.01101	.01046	.00997	.00950
11	.01662	.01566	.01478	.01398	.01324	.01257	.01195	.01137	.01085	.01036
12	.01791	.01690	.01597	.01513	.01435	.01364	.01298	.01238	.01182	.01131
13	.01926	.01820	.01722	.01634	.01552	.01477	.01408	.01344	.01285	.01231
14	.02059	.01948	.01846	.01752	.01667	.01588	.01515	.01448	.01386	.01328
15	.02189	.02072	.01965	.01867	.01777	.01694	.01617	.01547	.01481	.01421
16	.02315	.02192	.02080	.01977	.01882	.01795	.01714	.01640	.01572	.01508
17	.02436	.02308	.02190	.02082	.01982	.01891	.01806	.01728	.01656	.01589
18	.02556	.02422	.02298	.02184	.02080	.01983	.01894	.01812	.01736	.01665
19	.02679	.02537	.02408	.02288	.02178	.02077	.01983	.01897	.01817	.01742
20	.02804	.02656	.02519	.02394	.02278	.02172	.02073	.01982	.01898	.01819
21	.02932	.02776	.02633	.02501	.02380	.02268	.02164	.02068	.01979	.01896
22	.03065	.02902	.02751	.02613	.02485	.02367	.02258	.02157	.02063	.01976
23	.03204	.03033	.02876	.02730	.02595	.02471	.02356	.02249	.02150	.02058
24	.03356	.03176	.03010	.02857	.02716	.02585	.02463	.02351	.02246	.02149
25	.03520	.03332	.03158	.02997	.02848	.02710	.02582	.02463	.02352	.02249
26	.03702	.03504	.03321	.03152	.02995	.02850	.02714	.02589	.02472	.02363
27	.03902	.03695	.03502	.03324	.03159	.03006	.02863	.02730	.02607	.02492
28	.04120	.03902	.03700	.03513	.03339	.03178	.03027	.02887	.02757	.02635
29	.04358	.04129	.03917	.03720	.03537	.03367	.03208	.03061	.02923	.02794
30	.04616	.04376	.04154	.03947	.03754	.03575	.03408	.03251	.03106	.02969
31	.04897	.04646	.04413	.04195	.03993	.03804	.03627	.03463	.03309	.03165
32	.05200	.04938	.04693	.04465	.04252	.04053	.03867	.03693	.03531	.03378
33	.05529	.05254	.04998	.04758	.04534	.04325	.04130	.03946	.03775	.03614
34	.05883	.05595	.05326	.05075	.04840	.04620	.04414	.04221	.04040	.03870
35	.06262	.05961	.05680	.05417	.05170	.04939	.04723	.04520	.04329	.04149
36	.06665	.06351	.06057	.05781	.05523	.05280	.05053	.04839	.04638	.04449
37	.07094	.06766	.06459	.06171	.05900	.05646	.05407	.05182	.04971	.04771
38	.07550	.07208	.06888	.06586	.06303	.06037	.05786	.05550	.05327	.05118
39	.08034	.07678	.07344	.07029	.06733	.06454	.06191	.05943	.05709	.05489
40	.08547	.08177	.07828	.07499	.07190	.06898	.06623	.06363	.06118	.05886
41	.09090	.08704	.08341	.07998	.07675	.07371	.07083	.06811	.06553	.06310
42	.09661	.09260	.08882	.08525	.08188	.07870	.07569	.07284	.07015	.06760
43	.10260	.09844	.09451	.09080	.08729	.08397	.08083	.07785	.07503	.07236
44	.10891	.10459	.10051	.09666	.09300	.08954	.08626	.08316	.08021	.07741
45	.11553	.11106	.10683	.10282	.09902	.09542	.09201	.08876	.08568	.08276
46	.12247	.11784	.11346	.10930	.10536	.10161	.09806	.09468	.09146	.08841
47	.12974	.12496	.12042	.11611	.11202	.10813	.10443	.10091	.09756	.09438
48	.13732	.13238	.12769	.12323	.11899	.11495	.11111	.10745	.10397	.10065
49	.14520	.14011	.13526	.13064	.12625	.12207	.11809	.11429	.11066	.10721
50	.15338	.14812	.14312	.13836	.13381	.12948	.12535	.12141	.11765	.11405
51	.16187	.15646	.15130	.14639	.14169	.13721	.13294	.12885	.12495	.12121
52	.17072	.16516	.15985	.15478	.14993	.14531	.14088	.13665	.13261	.12873
53	.17993	.17422	.16876	.16353	.15854	.15377	.14920	.14482	.14064	.13662
54	.18949	.18362	.17801	.17264	.16750	.16258	.15787	.15335	.14902	.14486

TABLE U(1)
BASED ON LIFE TABLE 80CNSMT
UNITRUST SINGLE LIFE REMAINDER FACTORS
APPLICABLE AFTER APRIL 30, 1989

ADJUSTED PAYOUT RATE

AGE	*8.2%*	*8.4%*	*8.6%*	*8.8%*	*9.0%*	*9.2%*	*9.4%*	*9.6%*	*9.8%*	*10.0%*
55	.19940	.19339	.18763	.18212	.17683	.17176	.16690	.16224	.15777	.15348
56	.20968	.20353	.19762	.19196	.18654	.18132	.17632	.17152	.16691	.16247
57	.22035	.21406	.20802	.20222	.19665	.19129	.18615	.18121	.17646	.17189
58	.23142	.22499	.21881	.21287	.20717	.20168	.19640	.19132	.18643	.18172
59	.24286	.23630	.23000	.22393	.21809	.21247	.20705	.20184	.19682	.19198
60	.25465	.24797	.24154	.23534	.22938	.22363	.21808	.21274	.20759	.20262
61	.26676	.25996	.25341	.24710	.24101	.23513	.22946	.22399	.21871	.21361
62	.27916	.27225	.26559	.25916	.25295	.24695	.24117	.23557	.23017	.22495
63	.29184	.28483	.27806	.27152	.26520	.25909	.25319	.24748	.24196	.23661
64	.30483	.29772	.29085	.28421	.27779	.27157	.26555	.25973	.25409	.24863
65	.31817	.31098	.30402	.29729	.29076	.28444	.27832	.27240	.26665	.26108
66	.33192	.32466	.31762	.31079	.30418	.29777	.29155	.28552	.27968	.27400
67	.34609	.33876	.33164	.32474	.31805	.31156	.30525	.29913	.29319	.28742
68	.36066	.35328	.34610	.33914	.33238	.32581	.31943	.31323	.30720	.30134
69	.37558	.36815	.36093	.35391	.34709	.34045	.33400	.32773	.32163	.31569
70	.39078	.38332	.37606	.36900	.36213	.35545	.34894	.34260	.33643	.33042
71	.40620	.39872	.39144	.38435	.37744	.37071	.36415	.35776	.35153	.34547
72	.42184	.41435	.40706	.39994	.39301	.38625	.37965	.37322	.36694	.36082
73	.43771	.43023	.42293	.41581	.40886	.40207	.39545	.38899	.38267	.37651
74	.45387	.44641	.43912	.43201	.42505	.41826	.41163	.40514	.39881	.39261
75	.47039	.46296	.45570	.44861	.44167	.43488	.42824	.42175	.41541	.40920
76	.48729	.47991	.47269	.46563	.45872	.45196	.44534	.43886	.43251	.42630
77	.50452	.49722	.49006	.48305	.47619	.46946	.46287	.45642	.45009	.44389
78	.52203	.51481	.50773	.50079	.49399	.48732	.48078	.47437	.46808	.46191
79	.53966	.53254	.52556	.51870	.51198	.50538	.49891	.49255	.48632	.48019
80	.55728	.55028	.54340	.53665	.53002	.52351	.51712	.51083	.50466	.49860
81	.57471	.56784	.56109	.55445	.54792	.54151	.53521	.52901	.52292	.51692
82	.59186	.58512	.57850	.57199	.56558	.55927	.55307	.54697	.54097	.53506
83	.60863	.60204	.59556	.58918	.58289	.57671	.57062	.56462	.55872	.55290
84	.62505	.61862	.61228	.60604	.59989	.59383	.58786	.58198	.57618	.57047
85	.64118	.63491	.62873	.62263	.61663	.61070	.60486	.59911	.59343	.58783
86	.65685	.65075	.64473	.63879	.63294	.62716	.62145	.61583	.61027	.60479
87	.67187	.66594	.66008	.65430	.64859	.64296	.63739	.63190	.62647	.62112
88	.68631	.68054	.67485	.66923	.66367	.65818	.65276	.64740	.64211	.63688
89	.70042	.69483	.68930	.68384	.67845	.67311	.66784	.66262	.65747	.65237
90	.71434	.70894	.70359	.69830	.69307	.68790	.68278	.67772	.67271	.66775
91	.72789	.72266	.71750	.71239	.70733	.70232	.69736	.69246	.68760	.68280
92	.74070	.73567	.73068	.72574	.72085	.71601	.71121	.70647	.70176	.69711
93	.75266	.74780	.74298	.73821	.73348	.72880	.72417	.71957	.71502	.71051
94	.76363	.75893	.75428	.74967	.74510	.74057	.73608	.73163	.72722	.72285
95	.77356	.76901	.76451	.76005	.75562	.75123	.74688	.74257	.73829	.73405
96	.78237	.77797	.77360	.76927	.76497	.76071	.75648	.75229	.74813	.74401
97	.79039	.78612	.78187	.77766	.77348	.76934	.76523	.76115	.75710	.75308
98	.79762	.79345	.78932	.78522	.78115	.77711	.77310	.76913	.76518	.76126
99	.80429	.80023	.79620	.79220	.78823	.78429	.78038	.77649	.77264	.76881
100	.81047	.80651	.80258	.79867	.79479	.79094	.78712	.78332	.77955	.77580
101	.81636	.81249	.80865	.80483	.80104	.79727	.79352	.78981	.78611	.78244
102	.82250	.81872	.81497	.81124	.80754	.80386	.80020	.79656	.79295	.78936
103	.82900	.82532	.82167	.81804	.81442	.81083	.80726	.80371	.80018	.79667
104	.83622	.83266	.82911	.82558	.82207	.81858	.81510	.81165	.80821	.80479
106	.85814	.85494	.85175	.84857	.84540	.84225	.83911	.83598	.83286	.82975
107	.87704	.87420	.87136	.86853	.86571	.86290	.86009	.85729	.85450	.85171
108	.90812	.90593	.90375	.90156	.89939	.89721	.89504	.89286	.89070	.88853
109	.95900	.95800	.95700	.95600	.95500	.95400	.95300	.95200	.95100	.95000

TABLE U(1)
BASED ON LIFE TABLE 80CNSMT
UNITRUST SINGLE LIFE REMAINDER FACTORS
APPLICABLE AFTER APRIL 30, 1989

ADJUSTED PAYOUT RATE

AGE	10.2%	10.4%	10.6%	10.8%	11.0%	11.2%	11.4%	11.6%	11.8%	12.0%
0	.01754	.01731	.01710	.01690	.01671	.01654	.01638	.01622	.01608	.01594
1	.00630	.00607	.00585	.00565	.00547	.00530	.00514	.00499	.00485	.00472
2	.00604	.00579	.00557	.00536	.00516	.00498	.00481	.00465	.00451	.00437
3	.00604	.00578	.00554	.00532	.00511	.00492	.00474	.00458	.00442	.00427
4	.00621	.00593	.00568	.00544	.00522	.00502	.00483	.00465	.00448	.00433
5	.00648	.00619	.00592	.00567	.00544	.00522	.00502	.00483	.00465	.00449
6	.00684	.00653	.00624	.00597	.00572	.00549	.00528	.00507	.00489	.00471
7	.00726	.00693	.00663	.00634	.00608	.00583	.00560	.00539	.00518	.00499
8	.00777	.00742	.00709	.00679	.00651	.00624	.00600	.00577	.00555	.00535
9	.00837	.00800	.00765	.00733	.00703	.00675	.00649	.00625	.00602	.00580
10	.00908	.00868	.00832	.00797	.00765	.00736	.00708	.00682	.00657	.00634
11	.00991	.00949	.00910	.00874	.00840	.00808	.00779	.00751	.00725	.00700
12	.01083	.01039	.00997	.00959	.00923	.00890	.00858	.00829	.00801	.00775
13	.01181	.01134	.01090	.01049	.01012	.00976	.00943	.00912	.00883	.00855
14	.01275	.01226	.01180	.01137	.01097	.01060	.01025	.00992	.00961	.00932
15	.01365	.01313	.01264	.01219	.01177	.01138	.01101	.01066	.01034	.01003
16	.01449	.01394	.01343	.01295	.01251	.01209	.01171	.01134	.01100	.01068
17	.01526	.01469	.01415	.01365	.01318	.01274	.01233	.01195	.01159	.01125
18	.01600	.01539	.01482	.01430	.01380	.01334	.01291	.01251	.01213	.01177
19	.01673	.01609	.01550	.01494	.01442	.01393	.01348	.01305	.01265	.01227
20	.01747	.01679	.01616	.01557	.01502	.01451	.01403	.01358	.01316	.01276
21	.01820	.01748	.01682	.01620	.01562	.01508	.01457	.01409	.01365	.01323
22	.01895	.01819	.01749	.01683	.01622	.01565	.01511	.01461	.01414	.01369
23	.01972	.01893	.01818	.01749	.01684	.01624	.01567	.01514	.01464	.01417
24	.02058	.01974	.01895	.01822	.01753	.01689	.01629	.01572	.01519	.01469
25	.02154	.02064	.01981	.01903	.01830	.01762	.01698	.01638	.01582	.01529
26	.02262	.02167	.02079	.01996	.01919	.01847	.01779	.01715	.01655	.01599
27	.02385	.02284	.02191	.02103	.02021	.01944	.01872	.01804	.01740	.01680
28	.02521	.02415	.02316	.02222	.02135	.02053	.01977	.01904	.01836	.01772
29	.02673	.02561	.02455	.02357	.02264	.02177	.02095	.02018	.01946	.01877
30	.02842	.02723	.02611	.02506	.02407	.02315	.02227	.02146	.02068	.01996
31	.03030	.02903	.02784	.02673	.02568	.02470	.02377	.02290	.02207	.02130
32	.03235	.03101	.02976	.02857	.02746	.02641	.02543	.02450	.02362	.02279
33	.03463	.03321	.03188	.03062	.02944	.02833	.02728	.02629	.02535	.02447
34	.03711	.03561	.03419	.03286	.03161	.03043	.02931	.02826	.02726	.02632
35	.03981	.03822	.03672	.03531	.03398	.03273	.03154	.03042	.02936	.02836
36	.04271	.04103	.03945	.03796	.03655	.03522	.03396	.03277	.03164	.03057
37	.04584	.04407	.04239	.04081	.03932	.03791	.03657	.03531	.03411	.03297
38	.04920	.04733	.04556	.04389	.04231	.04082	.03940	.03806	.03679	.03558
39	.05280	.05083	.04897	.04721	.04554	.04396	.04246	.04103	.03968	.03840
40	.05667	.05459	.05263	.05077	.04901	.04733	.04575	.04424	.04280	.04144
41	.06080	.05861	.05655	.05459	.05272	.05096	.04928	.04768	.04617	.04472
42	.06518	.06289	.06071	.05864	.05668	.05482	.05305	.05136	.04975	.04822
43	.06982	.06742	.06513	.06296	.06089	.05893	.05706	.05528	.05358	.05196
44	.07475	.07223	.06983	.06754	.06537	.06330	.06133	.05945	.05766	.05595
45	.07998	.07733	.07481	.07242	.07014	.06796	.06588	.06390	.06202	.06021
46	.08550	.08273	.08010	.07758	.07519	.07290	.07072	.06864	.06665	.06474
47	.09134	.08845	.08569	.08306	.08055	.07815	.07586	.07367	.07157	.06957
48	.09748	.09446	.09158	.08882	.08619	.08368	.08128	.07898	.07678	.07467
49	.10391	.10076	.09775	.09487	.09212	.08949	.08697	.08456	.08225	.08003
50	.11062	.10734	.10420	.10120	.09832	.09557	.09293	.09041	.08798	.08566
51	.11764	.11423	.11096	.10783	.10483	.10195	.09919	.09655	.09401	.09158
52	.12503	.12148	.11807	.11481	.11168	.10868	.10581	.10304	.10039	.09784
53	.13278	.12909	.12556	.12216	.11891	.11578	.11278	.10989	.10712	.10445
54	.14088	.13706	.13339	.12986	.12648	.12322	.12009	.11709	.11419	.11141

TABLE U(1)
BASED ON LIFE TABLE 80CNSMT
UNITRUST SINGLE LIFE REMAINDER FACTORS
APPLICABLE AFTER APRIL 30, 1989

ADJUSTED PAYOUT RATE

AGE	10.2%	10.4%	10.6%	10.8%	11.0%	11.2%	11.4%	11.6%	11.8%	12.0%
55	.14936	.14540	.14159	.13793	.13442	.13103	.12778	.12464	.12163	.11872
56	.15821	.15412	.15018	.14639	.14274	.13923	.13584	.13258	.12944	.12642
57	.16749	.16326	.15918	.15526	.15148	.14784	.14433	.14094	.13768	.13453
58	.17719	.17282	.16862	.16456	.16065	.15688	.15324	.14973	.14634	.14306
59	.18731	.18281	.17847	.17429	.17025	.16634	.16258	.15894	.15543	.15203
60	.19782	.19319	.18872	.18440	.18023	.17621	.17231	.16855	.16491	.16139
61	.20869	.20393	.19934	.19489	.19060	.18644	.18242	.17854	.17477	.17113
62	.21990	.21502	.21029	.20573	.20131	.19703	.19289	.18887	.18499	.18123
63	.23144	.22644	.22159	.21690	.21236	.20796	.20370	.19956	.19556	.19167
64	.24335	.23823	.23326	.22845	.22379	.21927	.21489	.21063	.20651	.20250
65	.25568	.25045	.24537	.24044	.23566	.23103	.22653	.22216	.21791	.21379
66	.26850	.26316	.25797	.25293	.24804	.24329	.23868	.23420	.22984	.22560
67	.28182	.27637	.27108	.26594	.26095	.25609	.25137	.24678	.24231	.23797
68	.29565	.29011	.28472	.27949	.27439	.26943	.26461	.25991	.25534	.25089
69	.30991	.30429	.29882	.29349	.28830	.28325	.27833	.27354	.26887	.26432
70	.32457	.31887	.31332	.30791	.30264	.29750	.29249	.28760	.28284	.27820
71	.33955	.33378	.32816	.32267	.31732	.31210	.30701	.30204	.29719	.29246
72	.35485	.34902	.34333	.33778	.33236	.32707	.32190	.31686	.31193	.30711
73	.37049	.36461	.35887	.35326	.34778	.34242	.33719	.33207	.32707	.32218
74	.38656	.38064	.37485	.36920	.36366	.35825	.35296	.34778	.34272	.33776
75	.40312	.39717	.39136	.38566	.38009	.37464	.36930	.36407	.35895	.35394
76	.42022	.41426	.40842	.40271	.39711	.39163	.38625	.38099	.37583	.37077
77	.43782	.43187	.42603	.42031	.41470	.40920	.40380	.39851	.39332	.38823
78	.45586	.44992	.44410	.43839	.43278	.42728	.42188	.41658	.41138	.40627
79	.47418	.46828	.46248	.45679	.45120	.44572	.44033	.43503	.42983	.42472
80	.49264	.48679	.48103	.47538	.46982	.46436	.45900	.45372	.44853	.44343
81	.51103	.50524	.49954	.49394	.48843	.48301	.47768	.47243	.46727	.46219
82	.52925	.52352	.51789	.51235	.50690	.50153	.49624	.49104	.48591	.48087
83	.54718	.54154	.53598	.53051	.52512	.51981	.51459	.50943	.50436	.49936
84	.56484	.55930	.55383	.54844	.54313	.53789	.53273	.52764	.52262	.51767
85	.58231	.57686	.57149	.56619	.56096	.55581	.55072	.54571	.54076	.53588
86	.59939	.59405	.58878	.58358	.57845	.57339	.56839	.56346	.55858	.55377
87	.61583	.61061	.60545	.60035	.59532	.59035	.58545	.58060	.57581	.57108
88	.63171	.62661	.62156	.61658	.61165	.60678	.60196	.59721	.59251	.58786
89	.64733	.64235	.63742	.63255	.62774	.62298	.61827	.61361	.60900	.60444
90	.66285	.65801	.65321	.64847	.64377	.63913	.63453	.62998	.62548	.62103
91	.67804	.67334	.66868	.66407	.65950	.65498	.65050	.64607	.64169	.63735
92	.69250	.68793	.68341	.67893	.67450	.67011	.66575	.66144	.65718	.65295
93	.70604	.70162	.69723	.69288	.68858	.68431	.68008	.67589	.67174	.66762
94	.71852	.71422	.70997	.70575	.70156	.69742	.69331	.68923	.68519	.68119
95	.72984	.72567	.72154	.71744	.71337	.70934	.70534	.70137	.69744	.69354
96	.73992	.73586	.73183	.72784	.72388	.71995	.71605	.71218	.70835	.70454
97	.74910	.74514	.74122	.73733	.73346	.72963	.72582	.72205	.71830	.71458
98	.75737	.75351	.74967	.74587	.74209	.73835	.73463	.73093	.72727	.72363
99	.76501	.76123	.75748	.75376	.75007	.74640	.74276	.73914	.73555	.73198
100	.77208	.76838	.76471	.76107	.75745	.75385	.75028	.74673	.74321	.73971
101	.77879	.77517	.77157	.76800	.76444	.76092	.75741	.75392	.75046	.74702
102	.78579	.78224	.77871	.77521	.77173	.76827	.76483	.76141	.75801	.75463
103	.79318	.78971	.78626	.78283	.77942	.77604	.77266	.76931	.76598	.76267
104	.80139	.79801	.79464	.79129	.78796	.78465	.78136	.77808	.77482	.77157
106	.82665	.82357	.82049	.81743	.81438	.81134	.80831	.80530	.80229	.79930
107	.84893	.84616	.84340	.84064	.83789	.83515	.83241	.82969	.82696	.82425
108	.88637	.88421	.88205	.87989	.87774	.87559	.87344	.87129	.86915	.86701
109	.94900	.94800	.94700	.94600	.94500	.94400	.94300	.94200	.94100	.94000

TABLE U(1)
BASED ON LIFE TABLE 80CNSMT
UNITRUST SINGLE LIFE REMAINDER FACTORS
APPLICABLE AFTER APRIL 30, 1989

ADJUSTED PAYOUT RATE

AGE	12.2%	12.4%	12.6%	12.8%	13.0%	13.2%	13.4%	13.6%	13.8%	14.0%
0	.01581	.01569	.01557	.01546	.01536	.01526	.01516	.01507	.01499	.01490
1	.00459	.00448	.00437	.00426	.00417	.00407	.00399	.00390	.00382	.00375
2	.00424	.00412	.00400	.00389	.00379	.00369	.00360	.00352	.00343	.00335
3	.00414	.00401	.00389	.00377	.00366	.00356	.00346	.00337	.00328	.00320
4	.00418	.00404	.00391	.00379	.00368	.00357	.00347	.00337	.00327	.00319
5	.00433	.00418	.00405	.00391	.00379	.00368	.00357	.00346	.00336	.00327
6	.00454	.00439	.00424	.00410	.00397	.00384	.00372	.00361	.00351	.00341
7	.00482	.00465	.00449	.00434	.00420	.00407	.00394	.00382	.00371	.00360
8	.00516	.00498	.00481	.00465	.00450	.00436	.00422	.00410	.00397	.00386
9	.00560	.00541	.00523	.00505	.00489	.00474	.00459	.00446	.00433	.00420
10	.00613	.00592	.00573	.00555	.00537	.00521	.00505	.00491	.00477	.00463
11	.00677	.00655	.00635	.00615	.00597	.00580	.00563	.00547	.00532	.00518
12	.00751	.00728	.00706	.00685	.00666	.00647	.00629	.00613	.00597	.00581
13	.00829	.00805	.00782	.00760	.00739	.00719	.00701	.00683	.00666	.00650
14	.00905	.00879	.00854	.00831	.00809	.00789	.00769	.00750	.00732	.00715
15	.00974	.00947	.00921	.00897	.00874	.00852	.00831	.00811	.00793	.00775
16	.01037	.01009	.00982	.00956	.00932	.00909	.00887	.00866	.00846	.00827
17	.01093	.01063	.01034	.01007	.00982	.00958	.00935	.00913	.00892	.00873
18	.01143	.01112	.01082	.01053	.01027	.01001	.00977	.00954	.00933	.00912
19	.01192	.01159	.01127	.01097	.01069	.01043	.01017	.00993	.00970	.00949
20	.01239	.01204	.01170	.01139	.01109	.01081	.01055	.01029	.01005	.00983
21	.01283	.01246	.01211	.01178	.01147	.01117	.01089	.01063	.01037	.01013
22	.01328	.01288	.01251	.01216	.01183	.01152	.01122	.01094	.01067	.01042
23	.01372	.01331	.01292	.01254	.01219	.01186	.01155	.01125	.01097	.01070
24	.01422	.01378	.01336	.01297	.01260	.01225	.01191	.01160	.01130	.01101
25	.01479	.01432	.01388	.01346	.01306	.01269	.01233	.01200	.01168	.01138
26	.01545	.01495	.01448	.01404	.01362	.01322	.01284	.01248	.01214	.01182
27	.01623	.01570	.01520	.01472	.01427	.01385	.01344	.01306	.01270	.01235
28	.01712	.01655	.01601	.01551	.01503	.01457	.01414	.01373	.01334	.01298
29	.01813	.01752	.01695	.01641	.01589	.01541	.01494	.01451	.01409	.01370
30	.01927	.01862	.01801	.01743	.01688	.01635	.01586	.01539	.01495	.01452
31	.02056	.01987	.01922	.01859	.01801	.01745	.01692	.01642	.01594	.01548
32	.02201	.02127	.02057	.01990	.01927	.01868	.01811	.01757	.01706	.01657
33	.02363	.02284	.02209	.02138	.02071	.02007	.01946	.01888	.01833	.01781
34	.02543	.02458	.02378	.02302	.02230	.02162	.02096	.02034	.01975	.01919
35	.02741	.02651	.02565	.02484	.02407	.02333	.02264	.02197	.02134	.02073
36	.02956	.02859	.02768	.02681	.02599	.02520	.02446	.02374	.02307	.02242
37	.03189	.03087	.02990	.02897	.02809	.02725	.02645	.02569	.02496	.02427
38	.03443	.03334	.03230	.03131	.03037	.02948	.02862	.02781	.02703	.02628
39	.03718	.03602	.03491	.03386	.03285	.03190	.03099	.03011	.02928	.02849
40	.04015	.03891	.03774	.03662	.03555	.03453	.03355	.03262	.03173	.03088
41	.04335	.04204	.04079	.03959	.03846	.03737	.03633	.03534	.03439	.03348
42	.04677	.04538	.04405	.04278	.04157	.04042	.03931	.03825	.03724	.03627
43	.05042	.04894	.04754	.04619	.04491	.04368	.04250	.04138	.04030	.03926
44	.05432	.05276	.05127	.04984	.04848	.04718	.04593	.04473	.04358	.04248
45	.05849	.05684	.05526	.05375	.05231	.05092	.04960	.04832	.04710	.04593
46	.06292	.06118	.05952	.05792	.05639	.05492	.05352	.05217	.05087	.04963
47	.06765	.06581	.06405	.06237	.06075	.05920	.05771	.05628	.05491	.05359
48	.07265	.07071	.06886	.06708	.06537	.06373	.06216	.06064	.05919	.05779
49	.07791	.07587	.07392	.07204	.07024	.06851	.06685	.06525	.06371	.06223
50	.08343	.08129	.07923	.07726	.07536	.07354	.07178	.07009	.06847	.06690
51	.08924	.08699	.08483	.08276	.08076	.07884	.07699	.07520	.07349	.07183
52	.09539	.09303	.09076	.08858	.08648	.08446	.08251	.08064	.07883	.07708
53	.10189	.09942	.09704	.09475	.09255	.09043	.08838	.08640	.08450	.08266
54	.10872	.10614	.10365	.10126	.09894	.09672	.09456	.09249	.09049	.08855

TABLE U(1)
BASED ON LIFE TABLE 80CNSMT
UNITRUST SINGLE LIFE REMAINDER FACTORS
APPLICABLE AFTER APRIL 30, 1989

ADJUSTED PAYOUT RATE

AGE	12.2%	12.4%	12.6%	12.8%	13.0%	13.2%	13.4%	13.6%	13.8%	14.0%
55	.11592	.11322	.11062	.10811	.10569	.10335	.10110	.09892	.09682	.09478
56	.12350	.12068	.11796	.11534	.11281	.11036	.10800	.10571	.10350	.10137
57	.13148	.12855	.12572	.12298	.12033	.11777	.11530	.11291	.11060	.10836
58	.13990	.13685	.13389	.13104	.12828	.12561	.12303	.12053	.11811	.11576
59	.14875	.14557	.14250	.13953	.13665	.13387	.13118	.12856	.12604	.12359
60	.15799	.15469	.15150	.14841	.14542	.14253	.13972	.13700	.13436	.13180
61	.16761	.16419	.16088	.15768	.15457	.15156	.14864	.14580	.14305	.14039
62	.17758	.17404	.17062	.16729	.16407	.16094	.15791	.15496	.15210	.14932
63	.18791	.18425	.18071	.17726	.17392	.17068	.16753	.16447	.16150	.15861
64	.19862	.19484	.19118	.18762	.18417	.18081	.17754	.17437	.17129	.16829
65	.20979	.20590	.20212	.19845	.19487	.19140	.18802	.18474	.18154	.17843
66	.22149	.21748	.21359	.20980	.20612	.20253	.19904	.19564	.19233	.18911
67	.23374	.22962	.22562	.22172	.21792	.21423	.21062	.20712	.20370	.20037
68	.24656	.24234	.23822	.23422	.23031	.22651	.22280	.21919	.21566	.21222
69	.25988	.25556	.25134	.24724	.24323	.23932	.23551	.23179	.22816	.22461
70	.27367	.26925	.26493	.26073	.25662	.25261	.24870	.24488	.24115	.23750
71	.28784	.28333	.27892	.27462	.27042	.26631	.26230	.25839	.25456	.25082
72	.30241	.29781	.29332	.28893	.28464	.28044	.27634	.27233	.26841	.26457
73	.31740	.31272	.30815	.30368	.29930	.29502	.29084	.28674	.28273	.27880
74	.33291	.32817	.32352	.31897	.31452	.31016	.30589	.30171	.29762	.29361
75	.34903	.34422	.33951	.33490	.33038	.32595	.32161	.31735	.31318	.30909
76	.36581	.36095	.35619	.35152	.34694	.34245	.33805	.33373	.32949	.32533
77	.38324	.37835	.37354	.36883	.36420	.35966	.35520	.35083	.34654	.34232
78	.40126	.39634	.39150	.38676	.38210	.37752	.37302	.36861	.36427	.36001
79	.41970	.41476	.40992	.40515	.40047	.39587	.39135	.38690	.38253	.37823
80	.43842	.43348	.42864	.42387	.41918	.41456	.41002	.40556	.40117	.39685
81	.45719	.45228	.44744	.44267	.43799	.43337	.42883	.42436	.41996	.41562
82	.47590	.47101	.46619	.46145	.45677	.45217	.44764	.44317	.43877	.43443
83	.49443	.48957	.48478	.48007	.47542	.47084	.46632	.46187	.45748	.45315
84	.51279	.50798	.50324	.49856	.49394	.48939	.48490	.48048	.47611	.47180
85	.53106	.52630	.52161	.51698	.51241	.50790	.50345	.49906	.49473	.49045
86	.54902	.54434	.53971	.53514	.53062	.52616	.52176	.51741	.51312	.50888
87	.56640	.56178	.55722	.55271	.54826	.54386	.53951	.53521	.53097	.52677
88	.58326	.57872	.57423	.56979	.56541	.56107	.55678	.55254	.54834	.54420
89	.59994	.59548	.59107	.58671	.58240	.57813	.57391	.56973	.56560	.56152
90	.61662	.61226	.60794	.60367	.59944	.59526	.59112	.58702	.58296	.57894
91	.63305	.62879	.62457	.62040	.61627	.61217	.60812	.60411	.60013	.59619
92	.64876	.64461	.64050	.63643	.63239	.62839	.62443	.62051	.61662	.61277
93	.66355	.65950	.65550	.65153	.64759	.64369	.63983	.63600	.63220	.62843
94	.67722	.67328	.66938	.66551	.66167	.65786	.65409	.65035	.64664	.64296
95	.68967	.68583	.68203	.67825	.67451	.67079	.66711	.66345	.65983	.65623
96	.70076	.69701	.69330	.68961	.68595	.68231	.67871	.67513	.67158	.66806
97	.71089	.70722	.70359	.69998	.69640	.69284	.68931	.68581	.68234	.67888
98	.72001	.71642	.71286	.70933	.70582	.70233	.69887	.69544	.69203	.68864
99	.72844	.72492	.72143	.71796	.71452	.71110	.70770	.70433	.70098	.69765
100	.73623	.73278	.72935	.72594	.72256	.71920	.71586	.71254	.70924	.70597
101	.74361	.74021	.73684	.73349	.73016	.72685	.72356	.72029	.71704	.71382
102	.75128	.74794	.74463	.74133	.73806	.73480	.73157	.72835	.72515	.72198
103	.75938	.75610	.75284	.74961	.74639	.74319	.74000	.73684	.73369	.73056
104	.76835	.76514	.76194	.75877	.75561	.75246	.74934	.74623	.74313	.74005
105	.77956	.77643	.77332	.77023	.76714	.76408	.76102	.75798	.75496	.75195
106	.79632	.79334	.79038	.78743	.78449	.78157	.77865	.77575	.77285	.76997
107	.82154	.81884	.81615	.81346	.81079	.80811	.80545	.80279	.80014	.79750
108	.86487	.86274	.86061	.85848	.85635	.85423	.85210	.84998	.84787	.84575
109	.93900	.93800	.93700	.93600	.93500	.93400	.93300	.93200	.93100	.93000

TABLE D
SHOWING THE PRESENT WORTH OF A REMAINDER INTEREST
POSTPONED FOR A TERM CERTAIN IN A CHARITABLE
REMAINDER UNITRUST
APPLICABLE AFTER APRIL 30, 1989

ADJUSTED PAYOUT RATE

YEARS	4.2%	4.4%	4.6%	4.8%	5.0%	5.2%	5.4%	5.6%	5.8%	6.0%
1	.958000	.956000	.954000	.952000	.950000	.948000	.946000	.944000	.942000	.940000
2	.917764	.913936	.910116	.906304	.902500	.898704	.894916	.891136	.887364	.883600
3	.879218	.873723	.868251	.862801	.857375	.851971	.846591	.841232	.835897	.830584
4	.842291	.835279	.828311	.821387	.814506	.807669	.800875	.794123	.787415	.780749
5	.806915	.798527	.790209	.781960	.773781	.765670	.757627	.749652	.741745	.733904
6	.773024	.763392	.753859	.744426	.735092	.725855	.716716	.707672	.698724	.689870
7	.740557	.729802	.719182	.708694	.698337	.688111	.678013	.668042	.658198	.648478
8	.709454	.697691	.686099	.674677	.663420	.652329	.641400	.630632	.620022	.609569
9	.679657	.666993	.654539	.642292	.630249	.618408	.606765	.595317	.584061	.572995
10	.651111	.637645	.624430	.611462	.598737	.586251	.573999	.561979	.550185	.538615
11	.623764	.609589	.595706	.582112	.568800	.555766	.543003	.530508	.518275	.506298
12	.597566	.582767	.568304	.554170	.540360	.526866	.513681	.500800	.488215	.475920
13	.572469	.557125	.542162	.527570	.513342	.499469	.485942	.472755	.459898	.447365
14	.548425	.532611	.517222	.502247	.487675	.473496	.459701	.446281	.433224	.420523
15	.525391	.509177	.493430	.478139	.463291	.448875	.434878	.421289	.408097	.395292
16	.503325	.486773	.470732	.455188	.440127	.425533	.411394	.397697	.384427	.371574
17	.482185	.465355	.449079	.433339	.418120	.403405	.389179	.375426	.362131	.349280
18	.461933	.444879	.428421	.412539	.397214	.382428	.368163	.354402	.341127	.328323
19	.442532	.425304	.408714	.392737	.377354	.362542	.348282	.334555	.321342	.308624
20	.423946	.406591	.389913	.373886	.358486	.343690	.329475	.315820	.302704	.290106

TABLE D
SHOWING THE PRESENT WORTH OF A REMAINDER INTEREST
POSTPONED FOR A TERM CERTAIN IN A CHARITABLE
REMAINDER UNITRUST
APPLICABLE AFTER APRIL 30, 1989

ADJUSTED PAYOUT RATE

YEARS	6.2%	6.4%	6.6%	6.8%	7.0%	7.2%	7.4%	7.6%	7.8%	8.0%
1	.938000	.936000	.934000	.932000	.930000	.928000	.926000	.924000	.922000	.920000
2	.879844	.876096	.872356	.868624	.864900	.861184	.857476	.853776	.850084	.846400
3	.825294	.820026	.814781	.809558	.804357	.799179	.794023	.788889	.783777	.778688
4	.774125	.767544	.761005	.754508	.748052	.741638	.735265	.728933	.722643	.716393
5	.726130	.718421	.710779	.703201	.695688	.688240	.680855	.673535	.666277	.659082
6	.681110	.672442	.663867	.655383	.646990	.638687	.630472	.622346	.614307	.606355
7	.638881	.629406	.620052	.610817	.601701	.592701	.583817	.575048	.566391	.557847
8	.599270	.589124	.579129	.569282	.559582	.550027	.540615	.531344	.522213	.513219
9	.562115	.551420	.540906	.530571	.520411	.510425	.500609	.490962	.481480	.472161
10	.527264	.516129	.505206	.494492	.483982	.473674	.463564	.453649	.443925	.434388
11	.494574	.483097	.471863	.460866	.450104	.439570	.429260	.419171	.409298	.399637
12	.463910	.452179	.440720	.429527	.418596	.407921	.397495	.387314	.377373	.367666
13	.435148	.423239	.411632	.400320	.389295	.378550	.368081	.357879	.347938	.338253
14	.408169	.396152	.384465	.373098	.362044	.351295	.340843	.330680	.320799	.311193
15	.382862	.370798	.359090	.347727	.336701	.326002	.315620	.305548	.295777	.286297
16	.359125	.347067	.335390	.324082	.313132	.302529	.292264	.282326	.272706	.263394
17	.336859	.324855	.313254	.302044	.291213	.280747	.270637	.260870	.251435	.242322
18	.315974	.304064	.292579	.281505	.270828	.260533	.250610	.241044	.231823	.222936
19	.296383	.284604	.273269	.262363	.251870	.241775	.232065	.222724	.213741	.205101
20	.278008	.266389	.255233	.244522	.234239	.224367	.214892	.205797	.197069	.188693

TABLE D
SHOWING THE PRESENT WORTH OF A REMAINDER INTEREST
POSTPONED FOR A TERM CERTAIN IN A CHARITABLE
REMAINDER UNITRUST
APPLICABLE AFTER APRIL 30, 1989

ADJUSTED PAYOUT RATE

YEARS	*8.2%*	*8.4%*	*8.6%*	*8.8%*	*9.0%*	*9.2%*	*9.4%*	*9.6%*	*9.8%*	*10.0%*
1	.918000	.916000	.914000	.912000	.910000	.908000	.906000	.904000	.902000	.900000
2	.842724	.839056	.835396	.831744	.828100	.824464	.820836	.817216	.813604	.810000
3	.773621	.768575	.763552	.758551	.753571	.748613	.743677	.738763	.733871	.729000
4	.710184	.704015	.697886	.691798	.685750	.679741	.673772	.667842	.661951	.656100
5	.651949	.644878	.637868	.630920	.624032	.617205	.610437	.603729	.597080	.590490
6	.598489	.590708	.583012	.575399	.567869	.560422	.553056	.545771	.538566	.531441
7	.549413	.541089	.532873	.524764	.516761	.508863	.501069	.493377	.485787	.478297
8	.504361	.495637	.487046	.478585	.470253	.462048	.453968	.446013	.438180	.430467
9	.463003	.454004	.445160	.436469	.427930	.419539	.411295	.403196	.395238	.387420
10	.425037	.415867	.406876	.398060	.389416	.380942	.372634	.364489	.356505	.348678
11	.390184	.380934	.371885	.363031	.354369	.345895	.337606	.329498	.321567	.313811
12	.358189	.348936	.339902	.331084	.322475	.314073	.305871	.297866	.290054	.282430
13	.328817	.319625	.310671	.301949	.293453	.285178	.277119	.269271	.261628	.254187
14	.301854	.292777	.283953	.275377	.267042	.258942	.251070	.243421	.235989	.228768
15	.277102	.268184	.259533	.251144	.243008	.235119	.227469	.220053	.212862	.205891
16	.254380	.245656	.237213	.229043	.221137	.213488	.206087	.198928	.192001	.185302
17	.233521	.225021	.216813	.208887	.201235	.193847	.186715	.179830	.173185	.166772
18	.214372	.206119	.198167	.190505	.183124	.176013	.169164	.162567	.156213	.150095
19	.196794	.188805	.181125	.173741	.166643	.159820	.153262	.146960	.140904	.135085
20	.180657	.172946	.165548	.158452	.151645	.145117	.138856	.132852	.127096	.121577

TABLE D
SHOWING THE PRESENT WORTH OF A REMAINDER INTEREST
POSTPONED FOR A TERM CERTAIN IN A CHARITABLE
REMAINDER UNITRUST
APPLICABLE AFTER APRIL 30, 1989

ADJUSTED PAYOUT RATE

YEARS	*10.2%*	*10.4%*	*10.6%*	*10.8%*	*11.0%*	*11.2%*	*11.4%*	*11.6%*	*11.8%*	*12.0%*
1	.898000	.896000	.894000	.892000	.890000	.888000	.886000	.884000	.882000	.880000
2	.806404	.802816	.799236	.795664	.792100	.788544	.784996	.781456	.777924	.774400
3	.724151	.719323	.714517	.709732	.704969	.700227	.695506	.690807	.686129	.681472
4	.650287	.644514	.638778	.633081	.627422	.621802	.616219	.610673	.605166	.599695
5	.583958	.577484	.571068	.564708	.558406	.552160	.545970	.539835	.533756	.527732
6	.524394	.517426	.510535	.503720	.496981	.490318	.483729	.477214	.470773	.464404
7	.470906	.463613	.456418	.449318	.442313	.435402	.428584	.421858	.415222	.408676
8	.422874	.415398	.408038	.400792	.393659	.386637	.379726	.372922	.366226	.359635
9	.379741	.372196	.364786	.357506	.350356	.343334	.336437	.329663	.323011	.316478
10	.341007	.333488	.326118	.318896	.311817	.304881	.298083	.291422	.284896	.278501
11	.306224	.298805	.291550	.284455	.277517	.270734	.264102	.257617	.251278	.245081
12	.274989	.267729	.260645	.253734	.246990	.240412	.233994	.227734	.221627	.215671
13	.246941	.239886	.233017	.226331	.219821	.213486	.207319	.201317	.195475	.189791
14	.221753	.214937	.208317	.201887	.195641	.189575	.183684	.177964	.172409	.167016
15	.199134	.192584	.186236	.180083	.174121	.168343	.162744	.157320	.152065	.146974
16	.178822	.172555	.166495	.160634	.154967	.149488	.144191	.139071	.134121	.129337
17	.160582	.154609	.148846	.143286	.137921	.132746	.127754	.122939	.118295	.113817
18	.144203	.138530	.133069	.127811	.122750	.117878	.113190	.108678	.104336	.100159
19	.129494	.124123	.118963	.114007	.109247	.104676	.100286	.096071	.092024	.088140
20	.116286	.111214	.106353	.101694	.097230	.092952	.088853	.084927	.081166	.077563

TABLE D
SHOWING THE PRESENT WORTH OF A REMAINDER INTEREST
POSTPONED FOR A TERM CERTAIN IN A CHARITABLE
REMAINDER UNITRUST
APPLICABLE AFTER APRIL 30, 1989

ADJUSTED PAYOUT RATE

YEARS	*12.2%*	*12.4%*	*12.6%*	*12.8%*	*13.0%*	*13.2%*	*13.4%*	*13.6%*	*13.8%*	*14.0%*
1	.878000	.876000	.874000	.872000	.870000	.868000	.866000	.864000	.862000	.860000
2	.770884	.767376	.763876	.760384	.756900	.753424	.749956	.746496	.743044	.739600
3	.676836	.672221	.667628	.663055	.658503	.653972	.649462	.644973	.640504	.636056
4	.594262	.588866	.583507	.578184	.572898	.567648	.562434	.557256	.552114	.547008
5	.521762	.515847	.509985	.504176	.498421	.492718	.487068	.481469	.475923	.470427
6	.458107	.451882	.445727	.439642	.433626	.427679	.421801	.415990	.410245	.404567
7	.402218	.395848	.389565	.383368	.377255	.371226	.365279	.359415	.353631	.347928
8	.353147	.346763	.340480	.334297	.328212	.322224	.316332	.310535	.304830	.299218
9	.310063	.303764	.297579	.291507	.285544	.279690	.273944	.268302	.262764	.257327
10	.272236	.266098	.260084	.254194	.248423	.242771	.237235	.231813	.226502	.221302
11	.239023	.233102	.227314	.221657	.216128	.210725	.205446	.200286	.195245	.190319
12	.209862	.204197	.198672	.193285	.188032	.182910	.177916	.173047	.168301	.163675
13	.184259	.178877	.173640	.168544	.163588	.158766	.154075	.149513	.145076	.140760
14	.161779	.156696	.151761	.146971	.142321	.137809	.133429	.129179	.125055	.121054
15	.142042	.137266	.132639	.128158	.123819	.119618	.115550	.111611	.107798	.104106
16	.124713	.120245	.115927	.111754	.107723	.103828	.100066	.096432	.092922	.089531
17	.109498	.105334	.101320	.097450	.093719	.090123	.086657	.083317	.080098	.076997
18	.096139	.092273	.088554	.084976	.081535	.078227	.075045	.071986	.069045	.066217
19	.084410	.080831	.077396	.074099	.070936	.067901	.064989	.062196	.059517	.056947
20	.074112	.070808	.067644	.064614	.061714	.058938	.056280	.053737	.051303	.048974

TABLE F(4.2)
WITH INTEREST AT 4.2 PERCENT,
SHOWING FACTORS FOR COMPUTATION
OF THE ADJUSTED PAYOUT RATE FOR CERTAIN
VALUATIONS APPLICABLE AFTER APRIL 30, 1989

1		2			
NUMBER OF MONTHS BY WHICH THE VALUATION DATE FOR THE FIRST FULL TAXABLE YEAR OF THE TRUST PRECEDES THE FIRST PAYOUT		FACTORS FOR PAYOUT AT THE END OF EACH PERIOD			
AT LEAST	*BUT LESS THAN*	*ANNUAL PERIOD*	*SEMIANNUAL PERIOD*	*QUARTERLY PERIOD*	*MONTHLY PERIOD*
....	1	1.000000	.989820	.984755	.981389
1	2	.996577	.986432	.981385	.978030
2	3	.993166	.983056	.978026	
3	4	.989767	.979691	.974679	
4	5	.986380	.976338		
5	6	.983004	.972996		
6	7	.979639	.969666		
7	8	.976286			
8	9	.972945			
9	10	.969615			
10	11	.966296			
11	12	.962989			
12	....	.959693			

TABLE F(4.4)
WITH INTEREST AT 4.4 PERCENT, SHOWING FACTORS
FOR COMPUTATION OF THE ADJUSTED PAYOUT RATE FOR CERTAIN
VALUATIONS APPLICABLE AFTER APRIL 30, 1989

1		2			
NUMBER OF MONTHS BY WHICH THE VALUATION DATE FOR THE FIRST FULL TAXABLE YEAR OF THE TRUST PRECEDES THE FIRST PAYOUT		FACTORS FOR PAYOUT AT THE END OF EACH PERIOD			
AT LEAST	*BUT LESS THAN*	*ANNUAL PERIOD*	*SEMIANNUAL PERIOD*	*QUARTERLY PERIOD*	*MONTHLY PERIOD*
....	1	1.000000	.989350	.984054	.980533
1	2	.996418	.985806	.980529	.977021
2	3	.992849	.982275	.977017	
3	4	.989293	.978757	.973517	
4	5	.985749	.975251		
5	6	.982219	.971758		
6	7	.978700	.968277		
7	8	.975195			
8	9	.971702			
9	10	.968221			
10	11	.964753			
11	12	.961298			
12	....	.957854			

TABLE F(4.6)
WITH INTEREST AT 4.6 PERCENT, SHOWING FACTORS FOR COMPUTATION OF THE ADJUSTED PAYOUT RATE FOR CERTAIN VALUATIONS APPLICABLE AFTER APRIL 30, 1989

1		2			
NUMBER OF MONTHS BY WHICH THE VALUATION DATE FOR THE FIRST FULL TAXABLE YEAR OF THE TRUST PRECEDES THE FIRST PAYOUT		FACTORS FOR PAYOUT AT THE END OF EACH PERIOD			
AT LEAST	*BUT LESS THAN*	*ANNUAL PERIOD*	*SEMIANNUAL PERIOD*	*QUARTERLY PERIOD*	*MONTHLY PERIOD*
....	1	1.000000	.988882	.983354	.979680
1	2	.996259	.985183	.979676	.976015
2	3	.992532	.981498	.976011	
3	4	.988820	.977826	.972360	
4	5	.985121	.974168		
5	6	.981436	.970524		
6	7	.977764	.966894		
7	8	.974107			
8	9	.970463			
9	10	.966832			
10	11	.963216			
11	12	.959613			
12	....	.956023			

TABLE F(4.8)
WITH INTEREST AT 4.8 PERCENT, SHOWING FACTORS FOR COMPUTATION OF THE ADJUSTED PAYOUT RATE FOR CERTAIN VALUATIONS APPLICABLE AFTER APRIL 30, 1989

1		2			
NUMBER OF MONTHS BY WHICH THE VALUATION DATE FOR THE FIRST FULL TAXABLE YEAR OF THE TRUST PRECEDES THE FIRST PAYOUT		FACTORS FOR PAYOUT AT THE END OF EACH PERIOD			
AT LEAST	*BUT LESS THAN*	*ANNUAL PERIOD*	*SEMIANNUAL PERIOD*	*QUARTERLY PERIOD*	*MONTHLY PERIOD*
....	1	1.000000	.988415	.982657	.978830
1	2	.996101	.984561	.978825	.975013
2	3	.992217	.980722	.975008	
3	4	.988348	.976898	.971206	
4	5	.984494	.973089		
5	6	.980655	.969294		
6	7	.976831	.965515		
7	8	.973022			
8	9	.969228			
9	10	.965448			
10	11	.961684			
11	12	.957934			
12	....	.954198			

TABLE F(5.0)
WITH INTEREST AT 5.0 PERCENT, SHOWING FACTORS FOR COMPUTATION OF THE ADJUSTED PAYOUT RATE FOR CERTAIN VALUATIONS APPLICABLE AFTER APRIL 30, 1989

1		2			
NUMBER OF MONTHS BY WHICH THE VALUATION DATE FOR THE FIRST FULL TAXABLE YEAR OF THE TRUST PRECEDES THE FIRST PAYOUT		FACTORS FOR PAYOUT AT THE END OF EACH PERIOD			
AT LEAST	*BUT LESS THAN*	*ANNUAL PERIOD*	*SEMIANNUAL PERIOD*	*QUARTERLY PERIOD*	*MONTHLY PERIOD*
....	1	1.000000	.987950	.981961	.977982
1	2	.995942	.983941	.977977	.974014
2	3	.991901	.979949	.974009	
3	4	.987877	.975973	.970057	
4	5	.983868	.972013		
5	6	.979876	.968069		
6	7	.975900	.964141		
7	8	.971940			
8	9	.967997			
9	10	.964069			
10	11	.960157			
11	12	.956261			
12	....	.952381			

TABLE F(5.2)
WITH INTEREST AT 5.2 PERCENT, SHOWING FACTORS FOR COMPUTATION OF THE ADJUSTED PAYOUT RATE FOR CERTAIN VALUATIONS APPLICABLE AFTER APRIL 30, 1989

1		2			
NUMBER OF MONTHS BY WHICH THE VALUATION DATE FOR THE FIRST FULL TAXABLE YEAR OF THE TRUST PRECEDES THE FIRST PAYOUT		FACTORS FOR PAYOUT AT THE END OF EACH PERIOD			
AT LEAST	*BUT LESS THAN*	*ANNUAL PERIOD*	*SEMIANNUAL PERIOD*	*QUARTERLY PERIOD*	*MONTHLY PERIOD*
....	1	1.000000	.987486	.981268	.977137
1	2	.995784	.983323	.977132	.973018
2	3	.991587	.979178	.973012	
3	4	.987407	.975050	.968911	
4	5	.983244	.970940		
5	6	.979099	.966847		
6	7	.974972	.962771		
7	8	.970862			
8	9	.966769			
9	10	.962694			
10	11	.958636			
11	12	.954594			
12	....	.950570			

TABLE F(5.4)
WITH INTEREST AT 5.4 PERCENT, SHOWING FACTORS FOR COMPUTATION OF THE ADJUSTED PAYOUT RATE FOR CERTAIN VALUATIONS APPLICABLE AFTER APRIL 30, 1989

1		2			
NUMBER OF MONTHS BY WHICH THE VALUATION DATE FOR THE FIRST FULL TAXABLE YEAR OF THE TRUST PRECEDES THE FIRST PAYOUT		FACTORS FOR PAYOUT AT THE END OF EACH PERIOD			
AT LEAST	*BUT LESS THAN*	*ANNUAL PERIOD*	*SEMIANNUAL PERIOD*	*QUARTERLY PERIOD*	*MONTHLY PERIOD*
..	1	1.000000	.987023	.980577	.976295
1	2	.995627	.982707	.976289	.972026
2	3	.991273	.978409	.972019	
3	4	.986938	.974131	.967769	
4	5	.982622	.969871		
5	6	.978325	.965629		
6	7	.974047	.961407		
7	8	.969787			
8	9	.965546			
9	10	.961323			
10	11	.957119			
11	12	.952934			
12	..	.948767			

TABLE F(5.6)
WITH INTEREST AT 5.6 PERCENT, SHOWING FACTORS FOR COMPUTATION OF THE ADJUSTED PAYOUT RATE FOR CERTAIN VALUATIONS APPLICABLE AFTER APRIL 30, 1989

1		2			
NUMBER OF MONTHS BY WHICH THE VALUATION DATE FOR THE FIRST FULL TAXABLE YEAR OF THE TRUST PRECEDES THE FIRST PAYOUT		FACTORS FOR PAYOUT AT THE END OF EACH PERIOD			
AT LEAST	*BUT LESS THAN*	*ANNUAL PERIOD*	*SEMIANNUAL PERIOD*	*QUARTERLY PERIOD*	*MONTHLY PERIOD*
..	1	1.000000	.986562	.979888	.975455
1	2	.995470	.982092	.975449	.971036
2	3	.990960	.977643	.971029	
3	4	.986470	.973214	.966630	
4	5	.982001	.968805		
5	6	.977552	.964416		
6	7	.973124	.960047		
7	8	.968715			
8	9	.964326			
9	10	.959958			
10	11	.955609			
11	12	.951279			
12	..	.946970			

TABLE F(5.8)
WITH INTEREST AT 5.8 PERCENT, SHOWING FACTORS FOR COMPUTATION OF THE ADJUSTED PAYOUT RATE FOR CERTAIN VALUATIONS APPLICABLE AFTER APRIL 30, 1989

1		2			
NUMBER OF MONTHS BY WHICH THE VALUATION DATE FOR THE FIRST FULL TAXABLE YEAR OF THE TRUST PRECEDES THE FIRST PAYOUT		FACTORS FOR PAYOUT AT THE END OF EACH PERIOD			
AT LEAST	*BUT LESS THAN*	*ANNUAL PERIOD*	*SEMIANNUAL PERIOD*	*QUARTERLY PERIOD*	*MONTHLY PERIOD*
..	1	1.000000	.986102	.979201	.974618
1	2	.995313	.981480	.974611	.970050
2	3	.990647	.976879	.970043	
3	4	.986004	.972300	.965496	
4	5	.981382	.967743		
5	6	.976782	.963206		
6	7	.972203	.958692		
7	8	.967646			
8	9	.963111			
9	10	.958596			
10	11	.954103			
11	12	.949631			
12	..	.945180			

TABLE F(6.0)
WITH INTEREST AT 6.0 PERCENT, SHOWING FACTORS FOR COMPUTATION OF THE ADJUSTED PAYOUT RATE FOR CERTAIN VALUATIONS APPLICABLE AFTER APRIL 30, 1989

1		2			
NUMBER OF MONTHS BY WHICH THE VALUATION DATE FOR THE FIRST FULL TAXABLE YEAR OF THE TRUST PRECEDES THE FIRST PAYOUT		FACTORS FOR PAYOUT AT THE END OF EACH PERIOD			
AT LEAST	*BUT LESS THAN*	*ANNUAL PERIOD*	*SEMIANNUAL PERIOD*	*QUARTERLY PERIOD*	*MONTHLY PERIOD*
..	1	1.000000	.985643	.978516	.973784
1	2	.995156	.980869	.973776	.969067
2	3	.990336	.976117	.969059	
3	4	.985538	.971389	.964365	
4	5	.980764	.966684		
5	6	.976014	.962001		
6	7	.971286	.957341		
7	8	.966581			
8	9	.961899			
9	10	.957239			
10	11	.952603			
11	12	.947988			
12	..	.943396			

TABLE F(6.2)
WITH INTEREST AT 6.2 PERCENT, SHOWING FACTORS FOR COMPUTATION OF THE ADJUSTED PAYOUT RATE FOR CERTAIN VALUATIONS APPLICABLE AFTER APRIL 30, 1989

1		2			
NUMBER OF MONTHS BY WHICH THE VALUATION DATE FOR THE FIRST FULL TAXABLE YEAR OF THE TRUST PRECEDES THE FIRST PAYOUT		FACTORS FOR PAYOUT AT THE END OF EACH PERIOD			
AT LEAST	*BUT LESS THAN*	*ANNUAL PERIOD*	*SEMIANNUAL PERIOD*	*QUARTERLY PERIOD*	*MONTHLY PERIOD*
..	1	1.000000	.985185	.977833	.972952
1	2	.995000	.980259	.972944	.968087
2	3	.990024	.975358	.968079	
3	4	.985074	.970481	.963238	
4	5	.980148	.965628		
5	6	.975247	.960799		
6	7	.970371	.955995		
7	8	.965519			
8	9	.960691			
9	10	.955887			
10	11	.951107			
11	12	.946352			
12	..	.941620			

TABLE F(6.4)
WITH INTEREST AT 6.4 PERCENT, SHOWING FACTORS FOR COMPUTATION OF THE ADJUSTED PAYOUT RATE FOR CERTAIN VALUATIONS APPLICABLE AFTER APRIL 30, 1989

1		2			
NUMBER OF MONTHS BY WHICH THE VALUATION DATE FOR THE FIRST FULL TAXABLE YEAR OF THE TRUST PRECEDES THE FIRST PAYOUT		FACTORS FOR PAYOUT AT THE END OF EACH PERIOD			
AT LEAST	*BUT LESS THAN*	*ANNUAL PERIOD*	*SEMIANNUAL PERIOD*	*QUARTERLY PERIOD*	*MONTHLY PERIOD*
..	1	1.000000	.984729	.977152	.972122
1	2	.994844	.979652	.972114	.967110
2	3	.989714	.974600	.967101	
3	4	.984611	.969575	.962115	
4	5	.979534	.964576		
5	6	.974483	.959602		
6	7	.969458	.954654		
7	8	.964460			
8	9	.959487			
9	10	.954539			
10	11	.949617			
11	12	.944721			
12	..	.939850			

TABLE F(6.6)
WITH INTEREST AT 6.6 PERCENT, SHOWING FACTORS FOR COMPUTATION OF THE ADJUSTED PAYOUT RATE FOR CERTAIN VALUATIONS APPLICABLE AFTER APRIL 30, 1989

1		2			
NUMBER OF MONTHS BY WHICH THE VALUATION DATE FOR THE FIRST FULL TAXABLE YEAR OF THE TRUST PRECEDES THE FIRST PAYOUT		FACTORS FOR PAYOUT AT THE END OF EACH PERIOD			
AT LEAST	*BUT LESS THAN*	*ANNUAL PERIOD*	*SEMIANNUAL PERIOD*	*QUARTERLY PERIOD*	*MONTHLY PERIOD*
..	1	1.000000	.984274	.976473	.971295
1	2	.994688	.979046	.971286	.966136
2	3	.989404	.973845	.966127	
3	4	.984149	.968672	.960995	
4	5	.978921	.963527		
5	6	.973721	.958408		
6	7	.968549	.953317		
7	8	.963404			
8	9	.958286			
9	10	.953196			
10	11	.948132			
11	12	.943096			
12	..	.938086			

TABLE F(6.8)
WITH INTEREST AT 6.8 PERCENT, SHOWING FACTORS FOR COMPUTATION OF THE ADJUSTED PAYOUT RATE FOR CERTAIN VALUATIONS APPLICABLE AFTER APRIL 30, 1989

1		2			
NUMBER OF MONTHS BY WHICH THE VALUATION DATE FOR THE FIRST FULL TAXABLE YEAR OF THE TRUST PRECEDES THE FIRST PAYOUT		FACTORS FOR PAYOUT AT THE END OF EACH PERIOD			
AT LEAST	*BUT LESS THAN*	*ANNUAL PERIOD*	*SEMIANNUAL PERIOD*	*QUARTERLY PERIOD*	*MONTHLY PERIOD*
..	1	1.000000	.983821	.975796	.970471
1	2	.994533	.978442	.970461	.965165
2	3	.989095	.973092	.965156	
3	4	.983688	.967772	.959879	
4	5	.978309	.962481		
5	6	.972961	.957219		
6	7	.967641	.951985		
7	8	.962351			
8	9	.957089			
9	10	.951857			
10	11	.946653			
11	12	.941477			
12	..	.936330			

TABLE F(7.0)
WITH INTEREST AT 7.0 PERCENT, SHOWING FACTORS FOR COMPUTATION OF THE ADJUSTED PAYOUT RATE FOR CERTAIN VALUATIONS APPLICABLE AFTER APRIL 30, 1989

1		2			
NUMBER OF MONTHS BY WHICH THE VALUATION DATE FOR THE FIRST FULL TAXABLE YEAR OF THE TRUST PRECEDES THE FIRST PAYOUT		FACTORS FOR PAYOUT AT THE END OF EACH PERIOD			
AT LEAST	*BUT LESS THAN*	*ANNUAL PERIOD*	*SEMIANNUAL PERIOD*	*QUARTERLY PERIOD*	*MONTHLY PERIOD*
....	1	1.000000	.983368	.975122	.969649
1	2	.994378	.977839	.969639	.964198
2	3	.988787	.972342	.964187	
3	4	.983228	.966875	.958766	
4	5	.977700	.961439		
5	6	.972203	.956033		
6	7	.966736	.950658		
7	8	.961301			
8	9	.955896			
9	10	.950522			
10	11	.945178			
11	12	.939864			
12	....	.934579			

TABLE F(7.2)
WITH INTEREST AT 7.2 PERCENT, SHOWING FACTORS FOR COMPUTATION OF THE ADJUSTED PAYOUT RATE FOR CERTAIN VALUATIONS APPLICABLE AFTER APRIL 30, 1989

1		2			
NUMBER OF MONTHS BY WHICH THE VALUATION DATE FOR THE FIRST FULL TAXABLE YEAR OF THE TRUST PRECEDES THE FIRST PAYOUT		FACTORS FOR PAYOUT AT THE END OF EACH PERIOD			
AT LEAST	*BUT LESS THAN*	*ANNUAL PERIOD*	*SEMIANNUAL PERIOD*	*QUARTERLY PERIOD*	*MONTHLY PERIOD*
....	1	1.000000	.982917	.974449	.968830
1	2	.994223	.977239	.968819	.963233
2	3	.988479	.971593	.963222	
3	4	.982769	.965980	.957658	
4	5	.977091	.960400		
5	6	.971446	.954851		
6	7	.965834	.949335		
7	8	.960255			
8	9	.954707			
9	10	.949192			
10	11	.943708			
11	12	.938256			
12	....	.932836			

TABLE F(7.4)
WITH INTEREST AT 7.4 PERCENT, SHOWING FACTORS FOR COMPUTATION OF THE ADJUSTED PAYOUT RATE FOR CERTAIN VALUATIONS APPLICABLE AFTER APRIL 30, 1989

1		2			
NUMBER OF MONTHS BY WHICH THE VALUATION DATE FOR THE FIRST FULL TAXABLE YEAR OF THE TRUST PRECEDES THE FIRST PAYOUT		FACTORS FOR PAYOUT AT THE END OF EACH PERIOD			
AT LEAST	*BUT LESS THAN*	*ANNUAL PERIOD*	*SEMIANNUAL PERIOD*	*QUARTERLY PERIOD*	*MONTHLY PERIOD*
....	1	1.000000	.982467	.973778	.968013
1	2	.994068	.976640	.968002	.962271
2	3	.988172	.970847	.962260	
3	4	.982311	.965088	.956552	
4	5	.976484	.959364		
5	6	.970692	.953673		
6	7	.964935	.948017		
7	8	.959211			
8	9	.953521			
9	10	.947866			
10	11	.942243			
11	12	.936654			
12	....	.931099			

TABLE F(7.6)
WITH INTEREST AT 7.6 PERCENT, SHOWING FACTORS FOR COMPUTATION OF THE ADJUSTED PAYOUT RATE FOR CERTAIN VALUATIONS APPLICABLE AFTER APRIL 30, 1989

1		2			
NUMBER OF MONTHS BY WHICH THE VALUATION DATE FOR THE FIRST FULL TAXABLE YEAR OF THE TRUST PRECEDES THE FIRST PAYOUT		FACTORS FOR PAYOUT AT THE END OF EACH PERIOD			
AT LEAST	*BUT LESS THAN*	*ANNUAL PERIOD*	*SEMIANNUAL PERIOD*	*QUARTERLY PERIOD*	*MONTHLY PERIOD*
....	1	1.000000	.982019	.973109	.967199
1	2	.993914	.976042	.967187	.961313
2	3	.987866	.970103	.961301	
3	4	.981854	.964199	.955451	
4	5	.975879	.958331		
5	6	.969940	.952499		
6	7	.964037	.946703		
7	8	.958171			
8	9	.952340			
9	10	.946544			
10	11	.940784			
11	12	.935058			
12	....	.929368			

TABLE F(7.8)
WITH INTEREST AT 7.8 PERCENT, SHOWING FACTORS
FOR COMPUTATION OF THE ADJUSTED PAYOUT RATE FOR
CERTAIN VALUATIONS APPLICABLE AFTER APRIL 30, 1989

1		2			
NUMBER OF MONTHS BY WHICH THE VALUATION DATE FOR THE FIRST FULL TAXABLE YEAR OF THE TRUST PRECEDES THE FIRST PAYOUT		FACTORS FOR PAYOUT AT THE END OF EACH PERIOD			
AT LEAST	*BUT LESS THAN*	*ANNUAL PERIOD*	*SEMIANNUAL PERIOD*	*QUARTERLY PERIOD*	*MONTHLY PERIOD*
....	1	1.000000	.981571	.972442	.966387
1	2	.993761	.975447	.966374	.960357
2	3	.987560	.969361	.960345	
3	4	.981398	.963312	.954353	
4	5	.975275	.957302		
5	6	.969190	.951329		
6	7	.963143	.945393		
7	8	.957133			
8	9	.951161			
9	10	.945227			
10	11	.939329			
11	12	.933468			
12	....	.927644			

TABLE F(8.0)
WITH INTEREST AT 8.0 PERCENT, SHOWING FACTORS
FOR COMPUTATION OF THE ADJUSTED PAYOUT RATE FOR
CERTAIN VALUATIONS APPLICABLE AFTER APRIL 30, 1989

1		2			
NUMBER OF MONTHS BY WHICH THE VALUATION DATE FOR THE FIRST FULL TAXABLE YEAR OF THE TRUST PRECEDES THE FIRST PAYOUT		FACTORS FOR PAYOUT AT THE END OF EACH PERIOD			
AT LEAST	*BUT LESS THAN*	*ANNUAL PERIOD*	*SEMIANNUAL PERIOD*	*QUARTERLY PERIOD*	*MONTHLY PERIOD*
....	1	1.000000	.981125	.971777	.965578
1	2	.993607	.974853	.965564	.959405
2	3	.987255	.968621	.959392	
3	4	.980944	.962429	.953258	
4	5	.974673	.956276		
5	6	.968442	.950162		
6	7	.962250	.944088		
7	8	.956099			
8	9	.949987			
9	10	.943913			
10	11	.937879			
11	12	.931883			
12	....	.925926			

TABLE F(8.2)
WITH INTEREST AT 8.2 PERCENT, SHOWING FACTORS FOR COMPUTATION OF THE ADJUSTED PAYOUT RATE FOR CERTAIN VALUATIONS APPLICABLE AFTER APRIL 30, 1989

1		2			
NUMBER OF MONTHS BY WHICH THE VALUATION DATE FOR THE FIRST FULL TAXABLE YEAR OF THE TRUST PRECEDES THE FIRST PAYOUT		FACTORS FOR PAYOUT AT THE END OF EACH PERIOD			
AT LEAST	*BUT LESS THAN*	*ANNUAL PERIOD*	*SEMIANNUAL PERIOD*	*QUARTERLY PERIOD*	*MONTHLY PERIOD*
....	1	1.000000	.980680	.971114	.964771
1	2	.993454	.974261	.964757	.958455
2	3	.986951	.967883	.958441	
3	4	.980490	.961547	.952167	
4	5	.974072	.955253		
5	6	.967695	.949000		
6	7	.961361	.942788		
7	8	.955068			
8	9	.948816			
9	10	.942605			
10	11	.936434			
11	12	.930304			
12	....	.924214			

TABLE F(8.4)
WITH INTEREST AT 8.4 PERCENT, SHOWING FACTORS FOR COMPUTATION OF THE ADJUSTED PAYOUT RATE FOR CERTAIN VALUATIONS APPLICABLE AFTER APRIL 30, 1989

1		2			
NUMBER OF MONTHS BY WHICH THE VALUATION DATE FOR THE FIRST FULL TAXABLE YEAR OF THE TRUST PRECEDES THE FIRST PAYOUT		FACTORS FOR PAYOUT AT THE END OF EACH PERIOD			
AT LEAST	*BUT LESS THAN*	*ANNUAL PERIOD*	*SEMIANNUAL PERIOD*	*QUARTERLY PERIOD*	*MONTHLY PERIOD*
....	1	1.000000	.980237	.970453	.963966
1	2	.993301	.973670	.963952	.957509
2	3	.986647	.967148	.957494	
3	4	.980037	.960669	.951080	
4	5	.973472	.954233		
5	6	.966951	.947841		
6	7	.960473	.941491		
7	8	.954039			
8	9	.947648			
9	10	.941300			
10	11	.934994			
11	12	.928731			
12	....	.922509			

TABLE F(8.6)
WITH INTEREST AT 8.6 PERCENT, SHOWING FACTORS FOR COMPUTATION OF THE ADJUSTED PAYOUT RATE FOR CERTAIN VALUATIONS APPLICABLE AFTER APRIL 30, 1989

1		2			
NUMBER OF MONTHS BY WHICH THE VALUATION DATE FOR THE FIRST FULL TAXABLE YEAR OF THE TRUST PRECEDES THE FIRST PAYOUT		FACTORS FOR PAYOUT AT THE END OF EACH PERIOD			
AT LEAST	*BUT LESS THAN*	*ANNUAL PERIOD*	*SEMIANNUAL PERIOD*	*QUARTERLY PERIOD*	*MONTHLY PERIOD*
....	1	1.000000	.979794	.969794	.963164
1	2	.993148	.973081	.963149	.956565
2	3	.986344	.966414	.956550	
3	4	.979586	.959793	.949996	
4	5	.972874	.953217		
5	6	.966209	.946686		
6	7	.959589	.940199		
7	8	.953014			
8	9	.946484			
9	10	.940000			
10	11	.933559			
11	12	.927163			
12	....	.920810			

TABLE F(8.8)
WITH INTEREST AT 8.8 PERCENT, SHOWING FACTORS FOR COMPUTATION OF THE ADJUSTED PAYOUT RATE FOR CERTAIN VALUATIONS APPLICABLE AFTER APRIL 30, 1989

1		2			
NUMBER OF MONTHS BY WHICH THE VALUATION DATE FOR THE FIRST FULL TAXABLE YEAR OF THE TRUST PRECEDES THE FIRST PAYOUT		FACTORS FOR PAYOUT AT THE END OF EACH PERIOD			
AT LEAST	*BUT LESS THAN*	*ANNUAL PERIOD*	*SEMIANNUAL PERIOD*	*QUARTERLY PERIOD*	*MONTHLY PERIOD*
....	1	1.000000	.979353	.969136	.962364
1	2	.992996	.972494	.962349	.955624
2	3	.986041	.965683	.955609	
3	4	.979135	.958919	.948916	
4	5	.972278	.952203		
5	6	.965468	.945534		
6	7	.958706	.938912		
7	8	.951992			
8	9	.945324			
9	10	.938703			
10	11	.932129			
11	12	.925600			
12	....	.919118			

TABLE F(9.0)
WITH INTEREST AT 9.0 PERCENT, SHOWING FACTORS
FOR COMPUTATION OF THE ADJUSTED PAYOUT RATE FOR
CERTAIN VALUATIONS APPLICABLE AFTER APRIL 30, 1989

1		2			
NUMBER OF MONTHS BY WHICH THE VALUATION DATE FOR THE FIRST FULL TAXABLE YEAR OF THE TRUST PRECEDES THE FIRST PAYOUT		FACTORS FOR PAYOUT AT THE END OF EACH PERIOD			
AT LEAST	*BUT LESS THAN*	*ANNUAL PERIOD*	*SEMIANNUAL PERIOD*	*QUARTERLY PERIOD*	*MONTHLY PERIOD*
....	1	1.000000	.978913	.968481	.961567
1	2	.992844	.971908	.961551	.954686
2	3	.985740	.964954	.954670	
3	4	.978686	.958049	.947839	
4	5	.971683	.951193		
5	6	.964730	.944387		
6	7	.957826	.937629		
7	8	.950972			
8	9	.944167			
9	10	.937411			
10	11	.930703			
11	12	.924043			
12	....	.917431			

TABLE F(9.2)
WITH INTEREST AT 9.2 PERCENT, SHOWING FACTORS
FOR COMPUTATION OF THE ADJUSTED PAYOUT RATE FOR
CERTAIN VALUATIONS APPLICABLE AFTER APRIL 30, 1989

1		2			
NUMBER OF MONTHS BY WHICH THE VALUATION DATE FOR THE FIRST FULL TAXABLE YEAR OF THE TRUST PRECEDES THE FIRST PAYOUT		FACTORS FOR PAYOUT AT THE END OF EACH PERIOD			
AT LEAST	*BUT LESS THAN*	*ANNUAL PERIOD*	*SEMIANNUAL PERIOD*	*QUARTERLY PERIOD*	*MONTHLY PERIOD*
....	1	1.000000	.978474	.967827	.960772
1	2	.992693	.971324	.960755	.953752
2	3	.985439	.964226	.953734	
3	4	.978238	.957180	.946765	
4	5	.971089	.950186		
5	6	.963993	.943242		
6	7	.956949	.936350		
7	8	.949956			
8	9	.943014			
9	10	.936123			
10	11	.929283			
11	12	.922492			
12	....	.915751			

TABLE F(9.4)
WITH INTEREST AT 9.4 PERCENT, SHOWING FACTORS FOR COMPUTATION OF THE ADJUSTED PAYOUT RATE FOR CERTAIN VALUATIONS APPLICABLE AFTER APRIL 30, 1989

1		2			
NUMBER OF MONTHS BY WHICH THE VALUATION DATE FOR THE FIRST FULL TAXABLE YEAR OF THE TRUST PRECEDES THE FIRST PAYOUT		FACTORS FOR PAYOUT AT THE END OF EACH PERIOD			
AT LEAST	*BUT LESS THAN*	*ANNUAL PERIOD*	*SEMIANNUAL PERIOD*	*QUARTERLY PERIOD*	*MONTHLY PERIOD*
....	1	1.000000	.978037	.967176	.959980
1	2	.992541	.970742	.959962	.952820
2	3	.985138	.963501	.952802	
3	4	.977790	.956315	.945695	
4	5	.970497	.949182		
5	6	.963258	.942102		
6	7	.956074	.935075		
7	8	.948942			
8	9	.941865			
9	10	.934839			
10	11	.927867			
11	12	.920946			
12	....	.914077			

TABLE F(9.6)
WITH INTEREST AT 9.6 PERCENT, SHOWING FACTORS FOR COMPUTATION OF THE ADJUSTED PAYOUT RATE FOR CERTAIN VALUATIONS APPLICABLE AFTER APRIL 30, 1989

1		2			
NUMBER OF MONTHS BY WHICH THE VALUATION DATE FOR THE FIRST FULL TAXABLE YEAR OF THE TRUST PRECEDES THE FIRST PAYOUT		FACTORS FOR PAYOUT AT THE END OF EACH PERIOD			
AT LEAST	*BUT LESS THAN*	*ANNUAL PERIOD*	*SEMIANNUAL PERIOD*	*QUARTERLY PERIOD*	*MONTHLY PERIOD*
....	1	1.000000	.977600	.966526	.959190
1	2	.992390	.970161	.959171	.951890
2	3	.984838	.962778	.951872	
3	4	.977344	.955452	.944628	
4	5	.969906	.948181		
5	6	.962526	.940965		
6	7	.955201	.933805		
7	8	.947932			
8	9	.940718			
9	10	.933560			
10	11	.926455			
11	12	.919405			
12	....	.912409			

TABLE F(9.8)
WITH INTEREST AT 9.8 PERCENT, SHOWING FACTORS FOR COMPUTATION OF THE ADJUSTED PAYOUT RATE FOR CERTAIN VALUATIONS APPLICABLE AFTER APRIL 30, 1989

1		2			
NUMBER OF MONTHS BY WHICH THE VALUATION DATE FOR THE FIRST FULL TAXABLE YEAR OF THE TRUST PRECEDES THE FIRST PAYOUT		FACTORS FOR PAYOUT AT THE END OF EACH PERIOD			
AT LEAST	*BUT LESS THAN*	*ANNUAL PERIOD*	*SEMIANNUAL PERIOD*	*QUARTERLY PERIOD*	*MONTHLY PERIOD*
....	1	1.000000	.977165	.965878	.958402
1	2	.992239	.969582	.958382	.950964
2	3	.984539	.962057	.950945	
3	4	.976898	.954591	.943565	
4	5	.969317	.947183		
5	6	.961795	.939832		
6	7	.954331	.932539		
7	8	.946924			
8	9	.939576			
9	10	.932284			
10	11	.925049			
11	12	.917870			
12	....	.910747			

TABLE F(10.0)
WITH INTEREST AT 10.0 PERCENT, SHOWING FACTORS FOR COMPUTATION OF THE ADJUSTED PAYOUT RATE FOR CERTAIN VALUATIONS APPLICABLE AFTER APRIL 30, 1989

1		2			
NUMBER OF MONTHS BY WHICH THE VALUATION DATE FOR THE FIRST FULL TAXABLE YEAR OF THE TRUST PRECEDES THE FIRST PAYOUT		FACTORS FOR PAYOUT AT THE END OF EACH PERIOD			
AT LEAST	*BUT LESS THAN*	*ANNUAL PERIOD*	*SEMIANNUAL PERIOD*	*QUARTERLY PERIOD*	*MONTHLY PERIOD*
....	1	1.000000	.976731	.965232	.957616
1	2	.992089	.969004	.957596	.950041
2	3	.984240	.961338	.950021	
3	4	.976454	.953733	.942505	
4	5	.968729	.946188		
5	6	.961066	.938703		
6	7	.953463	.931277		
7	8	.945920			
8	9	.938436			
9	10	.931012			
10	11	.923647			
11	12	.916340			
12	....	.909091			

TABLE F(10.2)
WITH INTEREST AT 10.2 PERCENT, SHOWING FACTORS FOR COMPUTATION OF THE ADJUSTED PAYOUT RATE FOR CERTAIN VALUATIONS APPLICABLE AFTER APRIL 30, 1989

1		2			
NUMBER OF MONTHS BY WHICH THE VALUATION DATE FOR THE FIRST FULL TAXABLE YEAR OF THE TRUST PRECEDES THE FIRST PAYOUT		FACTORS FOR PAYOUT AT THE END OF EACH PERIOD			
AT LEAST	*BUT LESS THAN*	*ANNUAL PERIOD*	*SEMIANNUAL PERIOD*	*QUARTERLY PERIOD*	*MONTHLY PERIOD*
....	1	1.000000	.976298	.964588	.956833
1	2	.991939	.968428	.956812	.949120
2	3	.983943	.960622	.949099	
3	4	.976011	.952878	.941448	
4	5	.968143	.945196		
5	6	.960338	.937577		
6	7	.952597	.930019		
7	8	.944918			
8	9	.937301			
9	10	.929745			
10	11	.922250			
11	12	.914816			
12	....	.907441			

TABLE F(10.4)
WITH INTEREST AT 10.4 PERCENT, SHOWING FACTORS FOR COMPUTATION OF THE ADJUSTED PAYOUT RATE FOR CERTAIN VALUATIONS APPLICABLE AFTER APRIL 30, 1989

1		2			
NUMBER OF MONTHS BY WHICH THE VALUATION DATE FOR THE FIRST FULL TAXABLE YEAR OF THE TRUST PRECEDES THE FIRST PAYOUT		FACTORS FOR PAYOUT AT THE END OF EACH PERIOD			
AT LEAST	*BUT LESS THAN*	*ANNUAL PERIOD*	*SEMIANNUAL PERIOD*	*QUARTERLY PERIOD*	*MONTHLY PERIOD*
....	1	1.000000	.975867	.963946	.956052
1	2	.991789	.967854	.956031	.948202
2	3	.983645	.959907	.948181	
3	4	.975568	.952025	.940395	
4	5	.967558	.944208		
5	6	.959613	.936455		
6	7	.951734	.928765		
7	8	.943919			
8	9	.936168			
9	10	.928481			
10	11	.920858			
11	12	.913296			
12	....	.905797			

TABLE F(10.6)
WITH INTEREST AT 10.6 PERCENT, SHOWING FACTORS FOR COMPUTATION OF THE ADJUSTED PAYOUT RATE FOR CERTAIN VALUATIONS APPLICABLE AFTER APRIL 30, 1989

1		2			
NUMBER OF MONTHS BY WHICH THE VALUATION DATE FOR THE FIRST FULL TAXABLE YEAR OF THE TRUST PRECEDES THE FIRST PAYOUT		FACTORS FOR PAYOUT AT THE END OF EACH PERIOD			
AT LEAST	*BUT LESS THAN*	*ANNUAL PERIOD*	*SEMIANNUAL PERIOD*	*QUARTERLY PERIOD*	*MONTHLY PERIOD*
....	1	1.000000	.975436	.963305	.955274
1	2	.991639	.967281	.955252	.947287
2	3	.983349	.959194	.947265	
3	4	.975127	.951174	.939345	
4	5	.966974	.943222		
5	6	.958890	.935336		
6	7	.950873	.927516		
7	8	.942923			
8	9	.935039			
9	10	.927222			
10	11	.919470			
11	12	.911782			
12	....	.904159			

TABLE F(10.8)
WITH INTEREST AT 10.8 PERCENT, SHOWING FACTORS FOR COMPUTATION OF THE ADJUSTED PAYOUT RATE FOR CERTAIN VALUATIONS APPLICABLE AFTER APRIL 30, 1989

1		2			
NUMBER OF MONTHS BY WHICH THE VALUATION DATE FOR THE FIRST FULL TAXABLE YEAR OF THE TRUST PRECEDES THE FIRST PAYOUT		FACTORS FOR PAYOUT AT THE END OF EACH PERIOD			
AT LEAST	*BUT LESS THAN*	*ANNUAL PERIOD*	*SEMIANNUAL PERIOD*	*QUARTERLY PERIOD*	*MONTHLY PERIOD*
....	1	1.000000	.975007	.962667	.954498
1	2	.991490	.966710	.954475	.946375
2	3	.983052	.958483	.946352	
3	4	.974687	.950327	.938299	
4	5	.966392	.942239		
5	6	.958168	.934221		
6	7	.950014	.926271		
7	8	.941930			
8	9	.933914			
9	10	.925966			
10	11	.918086			
11	12	.910273			
12	....	.902527			

TABLE F(11.0)
WITH INTEREST AT 11.0 PERCENT, SHOWING FACTORS FOR COMPUTATION OF THE ADJUSTED PAYOUT RATE FOR CERTAIN VALUATIONS APPLICABLE AFTER APRIL 30, 1989

1		2			
NUMBER OF MONTHS BY WHICH THE VALUATION DATE FOR THE FIRST FULL TAXABLE YEAR OF THE TRUST PRECEDES THE FIRST PAYOUT		FACTORS FOR PAYOUT AT THE END OF EACH PERIOD			
AT LEAST	*BUT LESS THAN*	*ANNUAL PERIOD*	*SEMIANNUAL PERIOD*	*QUARTERLY PERIOD*	*MONTHLY PERIOD*
....	1	1.000000	.974579	.962030	.953724
1	2	.991341	.966140	.953700	.945466
2	3	.982757	.957774	.945442	
3	4	.974247	.949481	.937255	
4	5	.965811	.941260		
5	6	.957449	.933109		
6	7	.949158	.925029		
7	8	.940939			
8	9	.932792			
9	10	.924715			
10	11	.916708			
11	12	.908770			
12	....	.900901			

TABLE F(11.2)
WITH INTEREST AT 11.2 PERCENT, SHOWING FACTORS FOR COMPUTATION OF THE ADJUSTED PAYOUT RATE FOR CERTAIN VALUATIONS APPLICABLE AFTER APRIL 30, 1989

1		2			
NUMBER OF MONTHS BY WHICH THE VALUATION DATE FOR THE FIRST FULL TAXABLE YEAR OF THE TRUST PRECEDES THE FIRST PAYOUT		FACTORS FOR PAYOUT AT THE END OF EACH PERIOD			
AT LEAST	*BUT LESS THAN*	*ANNUAL PERIOD*	*SEMIANNUAL PERIOD*	*QUARTERLY PERIOD*	*MONTHLY PERIOD*
....	1	1.000000	.974152	.961395	.952952
1	2	.991192	.965572	.952927	.944559
2	3	.982462	.957068	.944534	
3	4	.973809	.948638	.936215	
4	5	.965232	.940283		
5	6	.956731	.932001		
6	7	.948304	.923792		
7	8	.939952			
8	9	.931673			
9	10	.923467			
10	11	.915333			
11	12	.907272			
12	....	.899281			

TABLE F(11.4)
WITH INTEREST AT 11.4 PERCENT, SHOWING FACTORS FOR COMPUTATION OF THE ADJUSTED PAYOUT RATE FOR CERTAIN VALUATIONS APPLICABLE AFTER APRIL 30, 1989

1		2			
NUMBER OF MONTHS BY WHICH THE VALUATION DATE FOR THE FIRST FULL TAXABLE YEAR OF THE TRUST PRECEDES THE FIRST PAYOUT		FACTORS FOR PAYOUT AT THE END OF EACH PERIOD			
AT LEAST	*BUT LESS THAN*	*ANNUAL PERIOD*	*SEMIANNUAL PERIOD*	*QUARTERLY PERIOD*	*MONTHLY PERIOD*
....	1	1.000000	.973726	.960762	.952183
1	2	.991044	.965005	.952157	.943655
2	3	.982168	.956363	.943630	
3	4	.973372	.947798	.935178	
4	5	.964654	.939309		
5	6	.956015	.930896		
6	7	.947452	.922559		
7	8	.938967			
8	9	.930557			
9	10	.922223			
10	11	.913964			
11	12	.905778			
12	....	.897666			

TABLE F(11.6)
WITH INTEREST AT 11.6 PERCENT, SHOWING FACTORS FOR COMPUTATION OF THE ADJUSTED PAYOUT RATE FOR CERTAIN VALUATIONS APPLICABLE AFTER APRIL 30, 1989

1		2			
NUMBER OF MONTHS BY WHICH THE VALUATION DATE FOR THE FIRST FULL TAXABLE YEAR OF THE TRUST PRECEDES THE FIRST PAYOUT		FACTORS FOR PAYOUT AT THE END OF EACH PERIOD			
AT LEAST	*BUT LESS THAN*	*ANNUAL PERIOD*	*SEMIANNUAL PERIOD*	*QUARTERLY PERIOD*	*MONTHLY PERIOD*
....	1	1.000000	.973302	.960130	.951416
1	2	.990896	.964440	.951389	.942754
2	3	.981874	.955660	.942728	
3	4	.972935	.946959	.934145	
4	5	.964077	.938338		
5	6	.955300	.929795		
6	7	.946603	.921330		
7	8	.937985			
8	9	.929445			
9	10	.920984			
10	11	.912599			
11	12	.904290			
12	....	.896057			

TABLE F(11.8)
WITH INTEREST AT 11.8 PERCENT, SHOWING FACTORS FOR COMPUTATION OF THE ADJUSTED PAYOUT RATE FOR CERTAIN VALUATIONS APPLICABLE AFTER APRIL 30, 1989

1		2			
NUMBER OF MONTHS BY WHICH THE VALUATION DATE FOR THE FIRST FULL TAXABLE YEAR OF THE TRUST PRECEDES THE FIRST PAYOUT		FACTORS FOR PAYOUT AT THE END OF EACH PERIOD			
AT LEAST	*BUT LESS THAN*	*ANNUAL PERIOD*	*SEMIANNUAL PERIOD*	*QUARTERLY PERIOD*	*MONTHLY PERIOD*
....	1	1.000000	.972878	.959501	.950651
1	2	.990748	.963877	.950624	.941855
2	3	.981582	.954959	.941828	
3	4	.972500	.946124	.933114	
4	5	.963502	.937370		
5	6	.954588	.928698		
6	7	.945756	.920105		
7	8	.937006			
8	9	.928337			
9	10	.919748			
10	11	.911238			
11	12	.902807			
12	....	.894454			

TABLE F(12.0)
WITH INTEREST AT 12.0 PERCENT, SHOWING FACTORS FOR COMPUTATION OF THE ADJUSTED PAYOUT RATE FOR CERTAIN VALUATIONS APPLICABLE AFTER APRIL 30, 1989

1		2			
NUMBER OF MONTHS BY WHICH THE VALUATION DATE FOR THE FIRST FULL TAXABLE YEAR OF THE TRUST PRECEDES THE FIRST PAYOUT		FACTORS FOR PAYOUT AT THE END OF EACH PERIOD			
AT LEAST	*BUT LESS THAN*	*ANNUAL PERIOD*	*SEMIANNUAL PERIOD*	*QUARTERLY PERIOD*	*MONTHLY PERIOD*
....	1	1.000000	.972456	.958873	.949888
1	2	.990600	.963315	.949860	.940960
2	3	.981289	.954260	.940932	
3	4	.972065	.945290	.932087	
4	5	.962928	.936405		
5	6	.953877	.927603		
6	7	.944911	.918884		
7	8	.936029			
8	9	.927231			
9	10	.918515			
10	11	.909882			
11	12	.901329			
12	....	.892857			

TABLE F(12.2)
WITH INTEREST AT 12.2 PERCENT, SHOWING FACTORS
FOR COMPUTATION OF THE ADJUSTED PAYOUT RATE FOR
CERTAIN VALUATIONS APPLICABLE AFTER APRIL 30, 1989

1 NUMBER OF MONTHS BY WHICH THE VALUATION DATE FOR THE FIRST FULL TAXABLE YEAR OF THE TRUST PRECEDES THE FIRST PAYOUT		2 FACTORS FOR PAYOUT AT THE END OF EACH PERIOD			
AT LEAST	*BUT LESS THAN*	*ANNUAL PERIOD*	*SEMIANNUAL PERIOD*	*QUARTERLY PERIOD*	*MONTHLY PERIOD*
....	1	1.000000	.972034	.958247	.949128
1	2	.990453	.962754	.949099	.940067
2	3	.980997	.953563	.940038	
3	4	.971632	.944460	.931063	
4	5	.962356	.935443		
5	6	.953168	.926512		
6	7	.944069	.917667		
7	8	.935056			
8	9	.926129			
9	10	.917287			
10	11	.908530			
11	12	.899856			
12	....	.891266			

TABLE F(12.4)
WITH INTEREST AT 12.4 PERCENT, SHOWING FACTORS
FOR COMPUTATION OF THE ADJUSTED PAYOUT RATE FOR
CERTAIN VALUATIONS APPLICABLE AFTER APRIL 30, 1989

1 NUMBER OF MONTHS BY WHICH THE VALUATION DATE FOR THE FIRST FULL TAXABLE YEAR OF THE TRUST PRECEDES THE FIRST PAYOUT		2 FACTORS FOR PAYOUT AT THE END OF EACH PERIOD			
AT LEAST	*BUT LESS THAN*	*ANNUAL PERIOD*	*SEMIANNUAL PERIOD*	*QUARTERLY PERIOD*	*MONTHLY PERIOD*
....	1	1.000000	.971614	.957623	.948370
1	2	.990306	.962195	.948340	.939176
2	3	.980706	.952868	.939147	
3	4	.971199	.943631	.930043	
4	5	.961785	.934484		
5	6	.952461	.925425		
6	7	.943228	.916454		
7	8	.934085			
8	9	.925030			
9	10	.916063			
10	11	.907183			
11	12	.898389			
12	....	.889680			

TABLE F(12.6)
WITH INTEREST AT 12.6 PERCENT, SHOWING FACTORS FOR COMPUTATION OF THE ADJUSTED PAYOUT RATE FOR CERTAIN VALUATIONS APPLICABLE AFTER APRIL 30, 1989

1		2			
NUMBER OF MONTHS BY WHICH THE VALUATION DATE FOR THE FIRST FULL TAXABLE YEAR OF THE TRUST PRECEDES THE FIRST PAYOUT		FACTORS FOR PAYOUT AT THE END OF EACH PERIOD			
AT LEAST	*BUT LESS THAN*	*ANNUAL PERIOD*	*SEMIANNUAL PERIOD*	*QUARTERLY PERIOD*	*MONTHLY PERIOD*
....	1	1.000000	.971195	.957000	.947614
1	2	.990159	.961638	.947583	.938289
2	3	.980416	.952175	.938258	
3	4	.970768	.942805	.929025	
4	5	.961215	.933527		
5	6	.951756	.924341		
6	7	.942390	.915245		
7	8	.933117			
8	9	.923934			
9	10	.914842			
10	11	.905840			
11	12	.896926			
12	....	.888099			

TABLE F(12.8)
WITH INTEREST AT 12.8 PERCENT, SHOWING FACTORS FOR COMPUTATION OF THE ADJUSTED PAYOUT RATE FOR CERTAIN VALUATIONS APPLICABLE AFTER APRIL 30, 1989

1		2			
NUMBER OF MONTHS BY WHICH THE VALUATION DATE FOR THE FIRST FULL TAXABLE YEAR OF THE TRUST PRECEDES THE FIRST PAYOUT		FACTORS FOR PAYOUT AT THE END OF EACH PERIOD			
AT LEAST	*BUT LESS THAN*	*ANNUAL PERIOD*	*SEMIANNUAL PERIOD*	*QUARTERLY PERIOD*	*MONTHLY PERIOD*
....	1	1.000000	.970777	.956379	.946860
1	2	.990013	.961082	.946828	.937403
2	3	.980126	.951484	.937372	
3	4	.970337	.941981	.928011	
4	5	.960647	.932574		
5	6	.951053	.923260		
6	7	.941554	.914040		
7	8	.932151			
8	9	.922842			
9	10	.913625			
10	11	.904501			
11	12	.895468			
12	....	.886525			

TABLE F(13.0)
WITH INTEREST AT 13.0 PERCENT, SHOWING FACTORS FOR COMPUTATION OF THE ADJUSTED PAYOUT RATE FOR CERTAIN VALUATIONS APPLICABLE AFTER APRIL 30, 1989

1		2			
NUMBER OF MONTHS BY WHICH THE VALUATION DATE FOR THE FIRST FULL TAXABLE YEAR OF THE TRUST PRECEDES THE FIRST PAYOUT		FACTORS FOR PAYOUT AT THE END OF EACH PERIOD			
AT LEAST	*BUT LESS THAN*	*ANNUAL PERIOD*	*SEMIANNUAL PERIOD*	*QUARTERLY PERIOD*	*MONTHLY PERIOD*
....	1	1.000000	.970360	.955760	.946108
1	2	.989867	.960528	.946075	.936521
2	3	.979836	.950795	.936489	
3	4	.969908	.941160	.926999	
4	5	.960079	.931623		
5	6	.950351	.922183		
6	7	.940721	.912838		
7	8	.931188			
8	9	.921753			
9	10	.912412			
10	11	.903167			
11	12	.894015			
12	....	.884956			

TABLE F(13.2)
WITH INTEREST AT 13.2 PERCENT, SHOWING FACTORS FOR COMPUTATION OF THE ADJUSTED PAYOUT RATE FOR CERTAIN VALUATIONS APPLICABLE AFTER APRIL 30, 1989

1		2			
NUMBER OF MONTHS BY WHICH THE VALUATION DATE FOR THE FIRST FULL TAXABLE YEAR OF THE TRUST PRECEDES THE FIRST PAYOUT		FACTORS FOR PAYOUT AT THE END OF EACH PERIOD			
AT LEAST	*BUT LESS THAN*	*ANNUAL PERIOD*	*SEMIANNUAL PERIOD*	*QUARTERLY PERIOD*	*MONTHLY PERIOD*
....	1	1.000000	.969945	.955143	.945359
1	2	.989721	.959975	.945325	.935641
2	3	.979548	.950107	.935608	
3	4	.969479	.940341	.925991	
4	5	.959514	.930675		
5	6	.949651	.921109		
6	7	.939889	.911641		
7	8	.930228			
8	9	.920667			
9	10	.911203			
10	11	.901837			
11	12	.892567			
12	....	.883392			

TABLE F(13.4)
WITH INTEREST AT 13.4 PERCENT, SHOWING FACTORS FOR COMPUTATION OF THE ADJUSTED PAYOUT RATE FOR CERTAIN VALUATIONS APPLICABLE AFTER APRIL 30, 1989

1		2			
NUMBER OF MONTHS BY WHICH THE VALUATION DATE FOR THE FIRST FULL TAXABLE YEAR OF THE TRUST PRECEDES THE FIRST PAYOUT		FACTORS FOR PAYOUT AT THE END OF EACH PERIOD			
AT LEAST	*BUT LESS THAN*	*ANNUAL PERIOD*	*SEMIANNUAL PERIOD*	*QUARTERLY PERIOD*	*MONTHLY PERIOD*
....	1	1.000000	.969530	.954527	.944611
1	2	.989575	.959423	.944577	.934764
2	3	.979260	.949422	.934730	
3	4	.969051	.939524	.924986	
4	5	.958949	.929730		
5	6	.948953	.920038		
6	7	.939060	.910447		
7	8	.929271			
8	9	.919584			
9	10	.909998			
10	11	.900511			
11	12	.891124			
12	....	.881834			

TABLE F(13.6)
WITH INTEREST AT 13.6 PERCENT, SHOWING FACTORS FOR COMPUTATION OF THE ADJUSTED PAYOUT RATE FOR CERTAIN VALUATIONS APPLICABLE AFTER APRIL 30, 1989

1		2			
NUMBER OF MONTHS BY WHICH THE VALUATION DATE FOR THE FIRST FULL TAXABLE YEAR OF THE TRUST PRECEDES THE FIRST PAYOUT		FACTORS FOR PAYOUT AT THE END OF EACH PERIOD			
AT LEAST	*BUT LESS THAN*	*ANNUAL PERIOD*	*SEMIANNUAL PERIOD*	*QUARTERLY PERIOD*	*MONTHLY PERIOD*
....	1	1.000000	.969117	.953913	.943866
1	2	.989430	.958873	.943831	.933890
2	3	.978972	.948738	.933854	
3	4	.968624	.938710	.923984	
4	5	.958386	.928788		
5	6	.948256	.918971		
6	7	.938233	.909257		
7	8	.928316			
8	9	.918504			
9	10	.908796			
10	11	.899190			
11	12	.889686			
12	....	.880282			

TABLE F(13.8)
WITH INTEREST AT 13.8 PERCENT, SHOWING FACTORS FOR COMPUTATION OF THE ADJUSTED PAYOUT RATE FOR CERTAIN VALUATIONS APPLICABLE AFTER APRIL 30, 1989

1		2			
NUMBER OF MONTHS BY WHICH THE VALUATION DATE FOR THE FIRST FULL TAXABLE YEAR OF THE TRUST PRECEDES THE FIRST PAYOUT		FACTORS FOR PAYOUT AT THE END OF EACH PERIOD			
AT LEAST	*BUT LESS THAN*	*ANNUAL PERIOD*	*SEMIANNUAL PERIOD*	*QUARTERLY PERIOD*	*MONTHLY PERIOD*
....	1	1.000000	.968704	.953301	.943123
1	2	.989285	.958325	.943087	.933018
2	3	.978685	.948056	.932982	
3	4	.968199	.937898	.922985	
4	5	.957824	.927849		
5	6	.947561	.917907		
6	7	.937408	.908072		
7	8	.927364			
8	9	.917428			
9	10	.907598			
10	11	.897873			
11	12	.888252			
12	....	.878735			

TABLE F(14.0)
WITH INTEREST AT 14.0 PERCENT, SHOWING FACTORS FOR COMPUTATION OF THE ADJUSTED PAYOUT RATE FOR CERTAIN VALUATIONS APPLICABLE AFTER APRIL 30, 1989

1		2			
NUMBER OF MONTHS BY WHICH THE VALUATION DATE FOR THE FIRST FULL TAXABLE YEAR OF THE TRUST PRECEDES THE FIRST PAYOUT		FACTORS FOR PAYOUT AT THE END OF EACH PERIOD			
AT LEAST	*BUT LESS THAN*	*ANNUAL PERIOD*	*SEMIANNUAL PERIOD*	*QUARTERLY PERIOD*	*MONTHLY PERIOD*
....	1	1.000000	.968293	.952691	.942382
1	2	.989140	.957778	.942345	.932148
2	3	.978399	.947377	.932111	
3	4	.967774	.937088	.921989	
4	5	.957264	.926912		
5	6	.946868	.916846		
6	7	.936586	.906889		
7	8	.926415			
8	9	.916354			
9	10	.906403			
10	11	.896560			
11	12	.886824			
12	....	.877193			

¶ 532 Ten-Percent Valuation Tables

Reproduced below are the 10-percent tables for valuing limited interests of decedents dying or gifts made after November 30, 1983, and before May 1, 1989 (see ¶ 530).[23]

TABLE A
SINGLE LIFE, UNISEX, 10 PERCENT—TABLE SHOWING THE PRESENT WORTH OF AN ANNUITY, OF A LIFE ESTATE, AND A REMAINDER INTEREST

Age (1)	*Annuity (2)*	*Life Estate (3)*	*Remainder (4)*	*Age (1)*	*Annuity (2)*	*Life Estate (3)*	*Remainder (4)*
0 ..	9.7188	.97188	.02812	52 ..	8.2969	.82969	.17031
1 ..	9.8988	.98988	.01012	53 ..	8.2028	.82028	.17972
2 ..	9.9017	.99017	.00983	54 ..	8.1054	.81054	.18946
3 ..	9.9008	.99008	.00992	55 ..	8.0046	.80046	.19954
4 ..	9.8981	.98981	.01019	56 ..	7.9006	.79006	.20994
5 ..	9.8938	.98938	.01062	57 ..	7.7931	.77931	.22069
6 ..	9.8884	.98884	.01116	58 ..	7.6822	.76822	.23178
7 ..	9.8822	.98822	.01178	59 ..	7.5675	.75675	.24325
8 ..	9.8748	.98748	.01252	60 ..	7.4491	.74491	.25509
9 ..	9.8663	.98663	.01337	61 ..	7.3267	.73267	.26733
10 ..	9.8565	.98565	.01435	62 ..	7.2002	.72002	.27998
11 ..	9.8453	.98453	.01547	63 ..	7.0696	.70696	.29304
12 ..	9.8329	.98329	.01671	64 ..	6.9352	.69352	.30648
13 ..	9.8198	.98198	.01802	65 ..	6.7970	.67970	.32030
14 ..	9.8066	.98066	.01934	66 ..	6.6551	.66551	.33449
15 ..	9.7937	.97937	.02063	67 ..	6.5098	.65098	.34902
16 ..	9.7815	.97815	.02185	68 ..	6.3610	.63610	.36390
17 ..	9.7700	.97700	.02300	69 ..	6.2086	.62086	.37914
18 ..	9.7590	.97590	.02410	70 ..	6.0522	.60522	.39478
19 ..	9.7480	.97480	.02520	71 ..	5.8914	.58914	.41086
20 ..	9.7365	.97365	.02635	72 ..	5.7261	.57261	.42739
21 ..	9.7245	.97245	.02755	73 ..	5.5571	.55571	.44429
22 ..	9.7120	.97120	.02880	74 ..	5.3862	.53862	.46138
23 ..	9.6986	.96986	.03014	75 ..	5.2149	.52149	.47851
24 ..	9.6841	.96841	.03159	76 ..	5.0441	.50441	.49559
25 ..	9.6678	.96678	.03322	77 ..	4.8742	.48742	.51258
26 ..	9.6495	.96495	.03505	78 ..	4.7049	.47049	.52951
27 ..	9.6290	.96290	.03710	79 ..	4.5357	.45357	.54643
28 ..	9.6062	.96062	.03938	80 ..	4.3659	.43659	.56341
29 ..	9.5813	.95813	.04187	81 ..	4.1967	.41967	.58033
30 ..	9.5543	.95543	.04457	82 ..	4.0295	.40295	.59705
31 ..	9.5254	.95254	.04746	83 ..	3.8642	.38642	.61358
32 ..	9.4942	.94942	.05058	84 ..	3.6998	.36998	.63002
33 ..	9.4608	.94608	.05392	85 ..	3.5359	.35359	.64641
34 ..	9.4250	.94250	.05750	86 ..	3.3764	.33764	.66236
35 ..	9.3868	.93868	.06132	87 ..	3.2262	.32262	.67738
36 ..	9.3460	.93460	.06540	88 ..	3.0859	.30859	.69141
37 ..	9.3026	.93026	.06974	89 ..	2.9526	.29526	.70474
38 ..	9.2567	.92567	.07433	90 ..	2.8221	.28221	.71779
39 ..	9.2083	.92083	.07917	91 ..	2.6955	.26955	.73045
40 ..	9.1571	.91571	.08429	92 ..	2.5771	.25771	.74229
41 ..	9.1030	.91030	.08970	93 ..	2.4692	.24692	.75308
42 ..	9.0457	.90457	.09543	94 ..	2.3728	.23728	.76272
43 ..	8.9855	.89855	.10145	95 ..	2.2887	.22887	.77113
44 ..	8.9221	.89221	.10779	96 ..	2.2181	.22181	.77819
45 ..	8.8558	.88558	.11442	97 ..	2.1550	.21550	.78450
46 ..	8.7863	.87863	.12137	98 ..	2.1000	.21000	.79000
47 ..	8.7137	.87137	.12863	99 ..	2.0486	.20486	.79514
48 ..	8.6374	.86374	.13626	100 ..	1.9975	.19975	.80025
49 ..	8.5578	.85578	.14422	101 ..	1.9532	.19532	.80468
50 ..	8.4743	.84743	.15257	102 ..	1.9054	.19054	.80946
51 ..	8.3874	.83874	.16126	103 ..	1.8437	.18437	.81563

[23] Reg. § 20.2031-7A(d)(6).

TABLE A
SINGLE LIFE, UNISEX, 10 PERCENT—TABLE SHOWING THE PRESENT WORTH OF AN ANNUITY, OF A LIFE ESTATE, AND A REMAINDER INTEREST

Age (1)	*Annuity* (2)	*Life Estate* (3)	*Remainder* (4)	*Age* (1)	*Annuity* (2)	*Life Estate* (3)	*Remainder* (4)
104 ..	1.7856	.17856	.82144	107 ..	1.3409	.13409	.86591
105 ..	1.6962	.16962	.83038	108 ..	1.0068	.10068	.89932
106 ..	1.5488	.15488	.84512	109 ..	.4545	.04545	.95455

TABLE B
TERM CERTAIN, UNISEX, 10 PERCENT—TABLE SHOWING THE PRESENT WORTH OF AN ANNUITY FOR A TERM CERTAIN, OF AN INCOME INTEREST FOR A TERM CERTAIN, AND OF A REMAINDER INTEREST POSTPONED FOR A TERM CERTAIN

(1) Number of Years	(2) Annuity	(3) Term Certain	(4) Remainder	(1) Number of Years	(2) Annuity	(3) Term Certain	(4) Remainder
1 ...	.9091	.090909	.909091	31 ...	9.4790	.947901	.052099
2 ...	1.7355	.173554	.826446	32 ...	9.5264	.952638	.047362
3 ...	2.4869	.248685	.751315	33 ...	9.5694	.956943	.043057
4 ...	3.1699	.316987	.683013	34 ...	9.6086	.960857	.039143
5 ...	3.7908	.379079	.620921	35 ...	9.6442	.964416	.035584
6 ...	4.3553	.435526	.564474	36 ...	9.6765	.967651	.032349
7 ...	4.8684	.486842	.513158	37 ...	9.7059	.970592	.029408
8 ...	5.3349	.533493	.466507	38 ...	9.7327	.973265	.026735
9 ...	5.7590	.575902	.424098	39 ...	9.7570	.975686	.024304
10 ...	6.1446	.614457	.385543	40 ...	9.7791	.977905	.022095
11 ...	6.4951	.649506	.350494	41 ...	9.7991	.979914	.020096
12 ...	6.8137	.681369	.318631	42 ...	9.8174	.981740	.018260
13 ...	7.1034	.710336	.289664	43 ...	9.8340	.983400	.016600
14 ...	7.3667	.736669	.263331	44 ...	9.8491	.984909	.015091
15 ...	7.6061	.760608	.239392	45 ...	9.8628	.986281	.013718
16 ...	7.8237	.782371	.217629	46 ...	9.8753	.987528	.012472
17 ...	8.0216	.802155	.197845	47 ...	9.8866	.988662	.011338
18 ...	8.2014	.820141	.179859	48 ...	9.8969	.989693	.010307
19 ...	8.3649	.836492	.163508	49 ...	9.9063	.990630	.009370
20 ...	8.5136	.851356	.148644	50 ...	9.9148	.991481	.008519
21 ...	8.6487	.864869	.135131	51 ...	9.9226	.992256	.007744
22 ...	8.7715	.877154	.122846	52 ...	9.9296	.992960	.007040
23 ...	8.8832	.888322	.111678	53 ...	9.9360	.993600	.006400
24 ...	8.9847	.898474	.101526	54 ...	9.9418	.994182	.005818
25 ...	9.0770	.907704	.092296	55 ...	9.9471	.994711	.005289
26 ...	9.1609	.916095	.083905	56 ...	9.9519	.995191	.004809
27 ...	9.2372	.923722	.076278	57 ...	9.9563	.995629	.004371
28 ...	9.3066	.930657	.069343	58 ...	9.9603	.996026	.003974
29 ...	9.3696	.936961	.063039	59 ...	9.9639	.996387	.003613
30 ...	9.4269	.942691	.057309	60 ...	9.9672	.996716	.003284

TABLE LN

Age X (1)	lx (2)	Age X (1)	lx (2)	Age X (1)	lx (2)	Age X (1)	lx (2)
0	100000	28	95586	56	84142	84	23638
1	97998	29	95448	57	83103	85	20908
2	97876	30	95307	58	81988	86	18282
3	97792	31	95158	59	80798	87	15769
4	97724	32	95003	60	79529	88	13407
5	97668	33	94840	61	78181	89	11240
6	97619	34	94666	62	76751	90	9297
7	97573	35	94482	63	75236	91	7577
8	97531	36	94285	64	73631	92	6070
9	97494	37	94073	65	71933	93	4773
10	97460	38	93843	66	70139	94	3682
11	97430	39	93593	67	68246	95	2786
12	97401	40	93322	68	66254	96	2068
13	97367	41	93028	69	64166	97	1511
14	97322	42	92712	70	61984	98	1087
15	97261	43	92368	71	59715	99	772
16	97181	44	91995	72	57360	100	542
17	97083	45	91587	73	54913	101	375
18	96970	46	91144	74	52363	102	257
19	96846	47	90662	75	49705	103	175
20	96716	48	90142	76	46946	104	117
21	96580	49	89579	77	44101	105	78
22	96438	50	88972	78	41192	106	52
23	96292	51	88315	79	38245	107	34
24	96145	52	87605	80	35285	108	22
25	96000	53	86838	81	32323	109	14
26	95859	54	86007	82	29375	110	0
27	95721	55	85110	83	26469		

¶ 534 Actuarial Factors vs. Actual Health

For estate tax purposes, the value of life and remainder interests must be determined from facts available at the time of the decedent's death. The fact that the life tenant may in fact survive the decedent by only a short period of time is not controlling. The actuarial tables at ¶ 531 and ¶ 532 reflect the deaths of those who die prematurely as well as those who enjoy lives of greater longevity.

Nonetheless, for the estates of decedents dying, and gifts made, after December 13, 1995, IRS regulations provide that the actuarial tables may not be used to determine the present value of a limited interest if it is known at the time of decedent's death, or at the time the gift is completed, that the individual who is a measuring life of the interest is terminally ill.[24] An individual who is known to have an incurable illness or other deteriorating physical condition is considered terminally ill if there is at least a 50-percent probability that the individual will die within one year. Under the regulations, a special actuarial factor must be computed that takes into account the projection of the actual life expectancy. However, if the individual survives for 18 months or longer after the date of the decedent's death, the individual shall be presumed to have not been terminally ill at the date of death unless the contrary is established by clear and convincing evidence. For purposes of the credit allowable to the transferee's estate for tax on a prior transfer, the value of the property shall be the value determined previously in the transferor's estate.

Prior to December 14, 1995, if it was known on the valuation date that a life tenant was afflicted with a fatal and incurable disease in its advanced stages such that death was clearly imminent, a departure from the actuarial tables may be made and the value of a life or remainder interest determined by reference to known facts based upon the expert testimony of a physician.[25] Generally, cases indicate a reluctance to depart from valuations determined through the use of actuarial tables unless an incurable or fatal disease exists *and* there is evidence indicating imminent death or a life expectancy so brief as to require a departure from such tables.[26] In the majority of cases permitting departures from such tables, the life tenant's maximum actual life expectancy was one year or less.[27] These principles apply in the valuation of interests for charitable and marital deduction purposes as well. They are also applicable for purposes of computing the allowable credit for tax on prior transfers. However, the Tax Court rejected the use of valuation tables for purposes of computing the credit in valuing a husband's usufruct interest in his wife's share of community property after their simultaneous deaths.[28]

---

[24] Reg. § 20.7520-3(b)(3) and Reg. § 25.7520-3(b)(3).

[25] *N.H. Jennings*, 10 TC 323, CCH Dec. 16,263 (Acq.). See *M.P. Fabric Est.*, 83 TC 932, CCH Dec. 41,667; *C. McDowell Est.*, 51 TCM 319, CCH Dec. 42,831(M), TC Memo. 1986-27.

[26] *Cont. Ill. Nat'l Bk. & Tr. Co. of Chicago*, CA-7, 74-2 USTC ¶ 13,034. *Mercantile-Safe Deposit & Trust Co.*, DC Md., 74-1 USTC ¶ 12,985, 368 FSupp 742.

[27] *Cont. Ill. Nat'l Bk. & Tr. Co. of Chicago*, CA-7, 74-2 USTC ¶ 13,034.

[28] *E.W. Marks Est.*, 94 TC 720, CCH Dec. 46,594. See also *A.P. Carter Est.*, CA-5, 91-1 USTC ¶ 60,054, 921 F2d 63, cert. denied.

¶ 535 Other Property Interests

The various other items reportable as "Other Miscellaneous Property" are valued as indicated below.

- *Debts Owed Decedent*

Debts owed to the decedent should be reported in the amount of the principal plus accrued interest. The executor possibly can establish a lower valuation.

- *Leasehold Interests*

The renewal value of leases is an important factor in valuing leaseholds.

- *Household Goods and Personal Effects*

Household goods and personal effects should be reported at the price that a willing buyer would pay a willing seller. A room-by-room itemization is desirable. All articles should be named separately. Items in the same room with individual values of not more than $100 may be grouped. A separate value should be given for each article named.[29]

The executor may furnish a sworn statement in lieu of the itemized list, however. This statement may set forth the aggregate value of the property as appraised by a competent appraiser or appraisers, or dealers in the kind of property involved (see ¶ 540).

If the estate includes articles of marked artistic or intrinsic value, such as jewelry, furs, silverware, works of art, oriental rugs or stamp collections, and any one article is valued in excess of $3,000 or any collection of articles is valued at more than $10,000, the appraisal of an expert or experts, under oath, must be filed with the return.[30]

- *Farm Products and Automobiles*

Farm products, growing crops (other than timber for which special use valuation is elected, see ¶ 290), livestock, farm machinery, and automobiles are valued at the price at which such items would change hands between a willing buyer and a willing seller. The fair market value is not to be determined by a forced sale price. All relevant facts and elements of value as of the applicable valuation date must be considered [31] (see ¶ 540).

Feed on hand at the date of the decedent's death but consumed by livestock during the elected alternate valuation period is includible in the gross estate at its value on the date of disposition—the date on which it was fed to the livestock.[32] The disposition price is to be used for any farm asset that is sold or disposed of during the alternate valuation period.[33]

- *Deferred Compensation Payments*

Many employees enter into contracts or agreements with their employers that provide for the payment of deferred compensation to the employee, usually upon the employee's retirement. These contracts also

---

[29] Reg. § 20.2031-6.

[30] Reg. § 20.2031-6.

[31] Reg. § 20.2031-1(b).

[32] Rev. Rul. 58-436, 1958-2 CB 366, modified by Rev. Rul. 64-289, 1964-2 CB 173.

[33] Rev. Rul. 68-154, 1968-1 CB 395.

usually provide for the payment of specified sums to a named beneficiary (commonly the employee's spouse) if the employee dies before retirement.

The IRS has attempted to include the commuted value of the latter payments (commonly called "death benefits") in the estates of deceased employees as property owned at death. However, most courts have held that these payments are not includible in a deceased employee's estate because the employee's interest in the employment contract is deemed to terminate at death.

The IRS has attempted to include death benefits of this type in decedents' estates under pre-1977 Code Sec. 2035 (as transfers in contemplation of death for gifts made prior to 1977) and under Code Sec. 2036 (transfers with retained life estate), Code Sec. 2037 (transfers taking effect at death), Code Sec. 2038 (revocable transfers), and Code Sec. 2039 (annuities) (see ¶ 733 for further details).

¶ 540 Retail Price and Auction Price

In general, the fair market value of property includible in a decedent's estate is the price at which it would change hands between a willing buyer and a willing seller, both having reasonable knowledge of relevant facts. However, if an item is generally available to the public in a particular market, the fair market value of the property is the price obtainable on the market in which it is most commonly sold to the public. If the item of property is generally obtainable by the public on the retail market, the fair market value of the item is the price at which that item or a comparable one will sell at retail in a particular geographical market.[34]

For example, the fair market value of a car (property generally obtained by the public on the retail market) is the price at which a car of the same make, model, age, and condition could be purchased by members of the public. Fair market value is *not* the price that a used-car dealer would pay for the decedent's car.

The price paid for an item in a decedent's gross estate at a public auction or in answer to a classified newspaper advertisement will also be considered its retail price.[35] There are two conditions, however. The sale must be made within a reasonable period after the applicable valuation date and there must not be a substantial change in market conditions during that period.

---

[34] Reg. § 20.2031-1(b).

[35] Rev. Proc. 65-19, 1965-2 CB 1002.

¶ 548 Filled-In Schedule F

Schedule F must be filed with Form 706 for all returns (see ¶ 73).

The filled-in Schedule F, Form 706 (Rev. July 1998), relates to the factual situation of a person who dies on January 1, 1998, with an estate tax return due within nine months (without extensions).

Form 706 (Rev. 7-98)

Estate of: James X. Diversey

SCHEDULE F — Other Miscellaneous Property Not Reportable Under Any Other Schedule

(For jointly owned property that must be disclosed on Schedule E, see the instructions for Schedule E.)
(If you elect section 2032A valuation, you must complete Schedule F and Schedule A-1.)

		Yes	No
1	Did the decedent at the time of death own any articles of artistic or collectible value in excess of $3,000 or any collections whose artistic or collectible value combined at date of death exceeded $10,000? ..... If "Yes," submit full details on this schedule and attach appraisals.		X
2	Has the decedent's estate, spouse, or any other person, received (or will receive) any bonus or award as a result of the decedent's employment or death? ..... If "Yes," submit full details on this schedule.		X
3	Did the decedent at the time of death have, or have access to, a safe deposit box? ..... If "Yes," state location, and if held in joint names of decedent and another, state name and relationship of joint depositor. State National Bank, Peterson and Pulaski Aves., Chicago, IL If any of the contents of the safe deposit box are omitted from the schedules in this return, explain fully why omitted.	X	

Item number	Description For securities, give CUSIP number.	Alternate valuation date	Alternate value	Value at date of death
1	Household goods and personal effects, including clothing, all located at home at 54 Fir Street, Homewood, IL. Value based on appraisal (Copy attached).			17,650
2	50% interest in City Windows Company, located at 175th and Park Ave., Homewood, IL. Partnership business operated by Robert Diversey. Value based on appraisal (Copy aatached).			225,000
3	Cadillac Seville, 1997 model. Value based on appraisal (Copy attached).			25,500
	Total from continuation schedules (or additional sheets) attached to this schedule			
	TOTAL. (Also enter on Part 5, Recapitulation, page 3, at item 6.)			268,150

(If more space is needed, attach the continuation schedule from the end of this package or additional sheets of the same size.) (See the instructions.)

Schedule F — Page 19

Chapter 15

TRANSFERS DURING LIFETIME

¶ 550 Scope of Estate Tax

If the estate tax law applied only to property in which the decedent had an interest at the time of death, the application of the estate tax to any estate could easily be prevented by lifetime transactions. State laws relating to trusts and other property rights make it easy to divest one's self of title to property. At the same time, one could retain either control or beneficial ownership for life. Likewise, when persons realized that they did not have long to live, they could dispose of any remaining property by outright gift, thereby removing such property from their gross estates.

In recognition of these possibilities, Congress included within the scope of the estate tax law various types of lifetime transfers that would otherwise permit complete escape from estate taxes. In prescribing that the value of certain lifetime property transfers are includible in the gross estate, Congress provided for almost every type of lifetime gift in which the decedent did not dispose of every consequential right. These transfers normally involve transfers to trusts.

¶ 555 Transfers Within Three Years of Death

Generally, the value of outright transfers (other than transfers of life insurance) made by a decedent within three years of death is not includible in a decedent's gross estate. However, the value of property is includible in a decedent's gross estate if, within three years of death, the decedent transferred an interest in or power over the property that, if retained by the decedent, would have caused the property to be includible in the decedent's gross estate under Code Sec. 2036 (transfers with retained life estate), Code Sec. 2037 (transfers taking effect at death), Code Sec. 2038 (revocable transfers), or Code Sec. 2042 (life insurance proceeds).[1] The exercise of a general power of appointment, as defined in Code Sec. 2041 (¶ 650), within three years of death does not require inclusion of the property subject to the power in the decedent's gross estate under Code Sec. 2035. In addition, for decedents dying after August 5, 1997, annual exclusion gifts made from a decedent's revocable trust within three years of the decedent's death are not includible in the decedent's gross estate.[2]

[1] Code Sec. 2035(a).

[2] Code Sec. 2035(e).

The value of any transfer made within three years of death is includible in the decedent's gross estate for the limited purpose of determining the estate's qualification for special use valuation (see ¶ 280), deferral of estate taxes (see ¶ 1672), and stock redemptions under Code Sec. 303. Additionally, the value of such a transfer is includible in the gross estate for purposes of determining property that is subject to estate tax liens.[3] This provision is designed to preclude deathbed transfers intended to qualify the estate for such favorable treatment by reducing the amount of nonqualifying property.[4] This provision also applies to transfers to a spouse within three years of death, even though an unlimited gift tax marital deduction is available for gifts made after 1981 (see ¶ 1001). Note that transfers within three years of death, as well as certain transfers within 10 years of death, are also includible for purposes of the qualified family-owned business deduction (¶ 1150).

- *Gifts for Which Gift Tax Return Not Required*

The value of transfers made within three years of death that are includible in the gross estate under exceptions to the general noninclusion rule of Code Sec. 2035 is includible even if no gift tax return was required to be filed with respect to the transfer.[5] In the case of a gift to a spouse within three years of death for which no gift tax return is required because of the unlimited gift tax marital deduction, the value of the gift is includible in the decedent's gross estate to a limited extent.

- *"Gross-Up" for Gift Tax Paid on Transfers Within Three Years of Death*

Gift taxes paid on transfers made within three years of a transferor's death are includible in the decedent's gross estate.[6] The amount subject to this rule includes the tax paid by the decedent or the decedent's estate on any gift made by the decedent or his or her spouse within the three-year period ending on the date of the decedent's death.

The "gross-up" rule does not apply to the gift tax paid by a spouse on a gift made by the decedent within three years of death that is treated as made one-half by the spouse under the gift-splitting provisions of Code Sec. 2513.

- *Transfer for Adequate Consideration*

Even though transferred within three years of the decedent's death, the value of property for which the decedent received a full and adequate consideration in money or money's worth is not includible in the gross estate.

¶ 565 Transfers Intended to Take Effect at Death

The estate tax law requires the inclusion in the gross estate of the value of lifetime "transfers intended to take effect at death." [7]

A transfer made by the decedent and taking effect at the decedent's death is one under which possession or enjoyment of the property can be obtained only by surviving the decedent. However, such a transfer is not

---

[3] Code Sec. 2035(c)(1)(C).

[4] *General Explanation of the Economic Recovery Tax Act of 1981*, Staff of the Joint Committee on Taxation, p. 262.

[5] Code Sec. 2035(c)(3).

[6] Code Sec. 2035(b).

[7] Code Sec. 2037.

treated as a transfer taking effect at death unless the decedent retained a reversionary interest in the property which immediately before the decedent's death had a value in excess of five percent of the value of the transferred property.[8] In determining whether or not a reversionary interest exceeds five percent of the value of the transferred property, the value of the reversionary interest is compared with the value of the transferred property, including interests therein that are not dependent upon survivorship of the decedent. For this purpose, a reversionary interest includes a possibility that property transferred by the decedent:

(1) may return to the decedent or to the decedent's estate, or

(2) may become subject to a power of disposition by the decedent.

If the interest is in income only, a decedent does not have a reversionary interest.[9]

This reversionary interest of the decedent may be expressly written into the instrument or it may arise by way of state law.[10] In other words, it may be explicit—"To A for life, remainder to B, but if B should predecease me, then the remainder to me or my heirs." It also may be implicit—"To A for life, remainder to B if B doesn't predecease me." In the second example, the entire fee interest has not been disposed of by the decedent. There is a possibility that B will not be eligible to take after A's life estate. Since the property is not otherwise disposed of, it will revert to the decedent by operation of law.

If, in either of these cases, the reversionary interest could be valued in excess of five percent of the value of the property, the value of the property (less the value of any outstanding, preceding interests in persons other than the transferor) would be included in the decedent's gross estate. Such a valuation in excess of five percent is quite possible if only one remainderman is named. The value of such an interest is to be determined by the usual methods of valuation, including the use of mortality tables and actuarial principles (see ¶ 530).

A transfer intended to take effect at death will not be included in the decedent's estate if possession or enjoyment of the property could have been obtained by any beneficiary during the decedent's lifetime through the exercise of a general power of appointment that was exercisable immediately before the decedent's death.[11]

- *Transfers Made Prior to October 8, 1949*

All transfers made prior to October 8, 1949, and intended to take effect at death, require the same estate tax consequences as those made after that date, with one exception. The reversionary interest must be expressly included in the instrument of transfer. If it arises by operation of law, the property is not included in the decedent's gross estate.[12]

---

[8] Reg. § 20.2037-1(a).

[9] Reg. § 20.2037-1(c).

[10] Reg. § 20.2037-1(c) and Rev. Rul. 82-24, 1982-1 CB 134.

[11] Reg. § 20.2037-1(b).

[12] Reg. § 20.2037-1(f).

¶ 570 Transfers with Possession or Enjoyment Retained

The gross estate includes the value of property or property interests transferred by a decedent, in trust or otherwise, if the decedent reserved or retained for life, or for any period not ascertainable without reference to the decedent's death, or for a period which does not in fact end before the decedent's death—

(1) the use, possession, right to the income, or other enjoyment of the transferred property, or

(2) the right, either alone or in conjunction with any other person, to designate the person or persons who will possess or enjoy the transferred property or the income therefrom.[13]

A reservation by the decedent for a period not ascertainable without reference to the decedent's death may be illustrated by the following:

> ***Example:*** Larry Collins reserved the right to receive the income from transferred property in quarterly payments on the condition that no part of the income between the last quarterly payment and the date of his death was to be received by him or his estate.

If the decedent retained or reserved one or more of these rights or interests as to all of the property he transferred, the amount includible in the gross estate is the value of the entire property transferred, less the value of any outstanding income interest which is not subject to the decedent's interest or right and which is actually being enjoyed by another person at the time of the decedent's death. If the decedent during life retained or reserved an interest or right as to only a part of the property transferred, the amount includible in the decedent's gross estate is only a corresponding portion of the entire value of the property.[14]

The use, possession, right to the income, or other enjoyment of the transferred property is considered as having been retained by or reserved to the decedent to the extent that it is to be applied toward the discharge of a legal obligation of the decedent or otherwise for the decedent's pecuniary benefit. The term "legal obligation" includes a legal obligation by the decedent during the decedent's lifetime to support a dependent.[15]

If the rights are retained for life, however, or for a period not ascertainable without reference to the decedent's death, the property will in all cases be includible unless one of the special exceptions noted below is applicable. With respect to their right to designate the person or persons who shall possess or enjoy the transferred property or income therefrom, the manner of making the transfer is immaterial. If these rights are retained, they are taxable whether made in trust or otherwise.[16] However, the Tax Court has held that the concept of a transfer with a retained life estate was not applicable to transfers that were deemed to have been made by a decedent under the Uniform Simultaneous Death Act. Thus, in a situation where a decedent and her husband died in a common accident, the proceeds of two policies of insurance on the husband's life that were

---

[13] Code Sec. 2036.

[14] Reg. § 20.2036-1(a).

[15] Reg. § 20.2036-1(b). See *E.E. German Est.*, CtCls, 85-1 USTC ¶ 13,610.

[16] Reg. § 20.2036-1(b)(3).

payable to a trust in which the decedent had a life income interest were not includible in her gross estate, even though she owned the policies and was deemed to have survived her husband under the Uniform Simultaneous Death Act. In the court's view, the Act is intended solely to provide rules for passage of property of both decedents to their beneficiaries.[17]

If the retained use is a natural one, however, such as the use with a spouse of a home that the decedent purchased for the spouse, rather than a use that has been reserved in the instrument of transfer or by a withholding of the property from the transferee, the transfer is not taxable in the absence of an understanding or agreement, expressed or implied. Continued occupancy in a residence, where the donor and donee are husband and wife, does not itself support an inference of an agreement or understanding as to retained possession or enjoyment by the donor.[18] Where the donor and donee are persons other than husband and wife, for example, a parent and child, the IRS has ruled that the continued occupancy of the transferred realty itself implies the existence of an agreement of retained enjoyment by the donor.[19] This IRS position has been sustained by an appellate court.[20]

Where the retention of a right to income was one which did not take effect until after the death of a primary life tenant and the decedent died before the primary life tenant, the entire value of the trust, less only the value of the outstanding life estate, is includible.[21] Unrequested income amounts that were irrevocably added to trust principal were includible in the gross estate of a life income beneficiary as a transfer with a retained life estate where the beneficiary had the right to income from the augmented trust principal.[22]

● *Effect of Consideration*

If the transfer was made for a consideration, the value of the consideration is deductible from the value of the property in determining the taxable value. As in the case of other transfers, the consideration is considered purely from the standpoint of monetary value. Sentimental attachments and sufficiency of consideration from a purely legal standpoint do not enter into the picture. If the value of the transferred property exceeds the value of the consideration, the difference is included in the decedent's gross estate.[23] Dispositions of life estates and remainder interests, discussed below, may not cause inclusion of the property if a seller receives the actuarial value of the interest.

● *Transfers of Stock in Closely Held Corporations*

The retention of the right to vote (either *directly or indirectly*) shares of stock in what is called "a controlled corporation," by a person who has irrevocably transferred the stock for other than full consideration after June 22, 1976, is treated as the retention of the enjoyment of the transferred shares; thus, retention of the right causes the transferred shares to

---

[17] *L. Goldstone Est.*, 78 TC 1143, CCH Dec. 39,138.

[18] Rev. Rul. 70-155, 1970-1 CB 189.

[19] Rev. Rul. 78-409, 1978-2 CB 234.

[20] *J.C. Guynn*, CA-4, 71-1 USTC ¶ 12,742, 437 F2d 1148, rev'g and rem'g DC, 70-1 USTC ¶ 12,661, 309 FSupp 233. But see *Est. of S.H. Roemer*, 46 TCM 1176, CCH Dec. 40,384(M), TC Memo. 1983-509 (no implied agreement between mother and daughter).

[21] Reg. § 20.2036-1(b).

[22] *S. Horner, Exr.*, CtCls, 73-2 USTC ¶ 12,956, 485 F2d 596.

[23] Reg. § 20.2043-1.

be includible in such a donor's estate at death.[24] A corporation is a "controlled corporation" for purposes of this rule if, at any time after the transfer of the stock and during the three-year period ending on the date of the decedent's death, the decedent *owned* (ownership being determined by applying the "constructive ownership" rules of income tax Code Sec. 318), or *had the right* (either alone or in conjunction with any person) to vote stock possessing at least 20 percent of the total combined voting power of all classes of stock.[25] If the stock is not in a "controlled corporation," the stock is not includible in the gross estate of a decedent even if the decedent directly held the power to vote the transferred shares.

In determining whether a transferor owns at least 20 percent of the stock in a corporation, the indirect or constructive ownership rules are applied.[26] Under these rules, stock owned by the members of a transferor's family (spouse, children, grandchildren, and parents) is treated as being owned by the transferor. These rules can also apply to stock that is owned by (1) partnerships and estates, (2) trusts, and (3) corporations in which the transferor has an interest.

These rules preclude the use of a formerly popular planning device sanctioned by a 1972 U.S. Supreme Court decision that a decedent who made this type of transfer did not retain the right to enjoy the transferred stock by reason of his voting control over it, and that he did not retain the right to designate the persons who would enjoy the income from the stock (see ¶ 580) by reason of his ability to control corporate dividends.[27] The decedent retained the power to (1) vote the stock held by a trust, (2) veto the transfer by the trustee of any of the stock, and (3) remove the trustee and appoint another corporate trustee.

● *Estate Freezes*

As part of the Revenue Act of 1987 (P.L. 100-203), Code Sec. 2036(c) was enacted in an attempt to prevent perceived valuation abuses involving a strategy known as an "estate freeze." The "estate freeze" was an estate planning device whereby an older owner of a closely held business would retain an income interest in the company, usually preferred stock and certain liquidation rights, and transfer to younger members of the family an interest in the company, usually common stock, that was likely to appreciate in value. The value of the retained interests (e.g., liquidation rights) could easily be inflated, thus lowering the value of the interest transferred and reducing the amount of the taxable gift. Under the provisions of Code Sec. 2036(c), the post-transfer appreciation in value of certain transferred property interests was includible in the transferor's gross estate.

The Revenue Reconciliation Act of 1990 (P.L. 101-508) repealed Code Sec. 2036(c) retroactive to its original effective date (December 17, 1987) and enacted the Chapter 14 special valuation rules,[28] effective for transfers after October 8, 1990 (see ¶ 2500). The special valuation rules take a

---

[24] Code Sec. 2036(b)(1). For an example of indirect retention of voting rights, see Rev. Rul. 80-346, 1980-2 CB 271.

[25] Code Sec. 2036(b)(2).

[26] Code Sec. 318.

[27] *M.A. Byrum, Exrx. (M.C. Byrum Will)*, SCt, 72-2 USTC ¶ 12,859, 408 US 125.

[28] Code Sec. 2701 through Code Sec. 2704.

more direct approach by providing rules for valuing the transferred interest for gift tax purposes rather than focusing on the transferor's estate.

● *Dispositions of Life Estates and Remainder Interests*

On the theory that estate tax liability for a transfer with a retained life estate arises at the time of the transfer, the U.S. Court of Appeals for the Tenth Circuit has held that the subsequent sale of the retained life interest at its fair market value only reduced the value of the taxable property.[29] There still would be included in the gross estate of the transferor the value of the property less the purchase money paid for the life estate. Accordingly, under this reasoning, to remove the transferred property from her gross estate, the transferor must have received full and adequate consideration for the interest which would otherwise be included in her gross estate.

The U.S. Court of Appeals for the Tenth Circuit later limited this theory to transfers of property solely owned by the decedent.[30] Following the decision of the U.S. Court of Appeals for the Seventh Circuit,[31] the Tenth Circuit held that the transfer with retained life estates of jointly held property for which the decedent furnished the entire consideration (and which, therefore, would have been includible in his gross estate to the extent of its entire value if held at his death) required only the inclusion in decedent's gross estate of the value of his one-half interest in the property transferred. See ¶ 502 for tax treatment of "qualified joint interests" created or recreated after 1976.

With respect to the issue of valuing an interest for purposes of the bona fide sale exception, the U.S. Court of Appeals for the Federal Circuit has held that where a decedent sold a remainder interest in property and retained a life interest, the payment of the actuarial value of the remainder interest did not satisfy the exception. Thus, the value of the transferred interest was includible in the decedent's gross estate (offset by the amount of consideration received, as provided under Code Sec. 2043).[32] However, the U.S. Court of Appeals for the Third Circuit reversed a decision by the Tax Court and found that the consideration paid for a remainder interest in certain shares of stock was full and adequate consideration.[33] Thus, no part of the value of the shares was includible in the decedent's estate because her retained life interest ended at death.

● *Pre-1931 and Pre-1932 Transfers*

Special exceptions exist in the case of transfers made before March 4, 1931. The exceptions concern any of the rights described above that were retained for life or for any period that does not in fact end before the decedent's death. Similar exceptions exist with respect to transfers made before June 7, 1932, under which the rights were retained for a period not

[29] *C. Allen, Exr. (Allen Est.)*, CA-10, 61-2 USTC ¶ 12,032, 293 F2d 916, cert. denied, 368 US 944.

[30] *E. Heasty, Exr. (King Est.)*, CA-10, 67-1 USTC ¶ 12,442, 370 F2d 525, aff'g DC Kan., 65-1 USTC ¶ 12,304, 239 FSupp 345.

[31] *H. Glaser, Jr., Admr.*, CA-7, 62-2 USTC ¶ 12,094, 306 F2d 57, aff'g and rev'g DC Ind., 61-2 USTC ¶ 12,031, 196 FSupp 47.

[32] *G.S. Gradow*, CA-FC, 90-1 USTC ¶ 60,010, 897 F2d 516, aff'g ClsCt, 87-1 USTC ¶ 13,711, 11 ClsCt 808.

[33] *R. D'Ambrosio Est.*, CA-3, 96-2 USTC ¶ 60,252, rev'g and rem'g TC, 105 TC 252, CCH Dec. 50,903. See also, *J.M. Wheeler*, CA-5, 97-2 USTC ¶ 60,278, 116 F3d 749, which noted that selling a remainder interest for its actuarial value does not deplete a seller's estate.

ascertainable without reference to the decedent's death. Such pre-1931 and pre-1932 transfers are not includible in the estate of a decedent unless there is some other basis for taxability, such as the retention of other rights as well.

¶ 580 Right Retained to Designate Who Shall Possess or Enjoy

The retention of income, possession, use, or enjoyment of property requires inclusion of the value of the transferred property in the gross estate under Code Sec. 2036. A transfer also will be taxed under Code Sec. 2036 if a decedent reserved or retained the right, either alone or in conjunction with any other person or persons, to designate the persons who shall possess or enjoy the property or the income therefrom. The requirements as to the period for which such designated person retains such rights are the same as if the decedent retained those rights.[34]

Similarly, the same exceptions as to pre-1931 and pre-1932 transfers and the same means of escaping the tax by relinquishing rights exist (see ¶ 570). In addition, transfers made before June 7, 1932, are excepted if the decedent's right to govern enjoyment was reserved to the decedent in conjunction with any other person or persons. The courts, however, are not in agreement as to whether the transfer contemplated by the statute is limited to irrevocable transfers made prior to the above dates.

If a grantor creates an irrevocable trust for the benefit of other persons and acts as trustee or co-trustee, and the trustees have the power to accumulate or distribute and add trust income to trust principal, the value of the trust property and the accumulated trust income will be included in the decedent's gross estate.[35] Each accumulation of income represented a taxable transfer. The grantor-trustee's power to deny the beneficiaries the immediate enjoyment of that income was a retention of the power to designate the persons who would enjoy the income.

The IRS has attempted to apply the rationale of this case to situations where the grantor-trustee has not directly retained the power to accumulate or distribute income but, instead, has retained only certain administrative and managerial powers over the trust. Frequently, these administrative powers are called "boiler-plate" powers. The two most common of the types of such powers causing trouble for estates are (1) the right to allocate receipts and disbursements between trust income and principal and (2) the right to invest in "non-legal" investments. Most courts have held that the existence of these powers does not give the decedent the right to designate the persons who shall possess or enjoy the transferred property.[36] The common denominator that has led the courts to exclude these trusts has been the existence of state laws governing the duties of trustees toward income beneficiaries and remaindermen.

The IRS will include the value of irrevocable trusts in a grantor's estate where the trustee is given the power to accumulate or distribute income to beneficiaries and the grantor retains the right to appoint a successor trustee which includes himself.[37] The Tax Court has agreed in at

---

[34] Reg. § 20.2036-1(b).

[35] *C.E. O'Malley*, SCt, 66-1 USTC ¶ 12,388, 383 US 627.

[36] For example, see *R. Budd Est.*, 49 TC 468, CCH Dec. 28,841 (Acq.).

[37] Rev. Rul. 73-21, 1973-1 CB 405.

least one case.[38] However, the Tax Court has refused to follow this rule in the case of a trust set up by a Texas resident who was legally incompetent at death.[39] The IRS will not include the value of the assets of such a trust in the grantor's gross estate where the grantor merely retains the right to appoint a successor corporate trustee that was not related or subordinate to the grantor after the original trustee has resigned or been removed by judicial process.[40]

The Tax Court has held that a corporate trustee's power to distribute income and principal was not attributable to the grantor simply because of the grantor's ability to remove and replace one corporate trustee with another corporate trustee, without cause. Noting that a trustee has a duty to display complete loyalty to the interests of the beneficiary, the court would not include the trust property in the grantor's estate without evidence of fraudulent collusion.[41] In another case, the U.S. Court of Appeals for the Eighth Circuit concluded that a decedent had not retained dominion and control over property that the decedent transferred to a trust by reason of his right to remove and replace trustees with successor trustees who were not related or subordinate to the decedent.[42] In view of these decisions, the IRS ruled that a grantor's reservation of an unqualified power to change corporate trustees will not result in the inclusion of the trust corpus in the grantor's gross estate.[43]

¶ 585 Revocable Transfers

Property transferred during lifetime is includible in the decedent's estate if, at the time of the decedent's death, the enjoyment of the property is subject to change through the exercise of a power to alter, amend, revoke, or terminate by the decedent alone or by the decedent in conjunction with another person. The retention of a power in conjunction with "any person" is not limited to nonbeneficiaries.

Taxation will result even though the only effect of the exercise of the decedent's power to revoke would have been to accelerate the enjoyment of principal by the beneficiaries.[44] No tax will result, however, if the power can be exercised only with the consent of all parties having an interest, vested or contingent, in the transferred property.[45]

• *Powers Resulting in Taxability*

The courts often have had to determine what is a power to alter, amend, revoke, or terminate. They have decided that the following powers result in taxability:

(1) power to revoke or terminate the trust, whether such power results in a return of corpus to the settlor or acceleration of enjoyment by the remaindermen;

---

[38] *J.A. Alexander Est.*, 81 TC 757, CCH Dec. 40,554.

[39] *R.T. Reid Est.*, 71 TC 816, CCH Dec. 35,883.

[40] Rev. Rul. 77-182, 1977-1 CB 273, modified by Rev. Rul. 95-58, 1995-2 CB 191.

[41] *H.S. Wall Est.*, 101 TC 300, CCH Dec. 49,330.

[42] *J. Vak Est.*, CA-8, 92-2 USTC ¶ 60,110, rev'g and rem'g TC, 62 TCM 942, CCH Dec. 47,674(M), TC Memo. 1991-503.

[43] Rev. Rul. 95-58, 1995-2 CB 191, revoking Rev. Rul. 79-353, 1979-2 CB 325, and Rev. Rul. 81-51, 1981-1 CB 458, and modifying Rev. Rul. 77-182, 1977-1 CB 273.

[44] *City Bank Farmers Trust Co.*, SCt, 36-1 USTC ¶ 9001, 296 US 85.

[45] Reg. § 20.2038-1(a)(2).

(2) power to control and manage the corpus, except where such power is concerned only with mechanics or details—the designation of funds as income or principal, investment policy, the issuance of voting proxies, or other matters which do not alter the rights or interests of the beneficiaries;

(3) power to change beneficiaries or to vary the amounts distributable (except where the transfer was made prior to March 3, 1931, and the power is applicable only to income during decedent's lifetime);

(4) power to appoint by will or to change shares by will;

(5) power to revoke which exists by virtue of state law; and

(6) power to invade the corpus of a trust created by another for whose benefit the decedent created a similar trust.

If the powers involved are applicable only to a part of the trust, only that part is taxable.[46]

The fact that the transferor will not benefit by exercise of the power is not important so long as the transferor can affect the interests of beneficiaries. This includes the power to distribute or accumulate trust income. Capital gains by the trust and additions to it traceable to the decedent have the same status as original corpus. Additions by a decedent to trusts created by others are governed by decedent's right over the trusts even though the original corpus may not be taxable in his estate.

The IRS maintains that when a donor transfers property to a minor under a state "Uniform Gifts to Minors Act" or a "Model Gifts of Securities to Minors Act" or a "Uniform Transfers to Minors Act," and is acting as custodian of the custodial property at the date of death, the custodial property is includible in the custodian's gross estate.[47] This position has been uniformly sustained by the courts because a custodian has the right, under most uniform acts, to terminate the custodianship by paying over the income and principal to the minor beneficiaries at any time. If a parent transfers property and serves as custodian, the custodial property is also includible in the parent's gross estate, under Code Sec. 2036, because the parent can apply custodial funds in satisfaction of the legal obligation of support.[48] This rule has also been applied where the decedent and the decedent's spouse made reciprocal transfers to each other in custodianship for their parents.[49]

● *Powers Not Resulting in Taxability*

The courts have decided that the following do not constitute powers sufficient to cause taxability under Code Sec. 2038:

(1) power in other than the grantor to revoke the transfer or to return part of it to the grantor (but such transfers may be taxed as transfers intended to take effect at death; see ¶ 565);

---

[46] Reg. § 20.2038-1.

[47] Rev. Rul. 57-366, 1957-2 CB 618, and Rev. Rul. 70-348, 1970-2 CB 193.

[48] *H. Prudowsky Est.*, 55 TC 890, CCH Dec. 30,671, aff'd per curiam, CA-7, 72-2 USTC ¶ 12,870, 465 F2d 62.

[49] *Exchange Bank and Trust Co. of Florida*, CA-FC, 82-2 USTC ¶ 13,505, aff'g ClsCt, 82-1 USTC ¶ 13,444, 694 F2d 1261.

(2) certain powers contingent upon the happening of a certain event;

(3) powers as to mechanics or details only, such as powers to direct issuance of voting proxies, to help determine investment policies, and to direct investment and reinvestment of funds;

(4) power to add to corpus; and

(5) power over trusts created by others with funds not derived from the decedent and not supported by similar trusts created by others.

If the decedent-transferor was unable to relinquish a power because of the existence of a mental disability for a continuous period beginning before October 1, 1947, and ending with death after August 16, 1954, the retained power to revoke or amend will not result in tax.

● *Split Gift Election*

Code Sec. 2038 contemplates a transfer by the decedent of the decedent's own property before death. Thus, individually owned securities transferred by the husband of a decedent to himself as custodian for his minor daughter under the Uniform Gifts to Minors Act and held by the decedent as successor custodian at the time of her death were not includible in the decedent's gross estate for estate tax purposes even though a split-gift election was made under Code Sec. 2513 and the decedent was considered a donor of half the value of the securities for gift tax purposes.[50]

¶ 590 Exercisability of Power

If the retained power comes within the scope of Code Sec. 2038, it is taxable whether exercisable by the decedent as trustee or as transferor, alone,[51] or in conjunction with trustees or outsiders. The transfer is taxable as long as any beneficiary, vested or contingent, is excluded from the group that, with the transferor, can exercise any of the powers.[52]

If the transfer was made on or before June 22, 1936, the value of an interest in property is not includible in the transferor's gross estate unless the power to alter, amend, revoke, or terminate was reserved at the time of transfer.[53] A power that is acquired by the decedent from the trustees by being appointed as a trustee some time after the transfer and not under provisions in the instrument of transfer will not result in taxability.

¶ 595 Relinquishment of Powers Within Three Years of Death

A retained power to alter, amend, revoke, or terminate a property interest that is relinquished after 1976 and within three years of the death of the holder of the power will require that the value of the property be included in the holder's gross estate.[54] However, effective for decedents dying after August 5, 1997, a transfer of property from a revocable trust

---

[50] Rev. Rul. 74-556, 1974-2 CB 300.

[51] See *S.A. Levin Est.*, 90 TC 723, CCH Dec. 44,706, holding that the retained power need not be exercisable by the decedent in his individual capacity; the ability to exercise it as a member of the board of directors of a company in which he held the controlling interest made it taxable.

[52] Reg. § 20.2038-1(a)(2).

[53] Reg. § 20.2038-1(c).

[54] Code Sec. 2035.

within three years of the transfer of such property to the trust will not be included in the decedent's gross estate.[55] Under prior law, the U.S. Court of Appeals for the Eighth Circuit had held that irrevocable fractional interests in the corpus of a revocable trust that were assigned by a decedent to her children within three years of death were not includible in the decedent's gross estate. The fractional interests portions of the trust functioned in the same way as if the decedent had withdrawn the fractions from the initial revocable trust and transferred them to a new irrevocable trust.[56]

¶ 600 Reciprocal Transfers

Estate taxation cannot be avoided through the use of reciprocal transfers whereby two taxpayers make transfers in trust to each other of similar economic rights under substantially identical terms. Thus, two persons cannot escape the estate tax by giving the other a right that would have resulted in an estate tax if the transferor had retained it for himself [57] (see ¶ 170). The U.S. Court of Appeals for the Sixth Circuit has held, however, that if the fiduciary powers provided to each transferee do not rise to the level of a retained economic benefit, then the value of the trusts is not included in the transferors' gross estates.[58]

¶ 605 Valuation Date

Property transferred by the decedent during life but included in the decedent's gross estate must be valued as of the date of the decedent's death or, if the alternate valuation date is chosen, in accordance with Code Sec. 2032 rules (see ¶ 105). If only a portion of the property is so transferred as to come within the terms of the statute, a corresponding proportion of the value of the property is included in the value of the gross estate. Because Code Sec. 2036 and Code Sec. 2038 overlap, the IRS will apply the Code section that results in the greatest amount being included in the gross estate.[59]

If the transferee makes additions or enhancements to the property, the enhanced value of the property at the valuation date due to such additions or enhancements is not includible. Because the additions were not made by the decedent, they are not deemed to be part of the transferred property. When only a portion of the value of the property is includible, the value of the whole must still be disclosed on Schedule G (Transfers During Decedent's Life) of Form 706 under the column headed "Description," together with an explanation of the proportionate inclusion.[60]

¶ 610 Transfers for a Consideration

The value of property transferred by a decedent during life for adequate and full consideration is not includible in the decedent's gross

---

[55] Code Sec. 2035(e), as amended by P.L. 105-34.

[56] *E. Kisling Est.*, CA-8, 94-2 USTC ¶ 60,176, rev'g and rem'g TC, 65 TCM 2956, CCH Dec. 49,097(M), TC Memo. 1993-262 (Acq.) (*H. McNeely*, CA-8, 94-1 USTC ¶ 60,155, followed).

[57] *J.P. Grace Est.*, SCt, 69-1 USTC ¶ 12,609, 395 US 316.

[58] *J. Green Est.*, CA-6, 95-2 USTC ¶ 60,216, 68 F2d 151, aff'g unreported decision.

[59] *H.B. Joy, Jr., Exr.*, CA-6, 69-1 USTC ¶ 12,570, 403 F2d 419, aff'g DC Mich., 67-2 USTC ¶ 12,482, 272 FSupp 544.

[60] Instructions for Form 706 (Rev. July 1998), p. 12.

estate. To constitute an exchange or sale for adequate and full consideration in money or money's worth, the exchange or sale must have been made in good faith. The price must have been an adequate and full equivalent and reducible to a money value. Transfers of property during lifetime made within three years of death (in the case of a decedent dying before 1982) or with rights retained (Code Sec. 2035 through Code Sec. 2038) and otherwise taxable powers of appointment (Code Sec. 2041) for less than full and adequate consideration are includible in the transferor's gross estate to the extent of the excess of the fair market value of the property (as of the valuation date) over the price or value of consideration received by the decedent.[61] The adequacy of the consideration received for a transfer is determined as of the date of the transfer and not at a later date, such as the date of the transferor's death.

For estate tax purposes (except for determining deductibility of claims against the estate; see ¶ 800), the relinquishment or promised relinquishment of dower, curtesy, a statutory estate created in lieu of dower or curtesy, or other marital rights in the decedent's property or estate is not consideration in money or money's worth.[62]

A release of support rights, pursuant to a divorce decree, is consideration to the extent of the value of the rights as determined on a case-by-case basis.[63] The IRS has ruled, in a National Office Technical Advice Memorandum, that a decedent's gross estate included the value of farmland transferred by him to his children pursuant to a property settlement agreement because the decedent had retained a life estate in the property and the transfer was not made for adequate consideration. The transfer of the remainder interest in the property to the children was deemed not to have been a part of the release of the decedent's obligation to support his minor children since the divorce decree already provided for child support payments that adequately satisfied the children's need for support. Accordingly, the IRS concluded that the transfer was not made for consideration, but, rather, was based upon the decedent's donative intent.[64]

Whether the consideration paid by a decedent to his father in conjunction with the father's transfer of stock into a trust naming the decedent as life beneficiary constituted a transfer with a retained life estate was decided by the U.S. Court of Appeals for the Sixth Circuit.[65] A payment made by a son in 1941 to his father in exchange for shares of stock, which were thereafter used to fund a trust for the benefit of the son for life and his wife and children after his death, constituted a purchase by the son of an undivided interest in approximately 11 percent of the value of the trust assets. Accordingly, the appellate court concluded that 11 percent of the value of the trust assets on the date of the son's death was includible in his gross estate as property transferred by him during his life subject to his retained life estate.

In determining, for estate tax purposes, whether the decedent received, in exchange for property transferred, property approximately

---

[61] Code Sec. 2043.

[62] Code Sec. 2043(b).

[63] Rev. Rul. 68-379, 1968-2 CB 414, Rev. Rul. 60-160, 1960-1 CB 374, and Rev. Rul. 80-82, 1980-1 CB 209. *J.H. Scholl Est.*, 88 TC 1265, CCH Dec. 43,918.

[64] IRS Technical Advice Memorandum 8526003, no date given, CCH IRS LETTER RULINGS REPORTS.

[65] *D.J. Mahoney, Jr., Exr.*, CA-6, 87-2 USTC ¶ 13,737, 831 F2d 641, rev'g DC Ohio, 86-1 USTC ¶ 13,653, cert. denied, 6-13-88.

equal to it in value, the transactions he made in the years just before his death are particularly subject to scrutiny. Agreements whereby the decedent has transferred property to another in return for a promise to support and care for the decedent have been found to be supported by adequate and full consideration.[66]

¶ 615 Valuation and Description on Return

Reportable lifetime transfers are, for the most part, listed on one special schedule—Schedule G (Transfers During Decedent's Life)—without regard to the kind of property transferred. Lifetime transfers of real property and certain lifetime transfers of insurance are reportable under this schedule, even though there are other schedules which are specifically concerned with the kind of property transferred. The other schedules are largely confined to property interests owned by the decedent at the time of death. Although various lifetime transfers are all reportable in the same schedule, the principles governing valuation and description of the transferred property are the same as those of the other schedules.

Copies of Form 709 (United States Gift (and Generation-Skipping Transfer) Tax Return) relating to the lifetime transfers should be attached to Schedule G. In addition, gift taxes paid on transfers made within three years of death are to be reported on the schedule (see ¶ 555).

¶ 625 Instruments Evidencing Transfers

If a transfer, by trust or otherwise, was made by a written instrument, a copy must be filed with the return. If the instrument is of public record, the copy should be certified; if not of record, the copy should be verified. The name of the transferee, date and form of the transfer, and a complete description of the property should be set forth in this schedule. Rents and other income must be included.

---

[66] *S.A. Bergan Est.*, 1 TC 543, CCH Dec. 12,954 (Acq.).

¶ 635 Filled-In Schedule G

The filled-in Schedule G, Form 706 (Rev. July 1998), relates to the fact situation of a person who dies on January 1, 1998, with an estate tax return due within nine months (without extensions). Schedule G must be filed only if the decedent made transfers of the type reportable on the schedule (see ¶ 73).

Form 706 (Rev. 7-98)

Estate of: James X. Diversey

SCHEDULE G — Transfers During Decedent's Life

(If you elect section 2032A valuation, you must complete Schedule G and Schedule A-1.)

Item number	Description For securities, give CUSIP number.	Alternate valuation date	Alternate value	Value at date of death
A.	Gift tax paid by the decedent or the estate for all gifts made by the decedent or his or her spouse within 3 years before the decedent's death (section 2035(b))	XXXXX		0
B.	Transfers includible under section 2035(a), 2036, 2037, or 2038:			
1	On Feb. 15, 1995, decedent transferred securities with a value of $24,000 in trust to the First National Bank of Homewood, Homewood, IL. The decedent retained the right to the income for life and directed that, at his death, the corpus was to be paid 1/2 to his sister (Ann Fagin) and 1/4 to each of his sons. On the date of death, the assets consisted of:			
	Securities			40,000
	Cash			10,768
	Dividends on above securities payable to holders of record on or before date of death			1,600
	Total from continuation schedules (or additional sheets) attached to this schedule			
	TOTAL. (Also enter on Part 5, Recapitulation, page 3, at Item 7.)			52,368

Chapter 16

POWERS OF APPOINTMENT

¶ 650 Powers of Appointment

The value of all property over which a decedent possessed a general power of appointment at death is includible in the decedent's gross estate.[1] The term "power of appointment" refers to a power given to the possessor by another, rather than to a power that has been created and retained by the same person. It authorizes the possessor of the power to control, with certain limitations, the ultimate disposition of the property subject to the power. The person who receives the power is usually referred to as the donee of the power.

Because, under some kinds of powers, the donee has almost as much authority over property as an owner of such property would have, the creation of a power of appointment could, in the absence of special tax treatment, afford an easy means of preventing the application of estate taxes to the estate of the donee—taxes that would be fully applicable if the property were the donee's own or had been given to the donee in fee. Code Sec. 2041 provides specifically for the taxing of property subject to powers of appointment, the provisions being based largely upon how nearly the power given to the donee resembles complete ownership of the property.

Only powers defined as "general powers of appointment" result in taxability, except in certain very special cases. Basically, for tax purposes, a "general power of appointment" is one that can be exercised by the donee in favor of the donee, the donee's estate, or the creditors of the donee or the donee's estate.[2] State law is applied in determining whether the decedent has a "general power of appointment."

"Power of appointment" is defined, for estate tax purposes, to include all powers that are in substance and effect powers of appointment, regardless of the wording used in creating the power and regardless of local property law connotations. Thus, a power in a life tenant to appropriate or consume the principal of a trust may be a power of appointment.

All property over which a decedent possessed a power of appointment must be reported on Schedule H (Powers of Appointment) of Form 706. Schedule H must be filed if the decedent's gross estate exceeds the applicable credit amount (see ¶ 73). If Schedule H is filed, certified or verified copies of the instrument granting the power and of any instrument by which the power was exercised or released must be attached to the Schedule. All powers of appointment must be reported even if the estate contends that property subject to a particular power is not includible in the gross estate.

---

[1] Code Sec. 2041.

[2] Reg. § 20.2041-1(c).

¶ 652 General Powers of Appointment

In general, only powers defined as *general* powers of appointment can result in tax. A "general power of appointment" is defined as "a power which is exercisable in favor of the decedent, his estate, his creditors, or the creditors of his estate."[3] However, there are exceptions, and a general power of appointment does *not* include:

(1) A power to consume, invade, or appropriate property for the benefit of the decedent, which is limited by an ascertainable standard relating to the health, education, support, or maintenance of the decedent.

(2) A power created on or before October 21, 1942, which is exercisable by the decedent only in conjunction with another person.

(3) A power created after October 21, 1942, which is exercisable by the decedent only in conjunction with the creator of the power, or with a person having a substantial interest in the property, subject to the power, where this interest is adverse to the exercise of the power in decedent's favor. If the power may be exercised both in favor of the decedent and of the persons whose consent the decedent must have, the power is general to the extent of the decedent's fractional interest in it.

A power of appointment created by will is, in general, considered as created on the date of the testator's death.[4] A power created by an instrument effective during the life of the creator is considered as created on the date the instrument takes effect. This is so even though at that time the power may not be exercisable, may be revocable, or the identity of the holder may not be ascertainable. If the holder of a power exercises it by creating a second power, the second power is considered as created at the time of the exercise of the first. Generally, property subject to a general power of appointment is includible in a decedent's gross estate even if at the time of death the decedent was an adjudicated incompetent, at least in the absence of a showing that the adjudication of incompetency barred exercise of the power by any person in any capacity.[5] Similarly, it has been held that property subject to a general power of appointment was includible in the decedent's gross estate even though the decedent, as a minor, was precluded by state law from exercising the power.[6]

It should be noted that the general power of appointment under Code Sec. 2041 is not necessarily equivalent to a power of appointment given to a decedent's surviving spouse in connection with a life estate. The IRS has ruled that property that passed to a trust for the benefit of a decedent's surviving spouse did not qualify for a marital deduction even though the spouse received a life estate in the trust corpus and a power to appoint the trust corpus to herself or her creditors because the trustee could prevent the spouse from exercising the power. Thus, for marital deduction pur-

---

[3] Reg. § 20.2041-1(c).

[4] Reg. § 20.2041-1(e).

[5] Rev. Rul. 75-350, 1975-2 CB 366; *W.R. Boeving*, CA-8, 81-2 USTC ¶ 13,415; *A.L. Gilchrist Est.*, CA-5, 80-2 USTC ¶ 13,378, 630 F2d 340; *F. Alperstein Est.*, CA-2, 80-1 USTC ¶ 13,326, 613 F2d 1213, cert. denied, 446 US 918; *Pennsylvania Bank and Trust Co., Exr.*, CA-3, 79-1 USTC ¶ 13,299, 597 F2d 382, cert. denied, 444 US 980; and IRS Technical Advice Memorandum 9344004, 7-13-93, CCH IRS LETTER RULINGS REPORTS.

[6] *N.E. Rosenblatt Est.*, CA-10, 80-2 USTC ¶ 13,374, 633 F2d 176.

poses, the power was not exercisable "alone and in all events." However, because the trustee did not have a substantial interest in the trust adverse to that of the spouse, the value of the trust corpus was includible in the spouse's gross estate as property subject to a general power of appointment.[7]

¶ 653 Powers Limited by Ascertainable Standard

A taxable general power does not include a power to consume, invade or appropriate income and corpus for the donee's benefit if the power is limited by an ascertainable standard relating to the health, education, support, or maintenance of the decedent.[8] In short, the holder's duty regarding use of the power must be reasonably measurable in terms of the holder's needs for health, education, or support—or any combination of them.

The words "support" and "maintenance" are considered synonymous. Their meaning is not limited to the bare necessities of life. For example, a power of appointment will be regarded as limited by the necessary standard if it is exercisable for the holder's (1) support, (2) support in reasonable comfort, (3) maintenance in health and reasonable comfort, (4) support in the holder's accustomed manner of living, (5) education, including college and professional education, (6) health, or (7) medical, dental, hospital and nursing expenses.

However, a power to use property for the comfort, welfare, or happiness of the holder of the power does not meet the required ascertainable standard for invasion. Under Illinois law, the word "comfort" was deemed to be an ascertainable standard that refers to maintaining someone in the station of life to which the person has become accustomed.[9] In determining the existence of an ascertainable standard, it is immaterial that the trust agreement may or may not require the beneficiary first to exhaust other income.[10]

Generally, the extent of a decedent's interest is governed by state law.[11] The U.S. Court of Appeals for the Tenth Circuit has held that a decedent's power to invade the corpus of a trust for her benefit "in case of emergency or illness" was not a general power of appointment, under New Mexico law, because its exercise was limited by an ascertainable standard. Accordingly, the court held that the value of the trust corpus was not includible in the decedent's gross estate.[12]

The U.S. Court of Appeals for the Sixth Circuit has held similarly that a decedent who was trustee and life beneficiary of a trust did not have a general power of appointment over the trust because her "right to encroach" upon the corpus was limited by an ascertainable standard under Tennessee law.[13] However, the U.S. Court of Appeals for the Seventh Circuit has held that decedent who was the trustee and one of the

---

[7] Rev. Rul. 82-156, 1982-2 CB 216.

[8] Reg. § 20.2041-1(c)(2).

[9] *V.I. Strauss Est.*, 69 TCM 2825, CCH Dec. 50,680(M), TC Memo. 1995-248.

[10] Reg. § 20.2041-1(c).

[11] But see IRS Technical Advice Memorandum 8339004, 6-14-83, CCH IRS LETTER RULINGS REPORTS (state supreme court decision not followed because the state court proceeding was not adversarial and, based on applicable case law and an analysis of the words used in the invasion clause, the decedent's power of appointment was general).

[12] *I.M. Sowell Est.*, CA-10, 83-1 USTC ¶ 13,526, 708 F2d 1564.

[13] *P.W. Finlay, Exr.*, CA-6, 85-1 USTC ¶ 13,604, 752 F2d 246.

beneficiaries of a trust established under the terms of her predeceased husband's will held a general power of appointment over the trust corpus because she was authorized to use so much of the principal as she deemed appropriate for her maintenance and support. Language giving the decedent the right to use the property "for whatever purpose she desires" was found by the court to negate any ascertainable standard under Wisconsin law.[14]

¶ 655 Taxable Powers Created After October 21, 1942

A general power created after October 21, 1942, and held by the donee will result in taxability of the subject property in the donee's estate, if the power is held until death, whether or not the donee exercises it by will. The exercise or release of the power during the donee's lifetime will be deemed a transfer for gift tax purposes.[15]

Estate tax liability will also result if the exercise or release was effected under circumstances which would have resulted in tax under Code Sec. 2035 through Code Sec. 2038 if the property had been the decedent's own.[16]

● *Release, Lapse and Disclaimer of Powers*

Release of a power of appointment created after October 21, 1942, will result in taxation just as completely as exercise of the power by will or possession at death of an unexercised power. A release of a power need not be formal or express in character. Failure to exercise a power of appointment within a specified time, so that the power lapses, is considered a release of the power.[17]

However, a lapse of the power in any calendar year during the decedent's life is considered a release for estate tax purposes only to the extent that the property over which the power existed exceeded the greater of $5,000 or five percent of the value, at the time of the lapse, of the assets out of which the exercise could have been satisfied.

> ***Example:*** In 1998, Jim Dorsey transferred $200,000 worth of securities in trust with provision for payment of income to his son, George, for life and the remainder to George's issue. George was also given a right to withdraw $15,000 a year from the trust fund (which neither increased nor decreased in value prior to George's death). The right is noncumulative, so that George can never withdraw more than $15,000 in any one year, even if he fails to withdraw the full amount in a preceding year.
>
> The failure to exercise his power of withdrawal in any single calendar year is considered a release to the extent that $15,000 exceeds five percent of the trust fund. Assuming that George fails to exercise his power of withdrawal for 1998, $5,000 ($15,000 – $10,000) is deemed to be a taxable transfer to the trust from George with a

---

[14] *Independence Bank Waukesha, N.A.*, CA-7, 85-1 USTC ¶ 13,613, 761 F2d 442. See also IRS Technical Advice Memorandum 8601003, 9-20-85, CCH IRS LETTER RULINGS REPORTS (decedent's right to invade the trust corpus for "any special need" that might arise was a general power of appointment).

[15] Code Sec. 2514(b).

[16] Code Sec. 2041(a)(2).

[17] Code Sec. 2041(b)(2).

retained right to income. (The $5,000 stays in the trust fund of which George is life income beneficiary.) The remaining $10,000 is not considered a release because it falls within the five-percent rule. The taxable proportion created by the release in 1998 at death is 1/40 ($5,000 ÷ $200,000) of the value of the trust corpus on the date of death (or alternate valuation date). If the value of the trust principal remained at $200,000 at George's death, $5,000 (1/40 × $200,000) would be included in his gross estate.

If the failure to exercise a power, such as a right of withdrawal, occurs in more than a single year, the proportion of the property over which the power lapsed, which is to be treated as a taxable disposition, must be determined separately for each year. Thus, in the Example above, if George had failed to exercise the power of withdrawal in three separate calendar years, $15,000 would be included in his gross estate, assuming the value of the corpus subject to the power remained at $200,000. The aggregate of the taxable proportions for all years is includible in the holder's gross estate, limited only by the aggregate value of the assets out of which an exercise of the power could have been satisfied on the applicable valuation date.[18] In addition, if in the year of death, the power has not been exercised and has not lapsed, the entire amount for which the power may be exercised is includible in the decedent's gross estate.

A widow's unexercised right, during the statutory period, to take against her husband's estate does not constitute an unexercised general power of appointment within the meaning of Code Sec. 2041 because the failure to assert the inchoate right constitutes a complete and effective disclaimer or renunciation of a power of appointment by operation of law.[19]

- *Post-1976 Disclaimers*

A post-1976 "qualified disclaimer" of a general power of appointment is not a release of the power and does not constitute a taxable gift. A "qualified disclaimer" is based on federal, rather than state, requirements [20] (see ¶ 2009 for details).

- *Pre-1977 Disclaimers*

A pre-1977 disclaimer or renunciation of a general power of appointment is not considered to be a release of the power.[21] In the absence of facts to the contrary, the failure to renounce or disclaim a power within a reasonable time after learning of its existence will be presumed to constitute an acceptance of the power. A disclaimer or renunciation of a power that is unequivocal and meets the requirements of local law will not result in a taxable gift.

- *Creation of New Power*

If a donee by will or by a lifetime transfer exercises a power of appointment (general or special) created after October 21, 1942, by creating another power, taxability will result. The property subject to the power will be included in the original donee's estate if, under local law, the power can be exercised to postpone the vesting of any estate or interest in

---

[18] Reg. § 20.2041-3(d)(5).

[19] Rev. Rul. 74-492, 1974-2 CB 298.

[20] Code Sec. 2046 and Code Sec. 2518.

[21] Reg. § 20.2041-3(d)(6).

such property, or suspend the absolute ownership or power of alienation of such property, for a period ascertainable without regard to the date of the creation of the first power.[22]

● *Avoidance of Tax*

A donee of a power of appointment does have some measure of control over whether the property subject to a general power will be included in the donee's gross estate at death. The donee may renounce or disclaim the power when it first comes to the donee's attention. If the donee follows either of these courses, the action will not create either estate or gift tax liability. The requirements for a federal "qualified disclaimer" are described at ¶ 2009.

A donee may escape estate tax liability by releasing or by exercising the power during life, only if the donee does not reserve rights that would cause a transfer of the donee's own property during life to be included in the gross estate. Generally, a release or exercise within three years of death will not result in inclusion of the property subject to the power in the decedent's gross estate in the case of decedents dying after 1981. For rules applicable to exercise or release of powers in the case of decedents dying in earlier years, see ¶ 555. When the donee seeks to keep the property out of the donee's own estate other than by a renunciation or disclaimer, the donee must consider the application of the gift tax law (see ¶ 2162) to his actions.[23]

¶ 665 Powers Created Before October 22, 1942

As to powers created on or before October 21, 1942, only general powers that are exercised can result in tax.[24] Under no circumstances is it necessary for the donee of the power to release it to keep it out of the estate.

If the donee does not exercise a pre-October 22, 1942 general power, and whether or not the donee exercises a limited or special power, no tax will result, except in one special case discussed below. Under a corresponding provision of the gift tax law (Code Sec. 2514), a complete release of a pre-October 22, 1942 general power will not result in gift tax liability or generation-skipping transfer tax consequences.[25]

If a general power of appointment created on or before October 21, 1942, is partially released so that it no longer is a general power of appointment, under certain circumstances the subsequent exercise of the power is not deemed to be the exercise of a general power of appointment. However, such partial release must have been made:

(1) before November 1, 1951; or

(2) if, on October 21, 1942, the donee of such power was under a legal disability to release the power, then within six months after the termination of such legal disability.

---

[22] Reg. § 20.2041-3(e).

[23] Code Sec. 2514.

[24] Code Sec. 2041(a).

[25] IRS Letter Ruling 9732034, 5-15-97, CCH IRS LETTER RULINGS REPORTS.

¶ 670 Instruments Granting Power

If the decedent at any time possessed a power of appointment, a certified or verified copy of the instrument granting the power, together with a certified or verified copy of any instrument by which the power was exercised or released, must be filed with the return. These copies must be filed even though the executor feels that the power is not a general power of appointment or that the property is not otherwise includible in the gross estate.[26]

[26] Instructions for Form 706 (Rev. July 1998), p. 12.

¶ 675 Filled-In Schedule H

Schedule H must be filed only if the decedent ever possessed, released or exercised any general power of appointment.

The filled-in Schedule H, Form 706 (Rev. July 1998), relates to the fact situation of a person who dies on January 1, 1998, with an estate tax return due within nine months (without extensions).

SCHEDULE H — Powers of Appointment

(Include "5 and 5 lapsing" powers (section 2041(b)(2)) held by the decedent.)

(If you elect section 2032A valuation, you must complete Schedule H and Schedule A-1.)

Item number	Description	Alternate valuation date	Alternate value	Value at date of death
1	Securities held by the Sixth National Bank of Chicago, IL in a testamentary trust created by William Diversey, decedent's father, who died Nov.10,1962. Decedent was granted a general power of appointment that he still possessed, unexercised, on the date of his death. Securities are listed on the attached supplement.			20,000
	Total from continuation schedules (or additional sheets) attached to this schedule			
	TOTAL. (Also enter on Part 5, Recapitulation, page 3, at item 8.)			20,000

(If more space is needed, attach the continuation schedule from the end of this package or additional sheets of the same size.)
(The instructions to Schedules G and H are in the separate instructions.)

Schedule G and H — Page 21

Chapter 17

ANNUITIES

¶ 700 General Requirements

Subject to certain limited exceptions (see ¶ 735, ¶ 737, and ¶ 739), all or a portion of an annuity or other payment receivable by any beneficiary by reason of surviving the decedent is includible in a decedent's gross estate.[1] The annuity or other payment is not taxable under the annuity rules unless it is payable under a contract or agreement and the following four factors exist:

(1) The contract or agreement is not a policy of insurance on the life of the decedent.

(2) The contract or agreement was entered into after March 3, 1931.

(3) The annuity or other payment is receivable by the beneficiary by reason of the beneficiary's having survived the decedent.

(4) Under the contract or agreement—

(a) an annuity or other payment was payable to the decedent, either alone or in conjunction with another, for the decedent's life or for any period not ascertainable without reference to the decedent's death or for any period which did not in fact end before the decedent's death, *or*

(b) the decedent possessed the right to receive the annuity or other payment, either alone or in conjunction with another, for the decedent's life or for any period not ascertainable without reference to the decedent's death or for any period which did not in fact end before the decedent's death.

The amount to be included in the gross estate is the value at the decedent's death of the annuity or other payment receivable by the survivor. It is immaterial whether the annuity or other payment to the survivor is payable in a lump sum or in installments. If payable in installments, it is immaterial whether the installments are in the same

[1] Code Sec. 2039(a); Reg. § 20.2039-1.

amount as, or in a greater or lesser amount than, the annuity or payments to the decedent.

Annuities may be includible under other provisions of the Internal Revenue Code. For example, if an annuitant retained the right to have any payments due after the annuitant's death paid to the annuitant's estate or to persons whom the annuitant might subsequently designate, the amounts payable could be included as property in which the annuitant had an interest at the time of death.[2] They could also be treated as transfers in which the annuitant had reserved the power to alter, amend or revoke.[3] The relinquishment of an annuitant's additional rights within three years of death would cause inclusion in the annuitant's gross estate.

¶710 "Annuity" Defined

The term "annuity" includes periodic payments for a specified period of time. The following are examples of contracts (but not necessarily the only forms of contracts) for payments that constitute annuities or other payments for the purpose of inclusion in Schedule I (Annuities): [4]

(1) A contract under which the decedent immediately before death was receiving or was entitled to receive, for the duration of the decedent's life, an annuity, or other stipulated payments that were to continue after the decedent's death to a designated, surviving beneficiary.

(2) A contract under which the decedent immediately before death was receiving or was entitled to receive, together with another person for their joint lives, an annuity or other stipulated payment to continue to the survivor following the death of either.

(3) A contract or agreement entered into by the decedent and the decedent's employer. Under the contract the decedent immediately before death and following retirement was receiving, or was entitled to receive, an annuity or other stipulated payment. Payments to the decedent were for the duration of the decedent's life. Thereafter, payments were to a designated beneficiary, if the beneficiary survived the decedent. (It is immaterial whether the payments after the decedent's death are fixed by the contract or subject to an option or election exercised or exercisable by the decedent.)

(4) A contract or agreement entered into by the decedent and the decedent's employer. At the decedent's death, prior to retirement or prior to the expiration of a stated period of time, an annuity or other payment was payable to a designated surviving beneficiary.

(5) A contract or agreement under which the decedent immediately before death was receiving or was entitled to receive an annuity or other payment for a stated period of time, with the annuity or other payment to continue to a designated, surviving beneficiary upon the decedent's death prior to the expiration of such period.

---

[2] Code Sec. 2033.

[3] Code Sec. 2038.

[4] Reg. § 20.2039-1(b).

¶715 Types of Payments Involved

In determining whether amounts payable under an annuity contract following the death of a primary annuitant are taxable under Code Sec. 2039, the exact method of payment following death is seldom important. It does not matter whether the payments that accrue following death are to be in the nature of:

(1) a continuing annuity to another person or persons;

(2) a periodic payment (whether fixed in number, duration, or total amount);

(3) a lump sum based upon the difference between the cost of the annuity and the total payments to the primary beneficiary; or

(4) a lump sum fixed in amount without regard to how much the primary annuitant received during the annuitant's lifetime.

The tests for includibility revolve around the rights of the primary annuitant. In addition to the annuitant's right to an annuity, the question of who paid for the annuity is important. The value of the benefits payable after the death of the primary annuitant will, however, vary with the nature of the payments.

Sometimes there are payments due that accrued to the primary annuitant before the annuitant's death. These payments generally become payable to the decedent's estate and are automatically included in the gross estate as property in which the decedent had an interest at the time of death. They are reported as miscellaneous property on Schedule F (Other Miscellaneous Property Not Reportable Under Any Other Schedule).

¶720 Primary Annuities Purchased by Decedent as Annuitant

Proceeds of an annuity contract payable after the death of the purchaser and primary annuitant are includible in the annuitant's gross estate for estate tax purposes. They are includible whether they are paid to the estate or to a named beneficiary. It is immaterial whether they represent payments due to the primary annuitant or payments due only after the annuitant's death. An annuity purchased by a deceased primary annuitant before March 4, 1931, is excludable from a decedent's gross estate under Code Sec. 2039.

- *Partial Payments by Others*

If the primary annuitant did not pay the entire purchase price of the annuity, that part of the value of amounts payable after the primary annuitant's death that is attributable to the part of the price paid by persons other than the primary annuitant may be excluded from the primary annuitant's gross estate.[5]

- *Death Before First Payment*

Even if the primary annuitant did not receive any payments under the annuity contract because of death prior to the date when the first payment was to be made, the payments after the annuitant's death are

[5] Reg. § 20.2039-1(c).

taxable. They are taxable to the same extent as if the annuitant had lived to receive the first payment. The amount payable after the annuitant's death is includible in the gross estate in the proportion in which the annuitant provided the purchase price for the annuities.

● *Partial Payment by Employer*

The portion (if any) of the purchase price paid by an employer or former employer, under a "nonqualified" benefit plan, is deemed to have been paid by the primary annuitant if made by reason of employment.[6] This results whether the employer made the payment directly or through an employee's trust or fund forming part of a pension, annuity, retirement, bonus, or profit-sharing plan. Totally voluntary payments made by a company to its employee's widow were not taxable as annuities because they were not payable to the employee during the employee's lifetime[7] (see ¶ 733).

See ¶ 735 and ¶ 737 for a discussion of the includibility of annuities payable under a qualified plan or trust, Keogh plan or an individual retirement account.

¶ 725 Annuities Not Purchased by Decedent

The annuity provisions of Code Sec. 2039 do not apply to annuities treated as having been purchased by someone other than the primary annuitant. Nor do they apply to portions of annuities purchased by another where the decedent, as primary annuitant, did pay a part of the purchase price. Such annuities, or parts of annuities, are governed by other provisions in the estate tax law.[8]

The taxability of any after-death payments under annuities, or portions of annuities, deemed purchased by persons other than the decedent depends upon the rights which the primary annuitant possesses (in addition to the right to receive an annuity for life). If the primary annuitant has no rights beyond the mere right to receive an annuity, any interest in the annuity contract or other property from which the payments stemmed ceases with the annuitant's death. Nothing remains to be taxed in the gross estate.

If any payments are to be made to the annuitant's estate after the annuitant's death, or to persons whom the annuitant names, these payments may be included in the annuitant's gross estate as property in which the annuitant had an interest at the time of death,[9] or as property over which the annuitant had a power of appointment.[10]

¶ 730 Service Member's Survivorship Annuities

The Tax Reform Act of 1984 (P.L. 98-369), repealed an exclusion, with respect to decedents dying after December 31, 1984, for the value of annuities receivable by a surviving spouse or certain child beneficiaries under the Retired Serviceman's Family Protection Plan or the Survivor Benefit Plan.[11] However, the repeal does not affect a decedent whose

---

[6] Reg. § 20.2039-1(c).

[7] *W.E. Barr Est.*, 40 TC 227, CCH Dec. 26,103 (Acq.).

[8] Reg. § 20.2039-1(a).

[9] Code Sec. 2033.

[10] Code Sec. 2041.

[11] Code Sec. 2039(c), prior to repeal by P.L. 98-369.

benefit was in pay status on December 31, 1984, and who, prior to July 18, 1984, made an irrevocable election to designate the form of the benefit distribution.[12]

¶733 Employees' Death Benefits

Many employers pay surviving spouses of employees sums of money that are commonly called death benefits. Such death benefits may be paid by reason of a contract with the employee or they may be paid by reason of a formal or informal company policy or plan, often on a case-by-case basis. The following comments apply to payments under "nonqualified" plans.

The inclusion of death benefits in the estates of deceased employees, as annuities, is dependent upon the terms of the particular employment contract or plan. Therefore, it is difficult to distill any general rules of law from court cases, which often seem contradictory despite the existence of common provisions in these plans or agreements. Here are a few examples of how the courts have ruled in these cases:

(1) Death benefits paid to a surviving spouse of an active employee were not includible in the employee's gross estate, as an annuity, where the employment contract provided for the payment of a salary and the death benefit, but did not provide for any retirement benefits.[13]

(2) Where the employment contract provided for annual payments for a period of 15 years starting with the employee's retirement or termination of employment and for the payment of these benefits to named beneficiaries if the employee died, the payments made to the beneficiaries were includible in the employee's gross estate where he died while employed by the company.[14] The payments were to continue so long as the decedent did not engage in certain acts that were detrimental to the operations of the company—a standard feature in many such contracts.

(3) Two courts have reached opposite conclusions concerning the inclusion of death benefits that were paid under employment contracts that provided for (a) the employment of the decedent at a fixed salary; (b) the payment of a salary to a decedent who had become disabled or ill; and (c) payments to the employees' surviving spouses after their death. (The terms of the contracts were slightly different, but both contained essentially the same standard provisions that are included in contracts of this type.) The U.S. Court of Claims (now, U.S. Court of Federal Claims) held that the "death benefit" paid to the surviving spouse was not included in the employee's gross estate because he had died before retirement.[15] A U.S. district court, on the other hand, held that the death benefit was includible in an active employee's gross estate.[16]

---

[12] Act Sec. 525(a), P.L. 98-369.

[13] *F.D. Fusz Est.*, 46 TC 214, CCH Dec. 27,944 (Acq.).

[14] *E.H. Wadewitz Est.*, CA-7, 65-1 USTC ¶12,277, 339 F2d 980, aff'g TC, 39 TC 925, CCH Dec. 26,015.

[15] *C. Kramer, Exrx.*, CtCls, 69-1 USTC ¶12,585, 406 F2d 1363.

[16] *J.C. Silberman, Exr.*, DC Pa., 71-2 USTC ¶12,814, 333 FSupp 1120.

(4) Payments made under nonqualified employees' plans have been included in the gross estates of deceased employees where the death benefits were vested or automatically payable to the beneficiaries at the employee's death. This rule has been applied in the case of a retired employee receiving a pension[17] and in the case of an employee who was not retired.[18] If the employee has more than one type of plan, the provisions of all the plans have been examined to determine whether an annuity is payable to a beneficiary at the decedent's death.[19] The U.S. Court of Appeals for the Second Circuit has held that a survivorship annuity payable to beneficiaries only if the decedent became totally disabled during employment was too dissimilar from a true annuity and too contingent to be aggregated with other plans covering the decedent for purposes of determining whether an annuity was payable to a beneficiary at death.[20] However, a U.S. district court in Georgia construed the same plans considered by the Second Circuit and concluded that the annuity payable to a decedent's beneficiaries was includible in the decedent's gross estate because the decedent had the right during his life to receive an annuity in the event that he became totally disabled.[21]

(5) Death benefits that were paid to the surviving spouse of an active employee were excludable from the employee's gross estate where the benefits were paid only after a company investigation into the circumstances of the employee's family and only with the approval of the board of directors.[22]

The IRS also has attempted to include death benefits under nonqualified plans or agreements as property owned at death under Code Sec. 2033 (see ¶ 535), as transfers with the right to govern enjoyment under Code Sec. 2036, as transfers taking effect at death under Code Sec. 2037, and as revocable transfers under Code Sec. 2038. The Tax Court and the U.S. Court of Appeals for the Second Circuit sustained the inclusion of death benefits as a transfer taking effect at death.[23] Three courts have ruled that death benefits paid pursuant to employment contracts are not includible in the gross estates of deceased employees as a revocable transfer or a transfer with the right to govern enjoyment.[24] However, the Tax Court has ruled that a post-mortem annuity payable to the surviving spouse of a decedent, the chairman of the board of directors and controlling shareholder of a closely held corporation, was includible in his gross estate as a revocable transfer.[25]

The amount includible in a deceased employee's estate is usually the present value of the payments to the beneficiary.

---

[17] *H.C. Beal Est.*, 47 TC 269, CCH Dec. 28,204 (Acq.).

[18] *J.W. Bahen Est.*, CtCls, 62-2 USTC ¶ 12,091, 305 F2d 827.

[19] *J.W. Bahen Est.*, CtCls, 62-2 USTC ¶ 12,091, 305 F2d 827; *J. Gray, Exr.*, CA-3, 69-1 USTC ¶ 12,604, 410 F2d 1094.

[20] *W.V. Schelberg Est.*, CA-2, 79-2 USTC ¶ 13,321, 612 F2d 25. See also *G.J. Van Wye Est.*, CA-6, 82-2 USTC ¶ 13,485, 686 F2d 425.

[21] *J.B. Looney, Admrx.*, DC Ga., 83-2 USTC ¶ 13,538, 569 FSupp 1569. Although the government prevailed in *Looney*, it moved to vacate the judgment of the district court when the estate appealed to CA-11, and this motion was granted on January 24, 1984.

[22] *W.E. Barr Est.*, 40 TC 227, CCH Dec. 26,103 (Acq.)

[23] *H. Fried Est.*, CA-2, 71-2 USTC ¶ 12,796, 445 F2d 979, aff'g TC, 54 TC 805, CCH Dec. 30,065, cert. denied, 404 US 1016.

[24] *C. Kramer, Exrx.*, CtCls, 69-1 USTC ¶ 12,585, 406 F2d 1363; *L.D. Hinze*, DC Calif., 72-1 USTC ¶ 12,842; *J.N. Harris*, DC Calif., 72-1 USTC ¶ 12,845.

[25] *S.A. Levin Est.*, 90 TC 723, CCH Dec. 44,706.

¶ 735 Annuities from Qualified Employees' Benefit Plans

The Tax Reform Act of 1984 (TRA 1984) (P.L. 98-369) repealed the $100,000 estate tax exclusion formerly available for certain retirement benefits payable under qualified plans, tax-sheltered annuities, individual retirement arrangements (see ¶ 737) and certain military retirement plans (see ¶ 730).[26] Thus, effective with respect to decedents dying after December 31, 1984, to the extent that retirement benefits payable under qualified plans fall within the annuity inclusion rules discussed at ¶ 700, such benefits are generally includible in a decedent's estate.

The exclusion with respect to qualified plans was unlimited prior to the $100,000 limitation imposed by the Tax Equity and Fiscal Responsibility Act of 1982 (P.L. 97-248). A transitional provision in TRA 1984, however, provided that the $100,000 limitation does not apply (thereby preserving the unlimited exclusion) to the estate of any decedent who was in a pay status on December 31, 1982, and who, prior to January 1, 1983, irrevocably elected the form of benefits that the beneficiary will receive under the plan. Section 1852(e)(3) of the Tax Reform Act of 1986 (TRA 1986) (P.L. 99-514) amended the transition rule of TRA 1984 by extending it to certain individuals who "separated from service" before January 1, 1985.

Section 1852(e)(3) of TRA 1986 does not deal specifically with the situation in which an individual participant in an employer-provided retirement plan who otherwise meets the requirements of the transition rule (i.e., separation from service prior to January 1, 1985, and no change in the form of the retirement or survivor benefits) transferred the proceeds from the plan to an IRA (see ¶ 737). According to the IRS, the TRA 1986 transition rule applies only to qualified pension plans and not to IRAs.[27]

¶ 737 Individual Retirement Accounts

The $100,000 estate tax exclusion for individual retirement arrangements has been repealed generally with respect to decedents dying after 1984. However, for decedents dying before 1985 and for certain other limited situations (see ¶ 735), retirement plan death benefits and annuities paid to beneficiaries of employees dying after 1976 under Keogh plans and individual retirement account plans (IRAs) are excludable from the employee's gross estate, subject to a $100,000 limitation after 1982.[28]

¶ 739 Lump-Sum Distributions

A lump-sum distribution will qualify for the estate tax exclusion (i.e., is not treated as a lump-sum distribution) if the recipient irrevocably elects to treat the lump-sum distribution as a taxable distribution, without applying the averaging method, for income tax purposes.[29] This election is made by filing an income tax return reflecting the distribution as taxable in the year of receipt. The election is reflected on Line A of Schedule I (Annuities) of Form 706. If the estate tax return is filed before the income tax return, the estate tax return nevertheless may reflect the election as if

---

[26] Act Sec. 525(a), P.L. 98-369.

[27] Rev. Rul. 92-22, 1992-1 CB 313.

[28] Code Sec. 2039(e), prior to repeal by P.L. 98-369.

[29] Code Sec. 2039(c) and Code Sec. 2039(f), prior to repeal by P.L. 98-369.

it had been made.[30] If the election is made, the estate must attach a written election made by each recipient. The recipient's name, address, and identification number (usually, the social security number) must also be listed on this attachment.

¶ 745 Annuities Combined with Life Insurance

Annuities are sometimes paired with life insurance in a combination type of contract. This combination is usually effected to enable a person who might otherwise be uninsurable to enter into a contract calling specifically for the payment of "life insurance" proceeds at death. A combination annuity contract and life insurance policy on a decedent's life that matured during the decedent's lifetime is taxed as an annuity.[31] In the case of a policy that has not matured, the policy is taxed as an insurance policy if the decedent dies before the reserve value equals the death benefit. If the reserve value equals the death benefit, the policy is taxed as an annuity [32] (see ¶ 415).

¶ 750 Annuities in Which Decedent Had No Beneficial Interest

If the decedent purchased or otherwise provided for an annuity for the benefit of another person, the rules for determining taxability are different. Taxability turns upon the circumstances surrounding the establishment of the annuity and upon the powers, if any, retained by the decedent.

If the annuity is provided for by will, it is fully taxable. If the annuity was purchased for another individual by the decedent within three years of death, it would be includible only to the limited extent that transfers within three years of death are still includible in the gross estate of a decedent who dies after 1981 [33] (see ¶ 555). If it was purchased more than three years before death, it cannot be included in the gross estate unless the decedent retained some control over the annuity.

Controls that would result in inclusion of an annuity in the estate include the right to change the beneficiary and the right to revoke the annuity, either by surrendering the contract for cash or by terminating it, if the interest is in a trust. The retention of controls that would require inclusion of any other types of lifetime transfers in the gross estate would similarly require the inclusion of annuities in the gross estate (see ¶ 570, ¶ 580, ¶ 585, and ¶ 590).

¶ 755 Special Rules for Trusts

If the decedent was an annuitant under a trust created by another person, no tax is due at the time of the decedent's death. The annuity ceases at the annuitant's death. However, tax consequences may result if the annuitant had certain rights in addition to the annuity or if the trust was reciprocal in nature.

The rights that can bring about inclusion of all or a portion of the fund from which the annuity stems are the same rights that would result in taxability of other interests. For example, a tax will result if the

---

[30] Reg. § 20.2039-4(d).

[31] Reg. § 20.2039-1(d).

[32] Reg. § 20.2039-1(d).

[33] Code Sec. 2035(d).

decedent is found to have a power of appointment that would require inclusion in the estate of any other property. The fact that the decedent had an annuity rather than some other type of interest does not influence the result.

If the decedent created the trust, the retention of an annuity from the trust will result in the inclusion of the value of the balance of the trust in the decedent's gross estate. Exceptions exist for certain instances if the trust was created before March 4, 1931 (see ¶ 570).

If a person creates an annuity interest in a trust that is to continue after the person's death, the fact that an annuity is created is of concern only if the remainder of the trust is deductible as a charitable interest or if the remainder, but not the annuity, is includible in the gross estate. In such instances, the value of the annuity must be determined before the amount of either the charitable deduction or the taxable remainder may be established (see ¶ 1122).

¶ 760 Valuation

The value of benefits under an annuity contract is determined as of the date of death of the primary annuitant. If the estate is valued under the alternate valuation method (¶ 105), the value of these benefits is little affected. Any lower value six months after the date of death is attributable to mere lapse of time.[34] The benefits paid out during the six months cannot be excluded from the evaluation.

Only that part of the value of the annuity or other payment receivable by the surviving beneficiary which the decedent's contribution to the purchase price of the contract or agreement bears to the total purchase price is actually includible in the gross estate.[35] Special annuity tables are to be used to value Civil Service temporary annuities payable to surviving children.[36]

• *Lump-Sum Payments*

If the benefits are payable in a lump sum, the amount payable is the value.

• *Installment Payments*

When the benefits are payable in installments—whether payable for a fixed period, payable in a fixed number, or payable for the life of the beneficiary—the valuation must be made on a commuted basis.

• *Insurance Company Contract*

If the payments are made under a contract issued by an insurance company, the value of a continuing annuity to the survivor is to be based on the cost of an annuity of a similar amount at the time of the decedent's death.

---

[34] *J.A. Hance Est.*, 18 TC 499, CCH Dec. 19,025 (Acq.).

[35] Reg. § 20.2039-1(c).

[36] Rev. Proc. 71-7, 1971-1 CB 671.

• *Fixed Payments*

If the payments to the survivor are fixed in duration or amount, it is likely that they will be valued as an annuity for a term certain. Tables used for this purpose are reproduced at ¶ 531 and ¶ 532.

• *Comparable Contract Method*

If the annuity is purchased by the decedent solely for the benefit of another but is includible in the decedent's gross estate, the value will be based strictly upon the cost of a comparable contract at the time of the decedent's death. If the annuity is payable from a trust or from any other source, except under a commercial annuity contract, the value is determined by applying factors obtained from tables reproduced at ¶ 531 and ¶ 532.

• *Lottery Payments*

The value of a decedent's interests in lottery payments will be includible in the gross estate for estate tax purposes. However, the method by which the interests would be valued was subject to debate. According to a district court in California, the decedent's interest would not be valued as a commercial annuity under Reg. § 20.2031-8, and departure from the private annuity Reg. § 20.2031-7 tables would be warranted if the tables produced substantially unrealistic and unreasonable results.[37]

¶ 770 Description on Return

The description of an annuity on Schedule I (Annuities) of Form 706 must include the name and address of the grantor. If the annuity was payable out of a trust or other fund, the description of the annuity must identify the payment and the trust. A description of an annuity payable for a term of years must include the duration of the term and the date on which it began. If the annuity is payable for the life of a person other than the decedent, the date of birth of that person should be given.

If the annuity is under a qualified plan, the ratio of the decedent's contribution to the total purchase price of the annuity must be reported. Similarly, the ratio of the amount paid for an annuity under an individual retirement account, annuity or bond that was not allowable as an income tax deduction under Code Sec. 219 (other than a rollover contribution) to the total amount paid for such account, annuity or bond must also be given.[38]

[37] *T. Shackleford Est.*, DC Calif., 98-2 USTC ¶ 60,230.

[38] Instructions for Form 706 (Rev. July 1998), p. 14.

¶772 Filled-In Schedule I

Schedule I must be filed if the decedent was receiving an annuity reportable on the schedule immediately before death.

The filled-in Schedule I, Form 706 (Rev. July 1998), relates to the fact situation of a person who dies on January 1, 1998, with an estate tax return due within nine months (without extensions).

Form 706 (Rev. 7-98)

Estate of: James X. Diversey

SCHEDULE I — Annuities

Note: Generally, no exclusion is allowed for the estates of decedents dying after December 31, 1984 (see page 13 of the instructions.)

		Yes	No
A	Are you excluding from the decedent's gross estate the value of a lump-sum distribution described in section 2039(f)(2)? .... If "Yes," you must attach the information required by the instructions.		

Item number	Description Show the entire value of the annuity before any exclusions.	Alternate valuation date	Includible alternate value	Includible value at date of death
1	Annuity contract No. X-16304, issued by Reliable Insurance Co., Jefferson City, MO, Jan. 15. 1962, payable in monthly installments of $100 to decedent for life then to his widow, Carrie Diversey, for life. Upon the death of the survivor, the excess cost over annuity payments is to be refunded to their son, Robert Diversey. Carrie Diversey was born Jan. 3, 1924. The decedent paid the entire cost of the annuity. Value obtained from issuing company.			12,300
2	Death benefit paid in a lump sum to the decedent's widow, Carrie Diversey, under the terms of an employees' trust qualified under Code Sec. 401(a) to which the decedent's employer, Siding Mfg. Co., Homewood, IL, contributed half the cost while the decedent contributed the other half.			25,000
	Total from continuation schedules (or additional sheets) attached to this schedule			
	TOTAL. (Also enter on Part 5, Recapitulation, page 3, at item 9.)			37,300

(If more space is needed, attach the continuation schedule from the end of this package or additional sheets of the same size.)

(The instructions to Schedule I are in the separate instructions.)

Schedule I — Page 22

Chapter 18

CERTAIN MARITAL DEDUCTION PROPERTY

¶ 773 Property Received Under Marital Deduction Rules

Property for which a marital deduction was allowed in the estate of a decedent dying after 1981 is includible in the surviving spouse's gross estate if the property is "qualified terminable interest property" (QTIP), as discussed at ¶ 1001.[1] The amount included in the gross estate of the surviving spouse is its fair market value on the date of death or alternate valuation date.

The main focus of litigation involving Code Sec. 2044 has been whether a particular interest is QTIP. The U.S. Court of Appeals for the Fifth Circuit, for example, has held that certain property interests the decedent received from his predeceased wife for which he elected QTIP treatment were includible in his gross estate despite the fact that neither the will nor state law expressly prohibited income accumulation. The court determined that the manifest intent of the will was not to accumulate income and, thus, the interest was QTIP.[2] In addition, the U.S. Court of Appeals for the Eleventh Circuit has held that a testamentary QTIP trust that did not entitle the surviving spouse to receive or appoint the trust income accumulating between the date of last distribution and the date of the surviving spouse's death was nonetheless QTIP. As such, the value of the interest at death was included in the surviving spouse's gross estate pursuant to Code Sec. 2044.[3]

QTIP property includible in a spouse's gross estate is considered as property passing from the spouse for estate and generation-skipping transfer tax purposes. Accordingly, such property may qualify for a marital deduction if it passes to the decedent's spouse, assuming that the spouse has remarried. Additionally, such property may qualify for a charitable deduction if it passes to a charitable organization. The basis of QTIP property acquired from a deceased spouse is its fair market value on the date of the spouse's death.[4]

If QTIP property from a prior estate is includible in a decedent's gross estate, this fact is to be indicated by answering "yes" to question 6 on page 2 of Form 706, Part 4 (Rev. July 1998). The property is to be reported on Schedule F (Other Miscellaneous Property Not Reportable Under Any Other Schedule).[5] Question 16 on page 3 of Form 706, Part 4, requires the executor to identify whether the decedent was the beneficiary of a QTIP trust for which a deduction was claimed by the predeceased spouse's estate and which is not otherwise reported on the decedent's Form 706.

---

[1] Code Sec. 2044, Reg. § 20.2044-1.

[2] *H.R. Cavenaugh Est.*, CA-5, 95-1 USTC ¶ 60,195, aff'g in part and rev'g in part TC, 100 TC 407, CCH Dec. 49,030.

[3] *L.P. Shelfer Est.*, CA-11, 96-2 USTC ¶ 60,238, rev'g TC, 103 TC 10, CCH Dec. 49,967.

[4] Code Sec. 2044(c).

[5] Instructions for Form 706 (Rev. July 1998), p. 6.

In construing Code Sec. 2044, the courts will apply a duty of consistency. Thus, for example, the Tax Court has held that the value of QTIP property that passed to a decedent from her predeceased husband was includible in her estate, even though the predeceased husband's estate had not made a QTIP election for the property but had claimed a marital deduction for it.[6] According to the court, the duty of consistency required inclusion in the decedent's estate because (1) the husband's estate made a factual representation in one year, (2) the IRS relied upon that fact in that year, and (3) the earlier year was closed by the statute of limitations and the decedent's estate attempted to change the earlier factual representations.

● *Right of Recovery for Estate Tax*

Additional estate tax liability attributable to taxation of the QTIP in the recipient spouse's gross estate is to be borne by the person or persons receiving the property unless the recipient spouse directs otherwise by will.[7]

---

[6] *M. Letts Est.*, 109 TC 15, CCH Dec. 52,368.

[7] Code Sec. 2207A.

Chapter 19

EXCESS RETIREMENT ACCUMULATIONS

¶ 775 Excess Retirement Accumulation Tax

Prior to repeal by the Taxpayer Relief Act of 1997 (P.L. 105-34), a 15-percent additional tax was imposed on the estate of any person who died after 1986 and before January 1, 1996, with "excess qualified retirement accumulation." In general, this excise tax was an additional estate tax and was calculated independently of the estate tax owed upon death.[1] Thus, the credits, deductions, exclusions or other special rules used to determine a decedent's estate tax did not affect the calculation of this excise tax. For example, the 15-percent tax could have applied, even though there was no estate tax liability. In that case, Form 706 would have been filed only to report the excise tax.

The following distributions were not subject to the tax: (1) any distribution received by any person with respect to an individual as a result of the death of that individual; (2) any distribution with respect to an individual that is received by an alternate payee under a qualified domestic relations order within the meaning of Code Sec. 414(p) that is includible in the payee's income; (3) distributions attributable to investment in the contract under Code Sec. 72(f); (4) a distribution not included in gross income by reason of rollover; and (5) a distribution for health or medical benefits under Code Sec. 401(h).[2] Additionally, the following types of distributions were excluded from the determination of excess distributions pursuant to the Technical and Miscellaneous Revenue Act of 1988 (TAMRA): (1) an annuity contract that is distributed to an individual and the value of which is not included in the individual's income when the contract is distributed; (2) excess deferrals as defined in Code Sec. 402(g)(2)(A)(ii); (3) excess contributions and related income as defined in Code Sec. 401(k)(8); (4) excess aggregate contributions and related income as defined in Code Sec. 401(m)(6); and (5) certain amounts withdrawn from an IRA before the due date of the return under Code Sec. 408(d)(4).

Any tax due under former Code Sec. 4980A(d) with respect to an estate on account of the decedent's excess accumulations was reported on Schedule S (Increased Estate Tax on Excess Retirement Accumulations) of Form 706.[3]

---

[1] See Temp. Reg. § 54.4981A-1T, Q&A d-9, for examples of the determination of the additional tax under Code Sec. 4981A(d).

[2] Temp. Reg. § 54.4981A-1T, Q&A a-4.

[3] Temp. Reg. § 54.4981A-1T(a). Schedule S was last included on the April 1997 version of Form 706.

Deductions

Chapter 20

FUNERAL AND ADMINISTRATION EXPENSES

¶ 780 Deductions Allowed

A deduction from the value of the gross estate is allowed for funeral and administration expenses allowable under the laws of the jurisdiction in which the estate is being administered. The deduction is allowable even if the jurisdiction is outside the United States.[1]

Deductions are allowable both for expenses incurred in administering property subject to claims and for expenses incurred in administering property *not* subject to claims. See ¶ 805 for the allowance of deductions where the amount of deductions exceeds the value of property subject to claims. Property not subject to claims must be included in the gross estate of the decedent, and the expenses must be paid within three years after the estate tax return is filed.

In the estate tax return, funeral expenses and the expenses incurred in administering property subject to claims are reported on Schedule J (Funeral Expenses and Expenses Incurred in Administering Property Subject to Claims) of Form 706. Expenses incurred in administering property not subject to claims are deducted on Schedule L (Net Losses During Administration and Expenses Incurred in Administering Property Not Subject to Claims).

Amounts allowable as expenses under Code Sec. 2053 or as losses under Code Sec. 2054 for federal estate tax purposes may not again be allowed as deductions in computing the taxable income of the decedent's estate. This rule also applies to trusts or any other person who might benefit from the expense, claim or loss item incurred. To secure a deduction for income tax purposes, a waiver of the right to claim the deductions for estate tax purposes must be filed (see ¶ 797).[2]

¶ 783 Trustees' Commissions

Trustees' commissions, if deductible, generally should be considered with expenses incurred in administering property not subject to claims. This is proper tax treatment whether the commissions are received by the executor acting as trustee or by a separate trustee.[3]

---

[1] Code Sec. 2053(a); Reg. § 20.2053-1(a)(1)(i).

[2] Code Sec. 642(g) and Reg. § 20.2053-1(d).

[3] Reg. § 20.2053-3(b).

¶ 785 Funeral Expenses

Deductible funeral expenses are those amounts actually expended by the executor or administrator. Under the laws of the local jurisdiction, expenses must be payable out of the decedent's estate.[4]

Included among the expenses deductible under this classification are reasonable expenditures for a tombstone, monument, or mausoleum, or for a burial lot (whether for the decedent or the decedent's family). These expenses must be allowable under local law. Also included as a funeral expense is the cost of transportation incurred by a person who brings the decedent's body to the place of burial. Amounts paid for perpetual care of a cemetery lot or mausoleum are deductible if allowable under local law.

If a decedent dies a resident of a state in which the spouse is responsible for the payment of funeral expenses, in the absence of contrary instructions in the decedent's will, funeral expenses are not deductible.[5] The deduction must be reduced by Social Security and Veterans Administration death benefits.[6] The funeral expense deduction must be reduced by any reimbursement that is received for such expenses under a state's wrongful death statute or by the reasonable value of such a claim filed for such expenses.[7]

In community property states, the extent of deductibility depends upon whether the funeral expenses are deemed to be an expense of the community estate or of the decedent's estate. If they are an expense of the community estate, only one-half the amount expended is deductible. If the expenses are allowable against the estate of the decedent, they are deductible to the extent so allowable (see ¶ 795).

¶ 790 Administration Expenses

To be deductible, administration expenses must be actually and necessarily incurred in the administration of the estate. They include those expenses incurred in: (1) collection of assets; (2) payment of debts; and (3) distribution among the persons entitled to share in the estate. These expenses, in turn, include executor's commissions, attorneys' fees, and miscellaneous expenses.[8]

Administration expense incurred for the individual benefit of the heirs, legatees, or devisees are never deductible. To be deductible, expenses must be incurred in connection with the transfer of estate property to the beneficiaries or to a trustee. Therefore, the expenses incurred in obtaining from the probate court the award of a support allowance for the widow during administration of the estate are not deductible.[9]

As to community property estates, see ¶ 795.

¶ 791 Executors' Commissions

Executors' and administrators' commissions are deductible in the amount actually paid or in an amount that, at the time the return is filed,

[4] Reg. § 20.2053-2.

[5] Rev. Rul. 76-369, 1976-2 CB 281.

[6] Rev. Rul. 66-234, 1966-2 CB 436.

[7] Rev. Rul. 77-274, 1977-2 CB 326.

[8] Reg. § 20.2053-3(a).

[9] *W.A. Landers Est.,* 38 TC 828, CCH Dec. 25,650.

is reasonably expected to be paid.[10] It is best that the fee be fixed by decree of the proper court. In the event that it has not been so fixed, the deduction will be allowed on the final audit of the return if:

(1) the District Director is reasonably satisfied that the commissions claimed actually will be paid;

(2) the amount claimed as a deduction is within the amount allowable by the laws of the jurisdiction in which the estate is being administered; and

(3) it is customary in that jurisdiction to allow such an amount in estates of similar size and character.

If the executor's commissions have not been paid at the time of the final audit of the return, the amount claimed as a deduction must be supported with an affidavit or statement signed under the penalty of perjury that the amount has been agreed upon and will be paid. If the deduction is not allowed in full at the time of the final audit, the amount disallowed may be later modified on the basis of subsequent events. If the deduction is allowed in full but actual commissions are less than the amount allowed, the difference should be reported. Any resulting increase in the tax should be paid, together with interest.

If the decedent, by will, fixes the compensation payable to the estate representative, that amount is deductible. It must not exceed the compensation allowable by local law or practice, however. If the will provides that the executor should receive a bequest or devise in lieu of commissions, no deduction is available for the amount of the bequest or devise.

Although the term "executor's commissions" may be taken to include administrator's commissions, it does not include trustee's commissions, even if received by the executor or administrator as trustee. Principal commissions paid with respect to trust property included in the gross estate are deductible as expenses in connection with property not subject to claims.

As to community property estates, see ¶ 795.

¶ 792 Attorneys' Fees

Attorneys' fees are deductible, at the time the return is filed, to the extent that they have been actually paid or to the extent that it is reasonably expected that they will be paid. If, when the return is finally audited, the fees claimed have not been awarded by the proper courts and paid, they still may be allowed. It must be shown to the satisfaction of the IRS that the amount claimed will be paid and that it is reasonable for the services rendered.[11]

If the fees claimed have not been paid at the time of the final audit of the return, the amount deducted must be supported by an affidavit, or statement signed under penalties of perjury, of the executor or the attorney stating that such amount has been agreed upon and will be paid. Even if part of the amount claimed is disallowed on final audit, subsequent adjustment may be made if warranted by the facts.[12] Deductible fees are

[10] Reg. § 20.2053-3(b).

[11] Reg. § 20.2053-3(c).

[12] Reg. § 20.2053-3(c).

those incurred for services that benefit the estate. Fees incurred by beneficiaries incident to litigation with regard to their interest are not deductible unless the litigation is essential to the proper settlement of the estate.[13]

The return, itself, can reflect only fees of which there is some knowledge at the time of preparation and filing. If there should later be litigation or other action requiring services of attorneys in finally establishing the amount of tax due, deductions on account of such fees should be claimed at the time of the contest. The IRS will not allow deductions for legal fees that are incurred in litigation and that are paid after a Tax Court decision becomes final and more than three years after the filing of the estate tax return.[14] The IRS will allow a deduction and refund in such cases only where the final decision of the Tax Court allows attorneys' fees as an additional deduction. The Tax Court has held that even where the estate tax was assessed against the transferees of the estate, thereby extending the statutory period for assessing the tax one year beyond the initial three-year period, a deduction will not be allowed for legal fees paid after such three-year period.[15]

Expenses incurred in contesting the inclusion of trust property in the gross estate are deductible as expenses incurred with respect to property not subject to claims. These expenses must be paid within three years after the final date for filing the return.

As to community property estates, see ¶ 795.

¶ 793 Miscellaneous Expenses

Deductible miscellaneous administration expenses are sufficiently broad in scope to include court costs, surrogate's fees, appraisers' fees, and clerk hire. They also include the cost of storing or maintaining estate property and other expenses necessary to the preservation and distribution of the estate. Brokers' and auctioneers' fees are also deductible if the sale of the property is necessary to pay debts or administration expenses, or to effect distribution.[16]

- *Selling Expenses*

Pursuant to IRS regulations, selling expenses (such as broker fees, survey fees, or transfer stamps) are deductible if the sale is necessary in order to pay the decedent's debts, expenses of administration or taxes, to preserve the estate, or to effect distribution.[17]

> ***Example:*** Robert Smith died on July 5, 1998. Because his estate did not have sufficient assets to pay his debts and taxes, the estate sold his residence. The selling expenses incurred in selling the residence are a deductible expense.

The Internal Revenue Code, however, allows a deduction for administration expenses that are allowable under local law.[18] The IRS has stated,

---

[13] *P.W. Reilly Est.*, 76 TC 369, CCH Dec. 37,691 (Acq.).

[14] Rev. Rul. 78-323, 1978-2 CB 240.

[15] *D.A. Gillum*, 49 TCM 240, CCH Dec. 41,654(M), TC Memo. 1984-631.

[16] Reg. § 20.2053-3(d).

[17] Reg. § 20.2053-3(d)(2).

[18] Code Sec. 2053(a).

and the courts have agreed,[19] that the expense must be both allowable under local law and necessary for the preservation and distribution of the decedent's estate.

● *Interest*

Interest on loans that were incurred by estates to pay estate and inheritance taxes are deductible as an administration expense where the loans are incurred to avoid "forced" sales of estate assets and are permitted by state probate laws.[20] However, the interest is deductible only as it accrues and, therefore, no deduction may be computed based upon an estimation of the interest expense.[21] Similarly, interest on deferred federal estate taxes (see ¶ 1672) is deductible only when accrued.[22] In addition, interest on deferred state death taxes is a deductible administration expense.[23] However, interest paid with respect to recapture tax was not deductible as an administration expense because it is separately imposed on the qualified heir(s) rather than the estate.[24]

Effective for the estates of decedents dying after 1997, interest payable on the installment payment of the estate tax is not deductible.[25]

¶ 794 Support of Dependents

No deduction is allowed for payments to support dependents. This does not prevent deduction of a spousal allowance in all cases. When the allowance to the surviving spouse under state law constitutes a vested right that will survive as an asset of the surviving spouse's estate in the event of remarriage or death, it will qualify for the marital deduction.

¶ 795 Community Property States

In community property states, the extent to which the administration expenses are deductible depends upon their treatment under state law. If they are deemed to be an expense of the entire community estate under state law, only one-half of the expenses are deductible, even if the decedent directs that his estate bear all the expenses.[26] If they are regarded as expenses of the decedent alone, the entire amount may be deducted. The usual limitations on deductions generally are applicable.

¶ 796 Execution of Schedule

Funeral expenses and expenses incurred in administering property subject to claims are itemized on Schedule J, Form 706. Funeral expenses less any amounts that were reimbursed, such as death benefits payable by the Social Security Administration and the Veterans Administration, are listed on Part A. The total deduction for executors' commissions should be

---

[19] *C. Swayne*, 43 TC 190, CCH Dec. 27,054; *D. Smith*, CA-2, 75-1 USTC ¶ 13,046, 510 F2d 479; *S. Marcus*, CA-11, 84-2 USTC ¶ 13,577, 5 ClsCt 362; *S.L. Payne, Exr.*, DC Fla., 75-1 USTC ¶ 13,059; *M.F. Park*, CA-6, 73-1 USTC ¶ 12,913, 475 F2d 73.

[20] *J.S. Todd Est.*, 57 TC 288, CCH Dec. 31,087 (Acq.); *F.M. Hipp, Admr.*, DC S.C., 72-1 USTC ¶ 12,824.

[21] Rev. Rul. 84-75, 1984-1 CB 193. See IRS Technical Advice Memorandum 8450003, 8-22-84, CCH IRS LETTER RULINGS REPORTS (timely filing of a claim for refund of estate taxes protected estate's right to a refund based upon interest paid on a long-term loan after the expiration of the limitations period); *M. Milliken Est.*, CA-6, 97-2 USTC ¶ 60,287.

[22] Rev. Rul. 80-250, 1980-2 CB 278.

[23] Rev. Rul. 81-256, 1981-2 CB 183.

[24] Rev. Rul. 90-8, 1990-1 CB 173. Also see IRS Technical Advice Memorandum 8902002, 9-26-88, CCH IRS LETTER RULINGS REPORTS.

[25] Code Sec. 2053(c)(1)(D).

[26] *D.A. Stapf*, 63-2 USTC ¶ 12,192, 375 US 118.

entered at Item 1, attorneys' fees should be entered at Item 2, accountant fees should be entered at Item 3, and miscellaneousadministration expenses should be itemized under Item 4 of the schedule. Schedule J must be filed only if the estate claims a deduction on item 13 of the Recapitulation (see ¶ 73).

An item may be entered for deduction even though the exact amount is not known at the time the return is filed. The item must be ascertainable with reasonable certainty and be expected to be paid. No deduction may be taken upon the basis of a vague or uncertain estimate. All vouchers and receipts should be reserved for possible inspection by the IRS.

¶ 797 Estate Tax vs. Income Tax Deduction

The executor or administrator of an estate has the choice of claiming administration expenses and casualty losses, under Code Sec. 2053 and Code Sec. 2054, as deductions on either the decedent's estate tax return or the fiduciary income tax return, but not on both.[27] This so-called double deduction prohibition also applies to such expenses or losses that are paid or incurred by trusts or other persons, instead of the estate. In addition, the rule against double deductions applies with respect to items that would be deductible in determining the taxable amount for taxable distributions and taxable terminations under the generation-skipping transfer tax.[28]

Administration expenses that are subject to the above double deduction prohibition include executors' commissions, attorneys' fees, and other expenses that are incurred in managing, maintaining and conserving estate assets, such as court costs, appraisal fees, custodial fees, investment counsel services, accountants' fees, etc. In addition, selling expenses may not be used to offset the sales price on a sale of property by an estate or trust in determining gain or loss on a fiduciary income tax return, if they have also been deducted as an administration expense for federal estate tax purposes.[29]

The rule against double deductions does not apply to deductions for taxes, interest, business expenses, and other items that are accrued at the date of a decedent's death, and that, therefore, are claims against his estate. These expenses can be claimed as an estate tax deduction and as a deduction in respect of a decedent for income tax purposes under Code Sec. 691.

The total amount of one deduction or of all deductions does not have to be treated in the same way. One deduction or portion of a deduction may be allowed for income tax purposes if the waiver is filed, while another deduction or portion is allowed for estate tax purposes. The election to treat administration expenses as income or estate deductions may be made on a year-to-year basis, if the required waiver is filed.[30]

If the executor decides to claim administrative expenses and casualty losses as estate tax deductions, the deductions are claimed on the estate tax return. On the other hand, if the executor decides on claiming such expenses and losses as income tax deductions, the estate must file a statement, in duplicate, with the IRS indicating that the amount has not

---

[27] Reg. § 1.642(g)-1 and Reg. § 20.2053-1(d).

[28] Code Sec. 642(g).

[29] Code Sec. 642(g).

[30] Rev. Rul. 70-361, 1970-2 CB 133.

already been claimed as an estate tax deduction and that it is waiving itsright to claim them as estate tax deductions.[31] A waiver of the right to the estate deduction cannot be revoked, even though it is later discovered that only a portion of the deducted expenses was of any income tax benefit. Although Reg. § 1.642(g)-1 indicates that failure to file the waiver statement precludes the allowance of an income tax deduction, the Tax Court has held that items previously deducted on a federal income tax return (where no waiver was filed) can be deducted as claims against the estate so long as they were personal obligations of the decedent at death.[32] An executor's decision to claim administration expenses or casualty losses as either income tax or estate tax deductions should be based on the course of action that will produce the greatest overall tax savings, after considering the beneficiaries and the provisions of the will.

---

[31] Reg. § 1.642(g)-1 and Reg. § 1.642(g)-2.

[32] *M. Love Est.*, 57 TCM 1479, Dec. 45,987(M), TC Memo. 1989-470.

¶798 Filled-In Schedule J

The filled-in Schedule J, Form 706 (Rev. July 1998), relates to the fact situation of a person who dies on January 1, 1998, with an estate tax return due within nine months (without extensions). Schedule J must be filed only if a deduction is claimed for amounts reportable on the schedule (see ¶ 73).

Form 706 (Rev. 7-98)

Estate of: James X. Diversey

SCHEDULE J — Funeral Expenses and Expenses Incurred in Administering Property Subject to Claims

Note: *Do not list on this schedule expenses of administering property not subject to claims. For those expenses, see the instructions for Schedule L.*

If executor's commissions, attorney fees, etc., are claimed and allowed as a deduction for estate tax purposes, they are not allowable as a deduction in computing the taxable income of the estate for Federal income tax purposes. They are allowable as an income tax deduction on Form 1041 if a waiver is filed to waive the deduction on Form 706 (see the Form 1041 instructions).

Item number	Description	Expense amount	Total amount
	A. Funeral expenses:		
1	Homewood Funeral Home, Homewood, IL: Funeral incidental expense.	5,000	5,000
2	Oak Ridge Cemetary, Oak Park, IL: Burial plot and marker.	1,175	1,175
	Total funeral expenses		6,175
	B. Administration expenses:		
1	Executor's commissions — amount ~~estimated/agreed upon~~/paid. (Strike out the words that do not apply.)		7,600
2	Attorney fees — amount ~~estimated/agreed upon~~/paid. (Strike out the words that do not apply.)		13,000
3	Accountant fees — amount estimated/agreed upon/paid. (Strike out the words that do not apply.)		6,500
		Expense amount	
4	Miscellaneous expenses: Roberts and Oaks, 542 James St, Homewood, IL: Appraisal of real estate and personal effects	1,500	
b	Probate Court -- Cook County, IL: Probate fees and incidental expenses	250	
c	Other administrative expenses: Hiring of clerk, collection of assets, etc.	300	
	Total miscellaneous expenses from continuation schedules (or additional sheets) attached to this schedule		
	Total miscellaneous expenses		2,050
	TOTAL. (Also enter on Part 5, Recapitulation, page 3, at item 13.)		35,325

(If more space is needed, attach the continuation schedule from the end of this package or additional sheets of the same size.) (See the instructions.)

Schedule J — Page 23

Chapter 21

DEBTS OF DECEDENTS

¶ 800 Claims Against the Estate

Claims against the estate that are allowable by the laws of the jurisdiction under which the estate is being administered are deductible.[1] Such claims, when founded upon a promise or agreement, are deductible to the extent that they are contracted in good faith and for adequate and full consideration. To the extent that they require the making of a contribution or gift to any charitable donee, they are deductible if similar transfers by will would qualify for deduction as a charitable transfer.

The amounts that are deductible as claims against a decedent's estate are those that represent personal obligations of the decedent existing at the time of his death. Interest that has accrued to the obligations at the time of death may be added. Only interest accrued to the date of decedent's death is deductible, even though the executor elects the alternate valuation method.[2]

If the claims represent personal obligations of the decedent at the time of his death, they are deductible whether or not they are then matured. Only claims enforceable against the estate are deductible, however. Interest accruing after a decedent's death on a claim is deductible as an administration expense if payment of the debt is postponed to benefit the estate and is allowable under state law.

Generally, a claim that becomes unenforceable (and that will not be paid) because of a creditor's failure to file as required under state law is not deductible.[3] However, the U.S. Court of Appeals for the Seventh Circuit has held that an amount owed to a creditor under a compromise agreement entered into with the decedent's estate was an enforceable, and therefore deductible, claim against the estate even though the creditor did not file a claim within the time period prescribed by state law.[4] Similarly, a U.S. district court in Illinois has allowed a deduction for late-filed claims because the enforceability of the claims at the time of death, rather than at the time of filing, was controlling.[5] However, the court denied a deduction for loans made to the decedent, the collection of which was barred by the state statute of limitations. A U.S. district court in Ohio held that a promissory note received by the executor of a decedent's estate from the decedent and payable at the decedent's death was valid and enforcea-

---

[1] Code Sec. 2053(a); Reg. § 20.2053-1(a)(1)(iii).

[2] Reg. § 20.2053-4.

[3] Rev. Rul. 60-247, 1960-2 CB 272. *F.G. Hagmann Est.*, CA-5, 74-1 USTC ¶ 12,996, 492 F2d 796.

[4] *B.L. Thompson*, CA-7, 84-1 USTC ¶ 13,568, 730 F2d 1071.

[5] *B. Greene, Exr. (A. Greene Est.)*, DC Ill., 78-1 USTC ¶ 13,240, 447 FSupp 885. See also *First Interstate Bank of Arizona, Pers. Rep.*, DC Ariz., 86-1 USTC ¶ 13,665.

ble on the date of death and, therefore, was deductible even though the executor failed to present the claim to the probate court for allowance as required under state law.[6] The Tax Court has held that the value of a decedent's obligation to pay an annuity was deductible as a claim against the estate even though the annuitant did not present a claim to the estate as required under state law.[7]

A claim that is enforceable against multiple sources of payment, but that is not asserted against the estate, is also not deductible.[8] A valid and enforceable claim that is informally presented to the executor within the period for presenting claims under state law and paid with the approval of the beneficiaries (in order to relieve the executor of personal liability) is deductible,[9] as is a claim that is not formerly paid where the creditor is also the sole beneficiary of the estate.[10] Life insurance proceeds paid to the decedent's former wife under a property settlement agreement incorporated in a divorce decree are deductible, even though the insurance company made such payment directly to the beneficiary and no claim was filed against the estate, where the executor would have been obligated to pay over such proceeds to the former wife if he had received such proceeds.[11]

The amount of the deduction is the value of the claim. This has led to some dispute as to whether events occurring after the decedent's death should be considered in determining the value of a claim. In the IRS view, post-death events should be considered in valuing claims against the estate.[12] However, the U.S. Court of Appeals for the Ninth Circuit has rejected the IRS position and has held that the amount of deduction allowable with respect to a lien on a parcel of real property was the amount of the claim that was due and owing on the date of the decedent's death, rather than a lower amount that was later paid in settlement of the claim.[13] Similarly, the Ninth Circuit has held that the executor of a decedent's estate properly determined, under actuarial tables, the amount of the allowable federal estate tax deduction for a claim consisting of an annuity payable to the decedent's ex-husband even though the total value of the annuity payments actually made was far less than the annuity's actuarial value because the ex-husband died seven months after the decedent's death.[14]

¶ 805 Claims Exceeding Assets Available for Payment

In the event that the claims against the estate exceed the value of property subject to the payment of claims, special rules apply. Deduction of such claims (together with funeral expenses, certain administration expenses, mortgages and liens) is disallowed to the extent they exceed the value of the property subject to the claims. Deductions for such amounts nevertheless will be allowed if they are actually paid before the date prescribed for filing the estate tax return.

---

[6] *R.C. Wilder, Exr. (C.H. Manley Est.),* DC Ohio, 83-2 USTC ¶ 13,546, 581 FSupp 86.

[7] *C. McDowell Est.,* 51 TCM 319, CCH Dec. 42,831(M), TC Memo. 1986-27.

[8] *Q.P. Courtney Est.,* 62 TC 317, CCH Dec. 32,639.

[9] Rev. Rul. 75-24, 1975-1 CB 306.

[10] Rev. Rul. 60-247, 1960-2 CB 272.

[11] *W.P. Gray, Exr. (Will of W.G. Robertson),* DC Cal., 74-2 USTC ¶ 13,019, 391 FSupp 693, and 78-1 USTC ¶ 13,244, 440 FSupp 684.

[12] Rev. Rul. 60-247, 1960-2 CB 272.

[13] *J.A. Propstra, Pers. Rep.,* CA-9, 82-2 USTC ¶ 13,475.

[14] *A.E. Van Horne Est.,* CA-9, 83-2 USTC ¶ 13,548, 720 F2d 1114, cert. denied, 5-14-84.

"Property subject to claims" is the property out of which the deductible amounts would be paid under applicable law upon the settlement of the estate. The value of such property must be reduced by any administration expenses deducted against such property.[15]

¶ 810 Deductible Claims

The following items are among those that have been held to be deductible as claims against the estate:

(1) alimony decreed by a court but past due (If payments are to continue periodically after the decedent's death, the commuted value of such payments is also deductible.[16]);

(2) commissions owed to trustee for services during decedent's lifetime;[17]

(3) the commuted value of support payments due a decedent's wife for her release of her support and maintenance rights under a valid separation agreement;[18]

(4) amounts due on judgments against the decedent, including tort liabilities;[19]

(5) amounts due under guarantees executed by the decedent and not collectible from primary obligator; and [20]

(6) amounts due on notes.[21]

Although, as noted at (4), above, amounts paid to satisfy judgments against the decedent are deductible, the IRS has ruled that a decedent's estate could not deduct amounts paid in satisfaction of a collusive lawsuit filed against the decedent by his son.[22] In so ruling, the IRS noted that the decedent's child filed the suit pursuant to a plan to reduce federal estate taxes that was devised by a financial planner. Even though the decedent did not contest the lawsuit and a judgment was awarded to the child under a consent decree, the amounts paid in satisfaction of the claim were not deductible because the lawsuit was without merit and was merely a device to allow the transfer of property free of estate and gift taxes.

¶ 813 Medical Expenses

The medical expenses resulting from a decedent's last illness are a deductible claim against the estate. In lieu of deducting these expenses on the estate tax return, the executor may deduct these expenses on the decedent's last income tax return. However, it may be preferable for the estate to deduct these expenses on the estate tax return because the tax rate schedule for estate tax is significantly higher than the tax rate schedule for income tax. Moreover, for estate tax purposes, the medical expenses are fully deductible. The medical expenses for income tax purposes are deductible only to the extent that such expenses exceed 7.5

---

[15] Code Sec. 2053(c)(2).

[16] Rev. Rul. 67-304, 1967-2 CB 224.

[17] *F.E. Baldwin Est.*, 44 BTA 900, CCH Dec. 11,878 (Acq.).

[18] Rev. Rul. 71-67, 1971-1 CB 271.

[19] *E.C. Moore, Exr.*, 21 BTA 279, CCH Dec. 6467 (Acq.).

[20] *E.L. Benz, Exr.*, CA-1, 37-2 USTC ¶ 9337, 90 F2d 747.

[21] *Security Tr. Co., Exr.*, 4 BTA 983, CCH Dec. 1647 (Acq.).

[22] Rev. Rul. 83-54, 1983-1 CB 229.

percent of the decedent's adjusted gross income. However, if the decision is made to deduct medical expenses on the decedent's last income tax return, a statement that such amount has not been claimed as a deduction on the estate's Form 706 and that the estate waives any right to do so in the future must be filed.[23]

In community property states, the deductibility of a decedent's medical expenses for estate tax purposes is dependent upon whether such costs are treated as an expense of the community estate or of the decedent's estate.[24] If such costs are a community expense, only one-half of the costs are deductible for estate tax purposes. If such costs are allowable against the decedent's estate, they are deductible to the extent so allowed.

¶ 815 Claims Founded on Promise or Agreement

A claim against the estate based upon a promise or agreement by the decedent to pay over certain property or a specified amount of money is subject to special treatment. It will be denied as a deduction except to the extent that it was contracted in good faith and for an adequate and full consideration in money or money's worth.[25]

Generally, the requirements as to consideration here are the same as those that apply in determining whether a lifetime transfer should escape inclusion in the gross estate. A special exception is provided with respect to claims made by charitable organizations. The consideration requirements are waived if the claimant is one to whom a testamentary transfer would be deductible as a charitable transfer.

• *Claims Under a Divorce Decree*

The consideration requirement applies to claims "founded on a promise or agreement." However, claims founded on a divorce decree are not founded on an agreement and, as such, are deductible without regard to the consideration requirement so long as they meet the general requirements for deduction.[26]

The obligation to transfer property to a former spouse of the decedent is deductible as a claim against the estate if the transfer is pursuant to an agreement satisfying the conditions for the gift tax exemption under Code Sec. 2516 (see ¶ 2165).[27] Thus, the deduction will be available if the transfer is pursuant to a written agreement between the spouses and if divorce occurred within the three-year period beginning one year before execution of the agreement. In the event the decedent dies before the divorce, the transfer would be eligible for the marital deduction (see ¶ 1000).

With respect to estates of decedents dying prior to July 18, 1984, the Tax Court has held that a decedent's estate could not deduct as a claim against the estate amounts paid to the decedent's ex-wife in settlement of her right to be named beneficiary of certain life insurance policies pursuant to a separation agreement. Although the parties were divorced and the

---

[23] Code Sec. 213(c); Reg. § 1.213-1(d).

[24] Rev. Rul. 78-242, 1978-1 CB 292.

[25] Code Sec. 2053(c)(1). Also see *M. Wedum Est.*, 57 TCM 219, Dec. 45,637(M), TC Memo. 1989-184.

[26] *W.E. Robinson Est.*, 63 TC 717, CCH Dec. 33,099 (Acq.), and *M.C. Watson Est.*, CA-2, 54-2 USTC ¶ 10,973, 216 FSupp 941.

[27] Code Sec. 2043(b).

separation agreement made part of the divorce decree, the court noted that because, under applicable state law (Missouri), the divorce court had no power to award the insurance policies to the ex-wife, the amounts were paid pursuant to the separation agreement rather than pursuant to the divorce decree. Because the estate could not show that support rights relinquished by the ex-wife and the couple's children were consideration for the insurance provision in the agreement, the court denied the deduction.[28]

The U.S. Court of Appeals for the Second Circuit, in a case involving a separation agreement under a Mexican divorce decree, has indicated its disagreement with the Tax Court's position as stated above.[29] In that case, the Second Circuit held that a decedent's estate could deduct as a claim against the estate an amount paid to the decedent's ex-wife pursuant to a separation agreement because the Mexican court had incorporated the agreement (which was executed in New York) into the divorce decree, as it was empowered to do by Mexican law. However, the Second Circuit noted that the payment would have been deductible even if it had been made pursuant to the agreement rather than to the divorce decree because the agreement was deemed made for full and adequate consideration under Code Sec. 2516, prior to amendment by the Tax Reform Act of 1984.[30] In the Second Circuit's view, such a holding was necessary in view of the U.S. Supreme Court's rulings that the estate and gift tax statutes are to be construed in a similar manner.[31]

¶ 820 Taxes

As a general rule, neither inheritance nor estate taxes payable on a decedent's estate are deductible, whether payable to the state, the federal government, or to a foreign government. State and foreign death taxes may give rise to credits against the federal estate tax, however. An exception is made in the case of death taxes paid on certain transfers for charitable purposes. An executor may elect to deduct such taxes on charitable transfers, rather than take the credit against the estate tax, if the decrease in the estate tax will inure solely to the benefit of the charitable transferee.[32]

Gift taxes due and payable on all post-1976 gifts made by a decedent dying after 1976 are subtracted from the estate tax.[33]

Property taxes are deductible only if they accrued under state law prior to the decedent's death.[34]

Excise taxes incurred in selling property of a decedent are deductible as expenses of administration if the sale is necessary to (1) pay the decedent's debts, taxes, or expenses of administration, (2) preserve the estate, or (3) effect distribution.

---

[28] *E. Satz Est.*, 78 TC 1172, CCH Dec. 39,151.

[29] *D.E. Natchez and P. Natchez, Exrs.*, CA-2, 83-1 USTC ¶ 13,519, 705 F2d 671.

[30] The decedent and his wife were divorced within two years after executing the separation agreement, as required under Code Sec. 2516.

[31] See, e.g., *C. Harris*, SCt, 50-2 USTC ¶ 10,786, 340 US 106, and *Merrill v. Fahs*, SCt, 45-1 USTC ¶ 10,180, 324 US 308.

[32] Code Sec. 2053(d).

[33] Code Sec. 2001.

[34] Reg. § 20.2053-6.

Unpaid income taxes are deductible if they are on income properly includible in an income tax return of the decedent for a period prior to his death. If a joint income tax return was filed, the portion of the joint liability (although entirely paid by the estate) that is deductible is the amount for which the estate would be liable under local law after enforcement of any effective right of reimbursement or contribution.[35]

Interest accruing after a decedent's death on his federal and state income tax deficiencies, which are contested by an executor or administrator, is deductible as an administration expense to the extent permitted by state law.[36] For decedents dying prior to 1998, interest payable by an estate on the unpaid balance of a decedent's federal estate tax, which the estate had elected to pay in installments pursuant to Code Sec. 6166 is also deductible as an administrative expense,[37] although only as the interest liability accrues.[38] For decedents dying after 1997, no deduction is allowable for interest payable pursuant to Code Sec. 6166.[39] Post-death interest on a decedent's gift tax liability is deductible while the gift tax liability is being contested along with the questions of whether such interest is an allowable expense under state law.[40]

¶ 825 Execution of Schedule

In claiming a deduction for claims against the estate, the claims should be itemized on Schedule K (Debts of the Decedent, and Mortgages and Liens) of Form 706. Notes unsecured by mortgage or other lien should be listed. Any indebtedness secured by a mortgage or other lien upon property of the gross estate should be listed separately under "Mortgages and Liens." Schedule K has to be filed only if the decedent had debts that are deductible on this schedule (see ¶ 73). A filled-in Schedule K is reproduced at ¶ 890.

If the amount of the debt is disputed or is the subject of litigation, only the amount that the estate representative concedes to be a valid claim is deductible. If the claim is contested, that fact must be stated on the schedule.

Full details must be included in the description of unsecured notes, including: (1) the name and address of the payee, (2) the face amount of the note, (3) the unpaid balance, (4) date and term of the note, (5) interest rate, and (6) the date to which interest was paid prior to death. Care must be taken to state the exact nature of the claim as well as the name of the creditor. If the claim is for services rendered over a period of time, the period covered by the claim should be stated. For example: Edison Electric Illuminating Co., for electric service during April 1998, $150.

If the amount of the claim is the unpaid balance due on a contract for the purchase of any property included in the gross estate, the schedule and item number at which the property is reported must be identified. If the claim represents a joint and several liability, the facts must be fully stated

[35] Reg. § 20.2053-6.

[36] Rev. Rul. 69-402, 1969-2 CB 176.

[37] Rev. Rul. 78-125, 1978-1 CB 292, revoking Rev. Rul. 75-239, 1975-1 CB 304.

[38] Rev. Rul. 80-250, 1980-2 CB 278; *Est. of E.H. Hoover*, 49 TCM 1239, CCH Dec. 42,031(M), TC Memo. 1985-183.

[39] Code Sec. 2053(c)(1)(D).

[40] *J. Webster*, 65 TC 968, CCH Dec. 33,661 (Acq.).

and the financial responsibility of the co-obligor explained. All vouchers or original records should be preserved for inspection by the IRS.

If the executor elects to take a deduction, rather than a credit, for state and foreign death taxes on certain charitable transfers, these taxes should be listed as a debt on the "Debts of the Decedent" portion of Schedule K.[41]

¶ 830 Community Property

If debts to be listed in the return are community debts, only one-half of the amount of such community debts should be listed. An appropriate explanation should be made.

[41] Instructions for Form 706 (Rev. July 1998), p. 14.

Chapter 22

MORTGAGES AND LIENS

¶ 850 Excluding Mortgages and Liens

The amounts of any mortgages and liens that are charges against the estate of the decedent or against any specific property in the estate and that date from before decedent's death are excluded from the taxable estate. If the charges are collectible against specific property only, they are excluded by including in the gross estate only the net value of the subject property. In other instances, the value of the property is first included in the gross estate in full. Then the mortgage or lien is taken as a deduction.[1]

¶ 855 Claiming Deductions on Schedule K

Only obligations secured by mortgages or other liens upon property included in the gross estate at its full value (undiminished by the amount of the mortgage or lien) are to be itemized as "Mortgages and Liens" on Schedule K (Debts of the Decedent, and Mortgages and Liens) of Form 706. If the decedent's estate is liable for the amount of the indebtedness secured by such mortgage or lien, the full value of the property subject to the mortgage or lien must be included in the gross estate under the appropriate schedule. The estate is considered liable for the indebtedness if it is enforceable against other property of the estate not subject to the mortgage or lien, or if the decedent was personally liable.[2] Schedule K need only be filed if the decedent has mortgages and/or liens that are deductible on this schedule.

There are instances where the decedent's estate is not liable for the amount of a debt secured by a mortgage or lien and the amount of the debt is greater than the value of the property subject to such mortgage or lien. In these situations, it is not possible to obtain a deduction for the full amount of the debt by entering the full value of the property as a part of the gross estate and then deducting the full amount of the debt under this schedule. Where the estate is not liable, only the redemption value (or the value of the property, less the mortgage or indebtedness) is reported as part of the gross estate.

Generally, the amount of mortgage liability on a decedent's property is available either as a deduction from the gross estate or as a reduction in the value of the property includible in the gross estate. However, the U. S. Court of Appeals for the Eleventh Circuit disallowed a deduction for the unpaid principal balances of mortgages on two parcels of real estate that were includible in the estates of a husband and wife because the decedents,

---

[1] Code Sec. 2053(a)(4); Reg. § 20.2053-1(a)(1)(iv).

[2] Reg. § 20.2053-7.

were mere accommodation parties to the mortgages and notes and, thus, were not primarily liable for the indebtedness.[3]

Notes and other obligations secured by the deposit of collateral, such as stocks and bonds, should also be listed under "Mortgages and Liens" on Schedule K. Each mortgage and lien should be identified by indicating in the "Description" column the particular schedule and item number at which the property subject to the mortgage or lien is reported. The description of the obligation should show: (1) the name and address of the mortgagee, payee, or obligee, (2) the date and term of the mortgage, note, or other agreement under which the indebtedness is established, (3) the face amount, (4) the unpaid balance, (5) the rate of interest, and (6) the date to which interest was paid prior to the decedent's death.

¶ 860 Limitations as to Amount

Mortgages on, or any indebtedness with respect to, property included in the gross estate are deductible only to the extent that the liability was contracted in good faith and for an adequate and full consideration in money or money's worth.[4] Only interest accrued to the date of the decedent's death is deductible, even though the estate representative elects the alternate valuation method.[5]

The IRS has ruled that a decedent's estate could claim a deduction for the full amount of a mortgage on the decedent's farmland, even though the farmland was included in the gross estate at its special use value (see ¶ 280 through ¶ 296).[6] The IRS noted that all of the property subject to the mortgage was included in the gross estate and that the estate was liable for payment of the mortgage. Generally, the amount of a mortgage for which a decedent's estate is liable is deductible from the gross estate if the full value of the property subject to the mortgage is included in the gross estate. Under the facts of the ruling, the full value of the decedent's farmland was included in the gross estate because, for estate tax purposes, the special use value of property is equivalent to its full value.

¶ 870 Community Property

If mortgages to be listed in the return are community obligations, such status should be made clear. Only one-half of the amount should be listed as an obligation of the estate.

---

[3] *C.F. Theis Est.*, CA-11, 85-2 USTC ¶ 13,639, 770 F2d 981.

[4] Reg. § 20.2053-7.

[5] Reg. § 20.2053-7.

[6] Rev. Rul. 83-81, 1983-1 CB 230.

¶ 890 Filled-In Schedule K

The filled-in Schedule K, Form 706 (Rev. July 1998), relates to the fact situation of a person who dies on January 1, 1998, with an estate tax return due within nine months (without extensions). Schedule K must be filed only if there are debts that are deductible on this schedule.

Form 706 (Rev. 7-98)

Estate of: James X. Diversey

SCHEDULE K — Debts of the Decedent, and Mortgages and Liens

Item number	Debts of the Decedent — Creditor and nature of claim, and allowable death taxes	Amount unpaid to date	Amount in contest	Amount claimed as a deduction
1	Richard LaForge,M.D., 633 East 81st St., Chicago, IL: Medical services with respect to decedent's last illness (Nov. 26,1997 to Jan. 1,1998).			3,200
2	St. Luke's Hospital, Chicago, IL: Hospitalization from Dec. 24, 1997 to Jan. 1, 1998 in connection with decedent's last illness (bill dated Jan. 10, 1998).			7,200
3	Telephone Co.: Telephone service from Nov. 26, 1997 to Jan. 1, 1998.			150
4	Public Service Company for Northern Illinois: Gas and electricity from Nov. 26, 1997 to Jan. 1, 1998.			500
	Total from continuation schedules (or additional sheets) attached to this schedule			
	TOTAL. (Also enter on Part 5, Recapitulation, page 3, at item 14.)			11,050

Item number	Mortgages and Liens — Description	Amount
1	Mortgage secured by house and lot, 402 Oceanview Drive, Tampa, FL (Schedule A, Item 2). The decedent was also personally liable. The Mortgagee is Home Mortgage Co., 71st and Ashland Aves., Chicago, IL. The mortgage is for 20 years, dated March 13, 1992, with a face amount of $170,000; interest at 10% per annum. Interest was paid through Dec. 31, 1997, prior to the decedent's death.	138,210
	Total from continuation schedules (or additional sheets) attached to this schedule	
	TOTAL. (Also enter on Part 5, Recapitulation, page 3, at item 15.)	138,210

(If more space is needed, attach the continuation schedule from the end of this package or additional sheets of the same size.)
(The instructions to Schedule K are in the separate instructions.)

Schedule K — Page 25

¶ 890. Filled-In Schedule K

SCHEDULE K—Debts of the Decedent, and Mortgages and Liens

Chapter 23

NET LOSSES DURING ADMINISTRATION

¶ 900 Claiming Losses

Casualty and theft losses that occur during settlement of the estate are deductible to the extent they are not compensated by insurance.[1] Losses with respect to an estate asset are not deductible if they occur after distribution of the asset to the beneficiary. The term "casualty losses" encompasses losses resulting from fire, storm, shipwreck and war. The loss contemplated is a loss with respect to tangible property.[2]

Depreciation in value of intangibles, even though occasioned by destruction, damage, or theft of underlying physical assets, is not deductible under Code Sec. 2054. Losses in value of intangibles can serve to reduce the taxable estate, but only if they occur within six months after death so that the intangibles may be included in the estate at their value as of a date six months after death.

Casualty and theft losses are not deductible for estate tax purposes if, at the time the return is filed, they had been claimed as an income tax deduction.[3]

¶ 901 Alternate Valuation

When the estate representative elects to value the estate as of a date six months after death, losses during this period are reflected in the value or absence of value of the damaged or lost property. Losses are shown in the values of the specific property rather than as a deductible item, except in unusual situations. The loss or theft cannot be reflected both as a deduction and in the valuation of the affected items of property.[4]

¶ 905 Execution of Schedule

Full details of the amount and cause of loss must be reported under "Net losses during administration" on Schedule L (Net Losses During Administration and Expenses Incurred in Administrating Property Not Subject to Claims) of Form 706. This schedule must be filed if the estate has deductible losses. In instances where insurance payments or other compensation is received on account of loss or theft, the amount received should be stated. The property on which loss is claimed should be identified by indicating the particular schedule and item number at which the property is reported.

¶ 906 Community Property

If losses have been incurred with respect to property that had been held as community property, only one-half of the amount of such losses may be listed. Such losses should be accompanied by an appropriate explanation.

---

[1] Code Sec. 2054.

[2] Reg. § 20.2054-1.

[3] Reg. § 20.2054-1.

[4] Reg. § 20.2032-1(g).

Chapter 24

EXPENSES FOR PROPERTY NOT SUBJECT TO CLAIMS

¶ 950 Expenses in Administration

Expenses of administering property that are included in the decedent's gross estate, but are not subject to claims against it, are deductible under certain circumstances. Such expenses are deductible if: (1) they would be allowed as deductions if the property being administered were subject to claims (see ¶ 780) and (2) they are paid before the expiration of the period of limitation for assessment (three years after the return was filed or at any time after such tax became due and before the expiration of three years after the date on which any part of such tax was paid).[1] Usually, such expenses include principal commissions paid with respect to trust property included in the gross estate and attorneys' fees incurred to contest the inclusion of trust property in the decedent's gross estate. However, they may also be incurred in connection with the collection of other assets, or the transfer or clearance of title to other property included in the decedent's gross estate but not included in the probate estate.

¶ 955 Execution of Schedule

Amounts representing expenses incurred in administering property included in the gross estate but not subject to claims should be itemized under "Expenses incurred in administering property not subject to claims" on the lower portion of Schedule L of Form 706.

The names and addresses of persons to whom the expenses are payable and the exact nature of the particular expense should be stated. The property with respect to which the expense was incurred should be identified by indicating the schedule and item number at which the property is reported.

An item may be entered for deduction, even though the exact amount is not known at that time. It must be ascertainable with reasonable certainty and expected to be paid before the expiration of the period of limitation for assessment (three years after the estate tax return is filed). No deduction may be taken upon the basis of a vague or uncertain estimate. All vouchers and receipts should be retained for inspection by the IRS.

---

[1] Code Sec. 2053; Reg. § 20.2053-1.

¶960 Filled-In Schedule L

The filled-in Schedule L, Form 706 (Rev. July 1998), relates to the fact situation of a person who dies on January 1, 1998, with an estate tax return due within nine months (without extensions). Schedule L must be filed only if there are losses that are deductible on this schedule.

Form 706 (Rev. 7-98)

Estate of: James X. Diversey

SCHEDULE L — Net Losses During Administration and Expenses Incurred in Administering Property Not Subject to Claims

Item number	Net losses during administration (Note: *Do not deduct losses claimed on a Federal income tax return.*)	Amount
1	Damage to house listed as Item 1 on Schedule A, Real Estate, resulting from high winds on April 30, 1998. Five windows were broken and siding on the upper half of the house required patching and repainting. Loss was not covered by insurance.	1,294
	Total from continuation schedules (or additional sheets) attached to this schedule	
	TOTAL. (Also enter on Part 5, Recapitulation, page 3, at item 18.)	1,294

Item number	Expenses incurred in administering property not subject to claims (indicate whether estimated, agreed upon, or paid.)	Amount
1	Commissions paid to the First National Bank of Homewood, Homewood, IL, with respect to trust listed as Item 1 on Schedule G, Transfers During Decdent's Life.	375
	Total from continuation schedules (or additional sheets) attached to this schedule	
	TOTAL. (Also enter on Part 5, Recapitulation, page 3, at item 19.)	375

(If more space is needed, attach the continuation schedule from the end of this package or additional sheets of the same size.)

Schedule L — Page 26 (The instructions to Schedule L are in the separate instructions.)

Chapter 25

MARITAL DEDUCTION

¶ 1000 Transfers to Surviving Spouse

An unlimited marital deduction is available for computing the taxable estate of an individual where any part of the deceased person's estate passes or has passed to the surviving spouse. The property so passing is deductible in computing the taxable estate to the extent that it is includible in the gross estate.[1] The amount of the allowable marital deduction depends on the year of death. For estates of decedents dying after 1981, the deduction is unlimited in amount. However, for estates of decedents dying after 1976 and before 1982, the deduction was limited to the greater of one-half of the adjusted gross estate or $250,000. The post-1981 rules are discussed at ¶ 1001. The pre-1982 rules are explained at ¶ 1005.

The marital deduction is allowed only with respect to property, the value of which is included in determining the gross estate. Thus, if the surviving spouse acquired property of the decedent during the decedent's life for full consideration in money or money's worth, no deduction will result from such interests.

Effective for the estates of decedents dying after November 10, 1988, a marital deduction is denied where property passes to a surviving spouse who is not a U.S. citizen.[2] However, in the case of a nonresident alien whose spouse is a U.S. citizen, the estate tax marital deduction will be

[1] Code Sec. 2056(a); Reg. § 20.2056(a)-1.

[2] Code Sec. 2056(d)(1).

allowed. An exception to the general rule denying a marital deduction for property passing to an alien spouse exists in the case of property passing by way of a qualified domestic trust (QDOT) (see ¶ 1004). However, if a surviving spouse becomes a U.S. citizen before the federal estate tax return is filed, property passing to the spouse will qualify for the marital deduction if the spouse was a U.S. resident at all times after the date of the decedent's death and before becoming a U.S. citizen.[3] The property qualifying for the marital deduction is listed on Schedule M (Bequests, etc., to Surviving Spouse) of Form 706.

¶ 1001 Amount of Deduction

In general, an unlimited marital deduction is allowed the estates of decedents dying after 1981. However, estates of decedents who died after 1981 but had executed a will or trust before 1982 containing a maximum marital deduction formula are subject to the law as in effect prior to amendment by the Economic Recovery Tax Act of 1981 (P.L. 97-34) (see ¶ 1005). Under prior law, the maximum estate tax marital deduction for property passing from the decedent to the surviving spouse was the greater of one-half of the decedent's gross estate or $250,000.

• *Terminable Interests*

Generally, transfers of terminable interests (such as life estates, terms for years, annuities, etc.) do not qualify for the marital deduction (see ¶ 1020 through ¶ 1029 for a detailed discussion of the terminable interest rule).[4] However, there is an exception to the terminable interest rule for "qualified terminable interest property" (see ¶ 1002). Under the exception, if certain conditions are met, a life interest granted to a surviving spouse will not be treated as a terminable interest. The entire property subject to such an interest will be treated as passing to the spouse and, accordingly, the entire value of the transferred property will qualify for a marital deduction.[5]

¶ 1002 Qualified Terminable Interest Property

An estate or gift tax marital deduction is allowed for the value of "qualified terminable interest property" if the donor or decedent's executor so elects. Qualified terminable interest property (QTIP) is property passing from the decedent to a spouse who is entitled to all income from the property (or a portion thereof) for life, payable at least annually. This income interest is known as a "qualifying income interest." The issue of whether an income interest for life fails to qualify when accumulated income for the period between the last distribution date and the date of the surviving spouse's death ("stub" income) is not distributed to the surviving spouse's estate or subject to the spouse's general power of appointment has been a subject of dispute. The Tax Court held that such an interest was not a qualifying interest,[6] but this decision was reversed by the U.S. Court of Appeals for the Ninth Circuit.[7] Later, the IRS issued final regulations that agreed with the position taken by the Ninth Circuit.[8] In a case decided after issuance of the final regulations, but arising prior to

---

[3] Code Sec. 2056(d)(4).

[4] Code Sec. 2056(b)(1).

[5] Code Sec. 2056(b)(7).

[6] *R. Howard Est.*, 91 TC 329, CCH Dec. 45,002.

[7] *R. Howard Est.*, CA-9, 90-2 USTC ¶ 60,033.

[8] Reg. § 20.2056(b)-7(d)(4).

their effective date, the Tax Court reasserted the position it took in *Howard,* but again was reversed, this time by the U.S. Court of Appeals for the Eleventh Circuit.[9]

With respect to the qualifying income interest requirement, the IRS has ruled that a decedent's estate could elect to treat a distribution from an individual retirement account as QTIP. In this instance the IRA distribution option required that the date of death balance in the IRA be paid in annual installments to a testamentary QTIP trust along with income earned on the undistributed balance. Income earned on both the distributed and undistributed portions of the IRA were to be paid currently to the surviving spouse. Because all of the IRA income for the calendar year was required to be distributed to the trust by the close of the year and the trust had to distribute all income currently to the surviving spouse, the income earned on the undistributed portion of the IRA was payable annually to the spouse as required by Code Sec. 2056(b)(7).[10]

In community property states, a nonparticipant spouse may be treated as having a vested community property interest in his or her spouse's qualified plan, IRA, or simplified employee pension (SEP) plan. Pursuant to the Taxpayer Relief Act of 1997 (P.L. 105-34), upon the death of a nonparticipant spouse, the nonparticipant spouse's survivorship interest in such a plan that is attributable to community property laws may be treated as QTIP.[11]

No person, including the spouse, can have the power to appoint any part of the property subject to the qualified income interest to any person other than the spouse during the spouse's life. However, creation or retention of any powers over all or a portion of the corpus is allowed, provided that all such powers are exercisable only on or after the spouse's death. Further, income interests granted for a term of years or a life interest subject to termination upon occurrence of a condition (such as remarriage) are not qualifying income interests.

● *Specific Portion*

The marital deduction is available when the spouse is entitled to all the income from the entire interest in the property or to the income from a specific portion of the property. For example, the right to receive 60 percent (or 3/5) of the income of a trust for life or the right to receive the income for life from 60 percent of a trust would qualify for QTIP treatment if all other requirements for QTIP treatment are satisfied.[12]

For most decedents dying after October 24, 1992, the term "specific portion" includes only amounts determined on a fractional or percentage basis, and not pecuniary amounts.

> ***Example:*** Alice Green's 1998 will provided for creation of a trust funded with $3,000,000 and providing for a benefit of $70,000 per year payable to her surviving spouse for life. Assume the trust assets are producing income of 7% per year. This is not a qualifying interest on $1,000,000 of the property despite the fact that $70,000 of

[9] *L. Shelfer Est.,* CA-11, 96-2 USTC ¶ 60,238, rev'g TC, 103 TC 10, CCH Dec. 49,967.

[10] Rev. Rul. 89-89, 1989-2 CB 231.

[11] Code Sec. 2056(b)(7)(C).

[12] Reg. § 20.2056(b)-5(c), as made applicable by Reg. § 20.2056(b)-7(b)(1)(ii).

income (given the 7% income level) could be translated into all of the income on $1,000,000 of property.

Under transitional rules, a pecuniary amount can still be a specific portion under certain circumstances for decedents dying after October 24, 1992.[13]

- *Annuities*

A survivor annuity includible in a decedent's gross estate under Code Sec. 2039 where only the surviving spouse has the right to receive payments before his or her death is treated as a qualifying income interest for life.[14] There is a presumption under the Code that a QTIP election is desired. Thus, an executor who does not intend QTIP treatment must elect out of the QTIP provision.[15]

Special rules apply in the case of a decedent dying with a will or trust executed on or before October 24, 1992, that provides the surviving spouse with a lifetime annuity interest payable from the trust or other assets passing from the decedent. In such cases, the surviving spouse's annuity interest is treated as a qualifying income interest for life if the decedent was under a mental disability to change the disposition of his property on October 24, 1992, and the decedent did not regain competence before death. The annuity interest will not be treated as a qualifying income interest for life if any person other than the surviving spouse may receive, during the surviving spouse's lifetime, any distribution of the property or its income from which the annuity is payable. For purposes of the marital deduction, the deductible interest is that *specific portion* of the property that, assuming the interest rate generally applicable for the valuation of annuities under Code Sec. 2031 and Code Sec. 7520, would produce income equal to the minimum amount payable annually to the surviving spouse.[16]

A usufruct interest for life under Louisiana law constitutes a qualifying income interest for QTIP purposes.[17] The QTIP election will be available for both consumable and nonconsumable property; however, in the case of consumable property, the value of the usufruct will be includible in the surviving spouse's gross estate under Code Sec. 2044 (see ¶ 773) rather than under Code Sec. 2033.

- *QTIP Election*

The election to treat property as QTIP property is made on Schedule M (Bequests, etc., to Surviving Spouse) of Form 706 by the estate's executor.[18] Once made, an election or failure to make an election is irrevocable.[19] A QTIP election is made on Form 706 by simply listing the qualified terminable interest property on Schedule M and deducting its value.

The election may be made for a portion of property that meets the QTIP requirements, provided that the election relates to a fractional or percentile share of the property. This fraction may be defined by means of a formula.[20]

---

[13] Reg. § 20.2056(b)-5(c)(3) and Reg. § 20.2056(b)-7(e).

[14] Code Sec. 2056(b)(7)(C).

[15] Code Sec. 2056(b)(7)(C)(ii).

[16] Reg. § 20.2056(b)-7(e).

[17] Code Sec. 2056(b)(7)(B)(ii).

[18] Reg. § 20.2056(b)-7(b)(3).

[19] Code Sec. 2056(b)(7)(B)(v).

[20] Reg. § 20.2056(b)-7(b)(1)(ii).

• *Contingent Income Interests*

Generally, an income interest will not qualify for QTIP treatment if it is contingent on the happening of some event. One exception to this rule is making the interest contingent on the election of QTIP treatment by the executor. Effective for estates whose returns are due after February 18, 1997, Reg. § 20.2056(b)-7(d)(3)(i) permits QTIP treatment to be contingent on the executor making a QTIP election. Prior to that time, the IRS successfully challenged several such contingent QTIP elections at the Tax Court,[21] only to be reversed each time.[22] The IRS finally acquiesced to this issue upon the Tax Court's abandonment of its position.[23] Certain estates of decedents whose estate tax returns were due on or before January 18, 1997, that did not make a QTIP election because the surviving spouse's interest was contingent on the executor making the election are granted an extension of time to make the election. To be eligible, the Code Sec. 6511(a) period of limitations for filing a claim for credit or refund must not have expired.[24]

• *Protective QTIP Election*

Executors may make a protective election in certain limited circumstances. Such an election is allowed only if, at the time the estate tax return is filed, the executor of the estate reasonably believes there is a bona fide issue as to whether an asset is includible in the gross estate or as to the nature of the property the surviving spouse is entitled to receive.[25]

• *Tax on Transfer of Interest*

Property for which a QTIP election is made will be subject to transfer taxes at the earlier of (1) the date on which the spouse disposes (by gift, sale or otherwise) of all or part of the qualifying income interest, or (2) the date of the spouse's death. If a spouse transfers the qualifying income interest during life, the entire value of the property, reduced by any amount received by the spouse upon disposition, is a taxable gift (see ¶ 2313).[26] Otherwise, the entire value of the property subject to the qualified income interest will be included in the spouse's gross estate at its fair market value on the date of death or on the alternate valuation date, if elected (see ¶ 773).[27]

The spouse or the spouse's estate may recover from the recipient of the property the gift tax paid on the remainder interest as a result of a lifetime transfer of the income interest, or the estate tax paid as a result of the inclusion of the value of the property in the spouse's gross estate, as well as any penalties or interest attributable to the additional estate or gift tax.[28]

---

[21] *A. Clayton Est.*, 97 TC 327, CCH Dec. 47,612; *W. Robertson Est.*, 98 TC 678, CCH Dec. 48,310; *J. Spencer Est.*, 64 TCM 937, CCH Dec. 48,546(M), TC Memo. 1992-579.

[22] *A. Clayton Est.*, CA-5, 92-2 USTC ¶ 60,121, 976 F2d 1486; *W. Robertson Est.*, CA-8, 94-1 USTC ¶ 60,153; *J. Spencer Est.*, CA-6, 95-2 USTC ¶ 60,188.

[23] *W. Clack Est.*, 106 TC 131, CCH Dec. 51,193 (Acq.).

[24] Reg. § 20.2056(b)-7(d)(3)(ii).

[25] Reg. § 20.2056(b)-7(c).

[26] Code Sec. 2519.

[27] Code Sec. 2044.

[28] Code Sec. 2207A.

¶ 1003 Split Gifts to Spouse and Charity

There is a special rule for transfers of interests in the same property to a spouse and a qualifying charitable organization. If an individual creates a qualified charitable remainder annuity trust or unitrust and the donor and his or her spouse are the only beneficiaries who are not a charitable beneficiary or an ESOP beneficiary, the prohibition on deduction of terminable interests (see ¶ 1020) does not apply. The individual (or his or her estate) receives a charitable deduction for the value of the remainder interest and a marital deduction for the value of the annuity or unitrust interest, and no transfer tax is imposed.[29]

If the individual transfers a qualified income interest to his or her spouse with a remainder to charity, the entire value of the property will be considered as passing to the surviving spouse, and will qualify for a marital deduction and no part of the value of the property qualifies for the charitable deduction.[30] Although, upon the spouse's death, the entire value of the property will be included in the spouse's gross estate, any property passing outright to charity may qualify for a charitable deduction.

¶ 1004 Qualified Domestic Trusts

Effective for estates of decedents dying after November 10, 1988, property passing to a surviving spouse who is not a U.S. citizen is not eligible for the estate tax marital deduction unless the property passes through a qualified domestic trust (QDOT). However, in the case of a nonresident alien whose spouse is a U.S. citizen, the marital deduction will be allowed for estate tax purposes.

In order to be considered a QDOT, the trust instrument must provide that at least one of the trustees be a U.S. citizen or domestic corporation and that any corpus distribution be subject to the U.S. trustee's right to withhold the estate tax imposed on such distribution. For trust instruments of decedents dying after November 10, 1988, if the instrument provides that all the trustees must be either U.S. citizens or domestic corporations, then the withholding requirement is deemed satisfied regardless of whether the withholding requirement is explicitly stated in the trust instrument. [31] The trust must also meet security requirements designed to ensure collection of the estate tax imposed on the trust. The trust instrument must require that at least one of the trustees be an individual citizen of the United States or a domestic corporation.[32] In addition, if the trust assets, as of the date of the decedent's death or, if applicable, the alternate valuations date, exceed $2,000,000, the trust's governing instrument must require that either:

(1) during the entire term of the QDOT, at least one U.S. trustee be a bank; or

(2) the U.S. trustee furnish a bond in favor of the IRS in an amount equal to at least 65 percent of the fair market value of the trust assets; or

---

[29] Code Sec. 2056(b)(8).

[30] Reg. § 20.2056(b)(9).

[31] Act Sec. 1303, Taxpayer Relief Act of 1997 (P.L. 105-34).

[32] Code Sec. 2056A(a)(1).

(3) the U.S. trustee furnish an irrevocable letter of credit issued by a U.S. branch of a foreign bank or by a foreign bank and confirmed by a U.S. bank, in an amount equal to 65 percent of the trust assets.[33]

If the fair market value of the trust assets as finally determined for federal estate tax purposes is less than $2,000,000, the QDOT need not meet any of the three requirements listed above if the trust instrument expressly provides that no more than 35 percent of the fair market value of the trust assets, determined annually, may be invested in real property located outside of the United States.[34]

In addition, the executor must make an irrevocable QDOT election on the estate tax return with respect to the trust. However, no election may be made on a return filed more than one year after the due date of such return, including extensions.[35]

An estate tax is imposed upon corpus distributions from the trust that are made prior to the date of the surviving spouse's death and upon the value of the property remaining in a QDOT upon the date of death of the surviving spouse. However, the estate tax will no longer be imposed on a QDOT after the surviving spouse becomes a U.S. citizen if: (1) the spouse was a U.S. resident at the time of the decedent's death and at all times thereafter, (2) no tax was imposed on a QDOT distribution before the spouse became a U.S. citizen or (3) the spouse elected to treat any distribution upon which tax had been imposed as a taxable gift made by the spouse (thereby reducing the unified credit available to the spouse) for the purpose of determining the spouse's future estate and gift tax liability.[36] In addition, the estate tax on distributions is itself a distribution subject to the estate tax.[37] Further, a distribution of corpus from a QDOT to a surviving spouse is excluded from the estate tax if the distribution is made "on account of hardship."[38] If no property other than the property passing to the surviving spouse is transferred to the QDOT, the trust need not otherwise qualify for the marital deduction. If the trust is funded with other property passing from the decedent, however, then all of the assets in the QDOT must qualify for the marital deduction.[39]

A special rule applies if more than one QDOT exists with respect to a decedent.[40] In such cases, the amount of estate tax imposed on the trusts is determined using the highest rate of tax in effect at the time of the decedent's death, unless a U.S. citizen or domestic corporation is responsible for filing all estate tax returns for such QDOTs and meets IRS regulatory requirements.

Another special rule states that estate tax is not imposed on distributions defined as income. However, the IRS is authorized to prescribe such regulations as necessary to determine when payments under an annuity would be treated as income for purposes of the estate tax on distributions. The IRS is also empowered to prescribe regulations under which an annuity or other payment, includible in a decedent's gross estate and payable for life or a term of years, may be treated as a QDOT.[41] Such

---

[33] Reg. § 20.2056A-2(d)(1)(i).

[34] Reg. § 20.2056A-2(d)(1)(ii).

[35] Code Sec. 2056A(d).

[36] Code Sec. 2056A(b)(12).

[37] Code Sec. 2056A(b)(11).

[38] Code Sec. 2056A(b)(3)(B).

[39] Reg. § 20.2056A-4(b)(1).

[40] Code Sec. 2056A(b)(2)(C).

[41] Code Sec. 2056A(e).

interests would include property interests that cannot be transferred to a QDOT under federal law, such as an interest in an IRA or qualified plan.[42]

Certain estate tax benefits, such as charitable and marital deductions, special use valuation, and extensions of time to pay estate tax, are allowed against the estate tax on QDOT distributions if such benefits would be allowable with respect to the estate of the surviving spouse.[43] In addition, property distributed from a QDOT during the surviving spouse's lifetime would receive a carryover basis. However, the carryover basis would be increased by an amount equal to the proportion of any QDOT estate tax paid that the net appreciation in the property bears to the distribution.[44]

● *Returns*

Form 706-QDT (U.S. Estate Tax Return for Qualified Domestic Trusts) is used to report the estate tax due with respect to taxable distributions from a QDOT, the death of the noncitizen surviving spouse, the trust's ceasing to qualify as a QDOT, and hardship distributions from the trust. Form 706-QDT must be filed within nine months following the date of the surviving spouse's death or the date that the trust ceases to qualify as a QDOT. The return is due by April 15 of the year following the year in which the taxable event or hardship distribution occurs.[45] (Form 706-QDT is at ¶ 1097.)

If the estate tax for the decedent spouse's estate has not been finally determined (such as in the case where a judicial determination of the tax is pending), a tentative tax is imposed using the highest estate tax rate in effect as of the date of the decedent's death. When a final determination is made, any amount of the tentative tax that is in excess of the additional estate tax that would have been imposed had the property been included in the decedent's estate is refundable if a claim is filed not later than one year after the date of final determination. A refund of tentative tax imposed pending final resolution of estate tax liability bears interest.[46]

A trustee is personally liable for the tax, but may discharge such liability.[47] The tax imposed on a QDOT is treated as an estate tax with respect to the decedent spouse's estate. Therefore, it qualifies as a previously paid tax for purposes of the Code Sec. 2103 credit for tax on prior transfers, determined without regard to the date of the decedent spouse's death.[48] In addition, there is a lien against the property giving rise to such tax for 10 years after the taxable event.

¶ 1005 Pre-1982 Marital Deduction Rules

For estates of decedents dying before 1982, the maximum estate tax marital deduction for property passing from the decedent to the surviving spouse was equal to the greater of one-half of the decedent's adjusted gross estate, or $250,000.[49] Thus, estates with adjusted gross estates of less than $500,000 were provided with an additional benefit. For example, assume a spouse had died in 1981 with an adjusted gross estate of $395,000 and had

[42] Conference Committee Report to the Revenue Reconciliation Act of 1989 (P.L. 101-239); Reg. § 20.2056A-4(b)(7); and Reg. § 20.2056A-4(c).

[43] Reg. § 20.2056A-6(b).

[44] Reg. § 20.2056A-12.

[45] Code Sec. 2056A(b)(5).

[46] Code Sec. 2056A(b)(2)(B).

[47] Code Sec. 2204.

[48] Reg. § 20.2056A-7.

[49] Code Sec. 2056(c), prior to its repeal by P.L. 97-34.

passed $250,000 in property to his or her surviving spouse that qualifies for the marital deduction. This left a net estate of $145,000 subject to estate tax. However, the unified credit exemption equivalent for 1981 (see ¶ 15) eliminated any estate tax liability. For the estates of decedents dying before 1977, the marital deduction was limited to 50 percent of the value of the adjusted gross estate.

- *Transitional Rule for Pre-1982 Marital Deduction Formula Clauses*

An unlimited marital deduction is allowed for estates of decedents dying after 1981 (see ¶ 1001). However, many wills and trusts that were executed prior to 1982 included maximum marital deduction formula clauses under which the amount of property transferred to the surviving spouse was to be determined by reference to the maximum allowable marital deduction. Because, with respect to estates of decedents dying before 1982, the maximum estate tax deduction was the greater of $250,000 or one-half of the adjusted gross estate, many individuals may not have intended any greater amount to pass to their surviving spouses as might be the case if the unlimited marital deduction were used in the computation of the marital deduction under the formula clause.

Under a transitional rule, the unlimited marital deduction is not applicable to transfers resulting from a will or trust executed before September 12, 1981, that contains a maximum marital deduction formula clause. The transitional rule applies provided that: (1) the decedent died after 1981, (2) the formula clause was not amended at any time after September 12, 1981 and before the death of the decedent to refer specifically to the unlimited marital deduction, and (3) there is no state law that would construe the formula clause as referring to the unlimited marital deduction.[50]

Whether a particular will or trust contains a maximum marital deduction formula has been a frequently litigated question. The mere appearance of a marital deduction formula clause in a will or trust will not satisfy the requirements of the transitional rule. Rather, the will or trust must contain a formula *expressly* providing that the surviving spouse is to receive the maximum amount of property qualifying for the marital deduction. Any additions to the formula that might further reduce the amount received by the spouse to ensure that the unified credit or other credits of the estate are fully utilized will not be a formula clause for purposes of the transitional rule.[51]

¶ 1015 Status as Surviving Spouse

The person receiving the decedent's property for which a marital deduction is claimed must qualify as a "surviving spouse" on the date of the decedent's death. A legal separation that has not terminated the marriage at the time of death does not change the status of the surviving spouse.[52] If an interest in property passes from the decedent to a person who was the decedent's spouse, but who was not married to the decedent at the time of death, the interest is not considered as passing to the surviving

[50] Act Sec. 403(e), P.L. 97-34.

[51] *L. Niesen Est.*, CA-8, 89-1 USTC ¶ 13,790, 865 F2d 162; *F.L. Bruning Est.*, CA-10, 89-2 USTC ¶ 13,821; *S.I. Levitt Est.*, 95 TC 289, CCH Dec. 46,873; IRS Technical Advice Memorandum 9206001, 12-7-91, CCH IRS LETTER RULINGS REPORTS.

[52] *M.S. Eccles*, 19 TC 1049, CCH Dec. 19,508, aff'd on other issues by CA-4, 54-1 USTC ¶ 9129, 208 F2d 769.

spouse. If a decedent's divorce from a prior spouse is declared invalid by a state court having jurisdiction, the IRS will not allow a marital deduction for the decedent's bequest of property to a subsequent spouse.[53]

A transfer by the decedent during his lifetime to an individual to whom he was not married at the time of the transfer but to whom he was married at the time of his death and who survives him is a transfer by the decedent to his surviving spouse with respect to gifts includible in a decedent's gross estate under Code Sec. 2035.[54]

¶ 1020 Life Estate or Other Terminable Interest

Generally, no marital deduction is allowed for property interests that are terminable interests.[55] A terminable interest is an interest in property that will terminate or fail on the lapse of time or on the occurrence, or the failure to occur, of some event or contingency. The purpose of the rule is to require that if property is transferred to the surviving spouse, it will be includible in the surviving spouse's estate unless disposed of or dissipated during the surviving spouse's lifetime.

• *Types of Terminable Interests*

Terminable interests include life estates, terms for years, annuities, patents and copyrights. However, a bond, note, or similar contractual obligation that would not have the effect of an annuity or a term for years, is not a terminable interest.[56] Whether or not an interest is a terminable interest is determined by state law[57] at the death of the decedent.[58]

• *Nondeductible Terminable Interests*

A terminal interest is nondeductible if:

(1) an interest in the same property has passed (for less than adequate and full consideration in money or money's worth) from the decedent to any person other than the surviving spouse or other than the estate of the surviving spouse; and

(2) by reason of its passing, such person or his heirs or assigns may possess or enjoy any part of the property after such termination or failure of the interest passing to the surviving spouse.

It is not necessary that the contingency or event occur or fail to occur in order to make the interest terminable.[59]

Example: Tom Atwood dies leaving stocks in trust, the income to pass to his wife, Sandy, for life, with the corpus to be distributed to his son, Jason, free of the trust when he reaches maturity. If Jason predeceases Sandy, the corpus is to be turned over to Sandy, free of the trust. There is also a gift over in the event of Jason's death after the date of Sandy's death but before the date of Jason's maturity. The

---

[53] Rev. Rul. 67-442, 1967-2 CB 65; *W.A. Steffke Est.*, CA-7, 76-2 USTC ¶ 13,145, 538 F2d 730, cert. denied; *L.J. Goldwater Est.*, CA-2, 76-2 USTC ¶ 13,146, 539 F2d 878, cert. denied.

[54] Rev. Rul. 79-354, 1979-2 CB 334.

[55] Code Sec. 2056(b)(1).

[56] Reg. § 20.2056(b)-1(b).

[57] *H.P. Shedd Est.*, CA-9, 56-2 USTC ¶ 11,614, 237 F2d 345.

[58] *M. Kellmann, Transferee*, DC Mo., 68-1 USTC ¶ 12,518, 286 FSupp 632.

[59] Reg. § 20.2056(b)-1.

interest passing to Sandy upon Tom's death is a nondeductible terminable interest.

An estate for the life of the surviving spouse is an interest that will terminate in all events. If conditions (1) and (2), described above, exist, it is immaterial whether the interest passing to the surviving spouse is considered a vested interest or a contingent interest. No marital deduction is allowed in any event if the life estate or terminable interest is to be acquired for the surviving spouse, pursuant to directions of the decedent, by his executor or by the trustee of a trust.[60]

If the decedent by will bequeaths a terminable interest for which a deduction is not allowed and the surviving spouse takes under the will, the marital deduction is not allowed. A deduction is denied, even though, under local law, the interest that the spouse could have taken against the will was a fee interest for which a deduction would be allowed.[61] Similarly, the marital deduction was disallowed for the interest passing to the surviving spouse as an income beneficiary or annuitant under a trust in which other persons have an interest if the surviving spouse has no power over the principal.[62]

The IRS has ruled that a cash bequest that a decedent's surviving spouse elected in lieu of a life income interest in a trust pursuant to a provision in the decedent's will qualified for an estate tax marital deduction because it was not a terminable interest. However, no such deduction was allowable for an additional amount that the spouse could demand from the trustee in order to assist the spouse in purchasing a new house. In the former situation, the spouse had an absolute right to the cash bequest as of the date of the decedent's death and the election in the will was a mere procedural requirement that did not constitute an event or contingency for marital deduction purposes. The additional amount that the spouse could demand from the trustee constituted a nondeductible terminable interest because it was conditioned upon the spouse's purchase of a new house.[63]

The interest of the surviving spouse is not considered a terminable interest merely because the spouse's possession or enjoyment may be affected by events not provided for by the terms of the bequest. These events are the surviving spouse's death, or loss of the property by fire, earthquake, condemnation or nonpayment of taxes, or the fact that the property may be used up in an indefinite period of time. However, interests in patents, copyrights, and annuity contracts that will be used up in a fixed length of time are terminable interests and are not deductible if an interest of a third person in the same property will outlast the termination of the interest of the surviving spouse.[64]

Although it formerly contested the matter, the IRS now agrees that the property passing to a decedent's spouse under an "equalization clause" governing a trust created for the spouse's benefit by the decedent is not a nondeductible terminable interest.[65] Under the clause, the trustee has the

---

[60] Reg. § 20.2056(b)-1(c) and (f).

[61] *E.J. Allen, Exr.*, CA-2, 66-1 USTC ¶ 12,393, cert. denied. See also IRS Letter Ruling 8236004, 5-23-82, CCH IRS LETTER RULINGS REPORTS.

[62] *C.H. Stockdick Est.*, DC Tex., 65-2 USTC ¶ 12,351.

[63] Rev. Rul. 82-184, 1982-2 CB 215.

[64] Reg. § 20.2056(b)-1(g).

[65] Rev. Rul. 82-23, 1982-1 CB 139; *C.W. Smith Est.*, 66 TC 415, CCH Dec. 33,862 (Acq.), aff'd per curiam, CA-7, 77-2 USTC ¶ 13,215, 565 F2d 455; and *V.S. Laurin Est.*, CA-6, 81-1 USTC ¶ 13,398, 645 F2d 8, aff'g TC, 72 TC 73, CCH Dec. 35,987 (Acq.).

power to select as the valuation date the date of death or the alternate valuation date, whichever produces the greatest tax savings, in order to determine the percentage of trust assets to be placed in the marital portion so as to equalize the estates of both spouses.

¶ 1023 Widow's Allowance—Dower Interest

An allowance to a surviving spouse for support during the period of settlement of a decedent's estate will qualify for the marital deduction if it is not classified as a terminable interest. Although a widow's (or widower's) allowance may fall within the terminable interest rule, a marital deduction can be obtained for any portion thereof which would, in any event, pass to the surviving spouse by operation of law or of the decedent's will.[66]

Whether or not a widow's allowance is a terminable interest is dependent upon the state statute that authorizes the support payments. If, under the authorizing state law, the widow's right to a support allowance is a vested one, her interest in the allowance will qualify for the estate tax marital deduction. If, however, the right would not survive her death or remarriage prior to the securing of an award by the court, her interest is considered a nondeductible terminable one.[67] The nature of the widow's interest in the allowance must be determined as of the date of the decedent's death.[68] The courts have ruled that widows' allowances in Illinois, Maine, Maryland, Michigan, Minnesota, Missouri, Ohio and Oklahoma qualify for the marital deduction. (Some of these cases were decided before the *Jackson* case and may not be followed.) Widows' allowances or awards have been held to be nondeductible terminable interests in the states of California, Connecticut, Florida, Georgia, Iowa, Massachusetts, Montana, Nebraska, Oregon, Tennessee, Texas and Wisconsin. (State laws should be consulted for possible changes that would permit a deduction.)

Dower and curtesy interests (or statutory estates in lieu thereof) may also qualify for a marital deduction, or they may not be deductible because of the terminable interest rule. The deductibility of such interests is also dependent upon state law. A deduction will be allowed if the surviving spouse has a fixed or vested right to the dower at the moment of the decedent's death and if the dower interest is an absolute interest.[69] A payment of the commuted value of a widow's dower, if requested and paid in accordance with applicable state law, also qualifies for the marital deduction if the right to it vests at the moment of the decedent-spouse's death, even though the payment is in lieu of a dower life estate in the decedent's property.[70]

Dower interests (or amounts awarded in lieu of such interests) in the states of Arkansas, Colorado, Florida, Hawaii, Illinois, Iowa, Kentucky, Montana, New York, North Carolina, South Carolina, Tennessee and Virginia have qualified for marital deductions. If the surviving spouse does not have such a vested interest under state law, the interest will not

---

[66] Rev. Rul. 82-23, 1982-1 CB 139; *C.W. Smith Est.*, 66 TC 415, CCH Dec. 33,862 (Acq.), aff'd per curiam, CA-7, 77-2 USTC ¶ 13,215, 565 F2d 455; and *V.S. Laurin Est.*, CA-6, 81-1 USTC ¶ 13,398, 645 F2d 8, aff'g TC, 72 TC 73, CCH Dec. 35,987 (Acq.).

[67] Rev. Rul. 83, 1953-1 CB 395.

[68] *L.R. Jackson*, SCt, 64-1 USTC ¶ 12,221, 376 U.S. 503.

[69] Rev. Rul. 72-8, 1972-1 CB 309.

[70] Rev. Rul. 72-7, 1972-1 CB 308, modified by Rev. Rul. 83-107, 1983-2 CB 159.

qualify for the marital deduction. The U.S. Court of Appeals for the Fifth Circuit has held that dower interests in Alabama do not qualify for the marital deduction, but that money received in lieu of dower may qualify.[71] The Tax Court has stated, by way of dictum, that dower in New Jersey also does not qualify for the deduction.[72]

¶ 1027 Life Interest with Power of Appointment

The terminable interest rule is designed primarily to prevent the allowance of a marital deduction with respect to property which, by the terms of the transfer, is likely to escape inclusion in the gross estate of the surviving spouse. Although there is a limited elective exception to this rule for qualified terminable interest property with respect to estates of decedents dying after 1981 (see ¶ 1002), this property is includible in the surviving spouse's gross estate by specific statutory provision.[73]

When a decedent gives to his or her spouse an interest for life, together with a general power of appointment, the possibility of exclusion from the surviving spouse's gross estate is substantially removed. Therefore, such transfers (which are usually made in the form of a "marital deduction" trust), are permitted to qualify for the marital deduction as exceptions to the terminable interest rule, so long as they meet certain conditions.[74]

● *All of the Income Requirement*

The surviving spouse must be entitled for life to all income from the property interest and have a general power of appointment over the property. Without disqualifying the property interest from the marital deduction, a surviving spouse may be entitled to the income from a specific portion of the property interest.[75] In general, for decedents dying after October 24, 1992, a "specific portion" is a portion of a property interest determined on a fractional or percentage basis only.[76]

Prior to the enactment of Code Sec. 2056(b)(10), the U.S. Supreme Court had held that "specific portion" included a fixed dollar amount.[77] Under a transitional rule, a right to a specific amount of income will qualify for the marital deduction if the interest was created under a will or revocable trust executed before October 24, 1992, if either (1) the decedent dies within three years after October 24, 1992, or (2) on October 24, 1992, the decedent was under a mental disability to change the disposition of his or her property and did not regain competence to dispose of such property before death. The transitional rule, however, does not apply if the will or trust is amended after October 24, 1992, to increase the amount of the transfer qualifying for the marital deduction or to alter the terms by which the interest passes.[78] Under the transitional rule, a specific sum payable annually, or at more frequent intervals, out of property and its income that is not limited by the income of the property is treated as the right to receive the income from a specific portion of the property. The specific

---

[71] *F.A. Crosby, Admr.*, CA-5, 58-2 USTC ¶ 11,808, 257 F2d 515; *M.I. Hiles, Exr.*, CA-5, 63-1 USTC ¶ 12,146.

[72] *J. Nachimson Est.*, 50 TC 452, CCH Dec. 28,993.

[73] Code Sec. 2044.

[74] Code Sec. 2056(b)(5).

[75] Reg. § 20.2056(b)-5.

[76] Code Sec. 2056(b)(10).

[77] *Northeastern Pennsylvania National Bank & Trust Co., Exr.*, SCt, 67-1 USTC ¶ 12,470, 387 US 213.

[78] Reg. § 20.2056(b)-5(c)(3).

portion is the portion of the property that, assuming the interest rate generally applicable for the valuation of annuities at the time of the decedent's death, would produce income equal to such payments.

● *Annual Income Requirement*

The surviving spouse must be entitled to receive the income annually, or at more frequent intervals. Such spouse must have the power, exercisable in favor of herself or himself or of her or his estate, to appoint the property interest or specific portion from which she or he has a right to the income. Such power must be exercisable by the spouse alone and in all events. It is not necessary that the surviving spouse have the right to exercise the power during lifetime if she or he can exercise it by will and in favor of her or his estate as well as in favor of other persons. The property must not be subject to a power in any other person to appoint to anyone other than the surviving spouse any of the property for which the deduction is sought. Nor is it necessary that the property be in trust.

In determining whether a transfer meets the above requirements, state law should be consulted. For example, if the transfer does not specify the frequency of income payments, the transfer may still qualify, if, under state law, income must be distributed at least annually.

● *Powers*

The IRS has issued rules that cover the power of a fiduciary to allocate income and expenses between income and principal and to provide depreciation reserves, without causing the loss or diminution of the marital deduction, where the spouse has a life estate and power of appointment.[79] A fiduciary may have these powers if state law or the governing instrument (1) prevents the fiduciary from favoring the other beneficiaries over the spouse; (2) gives the spouse enforceable rights to enjoy the trust; and (3) limits the fiduciary from making allocations, based on the composition of the assets, that would deprive the spouse of enjoyment. A fiduciary may also have discretionary powers to retain trust cash without investing it and to determine in what form distributions are to be made. These powers are permissible if the governing instrument or state law provides reasonable limitations.

A surviving spouse does not have a power of appointment exercisable by the survivor alone and in all events over that portion of a marital trust that an executor has the authority to use to pay death taxes to the federal or state government.[80] In one situation, the IRS denied a marital deduction for property that passed to a trust for the benefit of a decedent's spouse, even though the spouse received a life estate in the trust and the power to appoint the trust corpus for herself or her creditors. The spouse did not have the power to exercise the power "alone and in all events" because the trustee could prevent exercise of the power in his sole discretion if the remainder beneficiaries of the trust objected to a proposed exercise. However, because the trustee did not have a substantial interest in the trust corpus adverse to that of the spouse, the value of the trust corpus was includible in her gross estate as property subject to a general power of appointment.[81] A testamentary power of appointment over a

---

[79] Rev. Rul. 69-56, 1969-1 CB 224.

[80] *M.S. Wycoff Est.*, CA-10, 74-2 USTC ¶ 13,037, 506 F2d 1144, cert. denied.

[81] Rev. Rul. 82-156, 1982-2 CB 216.

trust was not exercisable by a surviving spouse alone and in all events where the trust agreement provided that the spouse's right to the income and principal of the trust and the testamentary general power of appointment terminated if the spouse became incompetent before either withdrawing the corpus or exercising the power of appointment.[82]

¶ 1028 Life Insurance and Annuities

The proceeds of life insurance, endowment or annuity contracts over which a surviving spouse is given a power of appointment may qualify for a marital deduction.[83] (Also, note the treatment of certain joint and survivor annuities as discussed at ¶ 1002.) The proceeds must be payable in installments or held by the insurer subject to an agreement to pay interest. The surviving spouse alone must have the right to receive all or a specific portion of the payments to be made during his or her lifetime. If held at interest, the proceeds, following termination of the period during which interest is to be paid, may be distributed in a lump sum or in installments. The distributions of interest or installments must be made at least annually and the first payment must be made not later than 13 months after the decedent's death.

The surviving spouse must have the power to appoint the entire proceeds or the portion from which he or she is entitled to receive installments or interest distributions. The power must be in favor of that person or that person's estate, regardless of whether he or she may also exercise the power in favor of others. There must be no power in any other person to appoint to any person other than the surviving spouse.

The power must also be exercisable in all events. Formal administrative restrictions on the survivor's right of withdrawal of the proceeds are considered to be for the convenience of the insurer and do not disqualify the survivor's interest from meeting the exercisable-in-all-events test.

¶ 1029 Interest of Spouse Conditioned on Survival for Limited Period

An interest passing to a surviving spouse will qualify for the marital deduction, so long as it is not terminable on other grounds, if it is conditioned upon (1) the surviving spouse's survival for six months after the death of the decedent and the spouse does not, in fact, die within this period; (2) the surviving spouse's not dying in a common disaster taking the lives of both spouses, which does not, in fact, occur; or (3) both events, and neither of them occurs.[84] The above rule does not apply to an ordinary life estate, such as a devise to the wife for her life, with remainder over to another because her death at *any* time will cause such termination or failure.

Otherwise qualifying marital bequests that are conditioned on survival to the final distribution of the decedent's estate, or to administration or settlement of the estate, are nearly always held to be terminable, even though the surviving spouse lives beyond this period. The U.S. Court of Appeals for the Second Circuit, however, has ruled that this rule had no

---

[82] *D. Walsh Est.*, 110 TC 393, CCH Dec. 52,733.

[83] Code Sec. 2056(b)(6).

[84] Reg. § 20.2056(b)-3.

application where state law vested real property in the surviving spouse at the date of the decedent's death.[85]

¶ 1030 Simultaneous Deaths of Joint Property Owners

For federal estate tax purposes, upon the decedent's death, any property that the decedent owned jointly with someone other than the surviving spouse is includible in the decedent's gross estate to the extent that the decedent paid for it. However, to the extent that such property passes to the surviving spouse, it qualifies for the marital deduction. If the decedent and his or her spouse are joint owners of property and it is determined that they have died simultaneously, the rule for distribution of such property may differ from general property rules, since most of the states have adopted the Uniform Simultaneous Death Act.

Section 3 of that Act provides that "Where there is no sufficient evidence that two joint tenants or tenants by the entirety have died otherwise than simultaneously the property so held shall be distributed one-half as if one had survived and one-half as if the other had survived . . . ." Thus, one-half of the property will pass to one decedent's heirs and the other half will pass to the spouse's heirs.

The general tax rule that property be included in the decedent's gross estate to the extent that the decedent furnished consideration for it does not apply in the case of "qualified joint interests" owned by husbands and wives. A "qualified joint interest" created and held by a husband and wife is divided equally between the spouses for estate tax purposes. A qualified joint interest is any property owned solely by spouses in joint tenancy or tenancy by the entirety (see ¶ 502).

¶ 1031 Interest Passing to Unidentified Persons

A marital deduction is not allowed for property interests that may pass to unidentified persons after the death of the spouse. If it is not possible to determine the particular person or persons to whom an interest may pass from the decedent, the interest is considered as having passed to a person other than the decedent's surviving spouse. This rule is inapplicable, however, to a spouse's life interest in connection with a qualifying power of appointment.[86]

> ***Example:*** Andrew Martin, by his will, devised the family real estate and home on Elm Street to his wife, Emily, for life and then to such of his grandchildren as survive Emily, but if none survive her, then to Emily's estate. No marital deduction is allowable for either the life estate or the contingent remainder to Emily's estate. An interest in the property is considered to pass to the grandchildren. Some of them may possess or enjoy the Elm Street property upon the death of Emily. It is immaterial that the grandchildren are not in being at the time of Martin's death.

---

[85] *W. Horton Est.*, CA-2, 68-1 USTC ¶ 12,503, 388 F2d 51.

[86] Reg. § 20.2056(c)-3.

¶ 1032 Interest in Unidentified Assets

If the interest passing to a spouse can be satisfied out of assets for which no marital deduction would be allowed, the marital deduction is affected.[87] The value of the interest passing to the spouse, for the purpose of the marital deduction, is reduced by the aggregate value of such assets.[88]

The assets out of which the interest passing to the surviving spouse may be satisfied are determined prior to payment of any general claims, but without including named property specifically bequeathed or devised.

> ***Example:*** Arthur Britton bequeathed $200,000 to his surviving spouse, Jean. The general estate includes a term for years interest (valued at $225,000 in determining the value of Britton's gross estate) in his country home and acreage—an interest retained by Britton after a gift of the realty to his son. If the bequest to Jean may be satisfied out of the term of years interest, the marital deduction with respect to the bequest of $200,000 is reduced to zero. It is immaterial whether Jean actually receives the term for years interest.

¶ 1033 Fiduciary's Powers to Distribute in Kind

The IRS has prescribed conditions under which the marital deduction will be allowed in cases of a pecuniary bequest in a will, or of a transfer in trust of a pecuniary amount, if the will or trust instrument either requires or permits the executor or trustee to satisfy the bequest in noncash properties selected at their values as finally determined for federal estate tax purposes.[89] The rules set out in the revenue procedure do not apply to transfers of fractional shares of the estate or to transfers of specific assets.

The marital deduction will not be allowed if the executor or trustee is required to, or has an option to, satisfy the pecuniary transfer in kind at estate tax values (and the property available for distribution includes assets that could fluctuate in value) *unless* applicable state law or the provisions of the will or trust instrument require the fiduciary to distribute to the surviving spouse either—

> (1) assets having an aggregate fair market value, on the dates of distribution, of not less than the amount of the pecuniary bequest or transfer in trust as finally determined for federal estate tax purposes, or
>
> (2) assets fairly representative of appreciation or depreciation in the value of all property available for distribution in satisfaction of the pecuniary bequest or transfer.

When condition (1) or (2) is not met, the IRS will consider the property interest passing from the decedent to the surviving spouse as unascertainable at the date of death, if the property available for distribution includes assets which could fluctuate in value.

With respect to wills and trust instruments executed prior to October 1, 1964, fiduciaries and surviving spouses were given an opportunity to

---

[87] Code Sec. 2056(b)(2).

[88] Reg. § 20.2056(b)-2.

[89] Rev. Proc. 64-19, 1964-1 CB (Part 1) 682.

preserve the marital deduction otherwise lost to the estate under the above policy by executing a "side agreement."

¶ 1035 "Interest" vs. "Property"

The terms "interest" and "property," as used in connection with the marital deduction, have separate and distinct meanings. The term "property" is the more comprehensive. It includes all objects or rights that are susceptible of ownership. The term "interest" refers to the extent of ownership of property, such as a life estate in a farm. The farm is the property; the life estate is the interest. A lease is an interest, and, if the lease is transferred from the decedent at death, an interest in property is so transferred.[90]

If a decedent devises acreage to his or her spouse for life with remainder to another, both devisees have an interest in the property. If the fee is devised to a son, subject to a charge of the rents to the surviving spouse for life, both the spouse and son have an interest in the same property.

¶ 1037 Joint and Mutual Wills

Joint and mutual wills of spouses fixing disposition of their respective estates rate a note of caution: The IRS contends that joint wills so restrict the survivor's right to dispose of the property as to create a terminable interest label for the survivor's otherwise nonterminable share, even if the property had been held in joint tenancy.[91] However, the courts have made state law a key factor in generally permitting the marital deduction under the reciprocal will arrangement. Generally, the deduction will be disallowed if the terms of the wills can be enforced under state law. An agreement between the spouses can also limit disposition and create a terminable interest.[92]

¶ 1040 Valuation of Deductible Property Interest

Only the net interest received is considered in determining the value of the interest passing to the surviving spouse for purposes of the marital deduction. Any burdens on the property passing, such as mortgages, liens, and death taxes, must be subtracted from the value of the property in determining the deductible amount.[93] Similarly, the marital deduction is allowable only to the extent that property bequeathed to the surviving spouse exceeds in value the property such spouse is required to relinquish. This principle has major application where, in community property states, the surviving spouse elects to take under the decedent's will and allows its terms to govern the disposition of the survivor's community interest.

Where death taxes are payable out of property bequeathed to the surviving spouse or passing to him or her under state intestate laws, the computation of the marital deduction may be dependent upon the computation of such taxes. In such event, an interdependent computation is

---

[90] Reg. § 20.2056(a)-2.

[91] See, e.g., IRS Technical Advice Memorandum 8105006, 9-26-80, and IRS Technical Advice Memorandum 9023004, 2-20-90, CCH IRS LETTER RULINGS REPORTS.

[92] *A.J. Batterton, Exr.*, CA-5, 69-1 USTC ¶ 12,584, 406 F2d 247, cert. denied.

[93] Reg. § 20.2056(b)-4. See also *V.H. Chiles, Exrx.*, CA-9, 88-1 USTC ¶ 13,763.

involved, which is accomplished most easily by means of algebraic procedures (see ¶ 1075). The unknowns involved will vary, depending upon the probate and death tax laws of the particular state and the provisions of the will.

If the decedent by will leaves the residue of his or her estate to his or her surviving spouse and the surviving spouse pays, or if the estate income is used to pay, claims against the estate so as to increase the residue, such increase in the residue is acquired by purchase and not by bequest. Accordingly, the value of any such additional part of the residue passing to the surviving spouse cannot be included in the amount of the marital deduction.

The value of the marital deduction must be reduced by death taxes that the executor is authorized by will to pay out of the marital trust even though the will does not require him to pay such expenses from the marital trust and, in fact, such payments are not made from the marital trust.[94] The U.S. Supreme Court has held, however, that the payment of administration expenses which, under state law (Georgia), could be allocated to principal or income and, in fact were allocated to income, did not affect the spousal share payable from principal at death. Therefore, the estate was not required to offset the marital deduction by the amount of expenses that could be, but were not, paid from marital deduction property.[95] The U.S. Court of Claims has held that the value of property passing to a marital trust under a decedent's will was to be reduced by the amount of the decedent's liability for unpaid federal gift taxes in order to determine the allowable marital deduction. This reduction was required because the property passing to the marital trust was the only source for payment of the gift tax liability available to the decedent's executors who, under applicable state law (New York), were empowered to use the property passing to the trust to pay the gift tax liability.[96]

Where the decedent's will does not clearly indicate what sources are to be used to pay death taxes and administration expenses, courts apply state law in determining whether marital deduction property is to be charged with these costs.[97] The Tax Court has also applied state law to determine that interest payable on federal estate tax and state inheritance tax, and on deficiencies with respect to these taxes, did not reduce the value of property passing to a surviving spouse.[98] State law provided that the interest did not have to be charged specifically to either income or principal. Thus, because a reduction of the principal by interest payments was contrary to the decedent's intent to obtain the maximum marital deduction as demonstrated by his will, the interest due was chargeable against the income of the estate.

● *Special Use Valuation Property*

In two separate IRS Technical Advice Memoranda relating to the same estate, the IRS ruled that an estate could claim a marital deduction for the full fair market value of property distributed to a marital trust

---

[94] *M.S. Wycoff Est.*, CA-10, 74-2 USTC ¶ 13,037, 506 F2d 1144. Rev. Rul. 79-14, 1979-1 CB 309.

[95] *O. Hubert Est.*, SCt, 97-1 USTC ¶ 60,261.

[96] *W.E. Murray, Exr.*, CtCls., 82-2 USTC ¶ 13,488, 687 F2d 386.

[97] *G.B. Phillips*, 90 TC 797, CCH Dec. 44,717. *See J.E. Reid Est.*, 90 TC 304, CCH Dec. 44,583.

[98] *W.E. Richardson Est.*, 89 TC 1193, CCH Dec. 44,388.

even though a portion of this property consisted of farmland that was included in the decedent's gross estate at its special use value (see ¶ 280 through ¶ 296).[99] The IRS National Office rejected the contention of its District Office that the allowable marital deduction should be reduced by the difference between the special use value and the fair market value of the farmland. However, the IRS ruled that the marital deduction claimed by the estate was allowable because the full value of the decedent's entire interest in the farmland was includible in his gross estate. In the second ruling, the IRS clarified this statement by defining the full value of the farmland to mean its special use value. Moreover, the allowance of a marital deduction based on the fair market value of the farmland did not violate the integrity of the marital deduction statute because the farmland would be includible in the spouse's gross estate at its fair market value upon her death.

However, in another Technical Advice Memorandum,[100] the IRS National Office determined that a marital bequest was overfunded when the executors used the special use value of the farm, as opposed to its fair market value when transferring property to the surviving spouse. The decedent's will directed that the spouse was to receive one-half of the adjusted gross estate but required the executor to use fair market value for transferring assets to satisfy the marital bequest. The effect of this ruling is to allow the executor to transfer less value to the surviving spouse and leave more property in the nontaxable residuary. The Tax Court has also ruled that farmland included in the decedent's gross estate at its special use value retained that value for purposes of calculating the marital deduction.[101]

¶ 1045 Passing of Interest in Property

For purposes of the marital deduction, an interest in property is considered as passing from the decedent to his or her spouse if:

(1) the interest is bequeathed or devised to the spouse by the decedent;

(2) the interest is inherited by the spouse from the decedent;

(3) the interest is the dower or curtesy interest (or statutory interest in lieu thereof) of the surviving spouse;

(4) the interest has been transferred to the spouse by the decedent at any time;

(5) the interest was, at the time of the decedent's death, held by the spouse and the decedent (or by them in conjunction with any other person) in joint ownership with right of survivorship, such joint ownership including joint tenancy, tenancy by the entirety, a joint bank account, or any other co-ownership with right of survivorship;

(6) the decedent had a power of appointment over such interest (either alone or in conjunction with another) which he exercised in

---

[99] IRS Technical Advice Memorandum 8314001, 9-22-82, and IRS Technical Advice Memorandum 8314005, 12-14-82, CCH IRS LETTER RULINGS REPORTS. See also IRS Technical Advice Memorandum 8509001, 11-13-84, CCH IRS LETTER RULINGS REPORTS.

[100] Technical Advice Memorandum 8708001, 5-6-86, CCH IRS LETTER RULINGS REPORTS.

[101] *H.M. Evers Est.*, 57 TCM 718, CCH Dec. 45,776(M), TC Memo. 1989-292.

favor of the spouse, or the spouse takes the interest in default upon release or nonexercise of the power; or

(7) the interest consists of proceeds of insurance upon the life of the decedent, receivable by the spouse, regardless of whether the decedent had previously assigned the policy or paid the premiums by way of gift.[102]

- *Settlement Agreements*

Property interests that a surviving spouse assigns or surrenders pursuant to a compromise agreement in settlement of a will contest are not deductible as an interest passing to the spouse.[103] Any interest received by the surviving spouse under a settlement will be regarded as having passed from the decedent to his surviving spouse if the settlement was based on an enforceable right, under state law, as properly interpreted. The U.S. Court of Appeals for the Eighth Circuit interpreted this test to mean that, where the constitutionality of a state dower statute was uncertain at the time of settlement, the Tax Court was required to make an independent determination as to the enforceability of the surviving spouse's dower claim.[104] Consent decrees will not necessarily be accepted as a bona fide evaluation of the rights of the spouse. The key factor is whether an interest passes from the decedent to his or her surviving spouse, so that the above rules also apply in the case of an intestate decedent where there is a dispute over the statutory share of the spouse.[105]

If a surviving spouse elects to take his or her share of the decedent's estate under local law instead of taking an interest under the will, the interest the surviving spouse takes under local law is considered as passing from the decedent.[106] The failure of a surviving spouse to elect to take an interest under the local law is not considered to any extent as a purchase of the interest the surviving spouse takes under the will.

An interest transferred to a surviving spouse, pursuant to an antenuptial agreement, is property passing from a decedent to his or her surviving spouse. A marital deduction will be allowed for it if all other requirements are met.[107]

¶ 1050 Disclaimers

A "qualified disclaimer" of property, as defined at ¶ 2009, may be made by a third person so that the property may pass to the decedent's surviving spouse and qualify for the marital deduction.[108] If the requirements are satisfied, refusals to accept property are given effect for estate tax purposes, even if local law does not characterize such refusals as "disclaimers." For requirements of a qualified disclaimer, see ¶ 2009.

Qualified disclaimers may be made with respect to transfers that created an interest in the person disclaiming and were made after December 31, 1976.

---

[102] Code Sec. 2056(c).

[103] Reg. § 20.2056(c)-2(d)(1).

[104] *G.M. Brandon Est.*, CA-8, 87-2 USTC ¶ 13,733, rev'g and rem'g TC, 86 TC 327, CCH Dec. 42,911.

[105] *V. Pastor, Admr.*, DC N.Y., 75-1 USTC ¶ 13,045, 386 FSupp 106.

[106] Reg. § 20.2056(c)-2(c).

[107] Rev. Rul. 68-271, 1968-1 CB 409.

[108] Code Sec. 2046, Code Sec. 2056, and Code Sec. 2518.

¶ 1055 Extensions for Future Interests

A six-month extension of time is provided for payment of estate tax on reversionary or remainder interests in property that are included in the value of the gross estate.[109] The extension is granted only for the part of the tax attributable to such interests. In determining the part of the tax attributable to the reversionary or remainder interests, proper effect must be given to any marital deduction allowed.

¶ 1060 Alternate Valuation Method

If the executor elects the alternate valuation method of valuing the estate (see ¶ 105), the amount of the marital deduction is governed by the value at the date of death. It is adjusted, however, for any difference in value (not due to mere lapse of time or the occurrence or nonoccurrence of a contingency) of the property as of the date six months after the date of death.[110] If the property was distributed, sold, exchanged, or otherwise disposed of during the alternate valuation period, it is to be valued as of the date of its first distribution, sale, exchange, or other disposition.

The alternate valuation election pertains only to valuation. It does not extend the time for determining the character of the interest passing to the surviving spouse.

> ***Example (1):*** Under Robert Babcock's will, a life estate is given to his surviving spouse, Ann, with remainder to Ann and to their son, Tom. No deduction results even though Tom dies within the six-month period after the decedent's death.
>
> ***Example (2):*** Tess Law's will directed the executor to sell certain described real estate and to purchase stock of X corporation with the proceeds. The executor was then to turn the stock over to Tess' widower. The value of the real estate at Tess' death was $100,000. It was sold by the executor prior to six months after Tess' death for $120,000. The stock was purchased for $120,000 but had a fair market value of $80,000 at the death of the decedent.
>
> If the gross estate is valued at the date of Tess' death, the marital deduction is $100,000 (the value of the real estate at the time of death). That value was the value of the interest included in determining the value of the gross estate. If the value of the gross estate is determined under the alternate valuation rule the marital deduction is $120,000, the value of the real estate at the time of sale within the six-month period.

¶ 1065 Execution of Schedule

The instructions to Form 706 specify items that should not be included in the marital deduction schedule, as well as the manner of listing those that may be included. Certain property interests that passed from the decedent to his or her surviving spouse are to be wholly or partially excluded from Schedule M (Bequests etc., to Surviving Spouse) of Form 706 (July 1998), as indicated below:

---

[109] Code Sec. 6163.

[110] Reg. § 20.2056(b)-4.

(1) When interests in the same property passed from the decedent both to his or her surviving spouse and (for less than an adequate and full consideration in money or money's worth) to some other person under such conditions that the other person may possess or enjoy any part of the property following the termination or failure of the interest therein that passed to the surviving spouse, the interest passing to the spouse must be excluded from the schedule (unless a QTIP election is made).

> ***Example (1):*** Property transferred by the decedent Bill Green in the following manner is excludable from Schedule M:
>
> (1) a bequest of property to his spouse for life, with remainder to his daughter, and
>
> (2) a bequest of property to his mother for life, with remainder to his spouse, if surviving, and, if not, to his daughter and her heirs.
>
> Under each bequest, the spouse's interest in the property may terminate or fail, and the daughter may thereafter possess or enjoy the property.

(2) If the decedent directs the executor or trustee to purchase for his or her surviving spouse an annuity, a life estate or estate for years in certain property, or any other property interest that may terminate or fail, the property to be used in the acquisition may not be included on the marital deduction schedule. The ownership of a bond, note, or other contractual obligation, the discharge of which would not have the effect of an annuity for life or for a term, is not considered to be a property interest which may terminate or fail.

(3) If any property passing from the decedent to his or her surviving spouse may be paid or otherwise satisfied out of a group of assets, the value of such property interest is, for the purpose of entry on the marital deduction schedule, to be reduced by the aggregate value of any assets that, if passing from the decedent to his surviving spouse, would be nondeductible terminable interests. Property interests that may be paid or otherwise satisfied out of any of a group of assets include bequests of the residue of the decedent's estate, or of a share of the residue, and cash legacies payable out of the general estate.

> ***Example (2):*** Carl Banks bequeathed $100,000 to his wife. His general estate includes a term for years (value of $10,000 in determining the value of his gross estate) in an office building. This interest was retained by Banks under a deed of the building by gift to his son. The portion of the value of the specific bequest to be entered on Schedule M is $90,000.

(4) Property interests are to be excluded from the marital deduction schedule to the extent that a deduction is taken for them under other, preceding schedules (Schedules J to L of Form 706, inclusive). Examples of interests to be so excluded are fees or commissions and payments made in satisfaction of a claim of the surviving spouse against the estate.

(5) When a property interest passing to the surviving spouse is subject to a mortgage or other encumbrance, or when an obligation is imposed upon the surviving spouse in connection with the passing of a property interest, only the net value of the interest after reduction by the amount of

the mortgage or other encumbrance, or obligation, should be included in the marital deduction schedule.

¶ 1067 Listings on Schedule M

Each property interest listed on Schedule M (Bequests etc., to Surviving Spouse) should be fully described. This includes otherwise nondeductible terminable interest property for which a QTIP election is intended. The items should be numbered in sequence. The description must indicate the instrument (including the clause or paragraph number of the instrument, if possible) or provision of law under which each item passed to the surviving spouse. The schedule and item number of the property interest as it appears in the schedules for reporting property includible in the gross estate should also be shown where possible. The value of each item listed on the schedule should be the value determined before taking into account the effect of federal and other death taxes.

If a residuary bequest is listed on Schedule M, a copy of the computation showing how the value of such item was determined should be submitted. The computation should include a statement showing:

(1) The value of all property that is included in the decedent's gross estate but is not part of the decedent's gross estate. This includes property transferred during life but taxed under Code Sec. 2035 through Code Sec. 2038, such as lifetime transfers, jointly owned property passing to the survivor on the decedent's death, and insurance payable to specific beneficiaries.

(2) The values of all specific and general legacies or devises, with an appropriate reference in each instance to the applicable clause or paragraph of the decedent's will or codicil. (In any case where legacies are made to each member of a class—for example, $1,000 to each of the decedent's employees—only the number of each class and the aggregate value of property received by them need be furnished.)

(3) The date of birth and the gender of all persons, the duration of whose lives may affect the value of the residuary interest passing to the surviving spouse.

(4) Any other information that may appear material, such as facts relating to any claim, not arising under the will, to any part of the estate.

¶ 1068 Adjustment for Death Taxes

The total of the values listed on Schedule M must be reduced by the amount of the federal estate tax, federal generation-skipping transfer tax and state or other death and generation-skipping transfer taxes that are payable out of, or chargeable against, the property interests involved at ¶ 1075. Such amounts of taxes should be entered in the designated spaces (Items (5a), (5b) and (5c)) of the schedule. Items (5b) and (5c) must be supported by an identification and computation of the amount of state or other death and generation-skipping transfer taxes shown.[111]

[111] Reg. § 20.2056(b)-4.

¶ 1069 Supplemental Documents

If property interests passing by the decedent's will are listed on Schedule M, a certified copy of the order admitting the will to probate must be submitted with the return. If, at the time the return is filed, the court of probate jurisdiction has entered any decree interpreting the will or any of its provisions affecting property interests listed on the schedule, a copy of the decree is also required. Additional evidence to support the deduction claim may be requested by the district director.

¶ 1075 Marital Deduction and Interrelated Death Taxes

The federal estate tax law contemplates that the marital deduction will be allowed only with respect to the net amount passing to the surviving spouse.[112] Any charges that reduce the amount actually passing to such spouse will reduce the deduction.

State death taxes payable out of residue, including those chargeable against the amounts passing to the surviving spouse, reduce the amount of the deduction. Because they are not deductible under the federal estate tax law, the amounts of these taxes are subject to federal estate taxes just as is any other property not passing to the surviving spouse.

Federal estate taxes payable out of the residue are also part of the taxable estate. Determination of the amount of the residue is dependent upon the marital deduction, which in turn is dependent upon the amounts of both the federal and state taxes. The computation problems may be minimized by making specific transfers to the surviving spouse and by shifting the burden of tax payment to other interests. Where it has not been feasible to prepare a will in a manner which will avoid the involved computation, special formulas must be used.

The IRS has issued Publication No. 904, "Interrelated Computations for Estate and Gift Taxes," [113] which illustrates how the allowable marital and charitable deductions may be computed in cases in which these deductions are interrelated with death taxes. A portion of Publication 904 is reproduced below.

The IRS National Office will furnish taxpayers with actuarial factors and assistance in the solution of interrelated tax computation problems. Taxpayers who have difficulty with tax computations may request assistance by writing to the IRS. The request should include sufficient supporting data to enable the IRS to make the computation. For most estates, copies of the will and relevant trust instruments, a schedule of assets and deductions, and a tentative computation of state tax should accompany the request.

In the event the estate includes community property, everything passing to the surviving spouse in excess of the surviving spouse's share of such community property should be listed in this schedule, regardless of whether such excess comes from the decedent's share of the community or from his or her separate property.

---

[112] Reg. § 20.2056(b)-4.

[113] IRS Publication No. 904, "Interrelated Computations for Estate and Gift Taxes" (Rev. May 1985), CCH IRS PUBLICATIONS REPORTS.

→ The example below is reproduced from IRS Publication 904, "Interrelated Computations for Estate and Gift Taxes" (Rev. May 1985), p. 15. ←

Example E

Algebraic Method

- **State death tax is interrelated.**
- **No adjusted taxable gifts are involved.**

In 1985 an individual died leaving a gross estate valued at $525,000. Debts and expenses of the estate were $40,000, and noncharitable bequests totaled $300,000. Thirty percent of the estate residue passed to a charity, and all death taxes were paid as a general charge against the residue.

The state death tax was 7% of the taxable estate for state purposes. State law allows deductions for debts and expenses, net charitable bequests, and an exemption of $10,000.

This example uses the alternate method.

1) Distribution of estate

Gross estate		$525,000.00
Minus:		
Debts and expenses	$ 40,000.00	
Bequests	300,000.00	
State death tax	S	
Federal estate tax	F	340,000.00 + (F + S)
Net residue		$185,000.00 − (F + S)
Times: Factor for charity		× .3
Charitable deduction in terms of F and S		$ 55,500.00 − .3(F + S)

2) Computation of state death tax

Gross estate		$525,000.00
Minus:		
Debts and expenses	$40,000.00	
Charitable deduction	55,500.00 − .3(F + S)	
Exemption	10,000.00	105,500.00 − .3(F + S)
Taxable estate for state		$419,500.00 − .3(F + S)
Times: Tax rate		× .07
State death tax in terms of F and S		$ 29,365.00 + .021(F + S)

3) Solve for S

The expression for the state death tax in terms of F and S may be expressed as an ordinary algebraic equation:

→ The example below is reproduced from IRS Publication 904, "Interrelated Computations for Estate and Gift Taxes" (Rev. May 1985), p. 15. ←

$$S = \$29,365.00 + .021(F+S)$$

Using this expression for the state death tax, derive an expression for the state death tax that is expressed solely in terms of F;

a) Eliminate the brackets by multiplication:

$$S = \$29,365.00 + .021F + .021S$$

b) Transpose to simplify the equation:

$$S - .021S = \$29,365.00 + .021F$$

c) Consolidate the S term:

$$.979S = \$29,365.00 + .021F$$

d) Divide both sides of the equation by the decimal coefficient (.979):

$$\frac{.979S}{.979} = \frac{\$29,365.00 + .021F}{.979}$$

e) This yields a value for the state death tax expressed in terms of F:

$$S = \$29,994.89 + .02145046F$$

4) Solve for charitable deduction

Using the expression for the charitable deduction derived earlier under *1) Distribution of estate,* substitute the expression for the state death tax, and derive a new expression for the charitable deduction that is stated solely in terms of F.

a) Charitable deduction = \$55,500.00 − .3(F+S)

b) Substitute the expression for the state death tax:

Charitable deduction = \$55,500.00 − .3(F + (\$29,994.89 + .02145046F))

c) Consolidate the F terms:

Charitable deduction = \$55,500.00 − .3(1.02145046F + \$29,994.89)

d) Eliminate the brackets by multiplication:

Charitable deduction = \$55,500.00 − .30643514F − \$8,998.47

→ The example below is reproduced from IRS Publication 904, "Interrelated Computations for Estate and Gift Taxes" (Rev. May 1985), p. 15. ←

e) Consolidate the equation:

Charitable deduction = $46,501.53 − .30643514F

5) Computation of federal estate tax

Gross estate		$525,000.00
Minus:		
Debts and expenses	$40,000.00	
Charitable deduction	46,501,53 − .30643514F	
		86,501.53 − .30643514F
Taxable interests		$438,498.47 + .30643514F
Times: Marginal rate from Table A, Column 4		× .34
Product		$149.089.48 + .10418795F
Minus: Subtractive term from Table A, Column 5		$14,200.00
Estate tax		$134,889.48 + .10418795F
Minus: Unified credit		121,800.00
Estate tax after unified credit		$ 13,089.48 + .10418795F
Minus: State death tax credit —		
Taxable estate	$438,498.47 + .30643514F	
Minus: $60,000	60,000.00	
Adjusted taxable estate	$378,498.47 + .30643514F	
Times: Marginal Rate from Table C, Column 4	× .032	
Product	$ 12,111.95 + .00980592F	
Minus: Subtractive term from Table C, Column 5	4,080.00	
State death tax credit		8,031.95 + .00980592F
Net federal estate tax		$ 5,057.53 + .09438203F

6) Solve for F

The expression for the federal estate tax in terms of F may be expressed as an ordinary algebraic equation:

F = $5,057.53 + .09438203F

Solve this equation for F to determine the federal tax.

a) Transpose to simplify the equation:

F − .09438203F = $5,057.53

→ The example below is reproduced from IRS Publication 904, "Interrelated Computations for Estate and Gift Taxes" (Rev. May 1985), p. 15. ←

b) Consolidate the F terms:

$$.90561797F = \$5{,}057.53$$

c) Divide both sides of the equation by the decimal coefficient (.90561797):

$$\frac{.90561797F}{.90561797} = \frac{\$5{,}057.53}{.90561797}$$

d) This yields the federal tax:

$$F = \$5{,}584.62$$

7) Determination of state death tax

Substitute the value for F in the expression for the state death tax, determined earlier under *3). Solve for S.*

$$S = \$29{,}994.89 + .02145046F$$

$$S = \$29{,}994.89 + .02145046\ (\$5{,}584.62)$$

$$S = \$29{,}994.89 + \$119.79$$

$$S = \$30{,}114.68$$

Proof

1) Distribution of estate

Gross estate		$525,000.00
Minus: Debts and expenses	$ 40,000.00	
Bequests	300,000.00	
State death tax	30,114.68	
Federal estate tax	5,584.62	375,699.30
Net residue		$149,300.70
Times: Factor for charity		× .3
Charitable deduction		$ 44,790.21

2) Computation of state death tax

Gross estate		$525,000.00
Minus: Debts and expenses	$ 40,000.00	
Charitable deduction	44,790.21	
Exemption	10,000.00	94,790.21
Taxable estate for state		$430,209.79
Times: Tax rate		× .07
State death tax		$ 30,114.69

→ The example below is reproduced from IRS Publication 904, "Interrelated Computations for Estate and Gift Taxes" (Rev. May 1985), p. 15. ←

3) Computation of federal estate tax

Gross estate		$525,000.00
Minus: Debts and expenses	$ 40,000.00	
Charitable deduction	44,790.21	84,790.21
Taxable interests		$440,209.79
Times: Marginal rate from Table A, Column 4		× .34
Product		$149,671.33
Minus: Subtractive term from Table A, Column 5		14,200.00
Estate tax		$135,471.33
Minus: Unified credit		121,800.00
Estate tax after unified credit		$ 13,671.33
Minus: State death tax credit—		
Taxable estate	$440,209.79	
Minus: $60,000	60,000.00	
Adjusted taxable estate	$380,209.79	
Times: Marginal rate from Table C, Column 4	× .032	
Product	$ 12,166.71	
Minus: Subtractive term from Table C, Column 5	4,080.00	
State death tax credit		8,086.71
Net federal estate tax		$ 5,584.62

Therefore, in Example E, the interrelated computation results in a charitable deduction of $44,790.21, a state death tax credit of $8,086.71, and a net estate tax of $5,584.62.

¶ 1095 Filled-In Schedule M

The filled-in Schedule M, Form 706 (Rev. July 1998), relates to the fact situation of a person who dies on January 1, 1998, with an estate tax return due within nine months (without extensions). Schedule M must be filed only if a marital deduction is claimed.

Form 706 (Rev. 7-98)

Estate of: James X. Diversey

SCHEDULE M — Bequests, etc., to Surviving Spouse

Election To Deduct Qualified Terminable Interest Property Under Section 2056(b)(7). — If a trust (or other property) meets the requirements to qualified terminable interest property under section 2056(b)(7), and

a. The trust or other property is listed on Schedule M, and

b. The value of the trust (or other property) is entered in whole or in part as a deduction on Schedule M,

then unless the executor specifically identifies the trust (all or a fractional portion or percentage) or other property to be excluded from the election, the executor shall be deemed to have made an election to have such trust (or other property) treated as qualified terminable interest property under section 2056(b)(7).

If less than the entire value of the trust (or other property) that the executor has included in the gross estate is entered as a deduction on Schedule M, the executor shall be considered to have made an election only as to a fraction of the trust (or other property). The numerator of this fraction is equal to the amount of the trust (or other property) deducted on Schedule M. The denominator is equal to the total value of the trust (or other property).

Election To Deduct Qualified Domestic Trust Property Under Section 2056A. — If a trust meets the requirements of a qualified domestic trust under section 2056A(a) and this return is filed no later than 1 year after the time prescribed by law (including extensions) for filing the return, and

a. The entire value of a trust or trust property is listed on Schedule M, and

b. The entire value of the trust or trust property is entered as a deduction on Schedule M,

then unless the executor specifically identifies the trust to be excluded from the election, the executor shall be deemed to have made an election to have the entire trust treated as qualified domestic trust property.

		Yes	No
1	Did any property pass to the surviving spouse as a result of a qualified disclaimer? *If "Yes," attach a copy of the written disclaimer required by section 2518(b).*		X
2a	In what country was the surviving spouse born? United States		
b	What is the surviving spouse's date of birth January 3, 1924		
c	Is the surviving spouse a U.S. citizen?	X	
d	If the surviving spouse is a naturalized citizen, when did the surviving spouse acquire citizenship?		
e	If the surviving spouse is not a U.S. citizen, of what country is the surviving spouse a citizen?		
3	**Election Out of QTIP Treatment of Annuities.** — Do you elect under section 2056(b)(7)(C)(ii) not to treat as qualified terminable interest property any joint and survivor annuities that are included in the gross estate and would otherwise be treated as qualified terminable interest property under section 2056(b)(7)(C)? (see instructions)		X

Item number	Description of property interests passing to surviving spouse		Amount
1	House and lot, 121 Oleander Ave., Tampa, FL, subject to devise in Paragraph 8 of decedent's will (Schedule A, Item 1)		336,000
2	Cadillac Seville (Schedule F, Item 3)		25,500
3	Cash (Schedule C, aggregate of Items 3 and 5)		2,312
4	Life insurance proceeds from National Service Life Insurance Co., Policy No. N-17-136-43 (Schedule D, Item 1)		10,000
5	Checking Account No.46835, State National Bank (1/2 of the amount listed on Schedule E, Part I, Item 2)		2,193
	Total from continuation schedules (or additional sheets) attached to this schedule		134,950
4	Total amount of property interest listed on Schedule M	4	510,955
5a	Federal estate taxes payable out of property interests listed on Schedule M	5a	0
b	Other death taxes payable out of property interests listed on Schedule M	5b	0,000
c	Federal and state GST taxes payable out of property interests listed on Schedule M	5c	0
d	Add items a, b, and c	5d	0
6	Net amount of property interests listed on Schedule M (subtract 5d from 4). Also enter on Part 5, Recapitulation, page 3, at item 20	6	510,955

(If more space is needed, attach the continuation schedule from the end of this package or additional sheets of the same size.) (See the instructions.)

Schedule M — Page 27

¶ 1096 Filled-In Continuation Schedule

The filled-in Continuation Schedule of Form 706 (Rev. July 1998) illustrates the use of the Continuation Schedule with respect to the entries that could not be entered on Schedule M because of lack of space. The Continuation Schedule may be used with respect to Schedules A–N and Schedule O. Assets or deductions from different schedules should not be combined on one Continuation Schedule—separate Continuation Schedules should be used.

Form 706 (Rev. 7-98) (Make copies of this schedule before completing it if you will need more than one schedule.)

Estate of: James X. Diversey

CONTINUATION SCHEDULE

Continuation of Schedule M
(Enter letter of schedule you are continuing.)

Item number	Description For securities, give CUSIP number.	Unit value (Sch. B, E, or G only)	Alternate valuation date	Alternate value	Value at date of death or amount deductible
6	Death benefit from qualified plan (Schedule I, Item 2)				25,000
7	Bequest, under Paragraph 3 of will, of household goods and personalty (Schedule F, Item 1)				17,650
8	Residence, 54 Fir Street, Homewood, IL (1/2 the value listed in Schedule E, Part 1, Item 1)				80,000
9	Annuity contract X-16304 (Schedule I, Item 1)				12,300
	TOTAL. (Carry forward to main schedule.)				134,950

See the instructions.

Continuation Schedule — Page 43

¶ 1097 Filled-in Form 706-QDT

The filled-in Form 706 QDT, U.S. Estate Tax Return for Qualified Domestic Trusts (Rev. January 1996), does not relate to the hypothetical estate of James X. Diversey illustrated elsewhere in this book. Form 706 QDT must be filed by either the trustee or a designated filer for any year in which the qualified domestic trust has a taxable event or makes a distribution on account of "hardship."

Form **706-QDT** (Rev. January 1996) Department of the Treasury Internal Revenue Service

U.S. Estate Tax Return for Qualified Domestic Trusts
Calendar Year 19 98
▶ See separate instructions.

OMB No. 1545-1212

Part I General Information

1a Name of surviving spouse (see "Definitions" in instructions) Corazon M. Costa	1b SSN of surviving spouse 491-23-8463
2a Name of designated filer/trustee (see instructions) Toni L. Costa (Trustee)	2b SSN or EIN of designated filer/trustee 484-26-1943
2c Address of designated filer/trustee 1428 Forest Ave., Northbrook, IL 60062	
3a Surviving spouse's date of death (if applicable)	3b Surviving spouse's current marital status
4a Name of decedent Jose D. Costa	4b SSN of decedent 480-29-1830
4c Service center where Form 706 for decedent's estate was filed Kansas City, MO 64999	4d Decedent's date of death 7-18-96

Part II Elections by the Designated Filer/Trustee (see instructions)

Please check the "Yes" or "No" box for each question.	Yes	No
1 Do you elect alternate valuation?		X
2 Do you elect special use valuation? If "Yes," you must complete and attach Schedule A-1 of Form 706.		X
3 Do you elect to pay the taxes in installments as described in section 6166? If "Yes," you must attach the additional information described in the instructions.		X
4 If the surviving spouse has become a U.S. citizen, does he or she elect under Code section 2056A(b)(12)(C) to treat all prior taxable distributions as taxable gifts and to treat any of the decedent's unified credit applied to the QDOT tax on those distributions as the surviving spouse's unified credit used under section 2505? (If not a U.S. citizen, enter "N/A")	N/	A

Part III Tax Computation

1	Current taxable trust distributions (total from Part II of Schedule A)	1	23,250
2	Value of taxable trust property at date of death (if applicable) (total from Part III of Schedule A)	2	0
3	Add lines 1 and 2	3	23,250
4	Charitable and marital deductions (see Schedule B instructions) (total from col. d, Part IV of Sch. A)	4	0
5	Net tentative taxable amount (subtract line 4 from line 3)	5	23,250
6	Prior taxable events (total from Part I of Schedule A)	6	0
7	Taxable estate of the decedent (see instructions)	7	781,168
8	Add lines 6 and 7	8	781,168
9	Add lines 5 and 8	9	804,418
10	Recomputation of decedent's estate tax based on the amount on line 9 (see instructions) (attach computation)	10	53,711
11	Recomputation of decedent's estate tax based on the amount on line 8 (see instructions) (attach computation)	11	45,760
12	Net estate tax (subtract line 11 from line 10)	12	7,951
13	Payment made with request for extension, if any, and credit under section 2056A(b)(2)(B)(ii)	13	0
14	TAX DUE — (If the amount on line 12 exceeds the amount on line 13, enter the difference here.) ▶	14	7,951
15	Overpayment — (If the amount on line 13 exceeds the amount on line 12, enter the difference here.)	15	0

Under penalties of perjury, I declare that I have examined this return, along with accompanying schedules and statements, and to the best of my knowledge and belief it is true, correct, and complete. Declaration of preparer (other than trustee or designated filer) is based on all information of which preparer has any knowledge.

Trustee's or designated filer's signature ▶ Toni L. Costa Date ▶ 4-10-99

Preparer's signature (other than trustee or designated filer) ▶ Date ▶

Preparer's address (other than trustee or designated filer) ▶

For Paperwork Reduction Act Notice, see page 1 of the separate instructions for this form. Form **706-QDT** (Rev. 1-96)

Form 706-QDT (Rev. 1-96) Page 2

SCHEDULE A — Complete Schedule A only if you are a designated filer filing this return for multiple trusts.

Part I. Summary of Prior Taxable Distributions

(a) Year	(b) Amount	(c) Year	(d) Amount
19___	$	19___	$
19___	$	19___	$
19___	$	19___	$
19___	$	19___	$
19___	$	19___	$
19___	$	19___	$
19___	$	19___	$
19	$	19	$
Total — Combine columns (b) and (d) ▶			

Part II Summary of Current Taxable Distributions

(a) EIN of QDOT	(b) Total Taxable Distributions for the Year	(c) EIN of QDOT	(d) Total Taxable Distributions for the Year
	$		$
	$		$
	$		$
	$		$
	$		$
	$		$
	$		$
	$		$
Total — Combine columns (b) and (d) ▶			23,250

Part III Summary of Property Remaining in QDOTs at Death of Surviving Spouse

(a) EIN of QDOT	(b) Alternate Valuation Date (if applicable)	(c) Value	(d) EIN of QDOT	(e) Alternate Valuation Date (if applicable)	(f) Value
		$			$
		$			$
		$			$
		$			$
		$			$
		$			$
		$			$
		$			$
Total — Combine columns (c) and (f) ▶					

Part IV Summary of Marital and Charitable Deductions

(a) EIN of QDOT	(b) Total Marital Deduction	(c) Total Charitable Deduction	(d) Total Deductions (add cols. (b) and (c))
	$	$	$
	$	$	$
	$	$	$
	$	$	$
	$	$	$
	$	$	$
	$	$	$
	$	$	$
Total ▶			

Form 706-QDT (Rev. 1-96) Page 3

SCHEDULE B

Part I General Information (see instructions)

1a Name of trust	1b EIN of trust
Joseph D. Costa Trust	21-3683414
2a Name of trustee	2b SSN or EIN of trustee
2c Address of trustee	
3 Name of designated filer, if applicable	
4a Name of surviving spouse	4b SSN of surviving spouse
4c Surviving spouse's date of death (if applicable)	4d Surviving spouse's current marital status (or at death, if applicable)
5a Name of decedent	5b SSN of decedent
5c Service center where Form 706 (or 706-NA) for decedent's estate was filed	5d Decedent's date of death

Part II Taxable Distributions From Prior Years

(a) Year	(b) Amount	(c) Year	(d) Amount
19 ___	$ ______	19 ___	$ ______
19 ___	$ ______	19 ___	$ ______
19 ___	$ ______	19 ___	$ ______
19 ___	$ ______	19 ___	$ ______
19 ___	$ ______	19 ___	$ ______
19 ___	$ ______	19 ___	$ ______
19 ___	$ ______	19 ___	$ ______
19 ___	$ ______	19 ___	$ ______
19	$	19	$
Total — Combine columns (b) and (d) . . . ▶			

Part III Current Taxable Distributions

(a) Date of Distribution	(b) Description	(c) Value	(d) Amount of Hardship Exemption Claimed (see instructions)	(e) Net Transfer (col. (c) minus col. (d))
9-12-98	500 shares of X Corp., common (traded principally on New York Stock Exchange) $46.50 per share, CUSIP No. XXXXX	23,250	0	23,250
TOTAL . . . ▶				23,250

Form 706-QDT (Rev. 1-96) Page 4

Schedule B (cont.)

Part IV **Taxable Property in Trust at Death of Surviving Spouse**

(a) Item No.	(b) Description	(c) Alternate Valuation Date	(d) Value
1			
TOTAL . . . . ▶			

Part V **Marital Deductions**

(a) Item No.	(b) Description of property interests passing to spouse	(c) Value
1		
TOTAL . . . . ▶		

Part VI **Charitable Deductions**

(a) Item No.	(b) Description	(c) Name and address of beneficiary	(d) Character of institution	(e) Amount
1				
TOTAL . . . . ▶				

Chapter 26

CHARITABLE, PUBLIC AND SIMILAR TRANSFERS

¶ 1100 Transfers

A charitable deduction is allowed for the value of property transferred by the decedent to or for the use of certain organizations.[1] The deduction is allowed, without limitation as to amount, for transfers of property (to the extent included in the gross estate) to or for the use of:

(1) any corporation organized and operated exclusively for: (a) religious; (b) charitable; (c) scientific; (d) literary; or (e) educational purposes, including the encouragement of art and the prevention of cruelty to children or animals;

(2) the United States, or any state or political subdivision thereof or the District of Columbia, for exclusively public purposes;

(3) any veterans' organization incorporated by Act of Congress, or of its departments or local chapters or posts;

(4) a trustee or trustees, or a fraternal society, order, or association operating under the lodge system if the contributions are to be used exclusively for the purposes enumerated in (1), above; or

(5) an employee stock ownership plan if the transfer qualifies as a qualified gratuitous transfer (see ¶ 1122).

A transfer to an individual member of a religious order will not qualify as a charitable contribution, even if the member has taken a vow of poverty requiring renunciation of any inheritance in favor of the order.[2] Bequests for masses qualify only if made directly to the church and not to a priest.[3] The IRS permits a charitable deduction for a bequest made to a church to say masses for previously deceased members of a decedent's family. In that situation, however, the masses would have been said even if the bequest had not been made, and the bequest became part of the general funds of the church.[4] A decedent's bequest in trust for the benefit of a nonprofit cemetery association did not qualify for an estate tax charitable deduction because the trust funds were not used for an exclu-

---

[1] Code Sec. 2055; Reg. § 20.2055-1.

[2] Rev. Rul. 55-760, 1955-2 CB 607.

[3] Rev. Rul. 68-459, 1968-2 CB 411.

[4] Rev. Rul. 78-366, 1978-2 CB 241.

sively charitable purpose. This was true because, under the decedent's will, the bequest was to be used to maintain the decedent's cemetery plot before it was used to maintain the cemetery in general.[5]

An estate tax deduction is not allowed for a bequest to a charity if the bequest is conditioned upon the approval of a third party.[6] Bequests to foreign governments and political subdivisions thereof that are used exclusively for charitable purposes are deductible.[7]

¶ 1101 Disqualifications

The transfer to any organization qualifying under category (1) or (3) (listed at ¶ 1100) will not be allowed as a deduction if any part of the net earnings of the organization inures to the benefit of any private stockholder or individual. A deduction is also denied where a substantial part of the transferee's activities involves the carrying on of propaganda or some other method of influencing legislation. A deduction is denied if the transferee participates or intervenes in (including the publishing or distributing of statements) any political campaign on behalf of or in opposition to any candidate for public office.[8] In any event, the amount of the deduction cannot exceed the portion of the contributed property included in the gross estate[9] (see ¶ 2305).

¶ 1102 Form of Transfer—Disclaimers

A charitable deduction is allowable only if the transfer is made by the decedent rather than by the decedent's estate or by the beneficiaries of the estate. The transfer may be made pursuant to a will or by means of a lifetime transfer.

However, a charitable deduction is available for property that is indirectly cast into a charitable transfer by means of a "qualified disclaimer." [10] If the qualified disclaimer requirements are satisfied, refusals to accept property are given effect for estate tax charitable deduction purposes even if local law does not characterize such refusals as "disclaimers." Qualified disclaimers may be made with respect to those transfers creating an interest in the person disclaiming. For requirements of a qualified disclaimer, see ¶ 2009.

The complete termination of a power to consume, invade or appropriate property for the benefit of an individual can also create a charitable deduction.[11] In order to qualify, the termination must occur before the due date of the estate tax return and before the power has been exercised.

¶ 1105 Qualifying Transferees

Transfers to organizations like the Red Cross, the Boy Scouts, the American Heart Fund, the American Cancer Society, the Salvation Army and other well-known charitable organizations clearly qualify for the

---

[5] *First National Bank of Omaha, Exr. (Est. of G. McIninch)*, CA-8, 82-2 USTC ¶ 13,474, cert. denied 1-10-83; see also *Mellon Bank N.A., Exr.*, CA-3, 85-1 USTC ¶ 13,615, cert. denied 2-24-86.

[6] Rev. Rul. 64-129, 1964-1 CB (Part 1) 329.

[7] Rev. Rul. 74-523, 1974-2 CB 304; IRS Technical Advice Memorandum 9842004, 7-7-98, CCH IRS LETTER RULINGS REPORTS.

[8] Code Sec. 2055(a).

[9] Code Sec. 2055(d).

[10] Code Sec. 2046 and Code Sec. 2518.

[11] Reg. § 20.2055-2(c).

deduction. Similarly, transfers made directly to a recognized school or church organization are deductible when the transfer is to be used for educational or religious purposes.

It is advisable to consult IRS Publication No. 78 (Cumulative List of Organizations Described in Section 170(c) of the IRC of 1986)) and its supplement before making charitable bequests or distributions. IRS Publication No. 78 is the official list of those organizations to which charitable contributions are deductible under Code Sec. 170 and Code Sec. 2055.[12] Failure to consult the list and contributing to a charity not listed may result in the denial of the charitable deduction. For example, a charitable deduction was denied for funds distributed to a private school that no longer had tax-exempt status.[13] According to the Tax Court, the trustees would have been aware of the revocation had they consulted IRS Publication No. 78.

Whether various types of indirect discretionary transfers are deductible is not so clear. The courts have indicated that even these transfers will qualify if the terms under which the discretionary powers may be exercised are sufficiently explicit to limit use of the funds to the purposes specified in the law. Thus, a transfer in trust can qualify, even if the trustee is given complete discretion in selecting the ultimate beneficiaries of the transferred property. In like manner, specific charitable bequests paid by a trustee of a testamentary trust can qualify for a deduction even if the trustee has complete discretion as to which assets will be used to pay the bequests.[14]

So long as it is clear that the trustee's or other third person's discretion is limited to choosing the charitable, religious, or educational organizations to receive the funds or so long as it is clear that he must expend the funds directly and only for the purposes specified in the estate tax law, the transfers may qualify. The IRS maintains that, where a trustee has the power to select the charitable beneficiaries, the deduction is available only if state law (1) upholds the validity of the charitable trust and (2) restricts the distribution of property to an organization that qualifies for an estate tax charitable deduction.[15]

No deduction is allowed for a transfer to or for the use of certain private foundations and foreign organizations. This matter is discussed for estate and gift tax purposes at ¶ 2305.

¶ 1110 State Law Effect

State law often plays a part in determining whether a particular transfer will qualify for the charitable deduction. If the transfer is one that is void under state law, the deduction will not be allowed.[16] No deduction will be allowed even if the heirs who would otherwise receive the property take action to permit it to go to the charitable transferees, unless they make a "qualified disclaimer" (see ¶ 1102). On the other hand, if the transfer is merely voidable under state law and the persons who have a

[12] IRS Publication No. 78 is available for sale from the Superintendent of Documents, U.S. Government Printing Office, Washington, D.C. 20402.

[13] *S.H. Clopton*, 93 TC 275, CCH Dec. 45,978.

[14] Rev. Rul. 81-20, 1981-1 CB 471, clarified by Rev. Rul. 90-3, 1990-1 CB 174.

[15] Rev. Rul. 69-285, 1969-1 CB 222; Rev. Rul. 71-441, 1971-2 CB 335.

[16] *H.V. Watkins, Sr., Exr.*, CA-5, 43-1 USTC ¶ 10,042, 136 F2d 578.

right to have the transfer voided fail to act, the deduction will be allowed.[17]

¶ 1115 Property Passing Under Power of Appointment

Property that is includible in the gross estate under Code Sec. 2041 (relating to powers of appointment, see ¶ 650) and that passes to a charitable beneficiary is considered to be a bequest by the decedent and is deductible as a charitable transfer.[18]

¶ 1120 Transfers Not Exclusively for Charitable Purposes

Special rules are provided for transfers that are not exclusively for charitable purposes.[19] An estate tax charitable deduction is allowed for the value of the charitable interest transferred to the extent that such interest is presently ascertainable and, thus, severable from the noncharitable interest. Transfers subject to a power to divert such property to noncharitable purposes are nondeductible.

Interests transferred for other than exclusively charitable purposes that are deductible include:[20]

(1) remainder interests in a charitable remainder annuity trust, a charitable remainder unitrust, or a pooled income fund;[21]

(2) remainder interests in a personal residence (This transfer does not have to be in trust and the Tax Court has held that the transfer to charity of proceeds from the sale of a residence after the life tenant's death qualifies for the deduction.);[22]

(3) remainder interests in a farm (This transfer does not have to be in trust.);

(4) a transfer of an undivided portion, not in trust, of the decedent's entire interest for the entire term of his interest;

Example: The decedent, Tom Sanders, transfers a life estate in an office building to his wife Lisa for her life, retains a reversionary interest in such building, and then transfers one-half of the reversionary interest to charity while Lisa is still alive. His estate is denied a charitable deduction because an interest in the same property has already passed from Tom for private purposes and the reversionary interest is not considered the decedent's entire interest in the property;

(5) guaranteed annuity interests (An interest, whether or not in trust, involving a right to receive a guaranteed annuity, that is defined as a determinable amount paid at least annually for a specified term or for the life or lives of an individual or individuals, each of whom is living at the date of the decedent's death and can be

---

[17] *M. Varick Est.*, 10 TC 318, CCH Dec. 16,258 (Acq.).

[18] Code Sec. 2055(b).

[19] Code Sec. 2055(e).

[20] Reg. § 20.2055-2.

[21] Code Sec. 2055(e)(2)(A).

[22] *E.W. Blackford Est.*, 77 TC 1246. CCH Dec. 38,477. The IRS acquiesced in the result in *Blackford;* however, in the IRS's view, the remainder would be deductible only if the governing state law followed the doctrine of equitable reconversion, under which the remainderman could elect to take the property in its original form. See Rev. Rul. 83-158, 1983-2 CB 159.

ascertained at such date. If not a trust, such interest must be paid by an insurance company or by an organization regularly engaged in issuing annuity contracts in order to qualify as a deductible charitable guaranteed annuity interest);

(6) unitrust income interests (An interest, whether or not in trust, involving the right to receive payment, not less often than annually, of a fixed percentage of the net fair market value, determined annually, of the property which funds the unitrust interest. Payments under a unitrust interest may be paid for a specified term or for the life or lives of an individual or individuals, each of whom must be living at the date of the decedent's death and can be ascertained at such date. If not in trust, such interest must be paid by an insurance company, or by an organization regularly engaged in issuing interests otherwise meeting the requirements of a unitrust interest, in order to qualify as a deductible charitable unitrust interest.);

(7) "conservation purpose" transfers (A deduction is also allowed for a bequest to a charitable organization exclusively for "conservation purposes" of (a) a "restriction" in perpetuity on the use of real property, e.g., easements, leases, restrictive covenants, etc., (b) remainder interests in real property, or (c) a decedent's entire interest in real property other than certain mineral rights.[23] "Conservation purposes" include the preservation of land, areas for public recreation, education, or scenic enjoyment, the preservation of historically important land or structures, or the preservation of natural environmental systems.); and

(8) artworks with retained copyrights (A charitable deduction will be allowed for the transfer of an artwork to charity even if the copyright covering the work is not so transferred.).[24]

¶ 1121 Split-Interest Transfers

Transfers involving property interests split between charitable and noncharitable beneficiaries may arise in a number of factual situations. The IRS has ruled that a decedent's estate was not entitled to an estate tax charitable deduction for the decedent's bequest of stock to charity because, under the terms of the will, the executor was to pay dividends from the stock to a noncharitable beneficiary during the period of estate administration.[25] In the IRS's view, this gave rise to a split-interest transfer because the noncharitable beneficiary's right to the dividends constituted a property right in the stock. Accordingly, the transfer was a split-interest transfer and no deduction was allowable because it was not in one of the forms required for such transfers (i.e., a charitable remainder annuity trust, charitable remainder unitrust, or pooled income fund).

Notwithstanding the position taken in the above ruling, the IRS has ruled that a decedent's bequest of the residue of his estate to charity was not a split-interest transfer even though, pursuant to a state court order, his surviving spouse was to receive a support allowance from the residue

---

[23] Code Sec. 170(f)(3)(B), Reg. § 1.170A-14 and Reg. § 20.2055-2(e)(2)(iv).

[24] Code Sec. 2055(e)(4).

[25] Rev. Rul. 83-45, 1983-1 CB 233.

during the period of estate administration.[26] The IRS allowed the deduction because the support allowance would be payable for only five years; the possibility that estate administration would last beyond five years was so remote as to be negligible. Because the charity was certain to receive an amount in excess of the present value of the support allowance, the IRS determined that only the charity had an interest in this amount of the residue, and, to the extent of this amount, the residuary bequest was not a split-interest transfer.

The U.S. Court of Appeals for the Eighth Circuit relied in part on this ruling in holding that a decedent's estate was entitled to an estate tax charitable deduction for a portion of the decedent's bequest to a trust having both charitable and noncharitable beneficiaries because the estate obtained a judicial modification of the trust to provide for immediate distributions to the charitable remainder beneficiaries.[27] The estate executors had a motive for the reformation, arising from state fiduciary law, that was independent of tax considerations; however, the court focused on the fact that the abuses calling for application of the split-interest transfer provisions were not a concern in the case because the charitable interests passed directly to the charities under the state court order. Also relying in part on the ruling, the Eighth Circuit allowed a charitable deduction for a decedent's bequest to charity of a remainder interest in a testamentary trust that was funded with the residue of his estate because his wife elected to take against his will, under which she was entitled to a life income interest in the trust.[28] The split-interest trust requirements did not apply to bar the deduction because the wife received an interest only in that portion of the residue necessary to fund an agreement in settlement of her election, while the charity was certain to receive the rest of the residue.

¶ 1122 Charitable Remainder Trusts

A deductible charitable remainder interest must be in the form of an annuity trust, a unitrust, or a pooled income fund.[29]

A charitable remainder annuity trust (CRAT) is a trust from which a sum certain or a specified amount (which is not less than five percent of the initial net fair market value of all property placed in trust) is to be paid to the income beneficiary or beneficiaries. The specified amount must be paid at least annually to the income beneficiary.[30]

A charitable remainder unitrust (CRUT) is a trust that specifies that the income beneficiary or beneficiaries are to receive payments (at least annually) based on a fixed percentage (which is not less than five percent) of the net fair market value of the trust's assets as determined each year. In the alternative, a qualified charitable remainder unitrust can provide for the distribution each year of five percent of the net fair market value of its assets (valued annually) or the amount of the trust income (other

---

[26] Rev. Rul. 83-20, 1983-1 CB 231.

[27] *W. Oetting, Exr.*, CA-8, 83-2 USTC ¶ 13,533, 712 F2d 358.

[28] *First National Bank of Fayetteville, Ark., Exr.*, CA-8, 84-1 USTC ¶ 13,558, 727 F2d 741.

[29] Code Sec. 2055(e)(2)(A); *E. La Mares Est.*, 98 TC 294, CCH Dec. 48,085.

[30] Reg. § 1.664-1 and Reg. § 1.664-2, respectively.

than capital gains), whichever is lower.[31] This payment requirement may not be discretionary with the trustee.

In addition, deficiencies in income (i.e., where the trust income was less than the stated amount payable to the income beneficiary) can be made up in later years when a CRUT's income exceeds the amount otherwise payable to the income beneficiary for that year. This is commonly referred to as a net income makeup charitable remainder unitrust (NIMCRUT). The determination of which items are trust income is to be made under state law and, therefore, cannot include such items as capital gains, which must be allocated to the trust principal. (No comparable rules are provided for CRATs.)

The Taxpayer Relief Act of 1997 (P.L. 105-34) imposed additional maximum payout and minimum charitable benefit requirements on both charitable remainder annuity trusts and charitable remainder unitrusts. Under the maximum payout limitation, a trust will fail to qualify as a charitable remainder trust if the annual payout exceeds 50 percent. Thus, a charitable remainder annuity trust cannot pay out in any year an amount in excess of 50 percent of the initial fair market value of the trust's assets. A charitable remainder unitrust may not make an annual payout in excess of 50 percent of the fair market value of the trust's assets determined annually. The 50-percent maximum payout limitation applies to transfers in trust made after June 18, 1997.[32]

A minimum 10-percent charitable remainder value rule applies to transfers in trust made after July 28, 1997. To satisfy the rule, the value of a remainder interest in a charitable remainder annuity trust must be at least 10 percent of the initial net fair market value of all property transferred to the trust. With respect to a charitable remainder unitrust, the 10-percent rule applies to each contribution of property to the trust. Under a grandfather provision, however, the 10-percent rule and the 50-percent limitation discussed above do not apply to transfers in trust under the terms of a will or other testamentary instrument executed on or before July 28, 1997, if the decedent (1) dies before January 1, 1999, without having republished the will or amended it by codicil or otherwise, or (2) was, on July 28, 1997, unable to change the disposition of the property due to a mental disability and did not regain competency before dying.[33]

Charitable remainder annuity trusts and unitrusts cannot have noncharitable remainder interests if a deduction is to be allowed. Furthermore, the remainder interest must pass to a charity upon the termination of the last income interest. There may be more than one noncharitable income beneficiary, either concurrently or successively, and the income interest may be a life estate or for a term of years, but the term of years cannot be in excess of 20 years (see, however, the exception for contingency provisions in charitable remainder trusts, noted above). Under the regulations, no deduction is allowable if a charitable unitrust interest is preceded by a noncharitable unitrust interest; however, the Tax Court has held the regulations invalid to the extent that they prohibit a deduction in such a

---

[31] Reg. § 1.664-1 and Reg. § 1.664-3, respectively.

[32] Code Sec. 664(d)(1)(A) and Code Sec. 664(d)(2)(A).

[33] Code Sec. 664(d)(1) and Code Sec. 664(d)(2); Act Sec. 1089(b)(6)(B) of the Taxpayer Relief Act of 1997 (P.L. 105-34).

situation.[34] In the court's view, Congress enacted the charitable trust rules to ensure that charities actually receive a benefit approximately equal to the amount of the deduction. The court found no evidence that Congress considered an intervening noncharitable unitrust interest to be a threat to the charity's benefit and, accordingly, held that the regulations were invalid, in part, because they were inconsistent with the intent of Congress. The trust cannot be invaded, amended or revoked for the benefit of any noncharitable income beneficiary. The trustee may be given these powers for the benefit of a charitable organization and may also have the discretionary power to make payments to such organization. A trustee cannot be restricted from investing the trust assets in a manner that could result in the annual realization of a reasonable amount of income or gain.

In a series of revenue procedures, the IRS has provided sample language in order to help taxpayers in drafting governing instruments for charitable remainder annuity trusts and charitable remainder unitrusts.[35]

● *Certain Transfers to Employee Stock Ownership Plans*

If a charitable remainder trust holds qualified employer securities transferred from a decedent dying before January 1, 1999, the securities transferred to an employee stock ownership plan in a "qualified gratuitous transfer" will qualify for the estate tax charitable deduction. The deduction is limited to the extent of the present value of the remainder interest in the trust.[36]

A transfer of qualified securities is treated as a qualified gratuitous transfer if: (1) the securities are transferred to the trust by a decedent dying before January 1, 1999; (2) the decedent and his family members owned no more than 10 percent of the value of the outstanding stock at the time of the transfer to the ESOP; (3) the ESOP owns at least 60 percent of the value of the stock after the transfer; (4) the ESOP was in existence on August 1, 1996; (5) the employer agrees to pay an excise tax on certain prohibited distributions and allocations of the securities; and (6) no income tax deduction is allowable for the transfer. Additionally, the ESOP must meet certain antidiscrimination, administrative and distribution and allocation requirements.[37]

¶ 1123 Trust Reformation Rules

A nondeductible charitable split-interest contribution can be reformed into a deductible split-interest contribution for purposes of the income, estate and gift tax charitable deductions.[38] No reformation occurs, however, unless a "reformable interest" is transformed into a "qualified interest" by means of a "qualified reformation."

● *Qualified Interest*

A qualified interest is an interest for which a charitable deduction is allowed under Code Sec. 2055(a).[39] If a qualified reformation occurs, the

---

[34] Reg. § 20.2055-2(e), held partially invalid in *M.L. Boeshore Est.*, 78 TC 523, CCH Dec. 38,902, appeal dismissed CA-7, 2-10-83. IRS has acquiesced in result only in this decision, Acquiescence Announcement, 1987-2 CB 1.

[35] Rev. Proc. 90-30, 1990-1 CB 534; Rev. Proc. 90-31, 1990-1 CB 539; Rev. Proc. 90-32, 1990-1 CB 546; and Rev. Rul. 92-57, 1992-2 CB 123.

[36] Code Sec. 2055(a)(5).

[37] Code Sec. 664(g).

[38] Code Sec. 2055(e)(3).

[39] Code Sec. 2055(e)(3)(D).

allowable charitable deduction is equal to the lesser of (1) the actuarial value of the charitable interest after the reformation, or (2) the actuarial value of the charitable interest before the reformation for which a deduction would have been allowable but for the disallowance rules of Code Sec. 2055(e)(2) (see ¶ 531 for actuarial tables).

• *Qualified Reformation*

A qualified reformation is a reformation, amendment, construction or other action pertaining to the governing instrument that changes a reformable interest (defined below) into a qualified interest.[40] A qualified reformation can be accomplished by any means permitted under applicable local law, provided that the change is binding on all relevant parties under applicable local law.[41]

A reformation will constitute a qualified reformation only if certain requirements are met:

(1) The difference between the actuarial value of the reformed charitable interest and the unreformed charitable interest cannot exceed five percent of the value of the interest prior to reformation. For purposes of this requirement, values are to be determined as of the date of the decedent's death.

(2) Charitable and noncharitable interests in charitable lead (income) trusts must terminate at the same time before and after reformation. The same is generally true with respect to charitable and noncharitable interests under a charitable remainder trust instrument, with the exception that a noncharitable interest for a term of years in excess of 20 years may be reduced to 20 years.

(3) The changes are made effective as of the date of the decedent's death.[42]

• *Reformable Interest*

A qualified reformation cannot occur unless the interest is "reformable." In order to be considered reformable, the following requirements must be met:

(1) The interest must be of a type that would have qualified for a charitable deduction except for the charitable split-interest rules of Code Sec. 2055(e)(2).

(2) The interest of the beneficiaries, before the remainder interest vests in possession, must be expressed as either a specified dollar amount or as a fixed percentage of the fair market value of the property, taking into account the rules of Code Sec. 664(d)(3).[43]

Requirement (2) does not apply if a judicial proceeding is commenced to change the remainder interest into a qualified interest no later than 90 days after:

(1) the last day for filing the estate tax return, including extensions, or

---

[40] Code Sec. 2055(e)(3)(B).

[41] Senate Finance Committee Report to the Tax Reform Act of 1984 (P.L. 98-369).

[42] Code Sec. 2055(e)(3)(B)

[43] Code Sec. 2055(e)(3)(C).

(2) if no estate tax return is required to be filed, the last date, including extensions, for the filing of the income tax return for the first tax year the trust is required to file a return.[44]

In deciding whether an action was commenced within the required 90-day period, the actual date that the judicial proceeding was instituted governs. Thus, a judicial proceeding instituted after this deadline will not be deemed to have a retroactive effect based on probate documents filed within the 90-day period that were not in the nature of pleadings sufficient to begin an action to amend the trust.[45]

The requirement that the interests of the beneficiaries be expressed as a specified dollar amount or fixed percentage of the property's fair market value does not apply to interests passing under wills or trusts executed before 1979, or for interests for which a timely judicial reformation proceeding is instituted.[46]

Application to Income and Gift Taxes. Rules similar to the estate tax deduction rules apply to the determination of the allowance of income and gift tax charitable deductions for split-interest contributions.

Statute of Limitations on Assessment. The period for assessment of any tax deficiency arising out of the application of the rules for reformation of charitable split-interest contributions will not expire before one year after the date on which the IRS is notified that the reformation has occurred.[47]

Death of Noncharitable Income Beneficiary. If, before the due date (including extensions) for filing the estate tax return upon which the charitable split-interest contribution is claimed, the reformable interest becomes a wholly charitable interest because of the death of all noncharitable income beneficiaries, or because of a termination or distribution of a trust in accordance with the terms of the trust instrument, a deduction for such interest is to be allowed as if it met the requirements of a split-interest trust on the date of the decedent's death.[48]

Remainder Interest in Personal Residence or Farm. A charitable (as well as a gift) deduction is available for the transfer of a remainder interest, not in trust, in a personal residence and farm.[49] The value of the deduction is the fair market value of the remainder interest, determined by the actuarial tables at the date of transfer, the date of death or the alternative valuation date.[50]

Contingency Provisions in Charitable Remainder Trusts. Generally, noncharitable interests in a charitable remainder trust (whether a charitable remainder annuity trust or a charitable remainder unitrust) must terminate at the end of specified lives in being or a term of years not to exceed 20 years. However, where a trust complies with the termination rule (i.e., the noncharitable interest must terminate at the end of lives in being or a term of years not exceeding 20 years), a contingency may be placed in the trust providing that the noncharitable interest is to terminate, and the charitable interest is to be accelerated, upon the happening

---

[44] Code Sec. 2055(e)(3)(C)(iii).

[45] *Z. Hall*, 93 TC 745, CCH Dec. 46,219.

[46] Code Sec. 2055(e)(3)(C)(iv).

[47] Code Sec. 2055(e)(3)(G).

[48] Code Sec. 2055(e)(3)(F).

[49] Reg. § 20.2055-2(e)(2).

[50] Code Sec. 7520.

of an event at an earlier time (e.g., the noncharitable interest may terminate upon the remarriage of an individual). In such a case, the value of the charitable remainder interest is determined without regard to the contingency.[51]

- *Effective Dates*

Code Sec. 2055(e)(3) applies to all reformations occurring after 1981.

- *Reformation to Comply with the Minimum Charitable Benefit Rule*

A trust that fails to qualify as a charitable remainder trust by reason of the failure to satisfy the 10-percent minimum charitable benefit requirement (see ¶ 1123) may be reformed to increase the value of the remainder interest. Generally, the remainder interest can be increased by reducing the payout percentage and/or shortening the trust term. If not reformed, the trust may be declared void as of its inception.[52]

¶ 1125 Charitable Bequests Not Governed by 1969 Tax Reform Act

Certain charitable bequests are not governed by the 1969 Tax Reform Act and, therefore, do not have to be an annuity trust or a unitrust. The trustee can be given the power to invade principal for a noncharitable income beneficiary. If there is a provision for invading the principal for the benefit of the life tenant, and the extent to which the principal can be so invaded is definitely ascertainable, the value of the remainder after making allowance for such invasion is deductible.[53] If the provision for invasion of principal is too liberal or vague to permit accurate measurement of the extent to which the principal can be so invaded, then no deduction is allowable.

Generally, a deduction is allowed if the trustee can invade only for the life tenant's support, maintenance, welfare and comfort, and there is evidence that the principal will not be invaded at the date of the decedent's death. This latter determination is made by examining the life tenant's health, age, mode of living and income and assets from other sources that he can use for living expenses.

¶ 1126 Valuation of Trust Interests

An estate can claim estate tax charitable deductions for the present value of income and remainder interests in property that is bequeathed or which otherwise passes to qualifying charities. A deduction is allowed for the fair market value of a partial interest at the appropriate valuation date for transfers not exclusively for charitable purposes. The fair market value of an annuity, life estate, term for years, remainder, reversion, or unitrust interest is its present value.

For transfers not exclusively for charitable purposes (involving guaranteed annuity trusts, unitrusts and pooled income funds—transfers (1), (5), and (6) of ¶ 1120 above) made by decedents dying after July 31, 1969, the rules for computing the present values of such interests for deduction purposes are as follows:

---

[51] Code Sec. 664(f).

[52] Code Sec. 2055(e)(3)(J).

[53] *Ithaca Tr. Co., Exr. (E.C. Stewart Est.)*, SCt, 1 USTC ¶ 386, 279 US 151.

(1) The present value of a remainder interest in a charitable remainder annuity trust is determined under income tax Reg. § 1.664-2(c).

(2) The present value of a remainder interest in a charitable remainder unitrust is determined under income tax Reg. § 1.664-4 or Reg. § 1.664-4A, depending on the valuation date.

(3) The present value of a remainder interest in a pooled income fund is determined under income tax Reg. § 1.642(c)-6.

(4) The present value of a guaranteed annuity interest is determined under either estate tax Reg. § 20.2031-7 or estate tax Reg. § 20.2031-7A, depending upon the date of the decedent's death (see ¶ 530), unless the annuity is issued by a company regularly engaged in the sale of annuities, in which case Reg. § 20.2031-8 should be used.

(5) The present value of a unitrust interest is determined by subtracting the present value of all interests in the transferred property other than the unitrust interest from the fair market value of the transferred property.[54]

The above regulations are applicable only where the interest is dependent upon one life.

With respect to pooled income funds in existence for less than three tax years preceding the tax year in which the transfer is made. Reg. § 1.642(c)-6(e)(3) provides the method for determining the rate of return for purposes of valuing a remainder interest in the fund.

For purposes of valuing charitable remainder interests in annuity trusts, unitrusts and pooled income funds that are dependent upon the death of the survivor of more than one life, the IRS has issued several publications providing special factors and tables (see ¶ 530 for a list of these publications).

Any claim for deduction in any return (income, estate or gift tax) for the value of a remainder interest in a trust or pooled income fund must be supported by a statement showing the computation of the present value of such interest. The IRS, upon request, may furnish a factor that can be used to value such interests.

¶ 1127 Contingent Gifts

If, as of the date of a decedent's death, a transfer to a charitable organization is dependent upon performance of an act or happening of an event (whether a condition precedent or subsequent) before it takes effect (or is divested), no charitable deduction will be allowed unless the possibility that the charity may not receive the property is so remote as to be considered negligible. The requirement of an "effective transfer"[55] makes it necessary that enjoyment of the benefits of the transfer accrue in fact to the charity, so it may be immaterial that the value of the contingent interest could have been computed actuarially.

Likewise, if a bequest to charities is wholly contingent, so that no present value is determinable from known data, no deduction can be

[54] Reg. § 20.2055-2(f)(2)(v).

[55] Reg. § 20.2055-2(b).

taken.[56] However, the fact that the remainder to charity is conditioned upon the life tenant's dying without issue does not make the remainder contingent if the possibility of issue is extinct,[57] as, for example, where the life tenant has reached an advanced age.[58]

¶ 1128 Transfers Out of Which Death Taxes Must Be Paid

Deductions for charitable bequests are limited to the amount actually received by the charitable organization.[59] For example, where taxes are to be paid from the residuary estate and the residuary estate is left to charity, the deduction for charitable bequests must be reduced by the amount of federal estate tax payable out of the residuary estate.[60] This computation may be accomplished algebraically or by application of the principle of the converging series, which is in general use by accountants in the determination of interdependent factors.

However, whether administration expenses *allocable to the income of an estate* reduce the amount of a marital or charitable deduction has been a matter of controversy among the U.S. Courts of Appeals for the Federal, Sixth and Eleventh Circuits and the Tax Court. The Federal and Sixth Circuits have held that administration expenses reduce the marital deduction regardless of whether the payment is allocated to income or to principal.[61] But the Tax Court and the Eleventh Circuit had declined to follow the reasoning of those appellate courts and had held that administration expenses allocable to the *income* of an estate do not reduce a decedent's estate's marital or charitable deduction provided that the decedent's will and applicable state law allow for the payment of administration expenses out of the estate's income.[62] Settling the split among circuits, the U.S. Supreme Court held in *O. Hubert Est.*[63] that the executor's or trustee's discretion, under the governing instrument and local law, to pay administration expenses out of principal or income reduces the marital deduction only if such discretion constitutes a material limitation on the spouse's right to receive income. In this case, the Court found that such discretion did not constitute a material limitation.

With respect to interest accruing on obligations payable from residuary principal or income, the IRS has ruled that it will not reduce the value of a residuary charitable bequest for purposes of determining the charitable deduction.[64] In light of this ruling and the results of several court decisions, the IRS revoked a prior ruling which held that the value of a decedent's bequest of his residuary estate to charity was reduced by an estimated amount of interest on deferred estate taxes because the interest was payable from the residue.[65]

---

[56] *A.L. Humes, Exr. (D.R. Gates Est.),* SCt, 1 USTC ¶ 298, 276 US 487.

[57] *Provident Trust Co., Exr. (G.T. Roberts Est.),* SCt, 4 USTC ¶ 1229, 291 US 272.

[58] *City Bank Farmers Trust Co., Exr. (T.B. Allen Est.),* CA-2, 35-1 USTC ¶ 9079, 74 F2d 692.

[59] Code Sec. 2055(c).

[60] Reg. § 20.2055-3.

[61] *G. Street Est.,* CA-6, 92-2 USTC ¶ 60,112, 974 F2d 723, rev'g in part TC, 56 TCM 774, CCH Dec. 45,201(M), TC Memo. 1988-553; *J. Burke,* CA-FC, 93-2 USTC ¶ 60,146, 944 F2d 1576.

[62] *O. Hubert Est.,* 95-2 USTC ¶ 60,209, aff'g TC, 101 TC 314, CCH Dec. 49,342, cert. granted; *F. Allen Est.,* 101 TC 351, CCH Dec. 49,346.

[63] *O. Hubert Est.,* SCt, 97-1 USTC ¶ 60,261.

[64] Rev. Rul. 93-48, 1993-2 CB 270, modifying Rev. Rul. 73-98, 1973-1 CB 407.

[65] Rev. Rul. 93-48, 1993-2 CB 270, revoking Rev. Rul. 82-6, 1982-1 CB 137; *W. Richardson Est.,* 89 TC 1193, CCH Dec. 44,388; *G. Street Est.,* CA-6, 92-2 USTC ¶ 60,112, 974 F2d 723; *R. Whittle Est.,* CA-7, 93-1 USTC ¶ 60,141, 994 F2d 379.

The amount of tax actually due and paid, rather than the present (date of death) value of such tax, is the proper amount of tax to be subtracted from the charitable interest.[66]

The deduction for charitable transfers allowed for federal estate tax purposes does not always correspond with state and foreign death tax exemptions or deductions for such transfers. In instances where a transfer is deductible under federal law but taxable under state or foreign law, the federal estate tax law authorizes a deduction for the state or foreign death taxes paid if the executor elects to take it.

In some instances, where the charitable transfer is reduced on account of state taxes and where the charitable transfer is a remainder interest, the complicated problem of interdependent taxes and deductions arises. This problem is identical in principle to the marital deduction situation at ¶ 1075. As in the case of the marital deduction, the problem can be avoided by providing for the payment of taxes out of other funds in the estate.

IRS Publication No. 904 (Interrelated Computations for Estate and Gift Taxes (Rev. May 1985)) contains examples for computing the charitable and marital deductions when these deductions are interrelated with the federal estate tax (see ¶ 1075 for sample computation). It is reproduced in the CCH FEDERAL ESTATE AND GIFT TAX REPORTER and is also available from the U.S. Government Printing Office.

¶ 1140 Execution of Schedule

Deductions authorized for charitable, public, and similar gifts and bequests should be claimed on Form 706, Schedule O (Charitable, Public, and Similar Gifts and Bequests). This schedule must be filed if the estate claims a charitable deduction and the gross estate exceeds the applicable exclusion amount. If the transfer was made by will, a certified copy of the order admitting the will to probate, in addition to the copy of the will, should be submitted with the return. If the transfer was made by any other written instrument, a copy of the instrument should be submitted with the return. If the instrument is of record, the copy should be certified. If not of record, the copy should be verified.[67]

If the transfer was made by will, the executor must answer questions 1a and 1b at the top of Schedule O, which deal with whether any action has been instituted to interpret or to contest the will or any provision affecting the charitable deduction and whether, according to his or her information and belief, any such action is designed or contemplated. If the executor answers "yes" to either of these questions, full details of the action or contemplated action must be submitted with the return.

If a charitable deduction is claimed for the value of a split-interest in property (see ¶ 1121), a copy of the computation of the deduction must be attached to the return. The computation must include the dates of birth of the life tenants or annuitants whose lives may affect the value of the interest passing to charity, and, in the case of a pooled income fund, the applicable yearly rate of return. If property passes to a charitable benefici-

---

[66] *J.G. Buchanan, Exr. (M.L. Gillespie Est.)*, CA-3, in unpublished decision aff'g DC Pa., 74-2 USTC ¶ 13,008.

[67] Reg. § 20.2055-1(c).

ary as a result of a "qualified disclaimer" (see ¶ 1102), a copy of the written disclaimer must be attached to Schedule O.

¶ 1141 Valuation of Residuary Transfer

If a claim is made for a deduction of the value of the residue of the estate or a portion of the residue passing to charity under the decedent's will, a copy of the computation determining the value should be submitted.[68] The computation, or supporting documents, should include:

(1) A statement showing the values of all specific and general legacies or devises, indicating whether they are for charitable or noncharitable uses. (Appropriate reference must be made to the applicable paragraph or section of the decedent's will or codicil. In any case where legacies are made to each member of a class, only the number in each class and the aggregate value of property received by them need be furnished.)

(2) The dates of birth of all life tenants or annuitants, the duration of whose lives may affect the value of the interest passing to charity under the decedent's will.

(3) A statement showing the value of all property that is included in the decedent's gross estate but does not pass under the will. (This includes jointly owned property which passed to the survivor on decedent's death and insurance payable to specific beneficiaries.)

(4) Any other information that may appear material, such as that relating to any claim, not arising under the will, to any part of the estate. This would include a spouse's claim to dower, curtesy or similar rights.

¶ 1142 Alternate Valuation

Even if the alternate valuation (see ¶ 105) is used, any charitable transfer deductible on Schedule O should be valued as of the date of the decedent's death. However, adjustment must be made for any difference in the value of the property six months after the decedent's death, or at the date of its sale or exchange within this period. No adjustment may take into account any difference in value due to mere lapse of time or to the occurrence or nonoccurrence of a contingency.[69] If a decedent gives a percentage of his adjusted gross estate to charity, and his executor elects to use the alternate valuation method, the amount of the allowable charitable deduction is determined by using the value of the decedent's adjusted gross estate as of the alternate valuation date.[70]

---

[68] Instructions for Form 706 (Rev. July 1998), p. 15.

[69] Reg. § 20.2032-1(g).

[70] Rev. Rul. 70-527, 1970-2 CB 193.

¶1145 Filled-In Schedule O

The filled-in Schedule O, Form 706 (Rev. July 1998), relates to the fact situation of a person who died on January 1, 1998, with an estate tax return due within nine months (without extensions). Schedule O must be filed only if a charitable deduction is claimed (see ¶ 73).

Form 706 (Rev. 7-98)

Estate of: James X. Diversey

SCHEDULE O — Charitable, Public, and Similar Gifts and Bequests

		Yes	No
1a	If the transfer was made by will, has any action been instituted to have interpreted or to contest the will or any of its provisions affecting the charitable deductions claimed in this schedule? If "Yes," full details must be submitted with this schedule.		X
b	According to the information and belief of the person or persons filing this return, is any such action planned? If "Yes," full details must be submitted with this schedule.		X
2	Did any property pass to charity as the result of a qualified disclaimer? If "Yes," attach a copy of the written disclaimer required by section 2518(b).		X

Item number	Name and address of beneficiary	Character of institution	Amount
1	American Heart Association, Chicago, IL 10 shares Public Service Corp., Common Stock (Schedule B, Item 2)	Heart Research	1,090
2	Homewood Trust and Savings, Homewood, IL in trust for the purpose of providing scholarships to worthy graduates of Homewood-Flossmoor High School in accordance with paragraph 8 of the decedent's will.	Trust Company	8,000

	Total from continuation schedules (or additional sheets) attached to this schedule		
3	Total	3	9,090
4a	Federal estate tax payable out of property interests listed above	4a	
b	Other death taxes payable out of property interests listed above	4b	
c	Federal and state GST taxes payable out of property interests listed above	4c	
d	Add items a, b, and c	4d	
5	Net value of property interests listed above (subtract 4d from 3). Also enter on Part 5, Recapitulation, page 3, at item 21	5	9,090

(If more space is needed, attach the continuation schedule from the end of this package or additional sheets of the same size.)
(The instructions to Schedule O are in the separate instructions.)

Schedule O — Page 31

Chapter 27

QUALIFIED FAMILY-OWNED BUSINESS DEDUCTION

¶ 1150 Qualified Family-Owned Business Deduction

In order to alleviate the impact of the estate tax on family-owned businesses, the Taxpayer Relief Act of 1997 (P.L. 105-34) created an exclusion for a portion of qualified family-owned business interests (QFOBIs) from a decedent's gross estate. However, because it was not clear whether Code Sec. 2033A excluded property or value from the gross estate, the Internal Revenue Service Restructuring and Reform Act of 1998 (P.L. 105-206) converted the exclusion into a deduction.[1] Effective for estates of decedents dying after December 31, 1997, the qualified family-owned business interests deduction, in combination with the applicable exclusion amount (unified credit), shields up to $1.3 million of qualified family-owned business interests from the estate tax.

If an estate qualifies and elects to take the deduction, up to $675,000 of the adjusted value of qualified interests may be deducted from the value of a decedent's gross estate. If the maximum $675,000 deduction is elected, the applicable exclusion amount (unified credit) is limited to $625,000, regardless of the date of death. In order to coordinate the deduction with the unified credit, if less than the maximum deduction is elected, the $625,000 applicable exclusion amount is increased by the excess of $675,000 over the amount of the deduction allowed. However, the applicable exclusion amount may not be increased above the amount that would apply to the estate if no QFOBI deduction had been elected.

> ***Example (1):*** Ruth Roth dies in 2000 when the applicable exclusion amount is $675,000. Roth's estate includes $600,000 of qualified interests and her estate qualifies for and elects a $600,000 deduction. Roth's estate will be entitled to a deduction of $600,000 and an applicable exclusion amount of $675,000. The estate is not entitled to a $700,000 applicable exclusion amount ($625,000 + ($675,000 − $600,000)) because the applicable exclusion amount cannot exceed the amount that would apply to the estate without regard to the deduction.

> ***Example (2):*** Adam Brook dies in 2006 when the applicable exclusion amount is $1,000,000. Brook's estate includes $1,000,000 of qualified interests and his estate qualifies for and elects to take a $600,000 deduction. Brook's estate will be entitled to a deduction of $600,000 and an applicable exclusion amount of $700,000 ($625,000 + ($675,000 − $600,000)).

In general, to qualify for the deduction the aggregate value of the decedent's qualified family-owned business interests that are passed to

---

[1] Code Sec. 2057.

qualified heirs must exceed 50 percent of the decedent's adjusted gross estate. In addition, the decedent must be a U.S. citizen or resident at the time of death, the executor must elect to make the deduction and file a recapture agreement signed by each person in being having an interest in the property, and certain other requirements must be met. The deduction is in addition to the special use valuation provisions (see ¶ 280), and the provisions for the installment payment of estate taxes attributable to a closely held business (see ¶ 1672).

¶ 1155 Ownership Requirement

A qualified family-owned business is any interest in a trade or business, regardless of form, with a principal place of business in the United States, the ownership of which is held at least (1) 50 percent by one family, (2) 70 percent by two families, or (3) 90 percent by three families. If held by more than one family, the decedent's family must own at least 30 percent of the trade or business.[2] A decedent is treated as engaged in a trade or business if any member of the decedent's family is engaged in the trade or business.

Members of the individual's family include: (1) the individual's spouse, (2) the individual's ancestors, (3) lineal descendants of the individual, of the individual's spouse, or of the individual's parents, and (4) the spouses of any such lineal descendants.[3]

In the case of a corporation, the ownership test is met if the decedent and family members own the requisite percentage of both the total combined voting power of all classes of voting stock and the total value of all shares of all classes of stock. In the case of a partnership, the decedent and family members are required to own the requisite percentage of the capital interest in the partnership. However, the Senate Committee Report to the Taxpayer Relief Act of 1997 indicates that an ownership in the profits interest of a partnership is also required. Special look-through rules apply in the case of a trade or business that owns an interest in another trade or business. Whether owned directly or indirectly, each trade or business owned by the decedent and members of the family must be separately tested to determine whether the trade or business meets the requirements of a qualified family-owned business.[4]

An interest in a trade or business does not qualify if the business's or a related entity's stock or securities were publicly traded at any time within three years of the decedent's death. In addition, the interest does not qualify if more than 35 percent of the adjusted ordinary gross income from the business for the year of the decedent's death was personal holding company income. The second restriction does not apply to banks and domestic building and loan associations.

¶ 1160 Valuation

The value of a trade or business qualifying as a family-owned business interest is reduced to the extent that the business holds certain passive assets or cash and marketable securities in excess of reasonably expected day-to-day working capital needed for the trade or business. In addition,

---

[2] Code Sec. 2057(e)(1).

[3] Code Sec. 2057(e)(2) and Code. Sec. 2057(i)(2).

[4] Code Sec. 2057(e)(3).

accumulations for capital acquisitions are not considered "working capital." Further, certain other passive assets are not considered in valuing qualified family-owned business interests.

The following assets are considered passive assets and are not included in the value of a qualified family-owned business: (1) assets that produce dividends, interest, rents, royalties, annuities and Code Sec. 543(a) personal holding company income; (2) assets that are interests in a trust, partnership or real estate mortgage investment conduit (REMIC) (as described in Code Sec. 954(c)(1)(B)(ii)); (3) assets that produce no income (as described in Code Sec. 954(c)(1)(B)(iii)); (4) assets that give rise to income from commodities transactions or foreign currency gains (as described in Code Sec. 954(c)(1)(C) and (D)); (5) assets that produce income equivalent to interest (as described in Code Sec. 954(c)(1)(E)); and (6) assets that produce income from notional principal contracts or payments in lieu of dividends (as described in Code Sec. 954(c)(1)(F) and (G)). However, with respect to regular dealers in property, such property is not considered to produce passive income and, therefore, is not considered a passive asset.[5]

¶ 1165 Qualifying Estates

In order to qualify for the QFOBI deduction, the decedent must have been a U.S. citizen or resident at the time of death and the aggregate value of the decedent's qualified family-owned business interests passing to qualified heirs must exceed 50 percent of the decedent's adjusted gross estate. For this purpose, qualified heirs include any individual who was actively employed by the trade or business for at least 10 years prior to the date of the decedent's death, as well as members of the decedent's family.

Property passing to a trust may be treated as having passed to a qualified heir if all of the beneficiaries of the trust are qualified heirs.[6] The decedent's qualified family-owned business interests passing to qualified heirs include lifetime gifts of such interests made by the decedent to members of the decedent's family to the extent that those interests are held by family members (other than the decedent's spouse) between the date of the gift and the date of the decedent's death.

- *Fifty-percent liquidity test*

Generally, a 50-percent liquidity test is used to determine if this requirement is met. Under this test, the total of all transfers of qualified family-owned business interests made by the decedent to qualified heirs at the time of the decedent's death, plus certain lifetime gifts to family members, is compared to the decedent's adjusted gross estate. If the decedent held qualified family-owned business interests in more than one trade or business, all such interests are aggregated for purposes of applying the 50-percent liquidity test.

To determine whether the decedent's qualifying interests comprise more than 50 percent of the decedent's adjusted gross estate, a percentage calculation using the following numerator and denominator is used.

The numerator is determined by aggregating the value of all qualified family-owned business interests that are includible in the decedent's gross

---

[5] Code Sec. 2057(e)(2).

[6] Code Sec. 2057(i)(3).

estate and that are passed from the decedent to a qualified heir, plus any lifetime transfers of such interests by the decedent to members of the decedent's family (other than the decedent's spouse), provided such interests have been continuously held by members of the family and were not otherwise includible in the decedent's gross estate. For this purpose, the qualified interests transferred to members of the family during the decedent's lifetime are valued as of the date of the transfer. This amount is then reduced by all the indebtedness of the estate, except for the following: (1) indebtedness on a qualified residence of the decedent, i.e., a residence that qualifies for the mortgage interest deduction under Code Sec. 163(h)(3); (2) indebtedness incurred to pay the educational or medical expenses of the decedent, the decedent's spouse, or the decedent's dependents; and (3) other indebtedness up to $10,000.[7]

The denominator is equal to the decedent's gross estate, reduced by any indebtedness of the estate and increased by the amount of the following transfers, to the extent not already included in the gross estate: (1) lifetime transfers of qualified business interests that were made by the decedent to members of the decedent's family (other than the decedent's spouse), provided such interests have been continuously held by members of the family, plus (2) transfers, other than *de minimis* transfers, from the decedent to the decedent's spouse that were made within 10 years of the date of the decedent's death, plus (3) any other transfers made by the decedent within three years of death, except nontaxable transfers made to members of the decedent's family.[8]

¶ 1170 Participation Requirements

The decedent, or members of the decedent's family, must have owned and materially participated in the trade or business for at least five of the eight years preceding the decedent's death in order to qualify for the QFOBI deduction.[9] In addition, a qualified heir is subject to a recapture tax if the heir, or a member of the qualified heir's family, does not materially participate in the trade or business for at least five years of any eight-year period within 10 years following the decedent's death. The definition of "material participation" provided in Code Sec. 2032A and Reg. § 20.2032A-3 pertaining to special use valuation applies. The principal factors to be considered include physical work and participation in management decisions. A qualified heir will not be treated as disposing of an interest in a trade or business by reason of ceasing to be engaged in a trade or business if any member of the qualified heir's family continues in the trade or business.[10] The material participation requirement will be met with respect to a qualified heir if the heir rents qualified property to a member of the qualified heir's family on a net cash basis, and that family member materially participates in the business.[11]

¶ 1175 Election

For the qualified family-owned business deduction to apply, the executor must make a Code Sec. 2057 election and file a written agreement

---

[7] Code Sec. 2057(d).

[8] Code Sec. 2057(b), (c), and (d).

[9] Code Sec. 2057(b)(1)(D).

[10] Code Sec. 2057(f)(3).

[11] Code Sec. 2057(b)(1)(D).

signed by each person in being having an interest in the property consenting to the application of the additional tax.[12]

- *Recapture tax*

An additional tax is imposed if any of the following recapture events occurs within 10 years of the decedent's death and before the qualified heir's death: (1) the qualified heir ceases to meet the material participation requirements; (2) the qualified heir disposes of any portion of his or her interest in the family-owned business, other than by a disposition to a member of the qualified heir's family or through a conservation contribution under Code Sec. 170(h); (3) the principal place of business of the trade or business ceases to be located in the United States; or (4) the qualified heir loses U.S. citizenship.

The recapture tax may be avoided if a qualified heir loses U.S. citizenship, provided the trade or business assets are placed into a qualified trust meeting the requirement similar to a QDOT under Code Sec. 2056A(a) or certain other security arrangements are met. The recapture period may be extended up to two years if the qualified heir does not begin to use the property for a period of up to two years after a decedent's death.

The recapture tax is a personal liability of each qualified heir to the extent of the portion of the additional tax that is imposed with respect to his or her interest in the qualified family-owned business.[13]

> ***Example:*** John, Beth and Sue Milton inherit equal qualified family-owned business interests from their father and the estate elects special tax treatment. Only Sue continues to materially participate in the family business. Such participation, as a family member, causes all three children to meet the participation requirements. However, during the fourth year following the decedent's death, Sue ceases to materially participate in the business and neither John nor Beth participates. As a result, each of the three children would be personally liable for the portion of the recapture tax attributable to his or her interest.

- *Amount of additional estate tax*

The additional estate tax is based upon when the recapture event occurs in relation to the decedent's death. If the recapture event occurs within the first six years of material participation, 100 percent of the reduction in estate tax attributable to the heir's interest plus interest is recaptured. Thereafter, the applicable percentage is 80 percent in the seventh year, 60 percent in the eighth year, 40 percent in the ninth year, and 20 percent in the 10th year.[14]

---

[12] Code Sec. 2057(h).

[13] Code Sec. 2057(f).

[14] Code Sec. 2057(f)(2)(B).

¶ 1180 Schedule T

Below is Schedule T, Form 706 (Rev. July 1998). The schedule is not filled in because the James X. Diversey estate did not own any qualified family-owned business interests.

Form 706 (Rev. 7-98)

Estate of:

SCHEDULE T. — Qualified Family-Owned Business Interest Deduction

For details on the deduction, including trades and businesses that do not qualify, see page 20 of the separate Instructions for Form 706.

Part 1. — Election

Note: *The executor is deemed to have made the election under section 2057 if her or she files Schedule T and deducts any qualifying business interests from the gross estate.*

Part 2. — General Qualifications

1 Did the decedent and/or a member of the decedent's family own the business interests listed on line 5 of this schedule for at least 5 of the 8 years immediately preceding the date of the decedent's death? . . . . ☐ Yes ☐ No

2 Were there any periods during the 8-year period preceding the date of the decedent's death during which the decedent or a member of his or her family:

	Yes	No
a Did not own the business interests listed on this schedule?		
b Did not materially participate, within the meaning of section 2032A(e)(6), in the operation of the business to which such interests relate?		

If "Yes," to either of the above, you must attach a statement listing the periods. If applicable, describe whether the exceptions of sections 2032A(b)(4) or (5) are met.

Attach affidavits describing the activities constituting material participation and the identity and relationship to the decedent of the material participants.

3 Check the applicable box(es). The qualified family-owned business interest(s) is:

☐ An interest as a proprietor in a trade or business carried on as a proprietorship.

☐ An interest in an entity, at least 50% of which is owned (directly or indirectly) by the decedent and members of the decedent's family.

☐ An interest in an entity, at least 70% of which is owned (directly or indirectly) by members of 2 families and at least 30% of which is owned (directly or indirectly) by the decedent and members of the decedent's family.

☐ An interest in an entity, at least 90% of which is owned (directly or indirectly) by members of 3 families and at least 30% of which is owned (directly or indirectly) by the decedent and members of the decedent's family.

4 Persons holding interests. Enter the requested information for each party who received any interest in the family-owned business. If any qualified heir is not a U.S. citizen, see the line 4 instructions beginning on page 20 of the separate instructions.

(Each of the qualified heirs receiving an interest in the business must sign the agreement that begins on page 40, and the agreement must be filed with this return.)

	Name	Address
A		
B		
C		
D		
E		
F		
G		
H		

	Identifying number	Relationship to decedent	Value of interest
A			
B			
C			
D			
E			
F			
G			
H			

Schedule T (Form 706) — Page 38

Form 706 (Rev. 7-98)

Part 3. — Adjusted Value of Qualified Family-Owned Business Interests

5 Qualified family-owned business interests reported on this return:
Note: *All property listed on line 5 must also be entered on Schedules A, B, C, E, F, G, or H, as applicable.*

A Schedule and item number from Form 706	B Description of business interest and principal place of business	C Reported value

6	Total reported value		6
7	Amount of claims or mortgages deductible under section 2053(a)(3) or (4) (see separate instructions)	7	
8a	Enter the amount of any indebtedness on qualified residence of the decedent (see separate instructions)	8a	
b	Enter the amount of any indebtedness used for educational or medical expenses (see separate instructions)	8b	
c	Enter the amount of any indebtedness other than that listed on line 8a or 8b, but do not enter more than $10,000 (see separate instructions)	8c	
d	Total (add lines 8a through 8c)	8d	
9	Subtract line 8d from line 7		9
10	Adjusted value of qualified family-owned business interests (subtract line 9 from line 6)		10

Part 4. — Qualifying Estate

11	Includible gifts of qualified family-owned business interests (see separate instructions):		
a	Amount of gifts taken into account under section 2001(b)(1)(B)	11a	
b	Amount of such gifts excluded under section 2503(b)	11b	
c	Add lines 11a and 11b		11c
12	Add lines 10 and 11c		12
13	Adjusted gross estate (see separate instructions).		
a	Amount of gross estate	13a	
b	Enter the amount from line 7	13b	
c	Subtract line 13b from line 13a	13c	
d	Enter the amount from line 11c	13d	
e	Enter the amount of transfers, if any, to the decedent's spouse	13e	
f	Enter the amount of other gifts	13f	
g	Add the amounts on lines 13d, 13e, and 13f	13g	
h	Enter any amounts from line 13g that are otherwise includible in the gross estate	13h	
i	Subtract line 13h from line 13g	13i	
j	Adjusted gross estate (add lines 13c and 13i)		13j
14	Enter one-half of the amount on line 13j		14
	Note: *If line 12 does not exceed line 14, stop here; the estate does not qualify for the deduction. Otherwise, complete line 15.*		
15	Net value of qualified family-owned business interests you elect to deduct (line 10 reduced by any marital or other deductions) — DO NOT enter more than $675,000 — (see instructions) (attach schedule) — enter here and on Part 5, Recapitulation, page 3, at item 22.		15

Schedule T — Page 39

Form 706 (Rev. 7-98)

Part 5. — Agreement to Family-Owned Business Interest Deduction Under Section 2057

Estate of:	Date of Death	Decedent's Social Security Number

There cannot be a valid election unless:

- The agreement is executed by each and every one of the qualified heirs, and
- The agreement is included with the estate tax return when the estate tax return is filed.

We (list all qualified heirs and other persons having an interest in the business required to sign this agreement)

____

____,

being all the qualified heirs and ____

____,

being all other parties having interests in the business(es) which are deducted under section 2057 of the Internal Revenue Code, do hereby approve of the election made by ____,

Executor/Administrator of the estate of ____,

pursuant to section 2057 to deduct said interests from the gross estate and do hereby enter into this agreement pursuant to section 2057(h).

The undersigned agree and consent to the application of subsection (f) of section 2057 of the Code with respect to all the qualified family-owned business interests deducted on Schedule T of Form 706, attached to this agreement. More specifically, the undersigned heirs expressly agree and consent to personal liability under subsection (c) of 2032A (as made applicable by section 2057(i)(3)(F) of the Code) for the additional estate tax imposed by that subsection with respect to their respective interests in the above-described business interests in the event of certain early dispositions of the interests or the occurrence of any of the disqualifying acts described in section 2057(f)(1) of the Code. It is understood that if a qualified heir disposes of any deducted interest to any member of his or her family, such member may thereafter be treated as the qualified heir with respect to such interest upon filing a new agreement and any other form required by the Internal Revenue Service.

The undersigned interested parties who are not qualified heirs consent to the collection of any additional estate tax imposed under section 2057(f) of the Code from the deducted interests.

If there is a disposition of any interest which passes or has passed to him or her, each of the undersigned heirs agrees to file the appropriate form and pay any additional estate tax due within 6 months of the disposition or other disqualifying act.

It is understood by all interested parties that this agreement is a condition precedent to the election of the qualified family-owned business deduction under section 2057 of the Code and must be executed by every interested party even though that person may not have received the estate tax benefits or be in possession of such property.

Each of the undersigned understands that by making this election, a lien will be created and recorded pursuant to section 6324B of the Code on the interests referred to in this agreement for the applicable percentage of the adjusted tax differences with respect to the estate as defined in section 2057(f)(2)(C).

As the interested parties, the undersigned designate the following individual as their agent for all dealings with the Internal Revenue Service concerning the continued qualification of the deducted property under section 2057 of the Code and on all issues regarding the special lien under section 6324B. The agent is authorized to act for the parties with respect to all dealings with the Service on matters affecting the qualified interests described earlier. This authority includes the following:

- To receive confidential information on all matters relating to continued qualification under section 2057 of the deducted interests and on all matters relating to the special lien arising under section 6324B.
- To furnish the Service with any requested information concerning the interests.
- To notify the Service of any disposition or other disqualifying events specified in section 2057(f)(1) of the Code.
- To receive, but not to endorse and collect, checks in payment of any refund of Internal Revenue taxes, penalties, or interest.
- To execute waivers (including offers of waivers) of restrictions on assessment or collection of deficiencies in tax and waivers of notice of disallowance of a claim for credit or refund.
- To execute closing agreements under section 7121.

(continued on next page)

Schedule T Part 5 — Page 40

Form 706 (Rev. 7-98)

Part 5. — Agreement to Family-Owned Business Interest Deduction Under Section 2057 (continued)

Estate of:	Date of Death	Decedent's Social Security Number

• Other acts (specify) ▶ ____________________

By signing this agreement, the agent agrees to provide the Service with any requested information concerning the qualified business interests and to notify the Service of any disposition or other disqualifying events with regard to said interests.

____________________	____________________	____________________
Name of Agent	Signature	Address

The interests to which this agreement relates arelisted in Form 706, United States Estate (and Generation-Skipping Transfer) Tax Return, along with their fair market value according to section 2031 (or, if applicable, section 2032A) of the Code. The name, address, social security number, and interest (including the value) of each of the undersigned in this business(es) are as set forth in the attached Schedule T.

IN WITNESS WHEREOF, the undersigned have hereunto set their hands at ____________________ .

this __________ day of ______________ .

SIGNATURES OF EACH OF THE QUALIFIED HEIRS:

Signature of qualified heir	Signature of qualified heir
Signature of qualified heir	Signature of qualified heir
Signature of qualified heir	Signature of qualified heir
Signature of qualified heir	Signature of qualified heir
Signature of qualified heir	Signature of qualified heir
Signature of qualified heir	Signature of qualified heir

____
Signature(s) of other interested parties

____
Signature(s) of other interested parties

Schedule T Part 5 — Page 41

Determination and Payment of Tax

Chapter 28

EXECUTOR ELECTIONS, GENERAL INFORMATION AND RECAPITULATION

¶ 1190 Executor Elections

Various federal estate tax elections that are available to the executor of a decedent's estate are to be made by marking the appropriate boxes on Part 3 of Form 706 (Rev. July 1998) (see ¶ 1225 for an example of a filled-in page 2, Form 706).

Executor elections include elections with respect to:

(1) alternate valuation;

(2) special use valuation;

(3) installment payment of tax; and

(4) deferred payment of tax attributable to certain remainder and reversionary interests.

Qualified terminable interest property (QTIP) elections are deemed to have been made by the executor if (1) QTIP property is listed on Schedule M and (2) the value of the property is entered as a deduction on Schedule M.

¶ 1195 General Information

Part 4 of Form 706 contains general information questions relating to the decedent's death certificate, the decedent's business or occupation, the decedent's marital status, the surviving spouse's name, and the identity of individuals (other than the surviving spouse), trusts, or other estates receiving benefits (and the amount of such benefits) from the decedent's estate.

Part 4 of Form 706 also contains questions concerning assets owned by the decedent during his life, such as whether the decedent received any QTIP property, owned any life insurance, possessed any retained powers, held an interest in a partnership or closely held business, etc. The purpose of this section is to alert the executor and the Internal Revenue Service to any assets that should be reported on the estate tax return or to remind the executor of possible elections to which the estate might be entitled. (See ¶ 1225 for an example of filled-in Parts 3 and 4 of Form 706.)

¶ 1200 Recapitulation

The Recapitulation, located in Part 5 of Form 706, brings together in one place the information reported in the schedules. This results in the determination of the size of the gross estate and the total allowable deductions.

With regard to the gross estate, Part 5 lists the value of the estate's interest in different assets, by way of the following Schedules: A—Real Estate, B—Stocks and Bonds, C—Mortgages, Notes and Cash, D—Insurance on the Decedent's Life, E—Jointly Owned Property, F—Other Miscellaneous Property, G—Transfers During Decedent's Life, H—Powers of Appointment, and I—Annuities. The total of these assets is then entered on line 10 of Part 5. The amount claimed for the qualified conversion on Schedule U is subtracted from the gross estate. The amount of the exclusion is shown on Line 11 and the net amount so determined is shown on Line 12 of Part 5 and on Line 1 of Part 2 (Tax Computation).

The second half of the Recapitulation lists deductions allowed the estate which are figured on the following Schedules: J—Funeral Expenses and Expenses Incurred in Administering Property Subject to Claims, K—Debts of the Decedent, and Mortgages and Liens, L—Net Losses During Administration and Expenses Incurred in Administering Property Not Subject to Claims, M—Bequests, etc. to Surviving Spouse, O—Charitable, Public, and Similar Gifts and Bequests, and T—Qualified Family-Owned Business Deduction.

- *Limitation on Deductions from Schedules J and K*

The amounts from Schedule J (Funeral Expenses and Expenses Incurred in Administering Property Subject to Claims) and Schedule K (Debts of the Decedent, and Mortgages and Liens) can be limited for purposes of determining the allowable deduction. This is the case when the sum of the items listed on Schedules J and K is more than the value (at the time of the decedent's death) of the property subject to claims. In such an instance, the amount deductible is limited to the value of the property that is subject to the claims. However, if the amount actually paid at the time the return is filed is more than the amount subject to the claims, the amount actually paid, rather than the amount subject to the claims, is deductible. The sum of the deductions allowable from Schedules J and K and the deductions from Schedules L, M, O, and T is then entered on line 23 of Part 5 and on line 2 of Part 2.

A sample Recapitulation section of Form 706 (filled in with respect to the estate of James X. Diversey) is reproduced at ¶ 1225.

¶ 1225 Filled-In Form 706—Elections, General Information and Recapitulation

The filled-in Form 706 (Rev. July 1998), pages 2 and 3 (relating to executor elections, certain general information questions and the Recapitulation), relates to the fact situation as it applies to the estate of a person who dies on January 1, 1998, with an estate tax return due within nine months (without extensions).

Form 706 (Rev. 7-98)

Estate of: James X. Diversey

Part 3. — Elections by the Executor

Please check the "Yes" or "No" box for each question. (See instructions beginning on page 3.)	Yes	No
1 Do you elect alternate valuation?		X
2 Do you elect special use valuation? If "Yes," you must complete and attach Schedule A-1.		X
3 Do you elect to pay the taxes in installments as described in section 6166? If "Yes," you must attach the additional information described on page 5 of the instructions.		X
4 Do you elect to postpone the part of the taxes attributable to a reversionary or remainder interest as described in section 6163?		X

Part 4. — General Information (Note: *Please attach the necessary supplemental documents.* You must attach the death certificate.) *(See instructions beginning on page 6.)*

Authorization to receive confidential tax information under Regulations section 601.504(b)(2)(i) to act as the estate's representative before the Internal Revenue Service, and to make written or oral presentations on behalf of the estate if return prepared by an attorney, accountant, or enrolled agent for the executor:

Name of representative (print or type)	State	Address (number, street, and room or suite no., city, state, and ZIP code)
William S. Oaks	IL	542 James St., Homewood, IL 60430

I declare that I am the ☒ attorney/ ☐ certified public accountant/ ☐ enrolled agent (you must check the applicable box) for the executor and prepared this return for the executor. I am not under suspension or disbarment from practice before the Internal Revenue Service and am qualified to practice in the state shown above.

Signature	CAF number	Date	Telephone number
William S. Oaks		9-14-98	(708)940-4600

1 Death certificate number and issuing authority (attach a copy of the death certificate to this return).
CX-12345 Cook County, IL

2 Decedent's business or occupation. If retired, check here ▶ ☐ and state decedent's former business or occupation.
Vice President, Siding Manufacturing Co., Inc., Homewood, IL 60430

3 Marital status of the decedent at time of death:
☒ Married
☐ Widow or widower — Name, SSN, and date of death of deceased spouse ▶
☐ Single
☐ Legally separated
☐ Divorced — Date divorce decree became final ▶

4a Surviving spouse's name	4b Social security number	4c Amount received (see page 6 of the instructions)
Carrie Diversey	322-43-8143	510,955

5 Individuals (other than the surviving spouse), trusts, or other estates who receive benefits from the estate (do not include charitable beneficiaries shown in Schedule O) (see instructions). For Privacy Act Notice (applicable to individual beneficiaries only), see the Instructions for Form 1040.

Name of individual, trust, or estate receiving $5,000 or more	Identifying number	Relationship to decedent	Amount (see instructions)
Robert Diversey	497-86-4763	Son	325,000
Richard Diversey	358-76-0957	Son	325,000
Martha Diversey	279-60-2763	Sister	75,000
Ann Fagin	343-44-6123	Sister	35,000
Katherine Diversey	352-54-6197	Granddaughter	50,000
All unascertainable beneficiaries and those who receive less than $5,000 ▶			
Total			810,000

Please check the "Yes" or "No" box for each question.	Yes	No
6 Does the gross estate contain any section 2044 property (qualified terminable interest property (QTIP) from a prior gift or estate) (see page 6 of the instructions)?		X

(continued on next page)

Page 2

Form 706 (Rev. 7-98)

Part 4. — General Information *(continued)*

Please check the "Yes" or "No" box for each question.	Yes	No
7a Have Federal gift tax returns ever been filed? If "Yes," please attach copies of the returns, if available, and furnish the following information:	X	
7b Period(s) covered: 1st quarter 1969 — 7c Internal Revenue office(s) where filed: Kansas City, MO		
If you answer "Yes" to any of questions 8 - 16, you must attach additional information as described in the instructions.		
8a Was there any insurance on the decedent's life that is not included on the return as part of the gross estate?	X	
b Did the decedent own any insurance on the life of another that is not included in the gross estate?		X
9 Did the decedent at the time of death own any property as a joint tenant with right of survivorship in which (a) one or more of the other joint tenants was someone other than the decedent's spouse, and (b) less than the full value of the property is included on the return as part of the gross estate? If "Yes," you must complete and attach Schedule E	X	
10 Did the decedent, at the time of death, own any interest in a partnership or unincorporated business or any stock in an inactive or closely held corporation?	X	
11 Did the decedent make any transfer described in section 2035, 2036, 2037, or 2038 (see the instructions for Schedule G beginning on page 9 of the separate instructions)? If "Yes," you must complete and attach Schedule G	X	
12 Were there in existence at the time of the decedent's death:		
a Any trusts created by the decedent during his or her lifetime?	X	
b Any trusts not created by the decedent under which the decedent possessed any power, beneficial interest, or trusteeship?	X	
13 Did the decedent ever possess, exercise, or release any general power of appointment? If "Yes," you must complete and attach Schedule H	X	
14 Was the marital deduction computed under the transitional rule of Public Law 97-34, section 403(e)(3) (Economic Recovery Tax Act of 1981)? If "Yes," attach a separate computation of the marital deduction, enter the amount on item 20 of the Recapitulation, and note on item 20 "computation attached."		X
15 Was the decedent, immediately before death, receiving an annuity described in the "General" paragraph of the instructions for Schedule I? If "Yes," you must complete and attach Schedule I	X	
16 Was the decedent ever the beneficiary of a trust for which a deduction was claimed by the estate of a pre-deceased spouse under section 2056(b)(7) and which is not reported on this return? If "Yes," attach an explanation		X

Part 5. — Recapitulation

Item number	Gross estate	Alternate value	Value at date of death
1	Schedule A — Real Estate		884,300
2	Schedule B — Stocks and Bonds		168,200
3	Schedule C — Mortgages, Notes, and Cash		36,553
4	Schedule D — Insurance on the Decedent's Life (attach Form(s) 712)		61,120
5	Schedule E — Jointly Owned Property (attach Form(s) 712 for life insurance)		147,193
6	Schedule F — Other Miscellaneous Property (attach Form(s) 712 for life insurance)		268,150
7	Schedule G — Transfers During Decedent's Life (attach Form(s) 712 for life insurance)		52,368
8	Schedule H — Powers of Appointment		20,000
9	Schedule I — Annuities		37,300
10	Total gross estate (add items 1 through 9)		1,675,184
11	Schedule U — Qualified Conservation Easement Exclusion		0
12	Total gross estate less exclusion (subtract item 11 from item 10). Enter here and on line 1 of the Tax Computation		1,675,184

Item number	Deductions	Amount
13	Schedule J — Funeral Expenses and Expenses Incurred in Administering Property Subject to Claims	35,325
14	Schedule K — Debts of the Decedent	11,050
15	Schedule K — Mortgages and Liens	138,210
16	Total of items 13 through 15	184,585
17	Allowable amount of deductions from item 16 (see the instructions for item 17 of the Recapitulation)	184,585
18	Schedule L — Net Losses During Administration	1,294
19	Schedule L — Expenses Incurred in Administering Property Not Subject to Claims	375
20	Schedule M — Bequests, etc., to Surviving Spouse	510,955
21	Schedule O — Charitable, Public, and Similar Gifts and Bequests	9,090
22	Schedule T — Qualified Family-Owned Business Interest Deduction	
23	Total allowable deductions (add lines 17 through 22). Enter here and on line 2 of the Tax Computation	706,299

Page 3

Chapter 29

DETERMINATION OF TAXABLE ESTATE

¶ 1250 Size of Taxable Estate

In the case of a U.S. resident or citizen, the computation of the taxable estate is accomplished on Part 2 (Tax Computation) of Form 706 (Rev. July 1998). Schedule B (Taxable Estate) of Form 706-NA (United States Estate (and Generation-Skipping Transfer) Tax Return, Estate of nonresident not a citizen of the United States) is used for this purpose by the estates of nonresidents not citizens.

¶ 1255 Residents and Citizens

If the decedent was a resident or a citizen of the United States, the taxable estate is determined by subtracting from the total gross estate (Line 1 of Part 2, Form 706) [1] the total allowable deductions (Line 2). A filled-in Part 2 of Form 706 appears at ¶ 1427.

¶ 1260 Nonresidents Not Citizens

As noted above, the taxable estate of a nonresident not a citizen of the United States is computed on Schedule B of Form 706-NA. The gross estate situated in the United States is entered on line 1, the gross estate situated outside of the United States is listed on line 2, and the sum of lines 1 and 2 is listed on line 3.[2] The value of the gross estate outside of the United States must be supported by proof (see ¶ 85).[3]

The total funeral, administrative expenses, debts of the decedent, mortgages, liens, and losses during the administration of the estate are entered on line 4. The allowable deduction for these expenses and debts is entered on line 5 and is computed by multiplying the total amounts of these expenses by the ratio of the gross estate within the United States (line 1) to the entire gross estate wherever situated (line 3).[4]

The amount of deductible charitable and marital transfers (line 6) is then added to the amount on line 5 to arrive at the total deductions shown on line 7. The total deductions are then subtracted from the gross estate within the United States (line 1) to arrive at the taxable estate shown on line 8.

Form 706-NA is used only for the estate of a nonresident not a citizen of the United States (see ¶ 1625). A filled-in Form 706-NA is reproduced at ¶ 1636.

---

[1] Form 706 (United States Estate (and Generation-Skipping Transfer) Tax Return) (Rev. July 1998).

[2] Form 706-NA (United States Estate (and Generation-Skipping Transfer) Tax Return, Estate of nonresident not a citizen of the United States) (Rev. September 1993); Code Sec. 2103; Reg. § 20.2103-1.

[3] Reg. § 20.6018-3(b).

[4] Code Sec. 2106; Reg. § 20.2106-1.

Chapter 30

CREDIT FOR TAX ON PRIOR TRANSFERS

¶ 1300 Effective Period of Credit

A credit is allowed against the estate tax for all or a part of the estate tax paid with respect to the transfer of property (including property passing as a result of the exercise or nonexercise of a power of appointment, see ¶ 650) to the present decedent by or from a person who died within 10 years before, or within two years after, the decedent.[1] The credit is computed on Schedule Q (Credit for Tax on Prior Transfers) of Form 706 after completing the worksheet provided in the instructions to Form 706. This schedule does not have to be filed if a credit is not claimed.

This credit can never be larger than it would have been if the present decedent had not received the property. Because the purpose of Code Sec. 2013 is to prevent diminution of an estate by successive taxes on the same property within a brief period, no credit is available for any gift tax that may have been paid with respect to the transfer of property to the present decedent. If the prior decedent (called the "transferor") predeceased the present decedent by more than two years, the credit allowable is reduced by 20 percent for each full two years by which the death of the transferor preceded the death of the decedent.[2] See ¶ 1325 for a table of the percentage allowable.

¶ 1310 General Requirements

The term "transferee" as used in Schedule Q for computing the credit for tax on prior transfers refers to the decedent for whose estate the return is filed.[3] It is not necessary that the property transferred be identified in or traced through the estate of the transferee. Nor is it necessary that the transferred property be in existence on the date of the transferee's death. It is sufficient for allowance of the credit that the transfer of the property was subject to federal estate tax in the estate of the transferor and that the specified period of time has not elapsed.[4] However, the credit cannot be waived, in whole or in part, and each transfer eligible for the credit must be taken into account in computing it.[5]

A credit may be allowed with respect to property received as the result of the exercise or nonexercise of a power of appointment. The credit is available if the property is included in the gross estate of the donee of

---

[1] Code Sec. 2013; Reg. § 20.2013-1.

[2] Reg. § 20.2013-1.

[3] Instructions for Form 706 (Rev. July 1998), p. 16.

[4] Reg. § 20.2013-1.

[5] Rev. Rul. 73-47, 1973-1 CB 397.

the power. If the transferee was the transferor's surviving spouse, no credit is allowed with respect to property received to the extent that a marital deduction was allowed the transferor's estate in connection with such property.

¶ 1315 "Property" Defined

The term "property" includes, for purposes of the credit, any beneficial interest received by the transferee,[6] including Louisiana usufruct interests.[7] The transferee is considered to be the beneficial owner of the property over which the transferee received a general power of appointment. "Property" does not include interests to which the transferee received bare legal title only, such as that of a trustee. Nor does it include an interest in property over which the transferee received a power that is not a general power of appointment under Code Sec. 2041 (see ¶ 652).

In addition to property interests in which the transferee received complete ownership, credit may be allowed for tax on annuities, life estates, terms for years, remainder interests (whether contingent or vested), and other future interests to the extent that the transferee became the beneficial owner of the interest. The credit is not available when the decedent "purchases" the property, as by electing to take a life estate in a spouse's community property and thereby relinquishing property greater in value than the property the decedent obtained.[8]

Additionally, the U.S. Courts of Appeals for the Fourth and Fifth Circuits have held that the credit is not available for a life estate where the transferor and the transferee die simultaneously in a common disaster.[9] The Tax Court has agreed with this conclusion with respect to a Louisiana usufruct interest passing from a husband to a wife upon their simultaneous deaths.[10]

¶ 1320 Maximum Amount of the Credit

The credit for tax on prior transfers is limited to the smaller of the following: [11]

(1) the amount of the estate tax of the transferor's estate pertaining to the transfer, or

(2) the amount by which (a) an estate tax on the transferee's estate (after deducting the unified tax credit and the credits for state death taxes, gift taxes, and foreign death taxes) determined without regard to the credit provided for in the schedule exceeds (b) an estate tax on the transferee's estate determined by excluding from the gross estate the net value of the transfer.

Where credit for a particular foreign death tax may be taken under either the statute or a death duty convention and the credit actually is

---

[6] Reg. § 20.2013-5.

[7] Rev. Rul. 66-271, 1966-2 CB 430.

[8] *I.M. Sparling Est.*, CA-9, 77-1 USTC ¶ 13,194, 552 F2d 1340, rev'g and rem'g TC, 60 TC 330, CCH Dec. 31,996 (Acq.).

[9] *G.A. Lion Est.*, CA-4, 71-1 USTC ¶ 12,745, 438 F2d 56, aff'g TC, 52 TC 601, CCH Dec. 29,646, cert. denied, and *A.P. Carter Est.*, CA-5, 91-1 USTC ¶ 60,054, rev'g DC La., 90-1 USTC ¶ 60,003, 929 F2d 699, cert. denied.

[10] *E.W. Marks, Jr., Est.*, 94 TC 720, CCH Dec. 46,594.

[11] Code Sec. 2013(c).

taken under the convention, credit for that foreign death tax may not be taken into consideration in computing estate tax (a) or estate tax (b).

The amounts in (1) and (2) are computed on the worksheet provided for Schedule Q (see ¶ 1345 and ¶ 1347).

¶ 1325 Percentage Reduction

If the transferor died within two years before or within two years after the transferee's death, the credit allowed for the tax on the prior transfer is 100 percent of the maximum amount allowable. If the transferor predeceased the transferee by more than two years, the credit allowed is a reduced percentage of the maximum amount allowable. The percentage allowable may be determined by using the following table:

Period of Time Exceeding	*Not Exceeding*	*Percent Allowable*
——	2 years	100
2 years	4 years	80
4 years	6 years	60
6 years	8 years	40
8 years	10 years	20
10 years	——	none

¶ 1330 Formula for Estimating Credit

The formula for estimating the credit is described below. For computation of the credit on the return, see ¶ 1345 and ¶ 1347.

(1) Determine the portion of the estate tax in the preceding estate for which the property transferred to the transferee was responsible. This portion is determined as follows:

$$\left[\text{Value of Property transferred to decedent} \div \left\{ \text{Taxable estate of prior decedent} - \text{Death tax on prior estate} \right\} \right] \times \text{Estate tax on prior estate}$$

For purposes of the above formula, "Death tax" includes state, federal and foreign taxes. "Estate tax" means the federal estate tax paid, increased by any credit allowed against such tax on account of gift taxes and any credit allowed on account of prior transfers to such prior decedent.

(2) Determine the estate tax (after deducting the unified credit and credits for state death taxes, gift taxes, and foreign death taxes) on the transferee's estate first including and then excluding the value of the property. If the difference between the two taxes is less than the amount computed under (1), above, the credit cannot exceed such difference.

(3) If the property previously taxed was transferred to the transferee more than two years before his or her death, reduce the lesser of (1) or (2) by 20 percent for each full two years by which the original transfer preceded the transferee's death so that, if the prior transfer occurred more than 10 years before the death, no credit would be allowed.

¶ 1335 Valuation

The value of the property transferred for purposes of the formula noted above is the value at which the property was included in the transferor's estate.[12] The interest received must be able to be valued under recognized valuation principles in order to claim the credit.[13] This value must be reduced by: (1) the amount of any lien or encumbrance thereon which was assumed by or imposed on the transferee at the time of acquisition; (2) the amount of death taxes which the transferee might have been required to pay; and (3) any marital deduction that might have been allowed upon the transfer to the transferee.

If any charitable deduction is allowed in the estate of the present decedent, that deduction must be reduced. Where the property transferred represents the residue, or a portion of the residue, administrative expenses (other than interest accruing on obligations payable from the residuary bequest), even if claimed as an income tax deduction, reduce the value of the property transferred, in whole or proportionately, for purposes of the credit.[14] Thus, the U.S. Court of Appeals for the Seventh Circuit held that in computing the credit for estate tax paid on prior transfers available to a deceased wife's estate, it was not necessary to reduce the value of the property she received from her predeceased husband by the amount of interest assessed and paid as a result of the husband's estate having elected to defer the payment of estate taxes under Code Sec. 6166.[15]

Property that, although difficult to value, is still capable of valuation will not result in loss of the credit. Thus, a trust provision requiring the termination of a transferee's life income interest in the event the transferee remarried did not result in the disallowance of the credit for the estate tax paid by the estate of the transferor-spouse. The Internal Revenue Service ruled that, because the possibility of termination of the life income interest upon the remarriage of the transferee could be taken into account as a valuation factor in determining the value of the annuity includible in the transferee's gross estate, the credit for tax on prior transfers should be allowed.[16]

See ¶ 530 for further rules that apply when a life estate or remainder interest is part of the property transferred.

¶ 1340 Treatment of Additional Tax on Recapture of Special-Use-Valuation Realty

If the gross estate of the transferor included farm or other closely held business realty for which the special use valuation election was made (see ¶ 280), and if the additional estate tax is imposed on the transferor's estate within two years of his death because of the termination of a qualified use (see ¶ 284), the additional tax on recapture of the special use valuation benefits is treated as a federal estate tax payable with respect to the estate of the transferor.[17]

---

[12] Code Sec. 2013(d) and *S. Pollock Est.*, 77 TC 1296, CCH Dec. 38,503.

[13] Rev. Rul. 67-53, 1967-1 CB 265.

[14] Rev. Rul. 93-48, 1993-2 CB 270, revoking Rev. Rul. 82-6, 1982-1 CB 137, modifying Rev. Rul. 73-98, 1973-1 CB 407, and Rev. Rul. 66-233, 1966-2 CB 428, and clarifying Rev. Rul. 80-159, 1980-1 CB 206.

[15] *R.M. Whittle Est.*, CA-7, 93-1 USTC ¶ 60,141, aff'g TC, 97 TC 362, CCH Dec. 47,623.

[16] Rev. Rul. 85-111, 1985-2 CB 196.

[17] Code Sec. 2013(f).

Further, the value of such property and the amount of the transferor's taxable estate are determined as if the special use valuation had not been elected.

¶ 1345 Computation of the Credit

The credit for tax on prior transfers is computed in two steps. First, a worksheet that is included in the instructions for Form 706 is used to determine the transferor's tax on prior transfers (Part I of the worksheet) and the transferee's tax on the prior transfers (Part II of the worksheet). Second, this information is transferred to Schedule Q, where the proper percentage (see ¶ 1325) is applied to the lesser of the transferor's tax or the transferee's tax on the transfers (see ¶ 1320) in order to compute the allowable credit.

Part I of the worksheet and Schedule Q provide for computation of the credit in situations involving up to three transferors. If there are more than three transferors, more than one worksheet and Schedule Q should be used and the totals for the appropriate lines should be combined.

¶ 1347 Worksheet for Schedule Q

The filled-in worksheet below is based on Form 706 (Rev. July 1998). The figures on the worksheet correspond to those used in the example on Schedule Q that appears at ¶ 1355. For purposes of the example, the transferor died in 1995.

Worksheet for Schedule Q — Credit for Tax on Prior Transfers

Part I Transferor's tax on prior transfers

Item	Transferor (From Schedule Q) A	B	C	Total for all transfers (*line 8 only*)
1. Gross value of prior transfer to this transferee	100,000			
2. Death taxes payable from prior transfer	0			
3. Encumbrances allocable to prior transfer	0			
4. Obligations allocable to prior transfer	0			
5. Marital deduction application to line 1 above, as shown on transferor's Form 706	0			
6. Total (*Add lines 2, 3, 4, and 5*)	0			
7. **Net value of transfers** (*Subtract line 6 from line 1*)	100,000			
8. **Net value of transfers** (*Add columns A, B, and C of line 7*)				100,000
9. Transferor's taxable estate	750,000			
10. Federal estate tax paid	55,500			
11. State death taxes paid	0			
12. Foreign death taxes paid	0			
13. Other death taxes paid	0			
14. Total taxes paid (*Add lines 10, 11, 12, and 13*)	55,500			
15. **Value of transferor's estate** (*Subtract line 14 from line 9*)	694,500			
16. Net Federal estate tax paid on transferor's estate	55,500			
17. Credit for gift tax paid on transferor's estate with respect to pre-1977 gifts (section 2012)	0			
18. Credit allowed transferor's estate for tax on prior transfers from prior transferor(s) who died within 10 years before death of decedent	0			
19. **Tax on transferor's estate** (*Add lines 16, 17, and 18*)	55,500			
20. Transferor's tax on prior transfers ((Line 7 ÷ line 15) × line 19 of respective estates)	7,991			

Part II Transferee's tax on prior transfers

Item			Amount
21. Transferee's actual tax before allowance of credit for prior transfers (*see instructions*)			109,407
22. Total gross estate of transferee (*from line 1 of the Tax Computation, page 1, Form 706*)			1,675,184
23. Net value of all transfers (*from line 8 of this worksheet*)			100,000
24. Transferee's reduced gross estate (*subtract line 23 from line 22*)			1,575,184
25. Total debts and deductions (not including marital and charitable deductions) (*items 17, 18, and 19 of the Recapitulation, page 3, Form 706*)		186,254	
26. Marital deduction (*from item 20, Recapitulation, page 3, Form 706*) (*see instructions*)		510,955	
27. Charitable bequests (*from item 21, Recapitulation, page 3, Form 706*)		9,090	
28. Charitable deduction proportion ([line 23 ÷ (line 22 − line 25)] × line 27)		611	
29. Reduced charitable deduction (*subtract line 28 from line 27*)		8,479	
30. Transferee's deduction as adjusted (*add lines 25, 26, and 29*)			705,688
31. (a) Transferee's reduced taxable estate (*subtract line 30 from line 24*)			869,496
(b) Adjusted taxable gifts			0
(c) Total reduced taxable estate (*add lines 31(a) and 31(b)*)			869,496
32. Tentative tax on reduced taxable estate		294,903	
33. (a) Post-1976 gift taxes paid	0		
(b) Unified credit	192,800		
(c) Section 2011 state death tax credit	26,136		
(d) Section 2012 gift tax credit	0		
(e) Section 2014 foreign death tax credit	0		
(f) Total credits (*add lines 33(a) from 33(e)*)		218,936	
34. Net tax on reduced taxable estate (*subtract line 33(f) from line 32*)			75,967
35. Transferee's tax on prior transfers (*subtract line 34 from line 21*)			33,440

Page 23

¶ 1355 Filled-In Schedule Q

The filled-in Schedule Q, Form 706 (Rev. July 1998), relates to the fact situation of a person who dies on January 1, 1998, with an estate tax return due within nine months (without extensions). Schedule Q must be filed only if a credit for a tax on prior transfers is claimed (see ¶ 73).

SCHEDULE Q — Credit for Tax on Prior Transfers

Part 1. — Transferor Information

	Name of transferor	Social security number	IRS office where estate tax return was filed	Date of death
A	Albert Smith	335-05-1234	Philadelphia, PA	2-20-95
B				
C				

Check here ▶ ☐ if section 2013(f) (special valuation of farm, etc., real property) adjustments to the computation of the credit were made (see page 16 of the instructions).

Part 2. — Computation of Credit (see instructions beginning on page 16)

Item	Transferor A	Transferor B	Transferor C	Total A, B, & C
1 Transferee's tax as apportioned (from worksheet, (line 7 + line 8) × line 35 for each column)	33,440			
2 Transferor's tax (from each column of worksheet, line 20)	7,991			
3 Maximum amount before percentage requirement (for each column, enter amount from line 1 or 2, whichever is smaller)	7,991			
4 Percentage allowed (each column) (see instructions)	80 %	%	%	
5 Credit allowable (line 3 × line 4 for each column) ..	6,393			
6 TOTAL credit allowable (add columns A, B, and C of line 5). Enter here and on line 19 of Part 2, Tax Computation				6,393

Schedules P and Q — Page 32 (The instructions to Schedules P and Q are in the separate instructions.)

Chapter 31

CREDIT FOR STATE DEATH TAXES

¶ 1370 State Death Tax Credit

A credit is allowed against the federal estate tax for any estate, inheritance, legacy, or succession taxes actually paid to any state of the United States or to the District of Columbia with respect to any property included in the decedent's gross estate.[1] This credit does not include, however, any taxes paid with respect to the estate of a person other than the decedent. The credit for state death taxes is available only to the extent that it does not exceed the estate's tax liability after reduction by the applicable credit amount.

Where the credit is used, it is applied to the adjusted taxable estate. For purposes of computing the credit for death taxes, the taxable estate is reduced by $60,000 (the amount of the specific estate tax exemption allowed prior to 1977) to produce the adjusted taxable estate. The adjusted taxable estate against which the death tax credit is applied is determined before reduction for any gift tax credit allowable. A graduated rate table (see ¶ 2630) under which the maximum amount of credit allowable for state death taxes is determinable is prescribed. The credit is allowed only on that part of the adjusted taxable estate that exceeds $40,000.

Because the credit is allowed only as to the amount of state taxes actually paid, care must be taken in claiming the credit to supply the required information in full. This is particularly important where a deposit is made with the state as security for the payment of the state tax, and where discounts or refunds may be allowed by the state. This information includes data tending to show the actual amount of tax due the state which may be regarded as having been paid by a deposit, the amount of tax reasonably expected to be paid, and the identity of the property in respect to which the state tax has been paid or is to be paid.

An estate tax computation involving the state death tax credit is illustrated below:

Taxable estate	$750,000
Less: $60,000	60,000
Adjusted taxable estate (see below)	$690,000

In order to determine the "adjusted taxable estate," the taxable estate is reduced by $60,000. The state death tax credit is computed on the basis of the adjusted taxable estate, while the estate tax is computed on the basis of the taxable estate before credits:

---

[1] Code Sec. 2011; Reg. § 20.2011-1. *J.B. Owen Est.*, 104 TC 498, CCH Dec. 50,607 (estate denied credit for state inheritance taxes paid with respect to gifts made by a decedent within three years of his death in 1986, because the gifts were not includible in the decedent's gross estate under Code Sec. 2035(d)(1)).

Estate tax on taxable estate	$248,300
Less: Unified credit for 1998	202,050
Less: State death tax credit	20,400
Tax payable	$ 25,850

Note that, in the above example, there are no taxable gifts to be considered. In addition, a state tax credit is available for any generation-skipping taxes that are reported on an estate tax return. See ¶ 2457 for further details concerning this credit.

¶ 1372 Four-Year Period of Limitations

The credit for state death taxes must be claimed within four years after the filing of the federal estate tax return. Exceptions apply where a petition has been filed with the Tax Court or where an extension of time for payment of tax or deficiency has been granted.[2]

An exception to the four-year period is made where the federal tax has been paid, a claim for credit or refund of federal estate taxes has been timely filed, and the claim is still pending upon expiration of the four-year period. Under these circumstances a claim for credit of state death taxes paid can be made within 60 days after the final disposition of the claim for credit or refund of federal estate taxes.

Additionally, the IRS has ruled that an estate that elected to pay federal estate and state death taxes over a period longer than four years from the date of the filing of its estate tax return could claim a credit for state death taxes paid before the end of the extended time period elected for payment of the federal estate taxes.[3] According to the IRS, the estate would be permitted to recompute the total remaining estate tax liability whenever it submitted certification of payment of additional state death tax and, upon payment in full of all state death and federal estate tax liabilities, a claim for a refund of any overpayment of estate tax could be made. However, in the event that an estate does not elect to extend the time for paying federal estate taxes, the IRS ruled that no extension of time within which to claim a refund based on the credit for state death taxes actually paid will be allowed, notwithstanding the fact that the state death taxes may be paid in installments over a period longer than four years.

¶ 1374 Taxes Paid to U.S. Possessions and Territories

Taxes paid to possessions of the United States do not qualify for the credit for state death taxes.[4] However, such taxes can qualify for the credit for foreign death taxes as described at ¶ 1401. Further, the credit is inapplicable for taxes paid to territories of the United States.[5]

¶ 1376 Deduction for Certain State Death Taxes

Although most charitable, religious, educational and public transfers are exempt from taxation at both the state and federal level, some states provide for the taxation of property so transferred. Because such state

---

[2] Code Sec. 2011(c).

[3] Rev. Rul. 86-38, 1986-1 CB 296.

[4] Code Sec. 2011(a).

[5] Code Sec. 2011(a).

taxes reduce the amount of the charitable deduction for purposes of the federal estate tax, the gross estate of a decedent would be increased to the extent of the state death tax, and, consequently, the federal estate tax would be increased.

To remedy this situation, a deduction is allowed for such state death taxes.[6] The deducted taxes, however, may not be included in those taxes upon which a credit is determined. The credit, in such cases, may not exceed the lesser of:

(1) the amount of state death taxes paid other than those on charitable transfers deductible under Code Sec. 2053(d),

(2) the amount of maximum credit for a taxable estate determined after deducting the death taxes under Code Sec. 2053(d), or

(3) that proportion of the amount of credit for a taxable estate, determined without regard to the deduction for state death taxes, as the amount of the taxes less those for which a deduction is allowed bears to the total amount of state taxes paid.[7]

---

[6] Code Sec. 2053(d).

[7] Reg. § 20.2011-2.

Chapter 32

CREDIT FOR GIFT TAXES

¶ 1380 Gifts Made After 1976

No credit is allowed for any gift tax paid on gifts made after 1976 because the gift tax payable on post-1976 gifts (includible in the gross estate) is automatically reflected in determining the estate tax liability under the unified transfer tax structure (see ¶ 11 and ¶ 12).[1]

¶ 1382 Gifts Made Before 1977

Credit is allowed against the estate tax for the federal gift tax paid on a gift by a decedent of property subsequently included in the gross estate.[2] The credit is allowable, even though the gift tax is paid after the decedent's death and the amount of the gift tax is deducted from the gross estate as a debt of the decedent.[3] The credit is allowed only when the gift tax has been paid on the transfer of non-probate assets and double taxation would result.

● *Limitation*

The credit is limited to the lesser of:

(1) the gift tax paid on the gift that is included in the gross estate, or

(2) the amount of estate tax attributable to the inclusion of the gift in the decedent's gross estate. This second limitation is computed as follows: [4]

$$\frac{\text{Gross estate tax, less credit for state death taxes and the unified credit}}{\text{The value of the gross estate, less all marital and charitable deductions allowable}} \times \text{The value of the gift (at the time of the gift or at time of death, whichever is lower)}$$

[1] Code Sec. 2012(e).

[2] Code Sec. 2012; Reg. § 20.2012-1.

[3] Reg. § 20.2012-1(a).

[4] Instructions for Form 706 (Rev. July 1998), p. 8.

Chapter 33

CREDIT FOR FOREIGN DEATH TAXES

¶ 1400 Double Taxation

The federal estate tax applies to the entire estate, wherever situated, of decedents who were either domiciled residents or citizens of the United States. Because many other countries levy death taxes on the transfer by nonresidents not citizens of property situated within their boundaries, the estates of many persons are subject to double taxation. The United States has entered into estate tax conventions with a number of foreign countries to provide relief from such double taxation (see ¶ 1420).

¶ 1401 Statutory Credit

To protect against double taxation, the law provides a foreign estate tax credit for U.S. citizens and residents.[1] The credit applies when double taxation arises from imposition by the United States of a tax on the entire estate and the imposition by a foreign country of an estate or other death tax on property situated within that country. For the purpose of this credit, U.S. possessions are classified as foreign countries.[2]

The foreign estate tax credit, in each case, is limited by apportionment. Only taxes attributable to property taxed in both countries may be allowed as a credit. In addition, the credit cannot exceed the portion of U.S. taxes attributable to the property taxed in both countries.

Although credits against the estate tax must be claimed within the later of four years after filing the estate tax return, before the date of any extension of time for paying the U.S. tax, or 60 days after a final Tax Court decision, an extended period within which to claim this credit is provided.[3] An extension is possible where payment of the estate tax attributable to a reversionary or remainder interest is postponed.

An executor is required to notify the IRS of any recovery of state or foreign death taxes for which credit has been claimed.[4] A redetermination of the federal estate tax on the basis of such recovery is authorized without regard to any statutory time limits that might otherwise apply.

¶ 1402 Reciprocity Requirement for Resident Aliens

Generally, the estates of resident aliens may take a credit for foreign inheritance and death taxes paid. However, the President may, by procla-

[1] Code Sec. 2014; Reg. § 20.2014-1.

[2] Code Sec. 2014(g).

[3] Code Sec. 2015.

[4] Code Sec. 2016.

mation, limit the availability of the credit if (1) the foreign country of which the resident aliens are citizens does not give U.S. citizens a reciprocal credit, (2) that country, when asked to do so, has not acted to provide such a credit, and (3) it is in the public interest to deny the credit. If a citizen or subject of such foreign country dies during the proclamation period, the credit will be allowed only if the foreign country allows a similar credit in the case of U.S. citizens who are residents of the foreign country at the time of their death.[5]

¶ 1405 Procedure for Claiming Credit

In the case of a citizen or resident of the United States, a credit is allowed for any estate, inheritance, legacy, or succession taxes paid to a foreign country or its possessions or political subdivisions with respect to property situated in that country and included in the gross estate. Credit is authorized by statute or by treaty. Unless otherwise provided by the treaty, a comparison is made to determine which of the following amounts is greater:

(1) the amount of the total credit authorized by the statute for all death taxes (national and local) imposed in the particular foreign country, and

(2) the amount of the total credit authorized by the treaty for death taxes imposed in such foreign country.[6]

● *Political Subdivisions*

When a credit for taxes imposed by a foreign country and one or more of its political subdivisions is involved, a third alternative to the credit allowed under the tax treaty or by statute is available. If it proves the most beneficial of the three, both a credit for the combined foreign death taxes allowable under the tax treaty *and* a credit under Code Sec. 2014 for death taxes paid to each political subdivision of the country (but only to the extent the taxes were not directly or indirectly creditable under the treaty) may be taken by the decedent's estate.

● *Multiple Foreign Countries*

If credit for death taxes paid in more than one foreign country is allowable, a separate computation of the credit must be made with respect to each foreign country. For purposes of the credit, each possession of the United States is considered as a foreign country. The copies of Schedule P (Credit for Foreign Death Taxes) on which the additional computations are made should be attached to the copy of Schedule P provided in the return.[7]

● *Limitations and Allowance*

The total amount of the credit allowable with respect of any property, whether subjected to tax by one or more than one foreign country, is limited to the amount of the estate tax attributable to such property. The anticipated amount of the credit may be computed on the return. The credit cannot be allowed until the foreign tax has been paid and a certificate on Form 706-CE (Certificate of Payment of Foreign Death Tax)

---

[5] Code Sec. 2014(h).

[6] Reg. § 20.2014-4.

[7] Reg. § 20.2014-5.

evidencing payment of the tax is furnished.[8] The Instructions to Form 706-CE contain procedures that should be followed in those cases where a foreign government refuses to certify Form 706-CE.

¶ 1410 Situs of Property

For purposes of the foreign death tax credit, a determination must be made as to whether a particular property is situated in the United States or a foreign country. This is made according to the same principles applicable in determining whether similar property of a nonresident not a citizen is situated within the United States for the purpose of the federal estate tax[9] (see ¶ 1620).

¶ 1415 Execution of Schedule P for Statutory Credit

Schedule P (Credit for Foreign Death Taxes) must be completed if an estate claims a credit for foreign death taxes paid. In addition, estates must attach Form 706-CE (Certificate of Payment of Foreign Death Tax) to support any credit claimed.

At item 1 on Schedule P, the amount of the estate, inheritance, legacy, and succession taxes paid to the foreign country and its possessions or political subdivisions attributable to property that (1) is situated in that country, (2) is subject to such taxes, and (3) is included in the gross estate should be entered. The amount entered at item 1 should not include any tax paid to the foreign country with respect to property not situated in that country. Nor should it include any tax paid to the foreign country with respect to property not included in the gross estate.

If only a part of the property subject to such foreign taxes is both situated in the foreign country and included in the gross estate, it will be necessary to determine the portion of the taxes that is attributable to such part of the property. The instructions for Schedule P indicate that an additional sheet showing the computation of the amount entered at item 1 must be attached.[10]

The value of the gross estate less the total of the deductions shown on lines 20 and 21 of Part 5, Recapitulation (the marital and charitable deductions, respectively) should be entered at item 2.

The value of the property situated in the foreign country that is subject to the foreign taxes and included in the gross estate, less those portions of the deductions on Schedules M (Bequests, etc., to Surviving Spouse) and O (Charitable, Public, and Similar Gifts and Bequests) that are attributable to such property, should be entered at item 3.

The amount shown at item 17, Part 2, Form 706, should be subtracted from the amount shown at item 16, Part 2, Form 706, and the result entered at item 4.

The amount of the federal estate tax attributable to the value of the property specified on line 3 is calculated at item 5.

The final entry at item 6—the smaller of item 1 or item 5—represents the credit that may be subtracted from the estate tax otherwise payable.

---

[8] Reg. § 20.2014-5.

[9] Reg. § 20.2014-1(a)(3).

[10] Instructions for Form 706 (Rev. July 1998), p. 16.

Schedule P must be filed if the estate claims a foreign death tax credit, and Form 706-CE must be filed for every such credit claimed.

¶ 1416 Example of Computation of Credit Under the Statute

The following is an example of how the foreign death tax credit is computed. A filled-in form relating to the Example is at ¶ 1418.

> ***Example:*** Tom Wilson was a citizen of, and domiciled in, the United States at the time of his death in 1998. The gross estate consisted of real property in Finland valued at $100,000; stocks of U.S. corporations, $500,000; bonds of corporations organized under the laws of Finland, $90,000; and stocks of corporations organized under the laws of Finland, $150,000. Debts and administration expenses totaled $25,000.
>
> The Finnish real property, which was valued at $100,000, and $100,000 of the U.S. stock were the only items that passed to Wilson's surviving spouse, and qualified for the marital deduction. The amount of the federal estate tax less the unified credit and the credit for state inheritance taxes was $27,950. The amount of the Finnish inheritance tax imposed on the surviving spouse's inheritance of $100,000 was $30,000. The stock in Finnish corporations, valued at $150,000, passed to Wilson's daughter, and the amount of Finnish inheritance tax imposed was $45,000. Finland did not impose inheritance tax on the bonds issued by the Finnish corporations.

¶ 1418 Filled-In Schedule P

Filled-in Schedule P, Form 706 (Rev. July 1998), relates to the fact situation of a person who dies on January 1, 1998, with an estate tax return due within nine months (without extensions). Filled-in Schedule P does not apply to the hypothetical estate of James X. Diversey illustrated elsewhere in this book.

Form 706 (Rev. 7-98)

Estate of:

SCHEDULE P — Credit for Foreign Death Taxes

List all foreign countries to which death taxes have been paid and for which a credit is claimed on this return.
FINLAND

If a credit is claimed for death taxes paid to more than one foreign country, compute the credit for taxes paid to one country on this sheet and attach a separate copy of Schedule P for each of the other countries.

The credit computed on this sheet is for the Finnish Inheritance Tax
(Name of death tax or taxes)
imposed in FINLAND
(Name of country)

Credit is computed under the U.S. - Finland Death Tax Convention
(Insert title of treaty or "statute")

Citizenship (nationality) of decedent at time of death

(All amounts and values must be entered in United States money.)

1 Total of estate, inheritance, legacy, and succession taxes imposed in the country named above attributable to property situated in that country, subjected to these taxes, and included in the gross estate (as defined by statute)	75,000
2 Value of the gross estate (adjusted, if necessary, according to the instructions for item 2)	640,000
3 Value of property situated in that country, subjected to death taxes imposed in that country, and included in the gross estate (adjusted, if necessary, according to the instructions for item 3)	150,000
4 Tax imposed by section 2001 reduced by the total credits claimed under sections 2010, 2011, and 2012 (see instructions)	61,950
5 Amount of Federal estate tax attributable to property specified at item 3. (Divide item 3 by item 2 and multiply the result by item 4.)	14,520
6 Credit for death taxes imposed in the country named above (the smaller of item 1 or item 5). Also enter on line 18 of Part 2, Tax Computation	14,520

¶ 1420 Execution of Schedule P for Credit Under Treaties

Where the provisions of a treaty apply to the estate of a citizen or resident of the United States, a credit is allowed for the payment of the foreign death tax or taxes specified in the treaty. Death tax conventions are in effect with the following countries:

Country	*Death Tax*
Australia	Commonwealth estate duty
Austria	Austrian inheritance and gift taxes
Canada	Canadian income tax on certain income, profits, and gains realized in the year of death and on certain gains deemed realized at death
Denmark	Duties on inheritance and gifts
Finland	Finnish inheritance tax, the communal tax on inheritances, bequests and devises, and the "poors percentage"
France	Duties on gifts and successions
Germany	German inheritance and gift taxes
Greece	Greek inheritance tax
Ireland	Irish estate tax duty
Italy	Italian estate and inheritance taxes
Japan	Japanese inheritance tax, including gift tax
Netherlands	Netherlands succession and transfer duties at death
Norway	Norwegian tax on inheritances, including death gifts
Union of South Africa	Union estate duty
Sweden	Swedish inheritance and gift taxes
Switzerland	Estate and inheritance taxes imposed by the cantons and their political subdivisions
United Kingdom	Capital transfer tax

Credit claimed under a treaty is, in general, computed on Schedule P (Credit for Foreign Death Taxes) in the same manner that credit is computed under the statute. The following principal exceptions apply:

(1) the situs rules contained in the treaty apply in determining whether property was situated in the foreign country;

(2) credit may be allowed only for payment of the death tax or taxes specified in the treaty;

(3) where specifically provided, the credit is proportionately shared for the tax applicable to property situated outside both countries, or that was deemed in some instances to be situated within both countries; and

(4) the amount entered as item 4 of Schedule P is the amount shown at line 16 in "Tax Computation" on page 1 of Form 706 (Rev. July 1998) less the total of the amounts shown at line 17 on that page.

If a credit is claimed for tax on prior transfers, it will be necessary to complete Schedule Q (Credit for Tax on Prior Transfers) before completing Schedule P.[11]

See CCH TAX TREATIES REPORTS for specific rules concerning the application of the treaties.

[11] Instructions for Form 706 (Rev. July 1998), p. 16.

Chapter 34

COMPUTATION OF TAX

¶ 1425 Unified Transfer Tax

The estate and gift tax rates are combined in a single rate schedule effective for the estates of decedents dying, and gifts made, after December 31, 1976. Lifetime gifts made after 1976 and transfers made at death are cumulated for estate tax purposes. Estate tax liability is determined by applying the unified transfer tax rate schedule to cumulated transfers and subtracting the gift taxes payable. The former $60,000 estate tax exemption was replaced by a unified credit (as determined by reference to an applicable credit amount for estates of decedents dying after 1997), which is subtracted after determining the decedent's estate tax liability. However, the benefits of the graduated rates and the unified credit are phased out beginning with cumulative transfers exceeding $10,000,000 but not exceeding $17,184,000 (see ¶ 16).

● *Unified Credit: 1977–1997*

The unified estate and gift tax credit and the exemption equivalent for the years 1977 through 1997 are as follows:

Year	*Amount of Credit*	*Amount of Exemption Equivalent*
1977	$ 30,000	$120,667
1978	34,000	134,000
1979	38,000	147,333
1980	42,500	161,563
1981	47,000	175,625
1982	62,800	225,000
1983	79,300	275,000
1984	96,300	325,000
1985	121,800	400,000
1986	155,800	500,000
1987–1997	192,800	600,000

● *Unified Credit: 1998–2006*

For the years 1998–2006, the unified credit is gradually increased to $345,800 by the Taxpayer Relief Act of 1997 (P.L. 105-34) and is determined by reference to the "applicable credit amount" and the "applicable exclusion amount" (formerly the exemption equivalent). The increase is phased in as follows:

Year	Applicable Credit Amount	Applicable Exclusion Amount
1998	$202,050	$ 625,000
1999	211,300	650,000
2000 and 2001	220,550	675,000
2002 and 2003	229,800	700,000
2004	287,300	850,000
2005	326,300	950,000
2006	345,800	1,000,000

¶ 1426 Computation of Tax

The basic steps in computing the tax on a post-1976 estate under the unified transfer tax system are as follows:

(1) Compute the decedent's taxable estate. The taxable estate of a U.S. citizen is determined by subtracting the total allowable deductions reported on the Recapitulation of Form 706 (United States Estate (and Generation-Skipping Transfer) Tax Return) (see ¶ 1225) from the total gross estate reported on the Recapitulation.

(2) Compute the "adjusted taxable gifts"—the aggregate post-1976 lifetime taxable gifts, other than post-1976 gifts which are includible in the decedent's gross estate. The Tax Court has held that the value of a decedent's gifts, as reported on his federal gift tax returns, could be revised even though the three-year statute of limitations period on the assessment of gift taxes had expired.[1] Although Code Sec. 2504(c) would prevent such a revaluation of prior taxable gifts for gift tax purposes, the Tax Court held that there is no corresponding provision in the estate tax area and, thus, the post-1976 lifetime gifts of the decedent could be revalued. However, for gifts made after August 5, 1997, the IRS is not permitted to revalue a gift if the three-year statute of limitations for gifts has expired.[2]

(3) Add (1) and (2).

(4) Determine the tentative tax by applying the rates in the unified rate schedule (see ¶ 1430) to the amount obtained in (3).

(5) Subtract the total gift tax paid on gifts made after 1976.

(6) Subtract the applicable credit amount to arrive at the estate tax payable.

See the example at ¶ 1428 for details of these basic steps, including how to compute gift tax on lifetime gifts.

The net estate tax payable is then computed by subtracting the following tax credits: the credit for state death taxes (see ¶ 1370); the credit for federal gift taxes on pre-1977 gifts that are includible in the decedent's gross estate (see ¶ 1382); the credit for foreign death taxes (see ¶ 1400); and the credit for prior transfer taxes (see ¶ 1300).

Two other types of taxes can be added to the net estate tax to arrive at the total amount of transfer taxes that is payable on a decedent's estate

---

[1] *F.R. Smith Est.*, 94 TC 872, CCH Dec. 46,648 (Acq.).

[2] Code Sec. 2001(f). For gifts made in calendar years ending after August 5, 1997, Code Sec. 6501(c)(9) provides that the statute of limitations will not run with respect to a gift that is not adequately disclosed on a gift tax return.

tax return: (1) the generation-skipping transfer tax on generation-skipping transfers made by the decedent at death, and (2) for decedents dying before 1997, the special estate tax that is payable on what are called "excess retirement accumulations." Only the net amount of the generation-skipping tax, as computed on Schedule R, is entered in the computation part (see ¶ 2475 for further details). The estate tax, if any, on excess retirement accumulations is computed on Schedule S of Form 706 (see ¶ 775 for further details).

● *Split Gifts*

If spouses have made split gifts, special rules apply for determining the amount of the adjusted taxable gifts includible in a decedent's estate and the amount of the gift tax offset that may be claimed on a decedent's estate tax return. These rules are dependent on whether the decedent was the donor or the consenting spouse. First, if the entire amount of the gift is includible in the donor spouse's gross estate, any gift tax paid by the consenting spouse on the gift can be claimed as part of the gift tax offset in determining the estate tax payable by the estate of the donor spouse.[3] Second, a gift is not included in the adjusted taxable gifts of a consenting spouse in those cases where the amount of the split gift was includible in the donor spouse's gross estate under Code Sec. 2035. Further, the gift tax paid by the consenting spouse is not included in the gift tax offset on the consenting spouse's estate tax return in computing the final estate tax to the extent that an offset had been used on the donor spouse's estate tax return.[4]

---

[3] Code Sec. 2001(d).

[4] Code Sec. 2001(e).

¶ 1427 Form 706 (Page One)

Page one of a filled-in Form 706, United States Estate (and Generation-Skipping Transfer) Tax Return (Rev. July 1998), of the hypothetical James X. Diversey estate is reproduced below.

Form **706** (Rev. July 1998) Department of the Treasury Internal Revenue Service

United States Estate (and Generation-Skipping Transfer) Tax Return

Estate of a citizen or resident of the United States (see separate instructions). To be filed for decedents dying after December 31, 1997, and before January 1, 1999. For Paperwork Reduction Act Notice, see page 1 of the separate instructions.

OMB No. 1545-0015

Part 1.—Decedent and Executor

1a Decedent's first name and middle initial (and maiden name, if any): James X.	1b Decedent's last name: Diversey		2 Decedent's social security no.: 241-24-3049
3a Legal residence (domicile) at time of death (county, state, and ZIP code, or foreign country): Cook County, IL 60430	3b Year domicile established: 1946	4 Date of birth: 11-14-16	5 Date of death: 1-1-98
6a Name of executor (see page 2 of the instructions): Carrie M. Diversey	6b Executor's address (number and street including apartment or suite no. or rural route; city, town, or post office; state, and ZIP code): 54 Fir Street, Homewood, IL 60430		
6c Executor's social security number (see page 2 of the instructions): 322-43-8143			
7a Name and location of court where will was probated or estate administered: Probate Court, Cook County, IL			7b Case number: 98-xx-xxx
8 If decedent died testate, check here ▶ [X] and attach a certified copy of the will.	9 If Form 4768 is attached, check here ▶ [ ]		
10 If Schedule R-1 is attached, check here ▶ [ ]			

Part 2.—Tax Computation

1	Total gross estate less exclusion (from Part 5, Recapitulation, page 3, item 12)			1	1,675,184
2	Total allowable deductions (from Part 5, Recapitulation, page 3, item 23)			2	706,299
3	Taxable estate (subtract line 2 from line 1)			3	968,885
4	Adjusted taxable gifts (total taxable gifts (within the meaning of section 2503) made by the decedent after December 31, 1976, other than gifts that are includible in decedent's gross estate (section 2001(b)))			4	0
5	Add lines 3 and 4			5	968,885
6	Tentative tax on the amount on line 5 from Table A on page 10 of the instructions			6	333,665
7a	If line 5 exceeds $10,000,000, enter the lesser of line 5 or $17,184,000. If line 5 is $10,000,000 or less, skip lines 7a and 7b and enter -0- on line 7c.	7a			
b	Subtract $10,000,000 from line 7a	7b			
c	Enter 5% (.05) of line 7b			7c	
8	Total tentative tax (add lines 6 and 7c)			8	333,665
9	Total gift tax payable with respect to gifts made by the decedent after December 31, 1976. Include gift taxes by the decedent's spouse for such spouse's share of split gifts (section 2513) only if the decedent was the donor of these gifts and they are includible in the decedent's gross estate (see instructions)			9	0
10	Gross estate tax (subtract line 9 from line 8)			10	333,665
11	Maximum unified credit against estate tax	11	202,050.00		
12	Adjustment to unified credit. (This adjustment may not exceed $6,000. See page 7 of the instructions.)	12			
13	Allowable unified credit (subtract line 12 from line 11)			13	202,050
14	Subtract line 13 from line 10 (but do not enter less than zero)			14	131,615
15	Credit for state death taxes. Do not enter more than line 14. Figure the credit by using the amount on line 3 less $60,000. See Table B in the instructions and attach credit evidence (see instructions)			15	31,458
16	Subtract line 15 from line 14			16	100,157
17	Credit for Federal gift taxes on pre-1977 gifts (section 2012) (attach computation)	17			
18	Credit for foreign death taxes (from Schedule(s) P). (Attach Form(s) 706-CE.)	18			
19	Credit for tax on prior transfers (from Schedule Q)	19	6,393		
20	Total (add lines 17, 18, and 19)			20	6,393
21	Net estate tax (subtract line 20 from line 16)			21	93,764
22	Generation-skipping transfer taxes (from Schedule R, Part 2, line 10)			22	0
23	Total transfer taxes (add lines 21 and 22)			23	93,764
24	Prior payments. Explain in an attached statement	24			
25	United States Treasury bonds redeemed in payment of estate tax	25			
26	Total (add lines 24 and 25)			26	
27	Balance due (or overpayment) (subtract line 26 from line 23)			27	93,764

Under penalties of perjury, I declare that I have examined this return, including accompanying schedules and statements, and to the best of my knowledge and belief, it is true, correct, and complete. Declaration of preparer other than the executor is based on all information of which preparer has any knowledge.

Carrie Diversey — Signature(s) of executor(s) — Date: 9-14-98

William S. Oaks — Signature of preparer other than executor — Address (and ZIP code): 542 James Street, Homewood, IL 60430 — Date: 9-14-98

¶ 1428 Example of Application of Unified Transfer Tax

The following Example illustrates application of the unified transfer tax.

Example (1): Nora Brown made the following taxable gifts to her son Carl.

1984	$300,000
1987	$200,000
1989	$600,000
1990	$700,000

In 1998, she died with a taxable estate of $1,000,000.

The total transfer taxes payable by Nora are calculated as follows:

1984

1. Taxable gift	$300,000
2. Prior taxable gifts	$ 0
3. Total taxable gifts	$300,000
4. Tentative tax on line 3 amount	$ 87,800
5. Less: Tentative tax on prior gifts	$ 0
6. Balance	$ 87,800
7. Maximum unified credit	$96,300
8. Less: Unified credit used in prior periods	$ 0
9. Available unified credit	$96,300
10. Unified credit used to reduce tax	($ 87,800)
11. Gift tax payable (line 6 minus line 10)	$ 0

1987

1. Taxable gift	$200,000
2. Prior taxable gifts	$300,000
3. Total taxable gifts	$500,000
4. Tentative tax on line 3	$155,800
5. Less: Tentative tax on prior taxable gifts	($ 87,800)
6. Balance	$ 68,000
7. Maximum unified credit	$192,800
8. Less: Unified credit used in prior periods	$ 87,800
9. Available unified credit	$105,000
10. Unified credit used to reduce tax	$ 68,000
11. Gift tax payable (line 6 minus line 10)	$ 0

1989

1. Taxable gift	$ 600,000
2. Prior taxable gifts	$ 500,000
3. Total taxable gifts	$1,100,000
4. Tentative tax on line 3	$ 386,800
5. Less: Tentative tax on prior taxable gifts	($ 155,800)
6. Balance	$ 231,000
7. Maximum unified credit	$ 192,800
8. Less: Unified credit used in prior periods	($ 155,800)
9. Available unified credit	$ 37,000
10. Unified credit used to reduce tax	$ 37,000
11. Gift tax payable (line 6 minus line 10)	$ 194,000

1990

1. Taxable gift	$ 700,000
2. Prior taxable gifts	$1,100,000
3. Total taxable gifts	$1,800,000
4. Tentative tax on line 3	$ 690,800
5. Less: Tentative tax on prior taxable gifts	($ 386,800)
6. Balance	$ 304,000
7. Maximum unified credit	$ 192,800
8. Less: Unified credit used in prior periods	$ 192,800
9. Available unified credit	$ 0
10. Unified credit used to reduce tax	$ 0
11. Gift tax payable	$ 304,000

Estate

1. Amount of taxable estate	$1,000,000
2. Plus adjusted taxable gifts	$1,800,000
3. Estate tax base	$2,800,000
4. Tentative tax on base	$1,184,800
5. Less: Gift tax payable	($ 498,000)
6. Balance	$ 686,800
7. Less: Unified credit	($ 202,050)
8. Estate tax payable	$ 484,750

Example (2): Assume the same facts as in Example (1), except that Nora dies in 1999.

Estate

1. Amount of taxable estate	$1,000,000
2. Plus adjusted taxable gifts	$1,800,000
3. Estate tax base	$2,800,000
4. Tentative tax on base	$1,184,800
5. Less: Gift tax payable	($ 498,000)
6. Balance	$ 686,800
7. Less: Unified credit	($ 211,300)
8. Estate tax payable	$ 475,500

¶ 1430 Rate Schedule Table for Unified Tax

The unified rate schedule applicable to the estates of decedents dying after 1983 (and gifts made after 1983) is as follows:

Unified Rate Schedule

Column A Taxable amount over	Column B Taxable amount not over	Column C Tax on amount in column A	Column D Rate of tax on excess over amount in column A Percent
0	$ 10,000	0	18
$ 10,000	20,000	$ 1,800	20
20,000	40,000	3,800	22
40,000	60,000	8,200	24
60,000	80,000	13,000	26
80,000	100,000	18,200	28
100,000	150,000	23,800	30
150,000	250,000	38,800	32
250,000	500,000	70,800	34
500,000	750,000	155,800	37
750,000	1,000,000	248,300	39
1,000,000	1,250,000	345,800	41
1,250,000	1,500,000	448,300	43
1,500,000	2,000,000	555,800	45
2,000,000	2,500,000	780,800	49
2,500,000	3,000,000	1,025,800	53
3,000,000	....	1,290,800	55

An additional five-percent tax is levied on amounts transferred in excess of $10 million but not exceeding $17,184,000.

The top rates in effect for decedents dying (and gifts made) in 1982 and 1983 are as follows:

Decedents Dying in 1982

Column A Taxable amount over	Column B Taxable amount not over	Column C Tax on amount in column A	Column D Rate of tax on excess over amount in column A Percent
$2,500,000	$3,000,000	$1,025,800	53
3,000,000	3,500,000	1,290,800	57
3,500,000	4,000,000	1,575,800	61
4,000,000	....	1,880,800	65

Decedents Dying in 1983

Column A Taxable amount over	Column B Taxable amount not over	Column C Tax on amount in column A	Column D Rate of tax on excess over amount in column A Percent
$2,500,000	$3,000,000	$1,025,800	53
3,000,000	3,500,000	1,290,800	57
3,500,000	....	1,575,800	60

● *Phaseout of Benefits*

The benefits of the graduated rates and the unified credit under the unified transfer tax system are phased out beginning with cumulative transfers rising above $10,000,000. This is accomplished by adding five percent of the excess of any transfer over $10,000,000 to the tentative tax computed in determining the ultimate transfer tax liability.

- *Decedents Dying and Gifts Made After 1987 and Before 1998*

For estates of decedents dying, and gifts made, after 1987 and before 1998, the tax is levied on amounts transferred in excess of $10,000,000 but not exceeding $21,040,000, in order to recapture the benefit of any transfer tax rate below 55 percent as well as the unified credit.[5]

- *Decedents Dying and Gifts Made After 1997*

Due to mistakes in the wording of the amendment to Code Sec. 2001(c)(2) by the Taxpayer Relief Act of 1997 (P.L. 105-34), the five-percent additional tax phases out the benefits of the graduated rates, but not the benefits of the unified credit (applicable credit amount), for estates of decedents dying, and gifts made, after 1997. Therefore, the additional tax is levied on amounts transferred in excess of $10,000,000 but not exceeding $17,184,000 for decedents dying after 1997. The applicable credit amount is not recaptured.

---

[5] Code Sec. 2001(c)(2).

Chapter 35

MEMBERS OF ARMED FORCES

¶ 1550 Special Exemption

A special exemption from estate taxation is available to the estates of members of the U.S. Armed Forces who were citizens or residents of the United States and who died while in active service as a member of the Armed Forces. This is qualified by the requirement that such person must either have been killed in action while serving in a combat zone, or have died as a result of wounds, disease, or injury suffered while serving in such combat zone. The wounds, disease, or injury must have been incurred in the line of duty and by reason of a hazard that was an incident of such service.[1]

The definition of "combat zone" is controlled by Code Sec. 112(c). That section defines the term to mean "any area which the President of the United States by Executive Order designates . . . as an area in which the Armed Forces of the United States are or have (after June 24, 1950) engaged in combat." For example, in 1991, the Arabian Peninsula was designated as a combat zone for Operation Desert Storm.[2] In addition, the Federal Republic of Yugoslavia (Serbia/Montenegro), Albania, the Adriatic Sea, and the Ionian Sea north of the 39th parallel (including all of their air spaces) were designated as a combat zone, effective March 24, 1999, for personnel serving in NATO Operation Allied Force.[3] Moreover, under legislation approved by Congress but not yet signed into law as we go to press, U.S. troops serving in this area are not required to file 1998 tax returns until 180 days after they finish their service in the area.[4] This extension is in addition to any other extensions for which the troops qualify. Combat zone tax treatment was also extended to those members of the Armed Forces serving in a qualified hazardous duty area.[5] Under P.L. 104-117, Bosnia, Herzegovina, Croatia, and Macedonia were designated qualified hazardous duty areas, effective November 21, 1995.

¶ 1560 Extent of Exemption

The estates of members of the Armed Forces qualifying for exemption are exempt from the "additional estate tax." Under the 1939 Code, the additional tax was the difference between the "tentative tax" and the "basic tax." For most estates, there is no longer an "additional tax," "tentative tax" or "basic tax." There is, instead, "the tax" and a "credit for state death taxes." The net tax is the difference between these two, less, of course, any other credits.

For purposes of the Armed Forces exemption, the "basic estate tax" is defined as 125 percent of the amount determined to be the maximum credit allowable for state death tax purposes.[6] The additional tax is the

[1] Code Sec. 2201; Reg. § 20.2201-1.

[2] Executive Order 12744, January 21, 1991.

[3] Act Sec. 1, P.L. 104-117.

[4] Executive Order, April 13, 1999.

[5] H.R. 1376, passed by the House and Senate on April 15, 1999.

[6] Code Sec. 2011(d).

difference between the regular estate tax and the basic estate tax, for military personnel dying after 1976.[7] Prior to 1977, the same rule applied, except that the separate estate tax rates were used.

¶ 1565 Execution of Return

The estate tax return form does not provide instructions concerning the Armed Forces exemption. The exemption should be reflected at line 8 on the first page of Form 706 (Rev. July 1998), and lines 4–7 can be left blank. A notation of the reason for variation is necessary, such as—"Am. Vet. killed in action" (Code Sec. 2201).

The amount shown as the "Gross estate tax" would be an amount equal to 125 percent of the maximum credit for state death taxes. In all other respects, the form would be filled out in the same manner as for any other decedent. The "General Information" portion of Form 706 (Part 4) should be supplemented with a statement concerning the basis for claiming the Armed Forces exemption.

[7] For computation of the estate tax liability of military persons "missing in action" declared "killed in action" after 1976, see Rev. Rul. 78-361, 1978-2 CB 246.

Chapter 36

NONRESIDENTS NOT CITIZENS

¶ 1600 Special Rules

There are a number of special requirements in the estate tax law that apply only to estates of persons who are neither residents nor citizens of the United States. They affect the definition of property subject to tax, the exemption, return requirements and deductions. Some of the requirements stem from the estate tax provisions of the Internal Revenue Code and apply to estates of all such persons, except to the extent modified by treaty. Others are based upon treaty provisions that limit their application to nonresidents not citizens who are residents of the country with which the treaty exists.

A number of these special requirements were discussed previously (see ¶ 85). Some are the subject of special instructions in the estate tax return form. The following material should be read in conjunction with specific requirements already covered.

¶ 1605 Residents of U.S. Possessions

Decedents who are citizens of the United States and residents of U.S. possessions at the time of their death are treated as "nonresidents not citizens of the United States," for estate tax purposes, if they acquired U.S. citizenship solely by reason of:

(1) being a citizen of the possession, or

(2) birth or residence within the possession.[1]

¶ 1615 Death Tax Conventions

If a death tax convention is applicable to the estate of a decedent who is a nonresident not a citizen, both the treaty and the regulations issued pursuant to the treaty should be consulted.[2]

Death duty conventions are in effect with each of the countries listed below. The provisions of a convention apply in the case of a decedent dying on or after the effective date shown.

---

[1] Code Sec. 2209; Reg. § 20.2209-1.

[2] See CCH TAX TREATIES REPORTS.

Country	*Effective Date*
Australia *	January 7, 1954
Austria	July 1, 1983
Canada (a revised protocol, signed March 17, 1995, to Income Tax Treaty)	November 10, 1995
Denmark	November 7, 1984
Finland	December 18, 1952
France	October 1, 1980
Germany (modified by protocol signed December 14, 1998)	January 1, 1979
Greece (modified by protocol (affecting situs of real property) signed February 12, 1964, which went into effect October 27, 1967)	December 30, 1953
Ireland	December 20, 1951
Italy	October 26, 1956
Japan	April 1, 1955
Netherlands	February 3, 1971
Norway	December 11, 1951
South Africa	July 15, 1952
Sweden	September 5, 1984
Switzerland	September 17, 1952
United Kingdom	November 11, 1979

* Note: The Commonwealth estate tax duty for Australia was abolished, effective for the estates of decedents dying after July 1, 1979.

¶ 1617 Gross Estate

The gross estate of a nonresident not a citizen of the United States is determined in the same manner as that of a U.S. citizen or resident. It includes not only all property beneficially owned by the decedent, but also joint estates with right of survivorship, tenancies by the entirety, community property, property transferred by the decedent during his lifetime, and property subject to the decedent's general power of appointment (see Chapter 6 through Chapter 19). However, the taxable estate is the part of the gross estate situated in the United States, less the authorized deductions.[3]

Only the part of the gross estate situated in the United States should be listed on the appropriate schedules (see ¶ 85 and ¶ 1620). The term "United States," when used in a geographical sense, includes only the states and the District of Columbia. Property transferred during the decedent's lifetime, and includible in the gross estate under one of the transfer provisions (Code Sec. 2035 through Code Sec. 2038), is deemed situated in the United States if it was so situated at the time of the transfer or at the time of death.

¶ 1620 Property Situated in the United States

Although the situs rules controlling the inclusion of property in estates of nonresidents not citizens may be modified under the provisions of an applicable death tax treaty with the United States, in general, only property located in the United States is includible in the gross estate of a

[3] Code Sec. 2106; Reg. § 20.2106-1.

nonresident not a U.S. citizen. Property located within the United States is reported on Schedule A of Form 706-NA. Schedules E (Jointly Owned Property), G (Transfers During Decedent's Life), and H (Powers of Appointment) of Form 706 must be attached to the return if the decedent transferred certain property or if the decedent possessed, exercised or released a general power of appointment in U.S. property (see ¶ 85 for further details).

● *Stocks and Bonds*

The notable exception to this general situs rule is the stock of domestic corporations. This stock is includible in the gross estate regardless of where located. Debt obligations (bonds, etc.) that are owned and held by a nonresident not a citizen are considered property located within the United States if the primary obligor is a domestic corporation or other U.S. person, the United States, a State, a political subdivision of a State, or the District of Columbia.[4]

For this purpose, it is immaterial whether the written evidence of the debt obligation is treated as being the property itself. Currency, however, is not to be considered a debt obligation.

If the obligation is a debt of a resident alien individual or domestic corporation that meets the 80-percent-foreign-business requirement, it will be treated as having a foreign situs.[5]

● *Deposits with U.S. Financial Institutions and Insurers*

Funds deposited by or for a nonresident alien in a U.S. bank (including a domestic banking branch of a foreign corporation), a savings and loan or similar association or held by a domestic insurance company under an agreement to pay interest are not includible in a decedent's gross estate if the monies are not effectively connected with the conduct of a trade or business within the United States by the decedent.[6] Deposits with a foreign branch of a domestic corporation or partnership, if such branch is engaged in the commercial banking business, are also excludable from the gross estate.[7]

A nonresident alien's U.S. bank deposits, chartered savings institution accounts, and amounts held by insurance companies will not be treated as property located within the United States for federal estate tax purposes, if the interest paid on these amounts would have been treated as nontaxable foreign-source income for federal income tax purposes. To be exempt from federal income tax as foreign-source income, the interest from these deposits must not be "effectively connected" with the conduct of a trade or business within the United States.[8]

● *Certain Other Properties*

Special rules exist for determining whether property is situated in the United States.

(1) Real property and tangible personal property are within the United States if physically located therein.

---

[4] Code Sec. 2104.

[5] Code Sec. 861(a)(1)(A).

[6] Code Sec. 2105(b).

[7] Code Sec. 2105(b).

[8] Code Sec. 864(c).

(2) Proceeds of insurance on the life of a nonresident not a citizen of the United States are not situated in the United States.[9]

(3) Works of art are not considered situated in the United States if they were: (a) imported into the United States solely for exhibition purposes, (b) loaned for such purposes to a public gallery or museum, no part of the net earnings of which inures to the benefit of any private stockholder or individual, and (c) on exhibit (or en route to or from exhibition) in such public gallery or museum at the time of the owner's death.[10]

¶ 1625 Deduction of Administration Expenses and Claims

Estates of nonresidents not citizens of the United States may deduct the following items: (1) funeral expenses; (2) administration expenses; (3) claims against the estate; (4) unpaid mortgages and other liens; and (5) losses incurred during the settlement of the estate arising from fires, storms, shipwrecks, or other casualties, or from theft, if such losses are not compensated for by insurance or otherwise.[11] However, the amount of the deduction is limited to the proportion of the nonresident noncitizen's gross estate located in the United States divided by the entire gross estate wherever it is located. This deduction is computed by completing lines 4 and 5 of Schedule B (Taxable Estate) of Form 706-NA (Rev. September 1993).

It is immaterial whether the amounts to be deducted were incurred or expended within or without the United States. However, no deduction may be taken unless the value of the entire gross estate wherever situated is entered on line 3 of Schedule B. The entire gross estate must be valued as of the date of the decedent's death. However, if the alternate valuation is adopted under Schedule A, such alternate valuation must be applied to the entire gross estate.

- *Substantiation*

Adequate proof in support of items 2 (gross estate outside the United States) and 4 (deductible expenses before limitation) of Schedule B must be submitted; otherwise, this deduction will be disallowed. With respect to line 2, a certified copy of the foreign death tax return should be submitted. If no such return was filed, a certified copy of the estate inventory, together with the schedule of debts and charges filed in conjunction with the estate administration proceedings or with the foreign probate court, should be submitted. Additional proof may be required in specific cases.

With respect to line 4, the exact nature and amount of each expense or claim, as well as the name of the creditor, must be fully described and, if relating to particular property, the property must be identified. Death taxes, taxes on income received after death, and property taxes accrued after death are not deductible. Deductions for debts and mortgages are limited to that part of the debt that was contracted in good faith for money or money's worth. Mortgages are deductible only if the full value of

---

[9] Code Sec. 2105(a).

[10] Code Sec. 2105(c).

[11] Code Sec. 2106.

the mortgaged property is included on line 3 (entire gross estate wherever located).[12]

¶ 1630 Charitable, Public and Similar Gifts and Bequests

Except as provided otherwise by treaty, a charitable deduction may be taken only if the transfer was to a corporation or association organized in the United States or to trustees for use in the United States.[13] If a charitable deduction is claimed, Schedule O (Charitable, Public, and Similar Gifts and Bequests) of Form 706 must be attached. In addition, if a charitable deduction is claimed under a treaty, the applicable treaty must be specified and a computation of the deduction attached.

● *Marital Deduction*

Effective for estates of decedents dying after November 10, 1988, the marital deduction will be allowed for estate tax purposes in the case of a nonresident alien whose spouse is a U.S. citizen, or, where the spouse is not a U.S. citizen, if the property passes by way of a qualified domestic trust.[14] Executors claiming the deduction should do so on line 6 on Schedule B of Form 706-NA (Rev. September 1993). Additionally, Schedule M of Form 706, and a statement showing the computation of the deduction, should be attached. The estates of nonresident aliens dying prior to November 11, 1988, could not claim marital deductions, unless the individual was a resident of a country that had entered into a treaty with the United States permitting his or her estate to claim a marital deduction.[15]

¶ 1635 Rates and Exemption

The gift and estate tax rates applicable to U.S. citizens also apply to the estate of a nonresident alien.[16] However, to reflect the fact that, in some cases, the estate of a nonresident noncitizen does not receive the same unified credit available to U.S. citizens, the additional five-percent rate imposed on decedents who died and on gifts made after 1987 is adjusted.[17] Accordingly, the additional five-percent rate applies to the taxable transfers of nonresident noncitizens in excess of $10 million only to the extent necessary to phase out the benefit of the graduated rates and unified credit actually allowed by statute or treaty.[18] Worksheets are provided on page 4 of the instructions to Form 706-NA (Rev. September 1993) to calculate the phaseout of these benefits when applicable.

Where permitted by treaty, the estate of a nonresident alien is allowed the unified credit available to a U.S. citizen multiplied by the proportion of the total gross estate situated in the United States. In other cases, a unified credit of $13,000 is allowed. The estate of a resident of a U.S. possession is entitled to a unified credit equal to the greater of (1) $13,000 or (2) $46,800 multiplied by the proportion that the decedent's gross estate situated in the United States bears to the total gross estate of the decedent wherever situated.[19] In the case of the estate tax provisions

---

[12] Instructions for Form 706-NA (Rev. September 1993), p. 3.

[13] Code Sec. 2106(a)(2)(A).

[14] Code Sec. 2056(d).

[15] Reg. § 20.2056(a)-1.

[16] Code Sec. 2101(b).

[17] Code Sec. 2101(b).

[18] Code Sec. 2101(b)(2).

[19] Code Sec. 2102(c)(2).

relating to expatriation to avoid estate tax, the credit allowable is $13,000.[20]

The executor of an estate of a nonresident who is not a citizen of the United States must file an estate tax return on Form 706-NA if that part of the gross estate that is located in the United States exceeds $60,000, reduced by (1) the total taxable gifts made by the decedent after December 31, 1976, and (2) the aggregate amount allowed as a specific exemption under Code Sec. 2521 (as in effect before its repeal by the Tax Reform Act of 1976) with respect to gifts made by the decedent after September 8, 1976, and before January 1, 1977.[21]

[20] Code Sec. 2107(c).

[21] Code Sec. 6018(a)(2); Instructions for Form 706-NA (Rev. September 1993), p. 1.

¶ 1636 Filled-In Form 706-NA

Reproduced below is Form 706-NA, United States Estate (and Generation-Skipping Transfer) Tax Return—Estate of nonresident not a citizen of the United States (Rev. September 1993), filled in for a hypothetical nonresident alien who died on February 1, 1998.

Form **706-NA** (Rev. September 1993) Department of the Treasury Internal Revenue Service

United States Estate (and Generation-Skipping Transfer) Tax Return

Estate of nonresident not a citizen of the United States

(See separate instructions. Section references are to the Internal Revenue Code.)

OMB No. 1545-0531 Expires 3 31 96

Attach supplemental documents and translations. Show amounts in U.S. dollars.

Part I Decedent, Executor, and Attorney

1a Decedent's first name and middle initial Rodney M.	b Decedent's last name Lodge		2 U.S. social security number (if any)
3 Place of death Washington, D.C.	4 Domicile at time of death Ontario, Canada	5 Citizenship (nationality) Canada	6 Date of death 2-1-98
7a Date of birth 1-4-43	b Place of birth Ontario, Canada	8 Business or occupation Television Reporter	

In United States	9a Name of executor Martin Lodge b Address 44 W. Elm Street Albany, NY 12207	10a Name of attorney for estate Michelle K. Murphy b Address 120 Ohio Avenue Washington, D.C. 20036
Outside United States	11a Name of executor Philip Lodge b Address 224 Foxmoor Drive Ontario, Canada	12a Name of attorney for estate Rutherford Harvey b Address 422 Covington Road Ontario, Canada

Part II Tax Computation

1	Taxable estate (from Schedule B, line 8)			1	331,415
2	Total taxable gifts of tangible or intangible property located in the U.S., transferred (directly or indirectly) by the decedent after December 31, 1976, and not included in the gross estate (see section 2511)			2	0
3	Total (add lines 1 and 2)			3	331,415
4	Tentative tax on the amount on line 3 (see instructions)			4	98,481
5	Tentative tax on the amount on line 2 (see instructions)			5	0
6	Gross estate tax (subtract line 5 from line 4)			6	98,481
7	Unified credit — enter smaller of line 6 amount or maximum allowed (see instructions)			7	13,000
8	Balance (subtract line 7 from line 6)			8	85,481
9	Credit for state death taxes (see instructions and attach credit evidence)			9	0
10	Balance (subtract line 9 from line 8)			10	85,481
11	Credit for Federal gift taxes (see sections 2102 and 2012 and attach computation)	11	0		
12	Credit for tax on prior transfers (attach Schedule Q, Form 706)	12	0		
13	Total (add lines 11 and 12)			13	0
14	Net estate tax (subtract line 13 from line 10)			14	85,481
15	Total generation-skipping transfer tax (attach Schedule R, Form 706)			15	0
16	Section 4980A increased estate tax (attach Schedule S, Form 706 (see instructions))			16	0
17	**Total transfer taxes** (add lines 14, 15, and 16)			17	85,481
18	Earlier payments (see instructions and attach explanation)	18	0		
19	U.S. Treasury bonds redeemed to pay estate tax	19	0		
20	Total (add lines 18 and 19)			20	0
21	Balance due (subtract line 20 from line 17) (see instructions)			21	85,481

Under penalties of perjury, I declare that I have examined this return, including any additional sheets attached, and to the best of my knowledge and belief, it is true, correct, and complete. I understand that a complete return requires listing all property constituting the part of the decedent's gross estate (as defined by the statute) situated in the United States.

Martin Lodge (Signature of executor) 8-28-98 (Date)

Michelle K. Murphy (Signature of preparer (other than executor)) 120 Ohio Avenue Washington, D.C. 20036 (Address) 8-28-98 (Date)

For Paperwork Reduction Act Notice, see page 1 of the separate instructions. Form 706-NA (Rev. 9-93)

Form 706-NA (Rev. 9-93) Page 2

Part III General Information

		Yes	No
1a	Did the decedent die testate?	X	
b	Were letters testamentary or of administration granted for the estate? *If granted to persons other than those filing the return, include names and addresses on page 1.*	X	
2	Did the decedent, at the time of death, own any:		
a	Real property located in the United States?	X	
b	U.S. corporate stock?	X	
c	Debt obligations of (1) a U.S. person, or (2) the United States, a state or any political subdivision, or the District of Columbia?		X
d	Other property located in the United States?		X
3	Was the decedent engaged in business in the United States at the date of death?	X	
4	At the date of death, did the decedent have access, personally or through an agent, to a safe deposit box located in the United States?	X	
5	At the date of death, did the decedent own any property located in the United States as a joint tenant with right of survivorship; as a tenant by the entirety; or, with surviving spouse, as community property? *If "Yes," attach Schedule E, Form 706.*		X
6a	Had the decedent ever been a citizen of the United States (see instructions)?		X
b	If "Yes," did the decedent lose U.S. citizenship within 10 years of death?		
7	Did the decedent make any transfer (of property that was located in the United States at either the time of the transfer or the time of death) described in sections 2035, 2036, 2037, or 2038 (see the instructions for Form 706, Schedule G)? *If "Yes," attach Schedule G, Form 706.*		X
8	At the date of death, were there any trusts in existence that were created by the decedent and that included property located in the United States either when the trust was created or when the decedent died? *If "Yes," attach Schedule G, Form 706.*		X
9	At the date of death, did the decedent:		
a	Have a general power of appointment over any property located in the United States?		X
b	Or, at any time, exercise or release the power? *If "Yes" to either a or b, attach Schedule H, Form 706.*		X
10a	Have Federal gift tax returns ever been filed?		X
b	Periods covered ▶		
c	IRS offices where filed ▶		
11	Does the gross estate in the United States include any interests in property transferred to a "skip person" as defined in the instructions to Schedule R of Form 706? *If "Yes," attach Schedules R and/or R-1, Form 706.*		X

Schedule A — Gross Estate in the United States (see instructions)

	Yes	No
Do you elect to value the decedent's gross estate at a date or dates after the decedent's death (as authorized by section 2032)?		X

To make the election, you must check this box "Yes." If you check "Yes," complete all columns. If you check "No," complete columns (a), (b), and (e). You may leave columns (c) and (d) blank or you may use them to expand your column (b) description.

(a) Item no.	(b) Description of property and securities For securities, give CUSIP number, if available.	(c) Alternate valuation date	(d) Alternate value in U.S. dollars	(e) Value at date of death in U.S. dollars
1	Condominium, 82 8th Street, Washington D.C.			140,000
2	2800 Shares of Power Co., Richmond, VA, $10 voting common, $75 per share on N.Y.S.E. at deate of death			210,000
3	Cash in safe deposit box, 1st Trust Bank, Alexandria, VA			7,774
	(If you need more space, attach additional sheets of same size.)			
Total				357,774

Schedule B — Taxable Estate

You must document lines 2 and 4 for the deduction on line 5 to be allowed.

1	Gross estate in the United States (Schedule A total)	1	357,774
2	Gross estate outside the United States (see instructions)	2	173,887
3	Entire gross estate wherever located (add amounts on lines 1 and 2)	3	531,661
4	Amount of funeral expenses, administration expenses, decedent's debts, mortgages and liens, and losses during administration (attach itemized schedule) (see instructions)	4	26,539
5	Deduction for expenses, claims, etc. (divide line 1 by line 3 and multiply the result by line 4) (see instructions)	5	17,859
6	Charitable deduction (attach Schedule O, Form 706) and marital deduction (attach Schedule M, Form 706, and computation)	6	8,500
7	Total deductions (add lines 5 and 6)	7	26,359
8	Taxable estate (subtract line 7 from line 1) (enter here and on line 1 of the Tax Computation)	8	331,415

Chapter 37

PAYMENT OF THE TAX

¶ 1650 Date of Payment

The estate tax is due and payable at the same time the return is due. Thus, payment is due nine months after the date of death. It must be paid within the time prescribed to avoid the assessment of various penalties. Extensions of time for payment may be granted, but such extensions, although preventing the application of certain penalties, do not entirely prevent the assessment of interest.[1]

The due date for payment is the same numbered day of the ninth month after the date of death as that day of the month in which death occurred. If there is no similarly numbered day in the ninth month, the tax is deemed to be due on the last day of that month. For example, if the date of death were May 31, 2000, the due date would be February 28, 2001.

¶ 1660 Place of Payment

The law requires that the tax be paid without any need for assessment or notice and demand to the internal revenue officer with whom the estate tax return is filed.[2] Unless the return is hand-carried to the office of the IRS District Director, it should be mailed to the IRS Service Center for the state in which the decedent was domiciled on the date of death. A list of these centers appears on page 2 of the Instructions for Form 706 (Rev. July 1998). If the decedent was a nonresident citizen, the return must be filed with the IRS Service Center, Philadelphia, Pennsylvania 19255, U.S.A. However, if the decedent is a nonresident alien, the estate must file Form 706-NA (United States Estate (and Generation-Skipping Transfer) Tax Return—Estate of Nonresident Not a Citizen of the United States).

¶ 1665 Method of Payment

The tax may be paid by check, draft, or money order made payable to the IRS.[3] Payment may also be made by credit or debit card for tax payments made after 1998 and through December 15, 2001.[4] The decedent's name, social security number and "Form 706" should be written on the check, draft, or money order in order to assist the IRS in posting it to the proper account. If the amount of tax paid with the return is different from the amount of the net estate tax payable as computed on the return, the executor should explain the difference in an attached statement. For example, the executor should indicate that he has made prior payments to the IRS in the statement.

---

[1] Reg. § 20.6161-1(c)(2).

[2] Code Sec. 6151.

[3] Reg. § 301.6311-1.

[4] Temp. Reg. § 301.6311-2T.

- *Flower Bonds*

Treasury bonds of certain issues (known as "flower" bonds) are redeemable at par (plus the accrued interest from the last preceding date to the date of redemption) upon the death of the owner, at the option of the representatives of, or persons entitled to, his estate. (Bonds issued after March 3, 1971, are not acceptable in payment of estate taxes at par value and accrued interest.) They may be redeemed for the purpose of having the proceeds applied in payment of the estate taxes on the decedent's estate. The bonds that are redeemable at par and accrued interest before the maturity or call redemption date are listed below.

The following U.S. Treasury bonds may be redeemed at par value in payment of federal estate taxes, including the additional estate tax excess retirement accumulations, but not the generation-skipping transfer tax. These bonds must be includible in the decedent's gross estate.[5]

Treasury Bonds

Series	Dated	Due
3's 1995	Feb. 15, 1955	Feb. 15, 1995
3½'s 1990	Feb. 14, 1958	Feb. 15, 1990
3½'s 1998	Oct. 3, 1960	Nov. 15, 1998
4's 1988-93	Jan. 17, 1963	Feb. 15, 1993
4⅛'s 1989-94	April 18, 1963	May 15, 1994
4¼'s 1987-92	Aug. 15, 1962	Aug. 15, 1992

Treasury obligations issued after March 3, 1971, will not be redeemable at par value in payment of estate taxes.[6]

¶ 1672 Estate Tax on Closely Held Business Interests

The estate of an individual who dies owning a closely held business interest may qualify for a special elective method of paying the estate tax attributable to the interest. Effective for estates of decedents dying after 1981, estate tax on a closely held business interest may be deferred for up to 14 years, with the estate making annual payments of interest only for the first four years and paying the balance in 10 annual installments of principal and interest. This deferral is permitted only if the value of the interest exceeds 35 percent of the decedent's adjusted gross estate.

- *Installment Payments*

If more than 35 percent of the adjusted gross estate is an interest in a farm or other closely held business, an executor may elect to defer payments of tax attributable to the interest for five years (paying interest only) and thereafter pay the tax in equal installments over the next 10 years.[7] The maximum payment period, however, is 14 rather than 15 years because the due date for the last payment of interest coincides with the due date for the first installment of tax. For purposes of the 35-percent rule, the adjusted gross estate consists of the gross estate less debts, expenses, claims, and losses deductible under Code Sec. 2053 or Code Sec. 2054.

For decedents dying prior to 1998, interest is payable at a special four-percent rate on the estate tax attributable to the first $1 million in value of a farm or other closely held business. For decedents dying after

---

[5] Code Sec. 6312, prior to repeal by P.L. 92-5.

[6] Act Sec. 4, P.L. 92-5.

[7] Code Sec. 6166.

1997, the four-percent rate is replaced with a two-percent rate that applies to the first $1 million of *taxable* value of a farm or closely held business. In addition, effective for estates of decedents dying after December 31, 1997, the $1,000,000 ceiling is indexed annually for inflation. (see ¶ 1680).[8]

For purposes of the 35-percent rule, an "interest in a closely held business" is defined as:

(1) an interest as a proprietor in a business carried on as a proprietorship;

(2) an interest as a partner in a partnership carrying on a trade or business (a) with no more than 15 partners or (b) where 20 percent or more of its assets help determine the decedent's gross estate; or

(3) stock in a corporation carrying on a trade or business (a) with no more than 15 stockholders or (b) where 20 percent of its voting stock is included in determining the decedent's gross estate.[9]

Property owned through a corporation, partnership, estate or trust is regarded as proportionately owned by shareholders, partners or beneficiaries. For purposes of this election, interests in two or more closely held businesses are treated as an interest in a single closely held business if 20 percent or more of the total value of each business is included in the decedent's gross estate.[10]

The election to defer and pay in installments estate tax attributable to a decedent's closely held business interest is made by attaching to a timely filed estate tax return a notice of election containing the following information:

(1) the decedent's name and taxpayer identification number as they appear on the estate tax return;

(2) the amount of tax to be paid in installments;

(3) the date selected for payment of the first installment;

(4) the number of annual installments, including the first installment, in which the tax is to be paid;

(5) the properties shown on the estate tax return that constitute the closely held business interest (identified by schedule and item number); and

(6) the facts supporting the conclusion that the estate qualifies for the deferral and installment election.

If it is not certain at the time for filing the estate tax return that the estate qualifies for the election, the estate may make a protective election. A final election notice is then filed within 60 days after it is determined that the estate qualifies for the election. The final notice must contain the information noted above.[11]

● *Holding Company Stock*

The stock of a holding company that directly or indirectly (through one or more other holding companies) owns stock in a closely held active

[8] Code Sec. 6601(j).

[9] Code Sec. 6166(b)(1).

[10] Code Sec. 6166(c).

[11] Reg. § 20.6166-1(d).

trade or business will be considered stock in the business company for purposes of Code Sec. 6166 and, thus, may qualify for installment payment of estate taxes.[12] A "holding company" is defined as any corporation holding stock in another corporation.[13] A "business company" is any corporation carrying on a trade or business.[14] The provisions relating to the installment payment of estate taxes for holding company stock generally are effective with respect to estates of decedents dying after July 18, 1984. However, if on June 22, 1984, and at all times prior to the decedent's death, a corporation has 15 or fewer shareholders, and the stock of the corporation is included in the decedent's gross estate, the stock of all wholly owned subsidiaries, at the executor's election, may be treated as one corporation.[15]

In order for holding company stock to qualify for the election, several requirements applicable to closely held business interests generally must be met. First, the interest that is held by the holding company must meet the general rule of Code Sec. 6166(b)(1)(C) requiring that: (1) a closely held business have 15 or fewer shareholders or (2) the decedent own 20 percent or more of the corporation's voting stock. Second, the value of the business interest held by the holding company must exceed 35 percent of the value of the decedent's adjusted gross estate. Only the portion of the holding company stock that represents direct or indirect ownership of non-readily tradable stock in a business company qualifies for the election.[16]

For purposes of determining whether the decedent, through holding company stock, owned at least 20 percent of the value of the voting stock of the business company, holding company stock will be treated as voting stock to the extent that the holding company's stock owns directly (or indirectly through one or more other holding companies) voting stock in the business company.[17]

Elections with respect to holding company stock are to be made by including on the notice of election a statement that such an election is being made and the facts forming the basis for the conclusion that the estate qualifies for such an election. If such an election is made, the special interest rate and the five-year deferral of principal payments provisions are not available. If the executor fails to state the amount of tax to be paid in installments or the number of installments, the election is presumed to be for the maximum amount payable and for payment thereof in 10 equal annual installments.[18]

• *Attribution of Ownership*

For installment payment purposes, all stock and partnership interests of a decedent and his family will be considered owned by the decedent.[19] Family members whose interests will be considered held by the decedent in order to meet these requirements are brothers and sisters, spouse, grandparents (ancestors), and children and grandchildren (lineal descendants).

---

[12] Code Sec. 6166(b)(8).

[13] Code Sec. 6166(b)(8)(D)(i).

[14] Code Sec. 6166(b)(8)(D)(ii).

[15] Act Sec. 1021(d), P.L. 98-369.

[16] Code Sec. 6166(b)(8)(B).

[17] Code Sec. 6166(b)(8)(C).

[18] Temporary Reg. § 301.9100-6T.

[19] Code Sec. 6166(b)(2)(D).

● *Special Attribution Election*

A special attribution-of-ownership rule applies if the executor of the estate so elects. This rule provides that all nonreadily tradable stock and all partnership capital interests of a decedent and the decedent's family will be considered owned by the decedent for purposes of determining whether 20 percent of the corporation or partnership is includible in the decedent's gross estate.[20] Family members whose interests will be considered as held by the decedent are brothers, sisters, spouse, ancestors and lineal descendants.

If the benefits of this rule are elected, the estate is deemed to have elected to pay the tax attributable to the business interest in 10 installments beginning on the due date for payment of the decedent's estate tax—there is no deferral period. Additionally, the special interest rate applied under the regular deferral and installment election is not available.[21]

It should be noted that the stock or partnership interest attributed to a decedent under this rule is attributed only for purposes of the 20-percent requirements. Thus, the value of the attributed stock or partnership interest is not included in the decedent's gross estate for purposes of the 35-percent rule.

● *Installment Payment Denied for Passive Assets*

In the case of all corporations and partnerships, only active business assets are considered for purposes of meeting the 35-percent-of-adjusted-gross-estate test discussed above as well as for determining the value of the business interest qualifying for the election.[22] However, this rule does not apply for purposes of the accelerated payment provisions (see below). Any asset other than an asset used in carrying on a trade or business constitutes a passive asset. This definition includes stock in another corporation unless (1) the stock is deemed to be held by the decedent by reason of the holding company rules of Code Sec. 6166(b)(8) (see above), and (2) the stock qualifies under the 35-percent-of-adjusted-gross-estate test.

An exception is provided for certain active corporations, whereby such corporations will be treated as one corporation if:

(1) a corporation owns at least 20 percent of the value of the voting stock of another corporation, or such corporation has no more than 15 shareholders; and

(2) at least 80 percent of the value of each such corporation is attributable to assets used in carrying on a trade or business.[23]

For purposes of applying the 80-percent-of-value test ((2), above) to the corporation holding stock in a second corporation, the second corporation's stock will not be considered.

---

[20] Code Sec. 6166(b).

[21] Code Sec. 6166(b)(7)(A)(iii).

[22] Code Sec. 6166(b)(9).

[23] Code Sec. 6166(b)(9)(iii).

- *Acceleration of Unpaid Taxes*

Under certain conditions, taxes that have been deferred under Code Sec. 6166 will become due. The following rules govern this acceleration of unpaid taxes: [24]

(1) Portions of an interest representing less than 50 percent of the value of the decedent's interest in a closely held business may be disposed of and/or withdrawn before payment of the balance of the estate taxes attributable to the interest will be accelerated. For this purpose, dispositions and withdrawals are aggregated.

(2) The transfer of the decedent's interest in a closely held business upon the death of the original heir, or upon the death of any subsequent transferee receiving the interest as a result of the prior transferor's death, will not cause acceleration of taxes if each subsequent transferee is a family member (within the meaning of Code Sec. 267(c)(4)) [25] of the transferor.

(3) A delinquent payment of interest or tax will accelerate the due date of the unpaid tax balance if the full amount of payment is not paid within six months of the original due date. However, the late payment will not be eligible for the special four-percent interest rate (see ¶ 1680), and a penalty of five percent per month of the amount of the payment will be imposed.

(4) If the estate has undistributed net income for any tax year ending on or after the due date for the first installment, the estate will pay an amount equal to any undistributed net income for any tax year in liquidation of the unpaid portion of the tax.

For purposes of acceleration of estate taxes deferred under Code Sec. 6166, all of the following will be considered as dispositions:

(1) disposition of any interest of holding company stock that was included in the decedent's gross estate;

(2) withdrawal of money or property from the holding company attributable to any interest included in determining the decedent's gross estate;

(3) disposition of any interest in the stock of the business company by the holding company; or

(4) withdrawal of money or property from such business company attributable to such stock by the holding company owning such stock.[26]

A redemption of stock to pay death taxes under Code Sec. 303 is not considered a disposition of a portion of the business interest for purposes of determining whether the installment election has been terminated.[27]

The installment payments are subject to the quarterly interest rates (see ¶ 1680).

---

[24] Code Sec. 6166(g)(1) and Code Sec. 6166(g)(2).

[25] An individual's family members include brothers and sisters (whether by whole or half blood), spouse, ancestors, and lineal descendants.

[26] Code Sec. 6166(g)(1)(E) and Code Sec. 6166(g)(1)(F).

[27] Code Sec. 6166(g)(1)(B).

¶ 1680 Discount, Interest and Penalties

No provision is made for the allowance of a discount for payment of the tax in advance of the last day for payment. If the tax is not paid when due, various interest and other penalties may be assessed, depending upon the extent and circumstances of the nonpayment.

● *Interest*

Interest must be paid on any amount of tax that is unpaid when the return is due, without regard to any extension of time for payment.[28] Interest rates paid on underpayments and overpayments of estate tax are determined on a quarterly basis and are based on the federal short-term rate.[29] In addition, the interest rates on overpayments of taxes are one percent less than those applicable for underpayments. Interest accruing is compounded daily.[30]

The interest rates for calendar quarters beginning in 1990 are as follows:

Calendar Quarter Beginning:	*Rate on Underpayments:*	*Rate on Overpayments:*
1/1/90	11	10
4/1/90	11	10
7/1/90	11	10
10/1/90	11	10
1/1/91	11	10
4/1/91	10	9
7/1/91	10	9
10/1/91	10	9
1/1/92	9	8
4/1/92	8	7
7/1/92	8	7
10/1/92	7	6
1/1/93	7	6
4/1/93	7	6
7/1/93	7	6
10/1/93	7	6
1/1/94	7	6
4/1/94	7	6
7/1/94	8	7
10/1/94	9	8
1/1/95	9	8
4/1/95	10	9
7/1/95	9	8
10/1/95	9	8
1/1/96	9	8
4/1/96	8	7
7/1/96	9	8
10/1/96	9	8
1/1/97	9	8
4/1/97	9	8
7/1/97	9	8
10/1/97	9	8
1/1/98	9	8
4/1/98	8	7
7/1/98	8	7
10/1/98	8	7
1/1/99	7	7
4/1/99	8	8

An exception to these interest rates applies in the case of a farm or closely held business that qualifies for the 14-year installment payment election (see ¶ 1672). For decedents dying prior to 1998, a special four-percent interest rate is allowed on the estate tax attributable to the first

[28] Code Sec. 6601 and Code Sec. 6611.

[29] Code Sec. 6621(b).

[30] Code Sec. 6622. See Rev. Proc. 95-17, 1995-1 CB 556, superseding Rev. Proc. 83-7, 1983-1 CB 583, for the uniform tables for computing interest using the Code Sec. 6622 daily compounding rules. The tables are effective for all interest computations made after December 31, 1994.

$1 million in value for such farm or business.[31] The maximum amount that may be subject to the lower four-percent rate is the lesser of: (1) $345,800 (the estate tax on $1 million), reduced by the amount of the allowable unified credit; or (2) the amount of estate tax that is attributable to the closely held business and that is payable in installments, as discussed at ¶ 1672. The current interest rates discussed above apply to the estate tax attributable to the value of property that exceeds $1 million.

● *Decedents Dying After 1997*

For decedents dying after 1997, the four-percent rate is replaced with a special two-percent rate that applies to the first $1,000,000 in *taxable* value (as indexed for inflation) of a closely held business.[32] For 1998, the maximum amount eligible for the two-percent rate is $410,000 (a $612,050 tentative tax on $1,625,000 less the applicable unified amount of $202,050). An executor of an estate of a decedent who died prior to 1998 may elect to apply the two-percent rate to the remaining installments.[33] The deferred estate tax in excess of the amount eligible for the two-percent rate is subject to a rate that is 45 percent of the federal underpayment rate.

Generally, interest is imposed on penalties and additions to tax only if such penalty or addition is not paid within 10 days after notice and demand, and then only for the period from the date of notice and demand to the date of payment. However, under an exception to the general rule, interest will be imposed on such additions to tax for failure to file or valuation understatements (see below), for the period beginning on the due date of the return (including extensions) and ending on the date of payment of the addition to tax.[34]

● *Late Filing and Late Payment Penalties*

The penalty for failure to timely file a return is five percent for the first month of such failure and an additional five percent for each month or part of a month thereafter. The penalty may not exceed 25 percent and applies only when there is an underpayment of tax.[35]

An addition to tax is also imposed for failure to pay estate and gift taxes when due, unless the failure is shown to be for reasonable cause. The addition is one-half of one percent if the failure to pay exists no longer than a month, with an additional one-half of one percent per month during the continuance of the failure to pay, up to a maximum of 25 percent.[36]

Fraud and negligence penalties will not apply in the case of a negligent or fraudulent failure to file a return. However, in the case of a fraudulent failure to file a return, the failure-to-file penalty is increased to 15 percent of the net amount of tax due for each month that the return is not filed, up to a maximum of five months, or 75 percent.[37]

● *Accuracy-Related Penalty*

Effective for returns due after December 31, 1989 (determined without regard to extensions), an accuracy-related penalty may be imposed

---

[31] Code Sec. 6601(j).

[32] Code Sec. 6601(j).

[33] Rev. Proc. 98-15, IRB 1998-4, 25.

[34] Code Sec. 6601(e)(2).

[35] Code Sec. 6651(a)(1).

[36] Code Sec. 6651(a)(2).

[37] Code Sec. 6651(f).

with respect to any portion of an underpayment that is attributable, among others, to negligence or disregard of rules and regulations or any substantial understatement of estate or gift tax valuation on an estate or gift tax return.[38] The penalty is equal to 20 percent of the portion of the understatement. For estate and gift tax purposes, there is a substantial estate or gift tax valuation understatement if the value of any property claimed on any return is 50 percent or less of the amount determined to be the correct amount of such valuation. The accuracy-related penalty does not apply to any portion of an underpayment that is attributable to fraud.

The penalty is increased to 40 percent for gross valuation misstatements. A gross valuation misstatement occurs if the value of the property claimed on an estate or gift tax return is 25 percent or less than the amount determined to be correct.[39] No penalty will be imposed for a substantial valuation understatement unless the portion of the underpayment attributable to substantial valuation understatement exceeds $5,000.[40]

● *Fraud Penalty Coordinated with Accuracy-Related Penalty*

The fraud penalty is imposed at the rate of 75 percent of the portion of any underpayment that is attributable to fraud. The 20-percent accuracy-related penalty will not apply to any portion of an underpayment on which the fraud penalty is imposed.[41] The accuracy-related penalty may be applied to any portion of the underpayment that is not attributable to fraud; however, the taxpayer must establish the portion not attributable to fraud by a preponderance of the evidence.[42]

¶ 1682 Special Lien Procedure

If the election to pay taxes in up to 10 installments after a deferral period (see ¶ 1672) is made, a special lien procedure is available that relieves the executor from personal liability for the entire installment period.[43]

The executor and all parties having any interest in the property to which the lien is to attach must file a written agreement consenting to creation of the lien in favor of the government, in lieu of bond. The agreement must designate a responsible person to deal with the IRS as an agent for the beneficiaries and any other parties who consented to the lien. The IRS may not require a bond except to the extent that there is no adequate security for the unpaid principal plus interest.[44]

Upon election of the installment payment provision, a lien attaches to real property, and other property with a long useful life, in the amount of the deferred taxes plus the aggregate amount of interest on those taxes for the first four years of the deferral period.[45]

---

[38] Code Sec. 6662; Reg. § 1.6662-1, Reg. § 1.6662-2, Reg. § 1.6662-3, and Reg. § 1.6662-7.

[39] Code Sec. 6662(h).

[40] Code Sec. 6662(g)(2).

[41] Code Sec. 6663.

[42] Code Sec. 6663(b).

[43] Code Sec. 6324A.

[44] Reg. § 301.6324A-1.

[45] Code Sec. 6324A.

¶ 1685 Extension of Time for Payment

The executor of an estate can obtain a general extension of time for payment of the estate tax for a period not to exceed 12 months from the date fixed for payment of the estate tax if he is able to show that "reasonable cause" exists for granting the extension.[46] In addition, a discretionary extension of time to pay may be allowed for reasonable cause. The time for payment of estate taxes may be deferred for a period not in excess of 10 years.[47] "Reasonable cause" will exist under any of the following circumstances: [48]

(1) the estate consists largely of a closely held business or farm and does not have sufficient funds to pay the tax on time;

(2) the estate is unable to gather sufficient liquid assets because of legal difficulties;

(3) the assets consist of annuities, royalties, contingent fees, or accounts receivable that are not collectible at the due date;

(4) litigation is required to collect assets in the decedent's estate;

(5) the estate must sell assets to pay the tax at a sacrifice price or in a depressed market; or

(6) the estate does not—without borrowing at a rate of interest higher than that generally available—have sufficient funds to pay the entire tax and at the same time also provide for the widow's and children's allowances and outstanding claims against the estate.

● *Application for Extension*

The above extension must be applied for, in writing, by the executor on Form 4768 (Application for Extension of Time to File a Return and/or Pay U.S. Estate (and Generation-Skipping Transfer) Taxes). The application should be submitted to the IRS office where the return will be filed and must state the period of extension requested, contain a statement of the reasonable cause for granting the extension, and include a declaration that it is made under penalties of perjury.[49]

The District Director may require the executor to furnish security for payment of the amount for which an extension is granted.[50] Such an extension does not prevent the running of statutory interest at the rate (see ¶ 1680) beginning nine months after the decedent's death, although it may extend the time in which state death taxes must be paid in order to qualify as a credit against the estate tax.

Special provision is made for extending the time for payment of the tax where existence of a remainder or reversionary interest causes the executor to elect to postpone paying the tax on such interest until six months after termination of the preceding property interests. A discretionary extension of time to pay the estate tax attributable to a remainder or

---

[46] Code Sec. 6161(a).

[47] Code Sec. 6161(a)(2).

[48] Reg. § 20.6161-1(a)(1).

[49] Reg. § 20.6161-1(b). Instructions for Form 4768 (Rev. October 1996), p. 2.

[50] Code Sec. 6165.

reversionary interest may be allowed for "reasonable cause" for additional periods not to exceed a total of three years.[51]

Notice of the exercise of this election to postpone payment of the tax in such instances must be filed with the District Director before the final date for paying the estate tax. Such notice should be accompanied by a certified copy of the will or other instrument creating the reversionary or remainder interest. Various other special requirements for this extension are set out in the regulations.

In the case of a deficiency, if "reasonable cause" is shown, an extension of time for payment may be granted under the regulations for a period not in excess of four years from the date otherwise fixed for the payment of the deficiency.[52] A satisfactory bond for not more than twice the deficiency may be required as a condition of such an extension, and the running of the statute of limitations for assessment and collection is suspended for the period of the extension. Interest at the current rate, as determined under Code Sec. 6621 (see ¶ 1680), is imposed until payment is made.

---

[51] Code Sec. 6163.

[52] Code Sec. 6161(b).

Chapter 38

REQUESTS FOR FACTORS, COMPUTATIONS AND RULINGS

¶ 1701 The Request

In the event that an actuarial factor (see ¶ 530), a computation, or a ruling is necessary to complete an estate or gift tax return, the estate representative, the donor, or the agent of either may request IRS assistance by writing to the Internal Revenue Service, Attn: CC:DOM:CORP:TSS, P.O. Box 7604, Ben Franklin Station, Washington, DC 20044.[1] If a private delivery service is used, the address is: 1111 Constitution Ave., Attn: CC:DOM:CORP:TSS, Room 6561, Washington, DC 20224.

The IRS is authorized to charge user fees for requests for rulings, determination and opinion letters, and similar requests. Pursuant to this authority, the IRS is presently imposing a $275 user fee for determination letters issued by District Directors with respect to estate, gift, and generation-skipping tax matters.[2]

It should be noted that the IRS has announced that it will not implement its so-called "comfort ruling" policy. Under the comfort ruling policy the IRS had proposed that it would no longer issue rulings with respect to issues that were clearly and adequately addressed by published authorities.[3] The IRS has decided to replace the comfort ruling policy with various other measures, including specific no-rule areas, model documents, published ruling checklists, and automatic action revenue procedures.[4]

¶ 1703 Information Necessary

The IRS annually issues a general checklist questionnaire that must be included with all ruling requests.[5] In addition, the IRS has issued a checklist specifically related to estate, gift, and generation-skipping transfer tax issues that is effective for all ruling requests made on or after March 13, 1991.[6] The issuance of the checklist was in response to the fact that many ruling requests did not include all of the information required for the IRS to consider them.

The estate and gift tax checklist includes the following questions:

(1) Have you read and complied with the requirements and procedures of the Associate Chief Counsel (Technical), including the checklist, as set forth in the "-1" revenue procedure of the current calendar year [e.g., Rev. Proc. 99-1, IRB 1999-1, 6]? The "-1" revenue procedure is published in the first IRB of the year.

(2) Have you read section 3 of the "-3" revenue procedure of the current calendar year, which sets forth issues on which the IRS will

---

[1] Rev. Proc. 99-1, IRB 1999-1, 6.

[2] Rev. Proc. 99-1, IRB 1999-1, 6.

[3] Rev. Proc. 89-34, 1989-2 CB 917, modified by Rev. Proc. 89-51, 1989-2 CB 632.

[4] Rev. Proc. 90-42, 1990-2 CB 420.

[5] Rev. Proc. 99-1, IRB 1999-1, 6, Appendix C.

[6] Rev. Proc. 91-14, 1991-1 CB 482.

not rule? The "-3" revenue procedure is published in the first IRB of the year.

(3) Is the requested ruling within the no-rule area in the "-3" revenue procedure?

(4) If the request involves a will, a trust instrument, a deed of conveyance, or a contract, is a copy of the document attached?

(5) If the answer to Item 4 is yes, and the document has not been executed, is a statement attached from the individual requesting the ruling that they have a present intention to execute the document?

(6) If the request involves an outright gift (as opposed to a gift in trust), is a copy of any deed of gift or other documents concerning the gift attached?

(7) If the request involves a disclaimer, is a copy of the disclaimer attached?

(8) If the request involves a disclaimer, is a complete description of the property to be disclaimed attached?

(9) If the request involves a decedent's estate tax and the estate tax return is due to be filed shortly, has a request for an extension of time to file the return been submitted to the District Director with jurisdiction over the return?

Gift Tax

Chapter 39

NATURE OF THE TAX

¶ 2000 Description of Gift Tax

Like the estate tax, the gift tax is an excise tax levied upon transfers of property made without adequate and full consideration. Because the gift tax is a tax on the transfer of property, rather than on the property itself, its application is generally not affected by the nature of the property or by any tax exemptions accorded to such property. An exception applies with respect to nonresidents who are not citizens of the United States.

The gift tax is levied during the transferor's lifetime and is cumulative in nature. The tax is paid annually, by means of a gift tax return, Form 709 (United States Gift (and Generation-Skipping Transfer) Tax Return). The return is due on or before April 15 of the year following the calendar year in which the taxable gifts were made.

Spouses who elect to split gifts of not more than $20,000 per year per donee may file Form 709-A (United States Short Form Gift Tax Return) annually (see ¶ 2240).

¶ 2005 Unified Rate Schedule

A single unified rate schedule applies both to gifts made, and to the estates of decedents dying, after December 31, 1976.[1] A "tentative tax" (before the unified credit (see ¶ 2007)) is levied under the unified rate schedules from a minimum rate of 18 percent to a maximum rate of 55 percent, which is applicable to taxable gifts and estates in excess of $3,000,000. A 53-percent rate applies to transfers between $2,500,000 and $3,000,000. For decedents dying prior to 1998, a five-percent surtax is imposed to phase out the graduated rates and unified credit with respect to taxable transfers between $10 million and $21,040,000. Due to mistakes in the wording of the amendment to Code Sec. 2001(c)(2) by the Taxpayer Relief Act of 1997 (P.L. 105-34,) the five-percent additional tax phases out the benefits of the graduated rates, but not the benefits of the unified credit (applicable credit amount), for estates of decedents dying, and gifts made, after 1997. Therefore, the additional tax is levied on amounts

[1] Code Sec. 2001.

transferred after 1997 in excess of $10,000,000 but not exceeding $17,184,000. The applicable credit amount is not recaptured.[2]

A separate unified estate and gift tax rate schedule applies to estates of, and gifts made by, nonresidents who are not citizens of the United States (see ¶ 2600).

The term "taxable gifts" means the gross amount of gifts less (1) the annual exclusion of $10,000 per gift and (2) any charitable or marital deductions that are available for the year (or quarter).

For gifts made before 1977, the separate gift and estate tax rates applied, with gift taxes set at three-fourths of estate taxes. However, taxable gifts before 1977 affect the rate at which post-1976 gifts are taxed (see ¶ 2008).

¶ 2007 Unified Credit

The unified credit is the amount that is subtracted from the taxpayer's gift or estate tax liability.[3] The unified credit for gifts made after 1987 and before 1998 is $192,800. For gifts made in 1998 and 1999, the unified credit is increased to $202,050 and $211,300, respectively. The unified credit is increased thereafter until it reaches $345,800 for gifts made in 2006 and later years (see ¶ 15). The amount of the unified credit that is available for gifts made in any one year must be reduced by the sum of the allowable credits in previous calendar periods. However, the allowable credit for any one year may not exceed the gift tax liability for that calendar period.[4] A chart indicating the applicable credit for years between 1977 and 1987 is at ¶ 2376.

A special transitional rule applied to gifts during the period September 9, 1976, through December 31, 1976. To the extent that use was made of the $30,000 lifetime exemption during this period, the allowable unified credit was reduced by an amount equal to 20 percent of the exemption. Thus, if the full $30,000 exemption was used during this period, a maximum reduction of $6,000 was made to the unified credit.

The amount of allowable credit for gifts made during the period January 1, 1977, to June 30, 1977, was limited to $6,000. However, over the full year 1977, a $30,000 credit was allowable. Thus, a donor could have used $6,000 of the credit during the first six months of 1977 and $24,000 of the credit during the second six months, for a total offset of $30,000 against gift taxes. In effect, any portion of the unified credit used against gift taxes will reduce the credit available to be used against the estate tax.

¶ 2008 Computing the Tax

The amount of gift tax payable for any calendar quarter or year, as appropriate, is determined by applying the unified rate schedule to cumulative lifetime taxable gifts and subtracting the taxes payable for prior periods.[5] Preceding periods are (1) calendar years 1932 (including only that portion of 1932 after June 6) and 1970 and all intervening calendar

---

[2] Code Sec. 2001(c)(2), as amended by P.L. 105-34.

[3] Code Sec. 2505.

[4] Code Sec. 2505(c).

[5] Code Sec. 2502 and Code Sec. 2505.

years, (2) the first calendar quarter of 1971 and all quarters between that quarter and the first quarter of 1982, and (3) all calendar years after 1981 and before the year for which the tax is being computed. Gifts made prior to 1977 are taken into account in the computation of post-1976 gifts (see example below). In computing the tax payable on post-1976 gifts, the reduction for taxes previously paid is calculated using the unified rate schedule. Then, to the extent allowable, the unified credit is used to offset the cumulative gift tax. (See ¶ 2378 for a discussion of the phaseout of the benefits of graduated rates and the unified credit for cumulative transfers exceeding $10,000,000.)

Example: In 1999, John Jones makes taxable gifts of $750,000. His only other taxable gifts were made prior to 1977 and amounted to $250,000. The unified transfer tax on the 1999 gifts is computed as follows:

1999 taxable gifts	$ 750,000
Pre-1977 taxable gifts	250,000
Total taxable gifts	$1,000,000
Unified transfer (tentative) tax on total gifts	$ 345,800
Less unified transfer (tentative) tax on pre-1977 gifts	70,800
Tentative tax on 1999 gifts	$ 275,000
Less applicable credit amount	211,300
Gift tax payable	$ 63,700

¶ 2009 Disclaimer

If a person makes a "qualified disclaimer," as defined below, for estate, gift, or generation-skipping transfer tax purposes, the disclaimed interest in property is treated as if it had never been transferred to the person making the qualified disclaimer.[6] Rather, it is considered as passing directly from the transferor of the property to the person entitled to receive the property as a result of the disclaimer. Thus, a person who makes a qualified disclaimer is not treated as having made a gift to the person to whom the disclaimed interest passes.

A qualified disclaimer is an irrevocable and unqualified refusal to accept an interest in property that satisfies the following four conditions:

(1) The refusal must be in writing.

(2) The written refusal must be received by the transferor, his legal representative, or holder of legal title, no more than nine months after the later of (a) the day on which the transfer creating the interest is made, or (b) the day on which the person making the disclaimer reaches age 21.

(3) The person making the disclaimer must not have accepted the interest or any of its benefits prior to the disclaimer.

(4) The interest must pass to a person other than the person making the disclaimer as a result of the refusal to accept the property. A surviving spouse may, under this rule, disclaim an interest in

[6] Code Sec. 2518.

property that, as a result and without direction on his or her part, passes to a trust in which he or she has an interest. A disclaimer is not unqualified if the disclaimant receives consideration in exchange for the disclaimer. A mere expectation or unenforceable hope that something will be received in the future does not rise to the level of consideration, however. To render the disclaimer invalid, the decision to disclaim must be part of a mutually bargained-for consideration.[7]

After 1981, a timely written transfer of the property by the person disclaiming the property to the person who would have received it under a disclaimer that is valid under local law is also considered a qualified disclaimer, assuming that the requirements of (2) and (3), above, have been met.[8]

A qualified disclaimer will apply for federal estate, gift and generation-skipping transfer tax purposes (see ¶ 1050 and ¶ 2465) even if local law does not characterize such a refusal as a disclaimer. The time limits prescribed for a qualified disclaimer also will supersede the time period prescribed by local law.

● *Joint Tenancy Interests*

In general, an individual must make a qualified disclaimer of the interest to which the disclaimant succeeds upon creation of the joint tenancy within nine months after the creation of the tenancy.[9] However, a qualified disclaimer of the survivorship interest must be made no later than nine months after the death of the first joint tenant to die. The timing for disclaiming the survivorship interest is not affected by the power of the disclaimant to unilaterally sever the tenancy under local law. The U.S. Court of Appeals for the Seventh Circuit has held that a surviving spouse's disclaimer of the survivorship interest in jointly held farmland within nine months of her husband's death was qualified, even though the joint tenancy was created 25 years earlier. According to the court, there was no "transfer" of the survivorship portion until the husband's death because, until that time, each tenant had the right under state law to partition the property.[10]

Similarly, the U.S. Court of Appeals for the Eighth Circuit has held that a surviving spouse's renunciation of her survivorship interest in several parcels of property that she had held in joint tenancy with her husband was timely when made within nine months of his death. On remand, the Tax Court concluded that the wife had made a qualified disclaimer and that no taxable gift resulted when the disclaimed joint interest passed to her children.[11]

With respect to a joint tenancy in real property created after July 13, 1988, between a donor and a noncitizen spouse, the surviving noncitizen spouse may disclaim any portion of the joint tenancy included in the decedent's gross estate under Code Sec. 2040.[12]

---

[7] *L.S. Monroe*, CA-5, 97-2 USTC ¶ 60,292, rev'g in part TC, 104 TC 352, CCH Dec. 50,539.

[8] Code Sec. 2518(c)(3).

[9] Reg. § 25.2518-2(c)(4)(i).

[10] *P.M. Kennedy*, CA-7, 86-2 USTC ¶ 13,699, rev'g TC, 51 TCM 232, CCH Dec. 42,804(M), TC Memo. 1986-3. Similarly, *J.O. Dancy Est.*, CA-4, 89-1 USTC ¶ 13,800, rev'g TC, 89 TC 550, CCH Dec. 44,184.

[11] *G.L. McDonald*, CA-8, 88-2 USTC ¶ 13,778, rev'g TC, 89 TC 293, CCH Dec. 44,118, cert. denied on another matter.

[12] Reg. § 25.2518-2(c)(4)(ii).

Special rules apply to disclaimers of joint tenancy interests in bank, brokerage, and investment accounts. The transfer creating the survivorship interest in a cotenant's contributions occurs on the death of the cotenant only if the cotenant possessed the right to unilaterally regain sole possession of the contributions. In such case, the surviving cotenant may make a qualified disclaimer within nine months of the deceased cotenant's death.[13] In addition, a joint tenant may not make a qualified disclaimer of any portion of the joint interest attributable to consideration furnished by that tenant.

● *Contingent Remainders*

A contingent remainder interest must be disclaimed within nine months after the interest becomes a completed gift for estate and gift tax purposes. In the case of a contingent remainder, a completed gift occurs when the contingent remainder interest vests.[14]

Prior to the enactment of the qualified disclaimer rules in 1986, a disclaimer of property transferred to an individual was effective for federal estate and gift tax purposes only if the disclaimer was made within a reasonable time after the individual became aware of the transfer. The U.S. Supreme Court held that an attempt to disclaim a contingent interest in a trust more than 30 years after the interest was created was invalid.[15] In the Court's view, the relevant transfer occurred when the interest was created, and not when the interest became possessory upon the death of the life tenant. The Supreme Court has also ruled, under the prior law, that a disclaimer must be made within a reasonable time after learning of the transfer that created the interest, regardless of when the interest vested, even if the original transfer in trust occurred prior to the enactment of the gift tax.[16]

● *Interests Created by Will: Statutory Shares*

A disclaimer of an interest created by a decedent's will must be made within nine months of the date of the decedent's death, not within nine months after the will was admitted to probate.[17]

The IRS has concluded that a surviving spouse's disclaimer of an undivided portion of an elected statutory share constituted a qualified disclaimer where both the election and the subsequent disclaimer occurred within nine months of the decedent's death.[18] Although the exercise of the statutory election was an affirmative act that vested title to the property in the surviving spouse, it was not considered to be an acceptance of the property or its benefits that would disqualify the disclaimer under Code Sec. 2518(c). However, such a disclaimer would not be timely if it was made more than nine months after the decedent's death, even if the disclaimer was made within nine months of the statutory election to take against the will.

---

[13] Reg. § 25.2518-2(c)(4)(iii).

[14] Reg. § 25.2518-2(c)(5), Example 6.

[15] *G.F. Jewett*, SCt, 82-1 USTC ¶ 13,453, 455 US 305.

[16] *J.O. Irvine*, SCt, 94-1 USTC ¶ 60,163.

[17] Reg. § 25.2518-2(c)(5), Example 5; *J.K. Fleming Est.*, CA-7, 92-2 USTC ¶ 60,113, aff'g TC, 58 TCM 1034, CCH Dec. 46,229(M), TC Memo. 1989-675.

[18] Rev. Rul. 90-45, 1990-1 CB 175.

¶ 2010 Transfers in Settlement of Support Obligations

An exclusion from the gift tax is provided with respect to certain transfers in settlement of support obligations.[19] The exclusion applies to transfers of property or property interests that are made under a written agreement between spouses in settlement of their marital and property rights or for the purpose of providing a reasonable allowance for the support of their children. Such transfers will be treated as having been made for full and adequate consideration, and will be exempt from gift tax under one condition—the divorce must occur within the three-year period beginning one year before the property settlement is entered into (see ¶ 2165).

¶ 2011 Taxable Gifts

A taxable gift may be any complete and irrevocable voluntary transfer to or for the benefit of another or others, whether in trust or otherwise, except to the extent that it is supported by full and adequate consideration in money or money's worth.[20] The gift tax is in addition to any other tax, such as federal income or generation-skipping transfer tax, paid or due on the transfer. The nature of the property transferred is not important except in the case of transfers by nonresidents who are not citizens.

The IRS has ruled that an executor or other fiduciary may waive his right to statutory fees and commissions without making a taxable gift.[21] In order to be effective, the waiver must evidence an intent to render a gratuitous service, and it must be executed within a reasonable time after appointment. Claiming a deduction for the fees on any tax return, however, will negate an intention to serve gratuitously.

¶ 2012 Valuation

Like the estate tax, the gift tax is measured by the value of property transferred at the date of the gift.[22] With certain exceptions, the methods of determining value for gift tax purposes are the same as those for estate tax purposes (see ¶ 2100 and following).

¶ 2013 Gift-Splitting

A married donor may elect, with his or her spouse, to treat all gifts made by either (other than gifts to the other spouse) as being made one-half from each. This has the effect of doubling the annual exclusion available for each donee ($20,000 as opposed to $10,000), and allows for the possibility of utilizing both spouses' unified gift tax credit.[23] The gift-splitting right is optional and may be taken or ignored in any calendar year.[24] In order to exercise the right, the spouses must consent, on an annual basis, to treat a gift made by either as a split gift. If the consent is effective, all gifts made by either spouse to any third party must be treated in the same way. A couple may not, therefore, elect to apply the gift-splitting privilege to some gifts but not others in the same calendar year (see ¶ 2200 and following).

---

[19] Code Sec. 2516 and Reg. § 25.2516-2.

[20] Code Sec. 2512.

[21] Rev. Rul. 66-167, 1966-1 CB 20.

[22] Code Sec. 2512.

[23] Code Sec. 2513.

[24] Reg. § 25.2513-1(c).

¶ 2014 Annual Exclusions

To prevent small gifts from being hampered by tax considerations, donors are allowed each year to exclude the first $10,000 ($3,000 for gifts made prior to 1982) in gifts made to any one donee, provided the gifts are not of future interests.[25] For transfers made after 1998, the annual exclusion is indexed for inflation. This exception is prompted by the belief that a gift of a future interest is more like a testamentary disposition of property than a current small gift to the donee. The future interest rule is strictly applied. A donor may also exclude gifts of up to $100,000 annually to his or her noncitizen spouse.[26] To facilitate the making of gifts to minors, however, Congress has specified certain types of gifts that will not be treated as gifts of future interests.[27]

¶ 2015 Deductions

Before applying the unified transfer tax rates, the donor may deduct the following from the value of the gifts he is required to report: (1) the allowable marital deduction for gifts to a spouse (see ¶ 2311); (2) transfers for public, charitable and religious uses (see ¶ 2305); and (3) any items that reduce the net value of the gift, such as partial consideration, mortgages and other charges against the specific property transferred. The tests and rules for determining the amounts of these various deductions are similar to those applied in determining the deductibility of corresponding items for estate tax purposes.

¶ 2016 Specific Exemption for Pre-1977 Gifts

In addition to the annual exclusion of $3,000 for gifts to each donee, a donor was entitled to a specific exemption of $30,000 for gifts made prior to 1977. The specific exemption was repealed, starting with gifts made in 1977, and was replaced by the unified credit (see ¶ 2007).

¶ 2017 Rates and Computation

The gift tax on gifts made after 1981 is reported and paid annually by filing Form 709 (United States Gift (and Generation-Skipping Transfer) Tax Return), which is due on April 15 of the year following the year in which the gifts are made (see ¶ 2052).

The specific steps to compute the gift tax are as follows: [28]

(1) Compute the tentative tax under the unified rate schedule on the total taxable gifts made in the current calendar period and all previous calendar periods, including periods before 1977.

(2) Compute the tentative tax under the unified rate schedule on the total taxable gifts for all calendar periods preceding the current calendar period.

(3) Subtract the tentative tax computed in step (2) from the tentative tax computed in step (1), to arrive at the gift tax before credit.

---

[25] Code Sec. 2503.

[26] Reg. § 25.2503-2(f).

[27] Code Sec. 2503(c).

[28] Reg. § 25.2502-1.

(4) Subtract the allowable unified credit, to arrive at the gift tax payable.

For purposes of this computation, calendar periods are (1) calendar years 1932 (including only that portion of 1932 after June 6) and 1970 and all intervening years, (2) the first calendar quarter of 1971 and all quarters between that quarter and the first quarter of 1982, and (3) all calendar years after 1981 and before the year for which the tax is being computed (see ¶ 2008).

Chapter 40
FORMS REQUIRED

¶ 2050 Filing by Donor

Donors are required to report gifts of present and future interests using Form 709 (United States Gift (and Generation-Skipping Transfer) Tax Return). This is the principal form that is used in the administration of the gift tax law. Spouses electing to split gifts of not more than $20,000 per year per donee may use Form 709-A (United States Short Form Gift Tax Return). Other forms and documents may be necessary, depending upon the circumstances (see ¶ 2120).

¶ 2052 Gift Tax Return Filing Requirements

Effective for gifts made after 1981, gift tax returns must be filed, and any gift tax must be paid, on an annual basis.[1] Generally, the due date for filing the annual gift tax return will be April 15. However, for the calendar year in which the donor dies, the gift tax return is required to be filed no later than the due date for filing the donor's estate tax return, including extensions.

● *Gifts in Excess of the Annual Exclusion*

Transfers of present interests in the amount of $10,000 or less to any donee are exempt from the gift tax and do not require a gift tax return, unless gift-splitting is elected (see ¶ 2013).[2] Donors making gifts that exceed $10,000 to a single donee are required to file an annual gift tax return in the year of such gifts. A return must be filed with respect to transfers in excess of $10,000 to a charitable organization if the gift is only partially deductible. However, a donor who makes a gift to charity in excess of the annual gift tax exclusion is not required to file a gift tax return if the *entire* value of the donated property qualifies for a gift tax charitable deduction.[3] A gift tax return must be filed for gifts of future interests, regardless of the amount of the gift.

A contributor making a contribution after August 5, 1997, to a qualified state tuition program (QSTP) that exceeds the annual exclusion limit may elect to have the contribution treated as if it were made ratably over five years.[4] A gift tax return must be filed with respect to any contribution in excess of the annual gift tax exclusion limit.

Example: In September 1998, Heinrich Neble contributes $50,000 to a qualified state tuition program, the designated beneficiary of which is his daughter, Gretchen. At Heinrich's election, the program treats the $50,000 as being paid ratably over a five-year

---

[1] Code Sec. 6075(b).

[2] Instructions for Form 709 (1998), pp. 1–2.

[3] Code Sec. 6019(3).

[4] Code Sec. 529(c)(2)(B).

period at $10,000 per year. Heinrich must make the election for the five-year averaging on his gift tax return.

- *Other Rules*

Married individuals who elect to split gifts (see ¶ 2013) must file a gift tax return, regardless of the amount of the gift.[5]

Only individuals are required to file returns. Where gifts are made by trusts, estates, partnerships or corporations, the trust beneficiaries, the partners or the stockholders become the donors and may incur a gift tax liability.[6]

Death of the donor before filing a gift tax return imposes the duty to file the return on the donor's executor or administrator. If a donor becomes legally incompetent before filing a gift tax return, the donor's guardian or conservator must file the return.[7]

Loans of qualified works of art (any archaeological, historic or creative tangible personal property) to a public charity or a private operating foundation are not treated as transfers subject to federal gift tax.

¶ 2056 Place for Filing Returns

Donors should file their gift tax returns with the IRS Service Center where their federal income tax returns would be filed. The instructions for Form 1040 (U.S. Individual Income Tax Return) contain a current list of filing locations.[8]

If a donor does not have a legal residence or a principal place of business in the United States, the gift tax return should be filed with the IRS Service Center in Philadelphia, Pennsylvania, or the Director of International Operations in Washington, D.C.[9]

¶ 2057 Description of Property

All property that is required to be listed on the return must be described in such a manner that it may be readily identified.[10] Thus, for example, pertinent information with respect to real estate would include a legal description, along with the street number, name and area (if the property is located in a city) and a short statement of any improvements made to the property.

¶ 2058 Supplemental Documents

A donor must provide information to support the value attributable to the gifts being made. For stock of closely held corporations or inactive stock, balance sheets of the corporation should be attached (particularly the most recent one), as should statements of net earning or operating results and dividends paid for each of the five preceding years. For every policy of life insurance listed on the return, the donor must obtain a statement by the insurance company which issued it on Form 712 (Life Insurance Statement). This form must then be filed with the return. If a

[5] Instructions for Form 709 (1998), pp. 3–4.

[6] Reg. § 25.6019-1(e).

[7] Reg. § 25.6019-1(g); Instructions for Form 709 (1998), p. 2.

[8] Instructions for Form 709 (1998), p. 3.

[9] IRS Publication 448, "Federal Estate and Gift Taxes" (Rev. August 1992), p. 31.

[10] Reg. § 25.6019-4.

gift was made by means of a trust, a certified or verified copy of the trust instrument must be submitted and the trust's identifying number must be entered on Schedule A (Computation of Taxable Gifts) of Form 709. Other special documents may also be required to substantiate the value shown for the property listed on the return[11] (see ¶ 2120).

¶ 2065 Signatures and Declarations

In addition to the taxpayer's signature and declaration, a second declaration must be executed by the firm or person that prepared the return. Declarations that the return is true, correct, and complete, under penalties of perjury, are made at the bottom of page 1 of Form 709 (1998).

¶ 2080 Penalties

Interest and penalties similar to those applicable to the estate tax apply to the failure to file a gift tax return and pay the tax when due (see ¶ 1680). Accordingly, there are penalties for late filing of the gift tax return,[12] and the late payment of any tax due.[13] There are also accuracy-related penalties that may apply to that portion of any underpayment attributable to negligence or disregard of rules and regulations.[14] Penalties may also be applicable where there is a substantial understatement of the value of any property shown on a gift tax return.[15] A fraud penalty may be imposed on any portion of any underpayment that is attributable to fraud. Interest must be paid on any amount of tax that is unpaid when the return is due even if the time for filing the return has been extended.

In addition to the civil penalties noted above, criminal penalties may apply.

The willful failure to pay any tax, make any return, or to keep any records or supply any information that is required under the gift tax laws or regulations constitutes a misdemeanor and may subject the donor to additional penalties.

Any person who willfully attempts in any manner to evade or defeat any gift tax is guilty of a felony. Upon conviction, such person may be fined not more than $100,000, or imprisoned for not more than five years, or both, and may be required to pay the costs of prosecution. Other penalties may also apply.[16]

Any person who willfully aids or assists in the preparation or presentation of a false or fraudulent notice or return, or procures, counsels, or advises the preparation or presentation of such notice or return (whether such falsity or fraud is with or without the knowledge or consent of the person required to make the notice or return) is guilty of a felony.

---

[11] Reg. § 25.6019-3 and Reg. § 25.6019-4. See Instructions for Form 709 (1998), p. 6.

[12] Code Sec. 6651(a)(1).

[13] Code Sec. 6651(a)(2).

[14] Code Sec. 6662.

[15] Code Sec. 6662(g) and Reg. § 1.6662-7.

[16] Code Sec. 7201.

Chapter 41
VALUATION

¶ 2100 Gift Date Controls

Like the estate tax, the gift tax is levied upon the value of the property transferred by gift. There are, however, no alternate valuation dates. The value is determined as of the date of the gift.

¶ 2105 Method of Valuation

Generally, the method of determining value for gift tax purposes is the same as that employed for estate tax purposes. Consequently, the paragraphs cited below, which explain the methods of valuation for estate tax purposes, are pertinent:

Real estate (¶ 270)
Stocks and bonds (¶ 318)
Interests in business (¶ 527)
Mortgages and notes (¶ 355)
Cash (¶ 365)
Household and personal effects (¶ 535)
Other property (¶ 535)
Annuities, life estates, remainders, and reversions (¶ 530)

Certain types of property interests, however, must be specifically valued for gift tax purposes. Other types of property are frequently subject to problems in valuation for gift tax purposes, and thus are discussed specifically from a gift tax standpoint. These include transfers conditioned on survivorship, tenancies by the entirety, and life insurance and annuity contracts. In addition, Code Sec. 2701 through Code Sec. 2704 provide special valuation rules with respect to gifts involving certain intrafamily transfers of corporate, partnership and trust interests (see ¶ 570).

The IRS will not issue advance rulings or determination letters with respect to actuarial factors for valuing prospective or hypothetical gifts of a donor.[1]

¶ 2106 Transfers Conditioned on Survivorship

Occasionally, a donor makes a gift of property in trust and retains no power over the trust corpus, but may, under certain contingencies, regain the corpus by surviving the various beneficiaries. An amount less than the entire value of the property transferred is taxable. The value of the gift is reduced by the present value of the donor's right to regain the corpus in

---

[1] Rev. Proc. 99-3, IRB 1999-1, 103.

the event all of the contingencies should occur, or fail to occur, as the case may be.[2] The value of such rights is determined in accordance with the actuarial tables at ¶ 531 or ¶ 532, depending upon the date of the transfer (see ¶ 530).

¶ 2107 Joint Tenancies Between Spouses

For estate tax purposes, a spouse's interest in any property owned in joint tenancy with right of survivorship is a qualified joint interest (see ¶ 502). Due to the unlimited gift tax marital deduction available for gifts made after 1981 (see ¶ 2311), the creation of a joint tenancy between spouses after 1981 is not a taxable gift.

● *Pre-1982 Tenancies in Real Property*

For tenancies created before 1982, a donor spouse may or may not have elected to treat the creation of a tenancy by the entirety in real property between the spouses as a gift. If the donor spouse elected not to treat the creation as a gift, the transaction was treated as a gift only in the event the tenancy was terminated other than by the death of one of the tenants. If the tenancy was terminated by death, its value was involved only in determining estate tax liability.[3] The above election applied only to real property and not to personal property. This election created, for joint interests created after 1976 and before 1982, a "qualified joint interest" for estate tax purposes, and such property was treated as belonging one-half to each spouse for estate tax purposes.

If the donor spouse elected not to treat the creation of a tenancy by the entirety as a gift, and the property was subsequently sold during the lives of both spouses, or if the tenancy was otherwise terminated during their joint lives, a gift was deemed to occur at the time of termination, as long as this event occurred before 1982. The termination resulted in a gift to the extent that the proportion of the total consideration furnished by the donor spouse multiplied by the value of the proceeds of termination exceeded the value of that part of the proceeds of termination received by him or her. However, the IRS has ruled that, due to the repeal of the rules governing the creation of joint tenancies in real property by spouses, a post-1981 termination of a tenancy by the entirety created before 1982 did not result in a gift to the spouse who had not contributed any of the consideration for the property, where the spouse who had purchased the property had not elected to treat the creation of the tenancy as a gift.[4] (See, also, ¶ 502 for decedent's treatment of pre-1977 spousal joint interests.)

● *Pre-1982 Tenancies in Personal Property*

In the case of personal property, creation of the joint interest before 1982 had to be a complete gift for gift tax purposes in order to be a "qualified joint interest." Joint bank accounts did not qualify because either co-owner could withdraw the entire amount. Therefore, the gift was incomplete.

The creation of a joint tenancy in personal property constituted a gift to the extent that a spouse's contribution exceeded his or her retained

---

[2] Reg. § 25.2511-1(e).

[3] Code Sec. 2515, prior to repeal by P.L. 97-34.

[4] Rev. Rul. 83-178, 1983-2 CB 171.

interest in the property.[5] Thus, in determining the amount of a gift where a joint tenancy in personal property was created after 1976 and before 1982, the retained interest of each spouse was considered to be one-half of the value of the personal property.

¶ 2108 Joint Tenancies Between Nonspouses

The creation by one person of a joint tenancy between that person and another in certain property that the first person owned, or for which he or she provided the entire consideration, normally constitutes a gift of one-half of the value of the transferred property.[6] In instances where each party provides part of the property or consideration, the gift is equal to one-half of the value of the difference between the contributions.

¶ 2109 Life Insurance Contracts

The value of a gift of life insurance is deemed to be equal to the cost of replacing the policy on the date of the gift. This cost may be obtained from the insurer.[7]

Sometimes, however, valuation through the sale value of a comparable contract is not readily ascertainable when the gift is of a policy that has been in force for some time and on which further premium payments are to be made. In these instances, the value may be approximated. The approximation is made by adding to the interpolated terminal reserve at the date of the gift the proportionate part of the last premium paid before the gift which covers the period extending beyond that date.

In cases where, because of the peculiar nature of the contract, approximation by this method is not close enough to the full value, some other method must be used. In no instance, however, may either the cash surrender or the loan value be used. The value should never be based upon the face value of the policy except, perhaps, in the case of certain endowment policies.

¶ 2110 Annuity Contracts

The value of a gift of an annuity for the primary benefit of a donee is the cost of the contract, if the annuity is purchased at the time of the gift.[8] If the annuity benefits are not to commence until the death of the donor, who is the primary annuitant, and if the donor has actually made a taxable gift of such secondary benefits, the value of the gift is the difference between the value of the donor's interest at the time of the gift and the value of the entire contract or trust in which the interest is created.

If the gift is of an interest in an annuity contract which has been in force for some time, the value must be based upon the cost of an annuity contract purchased at the time of the gift with the same provision for payment in the future.

---

[5] Code Sec. 2515A(a), prior to repeal by P.L. 97-34.

[6] Reg. § 25.2511-1(h)(5).

[7] Reg. § 25.2511-1(h)(8) and Reg. § 25.2512-6(a).

[8] Reg. § 25.2512-6(a).

Annuities not involving any formal contract with an insurance company are valued in the same manner as for estate tax purposes (see ¶ 530 through ¶ 532).

¶ 2112 Stock Options

The IRS has provided a safe-harbor methodology for the estate or gift tax valuation of certain stock options.[9] This revenue procedure applies only to the transfer tax valuation of nonpublicly traded compensatory stock options (that is, stock options that are granted in connection with the performance of services, including stock options that are subject to the provisions of Code Sec. 421), on stock that, as of the valuation date, is publicly traded on an established securities market. The options to which this revenue procedure applies are referred to as "compensatory stock options."

The procedure allows for use of an option pricing model that takes into account specific factors that are similar to those established by the Financial Accounting Standards Board in "Accounting for Stock-Based Compensation," Statement of Financial Accounting Standards No. 123 (Financial Accounting Standards Board 1995) (SFAS 123). Under SFAS 123, the fair value of a stock option granted by a public entity is estimated using an option pricing model (for example, the Black-Scholes model or a binomial model) that takes into account as of the option grant date: (1) the exercise price of the option; (2) the expected life of the option; (3) the current price of the underlying stock; (4) the expected volatility of the underlying stock; (5) the expected dividends on the underlying stock; and (6) the risk-free interest rate for the expected term of the option.

¶ 2115 Transfers for Consideration

The gift tax not only applies to transfers without consideration, but it also applies to sales and exchanges for less than adequate and full consideration in money or money's worth.[10] In the case of a transfer of property for less than adequate and full consideration in money or money's worth, the amount by which the value of the property exceeds the value of the consideration is a gift. Consideration that is not reducible to a money value, such as love and affection or a promise of marriage, is disregarded.

A bona fide sale, exchange, or other transfer of property in the ordinary course of business and free from any donative intent is considered to have been made for adequate and full consideration in money or money's worth.

¶ 2116 Transfers in Settlement of Marital Rights

If a husband and wife enter into a written agreement concerning their marital and property rights, transfers made pursuant to such an agreement may, under certain circumstances, be deemed to have been made for full and adequate consideration in money or money's worth. Transfers made on or before July 18, 1984, qualify under this rule if the parties obtained a final decree of divorce from each other within two years after

---

[9] Rev. Proc. 98-34, IRB 1998-18, 15.

[10] Code Sec. 2512(b).

entering into the settlement agreement.[11] For transfers occurring after July 18, 1984, the exemption will apply if divorce occurs within the three-year period beginning one year before the property settlement is entered into.[12] Thus, the divorce may precede the settlement agreement by as much as one year under this rule.

It is not necessary that the agreement be approved by the divorce decree. It is necessary, however, that the transfers made be in settlement of the transferee spouse's marital or property rights, or that the transfers be made to provide a reasonable allowance for the support of minor children of the marriage.

¶ 2117 Payment of Gift Tax by Donee

Although a donor is primarily liable for the gift tax, many donors transfer property with the understanding that the donee will pay the tax or that the tax will be paid from the transferred property. Gifts of this type are commonly called "net gifts." The gift tax paid by the donee may be deducted from the value of the transferred property, to compute the donor's gift tax, where it is expressly shown or implied that the payment of the tax by the donee or from the property itself is a condition of the transfer.[13] However, the value of the gift is not reduced by the amount of the donor's available unified credit that is applied to the tentative gift tax liability.[14] Any state gift tax paid by the donee pursuant to such a condition may also be deducted from the value of the gift for federal gift tax purposes to the extent that the donor would have been liable for payment of the state gift tax.[15] Special formulas must be used to compute the donor's gift tax liability, and the donor's, rather than the donee's, unified credit must be applied.[16]

The U.S. Supreme Court has held that, to the extent that the gift tax paid by the donee in a net gift situation exceeds the donor's basis in the transferred property, the donor recognizes gain on the transaction for income tax purposes.[17] Prior to that decision, several courts had ruled that the transfer of property subject to the donee's paying any gift taxes did not result in any gain being realized by the donor.[18]

¶ 2120 Supplemental Documents Required

Any documents required for an adequate explanation of the value or the basis of valuation of each gift should be filed with the return. Otherwise, full information as to the basis of valuation used should be set out in Schedule A (Computation of Taxable Gifts) of Form 709.

● *Closely Held Stock*

Stock of a closely held corporation and stock not listed on an exchange or actively traded should be valued in accordance with estate tax principles (see ¶ 326). Various supplemental documents are required to be filed in connection with valuation of such stock. The donor must submit (1)

---

[11] Code Sec. 2516, prior to amendment by P.L. 98-369.

[12] Code Sec. 2516, as amended by P.L. 98-369.

[13] Rev. Rul. 75-72, 1975-1 CB 310.

[14] Rev. Rul. 81-223, 1981-2 CB 189.

[15] Rev. Rul. 80-111, 1980-1 CB 208.

[16] IRS Letter Ruling 8035004, 11-16-79, CCH IRS LETTER RULINGS REPORTS.

[17] *V.P. Diedrich*, SCt, 82-1 USTC ¶ 9419, 457 US 191.

[18] See, for example, *R.H. Turner*, CA-6, 69-1 USTC ¶ 9416, 410 F2d 752 (Nonacq.).

balance sheets of the corporation, particularly the most recent one, (2) profit and loss statements for each of the five years preceding the date of the gift, and (3) statements of dividends paid during the same five-year period.

- *Life Insurance*

For every life insurance policy listed on the return, the donor must file Form 712 (Life Insurance Statement) with the return.

- *Real Estate*

A copy of the appraisal, if available, should be submitted with the return where the gift consists of real estate.

- *Transfers in Trust*

If the gift was made by means of a trust, a certified or verified copy of the trust instrument must be submitted and the trust's identifying number must be entered on Schedule A of Form 709.

- *Valuation Discounts*

If the value of any gift reflects a discount for lack of marketability, minority interest, fractional interest in real estate, blockage, market absorption, or any other reason, an explanation of the discount must be attached to Schedule A of Form 709.[19]

¶ 2125 IRS Statement Explaining Gift Valuation

Upon written request by a donor, the IRS is required to furnish a written statement explaining any determination or proposed determination of the value of gift property.[20] The IRS valuation statement must be furnished within 45 days after the request or the date of determination or proposed determination of value.

The method and computation used in arriving at the valuation is not binding on the IRS.

A request for such a statement must be filed no later than the deadline for filing a claim for refund of the tax with regard to which the valuation was made.[21]

A taxpayer may also request a statement of value for art objects from the IRS.[22] The taxpayer may rely upon the valuation of the art objects when filing an income, estate or gift tax return. Statements of value will be given for art objects that have been appraised at $50,000 or more. The IRS will issue a statement of value for items appraised at less than $50,000 if at least one item is appraised at $50,000 or more.

---

[19] Instructions for Form 709 (1998), p. 4.

[20] Code Sec. 7517.

[21] Reg. § 301.7517-1(a).

[22] Rev. Proc. 96-15, 1996-1 CB 627.

Chapter 42

TAXABLE GIFTS

¶ 2150 Imposition of Tax

The gift tax is an excise tax that is imposed on lifetime transfers of property for less than full and adequate consideration in money or money's worth.[1]

The tax applies "whether the transfer is in trust or otherwise, whether the gift is direct or indirect, and whether the property is real or personal, tangible or intangible; but, in the case of a nonresident not a citizen of the United States, shall apply to a transfer only if the property is situated within the United States." [2]

Gifts by U.S. citizens who are residents of U.S. possessions and who acquired their U.S. citizenship completely independent of their connections with the possessions are treated in the same manner as gifts made by resident citizens of the United States.[3] Gifts made by other citizen-residents of U.S. possessions are treated as gifts made by nonresidents not citizens of the United States.

¶ 2155 Elements of a Gift

By property law definition, a gift is a voluntary inter vivos transfer (in any form or manner) of property (of any kind or nature) by one person to another without consideration or compensation therefor. It is a gratuity that requires the fulfillment of three essential elements: (1) intent on the part of the donor to make a gift; (2) delivery by the donor of the subject matter of the gift; and (3) acceptance of the gift by the donee.

The presence of these elements in connection with any given transaction is determined in light of property law requirements rather than by the application of gift tax requirements. If a transfer is a gift within the meaning of property law, it is a gift for gift tax purposes as well, unless it is specifically excluded.

The property law definition of a gift is somewhat extended for gift tax purposes. Even transfers that, under contract law, constitute transfers in

---

[1] Code Sec. 2501 and Reg. § 25.2512-8.

[2] Code Sec. 2511(a).

[3] Reg. § 25.2501-1(c).

fulfillment of a contractual obligation rather than gifts may be treated as gifts, at least in part, for gift tax purposes. They are deemed to be gifts to the extent that the value of the property transferred exceeds the value of the consideration received. The value used in determining the adequacy of the consideration is monetary value. Exceptions are made, however, for arm's-length business transactions and certain settlements in connection with divorces.

Although Congress dispensed with the requirement of donative intent, the courts have required that the transfer be donative in nature. In fact, except for the matter of inadequacy of consideration, the courts have generally required the property law elements of a gift to be present before a transfer may be taxed as a gift.[4] Thus, if there has been no delivery, there is no taxable gift.[5] This is so even though the taxpayer may have announced an intention to make a gift. Similarly, if the taxpayer is incompetent, and therefore incapable of understanding the nature of the transaction or of possessing the intention to make a gift, a transfer by him does not constitute a taxable gift. Nor is there a taxable gift of corpus until the donor relinquishes dominion and control.

¶ 2160 Specific Types of Transfers

Most types of transfers clearly fall into gift or nongift categories. In addition to direct deliveries of specific property to a donee, gifts (in the absence of consideration) include: [6]

(1) the irrevocable transfer of property pursuant to a declaration of trust;

(2) the forgiveness of a debt;

(3) the assignment of a judgment;

(4) the assignment of benefits under an insurance contract or the transfer of ownership of a policy of insurance;

(5) the payment of insurance premiums on policies owned by others and in which the donor has no interest as a beneficiary; and

(6) the purchase of an annuity contract for the benefit of another, where no control over such annuity is retained by the donor. This may extend also to secondary rights in an annuity contract under which the donor is primary beneficiary.

• *Gifts to Political Organizations*

Transfers of money or other property to a qualified political organization are not subject to the gift tax.[7] A "qualified political organization" is a party, committee, association, fund, or other organization (whether or not incorporated) that is organized and operated primarily for the purpose of directly or indirectly accepting contributions or making expenditures, or both, in order to influence or to attempt to influence the selection, nomination, election or appointment of any individual to any public office or to any office in a political organization.[8]

---

[4] See, e.g., *W.H. Wemyss*, SCt, 45-1 USTC ¶ 10,179, 324 US 303.

[5] Reg. § 25.2511-2.

[6] Reg. § 25.2511-1(a).

[7] Code Sec. 2501(a)(5).

[8] Code Sec. 527(e).

- *Disclaimers*

A person who is a beneficiary, heir, or next-of-kin may refuse to accept ownership of property that would otherwise pass to him or her without being subject to the gift tax. However, the refusal to accept the property must be made in the form of a "qualified disclaimer" (see ¶ 2009).[9]

- *Interspousal Transfers*

The payment of income taxes due on a joint income tax return by one spouse is not a taxable gift. The same rule applies to the payment of gift taxes in the case of a husband and wife who have elected the gift-splitting provisions of Code Sec. 2513 (see ¶ 2200).

- *Transfers Subject to Adjustment*

The IRS and the courts have disregarded adjustment clauses included in instruments of transfer that were designed to prevent the imposition of gift tax upon an IRS determination that gift taxes were due.

The U.S. Court of Appeals for the Fourth Circuit has held that a trust provision nullifying a transfer that would otherwise be subject to gift tax was void as against public policy.[10] A settlor provided in a trust instrument that if any portion of the transfer in trust were subject to gift tax as determined by "final judgment or order of a competent federal court of last resort" then the property subject to the tax was not to be included in the transfer and remained the property of the settlor. The court stated that the gift tax may not be avoided in such a manner and that the condition subsequent was contrary to public policy.

Similarly, the IRS has ruled that the value of a gift of real estate was to be determined without regard to an adjustment clause in the transfer deed that provided for a recharacterization of the transfer depending on the IRS's valuation of the transferred property.[11] The IRS disregarded both an adjustment clause reconveying to the donor a fractional share of real property sufficient to reduce its value to the amount of the gift tax exclusion and one providing that the donee would transfer to the donor consideration equal to the excess of the property's value over the amount of the annual gift tax exclusion.

The IRS noted that such provisions operated to defeat what would otherwise be a gift and, thus, interfered with its enforcement of the gift tax regulations. In both cases, the IRS reasoned that the purpose of the adjustment clause was not to preserve or implement the original, bona fide intent of the parties, but, rather, to recharacterize the nature of the transaction in the event of a future adjustment to the donor's gift tax return by the IRS. Therefore, the value of the gifts was determined without regard to the adjustment clauses.

---

[9] Code Sec. 2518.

[10] *F.W. Procter*, CA-4, 44-1 USTC ¶ 10,110, 142 F2d 824, reh'g denied, CA-4, 44-1 USTC ¶ 10,123, 142 F 2d 828, cert. denied, 323 US 756.

[11] Rev. Rul. 86-41, 1986-1 CB 300.

¶2161 Below-Market Interest Loans

The U.S. Supreme Court has held that an interest-free demand loan between family members constitutes a taxable gift because such loans represent the transfer of a property right consisting of the use of money.[12] The Court did not, however, address the question of how to value the gift, nor did it determine the income tax consequences, if any, arising from such a transfer. In 1985, Congress established a set of rules under which both income and gift tax liability may be imposed on loans that are either interest-free or payable at a rate lower than the applicable federal interest rate established by statute.[13] This type of loan is known as a below-market interest loan.

Any transfer of money that provides the transferor with a right to repayment either upon demand or over a period of time may be subject to the rules of Code Sec. 7872. A demand loan is considered to be a below-market interest loan and, thus, is subject to Code Sec. 7872 rules if the interest payable on it is at a rate less than the applicable federal interest rate. A term loan is considered to be below market if the amount loaned exceeds the present value of all payments due under the loan. Although Code Sec. 7872 enumerates five types of demand or term loans that come within its purview, the discussion here will be limited to the rules applicable to gift loans, i.e., those in which the lender's forgoing of interest is in the nature of a gift to the borrower.[14]

Generally, interest-free and below-market interest loans are recharacterized as arm's-length transactions in which the lender is deemed to have made the loan to the borrower at a statutory interest rate and the borrower is deemed to have paid the interest to the lender. These transactions can have both income and gift tax consequences. Thus, in the gift loan situation, the deemed interest is includible in the lender's income, may be deductible by the borrower if he itemizes his nonbusiness deductions, and may be characterized as a gift to the borrower.

• *Applicable Federal Rates*

To determine whether a loan is a below-market interest loan subject to the rules of Code Sec. 7872, it is first necessary to compare the interest rate stated in the loan with a rate published by the IRS called "the applicable federal rate." The applicable federal rate is as follows: [15]

Term of loan	Applicable federal interest rate
Three years or less	Federal short-term rate
More than three but no more than nine years	Federal mid-term rate
More than nine years..................	Federal long-term rate

Because a demand loan is treated as a series of one-day term loans, the applicable federal rate is the federal short-term rate in effect for the period during which the forgone interest on the loan is being computed.[16]

---

[12] *E.C. Dickman*, SCt, 84-1 USTC ¶13,560, 465 US 330.

[13] Code Sec. 7872.

[14] Code Sec. 7872(f)(3).

[15] Code Sec. 1274(d).

[16] Code Sec. 7872(f)(2)(B).

Through 1985, the IRS determined the applicable federal rates for six-month periods, beginning on January 1 and July 1. Beginning with January 1985, the IRS, acting under its regulatory authority, began issuing alternative applicable federal rates on a monthly basis. The 1985 Imputed Interest Simplification Act (P.L. 99-121) made the monthly rates the sole factors to be used in imputing interest. The rates are based on the average market yields on outstanding marketable obligations of the United States during the one-month period ending on the 14th day of the preceding month. The applicable federal rate is the lower of the rates for the current or two preceding months.[17]

Once it has been determined that a loan is subject to the below-market interest loan rules, then the amount of forgone interest that is treated as a gift must be computed by using the applicable federal rate. In some cases a simplified rate, called the blended annual rate, applies. This rate is published annually, along with the applicable federal short-term, mid-term and long-term rates for the month of July, and applies in the case of a below-market demand loan of a fixed principal amount that remains outstanding for the entire calendar year. The blended annual rate established for 1998 is 5.63 percent.[18] Forgone interest on a below-market demand loan of a fixed principal amount that remains outstanding for the entire year of 1998, therefore, is equal to the excess of 5.63 percent of the principal amount over any interest payable on the loan that was properly allocable to 1998.

> ***Example:*** Harriet Sheldon makes a demand loan in the amount of $1,000,000 to her son, Nick, on January 1, 1998. The interest rate on the loan is three percent. The amount of forgone interest on the loan, as of December 31, 1998, is $28,500 (the excess of $56,300 (5.63 percent of $1,000,000) over $30,000 (three percent of $1,000,000, the amount of interest payable on December 31, 1998)).

● *Below-Market Gift Loans*

A gift loan is any below-market loan in which the lender's forgoing of interest is in the nature of a gift. Generally, any below-market interest loan that is not made in the ordinary course of business (i.e., in a bona fide, arm's-length transaction that is free from donative intent) is considered made for less than full and adequate consideration and is treated as a gift loan. Although most of these loans are made between related parties, the Conference Committee Report to the Tax Reform Act of 1984 (P.L. 98-369) clearly states that a below-market interest loan between unrelated parties may be considered a gift loan for purposes of Code Sec. 7872.

A below-market gift loan may generate both income tax and gift tax liability. One set of rules governs the gift taxation of such loans, and another set covers the income tax consequences arising from such transactions. However, there are certain statutory provisions that limit or prevent the imposition of the gift and income tax on these loans, and these exceptions are noted below.

● *Gift Tax Liability*

The extent of a lender's federal gift tax liability on a below-market interest gift loan is dependent upon whether the loan is a demand or a

---

[17] Reg. § 1.1274-4.

[18] Rev. Rul. 98-33, IRB 1998-27, 26.

term loan. If a demand loan is involved, the lender is deemed to have made a gift to the borrower on the last day of each year the loan is outstanding.[19] Thus, there may be annual gift tax consequences if the demand loan continues beyond one calendar year. The amount of the gift is calculated on December 31, and is equal to the amount of interest forgone during the year.

With respect to any tax period, forgone interest is defined as an amount equal to the excess of: (1) the amount of interest that would have been payable on the loan for the tax period if interest had accrued at the applicable federal rate and was payable annually on the last day of each calendar year over (2) any interest payable on the loan properly allocable to that period.[20]

In the case of a term loan, the lender is deemed to have made a cash gift to the borrower on the date the loan was made. The amount of cash deemed transferred is equal to the excess of the amount loaned over the present value of all payments that are required to be made under the terms of the loan.[21] The present value of the payments is computed as of the date of the loan by using a discount rate equal to the applicable federal rate in effect on that date, compounded semiannually. Therefore, in this situation, there will be only one taxable gift, because the amount is determined as of the date of the loan.

● *Income Tax Liability*

For federal income tax purposes, the lender in a below-market gift loan (whether term or demand) is deemed to have transferred any interest forgone to the borrower, and the borrower is then deemed to have retransferred an identical amount as interest to the lender. The transfer and retransfer of any forgone interest attributable to periods during any calendar year are deemed to have taken place on the last day of such calendar year.[22]

● De Minimis *Exception*

In the case of a gift loan between individuals, no interest will be imputed to either the borrower or the lender for any day on which the aggregate outstanding amount of loans between such individuals does not exceed $10,000.[23] However, if the loan balance exceeds $10,000 on any given date, the rules of Code Sec. 7872 will apply to the entire amount of the loan, and not just the amount in excess of $10,000. This *de minimis* exception does not apply where the loan proceeds may be directly attributed to the purchase or carrying of income-producing assets. For purposes of this exception, as well as all other provisions of Code Sec. 7872, a husband and wife are treated as one person.[24]

● *Special Rules for Gift Loans*

If the balance of all outstanding gift loans between individuals exceeds $10,000 but is not more than $100,000, the interest imputed as paid by the borrower will be limited to the borrower's net investment income for the year, provided that the loan's interest arrangement does not

---

[19] Code Sec. 7872(a)(2).

[20] Code Sec. 7872(e)(2).

[21] Code Sec. 7872(b).

[22] Code Sec. 7872(a).

[23] Code Sec. 7872(c)(2).

[24] Code Sec. 7872(f)(7).

have tax avoidance as one of its principal purposes.[25] In determining the borrower's net investment income for purposes of this rule, the borrower is deemed to have no investment income for any year in which his net investment income is $1,000 or less. If the borrower has two or more outstanding gift loans, he must allocate his net investment income among such loans in proportion to the respective amounts that would be treated as retransferred to the lender without regard to the net investment income limitation.

For purposes of this exception, net investment income has the same meaning as that given under Code Sec. 163(d). Thus, the borrower must take into account all investment income from any source after offsetting for investment expenses (except interest) that are attributable to such income. Investment income includes gross income from interest, dividends, rents and royalties, net short-term capital gains from investment property, and amounts recaptured as ordinary income from the sale of investment property. The above rules apply to term loans made, renegotiated, extended or revised after June 6, 1984, and demand loans outstanding after June 6, 1984.

¶ 2162 Transfers Subject to Special Rules

Special rules apply with respect to certain types of transfers, including the following: [26]

(1) When a donor, with his or her own funds, creates a joint bank account in his or her name and in another's name and grants the other person the right to make withdrawals, each withdrawal by the other person constitutes a gift at the time it is made.

(2) When a joint tenancy with rights of survivorship is created in property, other than a joint bank account, the transaction constitutes a gift if the contributions of the joint tenants are unequal. The amount of the gift is a fractional share or shares of the amount by which the contribution of one joint tenant exceeds the contributions of each of the others. If there are to be two joint tenants, one-half of the excess is treated as a gift. If there are three joint tenants, two-thirds of the excess, or one-third of the excess of each, will be the subject of a gift.

(3) When community funds are used to purchase insurance on the life of one spouse and a third person is revocably named as beneficiary, the death of the insured spouse results in a taxable gift by the surviving spouse of one-half of the proceeds of such insurance.

¶ 2163 Powers of Appointment

Transferred property need not belong to the person deemed to be the donor in order for a taxable gift to occur. If the property was transferred by some other person and the taxpayer was given a general power of appointment over the property, a taxable gift occurs if the taxpayer exercises the power during his lifetime. Further, if the general power was

[25] Code Sec. 7872(d).

[26] Reg. § 25.2511-1(h).

created after October 21, 1942, the mere release of the power will constitute a taxable gift.[27]

The meaning of the term "general power of appointment" is the same for gift tax purposes and estate tax purposes. The rules for determining the date of creation of a power are also the same (see ¶ 652).

¶ 2164 Real Estate Jointly Held by Husband and Wife

The creation between husband and wife of a tenancy by the entirety or joint tenancy with right of survivorship in real property is not a taxable gift if the tenancy is created after 1981. However, in the case of a tenancy created before 1982, the donor spouse could have elected to treat the creation of the tenancy as a gift by filing a timely gift tax return for the period during which the tenancy was created.[28] Also see ¶ 502 for special rules involving the transfer tax treatment of joint tenancies created prior to 1977.

¶ 2165 Transfers Incident to Divorce or Separation

Transfers of property or property interests under a written agreement between spouses settling their marital and property rights are considered to be made for adequate and full consideration and are exempt from the gift tax provided divorce occurs within the three-year period beginning one year before the property settlement is entered into.[29] Thus, the divorce may precede the settlement agreement by as much as one year. The condition applies regardless of whether the divorce decree approves the written settlement agreement of the spouses.

Transfers made under the settlement agreement to provide reasonable allowance for the support of minor children of the marriage will also be exempt from gift tax.

¶ 2166 Life Insurance

Gratuitous transfers of life insurance are generally subject to the same rules as other gifts. An insured who relinquishes rights under an insurance policy in favor of another for less than full and adequate consideration makes a gift. If, however, the insured relinquishes only some rights, there is no gift unless the rights that are retained give the insured no control over the policy or the proceeds thereof.

> ***Example:*** Betty Williams gratuitously transfers a policy of insurance on her life to her daughter, Barbara. In transferring ownership of the policy, Williams relinquishes all of her rights except the right to change the beneficiary under certain circumstances. There is no gift for gift tax purposes.

The mere naming of a person as a beneficiary under a policy of insurance on one's life does not, by itself, constitute a gift for gift tax purposes. An irrevocable naming of the beneficiary does not constitute a gift if the insured reserves the right to surrender the policy for cash or to borrow against its cash surrender value. On the other hand, one may make

---

[27] Code Sec. 2514.

[28] Code Sec. 2515, prior to repeal by P.L. 97-34.

[29] Code Sec. 2516.

a gift for gift tax purposes without disposing of every "incident of ownership" in the policy, with the result that the proceeds will be included in the insured's gross estate (see ¶ 430).

A gift of life insurance is complete when the insured disposes of all control over the policy or its reserves.[30] If the insured retains a possibility of reverter, the gift may be complete even though the value of the possibility exceeds five percent of the value of the policy, which would require the inclusion of the proceeds in the insured's gross estate for estate tax purposes. The value of that possibility of reverter, however, may be excludable from the value of the gift for gift tax purposes.

The payment of premiums on policies of life insurance owned by another constitutes a gift whether the policy is on the life of the donor or on the life of some other person. The value of the gift is the amount of the premiums paid in the calendar year, less any dividends received by the donor as a partial return of premiums. If the premiums are paid on policies under which the donor owns rights, the premiums will not constitute gifts.

Life insurance policies may be given in trust either before or after they are paid for, or at any intermediate stage. If the trust is irrevocable, and if no strings are attached to the transfer of insurance to the trust, there is a gift of the value of the insurance at the time of the transfer. Likewise, any premium payments by the donor after the insurance has been transferred to the trust constitute gifts. If the trustee pays the premiums out of income from other assets held in trust or reinvests some of the other assets in the insurance by selling them to pay the premiums, the payment of premiums does not amount to a gift.

¶ 2167 Annuities

A transferor who irrevocably creates an annuity for the benefit of another makes a gift to the extent that the transfer is not supported by full and adequate consideration in money or money's worth.[31] Therefore, the gratuitous purchase of an annuity contract for another constitutes a gift if the purchaser retains no rights in the contract. Similarly, the creation of an annuity in a trust or other property constitutes a taxable gift. A taxable gift is also made when a person establishes an annuity for his or her own benefit and irrevocably names another to receive certain benefits that may be payable after the annuitant's death.

• *Qualified Employee's Annuity Plans*

Effective for transfers made after October 22, 1986, there is no longer a blanket gift tax exclusion where an employee designates a survivor beneficiary in a qualified employee benefit plan.[32] For transfers made before October 23, 1986, an employee was allowed to designate a survivor beneficiary under a qualified pension plan, stock bonus plan, profit-sharing plan, or individual retirement account or annuity without incurring a gift tax as to any portion of the benefits attributable to contributions regarded as being made by the employer. However, this gift tax exclusion did not

---

[30] Reg. § 25.2511-1(h)(8).

[31] See, for example, Rev. Rul. 69-74, 1969-1 CB 43.

[32] Code Sec. 2517, repealed by P.L. 99-514.

apply to the extent that designated benefits were attributable to contributions made by the employee.

- *Waiver of Survivor Benefits*

The waiver of a joint and survivor benefit or a qualified preretirement survivor benefit or the right to such a benefit by a nonparticipant spouse prior to the death of the participant does not result in the imposition of the gift tax.[33]

¶ 2168 U.S. Savings Bonds

The IRS has issued comprehensive rules for determining whether purchases of U.S. savings bonds are taxable transfers.[34] Bonds that are purchased with an individual's own funds and registered in the purchaser's name, but that are payable to another person on the purchaser's death, are not taxable gifts. A taxable gift is made when the purchaser has the bonds registered in another person's name. Bonds that are purchased with an individual's own funds and registered in the names of the purchaser and another person as co-owners are not taxable gifts at the date of purchase. A taxable gift will result if the other co-owner cashes them. A person who purchases bonds and names two other persons as co-owners makes a gift of one-half of the purchase price to each of the co-owners.

¶ 2170 Donor's Dominion and Control

Before the gift tax may be imposed on any transaction, the gift must be complete. If the intention to make a gift is expressed at one time, but the delivery of the property and acceptance of the gift take place at a later date, the later date governs. It is only at that time that the gift is completed. A promise to make a gift is not a gift. Even the execution of a trust instrument in itself will not constitute a gift. The property subject to such a trust must be transferred without retention of powers by the donor.[35]

A transfer in trust is not complete for gift tax purposes if the trustee is given such broad powers to invade income and corpus for the grantor's benefit that there is no assurance, at the time of the transfer, that anything of value will be paid to any other beneficiary. Such a transfer will not result in a taxable gift even though the value of the trust property is large in amount. Similarly, if creditors of the grantor can reach the trust assets under applicable state law, the transfer in trust is not a taxable gift.[36]

¶ 2171 Cessation of Dominion and Control

A gift is incomplete unless the donor has parted with dominion and control and, thus, is without power to change the disposition of the transferred property—whether for the donor's benefit or for the benefit of another. A gift is incomplete in every instance where a donor reserves the power to reassume the beneficial title to the property. It is also incomplete

---

[33] Code Sec. 2503(f).

[34] Rev. Rul. 68-269, 1968-1 CB 399.

[35] Reg. § 25.2511-2.

[36] *M.M. Outwin*, 76 TC 153, CCH Dec. 37,645 (Acq.).

when a donor reserves the power to name new beneficiaries or to change the interests of the various beneficiaries.[37]

A gift will not be incomplete merely because the donor reserves the power to change the manner or time of enjoyment thereof. Also, it will not be incomplete as to an intermediate vested interest, such as a life estate or an estate for years, merely because it will return to the donor at a later date.

A donor is considered to retain a power if the donor may exercise that power in conjunction with any person not having a substantial adverse interest in the disposition of the transferred property or the income therefrom. A trustee who has no other interest in the trust is not a person having an adverse interest in the disposition of the trust property or its income.

The relinquishment or termination of a power to change the disposition of the transferred property, occurring otherwise than by the death of the donor, is regarded as the event that completes the gift and causes the tax to apply. However, if a donor retains the power to change the amount of the beneficiaries' interests or to designate the beneficiary of the trust corpus, any income that is transferred to the beneficiaries before the donor designates a recipient of the corpus is not a part of the property disposed of by the designation. The income received by the beneficiaries is a taxable gift at the time the gift is completed.[38]

¶ 2175 Transfers by Nonresidents Not Citizens

Blanket exemption from federal gift taxation is provided for all gifts by nonresidents who are not U.S. citizens of intangible property having a situs within the United States, e.g., stocks and bonds.[39]

Transfers by U.S. citizens who are residents of a U.S. possession but who acquired their U.S. citizenship solely by reason of being a citizen of the possession or by reason of birth or residence within the possession will be treated as transfers made by nonresidents who are not citizens of the United States.

¶ 2180 Manner of Reporting Gifts on Return

Gifts that are subject only to the gift tax are reported in Part 1 of Schedule A (Computation of Taxable Gifts) of Form 709 (1998). These gifts include charitable, public and similar gifts. Gifts that are direct skips and are subject to both the gift tax and the generation-skipping transfer tax are reported in chronological order on Part 2 of Schedule A. Gifts to political organizations and for medical and educational purposes are exempt from the gift tax and, thus, do not have to be reported.

If the total gifts of present interests to any donee are more than $10,000 in any calendar year, the donor must enter all such gifts that he made during that year to or on behalf of that donee, including those gifts that will be excluded under the annual exclusion. If the total is $10,000 or less, the donor need not enter on Schedule A any gifts (except gifts of

---

[37] Reg. § 25.2511-2.

[38] Reg. § 25.2511-2(f).

[39] Code Sec. 2501(a)(2).

future interests made to that donee). Gifts of future interests made during a calendar year must be reported on Schedule A regardless of their value.[40]

Where one transfer results in gifts to two individuals (such as a life estate to one person with the remainder to another person), the gift to each individual must be listed separately. Gifts made by a donor to his or her spouse should be reflected on Schedule A only if they are gifts of terminable interests. All terminable interests that pass to the spouse should be reported regardless of whether they qualify for the gift tax marital deduction (see ¶ 2313).

An annual Form 709 need not be filed if the donor's gifts consisted solely of:

(1) transfers of present interests not in excess of the annual gift tax exclusion (see ¶ 2250),

(2) qualified transfers for educational or medical expenses (see ¶ 2250), or

(3) transfers to the donor's spouse that qualify for the unlimited marital deduction (see ¶ 2311).[41]

To report gifts on Schedule A whenever spouses elect to treat gifts to third parties as being made one-half by each of them (see ¶ 2200): [42]

(1) If only one spouse makes gifts for which a return is required, the full value of all gifts made by the spouse filing the return must be included on Schedule A, Part 3. One-half of the full value of all gifts to third-party donees is then deducted on line (2) and no entry is made on line (4) of Schedule A, Part 3.

(2) If only one spouse makes gifts for which a return is required, but the second spouse is considered to have made gifts for which a return is required because he or she consented to gift-splitting, the full value of all gifts made by the donor spouse must be included on the donor spouse's return. One-half of the full value of all gifts to all third-party donees is deducted on line (2) and no entry is made on line (4) of the donor spouse's return. The amount from line (2) of the donor spouse's return is entered on line (4) of the return filed for the consenting spouse, but is excluded from lines (1), (2) and (3) of the return filed for the consenting spouse.

(3) If each spouse makes gifts for which a return is required, the full value of all gifts made by each is included on the separate return filed by each spouse. Each spouse then deducts one-half of the full value of all gifts that he or she has made to all third-party donees on line (2) of the separate return filed for each spouse. The respective amount deducted on line (2) of one return is entered on line (4) of the other return.

In order to facilitate the computations for lines (2) and (8), the gifts should be grouped into the following categories: (1) gifts to spouse, (2) gifts to third parties that are to be split, (3) gifts for charitable uses if gift-splitting is not elected, and (4) all other gifts. In all cases in which it is not

[40] Reg. § 25.6019-1.

[41] Instructions for Form 709 (1998), pp. 1–3.

[42] Instructions for Form 709 (1998), pp. 3–4 and 6–7.

apparent how the amounts entered at lines (2) and (8) were computed, additional sheets of the same size as the return should be attached and the computations set forth thereon in detail. To avoid correspondence from the IRS, where both spouses must file a gift tax return, both returns should be filed together in the same envelope.

¶ 2181 Description of Property on Return

The property comprising the gifts listed in Schedule A (Computation of Taxable Gifts) of Form 709 (reproduced at ¶ 2390) should be described in enough detail to be easily identified. For interests in property based on the duration of a person's life, the date of birth of that person should be included in the description.[43]

● *Real Estate*

A legal description should be given for each parcel of real estate. If the property is located within a city, the name of the street, the street number, and the area of the city should be given. A short statement of any improvements to the realty should also be furnished.

● *Bonds*

A description of bonds transferred should include: (1) the number of bonds transferred, (2) the principal amount, (3) the name of the obligor, (4) the maturity date, (5) the rate of interest, (6) the date or dates when interest is payable, (7) the series number, if there is more than one issue, (8) the exchange upon which the bond is listed, and (9) the CUSIP number, if available (see ¶ 313). If the bond is not listed on an exchange, the address of the principal business office of the corporation should be given.

● *Stocks*

A description of a gift of stock should include: (1) the number of shares transferred; (2) a designation of the shares as common or preferred stock; (3) if a listed security, the principal exchange on which it is sold; and (4) the CUSIP number, if available (see ¶ 313). If the stock is not listed on an exchange, the description should give the location of the corporation's principal business office, the state in which the corporation was incorporated, and the date of incorporation. If the gift is of preferred stock, the description should contain the issue, the par value of the stock, the quotation at which returned, and the exact name of the corporation.

● *Insurance Policies*

A description of life insurance policies should include the name of the insurer and the policy number.

---

[43] Instructions for Form 709 (1998), p. 6.

Chapter 43

GIFT-SPLITTING

¶ 2200 Practical Effect

A gift made by a husband or wife to a third person may be treated as made one-half by each, if both spouses consent.[1] This right is an optional one that is effective only for the calendar year, or quarter for certain prior periods, for which the election is made. If the consent is effective, all gifts by the husband and wife to third persons during that calendar year or quarter must receive the same treatment. By signifying their consent, the donor and his or her spouse become jointly and severally liable for the entire gift tax for that calendar year or quarter. See ¶ 2180 for guidelines concerning the manner of reporting these gifts on Schedule A (Computation of Taxable Gifts) of Form 709.

If a donor and the donor's spouse elect to split gifts of not more than $20,000 per year for each third-party donee, they may file a Form 709-A (United States Short Form Gift Tax Return). The short form is filed annually. A filled-in Form 709-A appears at ¶ 2240.

Although the Code does not limit gift-splitting treatment to separately owned property, such treatment has no significance except in the case of separate property. The purpose of gift-splitting, in fact, is to equalize the effect of the gift tax as between community and separate property.

> ***Example (1):*** On March 5, 1998, Tony Shaeffer made a gift to his son, Roger, of bonds worth $30,000, representing his separate property. Shaeffer and his spouse signed the required consent form. The gift is treated as one of $15,000 by Shaeffer and one of $15,000 by his spouse.

> ***Example (2):*** On February 6, 1998, Patricia Rey made a gift to her grandson, Louis, of stock worth $20,000, representing community property. Whether the consent was filed or not, the gift is one of $10,000 by Rey and one of $10,000 by her husband (see ¶ 2220).

The gift-splitting benefit is not available unless the donor is married at the time of the gift and does not become married to a different person before the close of the calendar year. In addition, each spouse must be a citizen or resident of the United States at the time of the gift. Finally, to qualify for the gift-splitting privilege, the spouse making the gift must not give the other spouse a general power of appointment over the property transferred.

If the spouse of the donor is given a partial interest in the property transferred, the gift-splitting privilege is available only for the value of the

[1] Code Sec. 2513.

property transferred to persons other than the spouse and only to the extent that these persons' interests are ascertainable at the time the gift is reported.

¶ 2205 Gift Tax Returns

When gift-splitting is elected, the donor spouse must file a return if annual gifts to any one donee exceed the amount of the gift tax exclusion. However, the consenting spouse must file a return only if he or she made gifts to any one donee in excess of the gift tax exclusion, including gifts attributable to the consenting spouse under the gift-splitting provisions.[2] The following examples illustrate this rule.

> ***Example (1):*** Gary Alto made gifts valued at $24,000 during 1998 to a third party, and his wife, Vicki, made no gifts during this time. Each spouse is required to file a return for 1998. Gary is required to file a return because the amount of the gift exceeds the amount of the annual exclusion ($10,000) by $14,000. Vicki is required to file because she is considered as having made a gift of $12,000 to the third party, which exceeds the annual gift tax exclusion by $2,000.

> ***Example (2):*** Mimi Bradley made gifts valued at $16,000 during 1998 to a third party, and her husband, John, made no gifts. Only Mimi is required to file a return for 1998 because John is considered as having made a gift of $8,000, which does not exceed the annual gift tax exclusion.

¶ 2210 Exclusions and Exemptions

All exemptions and exclusions that are available to each spouse are applicable to a single gift when gift-splitting is elected, resulting in a doubling of the exemptions and exclusions applicable to the transfer. Gifts of present interests in the amount of $20,000 annually may be made to each donee without incurring a tax, because each spouse may claim a $10,000 exclusion with respect to each donee. Note that the annual exclusion will be indexed for inflation after 1998.

¶ 2215 Consent of Both Spouses

The privilege of dividing a gift between husband-and-wife donors is granted only if both signify their consent to such division. When one spouse consents to have gifts made by the other treated as having been made one-half by each of them, gifts made by the consenting spouse must also be treated as having been made one-half by each spouse.[3]

¶ 2220 Community Property

The gift-splitting privilege does not apply to gifts of community property. Gifts of community property are automatically treated as being one-half from each spouse.[4] There is, consequently, no need to obtain consents with respect to gifts of community property.

---

[2] Reg. § 25.2513-1 and Reg. § 25.6019-2.

[3] Rev. Rul. 146, 1953-2 CB 292.

[4] Instructions for Form 709 (1998), p. 2.

¶ 2225 Time of Consent

Consent to split gifts must be given on or before April 15 of the year following the year in which the gifts were made.[5]

Consent to split-gift treatment may not be given after a deficiency notice with respect to tax in that year has been sent to either spouse.[6] Similarly, spouses may not consent to the election after the donor spouse has filed a gift tax return reporting the gifts and after the due date for the return has passed.[7] A consent, once given, may be revoked before the last day for filing the consent by filing a duplicate written notice with the IRS officer with whom the return was filed.[8]

The executor or administrator of the estate of a deceased spouse may give consent to gift-splitting treatment. The guardian or committee of a legally incompetent person may also give such consent.

¶ 2230 Form of Consent

In order to be effective, the consent to taxation to each spouse of one-half of the gifts must be signified by both husband and wife. The consent should be signified, by the spouse filing the return, by answering "Yes" on line 12, part 1, on the face of Form 709 (Rev. December 1996) (reproduced at ¶ 2390) and, by the other spouse, by executing the "Consent of Spouse" appearing in part 1, line 18, of the same return.

---

[5] Code Sec. 2513(b).

[6] Code Sec. 2513(b).

[7] Rev. Rul. 80-224, 1980-2 CB 281.

[8] Code Sec. 2513(c); Reg. § 25.2513-3.

¶ 2240 Filled-In Form 709-A

Reproduced below is Form 709-A (Rev. December 1996), filled in for gifts made in 1998.

Form **709-A** (Rev. December 1996) Department of the Treasury Internal Revenue Service

United States Short Form Gift Tax Return
(For "Privacy Act" notice, see the Form 1040 instructions)
Calendar year 19 98

OMB No. 1545-0021

1 Donor's first name and middle initial	2 Donor's last name	3 Donor's social security number
George O.	Anderson	201-20-3608
4 Address (number, street, and apartment number)		5 Legal residence (domicile)
4073 Rodney Place		Chicago, IL
6 City, state, and ZIP code		7 Citizenship
Chicago, Il 60618		U.S.A.

8 Did you file any gift tax returns for prior periods? .... ☐ Yes ☒ No

If "Yes," state when and where earlier returns were filed ▶

9 Name of consenting spouse	10 Consenting spouse's social security number
Sandra M. Anderson	330-24-1049

Note: *Do not use this form to report gifts of closely held stock, partnership interests, fractional interests in real estate, or gifts for which the value has been reduced to reflect a valuation discount. Instead, use Form 709.*

List of Gifts

(a) Donee's name and address and description of gift	(b) Donor's adjusted basis of gift	(c) Date of gift	(d) Value at date of gift
(1) 10 shares of Qualico Corporation common stock (traded principally on the New York Stock Exchange) to son: Harold Anderson 1401 N. Baldwin Ave. Chicago, IL 60628	$6,200	6/18/98	$19,000
(2) Cash to daughter: Sharon Anderson 6650 W. Pine Street Chicago, IL 60613	$19,000	6/23/98	$19,000

Consent I consent to have the gifts made by my spouse to third parties during the calendar year considered as made one-half by each of us.

Consenting spouse's signature ▶ *Sandra M Anderson* Date ▶ 4/2/99

Under penalties of perjury, I declare that I have examined this return, and to the best of my knowledge and belief it is true, correct, and complete. Declaration of preparer (other than donor) is based on all information of which preparer has any knowledge.

Donor's signature ▶ *George O Anderson* Date ▶ 4/2/99

Preparer's signature (other than donor's) ▶ ________ Date ▶ ________

Preparer's address (other than donor's) ▶

For Paperwork Reduction Act Notice, see the instructions on the reverse side of this form. Form **709-A** (Rev. 12-96)

Chapter 44
ANNUAL EXCLUSIONS

¶ 2250 Exclusions Available

The first $10,000 ($20,000 where gift-splitting is elected) of gifts of present interests made to any donee during the tax year is excluded in determining the amount of taxable gifts.[1] The annual exclusion is indexed for inflation after 1998. Indexing will be rounded to the next lowest multiple of $1,000. However, the inflation adjustment for 1998 was not enough to increase the annual exclusion above $10,000 for gifts made in 1999.[2] The annual exclusion is not limited in the number of donees for whom it may be taken or for the number of years in which it may be taken. However, it is limited to gifts of present, rather than future, interests (see ¶ 2265). Prior to 1982, the annual exclusion was $3,000.

In the case of gifts in trust, the trust beneficiaries, rather than the trust or trustees, are treated as the donees for the purpose of determining the number of annual exclusions allowable to the donor.

● *Unlimited Educational and Medical Expense Exclusion*

An unlimited gift tax exclusion is available for amounts paid on behalf of a donee directly to an educational organization, provided that such amounts constitute tuition payments.[3] In addition, amounts paid to health care providers for medical services on behalf of a donee qualify for an unlimited exclusion. The exclusions for qualifying educational expenses and medical expenses are available without regard to the relationship between the donor and donee and are available in addition to the annual exclusion. Transfers to educational organizations and for medical expenses do not have to be reported as gifts on Schedule A (Computation of Taxable Gifts) of Form 709.

Qualifying medical expenses, for purposes of the exclusion, are defined by reference to Code Sec. 213(d) (relating to the deductibility of medical and dental expenses for income tax purposes). The exclusion is not available to the extent that the amounts paid are reimbursed by insurance.

● *Contributions to Qualified State Tuition Programs*

Effective for transfers made after August 5, 1997, any contribution to a qualified state tuition program (QSTP) is treated as a completed gift of a present interest from the contributor to the beneficiary at the time of the contribution. Annual contributions are eligible for the gift tax exclusion ($10,000 for an individual, $20,000 for a married couple electing gift-

---

[1] Code Sec. 2503.

[2] Rev. Proc. 98-61 (Section 3.16), IRB 1998-52, 18.

[3] Code Sec. 2503(e).

splitting). However, contributions to a QSTP are not considered qualifying transfers under the rules providing an unlimited annual exclusion with respect to payments for educational and medical expenses.[4]

A contributor making a contribution in excess of the exclusion limit may elect to have the contribution treated as if it were made ratably over five years.[5] A gift tax return must be filed with respect to any contribution in excess of the annual gift tax exclusion limit (¶ 2052).

If a beneficiary's interest is rolled over to another beneficiary or there is a change in beneficiary, no gift tax consequences result, provided that the new beneficiary is assigned to the same generation as the old beneficiary.[6] Although the rollover of a beneficiary's interest to a beneficiary in a lower generation (e.g., parent to child or aunt to niece) will be treated as a taxable gift, the five-year averaging rule may be applied to exempt up to $50,000 ($100,000, if gift-splitting is elected) of the transfer.[7]

● *Completion of Gift; Transfer by Check*

A gift tax annual exclusion is available only in the year that the gift is completed—that is, the year in which the donor effectively parts with dominion and control over the transferred property. Problems may arise when a donor makes a gift by check in one year, but the check is not paid by the donor's bank until the following year. The IRS has taken the position that completion of a gift of a check to a noncharitable donee will relate back to the earlier of the date on which the donor no longer has the power to change the disposition of the check or the date on which the donee deposited, cashed, or presented the check if (1) the drawee bank paid the check when it was first presented, (2) the donor was alive when the bank paid the check, (3) the donor intended to make a gift, (4) delivery was unconditional, and (5) the check was deposited, cashed or presented by the donee in the year in which gift tax treatment is sought.[8]

¶ 2255 Gifts in Prior Years

The annual exclusion is available only for gifts made after 1981. Although the annual exclusion was $3,000 for all years beginning with 1943 and ending with 1981, larger exclusions were allowed for 1942 and earlier years. These exclusions are sometimes important in determining the tax for a current year. Gifts of prior years play a part in determining the tax for the current years because of the cumulative nature of the tax.

¶ 2260 Gifts by Married Persons

When a husband and wife have agreed to treat gifts to third persons made by either of them as being made one-half by each, they double the number of annual exclusions available with respect to their gifts. Each may claim an exclusion for each third-party donee, provided, of course, that the gifts are of present interests (see ¶ 2200 through ¶ 2240).

---

[4] Code Sec. 529(c)(2)(A).

[5] Code Sec. 529(c)(2)(B).

[6] Code Sec. 529(c)(5).

[7] Code Sec. 529(c)(2)(B).

[8] Rev. Rul. 96-56, 1996-2 CB 161, modifying Rev. Rul. 67-396, 1967-2 CB 351; however, see *S. Newman Est.*, 111 TC 81, CCH Dec. 45,056, for situation in which decedent died before checks were presented.

¶ 2265 Future Interests

The annual exclusion is not allowed for gifts of future interests.[9] Denial of the exclusion results from difficulty in determining the number of eventual donees and the values of their respective shares. This difficulty is especially significant where contingent remainders are involved. Rather than attempt to set up many fine-line distinctions, Congress chose to deny the exclusion with respect to all gifts of future interests in property.

"Future interests" refers to the interest taken by the donee. They are interests, whether vested or contingent, "limited to commence in use, possession, or enjoyment at some future date or time."[10] Thus, all gifts of remainder interests, whether vested or contingent, are gifts of future interests. However, a gift in trust of a remainder interest in personal property to a donee who is an income beneficiary of the trust is a gift of a present interest. Such a gift qualifies for the exclusion in those states whose laws provide for the merger of the interests and the termination of the trust.[11]

Gifts of income that commence immediately are gifts of present interests. If, however, the income is to be accumulated and paid over at a later time, the gift of the income is a gift of a future interest. This is so even if, upon some specified contingency, some portion or all of the income may be paid over earlier.[12] The IRS will not allow an exclusion for a gift of property in trust that provides that all income must be paid to a beneficiary, but permits corpus to be invested in non-income-producing property and life insurance.[13] However, a gift to a minor is not a future interest if the property and its income may be expended for the benefit of the minor before the minor attains age 21 and may be distributed to the minor at that time or to the minor's estate if the minor dies before reaching age 21.[14]

The IRS has ruled that transfers by a donor of specified portions of real property equal in value to the annual exclusion constituted gifts of present interests that were eligible for the annual exclusion.[15] According to the IRS, the donees received the present, unrestricted right to the immediate use, possession and enjoyment of an ascertainable interest in the real property.

A partner's gift to the partnership accounts of other partners has been held to qualify for the annual exclusion where the donee partners had the immediate and unrestricted right to possess and enjoy the transferred amounts.[16] Under the Uniform Partnership Act, as adopted in Indiana, each partner was entitled to receive amounts from his or her capital account on demand, since the underlying partnership agreement did not contain a provision to the contrary.

---

[9] Reg. § 25.2503-3.

[10] *A. Pelzer*, SCt, 41-1 USTC ¶ 10,027, 312 US 399; Reg. § 25.2503-3.

[11] Rev. Rul. 78-168, 1978-1 CB 298.

[12] *E.F. Fondren*, SCt, 45-1 USTC ¶ 10,164, 324 US 18.

[13] Rev. Rul. 69-344, 1969-1 CB 225.

[14] Code Sec. 2503(c).

[15] Rev. Rul. 83-180, 1983-2 CB 169.

[16] *J.P. Wooley, Exr.*, DC Ind., 90-1 USTC ¶ 60,013.

● Crummey *Trusts*

A gift of the right to demand a portion of a trust corpus is a gift of a present interest,[17] as long as the donee-beneficiary is aware of the right to make the demand.[18] The Tax Court held that transfers of property to a trust constituted a present interest where the trust beneficiaries (the grantor's grandchildren) had the right to withdraw an amount equal to the annual gift tax exclusion within 15 days of the transfer even though the only other interests the grandchildren had in the trust were contingent remainder interests.[19] In so holding, the Tax Court applied the present-interest test enunciated by the U.S. Court of Appeals for the Ninth Circuit in *D.C. Crummey,*[20] concluding that the grandchildren's withdrawal rights, if exercised, could not be legally resisted by the trustees.

¶ 2270 Gifts for the Benefit of a Minor

A gift of property to a minor in trust may qualify for the annual exclusion if certain statutory requirements are met. No part of a transfer for the benefit of a minor will be considered to be a future interest (which would not qualify for the exclusion) if the transfer meets the conditions specified in Code Sec. 2503(c):

> (1) Both the property and its income may be expended by, or for the benefit of, the minor donee prior to his attaining the age of 21. To the extent the property and income were not so expended, they will pass to the donee at that time.
>
> (2) In the event of the donee's death prior to reaching 21 years of age, the property and income not expended will pass to the donee's estate or to persons appointed by him under the exercise of a general power of appointment.

Persons drafting trust provisions for minor beneficiaries should include both of the above conditions in the trust instrument. The absence of one of the above provisions will cause the loss of annual gift tax exclusions for the trusts, and the courts have not permitted the donors to change the trust provisions in a later year in order to obtain annual exclusions.[21] In addition, the right of the trustees to expend property and income for the benefit of the minor beneficiaries should not be limited to a specific purpose or subject to a substantial restriction.[22] For example, the courts have disallowed annual exclusions where the trustees could expend property or income for a minor beneficiary's medical care only. However, it would appear that a trust could limit categories of expenditure to those allowed guardians under the law of the state where the gift was made.

A gift of an income interest in a trust to a minor may qualify for the annual exclusion even though the gift of the trust corpus does not qualify,

---

[17] Rev. Rul. 80-261, 1980-2 CB 279.

[18] Rev. Rul. 81-7, 1981-1 CB 474.

[19] *M. Cristofani Est.*, 97 TC 74, CCH Dec. 47,491 (Acq.), and *L. Kohlsaat Est.*, 73 TCM 2732, CCH Dec. 53,031(M), TC Memo. 1997-212. But see Technical Advice Memorandum 9628004, 4-1-96, CCH IRS LETTER RULINGS REPORTS and Technical Advice Memorandum 9731004, 4-21-97, CCH IRS LETTER RULINGS REPORTS.

[20] *D.C. Crummey*, CA-9, 68-2 USTC ¶ 12,541, 397 F2d 82.

[21] *S.S. Davis*, 55 TC 416, CCH Dec. 30,455; *A. Van Den Wymelenberg*, CA-7, 68-2 USTC ¶ 12,537, 397 F2d 443, cert. denied; *E.D. Harris*, CA-5, 72-1 USTC ¶ 12,853, 461 F2d 554.

[22] *S.L. Faber*, CA-6, 71-1 USTC ¶ 12,760, 439 F2d 1189; *J.T. Pettus, Jr.*, 54 TC 112, CCH Dec. 29,926.

or even though the minor does not have any interest in the corpus at all.[23] This is true because income interests payable to minor beneficiaries qualify as separate property interests apart from the corpus. An annual gift tax exclusion will be allowed for an income interest if: (1) the income may be used for the beneficiary's benefit during minority; (2) the accumulated income will be distributed to him or her at age 21; and (3) the accumulated income is payable to the beneficiary's estate, or to persons designated in his will, if he dies before reaching age 21.[24] An annual exclusion for the income interest may be lost where the trustee has power to allocate income and expenses between corpus and income.

> ***Example:*** Ron Kovak created a trust for his granddaughter, Cindy, who was to receive the income until she reached the age of 30, when she would receive the entire trust principal. The trustee was given discretion to use the principal for the benefit of the beneficiary and to accumulate income not used. The accumulated income was to be paid to Cindy when she reached majority or to her estate in the event of her death before that time. The gift property is separable into its several interests. In light of this division, the gift of a right to income until age 21 qualifies for the annual exclusion. The gifts of principal and income payable after majority to age 30 do not qualify.

The annual exclusion is available where a minor beneficiary has, upon reaching age 21, either (1) a continuing right to compel immediate distribution of the trust corpus by giving written notice to the trustee, or to permit the trust to continue by its own terms, or (2) a right during a limited period to compel immediate distribution of the trust corpus by giving written notice to the trustee—a right which, if not exercised, will permit the trust to continue by its own terms.[25]

¶ 2272 Uniform Transfers to Minors Act: Custodianship

A transfer of property for the benefit of a minor pursuant to the Uniform Transfers to Minors Act or one of its predecessors, the Uniform Gifts to Minors Act or the Model Gifts of Securities to Minors Act, is considered to be a complete gift of the full fair market value of the property. No taxable gift occurs by reason of a subsequent resignation of the custodian or termination of the custodianship for federal gift tax purposes. Such a gift also qualifies for the annual gift tax exclusion.

The value of the property transferred under the "Uniform" or the "Model" Act may be includible in the gross estate of the donor (with a credit against estate tax for prior gift taxes paid) if the donor appoints himself as custodian of the property and dies while serving in that capacity before the minor donee attains majority. The income from such property, to the extent it is used for the support of the minor donee, is includible in the gross income of any person who is legally obligated to support the minor donee.[26]

---

[23] *A.I. Herr*, 35 TC 732, CCH Dec. 24,652 (Acq.), aff'd by CA-3, 62-2 USTC ¶ 12,079, 303 F2d 780; Rev. Rul. 68-670, 1968-2 CB 413.

[24] Many states have lowered the age at which custodian property must be distributed to the minor from 21 to 18 years. The IRS has ruled that the annual exclusion still will be available in those states that have lowered the distribution age from 21 to 18 (Rev. Rul. 73-287, 1973-2 CB 321).

[25] Rev. Rul. 74-43, 1974-1 CB 285, revoking Rev. Rul. 60-218, 1960-1 CB 378.

[26] Rev. Rul. 59-357, 1959-2 CB 212.

¶ 2275 Present Interest with Possibility of Reduction

If a donor makes a gift of a present interest in property, the possibility that the interest may be diminished by an exercise of a power is disregarded in determining whether the interest qualifies for the annual exclusion if no part of the interest will at any time pass to any other person.[27]

¶ 2280 Reporting Exclusions on Gift Tax Return

After reporting all gifts by the donor on the gift tax return form, subtracting the portion, if any, reported by the donor's spouse on a separate return, and adding the portion of the spouse's gifts being taxed to donor, the annual exclusions are subtracted from the resulting "Total gifts," resulting in the "Total included amount of gifts" (lines 5, 6 and 7, Part 3 of Schedule A of Form 709 (1998)) (see ¶ 2390).

[27] Reg. § 25.2503-3(b).

Chapter 45

DEDUCTIONS AND EXEMPTIONS

¶ 2300 Reductions to Taxable Amount

In addition to the annual exclusion (see ¶ 2250) available to a donor for gifts of present interests made to each donee, the gift tax law provides for various deductions. Their total serves to reduce the "Total included amount of gifts" (line 7, Part 3 of Schedule A of Form 709 (1998)) to the ultimate amount of taxable gifts for the calendar quarter upon which the tax is to be paid. Allowable deductions include the deduction for charitable, public and similar gifts and the marital deduction.

For gifts made prior to 1977, a specific exemption of $30,000 was allowed, in addition to the above-noted reductions.

¶ 2305 Charitable, Public and Religious Transfers

Various gifts for charitable, public and religious purposes are deductible in determining net gifts subject to tax. Specifically, there may be deducted the value of gifts to or for the use of the following:

(1) The United States, any state, territory, or any political subdivision thereof, or the District of Columbia, for exclusively public purposes.

(2) Any corporation, trust, community chest, fund, or foundation, organized and operated exclusively for religious, charitable, scientific, literary, or educational purposes, including the encouragement of art and the prevention of cruelty to children or animals. No part of the net earnings of such organization may inure to the benefit of any private shareholder or individual. Furthermore, the organization may not attempt to influence legislation or participate in, or intervene in (including the publishing or distributing of statements), any political campaign on behalf of (or in opposition to) any candidate for public office.

(3) A fraternal society, order, or association, operating under the lodge system, provided such gifts are to be used by such fraternal society, order, or association exclusively for one or more of the purposes enumerated in (2), above.

(4) Any organization of war veterans or auxiliary unit or society thereof if such organization, auxiliary unit, or society thereof is

organized in the United States or any of its possessions. No part of its net earnings may inure to the benefit of any private shareholder or individual.[1]

The charitable deduction is not limited to gifts for use within the United States, or to gifts to or for the use of domestic corporations, trusts, community chests, funds, or foundations, or fraternal societies, orders, or associations operating under the lodge system. The exercise or release of a power of appointment that results in the passing of the property subject to the power to or for the use of any of the organizations listed above is a transfer by gift for purposes of the deduction.

Contributions to a political party or to a candidate for public office do not constitute a gift "to or for the use of the United States, any State, Territory, or any political subdivision thereof" for "exclusively public purposes" and, therefore, do not qualify as deductible charitable contributions. Contributions to political organizations are not subject to the gift tax.[2]

● *Disallowance of Deduction in Certain Cases*

Charitable deductions (both estate and gift tax) will be denied for otherwise deductible bequests and gifts to an organization upon which the Code Sec. 507 private foundation termination tax has been imposed. General contributors will be denied deductions after the organization is notified of the loss of its private foundation status.[3] Substantial contributors (generally, persons contributing more than $5,000 and whose contributions exceed two percent of the fund's year-end total) will be denied deductions in the year when the IRS takes action to terminate the private foundation status of an organization. Deductions are also denied for bequests and gifts to any private foundation or split-interest trust if such an entity or organization fails to meet these requirements.

The governing instrument of a private foundation must require the organization to distribute income currently and prohibit it from engaging in self-dealing, from retaining any excess business holdings, from making any speculative investments and from making taxable expenditures to government officials (for propaganda purposes or to influence legislation). Violations of these requirements by a donor and the entity may also cause the disallowance of deductions.[4]

● *Partial Interests in Property*

The allowance of gift tax deductions for split-interest gifts (where there are charitable and noncharitable donees) is limited to remainder interests in annuity trusts and unitrusts, to remainder interests in pooled income funds, to other interests that are payable in the form of a guaranteed annuity or a fixed percentage of the fair market value of the property distributed yearly, to remainder interests in nontrust transfers of residences and farms, and to nontrust transfers of an undivided portion of a donor's entire interest in property.

If the donor gives his entire interest to recognized charities, even though the interest is split among different charities, the gifts are not

---

[1] Reg. § 25.2522(a)-1.

[2] Code Sec. 2501(a)(5).

[3] Reg. § 25.2522(c)-2(a).

[4] Code Sec. 508(e).

subject to the above rules and a charitable deduction may be claimed for the entire value of the property transferred[5] (see ¶ 1120 for further details).

Whether a transfer to a pooled income fund (Code Sec. 642(c)(5)) or to an inter vivos charitable remainder trust (Code Sec. 664) qualifies for a charitable deduction under Code Sec. 2522(c)(2)(A) are questions upon which the IRS ordinarily will not issue an advance ruling or determination.[6]

● *Nonresidents Not Citizens*

If the donor is a nonresident who is not a U.S. citizen, the basic rules for determining whether or not a transfer qualifies for the charitable deduction are the same as those for citizens or residents.[7] In addition, the following requirements apply:

(1) If the gift is to or for the use of a corporation, such corporation must be one that is created or organized under the laws of the United States or of any State or Territory thereof.

(2) If the gift is made to or for the use of a trust, or community chest, fund, or foundation, or a fraternal society, order, or association, operating within the lodge system, the gift must be for use within the United States exclusively for religious, charitable, scientific, literary, or educational purposes, including the encouragement of art and the prevention of cruelty to children or animals.

The above requirements are, of course, subject to any special arrangements that may be made with the country of which such a donor is a citizen or resident.

● *Claiming Deduction on Gift Tax Return*

The values of all charitable, public and religious gifts listed in Schedule A (Computation of Taxable Gifts) of Form 709 (1998) should be totaled and then reduced by the total exclusions claimed on Schedule A with respect to the gifts. The difference should then be entered on Part 3, line 11 (see ¶ 2390).

● *Income Tax Deductions: Alternative Minimum Tax*

Prior to the Revenue Reconciliation Act of 1993 (P.L. 103-66), the contribution of appreciated property to charity could trigger alternative minimum tax (AMT) liability for the donor. However, the difference between the fair market value of donated appreciated property and the adjusted basis of such property is no longer treated as a tax preference item.[8] If a donor makes a gift of property to charity and use of the donated property is related to that charity's tax-exempt purpose, the donor may now claim a deduction, for both regular income tax and AMT purposes, in the amount of the property's fair market value. Deductions for charitable contributions are still subject to percentage limitations and restrictions apply with regard to contributions of inventory or other ordinary income property, short-term capital gain property and certain gifts to private foundations.

---

[5] Code Sec. 2522(c); Reg. § 25.2522(c)-3(c).

[6] Rev. Proc. 99-3, IRB 1999-1, 103.

[7] Code Sec. 2522(b); Reg. § 25.2522(b)-1.

[8] Code Sec. 57.

¶ 2311 Unlimited Marital Deduction

The monetary ceiling on the gift tax marital deduction was eliminated for gifts made after 1981.[9] Thus, unlimited amounts of property, except for certain terminable interests (see ¶ 2318), may be transferred between spouses free of gift taxes. In accord with this unlimited deduction, the limitations on the marital deduction with respect to community property (see ¶ 2322) that applied to gifts made before 1982 have also been repealed.

● *Alien Spouses*

The first $100,000 ($101,000 for gifts in 1999) of gifts per year to an alien spouse will not be taxed. To the extent that gifts are made in excess of this amount, no marital deduction will apply to reduce the gift tax.[10] However, the annual exclusion for transfers by gift to a noncitizen spouse is allowed only for transfers that would qualify for the marital deduction if the donee were a U.S. citizen. For example, a gift in trust would not qualify for the annual exclusion unless it fell within one of the exceptions to the terminable interest rule.

Effective for gifts made on or after July 14, 1988, it is no longer required that the donor spouse be a U.S. citizen or a resident in order for a gift to qualify for the marital deduction if the surviving spouse is a U.S. citizen. However, this does not change the rule stipulating that the gift tax marital deduction will apply only if the donee spouse is a U.S. citizen.[11] For further discussion of the availability of the marital deduction for property passing to non-U.S. citizen spouses, see ¶ 1000 and ¶ 1004.

¶ 2313 Qualified Terminable Interests

Generally, transfers of terminable interests (such as life estates, terms for years, annuities, etc.) do not qualify for the marital deduction (see ¶ 2318). However, there is a major exception to the terminable interest rule for "qualified terminable interest property" (QTIP).[12] This type of property is also eligible for the estate tax marital deduction. The definition of such property is discussed at ¶ 1001. Briefly, under these rules, a life interest granted to a spouse will not be treated as a terminable interest and the entire value of property in which the spouse is granted the interest will qualify for the marital deduction.

If a spouse disposes of all or part of a qualifying interest for life in QTIP property for which a marital deduction was allowed, that spouse is deemed to have made a transfer of all interest in the property, other than the qualifying income interest, that is subject to the gift tax.[13] (The gift of the income interest itself is governed by the rules applicable to a gift of income interests.) The amount of the gift is the entire value of the property, less any amounts received upon disposition.

In addition, the spouse making such a transfer may recover the gift tax, including penalties and interest, on the remainder interest from the recipients of the property.[14] If the property is not transferred during the

---

[9] Code Sec. 2523(a).

[10] Code Sec. 2523(i) and Rev. Proc. 98-61 (Section 3.16), IRB 1998-52, 18.

[11] Reg. § 25.2523(i)-1.

[12] Code Sec. 2523(f).

[13] Code Sec. 2519.

[14] Code Sec. 2207A(b).

spouse's lifetime, the entire value of the QTIP property is included in the donee's gross estate upon his or her death.

Further, it should be noted that, generally, the transfer to a spouse of an interest in a joint and survivor annuity in which only the spouses have the right to receive payments prior to the death of the surviving spouse qualifies for the marital deduction. However, such a transfer does not qualify for a gift tax marital deduction if either the donor or the executor irrevocably elects out of QTIP treatment.[15] The donee's subsequent transfer of an interest in the annuity is treated as a transfer of all interest in the annuity other than the donor's interest. If the donee dies before the donor, no amount with respect to the annuity is includible in the estate of the donee.

¶ 2314 Split Gifts to Spouse and Charity

A special rule is provided for transfers of interests in the same property made after 1981 to a spouse and a qualifying charitable organization. If an individual creates a qualified charitable remainder annuity or unitrust and if the donor and his or her spouse are the only noncharitable beneficiaries, the prohibition on deduction of terminable interests (see ¶ 2318) does not apply. The individual receives a charitable deduction for the value of the remainder interest and a marital deduction for the value of the annuity or unitrust income interest, and no transfer tax is imposed.[16]

If the individual transfers a qualified income interest (see ¶ 1001 and ¶ 2313) to a spouse with a remainder to charity, the entire value of the property will be considered as passing to the spouse and will qualify for a marital deduction.

¶ 2316 Pre-1982 Gift Tax Marital Deduction

For gifts made after 1976 and before 1982, a marital deduction was allowed for the first $100,000 of lifetime gifts to the donor's spouse.[17] The next $100,000 of lifetime gifts was fully taxable (that is, gifts ranging from $100,000 to $200,000). A 50-percent deduction applied to lifetime gifts to a spouse in excess of $200,000. The $100,000 lifetime marital deduction was in addition to the $3,000 annual exclusion. Thus, an annual gift of $3,000 to the donor's spouse did not count for purposes of the $100,000 lifetime exclusion for transfers between spouses.

For gifts made prior to 1977, the gift tax marital deduction was limited to 50 percent of the value of the property transferred to the spouse.

¶ 2317 Income to One Other Than Spouse

A gift of a vested remainder interest in property to a donor's spouse qualifies for the marital deduction.[18] It qualifies even though the income from the property is made payable to the donor or a third person. The two interests in the one property are separate and distinct.

---

[15] Code Sec. 2523(f)(6).

[16] Code Sec. 2523(g).

[17] Code Sec. 2523(a), prior to amendment by P.L. 97-34.

[18] Rev. Rul. 54-470, 1954-2 CB 320.

¶2318 Life Estate or Other Terminable Interest

Except as discussed at ¶2313 for certain interests transferred after 1981, the gift tax marital deduction is not allowed for transfers of "terminable interests." [19] If the transfer is of an interest that will terminate or fail upon lapse of time or the occurrence of an event or contingency, or upon the failure of an event or contingency to occur, a deduction is not allowed if (a) the reversionary or remainder interest is in the donor or any transferee, other than the spouse, who has acquired the interest for less than an adequate and full consideration in money or money's worth, or (b) the donor or transferee may thereby possess or enjoy any part of the property after such termination or failure of the interest transferred to the spouse.[20]

An exercise or release at any time by the donor (either alone or in conjuction with any person) of a power to appoint an interest in property is deemed to be a transfer by the donor. If the exercise or release is made in favor of a person other than the donor's spouse, a marital deduction will not be allowed.

¶2319 Interest in Unidentified Assets

The marital deduction is reduced by the value of assets transferred in trust from which a marital gift may be satisfied and for which a marital deduction would not be allowed if they were transferred by gift to the donor's spouse.[21] This provision has particular application to gifts in trust under which the donor's spouse has the remainder interest or the trust income and a power to appoint to himself or his estate.

> ***Example:*** David Strom gave his wife, Shirley, an interest valued at $500,000 in a group of assets, most of which qualify for the marital deduction, but one of which does not. The item that does not qualify (an interest in the residual value of an estate) is worth $100,000. For purposes of computing the marital deduction, the value of the interest passing to Shirley Strom is reduced by $100,000.

¶2320 Joint Ownership

Gifts by the donor to his or her spouse as joint tenant with the donor or as tenant by the entirety are exempt from the terminable interest provisions (see ¶2318) and will qualify for the marital deduction.[22] The possibility of the reacquisition of the property through survivorship or severance of the tenancy will not defeat the deduction.

¶2321 Power of Appointment

Life estates accompanied by certain powers of appointment are also exempt from terminable interest status.[23] If the donee spouse receives a power of appointment over property held in trust or otherwise, in addition to other interests in the transferred property, a deduction may be allowable. The donee spouse must be able to exercise the power in favor of

---

[19] Code Sec. 2523(b).

[20] Code Sec. 2523(b).

[21] Code Sec. 2523(c).

[22] Code Sec. 2523(d).

[23] Code Sec. 2523(e).

himself or his estate in all events. No one else may have the power to appoint any portion of the interest to anyone other than a donee spouse.

It is not essential that the life estate or the power exist with respect to the entire property involved. It is necessary only that the income be from all or a specific portion of the property transferred and that the power be coextensive with the deductible amount. When the income and power relate only to a portion of the transferred property, only that portion qualifies for the deduction. These requirements are substantially the same as the estate tax requirements.

¶ 2322 Gifts of Community Property

A gift of a donor's interest in community property qualifies for the marital deduction in the case of gifts made after 1981. For gifts made before 1982, no marital deduction was allowable for gifts of such interests or of interests in certain separate property that was considered to be community property for marital deduction purposes.[24]

¶ 2323 Limits on Deductions

The gift tax charitable and marital deductions are allowable only to the extent that the gifts with respect to which those deductions are authorized are included in the total amount of gifts made during the calendar year.[25] This means that both deductions are determined after the annual exclusion is deducted.

> ***Example:*** In 1998, Lisa Lake makes a cash gift of $17,000 to charity. The entire $17,000 would qualify for the charitable deduction. However, the annual exclusion of $10,000 is deducted first, and, therefore, only $7,000 is included in the total amount of gifts. Lake is entitled to a charitable deduction of $7,000.

¶ 2330 Specific Exemption for Pre-1977 Gifts

In determining the amount of taxable gifts made before 1977 for the calendar quarter, donors who were U.S. citizens or residents at the time the gifts were made were entitled to a specific exemption of $30,000. This amount was reduced by the sum of the amounts claimed and allowed as an exemption in prior calendar years and quarters.[26]

The donor had the option of taking the exemption in its entirety in a single calendar quarter or spreading it over a period of calendar quarters in such amounts as he saw fit. However, after the limit had been reached, no further exemption was allowable.

¶ 2331 Reporting Deductions on Gift Tax Return

The marital and charitable deductions that are allowed to a donor are subtracted from "Total included amount of gifts" (lines 7 through 13 on Part 3, Schedule A (Computation of Taxable Gifts) of Form 709 (1998)) (see ¶ 2390).

---

[24] Code Sec. 2523(f), prior to repeal by P.L. 97-34.

[25] Code Sec. 2524.

[26] Code Sec. 2521, prior to repeal by P.L. 94-455.

Chapter 46

COMPUTATION

¶ 2350 Cumulative Effect of Tax

The gift tax is cumulative in nature. As a result, prior years' and quarters' gifts push the current year's gifts into higher tax brackets.

The gift tax for each year (quarter for pre-1982 gifts) is determined by computing a tax on the taxable gifts made in that year or quarter plus taxable gifts made in all prior years beginning with June 6, 1932, and in all prior quarters beginning with the first quarter of calendar year 1971. In computing the tax on gifts made after 1981, gifts made in all years after 1981 and before the year for which the tax is being computed are also added. There is then subtracted from the resulting figure a tax computed only on the taxable gifts made in prior calendar periods (years and quarters). The unified transfer tax rate schedules (see ¶ 2600) are used in both of these computations for gifts made after 1976. The difference between the two amounts, as computed above, is the amount of gift tax payable for the year or quarter less the unified credit (see ¶ 2007) to the extent it has not been used in preceding calendar periods. For an example of the method of computing the gift tax and estate tax and of using the unified credit, see ¶ 1428.

Taxable gifts made after 1981 are reported on an annual return that is due April 15 of the year following the year of the gift.

Because of the method used to compute gift taxes for a given year, it is necessary on the gift tax return not only to determine the amount of taxable gifts for the year covered by the return but also to report the amount of taxable gifts determined for all prior calendar periods, beginning with 1932.

¶ 2355 Gifts for Prior Periods

Before the gift tax for a particular calendar year may actually be computed, it is necessary to take into account the taxable gifts made in prior calendar quarters and years. These gifts for prior quarters and years are presently recorded on Schedule B (Gifts From Prior Periods) of Form 709 (see ¶ 2390).

The donor's name as used in each return filed for preceding quarters and years should be shown on the current Schedule B if there has been a change in name on the current return or any prior return. Any variation in name (e.g., the use of the full given name instead of initials used previously) should be noted.

The amount of the specific exemption claimed for periods prior to 1977 must be entered in column D of Schedule B. The amount of unified credit claimed in prior quarters is entered in column C.

If a tax has been assessed and paid with respect to prior taxable gifts reported on a gift tax return, the IRS may not increase the valuation of such prior gifts once the statutory period of limitation for assessing a deficiency on the gifts has expired.[1] Although the Tax Court has held that this rule does not apply when computing the amount of adjusted taxable gifts for estate tax purposes for gifts made after August 15, 1997, the IRS is not permitted to revalue a gift for estate tax purposes if the three-year statute of limitations has expired on an adequately disclosed gift[2] (see ¶ 1426).

¶ 2375 Unified Rate Schedule for Computing Gift Tax

The amount of gift tax payable on post-1976 gifts (for any calendar quarter or year) is determined by applying the unified rate schedule to the cumulative lifetime taxable transfers and then subtracting the taxes payable on the lifetime transfers made for past tax periods (including pre-1977 taxable gifts). In computing the tax payable, the subtraction for taxes previously paid is based upon the unified rate schedule.

The unified transfer tax rate schedule, which applies for both estate and gift tax purposes, is reproduced at ¶ 1430.

¶ 2376 Unified Gift Tax Credit

For post-1976 gifts made during the donor's lifetime and at-death transfers, a single unified credit is subtracted after the determination of the taxpayer's gift or estate tax liability (see ¶ 1430 and ¶ 2375, above). The use of the unified credit against the tentative gift tax is mandatory.[3] In the case of gift taxes, the unified credit replaced the pre-1977 $30,000 specific exemption. A chart indicating the applicable credit and "exemption equivalent" for 1977 and later years is reproduced below. For 1987 through 1997, the credit is $192,800.

Unified Credits and "Exemption Equivalents"

Year	*Unified Credit*	*Exemption Equivalent*
Jan. 1, 1977–June 30, 1977	$ 6,000	
July 1, 1977–Dec. 31, 1977	30,000	$120,666
1978	34,000	134,000
1979	38,000	147,333
1980	42,500	161,563
1981	47,000	175,225
1982	62,800	225,000
1983	79,300	275,000
1984	96,300	325,000
1985	121,800	400,000
1986	155,800	500,000
1987–1997	192,800	600,000

[1] Code Sec. 2504(c).

[2] *F.R. Smith Est.*, 94 TC 872, CCH Dec. 46,648 (Acq.); Code Sec. 2001(f) and Code Sec. 2504(c).

[3] Rev. Rul. 79-398, 1979-2 CB 338.

Beginning in 1998, the unified credit is determined by reference to the "applicable credit amount" and "the applicable exclusion amount" (formerly the exemption equivalent). The unified credit increase enacted in the Taxpayer Relief Act of 1997 (P.L. 105-34) is phased in as follows:

Year	*Applicable Credit Amount*	*Applicable Exclusion Amount*
1998	$202,050	$ 625,000
1999	211,300	650,000
2000 and 2001	220,550	675,000
2002 and 2003	229,800	700,000
2004	287,300	850,000
2005	326,300	950,000
2006	345,800	1,000,000

A special adjustment (transitional) rule applied with respect to gifts made during the period September 9, 1976, through December 31, 1976. To the extent that use was made of the $30,000 lifetime exemption during this period, the allowable unified gift tax credit is reduced by an amount equal to 20 percent of the exemption. Thus, if the full $30,000 exemption was used during this period, a maximum reduction of $6,000 would be made to the unified credit.

However, the amount of the credit allowed may not exceed the amount of the gift tax imposed on the donor for the particular calendar quarter or year. In addition, the amount of the credit that is available for gifts made in one of the above years must be reduced by the sum of the amounts allowable as a credit to the donor for all preceding calendar quarters or years.

Example: Dawn Turner made taxable gifts in the years 1978, 1979, 1981 and 1982. Her tentative gift tax liabilities on these gifts amounted to $10,000 in 1978, $30,000 in 1979, $10,000 in 1981, and $20,000 in 1982. Turner's gift tax credit in 1978 would amount to $10,000—the amount of her gift tax liability.

In 1979, Turner could claim a gift tax credit of $28,000 ($38,000 credit for 1979 less $10,000 credit claimed in 1978). In 1981, Turner could take a gift tax credit of $9,000 ($47,000 credit for 1981 less credits claimed in 1978 and 1979 of $38,000). In 1982, Turner could claim a credit of $15,800 ($62,800 credit for gifts made in 1982 less credits claimed in the years 1978-1979 and 1981 of $47,000). If Turner were to make a gift after 1986 and before 1998, she would have already used $62,800 of the $192,800 credit available for gifts made in 1987 or after. Therefore, $130,000 would be available to offset any gift tax liability after 1986. For 1998 gifts, $139,250 of the credit would be available ($202,050 applicable credit amount less $62,800). For 1999 gifts, $148,500 of the credit would be available ($211,300 applicable credit amount less $62,800).

The IRS has ruled that an adjustment could be made to increase the aggregate sum of a donor's taxable gifts, thereby increasing the rate of tax applicable to a gift made in 1982, even though no gift tax could be assessed for an undervalued 1977 gift of stock because the period of limitations on assessment had expired.[4] According to the IRS, the donor's use of the unified credit to eliminate tax liability on the 1977 gift did not result in a payment or assessment of gift tax that would preclude an adjustment to the value of the gift for purposes of the unified credit. Similarly, see ¶ 1426 regarding revaluation of prior gifts for estate tax purposes where the period of limitations has expired.

A husband and wife may each claim separate unified gift tax credits in the amounts specified above for gifts made by each of them, even though these gifts may have resulted from the gift-splitting provisions of Code Sec. 2513 (see ¶ 2013). Thus, married couples may give away substantial amounts to their children or other donees without incurring any gift tax liability.

¶ 2378 Benefits of Graduated Rates and Unified Credit Phased Out

The benefits of the graduated rates and the unified credit under the unified transfer tax system are phased out beginning with cumulative transfers rising above $10,000,000. This is accomplished by adding five percent of the excess of any transfer over $10,000,000 to the tentative tax computed in determining the ultimate transfer tax liability. For estates of decedents dying and gifts made after 1987 and before 1998, the tax is levied on amounts transferred in excess of $10,000,000 but not exceeding $21,040,000, in order to recapture the benefit of any transfer tax rate below 55 percent as well as the unified credit.

Due to mistakes in the wording of the amendment to Code Sec. 2001(c)(2) by the Taxpayer Relief Act of 1997 (P.L. 105-34,) the five-percent additional tax phases out the benefits of graduated rates, but not the benefits of the unified credit (applicable credit amount), for estates of decedents dying, and gifts made, after 1997. Therefore, the additional tax is levied on amounts transferred after 1997 in excess of $10,000,000 but not exceeding $17,184,000. The applicable credit amount is not recaptured.

Although the provision of the Revenue Act of 1987 (P.L. 100-203) that added the phaseout rules is effective with respect to transfers made after 1987, the Conference Committee Report to that Act states that pre-effective-date gifts are included in cumulative transfers for purposes of determining the adjustment for transfers made after the effective date; however, the tax rate on the earlier gifts remains unchanged. Thus, according to the Report, if a person makes a $9 million gift before 1988, and an additional $4 million gift after 1987, $3 million of the latter transfer will be subject to the additional tax under the phaseout.

¶ 2380 Generation-Skipping Transfers

Generation-skipping transfers made during a calendar year are subject to the normal gift tax and to the generation-skipping transfer tax. The gift tax on such transfers is computed in the usual manner as described at ¶ 2350 through ¶ 2376, above.

However, the generation-skipping transfer tax is computed separately from the gift tax and, if applicable, represents an additional tax that must

[4] Rev. Rul. 84-11, 1984-1 CB 201.

be paid on Form 709. The generation-skipping transfer tax is computed on Schedule C (Computation of Generation-Skipping Transfer Tax) of Form 709.

¶ 2382 Gift Tax Treaties

Gift tax treaties are in force between the United States and Australia, Austria, Denmark, France, Germany, Japan, Sweden and the United Kingdom. For specific information, the applicable treaty should be consulted.

¶ 2390 Filled-In Form 709

Reproduced below is 1998 Form 709, United States Gift (and Generation-Skipping Transfer) Tax Return, filled in with respect to the hypothetical donor Robert A. Simon for the calendar year 1998.

Form **709** — Department of the Treasury, Internal Revenue Service

United States Gift (and Generation-Skipping Transfer) Tax Return

(Section 6019 of the Internal Revenue Code) (For gifts made after December 31, 1997)

▶ See separate instructions. For Privacy Act Notice, see the Instructions for Form 1040.

OMB No. 1545-0020 — **1998**

Part 1 — General Information

1 Donor's first name and middle initial	2 Donor's last name	3 Donor's social security number
Robert A.	Simon	362-54-7878
4 Address (number, street, and apartment number)		5 Legal residence (domicile) (county and state)
4700 N. Michigan		Cook County IL
6 City, state, and ZIP code		7 Citizenship
Chicago IL 60606		U.S.A.

		Yes	No
8	If the donor died during the year, check here ▶ ☐ and enter date of death ______ , ____ .		
9	If you received an extension of time to file this Form 709, check here ▶ ☐ and attach the Form 4868, 2688, 2350, or extension letter		
10	Enter the total number of separate donees listed on Schedule A — count each person only once. ▶		
11a	Have you (the donor) previously filed a Form 709 (or 709-A) for any other year? If the answer is "No," do not complete line 11b	x	
11b	If the answer to line 11a is "Yes," has your address changed since you last filed Form 709 (or 709-A)?		x
12	Gifts by husband or wife to third parties. — Do you consent to have the gifts (including generation-skipping transfers) made by you and by your spouse to third parties during the calendar year considered as made one-half by each of you? (See instructions.) (If the answer is "Yes," the following information must be furnished and your spouse must sign the consent shown below. **If the answer is "No," skip lines 13 - 18 and go to Schedule A.**)		x
13	Name of consenting spouse — 14 SSN		
15	Were you married to one another during the entire calendar year? (see instructions)		
16	If the answer to 15 is "No," check whether ☐ married ☐ divorced or ☐ widowed, and give date (see instructions) ▶		
17	Will a gift tax return for this calendar year be filed by your spouse?		
18	**Consent of Spouse** — I consent to have the gifts (and generation-skipping transfers) made by me and by my spouse to third parties during the calendar year considered as made one-half by each of us. We are both aware of the joint and several liability for tax created by the execution of this consent.		

Consenting spouse's signature ▶ Date ▶

Part 2 — Tax Computation

		Line	Amount
1	Enter the amount from Schedule A, Part 3, line 15	1	3,050,000
2	Enter the amount from Schedule B, line 3	2	500,000
3	Total taxable gifts (add lines 1 and 2)	3	3,550,000
4	Tax computed on amount on line 3 (see Table for Computing Tax in separate instructions)	4	1,593,300
5	Tax computed on amount on line 2 (see Table for Computing Tax in separate instructions)	5	155,800
6	Balance (subtract line 5 from line 4)	6	1,437,500
7	Maximum unified credit (nonresident aliens, see instructions)	7	202,050.00
8	Enter the unified credit against tax allowable for all prior periods (from Sch. B, line 1, col. C)	8	155,800
9	Balance (subtract line 8 from line 7)	9	46,250
10	Enter 20% (.20) of the amount allowed as a specific exemption for gifts made after September 8, 1976, and before January 1, 1977 (see instructions)	10	0
11	Balance (subtract line 10 from line 9)	11	46,250
12	Unified credit (enter the smaller of line 6 or line 11)	12	46,250
13	Credit for foreign gift taxes (see instructions)	13	0
14	Total credits (add lines 12 and 13)	14	46,250
15	Balance (subtract line 14 from line 6) (do not enter less than zero)	15	1,391,250
16	Generation-skipping transfer taxes (from Schedule C, Part 3, col. H, Total)	16	550,000
17	Total tax (add lines 15 and 16)	17	1,941,250
18	Gift and generation-skipping transfer taxes prepaid with extension of time to file	18	0
19	If line 18 is less than line 17, enter BALANCE DUE (see instructions)	19	1,941,250
20	If line 18 is greater than line 17, enter AMOUNT TO BE REFUNDED	20	0

Attach check or money order here.

Under penalties of perjury, I declare that I have examined this return, including any accompanying schedules and statements, and to the best of my knowledge and belief it is true, correct, and complete. Declaration of preparer (other than donor) is based on all information of which preparer has any knowledge.

Donor's signature ▶ Robert A. Simon — Date ▶ 4-15-99

Preparer's signature (other than donor) ▶ — Date ▶

Preparer's address (other than donor) ▶

For Paperwork Reduction Act Notice, see page 8 of the separate instructions for this form. — Form 709 (1998)

Form 709 (1998) Page 2

SCHEDULE A Computation of Taxable Gifts

A Does the value of any item listed on Schedule A reflect any valuation discount? If the answer is "Yes," see instructions .... Yes ☐ No ☒

B ☐ ◄ Check here if you elect under section 529(c)(2)(B) to treat any transfers made this year to a qualified state tuition program as made ratably over a 5-year period beginning this year. See instructions. Attach explanation.

Part 1 — Gifts Subject Only to Gift Tax. *Gifts less political organization, medical, and educational exclusions — see instructions*

A Item number	B • Donee's name and address • Relationship to donor (if any) • Description of gift • If the gift was made by means of a trust, enter trust's identifying number and attach a copy of the trust instrument • If the gift was of securities, give CUSIP number	C Donor's adjusted basis of gift	D Date of gift	E Value at date of gift
1	Cash to daughter, Deborah Miller, 500 Manda Lane, Wheeling IL 60090	510,000	3-15-98	510,000
Total of Part 1 (add amounts from Part 1, column E) ►				510,000

Part 2 — Gifts That are Direct Skips and are Subject to Both Gift Tax and Generation-Skipping Transfer Tax. You must list the gifts in chronological order. *Gifts less political organization, medical, and educational exclusions — see instructions. (Also list here direct skips that are subject only to the GST tax at this time as the result of the termination of an "estate tax inclusion period." See instructions.)*

A Item number	B • Donee's name and address • Relationship to donor (if any) • Description of gift • If the gift was made by means of a trust, enter trust's identifying number and attach a copy of the trust instrument • If the gift was of securities, give CUSIP number	C Donor's adjusted basis of gift	D Date of gift	E Value at date of gift
1	Cash to grandson, Matthew Miller, 3907 Cleveland St., Skokie IL 60097	1,010,000	3-15-98	1,010,000
2	Cash to granddaughter, Mary Miller, 4701 Oxnam, Norridge, IL 60656	1,010,000	3-15-98	1,010,000
Total of Part 2 (add amounts from Part 2, column E) ►				2,020,000

Part 3 — Taxable Gift Reconciliation

1	Total value of gifts of donor (add totals from column E of Parts 1 and 2)		1	2,530,000
2	One-half of items ______ attributable to spouse (see instructions)		2	0
3	Balance (subtract line 2 from line 1)		3	2,530,000
4	Gifts of spouse to be included (from Schedule A, Part 3, line 2 of spouse's return — see instructions)		4	0
	If any of the gifts included on this line are also subject to the generation-skipping transfer tax, check here ► ☐ and enter those gifts also on Schedule C, Part 1.			
5	Total gifts (add lines 3 and 4)		5	2,530,000
6	Total annual exclusions for gifts listed on Schedule A (including line 4, above) (see instructions)		6	30,000
7	Total included amount of gifts (subtract line 6 from line 5)		7	2,500,000
Deductions (see instructions)				
8	Gifts of interests to spouse for which a marital deduction will be claimed, based on items ______ of Schedule A	8 — 0		
9	Exclusions attributable to gifts on line 8	9 — 0		
10	Marital deduction — subtract line 9 from line 8	10 — 0		
11	Charitable deduction, based on items ______ less exclusions	11 — 0		
12	Total deductions — add lines 10 and 11		12	0
13	Subtract line 12 from line 7		13	2,500,000
14	Generation-skipping transfer taxes payable with this Form 709 (from Schedule C, Part 3, col. H, Total)		14	550,000
15	Taxable gifts (add lines 13 and 14). Enter here and on line 1 of the Tax Computation on page 1		15	3,050,000

(If more space is needed, attach additional sheets of same size.)

Form 709 (1998) Page 3

SCHEDULE A Computation of Taxable Gifts *(continued)*

16 Terminable Interest (QTIP) Marital Deduction. (See instructions for line 8 of Schedule A.)

If a trust (or other property) meets the requirements of qualified terminable interest property under section 2523(f), and

a. The trust (or other property) is listed on Schedule A, and

b. The value of the trust (or other property) is entered in whole or in part as a deduction on line 8, Part 3 of Schedule A,

then the donor shall be deemed to have made an election to have such trust (or other property) treated as qualified terminable interest property under section 2523(f).

If less than the entire value of the trust (or other property) that the donor has included in Part 1 of Schedule A is entered as a deduction on line 8, the donor shall be considered to have made an election only as to a fraction of the trust (or other property). The numerator of this fraction is equal to the amount of the trust (or other property) deducted on line 10 of Part 3, Schedule A. The denominator is equal to the total value of the trust (or other property) listed in Part 1 of Schedule A.

If you make the QTIP election (see instructions for line 8 of Schedule A), the terminable interest property involved will be included in your spouse's gross estate upon his or her death (section 2044). If your spouse disposes (by gift or otherwise) of all or part of the qualifying life income interest, he or she will be considered to have made a transfer of the entire property that is subject to the gift tax (see Transfer of Certain Life Estates on page 3 of the instructions).

17 Election Out of QTIP Treatment of Annuities

☐ ◀ Check here if you elect under section 2523(f)(6) NOT to treat as qualified terminable interest property any joint and survivor annuities that are reported on Schedule A and would otherwise be treated as qualified terminable interest property under section 2523(f). (See instructions.) Enter the item numbers (from Schedule A) for the annuities for which you are making this election ▶

SCHEDULE B Gifts From Prior Periods

If you answered "Yes" on line 11a of page 1, Part 1, see the instructions for completing Schedule B. If you answered "No," skip to the Tax Computation on page 1 (or Schedule C, if applicable).

A Calendar year or calendar quarter (see instructions)	B Internal Revenue office where prior return was filed	C Amount of unified credit against gift tax for periods after December 31, 1976	D Amount of specific exemption for prior periods ending before January 1, 1977	E Amount of taxable gifts
1986	IRS Service Center Kansas City, MO 64999	155,800	0	500,000

1	Totals for prior periods (without adjustment for reduced specific exemption)	1	155,800	0	500,000
2	Amount, if any, by which total specific exemption, line 1, column D, is more than $30,000			2	0
3	Total amount of taxable gifts for prior periods (add amount, column E, line 1, and amount, if any, on line 2). (Enter here and on line 2 of the Tax Computation on page 1.)			3	500,000

(If more space is needed, attach additional sheets of same size.)

Form 709 (1998) Page 4

SCHEDULE C Computation of Generation-Skipping Transfer Tax

Note: *Inter vivos direct skips that are completely excluded by the GST exemption must still be fully reported (including value and exemptions claimed) on Schedule C.*

Part 1 — Generation-Skipping Transfers

A Item No. (from Schedule A, Part 2, col. A)	B Value (from Schedule A, Part 2, col. E)	C Split Gifts (enter ½ of col. B) (see instructions)	D Subtract col. C from col. B	E Nontaxable portion of transfer	F Net Transfer (subtract col. E from col. D)
1	1,010,000	0	1,010,000	10,000	1,000,000
2	1,010,000	0	1,010,000	10,000	1,000,000
3					
4					
5					
6					

	Split gifts from spouse's Form 709 (enter item number)	Value included from spouse's Form 709	Nontaxable portion of transfer	Net transfer (subtract col. E from col. D)
If you elected gift splitting and your spouse was required to file a separate Form 709 (see the instructions for "Split Gifts"), you must enter all of the gifts shown on Schedule A, Part 2, of your spouse's Form 709 here.	S-			
In column C, enter the item number of each gift in the order it appears in column A of your spouse's Schedule A, Part 2. We have preprinted the prefix "S-" to distinguish your spouse's item numbers from your own when you complete column A of Schedule C, Part 3.	S-			
	S-			
	S-			
	S-			
In column D, for each gift, enter the amount reported in column C, Schedule C, Part 1, of your spouse's Form 709.	S-			
	S-			
	S-			

Part 2 — GST Exemption Reconciliation (Section 2631) and Section 2652(a)(3) Election

Check box ▶ ☐ if you are making a section 2652(a)(3) (special QTIP) election (see instructions)

Enter the item numbers (from Schedule A) of the gifts for which you are making this election ▶ ____________

		Line	Amount
1	Maximum allowable exemption	1	$1,000,000
2	Total exemption used for periods before filing this return	2	0
3	Exemption available for this return (subtract line 2 from line 1)	3	1,000,000
4	Exemption claimed on this return (from Part 3, col. C total, below)	4	1,000,000
5	Exemption allocated to transfers not shown on Part 3, below. **You must attach a Notice of Allocation.** (See instructions.)	5	0
6	Add lines 4 and 5	6	1,000,000
7	Exemption available for future transfers (subtract line 6 from line 3)	7	0

Part 3 — Tax Computation

A Item No. (from Schedule C, Part 1)	B Net transfer (from Schedule C, Part 1, col. F)	C GST Exemption Allocated	D Divide col. C by col. B	E Inclusion Ratio (subtract col. D from 1.000)	F Maximum Estate Tax Rate	G Applicable Rate (multiply col. E by col. F)	H Generation-Skipping Transfer Tax (multiply col. B by col. G)
1	1,000,000	500,000	0.500	0.500	55% (.55)	0.275	275,000
2	1,000,000	500,000	0.500	0.500	55% (.55)	0.275	275,000
3					55% (.55)		
4					55% (.55)		
5					55% (.55)		
6					55% (.55)		
					55% (.55)		
					55% (.55)		
					55% (.55)		
					55% (.55)		
Total exemption claimed. Enter here and on line 4, Part 2, above. May not exceed line 3, Part 2, above		1,000,000	**Total generation-skipping transfer tax.** Enter here, on line 14 of Schedule A, Part 3, and on line 16 of the Tax Computation on page 1				550,000

(If more space is needed, attach additional sheets of same size.)

Chapter 47
PAYMENT OF TAX

¶ 2400 Due Date

The gift tax is generally paid at the same time the return is required to be filed.[1] The annual gift tax return is due by April 15 of the year following that in which the gifts were made. The gift tax should be paid to the IRS Service Center where the gift tax return is filed.

An extension of time to file an income tax return also is deemed to be an extension of time to file an annual gift tax return. On line 4 of Form 4868 (Application for Automatic Extension of Time to File U.S. Individual Income Tax Return), a taxpayer requesting an extension of time to file an individual return indicates whether the taxpayer or the taxpayer's spouse plans to file a gift tax return (Form 709 or 709-A) for the year. The amount of gift or generation-skipping tax paid with the form is then entered on line 5a or 5b. Payment in full of gift and generation-skipping taxes with the extension application avoids interest and penalties. If paying the taxes in full with Form 4868 would cause undue hardship, the taxpayer should attach an explanation to the completed form.

A donor who fails to pay the tax is liable for a penalty of one-half of one percent of the amount of such tax for each month that the tax remains unpaid up to a maximum of 25 percent.[2] In addition, a lien attaches to the transferred property and the donee may be held personally liable.[3]

¶ 2405 Payment by Check or Money Order

Money orders and checks drawn on any bank or trust company incorporated under the laws of the United States, a state, territory or possession of the United States may be accepted by the appropriate IRS officer in payment of gift taxes. The check or money order in payment of the tax should be made payable to the "Internal Revenue Service." The donor's social security number, along with the number of the accompanying form and the applicable year, should be written on the check or money order.

¶ 2410 Discount and Interest

No discount is allowed for payment of the gift tax in advance of the last day for payment of the tax. If the tax is not paid when due, interest and various penalties may be assessed. If the tax required to be shown on the return is simply not paid when due, interest at the current rate (see ¶ 1680) is charged from the last date for payment to the date when paid.[4] Under other circumstances, more serious penalties can apply.[5]

Extensions of time for payment of up to six months may be granted.[6]

---

[1] Code Sec. 6151.

[2] Code Sec. 6651(a)(2).

[3] Code Sec. 6901 and Code Sec. 6902.

[4] Code Sec. 6601(a) and Code Sec. 6601(b).

[5] Code Sec. 6651.

[6] Code Sec. 6161(a).

Generation-Skipping Transfer Tax

Chapter 48

GENERAL RULES

¶ 2430 Purpose and Nature of the Tax

Property that is transferred to an heir or donee and eventually transferred to such person's own heirs or donees is generally exposed twice to federal estate or gift taxes. To avoid the second round of taxation, grantors sometimes have created life interests, with remainder interests reserved for members of subsequent generations. Generally, a generation-skipping transfer (GST) tax is imposed upon such trusts or trust equivalents (see ¶ 2431). The GST tax is designed to tax this means of transferring accumulated wealth to successive generations in much the same way that a gift or estate tax would have taxed the outright transfer of the property by gift or inheritance.

The GST tax [1] attempts to simplify compliance and administration by applying the tax to direct beneficial interests only (powers over trust property are not subject to taxation). Additionally, the tax is applied to direct skips, as well as to taxable terminations and distributions (see ¶ 2433).

¶ 2431 What Is a Generation-Skipping Transfer?

The GST tax applies to direct skips (for example, a transfer from a grandparent to a grandchild), as well as to taxable distributions and terminations (see ¶ 2433) of generation-skipping trust property.[2] The tax does not apply to any transfer (other than a direct skip) from a trust if the transfer was subject to estate or gift tax with respect to a person in the first generation below that of the grantor.

Gifts reported on Schedule A of Form 709 (Computation of Taxable Gifts) that are also generation-skipping transfers may be subject to both gift and generation-skipping transfer taxes. On the other hand, with one exception, if a transfer is excluded from the gift tax, then it is not subject to the generation-skipping transfer tax. For example, an *inter vivos* transfer that is not subject to gift tax due to the exclusion from the gift tax of certain transfers for educational or medical expenses [3] is not a generation-skipping transfer. An exception exists where there is a nontaxable gift to a trust that is also a direct skip. In that situation, the transfer is subject to the generation-skipping transfer tax unless no corpus or income may be

[1] Code Sec. 2601 through Code Sec. 2663.

[2] Code Sec. 2611.

[3] Code Sec. 529(c)(2), Code Sec. 2503(e), and Code Sec. 2611(b).

distributed to anyone other than the beneficiary and the trust assets are includible in the beneficiary's estate if the beneficiary dies during the trust term.

- *Property Subject to Tax Only Once*

Also excluded from the category of a taxable transfer is any transfer to the extent that the property transferred was previously subject to the GST tax.[4] However, the transferee in the prior transfer must have been a member of the same or a lower generation than the transferee in the later transfer. Additionally, the effect of the transfer must not be to avoid the GST tax entirely.

- *Distributions from Trust Income Taxed*

Distributions from a trust that qualify as generation-skipping distributions are subject to tax whether the distributions are from the trust income or the trust corpus. However, where the distribution is from the trust income, the recipient is entitled to an income tax deduction [5] for the amount of the GST tax paid.

¶ 2433 Taxable Terminations and Distributions; Direct Skips

The terms "direct skip," "taxable distribution," and "taxable termination" have special meanings for GST tax purposes. The occurrence of any of these three situations can result in the imposition of the generation-skipping transfer tax. However, there is a $1 million per-transferor exemption (see ¶ 2455) for all these transfers.

- *Direct Skip*

Two types of transfers are considered direct skips: (1) a transfer outright for the benefit of a "skip person," and (2) a transfer of property to a trust for one or more such beneficiaries.[6] The transfer may occur during the transferor's lifetime or at death. Generally, a "skip person" is any beneficiary assigned to a generation that is two or more generations below that of the grantor. The term is further defined at ¶ 2435.

A $1 million exemption ($1,010,000 for 1999) is provided for each person making a generation-skipping transfer.[7]

An exemption is also allowed for direct skips to grandchildren of a transferor when the grandchild's parent who is a lineal descendant of the transferor is deceased.[8] In such a case, the grandchild and all succeeding lineal descendants of the grandchild are "moved up" a generation, so that transfers to such grandchildren are not subject to the GST tax. For purposes of this exemption, a descendant who dies within 90 days after a transfer is treated as having predeceased the transferor if applicable state law or the governing instrument so provides.[9]

The Taxpayer Relief Act of 1997 (P.L. 105-34) extended the predeceased parent exception to collateral heirs of the transferor. However, for a transfer to a collateral heir to qualify for the exception the transferor

---

[4] Code Sec. 2611(b).

[5] Code Sec. 164(a)(4).

[6] Code Sec. 2612(c) and Code Sec. 2613.

[7] Code Sec. 2631; Rev. Proc. 98-61 (Section 3.16), IRB 1998-52, 18.

[8] Code Sec. 2612(c)(2).

[9] Reg. § 26.2612-1(a)(2)(i).

must have no lineal descendants. Additionally, the parent of the collateral heir who is a descendant of a parent of the transferor must predecease the transferor. A collateral heir is a person who is a lineal descendant of the parent of the transferor. The Act also extended the predeceased parent exception to taxable terminations and taxable distributions, provided that the parent of the relevant beneficiary was dead at the earliest time that the transfer (from which the beneficiary's interest in the property was established) was subject to estate or gift tax.[10]

- *Taxable Distribution*

A "taxable distribution" occurs whenever there is a distribution from a generation-skipping trust to a skip person.[11]

> ***Example:*** Lorna Lane establishes a discretionary trust for the benefit of Lilly and Lorenzo, her daughter and grandson. Lorenzo is a "skip person" because he is two or more generations younger than Lorna. If the trustee makes a distribution of trust corpus to Lorenzo, it will be a taxable distribution.

- *Taxable Termination*

A "taxable termination" occurs upon the termination of an interest in property held in trust. However, no taxable termination will occur if a non-skip person has an interest in the property immediately after such termination or if a distribution may not be made from the trust to a skip person at any time after the termination.[12] Such a termination usually occurs upon the death of the person holding a life interest in the trust or upon the lapse of time in a case where the grantor created an estate for years.

A partial termination of a trust is taxable if, upon the termination of an interest in property held in a trust, a specified portion of the trust assets is distributed to skip persons who are lineal descendants of the holder of the interest (or to one or more trusts for the exclusive benefit of such persons).

¶ 2435 Skip Person and Non-Skip Person Defined

A "skip person" is a natural person assigned to a generation that is two or more generations below the generation of the transferor.[13]

> ***Example (1):*** Jim Feldman's grandchild, Sam, is a "skip person" for purposes of the GST tax, as is his great-grandchild, Sally. Sam is in a generation that is two generations below that of his grandfather, Jim. Sally's generation is three generations below that of Jim. (See ¶ 2437 for a discussion of assignment of generations.)

The term "skip person" refers to a trust if (1) all interests in the trust are held by skip persons, or (2) there is no non-skip person holding an interest in such trust, and at no time after the generation-skipping transfer may a distribution be made from the trust to a non-skip person.

> ***Example (2):*** Maria Jacobs creates a testamentary trust wherein income will be distributed to her husband for his life and, at his death, the remainder will be split between Maria's daughter and

[10] Code Sec. 2651(e).

[11] Code Sec. 2612(b).

[12] Code Sec. 2612(a).

[13] Code Sec. 2613.

her grandson. The trust would not be a "skip person" because two "non-skip persons" hold an interest in the trust: Maria's husband and her daughter.

A direct skip (see ¶ 2433) transfer to a transferor's grandchild will not be taxable, however, if the child of the transferor who was that grandchild's parent is deceased at the time of the transfer. In such a situation, the grandchild and all succeeding lineal descendants are "moved up" a generation.[14] A descendant who dies within 90 days after a transfer is treated as having predeceased the transferor, if state law or the governing instrument so provides.[15]

¶ 2437 Assignment of Generations

Generally, assignment of generations is determined along family lines. For example, a transferor, the transferor's spouse, and the transferor's brothers and sisters are one generation. Their children constitute the next generation, and the transferor's grandchildren are two generations below that of the transferor.

- *Persons Who Are Not Lineal Descendants*

An individual who is not a lineal descendant is assigned to a generation on the basis of that individual's date of birth (subject, however, to the rules for treatment of legal adoptions, etc., discussed below).[16] An individual born within 12½ years of the date of the transferor's birth is assigned to the same generation as the transferor. An individual born more than 12½ years after but within 37½ years of the transferor's birth is assigned to the first generation younger than the transferor. Subsequent generation assignments are similarly made on the basis of 25-year periods.

- *Marriage, Legal Adoptions and Half-Blood Relationships*

For purposes of the GST tax, a relationship by legal adoption or half-blood is equivalent to a relationship by whole-blood.[17] An individual who is married at any time to a transferor is assigned to the transferor's generation. Similarly, an individual who is married at any time to a lineal descendant of the transferor is assigned to the same generation as the descendant.[18]

- *Other Special Rules*

Unless otherwise provided in regulations, an individual who could be assigned to more than one generation is assigned to the youngest such generation.[19]

If an estate, trust, partnership, corporation or other entity has an interest in property, each individual having a beneficial interest in such entity is treated as having an interest in the property and is assigned to a generation as discussed above. A charitable organization or a charitable trust is assigned to the transferor's generation.[20]

---

[14] Code Sec. 2612(c)(2).

[15] Reg. § 26.2612-1(a)(2)(i).

[16] Code Sec. 2651(d).

[17] Code Sec. 2651(b)(3).

[18] Code Sec. 2651(c).

[19] Code Sec. 2651(f).

[20] Code Sec. 2651(f)(3).

¶ 2439 Other Definitions

The following definitions apply with respect to the GST tax.

- *"Interest"*

A person has an interest in property held in trust if (at the time the determination is made) that person is a mandatory or permissible recipient of distributions from the trust.[21] A beneficiary of a charitable remainder annuity trust, a charitable remainder unitrust [22] or a pooled income fund [23] also has an interest in trust property. Certain "interests" used primarily to avoid the GST tax are disregarded.

Additionally, the fact that income or corpus of the trust may be used to satisfy an obligation of support arising under state law is disregarded in determining if a person has an interest in a trust, if (1) such use is discretionary or (2) such use is pursuant to a state law substantially like the Uniform Gifts to Minors Act.[24]

- *"Transferor"*

A decedent is the "transferor," for purposes of the GST tax, when the transfer is of any property that would be subject to the estate tax. The donor is the transferor when the transfer is of any property that would be subject to the gift tax.[25] In addition, the Tax Court has held that the holder of a general power of appointment over property includible in the estate of the holder for estate tax purposes is a transferor for purposes of the GST tax.[26]

- *"Trust" and "Trustee"*

The term "trust" includes any arrangement (other than an estate) that has substantially the same effect as a trust.[27] In such a case, the "trustee" is the person in actual or constructive possession of the property subject to such an arrangement. Examples of arrangements to which these definitions apply include life estates and remainders, estates for years, and insurance and annuity contracts.[28]

- *Special Election Available*

If property qualifies for estate [29] or gift [30] tax qualified terminable interest property (QTIP) treatment, the estate of the decedent or the donor spouse may elect to treat such property as if the QTIP election had not been made, for purposes of the GST tax. Once made, however, the "reverse QTIP election" is irrevocable.[31]

¶ 2440 Applicable Provisions

All of the Internal Revenue Code provisions on procedure and administration, including penalties (Subtitle F) that apply to estate and gift

[21] Code Sec. 2652(c).

[22] Code Sec. 664.

[23] Code Sec. 642(c)(5).

[24] Code Sec. 2652(c)(3).

[25] Code Sec. 2652(a)(1).

[26] *E. Peterson Marital Trust*, CA-2, 96-1 USTC, ¶ 60,225, aff'g TC, 102 TC 790, CCH Dec. 49,935.

[27] Code Sec. 2652(b)(1).

[28] Code Sec. 2652(b)(3).

[29] Code Sec. 2056(b)(7).

[30] Code Sec. 2523(f).

[31] Reg. § 26.2652-2.

taxation, are applicable to the GST tax.[32] Estate tax rules govern transfers occuring as a result of death; gift tax rules apply to *inter vivos* transfers.

¶ 2441 Effective Dates

The rules affecting generation-skipping transfers are generally applicable to transfers made after October 22, 1986. However, certain transfers from trusts that were irrevocable prior to that date are not subject to the GST tax. Consequently, care must be taken when a transfer is contemplated from such a trust. In general, the following exceptions to the effective date rules apply: [33]

(1) The GST tax does not apply to any generation-skipping transfer under a trust that was irrevocable on September 25, 1985, but only to the extent that such transfer was not made out of corpus added to the trust after that date. This exception was amended by the Technical and Miscellaneous Revenue Act of 1988 (P.L. 100-647) to clarify that the exception regarding irrevocable trusts applies without regard to whether or not income received from corpus contributions made before September 26, 1985, is distributed or accumulated.[34] The exercise of a limited power of appointment over a trust that was irrevocable on September 5, 1985, does not cause property subject to the power to lose its exemption from the GST tax if the power may not be exercised to postpone or suspend the vesting, absolute ownership, or power of alienation of an interest in the property for the longer of (1) 90 years as provided by the Uniform Rule Against Perpetuities or (2) 21 years after the death of any life in being when the irrevocable trust was created.[35] However, assets that were transferred from a marital trust that was irrevocable prior to the effective date of the GST tax were subject to the GST tax because the transfer was treated as being made from property constructively added after the effective date of the GST tax, because a spouse had a testamentary general power of appointment over the property.[36]

(2) Any generation-skipping transfers occurring under wills or revocable trusts executed before October 22, 1986, are not subject to the tax, provided that the following conditions are met: (a) the document in existence on October 21, 1986, was not amended after that date in a manner that resulted in the creation of, or an increase in the amount of, a generation-skipping transfer; (b) in the case of a revocable trust, no addition was made to the trust after October 21, 1986, that resulted in the creation of, or increase in the amount of, a generation-skipping transfer; and (c) the decedent died before January 1, 1987.[37]

Furthermore, revocable trusts which became irrevocable due to the transferor's death between September 25, 1985, and October 23, 1986, are also excluded from the category of taxable transfers.[38]

---

[32] Code Sec. 2661.

[33] Reg. § 26.2601-1(b).

[34] Act Sec. 1014(h) of P.L. 100-647, amending Act Sec. 1433(b) of P.L. 99-514.

[35] Reg. § 26.2601-1(b)(1)(v)(B)(*2*).

[36] *E. Peterson Marital Trust*, CA-2, 96-1 USTC ¶ 60,225, aff'g TC, 102 TC 790, CCH Dec. 49,935.

[37] Reg. § 26.2601-1(b)(2).

[38] Reg. § 26.2601-1(a)(4).

(3) Any generation-skipping transfer occurring under a trust (to the extent that such trust consists of property, or proceeds thereof, the value of which was included in a decedent's gross estate) or which is a direct skip occurring by reason of a decedent's death is not subject to the tax if the decedent was legally incompetent on October 22, 1986, and at all times thereafter until death. However, the exception does not apply to property transferred to such incompetent decedent (or to a trust) by gift or by reason of the death of another person, after August 3, 1990.[39]

The delays in effective dates were adopted to permit a reasonable period of time for individuals to re-execute their wills to reflect the extension of the GST tax to direct skips. Comparable delays were not provided for generation-sharing transfers because those transfers were subject to tax under prior law.

[39] Act Sec. 11703(c) of P.L. 101-508; Reg. § 26.2601-1(b)(3).

Chapter 49

COMPUTATION OF TAX

¶ 2450 Amount of Tax

In general, the generation-skipping transfer (GST) tax imposes a flat tax at the "applicable rate" (see ¶ 2459) on the taxable amount of a generation-skipping transfer. For purposes of determining the taxable amount of a direct skip, taxable distribution or taxable termination, the following exemptions from the tax are provided: (1) a $1 million per transferor exemption that may be allocated among several generation-skipping transfers (see ¶ 2455), and (2) an exemption that applies to a direct skip if a certain member of the skipped generation is deceased at the time of the transfer (see ¶ 2433).

¶ 2451 Determination of Tax Base

In general, the method of computing the tax base or the taxable amount of a generation-skipping transfer depends on whether a taxable distribution, a taxable termination, or a direct skip is involved. Unless a trust instrument specifically referring to the GST tax directs otherwise, the tax imposed on a generation-skipping transfer is charged to the property being transferred.[1]

● *Taxable Distributions*

In the case of taxable distributions, the amount subject to the GST tax is the amount received by the transferee.[2] This amount is reduced by any expenses incurred in connection with the determination, collection or refund of the tax. As discussed at ¶ 2470, the transferee pays the tax on the taxable distribution. If the trustee pays any amount of the tax, the trustee is treated as having made an additional taxable distribution of that amount.[3]

● *Taxable Terminations*

In the case of a taxable termination, the amount subject to tax is the value of the property with respect to which the termination occurred.[4] A deduction is allowed for expenses, indebtedness and taxes (similar to that discussed at ¶ 800 through ¶ 820) for amounts attributable to the property with respect to which the termination has occurred. The trustee pays any tax due on a taxable termination.

● *No Double Deductions for Expenses, Indebtedness and Taxes*

Administration expenses, indebtedness and taxes may be taken either as an income tax deduction on Form 1041 or as a deduction in determining

---

[1] Code Sec. 2603(b).

[2] Code Sec. 2621.

[3] Code Sec. 2621(b).

[4] Code Sec. 2622.

taxable distributions and taxable determinations for GST tax purposes. These amounts may not be deducted twice, however. To deduct them from an estate's taxable income, the fiduciary must file a waiver electing not to deduct the amounts for GST tax purposes.[5]

● *Direct Skips*

The taxable amount on a direct skip is the value of the property received by the transferee.[6] If the direct skip is made from a trust, the tax is paid by the trustee; otherwise, it is paid by the transferor. This means that the tax base is the amount actually received by the skip person after reduction for the amount of GST tax paid on the transfer. This means that a direct skip is tax-exclusive.

To calculate the amount of GST tax payable, an interrelated computation is necessary. The tax is 55 percent of the amount left after the amount of GST tax payable is removed from the tax base.

This tax-exclusive rate (TER) is calculated according to the following formula:

$$\text{TER} = \frac{\text{TIR (tax-inclusive rate)}}{1 + \text{TIR}}$$

Thus, for a 55-percent tax-inclusive rate the tax-exclusive rate would be .55/1.55 = 11/31 = .3548387. This rate is then applied to the amount subject to the GST tax to arrive at the amount of GST tax due. (Form 706, Schedule R (Rev. July 1998), Part 2, line 8, accomplishes the same result by dividing the amount subject to the GST tax by 2.818182, to arrive at the amount of GST tax due.)

Example (1): David Green died, leaving all his assets to his grandson, Nick. Assume that, after payment of the estate tax, the amount left is $3,000,000. The full $3,000,000 is not subject to the GST tax, but only the amount that Nick will receive after payment of the GST tax by the estate.

Accordingly, under the facts of this example, the GST tax would be 11/31 times $3,000,000, which equals $1,064,516.10.

The rules applicable to a lifetime direct skip are the same as those applicable to a testamentary direct skip. The GST tax is paid by the transferor, and the transfer is tax-exclusive. However, the treatment of a lifetime direct skip resembles that of a tax-inclusive transfer because of the "gross-up" rule.[7] Under this rule, the amount of any taxable gift that is also a direct skip is increased by the amount of GST tax payable on the transaction.

Example (2): Laura Green makes a gift of $3,000,000 to her grandson, Paul. (Assume that the whole value of the gift is in the 55-percent marginal bracket and that the unified credit has been used up.) The GST tax on the gift is .55 times $3,000,000, which equals $1,650,000. This amount is then added to the amount of the tax base for purposes of calculating the gift tax. Thus, the gift tax base is $4,650,000, and the gift tax payable is $2,557,500. This means that the total transfer tax on a gift of $3,000,000 is $4,207,500.

---

[5] Code Sec. 642(g).

[6] Code Sec. 2623.

[7] Code Sec. 2515.

Note that in the case of lifetime direct skips, the GST tax payable because of the gift is not itself subject to GST tax, but is subject to the gift tax. This makes the taxation of such transfers similar to a tax-inclusive treatment of taxable distributions and taxable terminations.

¶ 2453 Valuation

Generally, property is valued at the time of the generation-skipping transfer.[8] If property is transferred as a result of the death of a transferor, the value of the property, for GST tax purposes, is its value for estate tax purposes. If an estate elects either alternate or special use valuation for the property, that value will be used to compute GST tax liability. Additionally, if one or more taxable terminations with respect to the same trust occur at the same time as, and as the result of, the death of an individual, an election may be made to value all of the property included in such terminations at its alternate value as set forth in Code Sec. 2032.[9]

For purposes of the valuation rules for generation-skipping transfers, the value of transferred property is reduced by the amount of any consideration provided by the transferee.[10]

¶ 2455 GST Exemption; Allocation

An exemption of $1 million is provided for each person making generation-skipping transfers. The exemption may be allocated by a transferor (or the transferor's executor) to property transferred at any time but, once made, is irrevocable. The $1 million dollar exemption is not transferable between spouses; however, married couples may elect to split a transfer and treat it as made one-half by each spouse pursuant to the gift-splitting rules under Code Sec. 2513 (see ¶ 2013 and ¶ 2200).[11] For generation-skipping transfers made after 1998, the GST tax exemption is indexed for inflation.[12] The inflation-adjusted figure for generation-skipping transfers in 1999 is $1,010,000.[13]

● *Allocation of Exemption*

The GST tax exemption may be allocated by a transferor or the transferor's executor to property transferred at any time.[14] The election is irrevocable once made and must be made on or before the due date for filing an estate tax return (with extensions), regardless of whether a return is required to be filed.

If an individual makes a direct skip (defined at ¶ 2433) during the individual's lifetime, any unused portion of the individual's exemption is deemed allocated to the transferred property to the extent necessary to reduce the inclusion ratio (defined at ¶ 2461) for such property to zero.[15] If the amount of the direct skip exceeds the unused portion of the exemption, the entire unused portion is allocated to the property transferred. However, a transferor may elect to have these allocation rules not apply to a

[8] Code Sec. 2624.

[9] Code Sec. 2624(c).

[10] Code Sec. 2624(d).

[11] Code Sec. 2652(a)(2).

[12] Code Sec. 2631(c), as added by P.L. 105-34.

[13] Rev. Proc. 98-61 (Section 3.16), IRB 1998-52, 18.

[14] Code Sec. 2631.

[15] Code Sec. 2632(b).

transfer. Once the election is made, it is irrevocable and cannot be modified after the date on which a timely filed Form 709 is due.[16]

- *Appreciation in Value of Exempt Property*

The House Ways and Means Committee Report to the Tax Reform Act of 1986 (P.L. 99-514) indicates that once the GST tax exemption is applied to a transfer of property, and the property (or a portion of it) is designated as exempt, all subsequent appreciation on the property (or that portion of it) is also exempt from tax. If only a portion of the property is initially exempt, any subsequent appreciation will be exempt in the same ratio as the initially exempt property bore to the total property.

Example (1): Elizabeth Davis establishes a $1 million trust fund for the benefit of her grandchildren and great-grandchildren. Davis allocates her entire GST tax exemption to the trust. The assets in the trust appreciate to $5 million. None of the appreciation is subject to tax because the initial transfer was fully exempt.

Example (2): Charles Duvall establishes a $2 million trust for the benefit of his children and grandchildren. Duvall allocates $500,000 (or 50%) of his GST tax exemption to the trust. The value of the trust appreciates to $8 million. Only one-quarter of the appreciation will be exempt because at the time of the transfer only one-quarter of the property qualified as exempt.

- *Allocation of Unused Exemption at Death*

Any portion of a decedent's $1 million GST tax exemption that has not been allocated at the decedent's death is allocated in the following order:

(1) to property that is the subject of a direct skip occurring at the decedent's death, and

(2) to trusts with respect to which the decedent is the transferor and from which a taxable distribution or termination may occur at or after the decedent's death.[17]

¶ 2457 GST Credit for State Taxes

If a generation-skipping transfer (other than a direct skip) occurs at the same time as, and as a result of, the death of an individual, a credit in the amount of the GST tax paid to any state is permitted against the federal GST tax.[18] However, the credit is limited to five percent of the amount of federal generation-skipping transfer tax imposed on the transfer.

¶ 2459 Applicable Rate

All generation-skipping transfers are subject to tax at a flat rate equal to the product of the maximum estate tax rate (currently, 55 percent) and the "inclusion ratio" (defined at ¶ 2461) with respect to the transfer.[19] The "maximum estate tax rate" is the maximum rate imposed by Code Sec.

---

[16] Reg. § 26.2632-1(b).

[17] Code Sec. 2632(c).

[18] Code Sec. 2604.

[19] Code Sec. 2641.

2001 on the estates of decedents dying at the time of the taxable distribution, taxable termination or direct skip.

It should be noted, however, that, in the case of a direct skip occurring at death, the effective GST tax rate will be considerably lower than the maximum estate tax rate in effect at the time. For any given rate, the tax exclusive, effective rate is calculated according to the following formula:

$$\frac{\text{Maximum Estate Tax Rate}}{1 + \text{Maximum Estate Tax Rate}}$$

A maximum estate tax rate of 55 percent yields the following result:

$$\frac{.55}{1.55} = \frac{11}{31} \quad \text{or} \quad .3548387$$

Example: Harry West dies in 1998 and his will leaves $5 million to his grandson, Jake.

Tax Base	$5,000,000
Tentative Estate Tax	2,390,800
Less: Unified Credit	(202,050)
Estate Tax	$2,188,750
GST Tax Base ($5,000,000 − $2,188,750)	$2,811,250
Less: GST Tax Exemption	(1,000,000)
Net GST Tax Base	$1,811,250
GST Tax Payable ($1,802,000 × .3548387)	642,702
Total Transfer Tax	$2,837,419 *

* Note that the net GST tax base less the amount of GST tax paid times 55% is equal to the GST tax payable. ($1,811,250 − $642,702 = $1,168,548; $1,168,548 × .55 = $642,702)

¶ 2461 Inclusion Ratio

The inclusion ratio for any property transferred in a generation-skipping transfer is the excess (if any) of one (1) over the "applicable fraction" determined for the trust from which a generation-skipping transfer is made or, in the case of a direct skip, the applicable fraction determined for such a skip.[20] Stated differently, 1 − (applicable fraction) = inclusion ratio.

• *Applicable Fraction*

The applicable fraction is determined as follows: The numerator is the amount of the GST exemption allocated to the trust or the property transferred in the direct skip. Its denominator is the value of the property transferred to the trust (or involved in the direct skip) reduced by the sum of any federal estate or state death tax attributable to the property that was recovered from the trust and any estate or gift tax charitable deductions allowed.[21]

[20] Code Sec. 2642.

[21] Code Sec. 2642(a)(2).

$$\text{applicable fraction} = \frac{\text{amount of GST exemption allocated to trust or property}}{\left(\begin{array}{c}\text{value of property}\\ \text{transferred}\end{array}\right) - \left[\begin{array}{c}\text{state and federal}\\ \text{estate taxes}\end{array} + \begin{array}{c}\text{charitable deductions allowed}\\ \text{under Code Sec. 2055 or 2522}\end{array}\right]}$$

Example (1): Upon James Anderson's death in 1998, $2.5 million is transferred to a trust for the benefit of his grandchildren. At the time of the transfer, the full $1 million GST tax exemption is allocated to this trust. Assuming that there are no estate/death tax and charitable deductions, the calculation of the GST tax would be as follows:

(1) Determination of the applicable fraction: $1 million exemption divided by $2.5 million in property equals applicable fraction of 0.4,

(2) Determination of the inclusion ratio: Subtract the applicable fraction from 1. Thus, the inclusion ratio is 1 minus 0.4, or 0.6.

The GST tax rate is the product of the inclusion ratio—in this case, 0.6—and the maximum federal estate tax rate at the time of the transfer—55%. Thus, the rate of tax on this transfer is 33%.

● *Gift for Which Gift Tax Return Filed or Deemed Allocation Made*

For purposes of the GST tax, the value of property is generally determined at the time of a transfer to the trust or at the time of a direct skip. However, if an allocation of the GST tax exemption (see ¶ 2455) is made on a timely filed gift tax return [22] or is deemed to be made under Code Sec. 2632(b)(1), the value of the transferred property is its value for gift tax purposes (and the allocation becomes effective on the date of such transfer).[23]

If any allocation of the GST tax exemption to any property not transferred as a result of the death of the transferor is not made on a timely filed gift tax return and is not deemed to have been made under Code Sec. 2632(b)(1), the value of the property will be determined as of the time the allocation is filed with the IRS.[24]

● *QTIP Trusts*

If the value of the property is included in the gross estate of a spouse as qualified terminable interest property (QTIP) for which a marital deduction was previously allowed [25] and if the spouse was the transferor of the property, the value of the property (for GST tax purposes) will be the same as its value for estate tax purposes.[26]

● *Treatment of Certain Nontaxable Gifts*

The inclusion ratio of a direct skip that is a nontaxable gift is zero. A nontaxable gift is one excluded from gift tax because of the annual exclusion or because it is a transfer for educational or medical expenses.[27]

---

[22] Code Sec. 6075(b).

[23] Reg. § 26.2632-1(b)(2)(ii)(A) and Reg. § 26.2642-2(a)(1).

[24] Code Sec. 2642(b)(3).

[25] Code Sec. 2044.

[26] Code Sec. 2642(b)(4).

[27] Code Sec. 2642(c).

However, this rule does not apply to any transfer to a trust for the benefit of an individual unless (1) during the lifetime of that individual, no portion of the corpus or income of the trust may be distributed to (or for the benefit of) any other person, and (2) if the trust does not terminate before the individual dies, the assets of the trust will be includible in that individual's gross estate.

- *Special Rules Where More Than One Transfer Is Made to a Trust*

If a transfer of property (other than a nontaxable gift) is made to a trust in existence before the transfer, the applicable fraction must be recomputed.[28] The numerator of this recomputed fraction is the sum of (1) the amount of the GST tax exemption allocated to the property involved in such a transfer plus (2) the nontax portion of the trust (as defined below) immediately before such transfer. The denominator is the sum of (1) the value of the property involved in the transfer (reduced by the sum of (a) any federal estate or state death tax paid and (b) any charitable deduction allowed) and (2) the value of all property in the trust immediately before the transfer.

For purposes of the special rule outlined above, the nontax portion of a trust is the product of the value of all of the property in the trust and the applicable fraction in effect for such trust.

> ***Example (2):*** Joseph Grant established a generation-skipping trust for the benefit of his descendants, which he initially funded with $1 million. However, he chose to allocate only $500,000 (or one-half) of his GST tax exemption to the trust. Assuming that there were no allocable deductions, his initial applicable fraction was 0.5 and his inclusion ratio was also 0.5.
>
> Two years later, Grant placed an additional $600,000 into the trust and allocated his remaining $500,000 GST tax exemption to it. This necessitated the following recalculation. Assume that no deductions are allowable and that the initial trust corpus has not appreciated in value.

$$\frac{\left(\text{amount of GST tax exemption allocated to property involved in transfer}\right) + \left[\left(\text{value of all property in trust before transfer}\right)\left(\text{applicable fraction}\right)\right]}{\left[\left(\text{value of property involved in transfer}\right) - \text{federal estate or state death taxes recovered from trust attributable to such property and any charitable deductions}\right] + \left(\text{value of property in trust before transfer}\right)} =$$

$$\frac{(500{,}000) + [(1{,}000{,}000) \times (.5)]}{(\$600{,}000 - 0) + \$1{,}000{,}000} =$$

$$\frac{\$1{,}000{,}000}{\$1{,}600{,}000} = .625$$

[28] Code Sec. 2642(d).

Thus, the new applicable fraction is 0.625. The new inclusion ratio is 1 minus 0.625, which equals 0.375.

If any allocation of the GST tax exemption to property transferred to a trust is not made on a timely filed gift tax return and there was a previous allocation with respect to property transferred to the same trust, the applicable fraction for the trust must be recomputed at the time of the allocation.

¶ 2463 Taxation of Multiple Skips

If there is a generation-skipping transfer of any property and immediately after the transfer the property is held in trust, subsequent transfers from the portion of the trust attributable to that property are treated as if the transferor of the property were assigned to the first generation above the highest generation of any person who has an interest in such trust immediately after the transfer.[29] In general, the inclusion ratio of the trust will not be affected. However, Code Sec. 2653(b) specifically provides that, under regulations prescribed by the IRS, adjustments to the inclusion ratio are to be made to take into account any GST tax borne by such a trust.

- *Pour-Over Trusts*

The inclusion ratio of a trust is affected if the generation-skipping transfer involves the transfer of property from one trust to another (i.e., a "pour-over" trust).[30] In such a case, the inclusion ratio for the pour-over trust is determined by treating the nontax portion of such distribution as if it were a part of a GST tax exemption allocated to such trust. The nontax portion of any distribution in this case is the amount of such distribution multiplied by the applicable fraction that applies to the distribution.

¶ 2465 Special Rules

The following special rules apply to the GST tax.

- *Basis Adjustments*

If property is transferred in a generation-skipping transfer, the basis of the property in the hands of the transferee is stepped up (but not above fair market value) to reflect GST taxes attributable to appreciation.[31] For this purpose, the amount of GST tax imposed is computed without regard to the credit for state death taxes. Stepped-up basis may not exceed fair market value. The GST tax basis adjustment is applied after the basis adjustment for gift tax paid.[32] Thus, the two adjustments combined must not increase the basis of the property transferred above its fair market value.[33]

Example (1): Henry Cooper transfers property with a fair market value of $3 million to his granddaughter. Immediately before the transfer, the adjusted basis of the property was $2 million. The gift tax applicable to the transfer (after application of the applicable

---

[29] Code Sec. 2653.

[30] Code Sec. 2653(b)(2).

[31] Code Sec. 2654(a)(1).

[32] Code Sec. 1015(d).

[33] Code Sec. 2654(a).

credit amount) is $1,703,000. The GST tax (after application of the $1 million GST tax exemption) is $1,100,000. The basis would then be adjusted upwards to $3 million to reflect the taxes paid. The basis would not be $4,803,000 because the stepped-up basis cannot exceed the fair market value.

- *Certain Transfers at Death*

If the property is transferred in a taxable termination that occurs at the same time as, and as a result of, the death of an individual, the basis of the property is adjusted in a manner similar to that provided for in Code Sec. 1014(a) (relating to basis of property received from a decedent). However, if the inclusion ratio of the property is less than one (1), any increase or decrease in basis is limited by multiplying the increase by the inclusion ratio.[34]

Example (2): Ilsa Kuhn created an *inter vivos* trust funded with property with a basis of $2 million. Kuhn was to receive the income from the trust for her life and, upon her death, the remainder was directed to her grandson. When Kuhn died, the trust property had a fair market value of $3.5 million. Kuhn's estate allocates all of the $1 million GST tax exemption to this taxable termination. The inclusion ratio would be .714286 (1 – ($1,000,000 ÷ $3,500,000)). Thus, the adjusted basis of the property transferred to Kuhn's grandson would be $3,071,429 ([($3,500,000 – $2,000,000) × .714286] + $2,000,000).

- *Certain Trusts Treated as Separate Shares*

For purposes of the GST tax, the portions of a trust attributable to transfers from different transferors shall be treated as separate trusts. Similarly, substantially separate and independent shares of different beneficiaries in a trust are treated as separate trusts.[35]

Example (3): Tom Johnson and Julie Kelly created a trust for the benefit of Johnson's grandson and Kelly's son, Michael. Johnson contributed property worth $1.2 million and Kelly contributed property worth $2 million. For purposes of the GST tax, the trust would be treated as one trust containing $1.2 million with Johnson as the grantor and one trust containing $2 million with Kelly as the grantor.

Example (4): Larissa Jenkins created a trust to benefit her son, Manuel, and her granddaughter, Natalie, equally. She contributed $800,000 to the trust. The trust will be treated as two separate trusts containing $400,000 for each of Manuel and Natalie for purposes of the GST tax.

- *Disclaimers*

For the effect of disclaimer, taxpayers are referred by statute[36] to Code Sec. 2518, which relates to gift tax disclaimers (see ¶ 2009). The triggering event for the nine-month disclaimer period is the direct skip, taxable termination or taxable distribution.

---

[34] Code Sec. 2654(a)(2).

[35] Code Sec. 2654(b).

[36] Code Sec. 2654(c).

- *Limitation on Liability of Trustee*

A trustee is not personally liable for any increase in the GST tax that is attributable to the fact that the exemption of certain nontaxable gifts[37] does not apply to a transfer to the trust that was made during the life of the transferor and for which a gift tax return was not filed.[38]

The trustee is also not personally liable when the inclusion ratio (see ¶ 2461) with respect to the trust is greater than the amount of the ratio as computed on the basis of the return on which an allocation of the GST tax exemption to the property transferred to the trust was made (or deemed made under Code Sec. 2632).[39] The above exception, however, will not apply if the trustee has knowledge of facts sufficient to reasonably conclude that a gift tax return was required to be filed or that the inclusion ratio was erroneous.

- *Nonresidents Not Citizens*

In the case of a generation-skipping transfer by a person who is neither a U.S. citizen nor a resident, the GST tax applies only to property that is subject to gift or estate tax at the time of a direct skip or transfer to a trust.[40] In other words, the GST tax applies only if the property is U.S. situs property (see ¶ 1620).

---

[37] Code Sec. 2642(c).

[38] Code Sec. 2654(d).

[39] Code Sec. 2654(d).

[40] Reg. § 26.2663-2(b).

Chapter 50
RETURN REQUIREMENTS

¶ 2470 Liability for Tax

Which party is liable for generation-skipping transfer (GST) tax depends on the type of generation-skipping transfer.

The transferor is liable for GST tax resulting from a direct skip other than one from a trust, the trustee is liable for tax resulting from a direct skip from a trust or a taxable termination, and the transferee is liable for tax resulting from a taxable distribution.[1] If the trustee pays any amount of the tax on a taxable distribution, the trustee is treated as having made an additional taxable distribution of that amount (see ¶ 2451).

Generally, unless a trust instrument specifically directs otherwise, the GST tax is charged to the property constituting the transfer.[2] The estate and gift tax provisions with respect to transferee liability, liens and related matters are applicable to the GST tax.[3] As a result, the donees of stock were liable as transferees for unpaid GST tax even though no assessment of the tax had been asserted against the donor-transferor who was primarily liable for the tax.[4]

For an explanation of the limitations on the personal liability of a trustee, see ¶ 2465. See ¶ 2451 for an explanation of the amount of the transfer that is subject to tax.

¶ 2471 Persons Required to File Return; Required Returns

Regulations detail who is required to file GST tax returns and the time and manner for filing such returns.[5] Generally, the person liable for the tax must file the return. The form of return is governed by the generation-skipping transfer involved.

- *Direct Skips*

In the case of a lifetime direct skip, the donor is required to file Form 709 (United States Gift (and Generation-Skipping Transfer) Tax Return).

If the direct skip occurs at death, the executor must file the return unless the direct skip is from a trust or with respect to property that continues to be held in trust.[6] The executor must file Form 706 (United States Estate (and Generation-Skipping Transfer) Tax Return) or Form

---

[1] Code Sec. 2603(a)

[2] Code Sec. 2603(b).

[3] Code Sec. 2661.

[4] *K. O'Neal II*, 102 TC 666, CCH. Dec. 49,810.

[5] Reg. § 26.2662-1.

[6] Reg. § 26.2662-1(c)(1)(iv), (v).

706-NA. The GST tax payable by the estate is computed on Schedule R (Generation-Skipping Transfer Tax) of Form 706.

If a direct skip occurring at death is payable from a trust, the trustee is liable for the GST tax.[7] The executor must use Schedule R-1 (Generation-Skipping Transfer Tax, Direct Skips From a Trust, Payment Voucher) of Form 706 to notify the trustee that such a tax is due. Filled-in Schedule R appears at ¶ 2475, and Schedule R-1 appears at ¶ 2477. Instructions for completing these forms appear at ¶ 2473.

A special rule applies to direct skips occurring at death with respect to property held in a "trust arrangement." [8]

For decedents dying on or after June 24, 1996, if the total value of the property involved in direct skips with respect to the trustee of that trust arrangement is less than $250,000, the executor is liable for the GST tax on the direct skip and is required to file Form 706 or Form 706-NA (and not Schedule R-1 of Form 706).[9] For decedents dying before June 24, 1996, the executor is liable for the tax and required to file Form 706 or 706-NA if the property involved in the direct skip with respect to the trustee of the trust arrangement is, in the aggregate, less than $100,000.[10] In any event, the executor who is subject to such liability may recover the tax attributable to the transfer from the trustee of the trust arrangement if the property continues in trust or from the recipient of the property if the property is distributed.[11] The limits on the personal liability of a trustee are described at ¶ 2465.

- *Taxable Distributions*

The distributee is liable for the GST tax in the case of a taxable distribution and must file Form 706-GS(D) (Generation-Skipping Transfer Tax Return for Distributions). The trustee of the trust involved in a taxable distribution must file Form 706-GS(D-1) (Notification of Distribution From a Generation-Skipping Trust). The trustee must send a copy of this form to each distributee. Filled-in Forms 706-GS(D-1) and 706-GS(D) appear at ¶ 2483 and ¶ 2485, respectively. Instructions for completing each of these forms appear at ¶ 2479.

- *Taxable Terminations*

The trustee is liable for the GST tax in the case of a taxable termination and is required to file Form 706-GS(T) (Generation-Skipping Transfer Tax Return for Terminations). A filled-in Form 706-GS(T) appears at ¶ 2490; instructions for filling in the form appear at ¶ 2487.

¶ 2473 Reporting Direct Skips Occurring at Death

Direct skips occurring at death are reported on Form 706 (United States Estate (and Generation-Skipping Transfer) Tax Return).

---

[7] Reg. § 26.2662-1(c)(1)(iv).

[8] Reg. § 26.2662-1(c)(2)(ii) states that the term "trust arrangement" includes any arrangement (other than an estate) which, although not an explicit trust, has the same effect as an explicit trust.

[9] Reg. § 26.2662-1(c)(2)(iii).

[10] Reg. § 26.2662-1(c)(2)(iv).

[11] Reg. § 26.2662-1(c)(2)(v).

The entire estate and GST tax must be paid on the due date of the return (within nine months of the decedent's date of death), unless an extension of time to pay has been granted.[12]

The estate tax is imposed on the value of the entire taxable estate regardless of who the distributees are. The GST tax is imposed on the value of property interests that actually pass to skip persons.

To report direct skips on Form 706, complete Schedules A through I in order to determine the property interests that are includible in the gross estate. Determine who the skip persons are. Then determine which skip persons are transferees of interests in property. Following these determinations, the direct skips to be reported must be divided between Schedules R and R-1, and these schedules must then be completed.[13]

Unless the Form 706 Instructions specifically provide otherwise, all generation-skipping transfers are reported on Schedule R.[14] For a direct skip to be reportable on Schedule R-1, the trust must be includible in the decedent's gross estate. The trustee, not the estate, is liable for the tax on direct skips from a trust. Schedule R-1 is to be used by the executor to notify the trustee that such a tax is due.

The estate tax value of the property interests subject to the direct skips are entered on Schedules R and R-1. If alternate valuation or special use valuation has been elected, those values must be entered on Schedules R and R-1. The allocation of the $1 million GST tax exemption is calculated using lines 4, 5, and 6 in Part 1 of Schedule R after completing Parts 2 and 3 of Schedule R, and Schedule R-1.

Part 2 of Schedule R is used to compute the GST tax on direct skips in which the property interests transferred bear the GST tax on the transfers.[15] The tax on transfers in which the property interests transferred do not bear the GST tax on the transfers is reported on Part 3.

---

[12] Instructions for Form 706 (Rev. July 1998), p. 2.

[13] Instructions for Form 706 (Rev. July 1998), p. 17.

[14] Instructions for Form 706 (Rev. July 1998), p. 18.

[15] Instructions for Form 706 (Rev. July 1998), p. 19.

¶ 2475 Filled-In Schedule R

The filled-in Schedule R, Form 706 (Rev. July 1998), relates to the fact situation of a person who died on January 1, 1998.

Form 706 (Rev. 7-98)

SCHEDULE R — Generation-Skipping Transfer Tax

Note: *To avoid application of the deemed allocation rules, Form 706 and Schedule R should be filed to allocate the GST exemption to trusts that may later have taxable terminations or distributions under section 2612 even if the form is not required to be filed to report estate or GST tax.*

*The GST tax is imposed on taxable transfers of interests in property located **outside the United States** as well as property located inside the United States.*

See instructions beginning on page 17.

Part 1. — GST Exemption Reconciliation (Section 2631) and Section 2652(a)(3) (Special QTIP) Election

You no longer need to check a box to make a section 2652(a)(3) (special QTIP) election. If you list qualifying property in Part 1, line 9, below, you will be considered to have made this election. See page 19 of the separate instructions for details.

1	Maximum allowable GST exemption	1	$1,000,000
2	Total GST exemption allocated by the decedent against decedent's lifetime transfers	2	0
3	Total GST exemption allocated by the executor, using Form 709, against decedent's lifetime transfers	3	0
4	GST exemption allocated on line 6 of Schedule R, Part 2	4	0
5	GST exemption allocated on line 6 of Schedule R, Part 3	5	50,000
6	Total GST exemption allocated on line 4 of Schedule(s) R-1	6	0
7	Total GST exemption allocated to intervivos transfers and direct skips (add lines 2 - 6)	7	50,000
8	GST exemption available to allocate to trusts and section 2032A interests (subtract line 7 from line 1)	8	950,000
9	Allocation of GST exemption to trusts (as defined for GST tax purposes):		

A Name of trust	B Trust's EIN (if any)	C GST exemption allocated on lines 2 - 6, above (see instructions)	D Additional GST exemption allocated (see instructions)	E Trust's inclusion ratio (optional — see instructions)
9D Total. May not exceed line 8, above		9D		

10	GST exemption available to allocate to section 2032A interests received by individual beneficiaries (subtract line 9D from line 8). You must attach special use allocation schedule (see instructions)	10	950,000

(The instructions to Schedule R are in the separate instructions.) **Schedule R — Page 33**

Form 706 (Rev. 7-98)

Estate of: James X. Diversey

Part 2. — Direct Skips Where the Property Interests Transferred Bear the GST Tax on the Direct Skips

Name of skip person	Description of property interest transferred	Estate tax value

1	Total estate tax values of all property interests listed above	1	0
2	Estate taxes, state death taxes, and other charges borne by the property interests listed above	2	0
3	GST taxes borne by the property interests listed above but imposed on direct skips other than those shown on this Part 2 (see instructions)	3	0
4	Total fixed taxes and other charges (add lines 2 and 3)	4	0
5	Total tentative maximum direct skips (subtract line 4 from line 1)	5	0
6	GST exemption allocated	6	0
7	Subtract line 6 from line 5	7	0
8	GST tax due (divide line 7 by 2.818182)	8	0
9	Enter the amount from line 8 of Schedule R, Part 3	9	0
10	Total GST taxes payable by the estate (add lines 8 and 9). Enter here and on line 22 of the Tax Computation on page 1	10	0

Schedule R — Page 34

Form 706 (Rev. 7-98)

Estate of: James X. Diversey

Part 3. — Direct Skips Where the Property Interests Transferred Do Not Bear the GST Tax on the Direct Skips

Name of skip person	Description of property interest transferred	Estate tax value
Katherine Diversey	Unimproved lot, Schaumburg, IL (Schedule A, Item 4). (Under paragraph 10 of the decedent's will, all federal estate and generation-skipping transfer taxes, as well as all state inheritance taxes, are payable from the residue).	50,000

1	Total estate tax values of all property interests listed above	1	50,000
2	Estate taxes, state death taxes, and other charges borne by the property interests listed above	2	0
3	GST taxes borne by the property interests listed above but imposed on direct skips other than those shown on this Part 3 (see instructions)	3	0
4	Total fixed taxes and other charges (add lines 2 and 3)	4	0
5	Total tentative maximum direct skips (subtract line 4 from line 1)	5	50,000
6	GST exemption allocated	6	50,000
7	Subtract line 6 from line 5	7	0
8	GST tax due (multiply line 7 by .55). Enter here and on Schedule R, Part 2, line 9	8	0

Schedule R — Page 35

¶ 2477 Schedule R-1

Reproduced below is Schedule R-1, Generation-Skipping Transfer Tax, Direct Skips From a Trust, Payment Voucher, Form 706 (Rev. July 1998), which serves as a notification from the executor to the trustee that a generation-skipping transfer tax is due. The schedule is not filled in because no direct skip was made from a trust that was includible in the estate of James X. Diversey.

SCHEDULE R-1 (Form 706)
(Rev. July 1998)
Department of the Treasury
Internal Revenue Service

Generation-Skipping Transfer Tax
Direct Skips From a Trust
Payment Voucher

OMB No. 1545-0015

Executor: File one copy with Form 706 and send two copies to the fiduciary. Do not pay the tax shown. See the separate instructions.
Fiduciary: See instructions on the following page. Pay the tax shown on line 6.

Name of trust		Trust's EIN
Name and title of fiduciary	Name of decedent	
Address of fiduciary (number and street)	Decedent's SSN	Service Center where Form 706 was filed
City, state, and ZIP code	Name of executor	
Address of executor (number and street)	City, state, and ZIP code	
Date of Decedent's death	Filing due date of Schedule R, Form 706 (with extensions)	

Part 1. — Computation of the GST Tax on the Direct Skip

Description of property interests subject to the direct skip		Estate tax value
1 Total estate tax value of all property interests listed above	1	
2 Estate taxes, state death taxes, and other charges borne by the property interest listed above	2	
3 Tentative maximum direct skip from trust (subtract line 2 from line 1)	3	
4 GST exemption allocated	4	
5 Subtract line 4 from line 3	5	
6 **GST tax due from fiduciary** (divide line 5 by 2.818182) **(See instructions if property will not bear the GST tax.)**	6	

Under penalties of perjury, I declare that I have examined this return, including accompanying schedules and statements, and to the best of my knowledge and belief, it is true, correct, and complete.

Signature(s) of executor(s) Date

Date

Signature of fiduciary or officer representing fiduciary Date

Schedule R-1 (Form 706) — Page 36

¶ 2479 Reporting Distributions

Forms 706-GS(D-1) and 706-GS(D) must be filed for trust distributions that are subject to the GST tax.

- *Form 706-GS(D-1)*

Form 706-GS(D-1) (Notification of Distribution From a Generation-Skipping Trust) is used by the trustee of a generation-skipping trust to report taxable distributions and to provide skip person distributees (see ¶ 2435) with information needed to compute the GST tax on the distribution. The form has two copies: Copy A (to be filed with the IRS) and Copy B (to be sent to the skip person distributee).

When to File. Form 706-GS(D-1) must be filed with the IRS (Copy A), and sent to the distributee (Copy B) no later than April 15 of the year following the calendar year in which the distributions were made.[16]

Where to File. Copy A should be sent to the IRS Service Center in which the settlor's estate or gift tax return is filed. Copy B is to be sent to the skip person distributee.

The distributee is to report on Part II (Distributions) of Form 706-GS(D) all taxable distributions occurring in the year having an inclusion ratio greater than zero.

Nonexplicit Trusts. An arrangement that has substantially the same effect as a trust is treated as a trust for purposes of the GST tax even though it is not an explicit trust. Arrangements treated as nonexplicit trusts include insurance and annuity contracts, life estates, remainders and estates for years. Decedents' estates are not classified as nonexplicit trusts for purposes of Form 706-GS(D-1).

The person in actual or constructive possession of the property held in a nonexplicit trust is considered to be the trustee and is liable for filing Form 706-GS(D-1).[17]

Separate Trusts. Portions of a single trust must be treated as separate trusts for purposes of Form 706-GS(D-1) where:

(1) there are portions of the trust that are attributable to transfers from different transferors; or

(2) there are substantially separate and independent shares of different trust beneficiaries.[18]

- *Form 706-GS(D-1)—Line-by-Line Instructions*

Part I—General Instructions. The identifying number of the skip person distributee (whether an individual or a trust) is entered on line 1a of Part I (General Information) of Form 706-GS(D-1). Enter the social security number of the individual distributee on line 1a; if the skip person distributee is a trust, the trust's employer identification number (EIN) is entered on line 1a. Enter the skip person distributee's name, address and ZIP code on line 1b.

---

[16] Reg. § 26.2662-1(d).

[17] Instructions for Form 706-GS(D-1) (Rev. March 1995), p. 1.

[18] Instructions for Form 706-GS(D-1) (Rev. March 1995), pp. 1–2.

The employer identification number of the trust from which the distribution was made is entered on line 2a, and the trust's name, address and ZIP code are entered on line 2b.

Part II—Distributions. Report all distributions from any given trust to a single skip person distributee during the calendar year on Part II. The following information is entered under the columns of line 3 for each distribution:

(Column a) Item number: Consecutive numbers should be assigned to each distribution made during the year. Properties having different inclusion ratios are listed separately. Properties having the same inclusion ratio may be included under a single item number, even if they were distributed at different times.

(Column b) Description of property: Each parcel of real estate should be described in enough detail so that it may be located for inspection and valuation. If the parcel is improved, the improvements should be described. Any personal property distributed must be described in enough detail that the IRS can ascertain its value.

Stocks: For stocks, the following information should be supplied:

—Number of shares

—Classification of stock; common or preferred

—Issue

—Par value (where needed for valuation)

—Price per share

—Exact name of corporation

—Principal exchange upon which the stock is sold

—CUSIP number, if available

Bonds: For bonds, the following information should be supplied:

—Quantity and denomination

—Name of obligor

—Date of maturity

—Principal exchange upon which the bond is listed

—Interest rate

—Interest due date

—CUSIP number, if available

If a stock or bond is not listed on an exchange, the company's principal business office should be listed.

(Column c) Date of distribution: The trustee must disclose the date of distribution.

(Column d) Inclusion ratio: The trustee must provide an inclusion ratio (see ¶ 2461) for every distribution.

(Column e) Value: The trustee's responsibility with respect to valuing the property depends on the type of the property distributed. The trustee is required to provide the value of property having an objectively identifiable value, such as cash, stocks or bonds. For other property, the trustee may provide a value but is only required to give the distributee all the information the trustee has that will help the distributee to determine the value of the distribution.

(Column f) Tentative transfer: The amount of the tentative transfer is the value, entered in column e, multiplied by the inclusion ratio, entered in column d.

Part III—Trust Information. Only Copy A (which goes to the IRS) contains Part III—Trust Information, which requires the trustee to answer the questions on lines 4 through 7.

If the trust for which the Form 706-GS(D-1) is filed is a nonexplicit trust, the trustee filing the form must check the box on line 4 and attach a statement describing the trust arrangement that is substantially similar to an explicit trust.

If property has been contributed to the trust since the last Form 706-GS(T) (Generation-Skipping Transfer Tax Return For Terminations) or 706-GS(D-1) was filed, a schedule must be attached showing how the inclusion ratio was calculated (line 5).

Line 6 questions whether any contributions were made to the trust since the last Form 706-GS(T) or 706-GS(D-1) was filed that were not included in calculating the trust's inclusion ratio. If the answer is "Yes," a statement explaining why the contribution was not included must be attached.

If any exemption has been allocated to the trust by reason of the deemed allocation rules, this is indicated on line 7.

Signature Required. Copy A of Form 706-GS(D-1) must be signed by the trustee or an authorized representative.

IRS Service Center. On Copy B of Form 706-GS(D-1), the copy sent to the skip person distributee, the trustee must enter the name and address of the IRS Service Center where the distributee should report the distribution on Form 706-GS(D). This is the IRS Service Center for the state where an estate or gift tax return of the settlor must be filed to report the most recent transfer to the trust. It is the same Service Center to which the trustee mails Copy A. If the settlor is (or was at death) a nonresident citizen or alien, the forms should be mailed to the IRS Service Center in Philadelphia.[19]

• *Form 706-GS(D)*

Form 706-GS(D) (Generation-Skipping Transfer Tax Return for Distributions) generally must be filed with respect to taxable trust distributions (see ¶ 2471).

The form is filed by the skip person (see ¶ 2435) recipients of the trust distributions. In preparing Form 706-GS(D), trust distributees will have to consult the applicable portions of the copy of the completed Form

---

[19] Instructions for Form 706-GS(D-1) (Rev. March 1995), p. 1.

706-GS(D-1) that the trustee of the generation-skipping trust is required to submit to them.

Time and Place of Filing. Form 706-GS(D) generally must be filed no later than April 15 of the year following the calendar year in which the distributions were made. Form 706-GS(D) should be filed at the IRS Service Center that the trustee has included at the bottom of Copy B, Form 706-GS(D-1), the distributee's copy.[20]

● *Form 706-GS(D)—Line-by-Line Instructions*

Part I, General Information. The name of the skip person distributee (whether an individual or a trust) is entered on line 1a of Part I, General Information, Form 706-GS(D). If the skip person distributee is an individual, that individual's social security number is entered on line 1b; if the skip person distributee is a trust, the trust's employer identification number (EIN) is entered on line 1c. In no case should numbers appear on both lines 1b and 1c.

The name and title of the person filing the return is entered on line 2a, but only if different from the name entered on line 1a. The trustee's name should be entered here if the skip person distributee is a trust. If the skip person distributee is a minor, or an adult under a disability that precludes the distributee from filing the return, the name of the person who is legally responsible for conducting the distributee's affairs, such as a parent or guardian, should be entered on line 2a. The parent's or guardian's title or relationship to the distributee should be included.

The address of the distributee or person filing the return is entered on line 2b.

Part II, Distributions. All taxable distributions with inclusion ratios greater than zero that the distributee received during the year are reported on Part II of Form 706-GS(D). If additional space is required, the distributee should attach an additional sheet of the same size and use the same format that is used in Part II to report any additional distributions.

(Column a) Trust EIN: The employer identification number of the distributing trust, from line 2a, Form 706-GS(D-1), is entered in column a of Part II.

(Column b) Item number: The same item number that was used for the corresponding distribution on Form 706-GS(D-1), line 3, column a, should be entered in column b. If the distributee receives distributions from more than one trust, the same item number may have to be repeated.

(Column c) Amount of transfer: The amount of transfer will usually be entered from line 3, column f, of Form 706-GS(D-1), unless the trustee has not entered any amount there or the distributee disagrees with the amount that the trustee has entered. If the distributee and the trustee disagree about the amount of the tentative transfer, the distributee should attach a statement to Form 706-GS(D) showing what the distributee considers the correct amounts and how they were computed.

The total tentative transfers from Part II and from any continuation sheet should be entered on line 3 of Part II. The distributee should also

---

[20] Instructions for Form 706-GS(D) (Rev. March 1995), p. 1.

attach to Form 706-GS(D) a copy of each Form 706-GS(D-1) received during the year.

Part III, Tax Computation. Enter the amount of total transfers on line 3 of Part II. Adjusted allowable expenses are deducted from the line 3 amount, and the resulting amount entered on line 5 which appears in Part III. For purposes of this deduction, expenses incurred in connection with the preparation of Form 706-GS(D), or any other expenses incurred in connection with the determination, collection or refund of the generation-skipping transfer tax reported on the return are totalled and multiplied by the inclusion ratio. The resulting product is the amount of the "adjusted allowable expenses." A distributee who has more than one inclusion ratio to report on Part II must prorate the total expense among them, based on the relative value of each distribution.

An expense item may be included in the total of line 4 allowable expenses even if it has not been paid at the time the return is filed, provided that the amount of the expense is clearly ascertainable at that time. If an additional allowable expense is incurred after Form 706-GS(D) is filed, a refund should be claimed on Form 843 (Claim for Refund and Request for Abatement (Rev. January 1997)).[21]

A credit for state GST taxes paid may be claimed on line 8 if the taxable distribution occurred at the same time as, and as a result of, the death of an individual and the distribution is reported on the same Form 706-GS(D). However, the credit for the state GST tax paid is limited to a maximum of five percent of the federal gross GST tax reported on line 7.

Signature Required. Form 706-GS(D) must be signed by the distributee or by the distributee's authorized representative.

¶ 2481 Facts for Hypothetical Taxable Distribution

For purposes of the filled-in Forms 706-GS(D-1) and 706-GS(D), appearing at ¶ 2483 and ¶ 2485, respectively, the following facts are assumed:

On his death, Able Smith's will established the Able Smith GST Trust for the benefit of his son, Baker, his grandson Charlie, and his granddaughter Delta. The trust provides that the income from the trust corpus of $5 million is to go to Baker for life, with the remainder to go to Charlie and Delta at Baker's death. In addition, the trustee is given the power to invade trust corpus for the benefit of Charlie and/or Delta. Ten months later, the trustee exercises the power, transferring $100,000 in cash to Charlie.

No Schedule R or R-1 was filed because the transfer was to a trust having at least one non-skip person beneficiary (hence the trust was a non-skip person).

---

[21] Instructions for Form 706-GS(D) (Rev. March 1995), p. 2.

¶ 2483 Filled-In Form 706-GS(D-1)

Form **706-GS(D-1)**
(Rev. March 1995)
Department of The Treasury
Internal Revenue Service

Notification of Distribution From a Generation-Skipping Trust
(Complete for each skip person distributee—see separate instructions.)
For calendar year 1998

OMB No. 1545-1143

Copy A—Send to IRS

Part I General Information

1a Skip person distributee's identifying number (see instructions)	2a Trust's employer identification number (see instructions)
123-45-6789	77-6654321
1b Skip person distributee's name, address, and ZIP code	**2b** Trust's name, address, and ZIP code
Charles Smith 1130 South Harvey Ave. Oak Park, IL 60304	Able Smith GSTT Trust Southern Trust Company 100 South Lake Street Oak Park, IL 60302

Part II Distributions

3 Describe each distribution below (see instructions).

a Item no.	b Description of property	c Date of distribution	d Inclusion ratio	e Value (see instructions)	f Tentative transfer (multiply col. e by col. d)
1	Cash; distribution from corpus of Able Smith GSTT Trust	12-28-98	.7140	100,000	71,400.00

Part III Trust Information (see instructions)

4 If this is not an explicit trust, check the box and attach a statement describing the arrangement that makes its effect substantially similar to an explicit trust ☐

		Yes	No
5	Has any property been contributed to this trust since the last Form 706-GS(T) or (D-1) was filed? If "Yes," attach a schedule showing how the trust's inclusion ratio has been refigured		X
6	Have any contributions been made to this trust since the last Form 706-GS(T) or (D-1) was filed that were not included in calculating the trust's inclusion ratio? If "Yes," attach a statement explaining why the contributions were not included		X
7	Has any exemption been allocated to this trust by reason of the deemed allocation rules?		X

Under penalties of perjury, I declare that I have examined this return, including accompanying schedules and statements, and to the best of my knowledge and belief, it is true, correct, and complete. Declaration of preparer other than trustee is based on all information of which preparer has any knowledge.

Signature of trustee ▶ Charles Smith Date ▶ 4-15-99

Signature of preparer other than trustee ▶ Dunderson Caylor III Date ▶ 4-15-99

Address ▶

For Paperwork Reduction Act Notice, see page 1 of the separate trustee's instructions. Form 706-GS(D-1) (Rev. 3-95)

Form **706-GS(D-1)**
(Rev. March 1995)
Department of The Treasury
Internal Revenue Service

Notification of Distribution From a Generation-Skipping Trust
(Complete for each skip person distributee—see separate instructions.)
For calendar year 1998

OMB No. 1545-1143

Copy B—For Distributee

Part I **General Information**

1a Skip person distributee's identifying number (see instructions)	2a Trust's employer identification number (see instructions)
123-45-6789	77-6654321
1b Skip person distributee's name, address, and ZIP code	2b Trust's name, address, and ZIP code
Charles Smith 1130 South Harvey Ave. Oak Park IL 60304	Able Smith GSTT Trust Southern Trust Company 100 South Lake Street Oak Park IL 60302

Part II **Distributions**

3 Describe each distribution below (see instructions).

a Item no.	b Description of property	c Date of distribution	d Inclusion ratio	e Value (see instructions)	f Tentative transfer (multiply col. e by col. d)
1	Cash; distribution from corpus of Able Smith GSTT Trust	12-28-98	.7140	100,000	71,400.00

Skip Person Distributee—To report this distribution, you must file Form 706-GS(D), Generation-Skipping Transfer Tax Return for Distributions, at the following Internal Revenue Service Center. ▶

For Paperwork Reduction Act Notice, see page 1 of the separate trustee's instructions. Form **706-GS(D-1)** (Rev. 3-95)

¶ 2485 Filled-In Form 706-GS(D)

Form **706-GS(D)** (Rev. March 1995) Department of the Treasury Internal Revenue Service

Generation-Skipping Transfer Tax Return For Distributions

For calendar year 19 98

OMB No. 1545-1144

Attach a copy of all Forms 706-GS(D-1) to this return.

Part I General Information

1a Name of skip person distributee	1b Social security number of individual distributee (see instructions)
Charles Smith	123-45-6789
2a Name and title of person filing return (if different from 1a, see instructions)	1c Employer identification number of trust distributee (see instructions)

2b Address of distributee or person filing return (see instructions) (number and street or P.O. box; city, town, or post office; state; and ZIP code)

1310 South Harvey Ave.
Oak Park, IL 60304

Part II Distributions

a Trust EIN (from line 2a, Form 706-GS(D-1))	b Item no. (from line 3, column a, Form 706-GS(D-1))	c Amount of Transfer (from Total Transfers, line 3, column f, Form 706-GS(D-1))
77-6654321	1	71,400
3 Total transfers (add amounts in column c)	3	71,400

Part III Tax Computation

Attach check or money order here

Line	Description			Line	Amount
4	Adjusted allowable expenses (see instructions)			4	178
5	Taxable amount (subtract line 4 from line 3)			5	71,222
6	Maximum Federal estate tax rate (see instructions)			6	55 %
7	Gross GST tax (multiply line 5 by line 6)			7	39,172
8	Creditable state GST tax (if any)	8	0		
9	Multiply line 7 by 5% (.05)	9	1,959		
10	Allowable credit (enter the smaller of line 8 or line 9)			10	0
11	Net GST tax (subtract line 10 from line 7)			11	39,172
12	Payment made with Form 2758			12	0
13	TAX DUE — If line 11 is larger than line 12, enter amount owed *(Make the check payable to the Internal Revenue Service.)*			13	39,172
14	Overpayment — If line 12 is larger than line 11, enter amount to be refunded.			14	0

Under penalties of perjury, I declare that I have examined this return, including accompanying schedules and statements, and to the best of my knowledge and belief, it is true, correct, and complete. Declaration of preparer other than taxpayer is based on all information of which preparer has any knowledge.

Please Sign Here Charles Smith — Signature of taxpayer or person filing on behalf of taxpayer — Date 4-15-99

Paid Preparer's Use Only Preparer's signature: Gunderson Cuyler III — Date 4-15-99
Firm's name (or yours if self-employed) and address: Gunderson Cuyler III, 1419 Granger Ave., Elk Grove, IL — ZIP code 60007

For Paperwork Reduction Act Notice, see page 1 of separate instructions. Form 706-GS(D) (Rev. 3-95)

¶ 2487 Reporting Terminations

Generation-skipping terminations are reported on Form 706-GS(T) (Generation-Skipping Transfer Tax Return for Terminations) (see ¶ 2471). The form is used by a trustee to compute and report the GST tax due with respect to certain trust terminations (see ¶ 2433).

Form 706-GS(T) must be filed at the IRS Service Center for the state where an estate or gift tax is filed, no later than April 15 of the year following the calendar year in which the termination occurred.

● *Non-explicit Trust*

An arrangement that has substantially the same effect as a trust is treated as a trust for purposes of the generation-skipping transfer tax even though it is not an explicit trust. Arrangements treated as non-explicit trusts include insurance and annuity contracts, life estates, remainders and estates for years. Decedents' estates are not classified as non-explicit trusts for purposes of Form 706-GS(T) (see ¶ 2439). The person in actual or constructive possession of the property held in a non-explicit trust is considered to be the trustee and is responsible for filing Form 706-GS.[22]

● *Separate Trusts*

Portions of a single trust must be treated as separate trusts for purposes of Form 706-GS(T) when:

(1) portions of the trust are attributable to transfers from different transferors, or

(2) substantially separate and independent shares are for different trust beneficiaries.

If a single trust is treated as separate trusts under the above rules, a single Form 706-GS(T) is filed, but a separate Schedule A must be filed with respect to each such separate trust.

● *Medical and Educational Exclusion*

Form 706-GS(T) need not be filed if the termination is not a generation-skipping transfer by reason of the gift tax exclusion for amounts paid for medical or educational expenses. This occurs if the property was distributed and used for medical or educational expenses of the transferee and would not have been subject to gift tax if the transfer had been made during an individual's lifetime.

● *Form 706-GS(T)—Line-by-Line Instructions*

The Form 706-GS(T) instructions (Rev. March 1995) indicate that the form is to be filled out in the following order: (1) Parts I and II, (2) Schedule A (through line 4), (3) Schedule B, (4) Schedule A (lines 5 through 14), and (5) Part III.

Part I, General Information. Enter the name of the trust and the trust's Employer Identification Number (EIN) on lines 1a and 1b of Part I, General Information, of Form 706-GS(T) (Rev. March 1995). Non-explicit trusts, as well as explicit trusts, must have an EIN. The name and

---

[22] Instructions for Form 706-GS(T) (Rev. March 1995), pp. 1–2.

the address of the trustee (or the person who is considered to be the trustee under the non-explicit trust rules) are entered on lines 2a and 2b.

Part II, Trust Information. The trustee is required to answer the questions on lines 3 through 8 of Part II.

Line 3 questions whether any exemption has been allocated to the trust by reason of the deemed allocation rules of Code Sec. 2632(b) and (c) (see ¶ 2455). If the answer is "Yes," the allocation must be described on an attachment to Schedule A, line 7, showing how the inclusion ratio (see ¶ 2461) was calculated.

If property has been contributed to the trust since the last Form 706-GS(T) or 706-GS(D-1) was filed, a schedule showing how the inclusion ratio was calculated should be attached (line 4).

If terminations occurred that were not reported because of payments relating to medical and educational exclusions or prior payment of the generation-skipping transfer tax, check the "Yes" box on line 5, and attach a statement describing the termination.

Line 6 asks whether any contributions were made to the trust that were not included in calculating the trust's inclusion ratio. If the answer is "Yes," a statement explaining why the contribution was not included must be attached.

If the special QTIP election with respect to Code Sec. 2652(a)(3) has been made for the trust, this is indicated on line 7.

If the trust to which the Form 706-GS(T) is filed is a non-explicit trust, check the box on line 8, and attach a statement describing the trust arrangement that makes it substantially similar to an explicit trust.

Schedule A. Separate copies of Schedule A will have to be filed for each terminating interest of a single trust that has a different inclusion ratio. Under line 1 are listed the names of the skip persons and their respective SSNs, EINs, and the item number from line 4 of Schedule A in which the interest is held. The terminating power or interest is described in the space provided at line 2. If the trustee is reporting separate trusts, the reason for treating parts of the trust as separate trusts should be included here.

If the trustee wishes to elect alternate valuation, the election is made on line 3 of Schedule A.

The following information must be entered under the columns of line 4 for each taxable termination:

(Column a) Item number: All property having the same termination date, valuation date, and unit price may be combined under the same item number. Otherwise, a separate item number should be assigned to each article of property.

(Column b) Description of property subject to termination: Each parcel of real estate should be described in enough detail so that it may be located for inspection and valuation. If the parcel is improved, the improvements should be described. Personal property should be described in enough detail so that the IRS can ascertain its value.

Stocks: For stocks, the following information should be supplied:

—Number of shares

—Classification of stock: common or preferred

—Issue

—Par value (where needed for valuation)

—Price per share

—Exact name of corporation

—Principal exchange upon which stock is sold

—CUSIP number, if available

Bonds: For bonds, the following information should be supplied:

—Quantity and denomination

—Name of obligor

—Date of maturity

—Principal exchange, if listed on an exchange

—Interest rate

—Interest due date

—CUSIP number, if available

If a stock or bond is not listed on an exchange, the company's principal business office should be listed.

(Column c) Date of termination: The trustee must disclose the date of termination.

(Column d) Valuation date: Unless the trustee elected the alternate valuation date, this date should be the same as the termination date.

(Column e) Value: The value of property to be reported on Schedule A should be entered, reduced by the amount of any consideration that was provided by the skip person. An explanation of how the values were determined should be included, along with copies of any appraisals.

Deductible Expenses. In determining the taxable amount for a taxable termination, certain expenses (under rules generally similar to those discussed at ¶ 780) may be deducted from the value of the property subject to the termination. These expenses are deducted on Schedule B(1) (General Trust Debts, Expenses, and Taxes) or Schedule B(2) (Specific Termination-Related Debts, Expenses, and Taxes).

Schedule B(1). Enter the item number, description and amount of expenses that are related to the entire trust in columns a, b, and c, respectively, of Schedule B(1). In addition to a description of the nature of the expenses listed in column b, the name and address of the persons to whom the expenses were paid should be included.

The percentage of the expenses allocable to the property involved in the termination is to be entered on line 2. This percentage is determined by way of a two-step computation, as follows:

(1) the value of the interest that was terminated is divided by the total value of the trust at the time of the termination; and

(2) the amount determined under (1), above, is to be multiplied by a fraction, the numerator of which is the number of days in the year through the date of the termination, and the demoninator of which is the total number of days in the year, or, if the entire trust was terminated during the year, the total number of days the trust was in existence during the year.

Schedule B(2). The item number, description and amount of expenses that are related solely to the interest that has terminated are entered in columns a, b, and c, respectively, of Schedule B(2). If the expense entered relates to more property than is involved in the termination, but less than the entire trust, only the amount attributable to the property involved in the termination is to be entered in column c. This amount is determined by multiplying the total expense by a fraction, the numerator of which is the value of the property involved in the termination and to which the expense pertains, and the denominator of which is the total value of the property to which the expense pertains.

Schedule A, lines 5–14. The amount of the total deductions applicable to the Schedule A (carried over from the corresponding Schedule B, line 5) is entered on line 5. The inclusion ratio (see ¶ 2461) must be calculated with respect to every termination, and entered on line 7. All terminations, or any parts of a single termination that have different inclusion ratios must be shown on a separate Schedule A. The product of the amount shown on line 7 (inclusion ratio) and the maximum federal estate tax rate shown (line 8) is the applicable rate entered on line 9. That applicable rate is then multiplied by the taxable amount (line 6) to obtain the gross generation-skipping transfer tax to be entered on line 10.

If the taxable termination occurs at the same time as, and as a result of, the death of an individual, the trustee may claim a credit for any state-imposed generation-skipping transfer tax with regard to property that was also included as a termination reported on Form 706-GS(T). If applicable, enter this amount on line 11, although the allowable credit (line 13) is limited to the greater of the actual state generation-skipping transfer taxes paid, and five percent of the gross generation-skipping transfer tax computed on line 12. The net federal generation-skipping transfer tax with respect to the termination reported on the Schedule A is computed by subtracting the amount on line 13 from the amount on line 10. This amount is entered on line 14 (and, in turn, entered also on line 9a, Part III of Form 706-GS(T)).

Signature Required. Form 706-GS(T) must be signed by the trustee or by his authorized representative.

¶ 2489 Facts for Hypothetical Taxable Termination

For purposes of the filled-in Form 706-GS(T) at ¶ 2490, the following facts are assumed:

> Frank Wood established the Frank Wood Trust on January 1, 1987, funded with $4,000,000. Frank's son, Sanford, was to receive the trust's income for life, with trust remainder to go to Glenn (Frank's grandson) at Sanford's death. Upon Sanford's death on November 15, 1998, the trust corpus of $4,000,000 was distributed to Glenn. Frank Wood elected to apply the full

amount of his $1,000,000 generation-skipping transfer tax exemption to the $4,000,000 transferred into the trust. Accordingly, the inclusion ratio reported on Form 706-GS(T) upon termination of the trust is computed as:

$$1 - \frac{1{,}000{,}000}{4{,}000{,}000} = 1 - 1/4 = .75$$

¶ 2490 Filled-In Form 706-GS(T)

Form **706-GS(T)** (Rev. March 1995) Department of the Treasury Internal Revenue Service

Generation-Skipping Transfer Tax Return For Terminations

For calendar year 19 98

OMB No. 1545-1145

Part I General Information

1a Name of trust	1b Trust's employer identification number (see instructions)
Frank Wood Trust	58-4343434

2a Name of trustee

Aldrich Wolcott

2b Trustee's address (number and street or P.O. box; apt. or suite no.; city, town or post office; state and ZIP code)

1234 W. Ridgeview, Oak Park, IL 60304

Part II Trust Information (see page 3 of the instructions)

		Yes	No	Sch. A number(s)
3	Has any exemption been allocated to this trust by reason of the deemed allocation rules of section 2632 (b) and (c)? If "Yes," describe the allocation on the line 7, Schedule A attachment showing how the inclusion ratio was calculated		x	
4	Has property been contributed to this trust since the last Form 706-GS(T) or 706-GS(D-1) was filed? If "Yes," attach a schedule showing how the inclusion ratio was calculated		x	
5	Have any terminations occurred that are not reported on this return because of the exceptions in section 2611(b)(1) or (2) relating to medical and educational exclusions and prior payment of GST tax? If "Yes," attach a statement describing the termination		x	
6	Have any contributions been made to this trust that were not included in calculating the trust's inclusion ratio? If "Yes," attach a statement explaining why the contribution was not included		x	
7	Has the special QTIP election in section 2652(a)(3) been made for this trust?		x	

8 If this is not an explicit trust (see page 1 of the instructions under Who Must File), check box and attach a statement describing the trust arrangement that makes its effect substantially similar to an explicit trust ▶ ☐

Part III Tax Computation

9a Summary of attached Schedules A (see instructions for line 9b on page 6)

Schedule A No.			Net GST tax (from Sch. A, line 14)
1		9a1	1,643,813
2		9a2	
3		9a3	
4		9a4	
5		9a5	
6		9a6	
9b	Total from all additional Schedules A attached to this form ▶	9b	
10	Total net GST tax (add lines 9a1 - 9b)	10	1,643,813
11	Payment made with Form 2758	11	0
12	TAX DUE — If line 10 is larger than line 11, enter amount owed	12	1,643,813
13	Overpayment — If line 11 is larger than line 10, enter amount to be refunded	13	0

Please Sign Here Under penalties of perjury, I declare that I have examined this return, including accompanying schedules and statements, and to the best of my knowledge and belief, it is true, correct, and complete. Declaration of preparer other than fiduciary is based on all information of which preparer has any knowledge.

Aldrich Wolcott — Signature of fiduciary or officer representing fiduciary — Date 4-15-99

Paid Preparer's Use Only Preparer's signature — Date

Firm's name (or yours if self-employed) and address — ZIP code

For Paperwork Reduction Act Notice, see page 1 of separate instructions. Form **706-GS(T)** (Rev. 3-95)

Form 706-GS(T) (Rev. 3-95) Page 2

Name of trust	EIN of trust
Frank Wood Trust	58-4343434

Schedule A No.

Note: *Make copies of this schedule before completing it if you will need more than one Schedule A.*

Schedule A — Taxable Terminations
(See page 3 of the instructions before completing this schedule.)

1 a Name of skip persons	b SSN or EIN of skip person	c Item no. from line 4 below in which interest held
Glenn Wood	321-45-9876	1

2 Describe the terminating power or interest. If you need more space, attach an additional sheet.

Glenn Wood has the sole remainder interest in the Frank Wood Trust, created on January 1, 1998, by Frank Wood, who is Glenn's grandfather. Upon the death of the income beneficiary (Sanford Wood, Glenn's father) on November 15, 1998, all trust assets ($4,000,000) were distributed to Glenn.

3 If you elect alternate valuation, check here (see page 4 of the instructions) ▶ ☐

4 Describe each taxable termination below (see page 4 of the instructions)

a Item no.	b Description of property subject to termination	c Date of termination	d Valuation date	e Value
1	Cash from Frank Wood Trust	11-15-98	11-15-98	4,000,000

Line	Description			Line	Amount
	Total ▶			4	4,000,000
5	Total deductions applicable to this Schedule A (from attached Schedule B, line 5)			5	15,000
6	Taxable amount (subtract line 5 from line 4)			6	3,985,000
7	Inclusion ratio (attach separate schedule showing computation)			7	.7500
8	Maximum Federal estate tax rate (see page 6 of the instructions)			8	55 %
9	Applicable rate (multiply line 7 by line 8)			9	.4125
10	Gross GST tax (multiply line 6 by line 9)			10	1,643,813
11	Creditable state GST tax, if any (attach credit evidence)	11	0		
12	Multiply line 10 by 5% (.05)	12	82,191		
13	Allowable credit (enter the smaller of line 11 or line 12)			13	0
14	Net GST tax (subtract line 13 from line 10) (enter here and on line 9, Part III, page 1)			14	1,643,813

Schedule A (Form 706-GS(T)) (Rev. 3-95)

Form 706-GS(T) (Rev. 3-95) Page 3

Name of trust	Schedule A No. ▶
Frank Wood Trust	EIN of trust 58-4343434

Note: *Make copies of this schedule before completing it if you will need more than one Schedule B.*

Schedule B(1) — General Trust Debts, Expenses, and Taxes
(Section 2622(b)) (Enter only items related to the entire trust; see page 4 of the instructions.)

a Item no.	b Description	c Amount
1	Trustee fees paid to Aldrich State Bank, Oak Park, IL	15,000

1 Total of Schedule B(1)	1	15,000
2 Percentage allocated to corresponding Schedule A	2	100 %
3 Net deduction (multiply line 1 by line 2)	3	15,000

Schedule B(2) — Specific Termination-Related Debts, Expenses, and Taxes
(Section 2622(b)) (Enter only items related solely to terminations appearing on corresponding Schedule A; see page 5 of the instructions.)

a Item no.	b Description	c Amount
1		

4 Total of Schedule B(2)	4	0
5 Total — Add lines 3 and 4 (enter here and on line 5 of the corresponding Schedule A)	5	15,000

Schedules B(1) and B(2) (Form 706-GS(T)) (Rev. 3-95)

Special Valuation Rules

Chapter 51

ESTATE FREEZES

¶ 2500 Special Valuation Rules for Estate Freezes

The special valuation rules of Code Sec. 2701 through Code Sec. 2704 were enacted to prevent the transfer tax avoidance achieved by certain transfers to younger generations. In such transfers, the value of the transferred interest was determined by subtracting the value of the retained interest from the total value of the property. The value of the retained interest was overstated in order to reduce the value of the transferred interest and, consequently, the amount of the taxable gift.

In general, the special valuation rules preclude the undervaluation of gifts by providing rules for valuing retained interests. Code Sec. 2701 provides special rules for determining the amount of a gift when an individual transfers an equity interest in a corporation or a partnership to a family member while retaining an interest in the entity (see ¶ 2505). Code Sec. 2702 provides rules for determining the amount of a gift when an individual makes a transfer in trust to or for the benefit of a family member while retaining an interest in the trust (see ¶ 2550). Code Sec. 2703 disregards certain rights and restrictions for transfer tax valuation purposes (see ¶ 2580). Code Sec. 2704 forestalls the use of lapsing rights and restrictions to reduce transfer taxes (see ¶ 2590).

¶ 2505 Function of Code Sec. 2701

The classic estate freeze of a closely held business transferred the business's future appreciation to a younger generation in a manner that reduced or eliminated the transferor's gift tax cost.

> ***Example (1):*** Ben Thompson owns all of the common stock in Famco, which is valued at $50,000. As a result of a recapitalization, Thompson receives common and preferred noncumulative voting stock. Because the preferred stock has a par value approximating the corporation's liquidation value and confers a right to put the stock at par value, Thompson values the preferred stock at $50,000. Thomp-

son then gives the common stock to Chuck, his son, and assigns no value to the gift. At Thompson's death, the value of the preferred stock included in Thompson's gross estate is $50,000, but the value of Chuck's common stock has appreciated to $200,000.

Code Sec. 2701 addresses estate freezes by revaluing the older generation's retained interests. By assigning zero value or a lower value to the retained interest and using the subtraction method to value the gift, a higher value is assigned to the gifted interest for gift tax purposes. When the transferor dies, a special valuation adjustment may apply to lower the transferor's estate tax. Post-transfer appreciation, however, is not includible in the transferor's estate.

Example (2): Assume the same facts as in Example (1), except that Code Sec. 2701 applies. Thompson's retained preferred stock is valued at zero, and the gift of common stock to Chuck is valued at $50,000. The $50,000 value of the preferred stock included in Thompson's gross estate may be offset by a special valuation adjustment.

¶ 2510 Application of Code Sec. 2701

The Code Sec. 2701 valuation rules apply when (1) an interest in a corporation or a partnership is "transferred" to a "member of the family" of the transferor and (2) the transferor or an "applicable family member" retains an "applicable retained interest."[1]

Members of the Transferor's Family. Members of the family of the transferor are generally members of the younger generation and include:

(1) the transferor's spouse;

(2) a lineal descendant of the transferor or the transferor's spouse; and

(3) the spouse of any such descendant.[2]

Applicable Family Members. Applicable family members are generally members of the older generation and include:

(1) the transferor's spouse;

(2) any ancestor of the transferor or the transferor's spouse; and

(3) the spouse of any such ancestor.[3]

● *Code Sec. 2701 Transfers*

The following types of transactions are transfers for purposes of Code Sec. 2701:

(1) transactions in which full and adequate consideration is given, but such consideration is less than the value of the transferred interest as determined under Code Sec. 2701 (such transactions would not otherwise be treated as taxable gifts under the gift tax provisions);[4]

---

[1] Code Sec. 2701(a)(1); Reg. § 25.2701-1(a)(1).

[2] Code Sec. 2701(e)(1); Reg. § 25.2701-1(d)(1).

[3] Code Sec. 2701(e)(2); Reg. § 25.2701-1(d)(2).

[4] Reg. § 25.2701-1(b)(1).

(2) capital contributions to a new or existing entity;[5]

(3) changes in capital structure, including redemptions and recapitalizations, in which (a) the transferor or an applicable family member receives an applicable retained interest, (b) the transferor or applicable family member who holds an applicable retained interest before the transaction surrenders a junior equity interest and receives property other than an applicable retained interest, or (c) the transferor or applicable family member who holds an applicable retained interest before the transaction surrenders an equity interest other than a junior interest and the fair market value of the applicable retained interest is increased;[6] and

(4) terminations of an indirect holding in an entity through a grantor trust, or, if through another type of trust, then to the extent the value of the indirectly held interest would have been included in the indirect holder's gross estate if the indirect holder died immediately prior to the termination.[7]

The following transactions are not treated as Code Sec. 2701 transfers:

(1) Capital structure transactions that do not substantially change the interests held by the transferor, applicable family members and members of the transferor's family (for example, an exchange of nonvoting common stock for common stock with nonvoting lapsing rights);

(2) The shift of rights resulting from the execution of a qualified disclaimer; and

(3) The shift of rights resulting from the exercise, release or lapse of a power of appointment (other than a general power under Code Sec. 2514) except to the extent that such exercise, release, or lapse would constitute a transfer under the gift tax provisions.[8]

● *Applicable Retained Interests*

An applicable retained interest is either an extraordinary payment right or a distribution right in a family controlled entity.[9]

Extraordinary payment rights include any put, call or conversion right, any right to compel liquidation, or any similar right, the exercise or nonexercise of which affects the value of the transferred interest.[10] Extraordinary payment rights do not include (1) mandatory payment rights, (2) liquidation participation rights, (3) rights to Code Sec. 707(c) guaranteed payments, or (4) nonlapsing conversion rights.[11]

A distribution right is the right to receive distributions with respect to an equity interest.[12] Distribution rights do not include (1) rights to receive distributions with respect to an interest that is of the same class as, or junior to, the transferred interest, (2) extraordinary payment rights, (3) mandatory payment rights, (4) liquidation participation rights, (5) rights

---

[5] Reg. § 25.2701-1(b)(2)(i)(A).

[6] Reg. § 25.2701-1(b)(2)(i)(B).

[7] Reg. § 25.2701-1(b)(2)(i)(C).

[8] Reg. § 25.2701-1(b)(3).

[9] Code Sec. 2701(b)(1).

[10] Code Sec. 2701(c)(2)(A); Reg. § 25.2701-2(b)(2).

[11] Reg. § 25.2701-2(b)(4).

[12] Code Sec. 2701(c)(1)(A).

to Code Sec. 707(c) guaranteed payments, or (6) nonlapsing conversion rights.[13]

For a distribution right to be considered an applicable retained interest, the entity must be family controlled.[14] Such control exists if at least 50 percent of the total voting power or fair market value of the equity interests in a corporation (or at least 50 percent of the capital or profits interests in a partnership) are owned by the transferor, applicable family members, or any lineal descendants of the transferor or the transferor's spouse. In the case of a limited partnership, control means the holding of any interest as a general partner.[15]

- *Exceptions to Application of Code Sec. 2701*

Code Sec. 2701 does not apply under the following circumstances:

(1) market quotations on an established securities market are readily available for the value of an applicable retained interest or for the transferred interest;

(2) the retained interest is of the same class as the transferred interest;

(3) the rights in the retained interest are proportionally the same as all the rights in the transferred interest, without regard to nonlapsing differences in voting power (or, for a partnership, nonlapsing differences with respect to management and limitations on liability);[16] or

(4) the transfer results in a proportionate reduction of each class of equity interest held by the transferor and all applicable family members in the aggregate immediately before the transfer.[17]

For purposes of (3), above, a right that lapses by reason of federal or state law is treated as a nonlapsing right unless the IRS issues a contrary regulation or ruling,[18] Thus, for example, the IRS has ruled that the interest of a general partner who made a gift of limited partnership interests while retaining an interest as a general partner was not treated as an applicable retained interest since the retained rights were identical to the rights of the interest transferred except for nonlapsing differences with respect to management and limitations on liability.[19]

¶ 2515 Valuation of Applicable Retained Interests

Extraordinary payment rights are valued at zero. Distribution rights are also valued at zero unless they are qualified payment rights. If a qualified payment right exists in conjunction with one or more extraordinary payment rights, it is presumed that each extraordinary payment right is exercised in a way that results in the lowest value for all such rights.[20] If an applicable retained interest does not contain rights that are

---

[13] Reg. § 25.2701-2(b)(3)-(4).

[14] Code Sec. 2701(b)(1)(A).

[15] Code Sec. 2701(b)(2); Reg. § 25.2701-2(b)(5).

[16] Code Sec. 2701(a)(2); Reg. § 25.2701-1(c)(1)-(3).

[17] Reg. § 25.2701-1(c)(4).

[18] Reg. § 25.2701-1(c)(3).

[19] IRS Letter Ruling 9415007, 1-12-94, CCH IRS LETTER RULINGS REPORTS.

[20] Code Sec. 2701(a)(3).

valued at zero or under the "lower of" rule, the retained interest is valued at its fair market value.[21]

- *Qualified Payments*

Qualified payments include the following:

(1) dividends payable on a periodic basis (at least annually) with respect to any cumulative preferred stock to the extent such dividends are determined at a fixed rate;

(2) other cumulative distributions payable on a periodic basis (at least annually) with respect to an equity interest to the extent they are determined at a fixed rate or as a fixed amount; and

(3) any distribution rights that the transferor has elected (or partially elected) to treat as qualified payments, provided that the amounts and times of payment specified in the election do not exceed the distributions authorized under the instrument.[22]

A payment rate is determined at a fixed rate if it bears a fixed relationship to a specified market interest rate.

A transferor holding a qualified payment right may elect (or partially elect) to treat all rights of the same class as not being qualified payment rights.[23]

Example: Betty Edson owns all of the common and preferred stock in Famco. Edson has the right to put all 200 shares of preferred stock having an annual cumulative dividend of $20 per share to Famco for $180,000. Assuming that the fair market value of Famco is $300,000 and the value of the cumulative dividend is $200,000, she transfers the common stock to her child and retains the preferred. Because Edson holds an extraordinary payment right (the put right) in conjunction with a qualified payment right (the right to cumulative dividends), the "lower of" rule applies and it is assumed that the put will be exercised immediately. The preferred stock is valued at $180,000 (lower of $180,000 or $200,000). Accordingly, the resulting gift is $120,000 ($300,000 minus $180,000). If Edson's put right did not exist, the applicable retained interest would consist only of a qualified payment right. Accordingly, the value of the preferred stock would be $200,000 and the resulting gift would be $100,000.

¶ 2520 Determination of Amount of Gift

After the amount of the retained interest has been determined, the subtraction method is used to determine the amount of the gift.[24] In general, the values of all family-held senior equity interests are subtracted from the fair market value of all family-held interests in the entity as determined immediately before the transfer. Although the values of senior equity interests are determined under the rules of Code Sec. 2701 if they are held by the transferor and applicable family members, other family-held senior equity interests are valued at their fair market value. The

[21] Reg. § 25.2701-2(a)(4).

[22] Code Sec. 2701(c)(3); Reg. § 25.2701-2(b)(6).

[23] Code Sec. 2701(c)(3)(C)(i); Reg. § 25.2701-2(c).

[24] Reg. § 25.2701-3.

resulting balance is allocated among the transferred interests and other family-held junior interests. Certain discounts and other reductions are allowed under appropriate circumstances.[25] A 10-percent minimum value rule also applies to the valuation of gifts of junior equity interests.[26]

Family-Held Interests. Family-held interests are interests held directly or indirectly by the transferor, applicable family members, and any lineal descendants of the parents of the transferor or the transferor's spouse.[27]

Senior Equity Interests. Senior equity interests are interests that carry a right to distributions of income or capital that is preferred in comparison to the rights of the transferred interest.[28]

Junior (Subordinate) Equity Interests. Junior equity interests are equity interests that are junior to the applicable retained interest.[29]

- *Four-Step Subtraction Method*

The amount of the gift is determined in the following four steps:

(1) Value Family-Held Interests. In general, determine the value of all family-held equity interests in the entity immediately after the transfer (under the assumption that they are held by one individual). In the case of a contribution to capital, determine the fair market value of the contribution.

(2) Subtract the Value of Senior Equity Interests. Subtract from the amount determined in Step (1), (a) the sum of the fair market value of all family-held senior equity interests (other than applicable retained interests held by the transferor or applicable family members) *plus* the fair market value of any family-held interests of the same class or a junior class to transferred interests held by persons other than the transferor, applicable family members, and members of the transferor's family, and (b) the value of all applicable retained interests held by the transferor or applicable family members, as adjusted (see below).

If the value in Step (1) was determined under the special rule for contributions to capital, the value of any applicable retained interest received in exchange for the contribution must be subtracted from that value.

Adjustment. The percentage of any class of applicable retained interest held by the transferor and applicable family members that exceeds the "family interest percentage" is treated as a family-held interest that is not held by the transferor or an applicable family member. The family interest percentage is the highest ownership percentage (based on relative fair market values) of family-held interests in any class of junior equity interest or all junior equity interests, valued in the aggregate.

(3) Allocate the Remaining Value. The amount remaining after Step (2) is allocated among the transferred interests and the

[25] Reg. § 25.2701-3(a)(1).

[26] Code Sec. 2701(a)(4); Reg. § 25.2701-3(c).

[27] Reg. § 25.2701-3(a)(2)(i).

[28] Reg. § 25.2701-3(a)(2)(ii).

[29] Reg. § 25.2701-3(a)(2)(iii).

other junior equity interests held by the transferor, applicable family members, and members of the transferor's family. If there is more than one class of family-held junior equity interests, the allocation begins with the most senior class of junior equity interests in a manner that most fairly approximates their value if all the rights valued at zero did not exist. Any amount not appropriately allocated in this manner is allocated to the interests in proportion to their fair market values without regard to Code Sec. 2701.

(4) **Determine the Amount of the Gift.** The amount allocated to the transferred interests in Step (3) is reduced to make such of the following adjustments as are applicable:

(a) **Reduction for Minority or Similar Discounts.** The amount of the gift is reduced by the excess, if any, of (1) a pro rata portion of the fair market value of the family-held interests of the same class (determined as if all voting rights conferred by family-held equity interests were held by one person), over (2) the value of the transferred interest (determined without regard to Code Sec. 2701).

(b) **Reduction for Transfers with Retained Interest.** The amount of the gift is reduced by the amount, if any, of the reduction required under Code Sec. 2702 to reflect the value of a retained interest (see ¶ 2550).

(c) **Reduction for Consideration.** The amount of the gift is reduced up to the amount of the gift determined without regard to Code Sec. 2701 by the amount, if any, of consideration received by the transferor. Consideration in the form of an applicable retained interest is determined under Code Sec. 2701, except that in the case of a contribution to capital, the value of such an interest is zero.[30]

● *Minimum Value Rule*

In addition to the four-step subtraction method, Code Sec. 2701 applies a minimum value rule in determining the amount of a gift. Under this rule, the value of a junior equity interest cannot be less than its pro rata portion of 10 percent of the sum of:

(1) the total value of all equity interests in the entity; and

(2) the total amount of any indebtedness the entity owes to the transferor and applicable family members.[31]

Example: Famco has 1,000 shares of nonvoting common stock and 1,000 shares of $1,000 par value voting preferred stock outstanding. Each share of preferred stock carries a cumulative annual dividend of 8% and a right to put the stock to Famco for its par value at any time. Jim Warner owns 60% of the preferred stock and 75% of the common stock. The balance of the preferred and common stock is owned by Mike Brooks, who is unrelated to Warner. Warner transfers all of his common stock to his daughter, Charlotte. Because the preferred stock confers both a qualified payment right and an extraordinary payment right, Warner's rights are valued under the

[30] Reg. § 25.2701-3(b).

[31] Code Sec. 2701(a)(4); Reg. § 25.2701-3(c).

"lower of" rule at $800 per share, taking into account Warner's voting rights.

The amount of Warner's gift is computed as follows:

Step 1: Assume that the value of all family-held interests in Famco, taking account of Warner's control of Famco, is $1 million.

Step 2: Subtract the value of the preferred stock held by Warner (.60 × $800,000 = $480,000, computed under the "lower of" rule of Reg. § 25.2701-2(a)(3)).

Step 3: The balance of $520,000 is allocated to the 750 shares of family-held common stock.

Step 4: No adjustments are made because no minority or similar discount is appropriate and no consideration was furnished for the transfer. The amount of the gift is $520,000.[32]

¶ 2525 Subsequent Valuations of Qualified Payment Rights

If a "taxable event" occurs with respect to any distribution right that was previously valued as a qualified payment interest (see ¶ 2515), the taxable estate or the taxable gifts of the individual holding the interest are increased.[33]

• *Taxable Event*

A taxable event occurs if a qualified payment interest is transferred by the individual in whose hands the interest was originally valued under Code Sec. 2701 (or by certain individuals treated in the same manner as the original interest holder).[34] The transfer could be made either during life or at death.

A taxable event also occurs on the termination of an individual's rights with respect to a qualified payment interest.[35] A taxpayer also may elect to treat a late payment of certain qualified payments as a taxable event.[36] A qualified payment is late if it is paid more than four years after it is due. Qualified payments made during the four-year grace period are treated as having been made on the actual due date.[37]

A transfer is not a taxable event to the extent that a marital deduction (see ¶ 1000) is allowable for the transfer.[38] In such a case, the transferee or surviving spouse is treated as the holder of the interest from the time it is received.[39] In addition, if the interest holder transfers the qualified payment interest to an applicable family member in a taxable event, the transferee will be treated from that time on in the same manner as the transferor with respect to late or unpaid qualified payments that are first due after the taxable event.[40]

• *Amount of Increase*

The taxable estate or taxable gifts of the interest holder are increased by the excess, if any, of:

---

[32] Reg. § 25.2701-3(d), Example 1.

[33] Code Sec. 2701(d).

[34] Code Sec. 2701(d)(3); Reg. § 25.2701-4(b)(3).

[35] Reg. § 25.2701-4(b)(1).

[36] Code Sec. 2701(d)(3)(A)(iii).

[37] Code Sec. 2701(d)(2)(C).

[38] Code Sec. 2701(d)(3)(B).

[39] Code Sec. 2701(d)(3)(B)(iii).

[40] Reg. § 25.2701-4(b)(3).

(1) the amount of the qualified payments payable during the period beginning on the date of the transfer to which Code Sec. 2701 applied and ending on the date of the taxable event; and

(2) the earnings on such payments determined as if each payment were paid on its due date and reinvested on that date at a yield equal to the appropriate discount rate;

over the sum of:

(1) the amount of the qualified payments actually paid during the same period;

(2) the earnings on those payments determined as if each payment were reinvested as of the date actually paid at a rate equal to the appropriate discount rate; and

(3) to the extent necessary to prevent double inclusion, an amount equal to the sum of (a) the portion of the fair market value of the qualified payment interest solely attributable to the right to receive unpaid qualified payments (determined as of the date of the taxable event), (b) the fair market value of any equity interest received in lieu of qualified payments, and (c) the amount of any increase in the individual's aggregate taxable gifts by reason of the failure to enforce the right to receive qualified payments.[41]

The appropriate discount rate is the discount rate that was applied in determining the value of the qualified payment at the time of the original Code Sec. 2701 transfer.[42]

Limitation. Except in the case of an election to treat nonpayment of qualified payments as a taxable event, the amount of the increase in the individual's taxable estate or taxable gifts is limited to the "applicable percentage" of the excess, if any, of:

(1) the sum of:

(a) the fair market value (determined as of the date of the taxable event) of all equity interests in the entity that are junior to any applicable retained interests and

(b) any amounts expended by the entity to redeem or acquire any such junior interests; over

(2) the fair market value of such junior equity interests on the date of the original Code Sec. 2701 transfer.

The applicable percentage is equal to the number of shares of the applicable retained interest held by the interest holder on the date of the taxable event divided by the total number of shares of such interests in the business on the same date.[43]

¶ 2530 Attribution Rules

Under the attribution rules of Code Sec. 2701, an individual is treated as holding an equity interest to the extent that interest is held indirectly by that individual through ownership of a corporation, partnership, trust

---

[41] Reg. § 25.2701-4(c).

[42] Reg. § 25.2701-4(c)(3).

[43] Reg. § 25.2701-4(c)(6), (d)(2).

or other entity.[44] If an individual is deemed to hold an interest in more than one capacity, the interest is treated as held in a manner that attributes the largest ownership interest to the individual.[45]

Corporations. An individual is deemed to own any equity interest held by or for a corporation in the proportion that the fair market value of the stock held by the individual bears to the fair market value of all the stock of the corporation.[46]

Partnerships. An individual is deemed to own any equity interest held by or for a partnership in the proportion that the fair market value of the larger of the individual's profits interest or capital interest bears to the fair market value of the total profits interest or capital interest of the partnership.[47]

Trusts and Estates. An individual is deemed to own any equity interest held by or for an estate or trust to the extent that the individual's beneficial interest may be satisfied by the equity interest or the income or proceeds from the equity interest. It is assumed that the fiduciary will exercise maximum discretion in favor of the individual. In the case of a grantor trust, the individual is deemed to hold 100 percent of any equity interest held by the trust. If the trust has multiple grantors, an individual grantor is deemed to own equity interests held by the trust to the extent of such individual's fractional share.[48]

¶ 2535 Mitigation of Double Taxation

If Code Sec. 2701 applies to reduce the value of a retained interest, double taxation would result if the retained interest were valued under generally applicable valuation rules when the transferor subsequently transfers the retained interest or the retained interest is included in the transferor's estate. Code Sec. 2701(e)(6) therefore provides that, if there is a subsequent transfer, or inclusion in the gross estate, of an applicable retained interest that was valued under Code Sec. 2701, appropriate adjustments are to be made for purposes of the transfer tax provisions to reflect the increase of amount of any prior taxable gift made by the transferor or decedent by reason of such valuation.

Regulations provide that, for purposes of determining the transferor's estate tax, the transferor's adjusted taxable gifts are reduced to reflect the increase of the transferor's taxable gifts under Code Sec. 2701.[49]

In general, the amount of the reduction is the lesser of: (1) the amount by which the transferor's gifts are increased as a result of the application of Code Sec. 2701 to the transfer, or (2) the amount by which the individual's transfers are increased as a result of not applying the valuation rules to the later transfer of the applicable retained interest.

The regulations also provide an adjustment for split gifts that are generally consistent with the general principles of transfer taxation so that each spouse is treated as the transferor for one-half of the initial transfer and is entitled to mitigation under Code Sec. 2701(e)(6).

---

[44] Code Sec. 2701(e)(3).

[45] Reg. § 25.2701-6(a)(1).

[46] Reg. § 25.2701-6(a)(2).

[47] Reg. § 25.2701-6(a)(3).

[48] Reg. § 25.2701-6(a)(4).

[49] Reg. § 25.2701-5.

Example: Ellen O'Brien owns 15,000 shares of $1,000 par value preferred stock of X Corp. and all of the 1,000 shares of common stock of X Corp. On January 15, 1995, when the fair market value of the common stock is $500,000 and the value of the preferred stock is $1,500,000, she transfers the common stock to her daughter, Sally. The fair market value of all of Ellen's interests prior to the transfer is $2,000,000. The Code Sec. 2701 value of the preferred interest is zero. The value of Ellen's taxable gift is $2,500,000 (the Code Sec. 2701 transfer and Ellen's other taxable gifts). Later in 1998, when the preferred stock has a value of $1,400,000, Ellen transfers all of the preferred stock to Sally. She is entitled to reduce the amount on which her tax is computed by $1,400,000.

¶ 2540 Statute of Limitations

Although the statute of limitations on the assessment of gift tax is three years after the return was filed, special rules apply under the special valuation rules.

The statute of limitations for assessment of gift tax is modified so that it will not run on an undisclosed or inadequately disclosed transfer, regardless of whether a gift tax return was filed for other transfers in the year in which the Code Sec. 2701 transfer occurred.[50]

¶ 2550 Function of Code Sec. 2702

Prior to the enactment of Code Sec. 2702, a transferor could transfer property and its future appreciation to younger family members at a fraction of the gift tax cost of an outright transfer by retaining various limited interests in the gifted property.

A popular form of transfer with a retained interest was the grantor retained interest trust (GRIT). In a typical GRIT, a grantor retains an income interest for a certain number of years, after which the remainder passes to specified beneficiaries. If the grantor dies during the term of the trust, the grantor's retained income interest causes the entire value of the trust property to be includible in the grantor's taxable estate, just as if the GRIT had never been created.[51]

The grantor is deemed to have made a taxable gift at the time the GRIT is funded. The GRIT lowers the value of the gift to the beneficiaries because the grantor retains an income interest in the gift property. There is the possibility that the property will not pass to the beneficiaries if the grantor dies before the end of the specified term, and the beneficiaries do not have use of the trust property before the end of the specified term. The value of the gift is equal to the present value of the actuarial value of the remainder interest, as determined under Code Sec. 7520 (see ¶ 530).

Example (1): Brian Foley transfers $1 million to a 10-year GRIT. At the end of the 10 years, the trust will be distributed to his daughter, Jill. At the time of the transfer, the applicable interest rate under Code Sec. 7520 is 9.6 percent, which results in the retained interest being valued at $600,152 and the gift being valued at $399,848. If Foley survives the 10-year period, $1 million is removed

---

[50] Code Sec. 6501(c)(9).

[51] Code Sec. 2036(a)(1).

from his estate at a gift tax cost of approximately four-tenths of the cost had $1 million been transferred outright.

Code Sec. 2702 limits the application of Code Sec. 7520 to the valuation of "qualified retained interests" and retained interests in personal residence trusts (see ¶ 2570).[52] All other retained interests are valued at zero.[53] The subtraction method is used to determine the value of the gift. If the value of the retained interest is zero, the value of the gift is increased to equal the value of the property transferred in trust.

> ***Example (2):*** Assume the same facts as in Example (1), except that Code Sec. 2702 applies. Because Foley's retained interest is not a qualified retained interest, it is valued at zero and the gift to his daughter Jill is valued at $1 million.

¶ 2555 Application of Code Sec. 2702

Code Sec. 2702 applies when (1) an interest in trust is transferred to a "member of the transferor's family" and (2) the transferor or "applicable family member" retains an interest in the trust.[54]

Members of the Transferor's Family. Members of the transferor's family include:

(1) the transferor's spouse;

(2) any ancestor or lineal descendant of the transferor or the transferor's spouse;

(3) any brother or sister of the transferor; and

(4) any spouse of the persons described in (2) and (3).[55]

Applicable Family Members. Applicable family members are generally members of the older generation and include:

(1) the transferor's spouse;

(2) any ancestor of the transferor or the transferor's spouse; and

(3) the spouse of any such ancestor.[56]

- *Transfers of an Interest in Trust*

Transfers in trust include transfers to a new or existing trust and assignments of an interest in an existing trust. They do not include the exercise, release, or lapse of a power of appointment that is not a transfer under the gift tax provisions or the execution of a qualified disclaimer.[57] A transfer of an interest in trust includes a transfer of an interest in property that results in the creation of one or more term interests.[58] A term interest is one of a series of successive interests, which includes a life interest or an interest for a term of years.[59]

The following interests are not treated as term interests:

---

[52] Code Sec. 2702(a)(2)(B) and Code Sec. 2702(a)(3)(A)(ii).

[53] Code Sec. 2702(a)(2)(A).

[54] Code Sec. 2702(a)(1); Reg. § 25.2702-1(a).

[55] Code Sec. 2702(e) and Code Sec. 2704(c)(2); Reg. § 25.2702-2(a)(1).

[56] Code Sec. 2701(e)(2); Reg. § 25.2701-1(d)(2).

[57] Reg. § 25.2702-2(a)(2).

[58] Code Sec. 2702(c)(1).

[59] Code Sec. 2702(c)(3).

(1) concurrent fee interests, such as those held by tenants in common, tenants by the entireties, or joint tenants with right of survivorship; and

(2) leasehold interests to the extent the lease was acquired for adequate consideration, provided a good faith effort was made to determine the fair rental value of the property.[60]

The joint purchase of interests in the same property by a taxpayer and a member of the taxpayer's family is a transfer in trust if the taxpayer acquires only a term interest in the property. The taxpayer will be treated as acquiring the entire property and transferring to the family members the interests they acquired. However, any consideration paid by the acquiring family members will be considered in determining the amount of any gifts deemed made by the taxpayer.[61]

Example: Arlene Ricci purchases a 15-year term interest in a commercial building, and her child, Carol, purchases the remainder interest. Arlene is treated as if she had acquired the entire property and then transferred the remainder interest to Carol.

● *Retained Interest*

A retained interest is an interest held by the same individual before and after a transfer in trust. If the transfer creates a term interest, the transferor is deemed to hold the interest both before and after the transfer[62] (see ¶ 2560).

● *Exceptions to Application*

Code Sec. 2702 does not apply to the following transfers:

(1) transfers treated as incomplete for gift tax purposes;

(2) transfers to a "personal residence trust" (see ¶ 2570);

(3) transfers to a charitable remainder trust;

(4) transfers to a charitable lead trust;

(5) transfers to a pooled income fund;

(6) transfers of a remainder interest if the only interest retained by the transferor or applicable family members is the right to income distributions in the sole discretion of an independent trustee; and

(7) transfers in trust incident to a divorce.[63]

¶ 2560 Valuation of Retained Interests

Retained interests are valued at zero unless:

(1) the interest is a "qualified retained interest" (see ¶ 2565);

(2) the interest is a retained interest in a personal residence trust or qualified personal residence trust (see ¶ 2570); or

(3) the interest is in certain nondepreciable tangible property.

---

[60] Reg. § 25.2702-4(a) and (b).

[61] Code Sec. 2702(c)(2); Reg. § 25.2702-4(c).

[62] Reg. § 25.2702-2(a)(3).

[63] Reg. § 25.2702-1(c).

● *Special Rule for Tangible Property*

A special valuation rule applies to interests in nondepreciable tangible property, such as land and works of art. The exception applies to transfers in trust of tangible property that would not be entitled to a depreciation or depletion deduction if the property were used in a trade or business or held for the production of income. In addition, the nonexercise of rights under a term interest must not increase the value of the remainder interest in the property. Depreciable improvements to property that would otherwise disqualify the property will be ignored if the fair market value of the improvements do not exceed five percent of the fair market value of the entire property.[64]

For such transfers, the value of the retained interest (other than a qualified interest) is the amount that the holder of the term interest establishes as the amount for which such interest could be sold to an unrelated party.[65] However, if the transferor cannot reasonably establish the value of the term interest, it will be valued at zero.[66] If tangible property is converted during the term of the interest into property that does not qualify for valuation under the special rule, for gift tax purposes, the conversion will be treated as a transfer of the value of the unexpired portion of the term interest for no consideration.[67]

¶ 2565 Qualified Retained Interests

There are three types of qualified retained interests that are not valued at zero under Code Sec. 2702. The trusts that correspond to these interests are:

(1) a grantor retained annuity trust (GRAT), which makes fixed payments to the grantor at least annually;

(2) a grantor retained unitrust (GRUT), which makes payments to the grantor at least annually, but the amount of the payments is a fixed percentage of the trust's assets determined annually; or

(3) a noncontingent remainder interest if all the other interests in the trust consist of interests described in (1) and (2).[68]

● *Qualified Annuity Interest*

A qualified annuity interest is an irrevocable right to receive a fixed amount payable to, or for the benefit of, the holder of the interest for each taxable year of the term. A fixed amount is either (1) a stated dollar amount, or (2) a fixed fraction or percentage of the initial fair market value of the property transferred to the trust. The amount must be payable at least annually. In valuing a qualified annuity interest, an amount will be considered only to the extent that it does not exceed 120 percent of the stated dollar amount or the fixed fraction or percentage payable in the preceding year.[69]

The governing instrument must:

---

[64] Reg. § 25.2702-2(c)(2).

[65] Code Sec. 2702(c)(4)(B).

[66] Reg. § 25.2702-2(c)(1).

[67] Reg. § 25.2702-2(c)(4)(i).

[68] Code Sec. 2702(b).

[69] Reg. § 25.2702-3(b)(1).

(1) prohibit distributions to or for the benefit of any person other than the holder of the interest during the term of the interest;

(2) fix the term of the interest for the life of the holder, for a specific term of years, or for the shorter of those periods;

(3) prohibit prepayment of the income interest;[70]

(4) if the annuity is stated in terms of a fraction or percentage of the initial fair market value of the trust property, require payment adjustments or repayments as a result of any incorrect determination of the fair market value of the property;

(5) require the pro rata computation of the annuity amount in the case of a short taxable year and the last taxable year of the term; and

(6) prohibit additional contributions to the trust.[71]

● *Qualified Unitrust Interest*

A qualified unitrust interest is an irrevocable right to receive payment, at least annually, of a fixed percentage of the net fair market value of the trust assets, determined annually. The unitrust amount must be payable to, or for the benefit of, the holder of the unitrust interest for each taxable year of the term. In valuing a qualified unitrust interest, a percentage will be considered a fixed percentage only to the extent that it does not exceed 120 percent of the fixed fraction or percentage payable in the preceding year.[72]

The governing instrument must meet requirements (1)–(5) enumerated above for instruments creating qualified annuity interests.[73]

● *Qualified Remainder Interest*

A remainder interest (which includes a reversion) is the right to receive all or a fractional share of trust property on the termination of all or a fractional share of the trust. Therefore, a right to receive an amount that is a stated or pecuniary amount would not be a remainder interest.[74] A remainder interest is a qualified remainder interest if (1) it is payable to the beneficiary or the beneficiary's estate in all events and (2) all interests in the trust, other than noncontingent remainder interests, are qualified annuity or unitrust interests. Therefore, the governing instrument cannot permit payment of income in excess of the annuity or unitrust amount to the holder of a qualified annuity or unitrust interest.[75]

¶ 2570 Personal Residence Trusts

The zero valuation rule (see ¶ 2560) does not apply to retained interests in personal residence trusts and qualified personal residence trusts. Instead, such interests are valued under Code Sec. 7520. Grantor retained interest trusts (GRITs), therefore, play a continued role in yield-

---

[70] Reg. § 25.2702-3(d)(2)-(4).

[71] Reg. § 25.2702-3(b)(2)-(4).

[72] Reg. § 25.2702-3(c)(1).

[73] Reg. § 25.2702-3(c)(2)-(3) and Reg. § 25.2702-3(d)(2)-(4).

[74] Reg. § 25.2702-3(f)(2).

[75] Reg. § 25.2702-3(f)(1).

ing transfer tax savings if they are used to transfer the grantor's personal residence.

● *Personal Residence Trust*

The governing instrument of a personal residence trust must prohibit the trust from holding any asset other than the personal residence of the term holder and "qualified proceeds" for the entire term of the trust.[76] Qualified proceeds refer to insurance proceeds received if the residence is damaged, destroyed or involuntarily converted during the term of the trust. The trust instrument must require that the proceeds and income thereon are reinvested in a personal residence within two years of receipt.[77]

A personal residence is the principal residence or the second residence (within the meaning of Code Sec. 280A(d)(1)) of the term holder.[78] A personal residence may include appurtenant structures used by the term holder for residential purposes. It may also include adjacent land to the extent such land is reasonably appropriate for residential purposes, given the residence's size and location.[79] The amount of land that can be included under this provision can be substantial. For example, in one private letter ruling, the IRS allowed 10 acres of land surrounding a very large residence to be included,[80] and, in another, allowed the inclusion of two lots across the street from the personal residence which provided the term holder with access to a bay and a view of the bay.[81] The personal residence may not be used by anyone other than the term holder or the holder's spouse or dependent and may not be sold or transferred, directly or indirectly, to the grantor, the grantor's spouse, or an entity controlled by the grantor or the grantor's spouse.[82] A personal residence may not be used for purposes other than as a personal residence unless such use is secondary (such as a home office). Use as a hotel or as a bed and breakfast is not considered secondary.[83]

● *Qualified Personal Residence Trust*

Unlike a personal residence trust, a qualified personal residence trust may hold property other than a personal residence. In other respects, the rules governing the definition of a personal residence and the use thereof with respect to qualified personal residence trusts are substantially similar to those governing personal residence trusts.[84] Cash may be added to or held by the trust for the following limited purposes:

(1) to pay trust expenses (including mortgage payments) already incurred or expected to be incurred within the next six months;

(2) to pay for improvements to the residence within the next six months;

(3) to purchase the initial or replacement residence pursuant to a contract within the next three months.[85]

Governing Instruments. The governing instrument of a qualified personal residence trust must require the following:

---

[76] Reg. § 25.2702-5(b)(1).

[77] Reg. § 25.2702-5(b)(3).

[78] Reg. § 25.2702-5(b)(2).

[79] Reg. § 25.2702-5(b)(2)(ii).

[80] IRS Letter Ruling 9442019, 7-19-94, CCH IRS LETTER RULINGS REPORTS.

[81] IRS Letter Ruling 9503025, 10-27-94, CCH IRS LETTER RULINGS REPORTS.

[82] Reg. § 25.2702-5(b)(1).

[83] Reg. § 25.2702-5(b)(2)(iii).

[84] Reg. § 25.2702-5(c)(1) and (2).

[85] Reg. § 25.2702-5(c)(5)(ii)(A)(1).

(1) any trust income must be distributed to the term holder at least annually;

(2) no principal may be distributed to a beneficiary other than the transferor during the term of the retained interest;

(3) the term holder's interest may not be prepaid;

(4) the trust may not hold any assets other than the personal residence of the term holder and the assets permitted by the regulations;

(5) the trustee must determine the amount of cash holdings allowed by the regulations and distribute the excess to the term holder at least quarterly and within 30 days of the termination of the term holder's interest;

(6) the trust will cease to be a qualified personal residence trust if the residence ceases to be used as a personal residence or if the residence is sold and the trust instrument prohibits the holding of sales proceeds;

(7) the trust will cease to be a qualified personal residence trust if (a) the personal residence is sold, damaged or destroyed and (b) a replacement residence is not acquired or the residence is not repaired within two years;

(8) if the trust ceases to be a qualified residence, the assets will be distributed to the term holder or converted into a qualified annuity interest for the benefit of the term holder within 30 days;[86] and

(9) the trust instrument must prohibit the trust from selling or transferring the residence, directly or indirectly, to the grantor, the grantor's spouse, or an entity controlled by either of them during the retained term interest or at any time thereafter in which the trust is a grantor trust.[87]

¶ 2575 Mitigation of Double Taxation

If the value of a retained interest is reduced to zero under Code Sec. 2702, double taxation results if the retained interest is subsequently transferred by gift or at death. To mitigate double taxation, the transferor's taxable gifts are reduced at the time of the subsequent lifetime transfer or in determining the transferor's estate tax.[88]

The amount of the reduction is the lesser of:

(1) the increase in taxable gifts on the original transfer due to the application of Code Sec. 2702; or

(2) the increase in taxable gifts or gross estate on the subsequent transfer of the retained interest.[89]

¶ 2580 Rights and Restrictions Disregarded Under Code Sec. 2703

The purpose of Code Sec. 2703 is to prevent possible distortions in value that might result if a transferor retained certain rights or imposed

---

86 Reg. § 25.2702-5(c)(5)(ii)(A)(2).

87 Reg. § 25.2702-5(c)(9).

88 Reg. § 25.2702-6(a).

89 Reg. § 25.2702-6(b)(1).

certain restrictions with respect to the transferred property without intending to exercise the rights or restrictions. Unless the taxpayer establishes that the right or restriction qualifies for an exception to Code Sec. 2703, options, restrictive sale agreements and buy-sell agreements will be disregarded for transfer tax valuation purposes.

● *Rights and Restrictions*

A right or restriction includes any option, agreement or other right to acquire or use property at a price that is less than fair market value, or any restriction on the right to sell or use the property. For example, a lease entered into between a parent and child, the terms of which are not comparable to leases relating to similar property between unrelated parties, would be disregarded in valuing the leased property.

The right or restriction may be part of a partnership agreement, corporate bylaws, or articles of incorporation, or may be implicit in the capital structure of an entity. However, Code Sec. 2703 will not apply to a qualified easement under Code Sec. 2522(d) or Code Sec. 2055(f).[90]

● *Exceptions*

A right or restriction will not be disregarded for valuation purposes if the taxpayer can establish that it is:

(1) a bona fide arrangement;

(2) not a device to transfer property to family members for less than full and adequate consideration; and

(3) comparable to similar arrangements entered into by persons in arm's-length transactions.[91]

For purposes of the second requirement, family members include applicable family members, lineal descendants of the parents of the transferor or the transferor's spouse, and any other individual who is a natural object of the transferor's bounty.[92] Each of the above requirements must be satisfied independently.[93]

● *Application*

Code Sec. 2703 applies to rights or restrictions that are created or substantially modified after October 8, 1990. A substantial modification includes any discretionary modification of a right or restriction, whether or not authorized by the terms of an agreement, that results in anything more than a *de minimis* change in the quality, value, or timing of the rights of any party with respect to the property that is subject to the right or restriction. The addition of a family member as a party to a right or restriction is treated as a substantial modification unless the addition is required under the terms of the right or restriction or the person is assigned to a generation no lower than the lowest generation of individuals who already are parties to the right or restriction.[94]

The following items are not treated as substantial modifications:

---

[90] Reg. § 25.2703-1(a).

[91] Code Sec. 2703(b); Reg. § 25.2703-1(b)(1).

[92] Reg. § 25.2703-1(b)(3) and Reg. § 25.2701-2(b)(5).

[93] Reg. § 25.2703-1(b)(2).

[94] Reg. § 25.2703-1(c)(1).

(1) modifications required by the terms of a right or restriction;

(2) discretionary modifications that do not change the right or restriction;

(3) modifications of a capitalization rate with respect to a right or restriction, if done in such a way that the rate bears a fixed relationship to a specified market rate; and

(4) modifications that result in an option price that more closely approximates fair market value.[95]

¶ 2590 Treatment of Lapsing Rights and Restrictions

Code Sec. 2704 was enacted to reduce or eliminate the use of lapsing rights and restrictions as a way of reducing transfer taxes.

> ***Example (1):*** During her life, Betty Smith owned 80% of the voting stock of Famco, and her children owned the remaining 20%. The bylaws of Famco provided that a shareholder's voting rights lapsed at death. Smith's will provided that, upon her death, all of her Famco stock would pass to her children. The value of Smith's stock with the voting rights is $750,000. However, the value of the same stock without the voting rights is $500,000. Prior to the enactment of Code Sec. 2704, Smith's estate would have been worth $250,000 less than it was when she was alive.

Under Code Sec. 2704(a), the lapse of a voting or liquidation right created after October 8, 1990, is treated as a transfer for transfer tax purposes if the holder of the lapsing right and members of the holder's family control the entity both before and after the lapse. The amount of the transfer is the excess, if any, of the value of the holder's interests in the entity immediately before the lapse over the value of such interests after the lapse.[96] Code Sec. 2704(b) covers the other side of lapsing rights—the restrictions placed on the transferor. Under Code Sec. 2704(b), if an interest in a corporation or partnership is transferred to, or for the benefit of, a member of the transferor's family, and the transferor and members of the transferor's family control the entity before the transfer, any "applicable restrictions" are disregarded in valuing the transferred interest.

> ***Example (2):*** Assume the same facts as in Example (1), except that Code Sec. 2704(a) applies. Smith is deemed to have made a transfer of $250,000, the difference between the value of the stock with voting rights and the value of the stock without the voting rights. The amount of the transfer plus the $500,000 value of the stock in Smith's estate equals the value of Smith's stock before she died.

● *Lapse of Voting and Liquidation Rights*

For purposes of Code Sec. 2704(a), a voting right is the right to vote with respect to any matter of the entity. The right of a general partner to participate in partnership management is a voting right.[97] A liquidation right is the right to compel the entity to acquire all or a portion of the holder's interest in the entity. It is not necessary that the exercise of the right result in the complete liquidation of the entity.[98]

---

[95] Reg. § 25.2703-1(c)(2).

[96] Code Sec. 2704(a).

[97] Reg. § 25.2704-1(a)(2)(iv).

[98] Reg. § 25.2704-1(a)(2)(v).

A voting or liquidation right lapses when a currently exercisable right is restricted or ceases to exist. The transfer of an interest conferring a right generally is not a lapse. However, a transfer that eliminates the transferor's right to compel the entity to acquire an interest retained by the transferor that is junior to the transferred interest is a lapse of a liquidation right with respect to the junior interest.[99]

A lapse of a liquidation right is not treated as a transfer (1) to the extent that the holder and members of the holder's family cannot, immediately after the lapse, liquidate an interest the holder could have liquidated before the lapse, (2) if the lapse was previously valued under Code Sec. 2701, or (3) if the lapse occurred by reason of a change in state law.[100]

● *Disregard of Applicable Restrictions*

An applicable restriction is a limitation on the ability to liquidate the entity that is more restrictive than the limitations that would apply under state law. A restriction is an applicable restriction only to the extent that (1) the restriction lapses after the transfer, or (2) the transferor or a member of the transferor's family has the right to remove the restriction immediately after the transfer.

Applicable restrictions do not include restrictions imposed by state or federal law or commercially reasonable restrictions on liquidation imposed by an unrelated person providing financing to the entity for trade of business operations. An unrelated person is any person who is not related to the transferor, the transferee, or any member of the family of either in a way specified by Code Sec. 267.[101] An option, right or agreement subject to Code Sec. 2703 is not an applicable restriction.[102]

● *Control Requirement*

Control has the same definition for purposes of Code Sec. 2704 as for purposes of Code Sec. 2701 (see ¶ 2510).[103] In the case of a corporation, it means at least 50 percent of the stock of the corporation, measured by vote or value. In the case of a partnership, it means at least 50 percent of the capital or profits interest and, in the case of a limited partnership, the holding of any interest as a general partner.[104]

Family Member. For purposes of Code Sec. 2704, the following are family members with respect to any individual:

(1) the individual's spouse;

(2) an ancestor or lineal descendant of the individual or the individual's spouse;

(3) a brother or sister of the individual; and

(4) a spouse of any individual described in (2) or (3) above.[105]

The attribution rules of Code Sec. 2701(e)(3) apply in determining the interest held by any individual (see ¶ 2510).[106]

---

[99] Reg. § 25.2704-1(b), (c)(1).

[100] Reg. § 25.2704-1(c)(2).

[101] An individual's family, under Code Sec. 267, includes brothers, sisters (whether by whole or half-blood), spouse, ancestors, and lineal descendants.

[102] Reg. § 25.2704-2(b).

[103] Code Sec. 2704(c)(1).

[104] Code Sec. 2701(b)(2).

[105] Code Sec. 2704(c)(2).

[106] Code Sec. 2704(c)(3).

APPENDICES

¶ 2600 UNIFIED RATES AND CREDIT

I. ESTATES OF U.S. CITIZENS AND RESIDENTS DYING AFTER 1976, AND GIFTS MADE AFTER 1976

Estate and gift tax rates are combined in a single rate schedule effective for the estates of decedents dying, and for gifts made, after December 31, 1976. For transfers occurring after 1983, the maximum tax rate is 55 percent, applicable to transfers in excess of $3,000,000. In addition, prior to 1998 a five-percent surtax was imposed to phase out the benefits of the graduated rates and the unified credit with respect to taxable transfers greater than $10 million but not exceeding $21,040,000. Due to mistakes in the wording of the amendment to Code Sec. 2001(c)(2) by the Taxpayer Relief Act of 1997 (P.L. 105-34,) the five-percent additional tax phases out the benefits of the graduated rates, but not the benefits of the unified credit (applicable credit amount), for estates of decedents dying, and gifts made, after 1997. Therefore, the additional tax is levied on amounts transferred after 1997 in excess of $10,000,000 but not exceeding $17,184,000. The applicable credit amount is not recaptured. Lifetime transfers and transfers made at death are cumulated for estate tax purposes.

- The estate tax liability is determined by applying the unified rate schedule to the cumulated transfers, calculating a tentative tax, and providing a credit for gift taxes payable. The cumulated transfers to which the tentative tax applies equal the sum of (1) the amount of the taxable estate and (2) the amount of the taxable gifts made by the decedent after 1976, other than gifts includible in the gross estate. Gift taxes to be credited include the aggregate gift tax payable on gifts made after December 31, 1976. Gift taxes payable on pre-1977 gifts are not subtracted from the estate tax.

- Gift tax liability for any calendar quarter (for gifts made after 1970 and before 1982) or year (for gifts made before 1971 and after 1981) is determined by applying the unified rate schedule to cumulative lifetime taxable transfers and subtracting the taxes payable for prior taxable periods. Preceding calendar periods are: (1) calendar year 1932 (after June 6) and 1970 and all intervening calendar years, (2) the first calendar quarter of 1971 and all quarters between that quarter and the first quarter of 1982, and (3) all calendar years after 1981 and before the year for which the tax is being computed. In computing cumulative taxable gifts for prior taxable periods, the donor's pre-1977 taxable gifts are to be taken into account, with the reduction for taxes previously paid to be based upon the unified rate schedule.

The unified rate schedule applying to estates of decedents dying after 1983 (and gifts made after 1983) appears below.

Table A—Unified Rate Schedule

Column A *Taxable amount over*	Column B *Taxable amount not over*	Column C *Tax on amount in column A*	Column D *Rate of tax on excess over amount in column A* *Percent*
$ 0	$ 10,000	$ 0	18
10,000	20,000	1,800	20
20,000	40,000	3,800	22
40,000	60,000	8,200	24
60,000	80,000	13,000	26
80,000	100,000	18,200	28
100,000	150,000	23,800	30
150,000	250,000	38,800	32
250,000	500,000	70,800	34
500,000	750,000	155,800	37
750,000	1,000,000	248,300	39
1,000,000	1,250,000	345,800	41
1,250,000	1,500,000	448,300	43
1,500,000	2,000,000	555,800	45
2,000,000	2,500,000	780,800	49
2,500,000	3,000,000	1,025,800	53
3,000,000	....	1,290,800	55

For estates of decedents dying and gifts made after 1976 but before 1982, the top tax rate was 70 percent and was applied to transfers in excess of $5,000,000. A 53-percent rate applied to transfers in the $2,500,000–$3,000,000 range; a 57-percent rate applied to transfers in the $3,000,000–$3,500,000 range; a 61-percent rate applied to transfers in the $3,500,000–$4,000,000 range; a 65-percent rate applied to transfers in the $4,000,000–$4,500,000 range; and a 69-percent rate to transfers in the $4,500,000–$5,000,000 range.

The top rates in effect for decedents dying (and gifts made) in 1982 and 1983 appear below.

Decedents Dying (and Gifts Made) in 1982

Column A *Taxable amount over*	Column B *Taxable amount not over*	Column C *Tax on amount in column A*	Column D *Rate of tax on excess over amount in column A* *Percent*
$2,500,000	$3,000,000	$1,025,800	53
3,000,000	3,500,000	1,290,800	57
3,500,000	4,000,000	1,575,800	61
4,000,000	....	1,880,800	65

Decedents Dying (and Gifts Made) in 1983

Column A *Taxable amount over*	Column B *Taxable amount not over*	Column C *Tax on amount in column A*	Column D *Rate of tax on excess over amount in column A* *Percent*
$2,500,000	$3,000,000	$1,025,800	53
3,000,000	3,500,000	1,290,800	57
3,500,000	....	1,575,800	60

Benefits of Graduated Rates and Unified Credit Phased Out.—The benefits of the graduated rates and the unified credit under the unified transfer tax system are phased out beginning with cumulative transfers rising above $10,000,000. This is accomplished by adding five percent of the excess of any transfer over $10,000,000 to the tentative tax computed in determining the ultimate transfer tax liability. For estates of decedents dying, and gifts made, after 1987 the tax is levied on amounts transferred in excess of $10,000,000 but not exceeding $21,040,000, in order to recapture the benefit of any transfer tax rate below 55 percent as well as the unified credit. Due to mistakes in the wording of the amendment to Code Sec. 2001(c)(2) by the Taxpayer Relief Act of 1997 (P.L. 105-34), the five-percent additional tax phases out the benefits of graduated rates, but not the benefits of the unified credit (applicable credit amount), for estates of decedents dying, and gifts made, after 1997. Therefore, the additional tax is levied on amounts transferred after 1997 in excess of $10,000,000 but not exceeding $17,184,000. The applicable credit amount is not recaptured.

Unified Credit

For estates of decedents dying after 1976 and gifts made after 1976, both the $60,000 estate tax exemption and the $30,000 lifetime gift tax exemption were replaced by a single unified credit. The amount of this credit is subtracted from the amount of the decedent's gross estate tax. In effect, the amount of the unified credit available at death will be reduced to the extent that any portion of the credit is used to offset gift taxes on lifetime transfers.

- Amounts allowed as lifetime exemptions on gifts made after September 8, 1976, but before January 1, 1977, reduce the unified credit allowable by 20 percent of the exemption used, to a maximum of $6,000.

- For estates of decedents dying in 1977 and thereafter, the credit was phased in as follows:

Year	*Amount of Credit*	*Amount of Exemption Equivalent*
1977	$ 30,000	$120,667
1978	34,000	134,000
1979	38,000	147,333
1980	42,500	161,563
1981	47,000	175,625
1982	62,800	225,000
1983	79,300	275,000
1984	96,300	325,000
1985	121,800	400,000
1986	155,800	500,000
1987–1997	192,800	600,000

For the years 1998–2006, the unified credit is gradually increased to $345,800 by the Taxpayer Relief Act of 1997 (P.L. 105-34) and is determined by reference to the "applicable credit amount" and the "applicable exclusion amount" (formerly the exemption equivalent). The increase is phased in as follows:

Year	Applicable Credit Amount	Applicable Exclusion Amount
1998	$202,050	$625,000
1999	$211,300	$650,000
2000 and 2001	$220,550	$675,000
2002 and 2003	$229,800	$700,000
2004	$287,300	$850,000
2005	$326,300	$950,000
2006	$345,800	$1,000,000

An illustration of the computation of federal gift and estate taxes under the unified transfer tax system is at ¶ 1428.

II. ESTATES OF NONRESIDENTS NOT CITIZENS

Effective for the estates of decedents dying after November 10, 1988, estate and gift tax rates applicable to U.S. citizens are also applicable to the estates of nonresident aliens.

The gift tax applies to transfers made by nonresidents not U.S. citizens only with respect to transfers of tangible property situated within the United States.

A separate estate tax rate schedule applies in the case of nonresidents not U.S. citizens dying after December 31, 1976, and before November 11, 1988. The amount of estate tax is determined by applying the unified rate schedule below to the cumulative lifetime and deathtime transfers subject to United States transfer taxes and then subtracting gift taxes payable on the lifetime transfers made after December 31, 1976.

If the amount is:	The tentative tax is:
Not over $100,000	6% of the taxable estate.
Over $100,000 but not over $500,000	$6,000, plus 12% of excess over $100,000.
Over $500,000 but not over $1,000,000	$54,000, plus 18% of excess over $500,000.
Over $1,000,000 but not over $2,000,000	$144,000, plus 24% of excess over $1,000,000.
Over $2,000,000	$348,000, plus 30% of excess over $2,000,000.

Credit

Effective for the estates of decedents dying after November 10, 1988, where permitted by treaty, the estate of a nonresident alien is allowed the same unified credit as a U.S. citizen multiplied by the proportion of the total gross estate situated in the United States. In other cases, the estate of a nonresident alien is allowed a unified credit of $13,000 (which exempts the first $60,000 of the estate from estate tax). The estate of a resident of a U.S. possession, dying after November 10, 1988, is entitled to a unified credit equal to the greater of (1) $13,000 or (2) $46,800 multiplied by the proportion of the decedent's gross estate situated in the United States.

A $30,000 estate tax exemption was available to the estates of nonresident aliens dying before January 1, 1977. Applicable for the estates of nonresident aliens dying after December 31, 1976, and before November 11, 1988, that exemption was eliminated and replaced by a credit of $3,600 that is allowed against the estate tax. In the case of residents of a possession of the United States (who are not considered citizens), dying after December 31, 1976, and before November 11, 1988, the credit allowable is the greater of $3,600 or that proportion of $15,075 that the value of that part of the decedent's property situated in the United States bears to the value of the entire gross estate wherever situated. The $15,075 figure was phased in over a five-year period. See ¶ 20.

Estates of nonresident noncitizens are allowed a $13,000 credit against the estate tax.

Any amount that had been allowed as a unified credit for any gift made by a decedent will reduce, dollar-for-dollar, the unified credit allowed to the estate.

¶ 2630 State Death Tax Credit Table[1]

A credit is allowed against the federal estate tax for any estate, inheritance, legacy, or succession taxes actually paid to any state of the United States or the District of Columbia with respect to any property included in the decedent's gross estate. The credit is applied against the adjusted taxable estate, which for this purpose is the taxable estate reduced by $60,000. The credit is available only if it does not exceed the estate's tax liability after reduction by the unified credit.

Estates of Decedents Dying After 1976

Adjusted Taxable Estate ("Adjusted Taxable Estate" is the decedent's taxable estate less $60,000) From	To	Credit =	+	%	Of Excess Over
0	$ 40,000	0		0	0
$ 40,000	90,000	0		.8	$ 40,000
90,000	140,000	$ 400		1.6	90,000
140,000	240,000	1,200		2.4	140,000
240,000	440,000	3,600		3.2	240,000
440,000	640,000	10,000		4	440,000
640,000	840,000	18,000		4.8	640,000
840,000	1,040,000	27,600		5.6	840,000
1,040,000	1,540,000	38,800		6.4	1,040,000
1,540,000	2,040,000	70,800		7.2	1,540,000
2,040,000	2,540,000	106,800		8	2,040,000
2,540,000	3,040,000	146,800		8.8	2,540,000
3,040,000	3,540,000	190,800		9.6	3,040,000
3,540,000	4,040,000	238,800		10.4	3,540,000
4,040,000	5,040,000	290,800		11.2	4,040,000
5,040,000	6,040,000	402,800		12	5,040,000
6,040,000	7,040,000	522,800		12.8	6,040,000
7,040,000	8,040,000	650,800		13.6	7,040,000
8,040,000	9,040,000	786,800		14.4	8,040,000
9,040,000	10,040,000	930,800		15.2	9,040,000
10,040,000	....	1,082,800		16	10,040,000

[1] The table below may not be used in computing taxes on estates of certain members of the Armed Forces.

¶ 2640 PRE-1977 ESTATE TAX RATES

I. EFFECTIVE FOR ESTATES OF U.S. CITIZENS AND RESIDENTS DYING BEFORE 1977 [2]

The federal estate tax on estates of U.S. citizens and residents is computed on a "taxable estate," after deduction of a $60,000 exemption, at the rates below. This amount is further reduced by a state death tax credit computed under Table III, below, or by the actual amount of state death taxes, whichever is less. (Credits are also available for foreign death taxes, certain gift taxes, and federal estate taxes on prior transfers.)

Taxable Estate (After deducting the $60,000 exemption) From	To	*Tax =*	*+*	*%*	*Of Excess Over*
0	$ 5,000	0		3	0
$ 5,000	10,000	$ 150		7	$ 5,000
10,000	20,000	500		11	10,000
20,000	30,000	1,600		14	20,000
30,000	40,000	3,000		18	30,000
40,000	50,000	4,800		22	40,000
50,000	60,000	7,000		25	50,000
60,000	100,000	9,500		28	60,000
100,000	250,000	20,700		30	100,000
250,000	500,000	65,700		32	250,000
500,000	750,000	145,700		35	500,000
750,000	1,000,000	233,200		37	750,000
1,000,000	1,250,000	325,700		39	1,000,000
1,250,000	1,500,000	423,200		42	1,250,000
1,500,000	2,000,000	528,200		45	1,500,000
2,000,000	2,500,000	753,200		49	2,000,000
2,500,000	3,000,000	998,200		53	2,500,000
3,000,000	3,500,000	1,263,200		56	3,000,000
3,500,000	4,000,000	1,543,200		59	3,500,000
4,000,000	5,000,000	1,838,200		63	4,000,000
5,000,000	6,000,000	2,468,200		67	5,000,000
6,000,000	7,000,000	3,138,200		70	6,000,000
7,000,000	8,000,000	3,838,200		73	7,000,000
8,000,000	10,000,000	4,568,200		76	8,000,000
10,000,000	....	6,088,200		77	10,000,000

[2] The table below may not be used in computing taxes on estates of certain members of the Armed Forces. See Code Sec. 2011(d) and Code Sec. 2201.

II. ESTATES OF NONRESIDENTS NOT CITIZENS DYING AFTER NOVEMBER 13, 1966 AND BEFORE JANUARY 1, 1977

The federal estate tax on estates of nonresidents not citizens dying after November 13, 1966 and before January 1, 1977, after deduction of the $30,000 exemption, but prior to any credit for state death taxes, gift taxes or taxes on prior transfers, is computed at the rates below.

Taxable Estate (After deducting the $30,000 exemption) From	To	*Tax =*	*+*	*%*	*Of Excess Over*
0	$ 100,000	0		5	0
$ 100,000	500,000	$ 5,000		10	$ 100,000
500,000	1,000,000	45,000		15	500,000
1,000,000	2,000,000	120,000		20	1,000,000
2,000,000	....	320,000		25	2,000,000

III. STATE DEATH TAX CREDIT

Taxable Estate (After deducting the applicable exemption) From	To	*Credit =*	*+*	*%*	*Of Excess Over*
0	$ 40,000	0		0	0
$ 40,000	90,000	0		.8	$ 40,000
90,000	140,000	$ 400		1.6	90,000
140,000	240,000	1,200		2.4	140,000
240,000	440,000	3,600		3.2	240,000
440,000	640,000	10,000		4	440,000
640,000	840,000	18,000		4.8	640,000
840,000	1,040,000	27,600		5.6	840,000
1,040,000	1,540,000	38,800		6.4	1,040,000
1,540,000	2,040,000	70,800		7.2	1,540,000
2,040,000	2,540,000	106,800		8	2,040,000
2,540,000	3,040,000	146,800		8.8	2,540,000
3,040,000	3,540,000	190,800		9.6	3,040,000
3,540,000	4,040,000	238,800		10.4	3,540,000
4,040,000	5,040,000	290,800		11.2	4,040,000
5,040,000	6,040,000	402,800		12	5,040,000
6,040,000	7,040,000	522,800		12.8	6,040,000
7,040,000	8,040,000	650,800		13.6	7,040,000
8,040,000	9,040,000	786,800		14.4	8,040,000
9,040,000	10,040,000	930,800		15.2	9,040,000
10,040,000	....	1,082,800		16	10,040,000

¶ 2650 PRE-1977 GIFT TAX RATES

The rate table below is applicable for gifts made in 1976 and prior years. See ¶ 2600 for unified rate table for gifts made after 1976. Gifts made prior to 1977 will be taken into account in the computation of the unified transfer tax generated by post-1976 gifts. In computing the tax payable on post-1976 gifts, the reduction for taxes paid previously is to be based upon the unified rate schedule. See illustration at ¶ 2008.

● "Taxable gifts," as noted in the table below, are determined by deducting the $30,000 specific exemption (allowed only once, but cumulative until used up) and by deducting an annual exclusion of $3,000 per donee of gifts of present interests. The $30,000 specific exemption is eliminated for post-1976 gifts.

Taxable Gifts From	To	Tax =	+ %	Of Excess Over
....	$ 5,000	0	2¼%	....
$ 5,000	10,000	$ 112.50	5¼%	$ 5,000
10,000	20,000	375	8¼%	10,000
20,000	30,000	1,200	10½%	20,000
30,000	40,000	2,250	13½%	30,000
40,000	50,000	3,600	16½%	40,000
50,000	60,000	5,250	18¾%	50,000
60,000	100,000	7,125	21 %	60,000
100,000	250,000	15,525	22½%	100,000
250,000	500,000	49,275	24 %	250,000
500,000	750,000	109,275	26¼%	500,000
750,000	1,000,000	174,900	27¾%	750,000
1,000,000	1,250,000	244,275	29¼%	1,000,000
1,250,000	1,500,000	317,400	31½%	1,250,000
1,500,000	2,000,000	396,150	33¾%	1,500,000
2,000,000	2,500,000	564,900	36¾%	2,000,000
2,500,000	3,000,000	748,650	39¾%	2,500,000
3,000,000	3,500,000	947,400	42 %	3,000,000
3,500,000	4,000,000	1,157,400	44¼%	3,500,000
4,000,000	5,000,000	1,378,650	47¼%	4,000,000
5,000,000	6,000,000	1,851,150	50¼%	5,000,000
6,000,000	7,000,000	2,353,650	52½%	6,000,000
7,000,000	8,000,000	2,878,650	54¾%	7,000,000
8,000,000	10,000,000	3,426,150	57 %	8,000,000
10,000,000	....	4,566,150	57¾%	10,000,000

CODE FINDING LIST

¶ 2700

This table lists all sections of the Internal Revenue Code that are cited as authority in this edition of *Federal Estate and Gift Taxes Explained.* The citations appear at the paragraphs indicated.

Code Sec.	Par. (¶)
57	2305
79	460
112(c)	1550
163(d)	2161
164(a)	2431
170(c)	1105
170(f)	1120
170(h)	257
213(c)	813
213(d)	2250
219	770
267	2590
267(c)	1672
280A(d)	2570
303	555, 1672
318	570
469	292
507	2305
508(e)	2305
527(e)	2160
529(c)	2052, 2255, 2431
642(c)	2305, 2439
642(g)	780, 797, 2451
664	2305, 2439
664(d)	1122, 1123
664(f)	1123
664(g)	1122
691	797
707(c)	2510
864(c)	1620
1014	121
1014(a)	296, 2465
1014(e)	121
1015(d)	2465
1016(c)	296
1031	286
1033	286
1040(a)	285
1040(c)	296
1223(12)	285
2001	11, 820, 2005, 2459
2001(a)	28
2001(b)	12, 15, 29, 36
2001(c)	11, 16, 35, 1430, 2005
2001(d)	1426
2001(e)	1426
2001(f)	1426
2010	15, 29, 36
2010(b)	18
2010(c)	22
2011	36, 1370
2011(a)	1374
2011(c)	1372
2011(d)	1560, 2640
2012	36, 1382
2012(e)	1380
2013	36, 1300
2013(c)	1320
2013(d)	1335
2013(f)	1340
2014	36, 1401, 1405
2014(g)	1401
2014(h)	1402
2015	1401
2016	1401
2031	30, 1002
2031(b)	325
2031(c)	253, 255, 257, 259
2032	105, 107, 605, 2453
2032(a)	107
2032(c)	105
2032(d)	105
2032A	50, 66, 73, 80, 109, 253, 285, 289, 292
2032A(a)	280, 281
2032A(b)	281, 284, 291, 292, 293
2032A(c)	284, 288
2032A(d)	289

FINDING LIST OF FORMS

¶ 2750

Index

References are to (¶) numbers.

E

F

G

H

I

N

P

S

T